A WORLD of IMPONDERABLES™

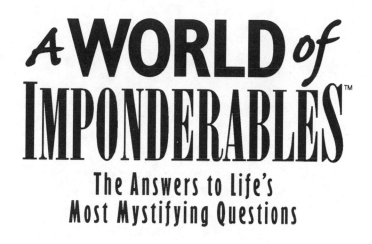

A WORLD *of* IMPONDERABLES™

The Answers to Life's Most Mystifying Questions

When Did Wild Poodles Roam the Earth?

Do Penguins Have Knees?

How Does Aspirin Find a Headache?

DAVID FELDMAN

GALAHAD BOOKS
NEW YORK

Contents

WHEN DID WILD POODLES ROAM THE EARTH?

An Imponderables™ Book

For Kassie Schwan

Contents

Preface

Are you thinking of buying this book? If so, take this simple quiz about food and nutrition. In each category, which question concerns you most, A or B?

> Vitamins. A) Does a well-balanced diet provide one with sufficient vitamins, or should one take a supplement? B) Why is there no Betty Rubble character in Flintstones multivitamins?
>
> Poultry. A) Are free-range chickens superior nutritionally to conventionally raised chickens? B) Has anyone ever seen a *live* Cornish game hen?
>
> Seafood. A) Are lobsters as high in cholesterol as beef? B) Are lobsters ambidextrous?
>
> Decaffeinated Coffee. A) Is there anything dangerous about the decaffeination process? B) Why do decaf pots in restaurants have orange rims?

If you answered A to three or more of the four questions, you are a normal, well-adjusted person, concerned about the important issues of our day. We're proud of you. Buy another book.

But if you are a B-type person, who lies awake wondering why, if moths are attracted to light, they don't fly toward the sun, you have found your spiritual home in this book. Imponderables are the little mysteries of life that drive you nuts until you find out their solution. That's precisely what we're trying to do (solve the mysteries, not drive you nuts).

This, our sixth *Imponderables* book, is a collaboration between our readers and us. Most of the Imponderables in this book came as suggestions from readers. In the Frustables section, our readers take a crack at answering Imponderables that have stumped us. In the Letters section, readers take a crack at our heads, enumerating our imperfections.

As a gesture of our appreciation, we offer an acknowledgment and a free, autographed copy of our next book to the first person who sends in an Imponderable or the best solution to a Frustable we use.

The last page of the book tells you how you can contribute to the enterprise. But for now, sit back and enjoy. There will be no more quizzes.

Imponderables

Are lobsters ambidextrous?

Have you ever noticed, while digging into a lobster, that one claw is significantly larger than the other, as if one claw was pumping iron and taking steroids, while the other claw was used only for riffling the pages of library books? The large claw is called the "crusher" and the smaller one the "cutter" (terms that sound like the members of a new tag team in the World Wrestling Federation). The crusher has broader and bigger teeth but moves relatively slowly. The cutter has tiny, serrated teeth and moves swiftly.

The two claws do not start out distinctly different. Lobsters shed their shells more often than Cher has plastic surgery—they undergo three molts in the larval stage alone. When lobsters are first hatched, the two claws look identical, but with each successive stage in their development, the differences become more pronounced. It isn't until their fifth molt, and second postlarval molt, that the two claws are truly differentiated.

As you may have guessed, the crusher claw is important for the defense of lobsters against predators, and the cutter particularly useful in eating. Claws of lobsters are often torn off in accidents and in fights. Although there are some differences among species of lobsters, most lobsters will regenerate severed claws.

Most bizarre of all, if the remaining claw of an injured lobster is a cutter, many species with "plastic dimorphism" will change the function of that claw from cutter to crusher, presumably because the crusher is more essential for survival. The next regenerated claw of that lobster is capable itself of shifting to the cutter function, so that the positions of the two claws are reversed.

According to Darryl Felder, chairman of the University of Louisiana, Lafayette, biology department, lobsters are not always right- or left-"handed." The crusher may be on the right or left side of a lobster.

The ultimate answer to this Imponderable depends upon how you define ambidextrous. Certainly, lobsters can use either cheliped (the scientific name for claw) with equal ease. Although their regenerative powers give lobsters a certain flexibility, the versatility of each claw is not as great as that of a switch hitter in baseball, who can swing the bat equally well from both sides, or the pickpocket who can pilfer skillfully with either hand.

Submitted by Danny Kotok of New York, New York.

Why is there no Betty Rubble character in Flintstones Multivitamins?

For reasons too unfathomable for even us to delve into, we are thrown this question periodically on radio phone-in shows but have never received it in a letter. Perhaps no one wants to take credit for asking this Imponderable. One radio host said that he

DAVID FELDMAN

had investigated the matter, and found that for technical reasons, it was difficult to manufacture a realistic Betty facsimile.

Ah, we wish that were true, but the real story is far sadder, far darker. We heard from William D. Turpin, director of consumer relations for Multivitamins' manufacturer, Miles, Inc.:

> The current group of Flintstones characters was selected based upon research of the popularity of each character with children. As a result of this research, it was determined that Betty Rubble is not as popular with the majority of the children as the other characters.

Thus, if you investigate the contents of a Flintstones Multivitamins jar carefully, you'll find seven different "characters." As expected, Wilma, Fred, and a lonely Barney are included. Bamm-Bamm, Pebbles, and Dino are there, too, to help round out the nuclear family. But the Flintmobile? Is a car really more popular with children than a fine specimen of womanhood? You'd better believe it.

Truth be told, Betty was never our favorite character either. In fact, we don't think she deserved a great catch like Barney. Nevertheless, her lack of charisma is hardly reason enough to break up the family units that helped make the Flintstones a television and multivitamin supplement institution.

What in the heck is a tumbleweed? Why does it tumble? And how can it reproduce if it doesn't stay in one place?

Three Imponderables for the price of one. The first part is easy. The most common form of tumbleweed, the one you see wreaking havoc in movie westerns, is the Russian thistle. But actually the term is applied to any plant that rolls with the wind, drops its seed as it tumbles, and possesses panicles (branched flower clusters) that break off.

Usually, the stems of tumbleweed dry up and snap away

from their roots in late fall, when the seeds are ripe and the leaves dying. Although tumbleweeds cannot walk or fly on their own, they are configured to move with the wind. The above-ground portion of the thistle is shaped like a flattened globe, so it can roll more easily than other plants.

In his March 1991 *Scientific American* article "Tumble-weed," James Young points out how tumbleweed has adapted to the arid conditions of the Great Plains. One Russian thistle plant can contain a quarter of a million seeds. Even these impressive amounts of seeds will not reproduce efficiently if dumped all at once. But the flowers, which bloom in the summer, are wedged in the axil between the leaves and the stem, so that their seeds don't fall out as soon as they are subjected to their first tumbles. In effect, the seeds are dispersed sparingly by the natural equivalent of time-release capsules, assuring wide dissemination.

Young points out that tumbleweed actually thrives on solitude. If tumbleweed bumps into another plant, or thick, tall grass, it becomes lodged there, and birds and small animals find and eat the seeds:

> Hence, successful germination, establishment of seedlings, and flowering depend on dispersal to sites where competition is minimal: Russian thistle would rather tumble than fight.

Although songs have romanticized the tumbleweed, do not forget that the last word in "tumbleweed" is "weed." In fact, if the Russian thistle had been discovered in our country in the 1950s rather than in the 1870s, it probably would have been branded a communist plot. Thistle was a major problem for the cowboys and farmers who first encountered it. Although tumbleweed looks "bushy," its leaves are spiny and extremely sharp. Horses were often lacerated by running into tumbleweed in fields and pastures, and the leaves punctured the gloves and pants worn by cowboys.

Tumbleweed has also been a bane to farmers, which explains how tumbleweed spread so fast from the Dakotas down to the Southwest. The seeds of tumbleweed are about the same

DAVID FELDMAN

size as most cereal grains. Farmers had no easy way to separate the thistle seeds from their grains; as "grain" moved through the marketplace, thistle was transported to new "tumbling ground."

Today, tumbleweed's favorite victims are automobiles and the passengers in them. We get into accidents trying to avoid it, trying to outrace it, and from stupid driving mistakes when simply trying to watch tumbleweed tumble.

Submitted by Plácido García of Albuquerque, New Mexico.

When a body is laid out at a funeral home, why is the head always on the left side from the viewer's vantage point?

Why are so many readers obsessed with this Imponderable? And why are so many of them from Pennsylvania?

We found no evidence that any religion cares one iota about the direction in which a body is laid out at a viewing. Discussions with many funeral directors confirmed that the arrangement has become a custom not because of religious tradition but because of manufacturing practice.

Caskets can be divided into two types: half-couches, which have two separate lids, either or both of which can be opened; and full couches, whose lids are one, long unit. Full couches are designed to display the entire body at the viewing; half-couches are intended to show the head and upper torso of the deceased, with the option that, if the second lid is opened, the full body can be displayed.

DAVID FELDMAN

The hinges of all caskets allow the lids to be opened only in one direction. When the lids are lifted, they move first up and then back away from the viewers, to allow an unobstructed view for the bereaved. In many viewing rooms, the raised lids rest against a wall during viewing, dictating the direction the casket will be placed in a viewing room.

According to Howard C. Raether, former executive director and now consultant to the National Funeral Directors Association, the half-couch caskets made in the United States are all manufactured so that "only the left side has an interior and pillow for positioning and viewing the body." The two sides of the half-couch are also not symmetrical and thus not totally interchangeable. The left side of the half-couch is shorter than the "leg side," and because it is not normally opened, the bottom of the right side of the casket is usually unfinished. The interiors of full-couch caskets are also designed for the head to be placed on the left side.

Occasionally, however, a funeral director may need to put the head on the right side of the casket, usually when an injury or disease has disfigured the "wrong" side of the deceased's face. Since American-made caskets are rarely tapered, it is easy to rearrange the pillows inside the casket and put the deceased in the opposite direction.

One of our sources, who has worked in the industry for over fifty years and has sense enough to want to remain anonymous, told *Imponderables* that more families are asking for full-body viewings these days. He singled out *Pennsylvania* (along with southern New Jersey and parts of Florida and Ohio) for special mention in their preference for full-couch caskets—everywhere else, half-couches predominate.

What's with these Pennsylvanians?

Submitted by Barbara Peters of Norwood, Pennsylvania. Thanks also to Bridget Hahn of Conneaut Lake, Pennsylvania; Carol Haten of Monroeville, Pennsylvania; Earle Heffley of Springfield, Illinois; Sandy Zak of Pittsburgh, Pennsylvania; and Jason Humble of Starks, Louisiana.

Has anyone ever seen a live Cornish game hen?

We've seen a few dead Cornish game hens in our time, usually on a plate in front of us—and always when we are ravenously hungry at a formal dinner, surrounded by folks we don't know. So we feel we have to eat the bird with a knife and fork. Without picking up the dead hen and eating it with our fingers, we are capable of extracting a good two or three mouthfuls' worth of edible meat before we give up on meeting our protein requirements for the day.

As you can see, we have more than a little hostility toward these little bitty particles of poultry, so we are going to expose a nasty scandal about Cornish game hens (aka Rock Cornish game hens): They are nothing more than chickens—preadolescent chickens, in fact.

That's right. Cornish game hens, despite their highfalutin moniker, are nothing more than immature versions of the same broilers or fryers you buy in the supermarket. A Rock Cornish game hen could theoretically grow up to be a Chicken Mc-Nugget. (At least a Chicken McNugget gets eaten.) We have *all* seen a live "Cornish game hen."

Federal regulations define a Rock Cornish game hen or Cornish game hen as

> a young immature chicken (usually 5 to 6 weeks of age) weighing not more than 2 pounds ready-to-cook weight, which was prepared from a Cornish chicken or the progeny of a Cornish chicken crossed with another breed of chicken.

In practice, most Cornish fowls are crossbred with Plymouth Rock fowls.

Dr. Roy Brister, director of research and nutrition at Tyson Food, Inc., told *Imponderables* that *all* the chicken we eat has the Cornish White Rock as one of its ancestors. Cornish fowl are prized because they are plump, large-breasted, and meaty. Other breeds are too scraggly and are better suited for laying eggs. Most of the Cornish game hens now sold in the United States are actually less than thirty days old and weigh less than one pound after they are cooked.

According to the USDA's *Agriculture Handbook*, Cornish game hens are raised and produced in the same way as broilers. But because they are sold at a smaller weight, the cost per pound to process is higher for the producer and thus for the consumer.

But let's face it. It's a lot easier to get big bucks for a product with a tony name like "Rock Cornish game hen" than it is for "chick" or "baby broiler." If veal were called "baby cow," its price would plummet overnight. Dr. Brister speculates that the creation of "Cornish Game Hens" was probably a marketing idea in the first place.

While we are pursuing our literary equivalent of "A Current Affair," one more scandal must be unleashed. Not all those Cornish game hens are really hens. Legally, they can be of either sex, although they are usually females, because the males tend to be larger and are raised to be broilers. In fact, if immature chicks get a little chubby and exceed the two-pound maximum weight, they get to live a longer life and are sold as broilers.

Submitted by an anonymous caller on the Mel Young Show, KFYI-AM, Phoenix, Arizona.

Why do boxer shorts have straight frontal slits and briefs have complicated "trap doors"?

All that infrastructure on the briefs is what keeps you from indecent exposure charges. Even though most briefs and boxers sold in the U.S. are made out of the same material (cotton-polyester blends), briefs are knitted and boxers are woven. The two techniques yield different wear characteristics.

Boxers are built for comfort and won't stretch unless elasticized bands are added. But as Janet Rosati of Fruit of the Loom's Consumer Services told *Imponderables*, briefs are intended as support garments and are designed to stretch. Without all the reinforcements, or "trap doors," as our correspondent so elegantly put it, the opening on briefs would tend to gape open at embarrassing and unfortunate times. 'Nuf said?

Submitted by Josh Gibson of Silver Spring, Maryland.

DAVID FELDMAN

Auto Design Heaven

FINS — PUSH-BUTTON GEAR — WING WINDOW

OH, YEAH! I REMEMBER THESE!

EDSEL

Why have auto manufacturers eliminated the side vents from front door windows?

As Frederick R. Heiler, manager of public relations for Mercedes-Benz of North America, put it, "Vent wings have gone the way of the starter crank handle." Sure, there are the occasional exceptions, such as the 1988 Mercury, which resurrected this feature. But on the whole, it has now been superseded by the vent setting on air-conditioning systems (the device that propels air onto your shins rather than onto your face).

Why the change? The main reason, believe it or not, is fuel economy. In order to meet the Environmental Protection Agency's fuel requirements, American car manufacturers will change just about anything in order to achieve a better aerodynamic design. Heiler remarks that "designers found they could do without the air turbulence of the extra window post and hardware." Especially at high speeds, air turbulence, including turbulence caused by leaving the "regular" windows down, lowers fuel economy significantly.

Representatives at Ford and Chrysler add that since most automobiles now come equipped with air conditioning and flow-through ventilation systems, the need for vent wings has been obviated (thus reducing the flak the companies received for eliminating them). Our cars are now like modern office buildings —often run without windows ever being opened.

An official at the National Highway Traffic Safety Administration, who preferred to remain anonymous, corroborated the above but listed two more reasons why auto manufacturers dumped vent wings: One, a single, bigger plate of glass costs less than a smaller piece with a vent wing; and two, the vent wing was the perfect place for thieves to insert the old coat hanger.

Submitted by Tom Ferrell of Brooklyn, New York. Thanks also to Ronald C. Semone of Washington, D.C.; H.J. Hassig of Woodland Hills, California; and Richard Nitzel of Daly City, California.

Why do the Oakland Athletics' uniforms have elephant patches on their sleeves?

The elephant may be the symbol of the Republican party, but partisan politics was the last thing on Connie Mack's mind when the legendary owner of the Philadelphia Athletics decided to adopt the white elephant as his team's insignia. Rival New York Giants manager John McGraw boasted that the Athletics, and the fledgling American League, to which they belonged, were unworthy competitors, and indicated that Mack had spent a fortune on a team of "white elephants."

Mack got the last laugh. The A's won the American League pennant in 1902. A few years later, the elephant's image appeared on the team sweater. In 1918, Mack first emblazoned the elephant on the left sleeve of game uniforms.

The elephant image became so popular that in 1920, Mack

DAVID FELDMAN

eliminated the "A" on the front of the jersey and replaced it with a blue elephant logo. Four years later, he changed it to a white elephant. After a few years of playing more like a bunch of thundering elephants than a pennant contender, Mack de-pachydermed his players' uniforms.

No A's uniform sported an elephant again until 1955, when the Kansas City A's added an elephant patch to their sleeves. But when the irascible Charlie Finley bought the A's in the early 1960s, he replaced the elephant with the image of an animal more befitting his own personality—the mule.

But you can't keep a good animal down. According to Sally Lorette, of the Oakland A's front office, the current owners of the A's resurrected the same elephant used by the Kansas City Athletics in time for the 1988 season. The mascot did the job for the Oakland A's just as it had for Connie almost a century ago. Since 1988, the A's have won three American League pennants and one championship.

Submitted by Anthony Bialy of Kenmore, New York. Thanks also to a caller on the Jim Eason Show, KGO-AM, San Francisco, California.

Why is the imperial gallon bigger than its American counterpart?

The English have never been particularly consistent in their standards of weights and measures. In fact, in the eighteenth and early nineteenth centuries, England changed its definition of a gallon about as often as Elizabeth Taylor changes wedding rings. (Before then, Kings Henry VII and VIII and Queen Elizabeth I had also changed the definition of a gallon.)

Colonialists in America adopted the English wine gallon, based on the size of then-used hogsheads (barrels) of 231 cubic inches. The English, who also recognized the larger ale gallon of 282 cubic inches, finally settled the mess in 1824 by eliminating the ale and wine gallons completely and instituting the imperial gallon, defined as the volume of ten pounds of water at the temperature of 62 degrees Fahrenheit, the equivalent of about 277.420 cubic inches.

Meanwhile, Americans were basking in the freedom of a

DAVID FELDMAN

participatory republic but were saddled with an anachronistic wine gallon. In both the English and American systems, one gallon equals four quarts and eight pints, but English portions were significantly larger.

To compound the standardization problem, the British decided to use the same system to measure liquid and dry substances. They redefined a bushel as eight gallons. In the U.S., bushels, pecks, and all those other measurements we hear in Broadway songs but not in everyday speech are used only to measure grains and other dry commodities.

Perhaps this was England's revenge for the American Revolution. By the time the English finally got their act together and laid out a simple, sensible system of measurement, Americans had already committed to the inferior, old English system.

Submitted by Simon Arnold of Los Angeles, California.

Why do painters wear white uniforms?

Often, when we confront practitioners of an industry with an Imponderable about their line of work, they are befuddled. "I'd never stopped to think about that" is a typical reply.

Such was not the case with painters we contacted about this mystery. Nobody seemed to know for sure how the practice started, but we were lavished with theories about why "whites" made sense. In fact, when we contacted the International Brotherhood of Painters & Allied Trades, we were stunned to find out that after they posed the same question to their membership, their *Journal* was filled with responses in the April and May 1985 issues. Our thanks to the many members of IBPAT and other painters we contacted for help in answering what, on the basis of our mailbag, is a burning question of the 1990s.

One advantage that just about everyone could agree on is that white connotes cleanliness. A painter, after all, removes dirt and crumbling plaster before applying paint. Many painters compared the purity of their "whites" to the uniforms of nurses, chefs, and bakers. Philadelphia painting contractor Matt Fox told *Imponderables* that a white uniform is like a badge that says, "There's no paint on me, so I'm doing my job." Obviously, it is as hard to hide paint smeared on a white uniform as it is to hide a ketchup stain on a chef's apron.

The white uniform is also a sign of professionalism, one that distinguishes painters from other craftspeople. One IBPAT member wrote that in the early twentieth century, his father often encountered part-time, nonunion workmen trying to horn in on the painting trade. These workers, usually moonlighting, wore blue bib overalls or other ordinary work clothes not related to the paint trade. By contrast, "Our men certainly looked professional in their white overalls, white jackets, and black ties." Even today, most professionals prefer crisp white uniforms (even if they've shed the tie), while odd-job part-timers might don blue jeans and a T-shirt.

Of course, a color other than white could still look clean and professional. And at first glance, white seems like precisely the wrong color—by wearing white, you "broadcast" any color you spill. True, but remember that the majority of the time (estimates are 70 to 80 percent), painters are dealing with white paint. And what other color uniform is going to look better when splattered with white paint?

Painters deal with other white substances more than likely to be deposited on their uniforms. Painter Jerry DeOtis presumes that the tradition of "whites" began in eighteenth-century England, when buildings were routinely whitewashed. Irving Goldstein of New York City adds:

> Plaster, lime, spackle, and compound are also white. Repairing and sanding existing walls creates a fine white powder; therefore wearing "painters whites" enables these materials to blend into the uniform.

The beauties of white as proper background even inspired one Local 277 member, Liz Weber, to burst into verse:

> . . . and although we strive for neatness,
> getting paint on our clothes is our one weakness.
> So what if those colors tend to cling—
> we're in style because . . .
>   White goes with everything!

Even if a painter isn't thrilled with pigment-stained whites, compared to other colored garb, they are a washroom delight. Traditionally, painters used bleach or lye to remove paint from their uniforms: Those that started with dark uniforms ended up with bleached-out, dingy, light-colored ones anyway.

Some other painters we consulted mentioned two other advantages of whites: They are cheaper than dyed fabrics and, because of their color, reflect light rather than absorb it, a small comfort to painters working in the sun-drenched great outdoors.

Submitted by Angelique Craig of Austin, Texas. Thanks also to Howard Livingston of Arlington, Texas; Laura Arvidson of Westville, Indiana; Cristie Avila of Houston, Texas; Tom Rodgers of Las Vegas, Nevada; Adam Rawls of Tyler, Texas; and Karen Riddick of Dresden, Tennessee.

HURRY UP! IT'S ALMOST TIME FOR THE HUMAN'S MIDNIGHT SNACK!!

Why do roaches run away when a light is turned on in a darkened room?

Just as a sunflower is genetically programmed to turn toward the sun, many plants and animals are phototropic—they are genetically programmed to turn away from and avoid the sun. Cockroaches are nocturnal animals, and most species instinctively scurry when exposed to light.

The urban roach has adapted well to its environment. While we are asleep, dreaming away, the roach is free to loot our kitchens as if they were no-cost supermarkets. By roaming at night, it also avoids the rodents that might eat it during the day. At night, the only foes roaches have to worry about are Raid and Combat.

It is impossible to know for sure, since we can't interview a roach, to what extent the roaches are bothered by the light per se, or whether the scurrying is a genetically programmed response to help roaches avoid predators. Randy Morgan, entomologist at the Cincinnati Insectarium, told us that the speed of a given roach's retreat is subject to many factors, including its species, the humidity, and how hungry it is.

　　　　　　　　　　　　DAVID FELDMAN

But why assume that the roach is running because of the light? Maybe it is running away from *you!* Cockroaches have poor eyesight; their main method of detecting danger is by sensing vibrations around them. Robin Roche, entomologist at the Insect Zoo in San Francisco, told *Imponderables* that roaches have two hornlike structures on their back called cerci. The cerci have hairs that are very sensitive to wind currents. So when you enter the kitchen for your midnight snack, chances are the roach senses you not from sight, or by sound, but by feeling the air currents your movement has generated.

At the very least, the roach knows something is moving around it; when you flip the light switch on, an automatic physiological response ensues. If it hasn't already bidden a hasty retreat, it decides that the better part of valor is to sneak back into the crevice it came from. When you go back to bed, it knows those bread crumbs will be right where you left them before, and it can snack away later in peaceful darkness.

Submitted by Jill Davies of Forest, Mississippi.

If moths are attracted to light, why don't they fly toward the sun?

There is one little flaw in the premise of this Imponderable. Even if they were tempted to fly toward the sun, they wouldn't have the opportunity—the vast majority of moths are nocturnal animals. When's the last time you saw one flitting by in daylight? Actually, though, the premise of this question isn't as absurd as it may appear. For details, see the next Imponderable.

Submitted by Joel Kuni of Kirkland, Washington. Thanks also to Bruce Kershner of Williamsville, New York.

Why are moths attracted to light? And what are they trying to do when they fly around light bulbs?

Moths, not unlike humans, spend much of their time sleeping, looking for food, and looking for mates. As we've already learned, most moths sleep during the day. Their search for dinner and procreation takes place at night. Unlike us, though, moths are not provided with maps, street signs, or neon signs flashing "EAT" to guide them to their feeding or mating sites.

Over centuries of evolution, moths have come to use starlight, and particularly moonlight, for navigation. By maintaining a constant angle in reference to the light source, the moth "knows" where to fly. Unfortunately for the insects, however, humans introduce artificial light sources that lull the moths into assuming that a light bulb is actually their natural reference point.

An English biologist, R.R. Baker, developed the hypothesis that when moths choose the artificial light source as their reference point, and try keeping a constant angle to it, the moth ends up flying around the light in ever-smaller concentric circles, until it literally settles on the light source. Baker even speculates that moths hover on or near the light because they are attempting to roost, believing that it is daytime, their regular hours. Moths have been known to burn themselves by resting on light bulbs. Others become so disoriented, they can't escape until the light is turned off or sunlight appears.

So don't assume that moths are genuinely attracted by the light. Sad as their fate may be, chances are what the moth "is trying to do" isn't to hover around a porch light—the only reason the moth is there is because it has confused a soft white bulb with the moon. The moth would far rather be cruising around looking for food and cute moths of the opposite sex.

Submitted by Charles Channell of Tucson, Arizona. Thanks also to Joyce Bergeron of Springfield, Massachusetts; Sara Anne Hoffman of Naples, Florida; Gregg Hoover of Pueblo, Colorado;

DAVID FELDMAN

Gary Moore of Denton, Texas; Bob Peterson, APO New York; and Jay Vincent Corcino of Panorama City, California.

Why do some nineteen-inch televisions say on the box: "20 IN CANADA"?

Do televisions grow when exposed to the clean air in Canada? Are Canadian rulers more generous? Do televisions bloat when transported over the border?

None of the above. What we have here are two bureaucratic mechanisms that have agreed to differ. In Canada, the size of a television is measured by determining the size of the picture tube from one corner to its opposite diagonal corner. But in the U.S., the *viewable* picture is measured: from one corner of the picture itself to its opposite along the diagonal. Those cropped corners on the monitors reduce the viewing size by approximately one inch.

The picture tube is always a little bigger than the measurable picture, which is why Canadians might think they are getting ripped off when they try to confirm the measurements of their sets. Steve Sigman, vice-president of consumer affairs for Zenith, told *Imponderables* that the television picture shrinks naturally with age. Luckily, the shrinkage materializes along the edges of the monitor. By supplying a little extra picture tube, the manufacturer insures that the consumer will get the whole image for a long time.

Submitted by Mary Mackintosh of Sacramento, California.

Why does an old person's voice sound different from a middle-aged person's?

To unravel this Imponderable, we spoke to our favorite speech pathologist, Dr. Michael J. D'Asaro, of Santa Monica, California, and Dr. Lorraine Ramig, who has published extensively on this very subject. Both of them named three characteristics of the aged voice and found physiological explanations for each:

1. The elderly voice tends to be higher in pitch. This characteristic is much more noticeable among men because hormonal changes at the onset of menopause work to lower the pitch of older women. As we age, soft tissues all over our body shrink in size. The vocal cords are no exception. As we learned in *Why Do Clocks Run Clockwise?*, there is a direct correlation between the mass of the vocal cords and pitch: The larger the vocal cords, the lower the pitch.

2. The elderly voice tends to be weaker in strength. D'Asaro points out that another characteristic of aging is increased stiffening of joints, which reduces amplitude of motion:

> In the voice mechanism, the result is reduced volume, especially if the respiratory system is also reduced in capacity. The shortness of breath reduces the motive power of the voice, the exhaled breath.

Ramig adds that the degeneration of vocal folds compounds the problem of creating enough air pressure to fuel a strong voice.

3. Many elderly people experience quavers or tremors in the voice. Again, many old people experience tremors in other muscle groups, as they age, as part of a decrease in nervous system control. Tremors in the laryngeal muscles produce the Katharine Hepburnish vocal quavers we associate with old age. Frequently, serious neurological disorders, such as Parkinson's disease, are also responsible for severe tremors in the voice.

Ramig told *Imponderables* that not every old person experiences these symptoms, so we asked her if there could be a psychological component to the stereotyped notion of the aged voice. She responded that in many cases, there very well might be. Certainly, the strong, unwavering voices of numerous elderly actors and singers betray their age. Do these young-sounding performers have different anatomical equipment than others of their age? Does their constant training and projection of their vocal equipment help maintain their laryngeal muscles in fighting trim? Or does their active lifestyle keep them from succumbing to the apathy of some of their age peers? These are the types of further Imponderables that will keep Ramig and her fellow researchers knee-deep in work for years to come.

Submitted by Herbert Kraut of Forest Hills, New York.

Why is there usually no organization in the shelving of soup cans in supermarkets?

Few grocery store experiences are as frustrating as trying to find your can of split pea soup amid a sea of red and white. Ninety percent or more of most soup sections are filled with Campbell Soup Company products, and our correspondent wondered why soup lovers weren't given a break.

Perhaps, our reader speculates, the soups could be arranged alphabetically. But then would cream of mushroom soup be filed under "C" or "M"?

No, organization by genre seems more logical. Indeed, this is what Campbell tries to do. Unfortunately, although Campbell suggests a shelving plan for retailers, grocers ultimately have "artistic control" over how and where the soup is shelved.

We had a long talk with Kevin Lowery, Campbell's manager of corporate communications, who offered us a primer on how the ideal soup section should be organized. A random check of

DAVID FELDMAN

our local supermarkets indicated that they were at least trying to follow the following golden rules:

Rule 1: *The Big 3 must go on the bottom shelf.* The Big 3, of course, are chicken noodle, cream of mushroom, and tomato soup, by far Campbell's best sellers. About 80 percent of cream of mushroom purchasers use it as an ingredient in cooking rather than as an eating soup, such as chicken noodle. Tomato soup is used by about half of all purchasers as an ingredient rather than an end product.

Lowery claims that the Big 3 are the three single fastest-moving dry (i.e., nonbeverage) items in an entire typical supermarket. The Big 3 are placed on the lowest shelves to ease the burden of grocery workers, who usually restock in case lots because of the quick turnover.

Rule 2: *New soups are stocked at eye level.* Eye level is the best placement for impulse purchasing. If you are in doubt about whether a variety is a new product, it can be identified with ease. Whenever Campbell markets a new variety of its regular "red and white" soups, the new product is given a "vignette label," with the contents pictured on the front of the can.

Rule 3: *Cooking soups should be segregated.* All these "cream of" soups should be stocked together.

Rule 4: *Eating soups are the biggest category, so poultry, beef, and vegetarian soups should be placed in separate sections.* In our experience, few markets even attempt this.

Rule 5: *Ready-to-serve and dry soups should be separated from all the others.*

Campbell's shelving plan theoretically produces the best of both worlds, allowing its soups to be organized by food type, preparation, and function, but the company's strategy is usually foiled in practice. How can you expect grocery stores to deploy sophisticated marketing schemes when they have great difficulty bagging your order?

Submitted by Louis Zelenka of Bainbridge, Georgia.

Why has Swanson stopped putting vent holes on the top of its pot pies?

The relentless rise of the microwave oven was responsible for the abolition of those vent holes. All frozen foods, including pot pies, have become popular items for the microwave.

Swanson introduced the first microwavable double-crusted pie on the market in 1989. While developing the product, Swanson determined that the pie baked better without the vent holes.

Joanne Marshall, of the Campbell Soup Company, told *Imponderables* that when a pot pie is prepared in a conventional oven, "We direct consumers to prick the top crust in order to ensure a crisp-textured pastry." One of the side benefits of eliminating the vent holes, if not the original rationale, is that it eliminates spillage of the filling during baking.

We'd add another reason. Even with the vent holes, fewer things are more capable of burning the roof of the mouth than the insides of a pot pie. Anything that allows the pot pie to "let off steam" can't be all bad.

Submitted by Randall Tada of Bellevue, Washington.

Why do TWIX cookie bars have holes in them?

Alas, while one company taketh away holes, another provideth them. We may have lost our beloved pot pie vents, but the folks at M&M/Mars have inserted them in their TWIX Bars.

We assumed that the answer to this Imponderable was that the ingredients in holes were considerably less expensive than those for the cookie bar itself. The more air in the product, the bigger the product seems, and the greater the value of the product is perceived to be (Cheerios and Ivory Soap certainly haven't suffered commercially from their airy constitutions).

DAVID FELDMAN

But it turns out we were paranoid. Hans Fiuczynski, external relations director of M&M/Mars, explains that the different ingredients in the TWIX cookie bar vary in their reaction to heat:

> As storage conditions in shops and in cupboards vary a bit, there is the chance that the topping on top of the cookie (such as caramel) would expand and create hairline cracks in the chocolate coating, thus allowing oxygen to enter the product. This would reduce the shelf life.
>
> To prevent this from happening, or at least to mitigate this effect, holes are put into the cookie so the topping can expand into the holes, internally, rather than crack the coating.

Submitted by Corrine Levering of Highland, Michigan.

What are those wavy marks on the bottom of Snickers bars?

What's with you guys? Holes in TWIXes? Wavy lines on Snickers? Don't you know you are supposed to be scarfing, not scrutinizing, candy bars?

We obtained Snickers specimens and found that, indeed, there were wavy marks on the bottom of each bar. The marks were not applied to the surface of the chocolate but were in the form of thin indentations, as if someone ran a needle through the epidermis of the chocolate on the bottom of the bar. To uphold our rigorous scientific principles, we also purchased a Milky Way bar. It, too, had markings on its bottom, but they formed a honeycomb pattern.

Despondent correspondent Jennifer Martz has been begging us to get to the bottom of this Snickers Imponderable for years, so we contacted M&M/Mars once again. We feared that we were risking overexposing Hans Fiuczynski to his growing legion of fans (but don't despair, Fiuczynski groupies—see the Letters section for Hans's bombshell announcement about

M&Ms), so we asked Marlene Marchut, external relations manager, for help.

She unlocked the mystery of the wavy lines. Marchut explained that there are two ways of preparing commercial chocolate bars: molding and enrobing. To mold a bar, the chocolatier pours liquid chocolate into a plastic or metal mold, where it conforms to the shape of the mold. Most solid chocolate bars are molded, because the process is simple and produces a bar of uniform shape and a pleasing, glossy finish. Although bars with fillings (e.g., caramel, nougat, nuts) can be produced by molding, most commercial candy bar makers use the enrobing process (M&M/Mars enrobes all of their bars except for the new solid chocolate Dove Bar). Enrobing is more complicated:

> The process begins with a filling, which is laid in a wide band on a continuous stainless steel belt. In the case of "layered" fillings, there are two bands, one on top of the other. The wide band is then sliced into long, continuous strips and eventually cut to the desired length, forming "centers." The actual enrobing process begins when these centers pass through a continuous curtain of liquid chocolate, which coats the top and sides of the bar. At the same time, a rotating chocolate-covered wheel beneath the mesh belt coats the base of the bar. To ensure an attractive, glossy, smooth coating, the chocolate must be at just the right temperature. The fully enrobed bar is then cooled and prepared for wrapping.

During enrobing, the chocolate is placed on a mesh belt rather than a solid one, so that excess liquid chocolate can be collected. In order for the chocolate to harden properly, it must pass through a cooling tunnel, where the cocoa butter crystallizes.

All fine and dandy, except for one potential problem: The liquid chocolate, once enrobed, does not transfer easily from the wire-mesh belt to the solid belt used to carry the bar through the cooling tunnel. Nothing could hold up the production line more annoyingly than splattered liquid chocolate. Mars came up with an elegant solution to clear the potential hurdle—one that coincidentally also creates the wavy lines. Marchut explains:

The solid belt [that picks up the chocolate from the enrober and sends it through the cooling tunnel] has a pattern on its surface which helps us to "pull" the wet bar off the wire belt. The patterns create a rough, irregular surface, just as the chains on tires help pull the car over wet surfaces.

When the chocolate bar has hardened, it is released from the patterned, solid belt as it is transferred to be wrapped. Once again, the pattern on the belt aids in the release of the bottom surface. The physics of the pattern allow the irregular surface to more easily "snap" off the belt than a completely smooth bottom, which has a tendency to create more suction.

Not all the bars of any given brand necessarily have exactly the same pattern (although we've never seen an unwavy Snickers bar)—it depends upon the individual plant or enrobing line.

From what we can tell, the folks at M&M/Mars aren't obsessed about the aesthetic pleasure offered by the bar bottoms. They just want their chocolate to melt in your mouth, not on their assembly line.

Submitted by Jennifer Martz of West Chester, Pennsylvania. Thanks also to Marguerite MacLeod of Braintree, Massachusetts; and Stacia Leary of Saunderstown, Rhode Island.

What is one hearing when one hears a house "settling" or creaking?

We like to think of a home as a bulwark, a refuge from the vicissitudes and capriciousness of the outside world. The infrastructure of a house consists of elements like beams, pillars, and foundations, words that connote steadiness, permanence, and immutability.

But architects we talked to soon disabused us of this notion. In fact, talking to an architect about the stability of houses is a little like talking to Norman Bates about shower safety. In particular, we were startled by a book called *How Buildings Work: The Natural Order of Architecture*, written by Edward Allen, and passed on to us by James Cramer, executive vice-president/ CEO of the American Institute of Architects. In one chapter, "Providing for Building Movement," Allen details the many ways in which buildings move, and if we weren't averse to

DAVID FELDMAN

clichés and bad puns, we would say that the opening rocked us to our very foundations:

A building, even a seemingly solid, massive one, is never at rest. Its motions are usually very small ones, undetectable by the unaided eye, but most of them are of virtually irresistible force, and would tear the building to pieces if not provided for in some way.

Allen states that in an average house, all of these components can and do move:

1. The soil underneath the foundation buckles under the weight of the new foundation.
2. Materials that are put in place while wet, such as mortar, concrete, and lime plaster, shrink as they harden.
3. Some dry materials, such as gypsum plaster, tend to expand and push against adjoining elements.
4. Most lumber used in houses is not completely dry when put in place. Wet lumber shrinks.
5. Structural elements that carry weight loads, such as beams, pillars, and columns, deflect under the weight.
6. Wind and earthquakes cause more "natural" deflection.
7. Wood and concrete sag.
8. Wood, in particular, tends to expand when exposed to high humidity and contract in dry conditions. When humidity decreases noticeably, such as when heat is put on to warm a room in winter, the wood creaks noticeably.
9. Any material adjoining another material with different movement characteristics is in danger of scraping against another or moving away from the other, which can cause movement and noise.
10. All of the above movements can and do cause noise, but the most common noise associated with "settling" is the actual expansion and contraction of the building. Allen explains:

Back-and-forth movements caused by thermal and moisture effects occur constantly. A building grows measurably larger in warm weather, and smaller in cold weather. A roof, heated by the sun, grows larger in the middle of the day while the cooler walls below stay the same size. At night the roof cools and shrinks.

And so on and so on. The architect's planning compensates for the inevitable movement of these materials. Or at least we hope that it does. Otherwise, the creaking noises might lead us to the same fate as Janet Leigh's in *Psycho*.

Submitted by Joanne Walker of Ashland, Massachusetts. Thanks also to Dr. Emil S. Dickstein of Youngstown, Ohio.

Why do dogs drool? And why do some dogs drool much more than other dogs?

In order to execute a proper drool, a dog must have two weapons at its disposal: a lot of saliva and a lot of lip. Getting a dog to salivate is as easy as exposing it to food—the smell of it, the taste of it, the anticipation of it, the consumption of it—and, as Pavlov proved, to any conditioned reflexes associated with feeding.

Drooling is simply the inability of a dog to dam the flood of saliva it manufactures. Salivation serves a useful function, helping the dog to swallow, and to lubricate the alimentary canal, the passageway from the mouth all the way through the esophagus and stomach that food must travel through before it is excreted. Individual dogs vary in their capacity to manufacture saliva, but some breeds manage to contain all saliva flow under normal conditions.

The dog experts we consulted agreed that some breeds drool more than others. Dogs with loose lips (and we're not talking about dogs who gossip too much), such as Saint Bernards, mastiffs, bloodhounds, and boxers, are prodigious droolers. The hanging parts of these dogs' lips, called flews, are usually the tell-tale sign of droolers. Dog breeder Fred Lanting reminded us of the old World War II slogan "Loose flews sink ships." Lanting says that the pushed-in faces of some breeds, such as bulldogs, create loose flews. He adds:

DAVID FELDMAN

Other breeds may drool because of poor breeding. . . . The looser and longer the lips, the more the loss of saliva outside rather than inside the throat.

Anatomist Robert Habel, of Cornell University's College of Veterinary Medicine, wrote *Imponderables* that medical problems can also cause excess drooling. Many drugs "artificially" stimulate salivation. Rabies can cause nerve damage leading to paralysis of the throat and tongue that prevents dogs from swallowing.

Habel reports that his own coonhound "slobbers foam when he is running a trail with his nose to the ground. I think that is the effect of gravity." He added: "Did you see the movie *Turner & Hooch?* You should, before you write about drooling."

Indeed. If you want a graduate course in drooling, drop this book and run to your local video store. We've heard they are doing a sequel to *Turner & Hooch*. It's called *Flews 2*.

Submitted by Catherine Price of New York, New York.

Why do dogs eat cat feces? Why do they sometimes eat their own feces?

And you thought the chapter about drooling was disgusting? Read on.

The nasty habit of eating feces is called "coprophagia" (wasn't that a Stephen King title?). Many puppies have a preoccupation with their own or their, pardon the expression, littermates', feces. But many canines continue to expand their culinary horizons as they get older, and experiment with the feces of other animals. Cat feces tend to be most easily available to domestic dogs, and more readily apparent to dog owners, but dogs won't stop with cat litter.

Why do dogs continue to eat food that, at best, gives them

bad breath, and at worst, leads to parasites and illnesses? Sometimes, undigested food can be found in animal stools. With their keen sense of smell, dogs can spot these "opportunities."

But more often, coprophagia is a symptom of a poor diet or nutritional deficiency. Carol Barfield, an official of the United Animal Owners Association, wrote *Imponderables* that her female Keeshond, Mattie, used to "clean up the cat litter box at any opportunity." After Barfield drastically upgraded Mattie's diet, the feces fetish disappeared almost immediately. Barfield is delighted that now she removes litter, rather than Mattie, from her cat litter box.

Our favorite lecturer on canine topics, Fred Lanting, sent us a delightful letter on the subject of coprophagia. Although he, too, mentioned nutritional deficiencies as an explanation for this habit, he has a simpler explanation for dogs' behavior:

> Dogs eat cat feces simply because they like the taste. Many animals eat (or at least sample) feces. They also lick urine markings to tell them something about the animal they are "researching," but the eating of feces is more than territorial data-gathering. It's also a gourmet delicacy—they think. Can you imagine a dog not liking ripe olives or oysters and wondering about that dumb human who's eating bitter berries and a mollusk that looks like snot? Sounds like a Gary Larson "Far Side" anthropomorphism, doesn't it?
>
> Dogs also eat the traces (droppings) of other species. They are positively *addicted* to rabbit "pellets," *love* deer "nuggets," horse "road apples," etc. On the other hand, they don't come more than a millimeter close to possum, goose, and many other droppings. They will pass up fox feces, as a rule.

Why do they eat their own feces? Or the feces of other dogs? Lanting continues:

> If they eat dog feces, it's due to a number of possible reasons: boredom; pancreatic insufficiency; or temperamental or hormonal problems in the dropper or droppee, depending on the details.
>
> Wild canids (chromosomally compatible with domestic dogs) also eat feces of other species. Sparrows feast on the undigested grain in horse feces. Dung beetles' only *raison d'être* is feasting

DAVID FELDMAN

on feces. Was it Cole Porter who said, "Birds do it, worms do it, dogs and fish and maybe cats do it . . ."? I doubt if anyone has made a study of the catholicity of coprophagy. Usually, pet owners want to know how to *stop* it, not who else is doing it.

Submitted by Nadia Norris of Saint Paul, Indiana. Thanks also to Vince Tassinari of Van Nuys, California.

HOW do they keep the water in water towers from freezing in the wintertime?

We were on the road promoting our last tome, *Do Penguins Have Knees?*, and radio host Mike Rosen was asking about one of the Imponderables in the book: Why are water towers built so high? We provided our concise, prefabricated answer, sounding, we hoped, as if the study of water towers was one of our driving passions in life.

When it came time to answer phone-in questions, and a caller asked about how they kept the water in towers from freezing, we replied with a resounding "Duh."

Callers soon pounced in with different theories. One caller was sure that there were heating elements in the water tower. Another swore that often water did freeze inside the tower. A third caller claimed that the constant movement of the water inside the tower kept it from freezing.

Time to contact our water tower sources again. Who would

DAVID FELDMAN

have ever thought there would be an Imponderable about water towers in successive books?

It turns out there isn't a single, simple answer to this Imponderable, but most of the time the third caller got it right. SUNY Professor Peter Black, affiliated with the American Water Resources Association, told *Imponderables* that in all but sparsely populated agricultural areas, water inside the tower is moving all the time. He added that wood is a good insulator, and that freezing is rarely a problem.

Thomas M. Laronge, whose Thomas M. Laronge, Inc., consults on water treatment and other environmental issues, isn't quite as sanguine. He points out that water usage tends to be lower in winter than in summer, especially in agricultural areas, and that evaporation consumption is much lower. If the demand is low enough so that water isn't constantly flowing within the tower, the water can easily freeze.

Many water towers are equipped with a cathodic protection system, designed to counteract corrosion. The natural corrosion tends to make the water inside the tower flow in one direction; the cathodic protection system acts as a bucking mechanism to send the current flow in the opposite direction. A byproduct of this system is the constant movement of water, and a cessation of any tendency toward freezing.

Even the first caller wasn't entirely wrong. Thomas Laronge says that in rare instances, in small water systems, water towers may be insulated and/or heated by a jacketing system, in which warm water flows on the outside of the jacket and cool water flows on the inside of the jacket to prevent freezing.

Even if the water in the tower does freeze, service may continue without any problems at all. Laronge explains:

> The density of water is greater than the density of ice. Therefore, if an ice plug forms, it will tend to form on the top of the water surface. Water can still flow through the bottom of the tower. Only the volume is restricted.
>
> Another reason why water towers may not freeze completely is that sometimes an insulating layer of ice forms within the tower.

The ice actually transfers heat slower than does the metal of the tower. Therefore, the ice barrier actually reduces the tendency for water towers to freeze.

Submitted by an anonymous caller on the Mike Rosen Show, KOA-AM, in Denver, Colorado.

Why do quarterbacks call the snap with the exclamation "hut"?

Put men in a uniform. Give them a helmet. And they all start speaking alike. At least, that's what all of our football sources claimed. Pat Harmon, historian at the College Football Hall of Fame, was typical:

> In Army drills, the drill sergeant counts off: "Hut-2-3-4." He repeats "Hut-2-3-4" until the men get in right. Football language has copied the drill sergeant.

We'll have to believe our football authorities, since no evidence exists that the "hut" barked by quarterbacks has anything to do with little thatched houses.

In fact, "hut" wasn't always used as the signal. Joe Horrigan, of the Pro Football Hall of Fame, sent us a photocopy of a section of the 1921 *Spalding's How to Play Football* manual that indicates that perhaps we aren't as hip as our forbears:

> When shift formations are tried, the quarter-back should give his signal when the men are in their original places. Then after calling the signal [he] can use the word "hip" for the first shift and then repeat for the players to take up their new positions on the line of scrimmage.

Our guess is that the only important virtue of "hut" is that it contains one syllable.

Submitted by Paul Ruggiero of Blacksburg, Virginia.

DAVID FELDMAN

Why are elections in the United States held on the first Tuesday after the first Monday in November rather than on the first Tuesday in November?

We had almost given up trying to answer this Imponderable when we contacted Professor Robert J. Dinkin, of California State University, Fresno, who specializes in the history of U.S. elections. Although Dinkin says he has never seen anything written on this subject, he does have an interesting conjecture.

Hallowmas, also known as All Saints' Day, was celebrated in most locales on November 1. Although candy companies have now insured that Hallow's Eve is the bigger holiday, All Saints' Day was a major celebration in the past. Therefore, as Dinkin speculates: "By making elections on the first Tuesday after the first Monday, no such scheduling conflict could occur." We could only find one other conjecture, from Megan Gillispie, of the League of Women Voters, who claims that the contorted "first Tuesday after the first Monday" language was simply an attempt to prevent elections from landing on the first day of the month "because merchants were busy closing their accounting books and courthouses were often busy with beginning of the month business."

No one seems able to find any primary sources to bolster their arguments. Can any of our enterprising readers?

Submitted by Barry Gluck of Rio de Janeiro, Brazil. Thanks also to Lynda Frank of Omaha, Nebraska.

How do dehumidifiers sense the humidity level in the air and "know" when to shut off automatically?

Not all dehumidifiers shut off automatically. But most that do work like this: Ambient air is drawn into a chamber or pipe via a fan. The outside air passes over a sensor in the humidistat, the device that determines whether or not the air exceeds the humidity you've set as your standard. If the air meets with your requirements, the air will pass through. But if the air in the room exceeds your desired humidity level, the air is heated by a hot-air dryer (or, less frequently, a desiccant chamber) before it is sent back into the room.

How does the humidistat determine the humidity of the ambient air? J. C. Laverick, technical director of dehumidifier manufacturer Ebac Ltd., explains:

> At the heart of the humidistat [behind the console] is a sensing element in the shape of an endless belt made from Nylon 6. This material has the characteristic of changing length in proportion to the amount of moisture it contains. At higher humidity levels its length expands, and it contracts at lower humidity levels. This change of length is converted into the force required to operate the [snap-action] microswitch and hence the dehumidifier.

Submitted by Alan Wright of Mansfield Center, Connecticut.

What do you call that little groove in the center of our upper lips?

Sorry, we can't answer this question. It is hardly an Imponderable, since it has been answered in scores of trivia books. Heck, this question has been posed by so many stand-up comedians on bad cable television shows, we refuse to answer on principle.

Submitted by too many readers.

DAVID FELDMAN

What is the purpose of the little indentation in the center of our upper lips?

If you rephrase your Imponderable in the form of a proper question, you can weasel just about anything out of us. How can we write about the indentation without mentioning its name? OK guys . . . it's called the *philtrum*. You'll be proud to know that we have a groove running down our upper lip for absolutely no good reason, as William P. Jollie, professor and chairman of anatomy at the Medical College of Virginia, explains:

> The indentation in the center of our upper lip is a groove, or raphe, that forms embryonically by merging paired right and left processes that make up our upper jaw. It has no function, just as many such midline merger marks, or raphes, have no function. We have quite a few merger-lines on our bodies: a raphe down the upper surface of our tongues; a grooved notch under the point of our chins; and a raphe in the midline of our palates. There are also several in the genital area, both male and female.
>
> Anatomically, the raphe on our upper lip is called the *philtrum*, an interesting word derived from the Greek word *philter*, which even in English means a love potion. I confess I don't see a connection, but many anatomical terms are peculiar in origin, if not downright funny.

Speaking of funny, it is our earnest hope that after the information in this chapter is disseminated, every stand-up comedian, standing before the inevitable brick wall, will stop doing routines about philtrums. Enough is enough.

Submitted by Bruce Hyman of Short Hills, New Jersey. Thanks also to three-year-old Michael Joshua Lim of Livonia, Michigan.

What happens to an ant that gets separated from its colony? Does it try to relocate the colony? Can it survive if it can't find the colony?

As we all learned in elementary school, ants are social animals, but their organization doesn't just provide them with buddies—it furnishes them with the food and protection they need to survive in a hostile environment.

All the experts we consulted indicated that an isolated worker ant, left to its own devices, would likely die a week or two before its normal three-week lifespan. And it would probably spend that foreshortened time wandering around, confused, looking for its colony.

Ants help each other trace the path between food sources and the colony by laying down chemical trails called pheromones. Our hypothetical solitary ant might try following pheromone trails it encounters, hoping they will lead it back home. Worker ants in a given colony are all the daughters of the original queen and can't simply apply for admission to a new colony.

Three dangers, in particular, imperil a lost ant. The first, and most obvious, is a lack of food. Ants are natural foragers but are used to receiving cues from other ants about where to search for food. A single ant would not have the capacity to store enough food to survive for long. Furthermore, ants don't always eat substances in the form they are gathered. Cincinnati naturalist Kathy Biel-Morgan provided us with the example of the leaf-cutter ant. The leaf-cutter ant finds plants and brings leaves back to the nest, where the material is ground up and used in the colony's fungus garden. The ants then eat the fruiting body of the fungus. Without the organizational assistance of the colony, a leaf does nothing to sate the appetite of a leaf-cutter ant.

The second danger is cold. Ants are ectotherms, animals that need heat but are unable to generate it themselves. When it is cold, ants in colonies will seek the protective covering of the nest. If left to its own devices, a deserted ant would probably try to find a rock or the crack of a sidewalk to use as cover, which

DAVID FELDMAN

may or may not be enough protection to keep it from freezing.

The third problem our lonesome ant would encounter is nasty creatures that think of the ant as their dinner fare. Collectively, ants help protect one another. Alone, an ant must fend off a variety of predators, including other ants. Biel-Morgan compared the vulnerability of the ant, on its own, to a single tourist in New York City. And that is vulnerable, indeed.

Submitted by Cary Hillman of Kokomo, Indiana.

Why is the color purple associated with royalty?

Although pagans once believed that purple dye was the creation of Satan, we actually have the Phoenicians to thank for the association of purple with royalty. Somehow, and we always wonder how anyone ever stumbles upon this sort of stuff, an anonymous Phoenician discovered that the spiny shell of the murex sea snail yielded a purple substance perfectly suited as a dye base. Phoenicians, the greatest traders and businessmen of the ancient world, soon developed purple cloth as one of their most lucrative trading commodities.

Since purple cloth was more expensive than other hues, only aristocrats could afford to wear it. But the Romans codified the practice, turning the color of clothing into a status symbol. Only the royal family itself could wear all-purple garments. Lesser aristocrats wore togas with purple stripes or borders to designate their rank—the more purple on the clothing, the higher the status.

The original "royal purple" was a different color than what we call purple today. It was a dark wine-red, with more red than blue. Many written accounts liken the color to blood. Indeed, the Phoenician dye was prized because it symbolized the unity, strength, and bonding of blood ties, and the continuity of royal families based on bloodlines. The spiritual quality supposedly imparted by the purple color is suggested by its Roman root, *purpureus* ("very, very holy").

The association of purple with royalty crossed many cultures and centuries. Greek legend explained royal purple as the color of Athena's goatskin dyed red. Kings in Babylonia wore a "lanbussu" robe of the same color. Mark's Gospel says that Jesus' robe was purple (although Matthew describes it as scarlet). In many churches, purple became the liturgical color during Lent, except for Good Friday. Consistently, in the succeeding centuries, the color purple was always identified with blood, as late as the time of Shakespeare, for the Bard himself referred to the "purpled hands" of Caesar's assassins, "stained with the most noble blood of all the world."

Curiously, marketing research indicates that today, purple is one of the least popular colors, which helps explain why it is so seldom used in packaging. Is the current aversion to purple stirred by a rejection of the patrician origins of the color, its close approximation to the color of blood, or a rejection of our contemporary purple royalty, Prince?

> *Submitted by Raymond Graunke of Huntersville, North Carolina. Thanks also to Sharon M. Burke of Los Altos, California; and Brian Dunne of Indianapolis, Indiana.*

Was Ben Gay?

We don't have the slightest idea. But we do know how the product got its name.

Ben-Gay was created by a French pharmacist, whose name was, conveniently enough, Dr. Ben Gué. He introduced his product in France in 1898, and called it *Baume Gué* (*baume* means "balm" *en français*).

When the analgesic was launched in the United States, it was decided that the unwashed masses of North America couldn't contend with a French word like *baume* or pronounce one of those nasty accent *acutes*. So marketers settled on naming their product after an Anglicization of its creator's name.

Submitted by Linda Atwell of Matthews, North Carolina.

Why are haystacks increasingly round rather than rectangular?

Everything old is new again. Round stacks were the fashion in the early twentieth century, as Oakley M. Ray, president of the American Feed Industry Association, explains:

> Fifty to one hundred years ago, it was the usual practice for the wheat farmer to "thresh" wheat (separate the grain from the straw). The threshing machine discharges the straw in one location for a given field so that the result was normally a round stack of straw.
>
> Some years later, the hay baler was invented, which compressed either hay or straw into a much smaller space, much as a household trash compactor does in many houses today. The bales were commonly three feet or so in length, perhaps eighteen inches wide, and perhaps eighteen inches high. They were held together by two wires or two strong pieces of twine. Each bale would weigh fifty to one hundred pounds, with the baler set in such a manner that all of the bales in a given field were essentially the same size.

Obviously, the uniform, rectangular shape made it easier to stack rectangular bales neatly and efficiently, first lengthwise in the wagons used to pick up the stacks, and then later in boxlike fashion in warehouses or barns.

But in the last fifteen to twenty years, "swathers" have gained popularity. These machines feature a sickle in front that cuts the hay and a belt that dumps the fodder in nice neat rows —a separate machine rolls it up—where it is left out in the sun to dry. The swather produces "wind-rowed" hay, which rarely blows away, a great advantage, considering the fact that wet hay gets moldy if moist. The ability to allow hay to cure before baling reduces spoilage.

Round bales are much larger than square ones, often about a thousand pounds, ten to twenty times heavier than rectangular bales, so they must be picked up by machine. Still, there are economies of scale achieved by assembling larger units of hay, and mechanically, there are fewer technical problems—there are fewer moving parts in the machinery that produces round bales. Kendell Keith, of the National Grain and Feed Association, told *Imponderables* that the wire and twine used to secure each bale of rectangular hay and the labor involved in packing and securing it were costlier than those for producing round haystacks.

Perhaps the most important advantage of "round hay" is that it weathers better than its compressed rectangular counterpart, as Gary Smith, of the University of Maryland's Agricultural Engineering department explains:

> The round bales shed the weather better. They reduce the need for storage space indoors, depending on what part of the country you are in, they can be left outdoors with minimum loss. Out West there is virtually no loss. In Maryland, there is about a 15% loss. This is cheaper than having to build storage for rectangular bales.

Submitted by Rosemary Arseneault of Halifax, Nova Scotia.

DAVID FELDMAN

Sno-Man   *Sno-Muffin*   *Sno-Tree*

What are the little white particles found on the bottom half of English muffins?

The particles are farina. Farina helps add to the taste of the product, but the main function of farina particles, and the reason why they are placed only on the bottom half of the muffin, is to prevent the ball of dough from sticking to the oven plate during cooking.

Submitted by Jessica Ahearne of Madawaska, Maine.

How do they assemble tall cranes without using another crane?

George O. Headrick, director of public relations and administrative services at the Construction Industry Manufacturers Association, was kind enough to direct us to several manufacturers of cranes. While they were uniformly generous in sharing their knowledge of how cranes are erected, they tended to provide us not with more than we wanted to know but a great deal more than we were capable of understanding. So we are indebted for the following explanation to the former secretary-treasurer of the Construction Writers Association, E.E. Halmos, Jr., who is now majordomo of Information Research Group, an editorial consulting group in Poolesville, Maryland:

> The tall cranes, which often carry booms (known to the trade as "sticks") of 120 feet or more, are assembled on the ground, at the construction site. If you'll notice, most of the tall booms are built as steel lattice-work structures, and are thus comparatively lightweight. Usually, the machine arrives on the scene on its own, carrying only the base stub of the boom.
>
> The sections for the full length of the boom usually arrive separately, via trailer-truck. At site, the stub of the boom is lowered to a horizontal position, and the sections of the finished boom laid out on the ground, attached together (much like a child's erector set), then mounted on the stub, and raised into position by cables attached to the crane body.

Likewise, extensions can be added when needed by laying the boom on the ground.

The use of these conventional rigs has been steadily declining, however, in favor of the "tower crane." These are the cranes that sit in the middle of a site and can be raised after they have been erected. The center column on which the control cab and the moving "head" sit is built up to three or four stories. As the building rises around the crane, added height is built onto the center column, and the whole top assembly is "jumped" upward.

Halmos reports that tower cranes have largely eliminated the need for elevators (known as "skips") and the lifting of loads from the ground by mobile cranes. "The tower crane operator can see not only what he's picking up, but can spot the load almost anywhere on the job, without a lot of elaborate signaling."

Submitted by Laura Laesecke of San Francisco, California. Thanks also to Paula Chaffee of Utica, Michigan; Lawrence Walters of Gurnee, Illinois; James Gleason of Collegeville, Pennsylvania; and Robert Williams of Brooklyn, New York.

What is "single-needle" stitching, and why do we have to pay more for shirts that feature it?

You'd think that at fifty dollars or more a pop, shirtmakers could afford another needle or two. Actually, they can.

"Regular" shirts are sewn with one needle working on one side of a seam and another needle sewing the other side. According to clothing expert G. Bruce Boyer, this method is cheaper and faster but not as effective because "Seams sewn with two needles simultaneously tend to pucker. Single-needle stitching produces flatter seams."

Submitted by Donald Marti, Jr., of New York, New York.

Why do dogs wiggle their rear legs when scratched on their belly or chest?

Maybe there is a Labrador retriever out there writing a book of canine Imponderables, trying to answer the mystery: Why do humans kick their legs up when you tap the area below their kneecaps? The leg wiggling of dogs is called the scratch reflex, the doggy equivalent of our involuntary knee-jerk reflex (or, as it is known to doctors, patellar reflex).

Anatomist Robert E. Habel, of Cornell University's College of Veterinary Medicine, wrote *Imponderables* that the scratch reflex allows veterinarians to diagnose neurological problems in dogs:

> Because the same spinal nerves pass all the way down to the midline of the chest and abdomen, you can stimulate the scratch reflex anywhere from the saddle region to the ventral midline. You can test the sensory function of many spinal nerves and the motor function of the nerves to the hind limb (they don't wiggle

DAVID FELDMAN

their forelimbs). If the dog moves the hind limb, it means the spinal cord is not severed between the origin of the nerve stimulated and the origins of the lumbar through first sacral nerves, but the cord may be injured above the level stimulated.

A dog is not necessarily injured if it doesn't exhibit the scratch reflex. In fact, Dr. Habel reports that his hound doesn't respond at all.

What function does the scratch reflex serve? Nobody knows for sure, but that doesn't stop dog experts from theorizing. Breeder and lecturer Fred Lanting believes that the wiggling might be a "feeble or partial attempt" to reach the area where you are scratching. Just as scratching ourselves sometimes causes the itch to migrate to other parts of the body, Lanting believes that scratching a dog may cause itchiness in other regions.

Dog expert and biology instructor Jeanette Hayhurst advances an even more fascinating theory, which is that the scratch reflex might help dogs survive. The movement of the back legs during the scratch reflex resembles the frantic movements of a puppy learning to swim. The scratch reflex might be an instinctive reaction to pressure on the abdomen, the method nature provides for a puppy to survive when thrown into the water. Newborn pups also need to pump their back legs in order to crawl to reach their mother's teat.

We'd like to think that our human knee-jerk reflex might also have a practical purpose, but we'll leave it to the dogs to solve this particular mystery.

Submitted by Shane Ellis of Mammoth Lakes, California.
Thanks also to Kurt Perschnick of Palatka, Florida; Sonya
Landholm of Boone, North Carolina; Alina Carmichael and Pat
Kirkland of Lake St. Louis, Missouri; Sherry-Lynn Jamieson of
Surrey, British Columbia; Sofi Nelson of Menomonie, Wisconsin;
and Scott Wolber of Delmont, Pennsylvania.

Whilst strolling alone in a garden, Robert quietly pulls out his notebook.

SUCH A CHARMING VERSE! AND — WHO'S TO KNOW ?!

THE BEST YET TO BE GROW OLD WITH ME

OOOOH!

Ideas

Why do so many sundials have Robert Browning's lines "Grow old along with me! The best is yet to be" inscribed on them?

Although not every sundial has a motto on it, most do; the tradition dates from antiquity. None of the many sundial makers and books about sundials we consulted could explain the reason for putting the motto on the sundial in the first place. Timothy Lynch, president of the sundial maker Kenneth Lynch & Sons, speculates that it was originally put there "for the personal gratification of either the maker or the receiver."

The sundial makers we spoke to have standard mottoes or will custom-inscribe a customer's personalized motto. They unanimously agreed with Lee Brown, a designer at Whitehall Products, who told *Imponderables* that virtually all mottoes refer to the passage of time.

Why are Browning's lines the most popular? (Their only competitor in popularity is *Tempus Fugit*—"time flies"—a pithier if less poetic motto.) Ben Brewster, president of Colonial Brass, the largest manufacturer of sundials in the United States, has a simple theory with which the other sources agreed: Most quotations about time are depressing, or at least downbeat. A look at some of the suggested inscriptions used by Colonial Brass will give you the idea:

> "Time takes all but memories."
> "Time waits for no man."
> "You ask the hour, meanwhile you see it fly."
> "Watch for ye know not the hour."
> "Time passeth and speaketh not."

Not the kind of words to send your losing football team bursting out of the locker room in renewed spirits, are they? But Browning's words are reassuring, making old age seem secure and downright romantic.

In her book *Sun-Dials and Roses of Yesterday,* Alice Morse writes:

> One almost unvarying characteristic of the sun-dial motto might be noted—its solemnity. A few are jocose, a few are cheerful, nearly all are solemn, many are sad, even gloomy. They teach no light lesson of life, but a regard of the passing of every day, every hour, as a serious thing.

Morse's book was written in 1922, when most mottoes were biblical quotations. (Her favorite was this far-from-upbeat citation from Chronicles: "Our days on earth are as a shadow, and there is none abiding.")

For better or worse, we live in a society that has a relentless need to find optimism in any situation. Perhaps our fondness for the Browning quote shows a deep-seated psychological need to evade not only death but some of the hardships of old age. After all, better to spout platitudes than to confront the pain in this actual motto sent to us by Brewster, who remarked that its message was a little less uplifting than Browning's bromide:

> What Cain did to Abel
> Brutus to Caesar was quick.
> What Kip B. and Esther's sister

Edith did to Esther and me
Was Torture—slow and fatal
May God forgive them.

Submitted by Sheryl Aumack of Newport Beach, California.

For a whole collection of sundial mottoes, see *The Book of Sun-Dials* by Mrs. Alfred Gatty.

Why do babies sleep so much? Why do they sleep so much more soundly than adults or older children?

This is Mother Nature's way of preserving the sanity of parents.

And there's an alternative, less cosmic, explanation. Dr. David Hopper, president of the American Academy of Somnology, told *Imponderables* that sleep is crucial to the brain development of infants. After birth, the average infant spends sixteen to eighteen hours asleep per day. Up to 60 percent of that time is spent in REM (rapid eye movement) sleep, more than twice the percentage of adults. What is the significance of their greater proportion of REM sleep? Dr. Hopper explains:

> REM sleep is the stage of sleep that dreams are associated with. Brain wave activity is very active during this stage and closely resembles an awake state. It is sometimes called paradoxical sleep because the brain is very active as if awake but the individual is deeply asleep. By one year of age, the brains of babies are sufficiently developed to begin cycling of four distinct NREM (non-rapid eye movement) sleep stages with REM sleep.

Although sleep researchers still do not understand precisely how this works, REM sleep seems crucial to the development of the central nervous system of infants. The NREM "quiet sleep" is far from a waste of time, though, for the pituitary hormones, crucial for growth, are released during this phase of sleep.

Parents will be glad to inform anyone willing to listen that their babies don't always sleep soundly, yet the cliché persists

DAVID FELDMAN

that anyone who can withstand interference from sound or light while snoozing is sleeping "like a baby." The solution to this paradox lies in the unique sleep cycle of newborns. The reason why babies sleep like a log much of the time, as we learned above, is because they are in REM sleep 50 to 60 percent of the time. It can be difficult to rouse an infant during REM sleep; yet the same baby might awaken quite easily when in any stage of NREM sleep.

The proportion of REM to NREM sleep gradually decreases during the first year of life, and babies sleep for longer periods at a stretch. Still, they may be fussier and wake up more easily, especially if they are being weaned from breast milk, which studies show truly does help babies "sleep like a baby."

Submitted by Father Gregory A. Battafarano of Niagara Falls, New York.

What causes the film that forms on the top of the chocolate pudding I cook? Does this film appear on any kind of pudding?

We went straight to the makers of Jell-O brand pudding. The General Foods Response Center replied:

> When pudding has been heated and then allowed to cool while directly exposed to air, the starch on the surface releases water. This evaporation hardens the texture of the top and causes a film to form on *any* pudding that requires cooking. Incidentally, if plastic wrap is placed directly on the surface of the pudding, while cooling, it prevents the water vapor from escaping and the film from forming.

General food researcher Noel Anderson told *Imponderables* that pudding film is actually a "starch gel," a combination of sugar and starch that forms a moisture barrier that will not break down unless subjected to intense heat.

Submitted by Linda Wiley of Berlin, New Jersey.

Why does milk obtain a skin when heated, while thicker liquids, like gravy, lose their skin when heated?

Proteins and starch react differently to heat. When heated, the protein in milk coagulates; the fat globules no longer can be suspended in water and, being lighter than water, float to the top. Bruce V. Snow, a dairy consultant, told us that the fat globules "adhere and form a surface skin when the liquid ceases to boil or simmer heavily."

But when gravy is heated, the starch, which has formed the skin in the first place, breaks down. Since starch is more soluble than protein, the result is that the ex-skin is reabsorbed into the rest of the gravy. The same process can be seen when soup is reheated after a skin has "grown" in the refrigerator.

Submitted by Beth Oakley of Ishpeming, Michigan.

Why do the tags on the left side of the right back pocket of Levi's jeans come in different colors? What is the code?

If you haven't noticed the different colors on the tags on the back pockets of Levi's jeans, you just haven't been looking at enough rear ends lately, or else it's time for that eye check-up you've been avoiding for the last five years or so. Actually, the folks at Levi Strauss & Co. call them "tabs," not tags.

Lynn Downey, the company historian, says that tabs were originally created to make Levi's stand out from the competition. Tabs were the brainchild of an in-house advertising manager in 1936, and have been on all Levi brand jeans ever since. The design of the tabs and their position on the jeans are registered trademarks of Levi Strauss & Co.

There are now four different colored tabs (red, orange, silver, and cream) and they do indeed signify something—the type of construction used to manufacture the jeans. Although the consumer may not be aware of it, Levi Strauss spokesperson Jill Novack told *Imponderables* that many stores place all of the red-tab Levi jeans together, the orange together, etc. Here, in descending order of sales, are the four different colored tabs and what they mean:

1. *Red*. Red-tab Levi's feature the classic, detailed construction: five high-sloped pockets; six rivets in the front pocket; single-needle work on the top stitching; double stitching on the back pocket, which flares slightly. All 501s have red labels, but so do many other popular styles: 505, 506, 509, 517, 550, 583, 584, etc.

2. *Orange*. Orange-tabs often look superficially like their red-tab counterparts. In fact, some lines, such as the 505 and 550, have both red- and orange-tab versions. But orange-tab jeans have slightly less expensive finishing and tend to cost a few dollars less than red-tab Levi's. Here's why: Orange-tabs have five rather than six rivets in front; more gradually sloping pockets; double-needle rather than single-needle work on the top stitching; and their pockets are simpler, with the stitching on the back pockets parallel rather than flared. Most of the 500 series not named above have orange tabs.

3. *Silver*. Levi's "fashion forward" contemporary jeans line features silver tabs. These jeans are identified by names rather than numbers, and are often available only on a seasonal basis. Baggy jeans, anti-fit, and sport jeans are all placed in the silver line. The silver line tends to contain the most expensive Levi jeans.

4. *Cream or Natural*. The rarest of the tabs is the so-called natural tab, with a cream color that is the untreated natural color of the tab fabric, with brown lettering. The natural tab can be found only on Levi's "Naturals" line, jeans that are, appropriately enough, naturally colored. Levi Strauss spokesperson Brad Williams told us that Naturals are softer to the touch than all their other jeans because they are the only ones that contain no dye. For technical reasons, starch must be used when applying dyes to jeans. As the consumer continues to wash most jeans, the starch gradually is eliminated from the garment. This lessening of the starch content is the reason why jeans get more comfortable after repeated washings.

Or course, *we* knew nothing about this color coding before we started researching this Imponderable. So the next time we

are in the market for 501's, we will undoubtedly become para-
lyzed with self-consciousness. Do we buy the red-tabs and prove
that we are fashion snobs of the worst order, demanding construction details that we never noticed in the first place? Or do
we try orange-tabs, and advertise to the rest of the world how
cheap we are?

*Submitted by Cathy Pearce and Heather McCausland of
Lakeland, Florida.*

How did Levi's 501 jeans get their number?

Levi Strauss (yes, there *was* a real Levi Strauss) was a dry goods
merchant in California and sold a wide range of products. The
original Levi jean was the 501, and this number was simply its
arbitrary stock number, according to Levi Strauss & Co. spokesperson Brad Williams.

Strauss disliked applying the word "jeans" to his garment,
so he promoted the 501 as "waist-high overalls." Just think, if
his company kept that name into the 1970s, chances are that
high-fashion designers like Gloria Vanderbilt and Calvin Klein
wouldn't have foisted "designer waist-high overalls" on a gulli-
ble public at triple the prices of Mr. Strauss.

*Submitted by Sharon Michele Burke of Los Altos, California.
Thanks also to John Hyatt of Boise, Idaho.*

Why do the bricks used in constructing houses come with three holes in them?

We have the feeling that when Lionel Richie and the Commo-
dores sang "Brick House," this wasn't what they had in mind. In

fact, we didn't even know there were holes in bricks until reader Sandra Sandoval brought this to our attention.

When we get a brick Imponderable, we know where to head —to the Brick Institute of America and its director of engineering and research, J. Gregg Borchelt. He informed us that these holes are known to brickophiles as "cores," and that there can be zero to twelve cores in a "unit," or individual brick. The main reason for the cores, according to Borchelt,

> is to improve the drying and firing process of the unit. The clay dries more easily and reaches a more uniform firing temperature with the cores present. Tests were conducted to show that the presence of cores does not reduce the overall strength of the brick.

But the cores serve many other purposes. Construction writer and consultant E.E. Halmos, Jr., of Poolesville, Maryland, told *Imponderables* that one of the main benefits of cores is that they provide a way for the mortar to penetrate the brick itself,

> thus making a better bond between layers (or courses) of brick, without the need for metal ties or other devices. A brick wall derives virtually no strength from the mortar—which is only to tie courses together. That's why the so-called Flemish or Belgian bonds were developed, to tie the outer and inner columns of brick (called "wythes") together in early construction—resulting in the interesting patterns you see in Williamsburg and older structures in other cities. The little holes provide a better vertical bond between the bricks.

Borchelt enumerated other advantages of cores: They lower the weight of the bricks without sacrificing strength; they are a receptacle for steel reinforcement, if needed; they make it easier to break units into brick bats; and they can aid in lifting large units. Bet you never guessed three holes could be so talented.

Submitted by Sandra Sandoval of San Antonio, Texas.

DAVID FELDMAN

Why do dogs eat standing up, while cats often eat sitting down?

No dog or cat would volunteer to answer this Imponderable, so we were forced to consult human experts. All agreed that the answer goes back to the ancestors of our pets, who lived in the wild.

Our most interesting response came from Dr. James Vondruska, research veterinarian and senior developmental scientist for pet food giant Quaker Oats Company. Vondruska reminds us that dogs are by nature pack animals. In the wild, they hunted in packs. In homes, they adopt the household as their pack and their owners as dominant members:

> In their prehistoric years, dogs lived with others of their type, and hunted or scavenged for food together. Many of their type, such as the African Cape Hunting Dog and the hyenas, still do. Scavenging dogs must compete with the pack members for their food, which often leads to fighting. For this reason, dogs will eat standing up, so that they can better protect their food. Even though they usually don't have to fight over their food anymore, the behavior persists in modern dogs.

Vondruska contrasts the dog's behavior in the wild with that of our house cat's ancestors. Most cats, even in the wild, are solitary creatures, and are hunters rather than scavengers. Susie Page, of the American Cat Association, compares the eating posture of cats to that of other hunting predators who "hunch" over their prey while devouring it.

With the exception of African lions, who live in prides, cats rarely had to contend with eating companions/rivals in the wild. This probably explains not only why cats today would feel secure eating in a more relaxed crouched or sitting position but also why cats eat languorously, while dogs eat at a pace that suggests that any meal might be their last.

Of course, cats as well as dogs often eat standing up, even while eating in comfortable surroundings from a bowl. Vondruska points out one big advantage to eating in a crouched position for both dogs and cats: "This is the only way in which they can use their paws to hold their food, and this is sometimes necessary when chewing bones."

Submitted by a caller on the Ray Briem Show, KABC-AM, Los Angeles, California.

DAVID FELDMAN

Christmas Cheer to light your Holidays

Wishing you a string of Christmas lights that stays lit all Yuletide through
MILDRED AND RALPH WATTS

Why do all the Christmas tree lights burn out when one burns out?

Many a Yuletide has been ruined by the blight of premature Christmas light burnout. So for those who have experienced the trauma of having one burnt-out bulb turning your rainbow of illumination into a cavelike darkness, we have one word of advice for you. Upgrade.

If you experience this problem, your Christmas lights are *series*-wired. In series wiring, each bulb acts like a fuse; if one bulb burns out, the circuit is broken. Some sets have a shunt wire that allows the electricity to pass into the next socket if one bulb burns out, but no series-wired set will work if a bulb is removed from its socket. If your set does not have a functioning shunt wire, all you need to do is locate the missing bulb and replace it in order to close the circuit.

E. H. Scott, of J. Hofert Co., a leading supplier of Christmas trees and decorations, told *Imponderables* that many consumers are confused about how to replace bulbs in series-connected sets. To find the appropriate bulb, you merely divide the voltage standard (120 volts) by the number of bulbs in the set. If you have a set of 20 lights, you would need a six-volt bulb.

Of course, most families keep Christmas lights originally bought during the Stone Age. Most contemporary Christmas light sets have forsaken series wiring for *parallel* wiring. In this configuration, each bulb burns independently, so that 120 volts are directed to each bulb. The current will flow even if one or more bulbs burn out.

Why did manufacturers use series wiring when parallel wiring was so much more convenient? Hy Greenblatt, representative of the Manufacturers of Illuminating Products, gave us the answer we expected: Parallel wiring is harder to manufacture and considerably more expensive to produce.

Submitted by O.J.J.R. Jennings of Henderson, Nevada. Thanks also to Gregg Gariepy of Muskego, Wisconsin.

Why are Yellow Freight System trucks painted orange?

Consistency is the refuge of small minds. Let Yellow Cab Companies all over North America paint their fleets yellow. Trucking giant Yellow Freight System has a more highly evolved imagination.

We got the answer to this Imponderable from Mark J. Spencer, a friendly man with an unlikely job—art curator for Yellow Freight. Spencer is also, as he puts it, "the unofficial archivist of the unofficial archives and thus the unofficial historian" of his company.

Yellow Freight was founded by A. J. Harrell, who ran a taxi service, the Yellow Cab Company of Oklahoma City, in the early 1920s. A.J. started the Yellow Cab Transit Co., a bus service, in 1924, and, more important for our purposes, opened a truck ter-

DAVID FELDMAN

minal in Oklahoma City. Starting with two trucks, what was then known as the Yellow Transit Company, and later Yellow Transit Freight Lines, gobbled up several other companies and became the Yellow Freight System, now one of the three largest freight companies in the United States, with more than 600 terminals and 30,000 employees.

So why did Harrell, who named all of his companies "Yellow," paint his trucks orange? The evidence indicates that at the very beginning of his freight company, the trucks were not painted any particular color. But Harrell was obsessed with safety, and in the late 1920s or early 1930s, he commissioned the E. I. Dupont Company to determine precisely which shade of color was most visible from the farthest distance. Dupont's answer: the "swamp holly orange" color you see on all of the tractors of Yellow Freight System.

Faithful readers of *Imponderables* already know that the amber and red shades found on traffic stoplights were selected for the same reason. Yellow Freight's orange looks like a blend of those two stoplight colors.

Submitted by Paola Sica of Lawrence, Kansas. Thanks also to Bethany Franko of Spring Valley, Ohio; and Jared Martin of Kokomo, Indiana.

Why has the orange-colored coffee pot become the symbol for decaffeinated coffee in restaurants?

Obviously, it behooves the customer and restaurateur to have easily identifiable coffee pots on hand, for no waiter or customer can discriminate visually between "regular" and decaffeinated coffee. But the orange rim on restaurant coffee pots is no accident—it is the color associated with Sanka brand decaffeinated coffee, the first and best-selling decaffeinated coffee in North America.

The developer of Sanka coffee, European coffee magnate

Ludwig Roselius, realized the commercial potential of a coffee that didn't produce nervousness, sleeplessness, and indigestion in caffeine-sensitive coffee drinkers, but his chemists could not devise a process to remove more than half the caffeine while retaining the richness of ordinary coffee.

Supposedly, when a shipment of coffee was traveling between South America and Europe, a storm flooded the coffee with sea water. Although the coffee was ruined for commercial purposes, Roselius's researchers discovered that the salt water had naturally leached the caffeine out of the coffee but kept the taste intact. Roselius soon marketed a 97 percent caffeine-free product under several different brand names throughout Europe and called the product Sanka (a contraction of *sans caffeine*— "without caffeine") in France.

When Roselius brought Sanka to the United States in the 1920s, the product was introduced in restaurants in New York City, and packaged Sanka was sold over the counter for home consumption. (Only later, when customer incredulity that the taste of a decaffeinated coffee could be palatable waned, was Sanka sold in grocery stores.) Institutional sales of Sanka have represented a substantial part of the brand's sales ever since. When General Foods bought the company from Roselius in 1932, it not only advertised to home consumers but aggressively marketed Sanka to restaurants, institutional food services, and offices.

General Food's Sanka food service division developed the orange pots you see in restaurants and in the coffee room in your office. Subliminally, General Foods hopes, you will equate orange with decaf. This identification is important enough to General Foods that, according to Nan Redmond, director of corporate affairs, the integrity of the color has been assured by trademarking the "Sanka Orange."

In many cases, Sanka/General Foods provides both the coffee maker and orange pots for free to institutions that buy Sanka brand coffee, ensuring that most of the time when we pick up a cup of Sanka brand outside our homes, the drink has been poured from a "Sanka orange" coffee pot. Although General

Foods wishes that every drop of decaffeinated coffee served in restaurants were Sanka brand, the company can't keep establishments from serving other brands in orange-rimmed pots. If you see a green-colored pot, it means that Folger Decaf has invaded Sanka territory.

Submitted by K. David Steidley of Short Hills, New Jersey. Thanks also to Craig Kirkland of Greenville, North Carolina, and April Williams of Richton Park, Illinois.

Why are "contemporary" or slightly risqué greeting cards invariably long and narrow in shape?

This size is known in the greeting card trade as a "studio" card because their earliest merchandisers were Greenwich Village artists who worked out of their studios. Studio cards emerged just after the end of World War II, created by returning veterans, and could be found in any greeting card section by the 1950s. The long, narrow configuration of the studio card attracted attention on the retail shelf; it differed drastically from the boxy, conventionally sized card. To this day, when we see a group of long, narrow greeting cards in a shop, we assume that they are "funny" or "contemporary."

Although no one seems to know the identity of the inventor of the studio card, chances are he or she was attracted to the size more by financial considerations than marketing ones. Product could be cut from conventional card stock with only one fold. Perhaps even more importantly, the studio card fit snugly into standard number 10 envelopes, which meant that the artists could obtain readily available envelopes inexpensively. Michael DeMent, product spokesperson for Hallmark, told *Imponderables* that many early artists sold studio cards to retail accounts without envelopes. With lower costs, artists could pass the savings on to their retail accounts, and consumers didn't mind—they simply placed the card in one of their own number 10 envelopes at home.

You can no longer assume that all funny cards are studio size. Hallmark has a division called Shoebox Greetings, which it facetiously calls "a tiny little division of Hallmark," which is like a guerrilla operation within the conservative giant. Although Shoebox cards are always humorous, their conventional size does not betray their offbeat attitude.

In a business totally dominated by Hallmark in the 1950s, artists saw a niche: greeting cards, heretofore, were almost exclusively a women's product. Even today, according to DeMent, about 90 percent of the products sold in Hallmark stores are bought by women. Hallmark's rival, American Greetings, was the first major card company to capitalize on the studio card format, with its Hi-Brows line, begun in 1956.

Many of the original studio cards were sarcastic in tone and often off-color in subject matter. Some featured unclad or scantily clad females, which gave any card of that size a risqué reputation that persists even today. That's why although you'll now see many humorous cards in conventional sizes, you'll never find that Mother's Day card, full of sweet roses on the outside and even sweeter verse inside, in the naughty studio size.

Submitted by Caryl Jost of Cleveland, Ohio.

What good does a "Falling Rock" sign do? How are we supposed to adjust our driving when we see a "Falling Rock" sign?

We know what Laurie Hutler means. Driving along a mountain pass and seeing a "Falling Rock" sign always leaves us with free-floating anxiety. Are we supposed to crane our necks and look up at the mountain to spot tumbling rocks? If so, how are we supposed to keep our eyes on the road?

"Falling Rock" signs are usually placed on roadways adjacent to rocky cliffs. You are supposed to worry about rocks on the road, not rocks tumbling down slopes.

Of course, traffic engineers know that we are going to be more anxious once we see a "Falling Rock" sign, and that is one of the reasons the sign is there in the first place. Anxious drivers proceed more slowly than complacent drivers. The chief of the traffic engineering division of the Federal Highway Administration told *Imponderables* that "By alerting the motorist to the

DAVID FELDMAN

potential hazard, the motorist should be able to react more quickly if a rock is encountered." If the motorist slows down, he or she can choose to drive over small rocks; at faster speeds, accidents are created when drivers swerve to avoid such obstacles. At slow speeds, the option of driving around a larger rock is more feasible.

The "Falling Rock" sign is one of the few warning signs for which there are no federal standards. Some jurisdictions use more accurately worded signs, such as "Caution Rocks May Be on Road" or "Watch for Rocks on Road." New York State chooses to use the wording "Fallen Rocks," which manages to be briefer than these other alternatives while simultaneously making it clear that the greater danger is rocks on the road rather than rocks from above.

The State of New York's Department of Transportation indicated how important brevity is in the effectiveness of warning signs. After reiterating the greater semantic precision of "Fallen" over "Falling," the director of the traffic and safety division, R. M. Gardeski, elaborates:

> Naturally we want sign legends to be as precise as possible, but absolutely precise legends often would be too long and complicated to be effective. Drivers have only a few seconds to read, understand, and react to each sign. Precision has to be balanced with the length and size of the legend to produce signs that can be read and understood quickly and easily. Even if it were more grammatically correct to do otherwise, we might still have chosen "Fallen" over "Falling" so the legend could be larger and more readable.

That's right. New York's "Falling" vs. "Fallen" decision was made partly because "Fallen" contains one less letter than "Falling."

Donald L. Woods, a research engineer at the Texas Transportation Institute, has a refreshing perspective on the problems with warning signs:

> Unfortunately, the public presses for warnings of all kinds and the tort liability situation forces government to install far too many warning signs. This results in far too many warning signs

being used on our nation's street and highway system. My favorites are "Church" and "Slow Children."

The "Church" warning sign must mean to watch out because that church is really something. Possibly Brother Swaggart's church should have had such a sign. The "Slow Children" warning sign completely mystifies me. Why should folks want to advertise that their children were not too bright?

Obviously, Mr. Woods's tongue was planted firmly in cheek, but his point is well taken. By oversigning, traffic planners risk desensitizing motorists to the danger implicit in the sign.

Submitted by Laurie Hutler of Boulder Creek, California.

Why is there no apostrophe on the flashing "DONT WALK" traffic signal?

Because an apostrophe just uses up space. If you can believe that one of the main reasons New York uses "Fallen Rocks" rather than "Falling Rocks" is because "Fallen" is one letter shorter, why wouldn't you believe that an apostrophe is dead weight?

After all, traffic signs are designed for motorists in moving vehicles who are some distance away. Research has shown that punctuation marks aren't even perceived from a distance. If a punctuation mark isn't noticed, then it is redundant. Any word, mark, or even letter that doesn't add to the meaning of the sign will be eliminated. By using "PED XING" rather than "PEDESTRIAN CROSSING" on signs, the letters can be made larger without a lessening of motorist comprehension.

According to Victor H. Liebe, director of education and

training for the American Traffic Safety Services Association, punctuation "is rarely used on any traffic sign or signal except for certain parking signs, which are usually read from a very slowly moving or stopped vehicle."

Submitted by Bruce W. Miller of Riverside, Connecticut.

DAVID FELDMAN

Why does rinsing with hot water "set" a stain? Why is rinsing with cold water more effective in eliminating the stain?

First the good news. As you increase the temperature of the water applied to a stain, the solubility of the stain also increases. Obviously, dissolving the stain is a good first step in eliminating the stain.

Now the bad news. In practice, most of the time, "dissolving" the stain translates into *spreading* the stain. Usually, hot water helps break up the stain, but it doesn't lift the stain; rather, it allows stains to penetrate deeper into the fiber. Oily stains, especially on synthetics, have this reaction. Once the stain sets deeply enough in a fabric, detergents or dry cleaning are often ineffective.

In other cases, hot water can actually create a chemical change in the stain itself that hampers removal. Protein stains are a good example of this problem, as Lever Brothers spokes-person Sheryl Zapcic illustrates:

> One common type of stain that can be set by hot water is a protein stain. If protein is a component of the stain, rinsing with hot water will coagulate the protein. For example, egg white, which is a protein, can be loosened with cold water without co-agulating; however, hot water will immediately coagulate the egg white. Technically, this is called denaturation of the protein. In any event, the stain becomes insoluble or set.

On some stains, it won't matter much whether hot or cold water is used.

Our own rule of thumb on this subject is: Nothing works. We have been in fancy French restaurants where our dining companions insist that "only club soda can get that stain out of your tie." Of course, we never have club soda at hand. To placate our true believer, we end up ordering a glass. And, *naturelle-ment,* the stain lingers as an enduring testament to our naïve belief that we will one day get a stain out of a garment success-fully.

Submitted by Pamela Gibson of Kendall Park, New Jersey.

Why is the bark of a tree darker than the wood inside?

Depends on how and where you slice it. Actually, there is more than one bark in a tree. A living inner bark, called the phloem, is relatively light in color and is composed of the same cells as wood. When the enzymes in phloem are exposed to air, oxida-tion darkens it, just as a peeled apple or banana discolors when exposed to air.

The outer bark of a tree, called the rhytidome, is dark. Dark and dead. The main purpose of the rhytidome is to protect the inside of the tree, so it contains tannins (acids used in tanning and in medicine), phenols, and waxes, which help form a barrier

DAVID FELDMAN

to protect the tree from invading fungi and insects. These protective substances are the source of the outer bark's dark color. The degree to which the color of outer and inner barks of trees compare to their wood varies considerably, as John A. Pitcher, of the Hardwood Research Council, explains:

> The concentration of tannins, waxes, and phenols varies from tree to tree and between species. Tannins are still extracted from bark for use in the leather curing process (e.g., genuine oak-tanned leathers). On the other hand, [lighter-colored] wine bottle corks come from the dead inner bark of the corkbark oak, *Quercus suber*. The bark is nearly the same color as the wood itself.

Submitted by Jill Davies of Forest, Mississippi.

Why do seven-layer cakes usually have fewer than seven layers?

We faced this investigation with the seriousness of Geraldo Rivera. But the bakers we spoke to laughed about the "scandal of the missing layers."

A survey of bakeries in the City of Brotherly Love, Philadelphia, yielded not only guffaws but the startling revelation that the true seven-layer cake is an endangered species. The baker at D'Elain Pastries simply said, "People call it seven-layer cake, but it's not seven layers. It's four or five." The closest the Swiss Bakery could come up with is a Dobosh cake, which has four layers of cake and three layers of frosting. Seven layers would "make too big of a cake." At least the Eclair Bake Shoppe makes true seven-layer cakes at Passover, but its spokesperson indicated that most other bakeries don't make them anymore. They take too much time to lay out.

We understand why, in the world of commerce, cakes might become inflated in price and deflated in layers, but even cookbooks designed for home bakers conspire to eliminate the purity of the seven-layer cake. In his book *Practical Baking*, William Sultan begins his recipe with "Prepare 7 sheet pans . . .", clearly indicating the intent of producing a true seven-layer pastry. But then why does the accompanying picture show a cake with only six layers?

At least Susan Purdy, author of *A Piece of Cake*, owns up to the confusion. Before presenting her recipe, she muses:

> . . . I remember, as a child, always counting the layers just to check, feeling triumphant when the number varied, as it often did and still does, from the seven we consider traditional to nine or even twelve, depending upon the whim of the chef. Now the choice is yours . . .

We really couldn't find anyone in the bakery trade who was upset about the misnamed seven-layer cake. Bakery engineering consultant Dr. Simon S. Jackel told us that most cakes have thick layers. The idea of the seven-layer cake was to create not a thicker cake but a normal-sized cake with extremely thin layers. To Jackel, all that is important in creating an authentic seven-layer cake is to make sure that each layer is separated by icing or filling.

May we offer a humble suggestion? How about bakeries simply calling their offerings "layer cakes"?

Submitted by Gerald Stoller of Spring Valley, New York.

Why is the part of bills that needs to be sent back by customers often too large for the envelope it is to be sent back in, forcing customers to fold the bill stub?

Harper Audio makes cassette versions of *Imponderables* books in a quiz format. A question is posed by Dave "Alex Trebek" Feldman, and three characters, A, B, and C, provide possible answers. Two of them are bluffs, and one is the correct answer.

The task of the listener is to identify which of the three alternatives is correct.

Obviously, in order to use an Imponderable on the tape, we need to conjure up two viable bluffs. This subject is a particular peeve of ours, and the fact that seven readers felt strongly enough about it to write to us indicates that it is plaguing men, women, and children throughout the Western world. One problem arose in using it on the tape: We couldn't think of two decent bluffs.

Why in the world would any company, a utility or phone company or credit card company, ever supply an envelope too small for the stub? The only sensible explanation we could come up with was that chintzy companies were trying to save money by not purchasing larger envelopes.

We are overjoyed. After consulting several business forms and stationery manufacturers, and all of the relevant trade associations, we are pleased to report that the answer to this Imponderable is simple: Our gut instinct was right—there *is* absolutely *no* reason for providing a stub that doesn't fit into the envelope (many envelopes provided for paying bills are also too small to accommodate a check without folding it over, but we'll let this pass). These companies have simply screwed up!

Not since we tackled the insanity of the issue of why there are ten hot dogs in a package but only eight hot dog buns in a package in *Why Do Clocks Run Clockwise?* have we encountered an Imponderable with less reason for being or that makes grown men and women look so silly.

Several of the authorities we contacted were as befuddled and frustrated by this incompetence as we are—for example, Maynard H. Benjamin, executive vice-president of the Envelope Manufacturers Association of America:

> The reason that the bills are larger than the envelopes is that the individuals who procure the envelopes sometimes do not talk to the individuals that work in the billing department. As a result, in some cases the bills are larger than the envelopes; in other cases, the envelopes are much larger than the bills. If we could ever get both of these individuals talking together, your question

would probably be unnecessary. Believe it or not, in most cases the envelopes and bills are designed and procured by the same person.

In the latter case, then, we hope that the "talking together" will not be out loud.

Is there any hope to end this crisis? The popularity of window envelopes is forcing forms analysts to size the bills properly; if they don't, the address won't show through the window. Otherwise, the only answer is education. One of our contacts, the Business Forms Management Association, Inc., provides continuing education on these types of subjects; its executive director, Andy Palatka, wrote us:

> The Business Forms Management Association, the international society for forms professionals, has existed since 1958 to provide the training, networking, and information needed to improve productivity in the workplace through forms-systems integration.

We have no idea what forms-systems integration means, but it sure sounds important, and although it is not our policy to endorse associations and their educational programs, we hope that every company that sends out bills (and, judging from our mail, there are a lot of them) hires folks with Ph.D.s in forms-systems integration. After all, it must take incredible savvy to design a stub small enough to fit into an actual envelope. Ain't this a wonderful world?

Submitted by Bert Garwood of Grand Forks, North Dakota. Thanks also to Dorothy Kiddie of Nashua, New Hampshire; Sharon Sherriff of Alameda, California; John Hevlow of Idaho Falls, Idaho; John Beton of Chicago, Illinois; Rev. Ken Vogler of Jeffersonville, Indiana; and John R. Green of Cincinnati, Ohio.

Why are men's neckties tapered at the bottom?

Neckties don't *have* to be tapered on the bottom. In fact, they weren't until the early twentieth century. Before then, ties were cut straight down from a piece of material. But now, the vast majority of silk ties are cut on a bias (on an angle to the floor). According to fashion writer G. Bruce Boyer, there are two main benefits to cutting on an angle: it produces a tie "more impervious to the rigors of knotting and maximizes the natural elasticity of the silk."

When the end of the necktie is finished, it is "trimmed square" (along the lines of the weave) so that the end forms a natural point. The larger point, the one presented to the outside world, is known as the "blade" or "apron" end, and the smaller, covered-up point is known as the "upper end."

Have you ever noticed that knitted ties are not tapered on

DAVID FELDMAN

the bottom? You may have figured out the reason already. Knitted ties (whether made out of yarn or silk) are cut and seamed straight across the blade end, rather than on a bias—circumstantial evidence that ties are tapered for purely functional rather than aesthetic reasons.

Submitted by Sonja Trojak of Brandon, Florida.

Why do stripes on neckties always run in the same direction? And why do American ties run in the opposite direction from English ties?

We don't mind our books being browsed and sampled in random dollops, in the bathroom or in more prestigious rooms of your castle, but if you haven't read the previous chapter, please read it. We'll wait for you.

Now that you have mastered the intricacies of tie cutting, you are ready for the simple answer. The reason why the stripes are all on the same angle is that the stripes on the bolt, before the material is cut, are in perfectly horizontal position. The angle is achieved by cutting on the bias.

Although the origin of the practice is lost in antiquity, American tiemakers traditionally cut their material face up, while the English cut it face down. We don't know whether this discrepancy has anything to do with squeamishness or prudishness on the Brits' part (a culture that gave us Johnny Rotten and Sheena Easton can't be *that* afraid of stripes) or some technical requirement of machinery. But we do know the end result: The stripe

DAVID FELDMAN

on an American tie will run from the right on top and downwards to the left, while the English will slant in the opposite direction.

The striped tie originated in England in 1890, where different stripes were used to identify particular military regiments and, later, schools and clubs. One expert recounts a theory that the English stripe stems from the left side so that it will "descend from the heart." Another source speculates that Americans consciously rebelled against English tradition. We've heard the latter theory used to explain everything from why we drive on the right side of the road to why we, unlike the British, put our fork down and switch hands when eating meat. But we think it's a tad preposterous to believe that long after the Civil War, American tiemakers were still trying to fight the revolutionary war.

Submitted by Mary Jo Hildyard of West Bend, Wisconsin. Thanks also to Jill Palmer of Leverett, Massachusetts; Ed Hawkins of Warner Robins, Georgia; and Fletcher Eddens of Wilmington, North Carolina.

What is the purpose of the oil found in the head of sperm whales?

Sperm whales lend a new dimension to the term "greasy." Their spermaceti oil is located in their "case," a trunk about five feet deep and ten to twelve feet long, and nearly the entire depth, breadth, and length of their heads. Surely, this odd anatomical arrangement must have a function. But what is it? In his 1991 book *Men and Whales*, Richard Ellis stated the problem:

> When some ancient Europeans first discovered a dead sperm whale on a beach (sperm whales are notorious stranders), they were unable to explain the clear amber liquid in its head, and guessed that it was the animal's seminal fluid. . . . Hundreds of years later we know the fluid is not the seed of the whale, but we do not know what the whale uses it for.

But this hasn't stopped aquatic researchers from theorizing over the last two centuries. Here are some of the more intriguing hypotheses:

1. *The oil provides buoyancy.* This is the "answer" found in most encyclopedias and books about whales. The lighter specific gravity of the oil allows the sperm whale to rise to the surface of the water with less effort, an obvious advantage to a mammal that must breath air. Buoyancy helps keep the whale's blow hole above the surface of the water, so that it can inhale and exhale without water constantly streaming into its respiration apparatus.

Why does a sperm whale need greater buoyancy than other whales? The main reason is that the sperm whale has a huge head, and its jaws contain the largest teeth not only of any whale but of any animal. Without the buoyancy lent by the oil, the weight of the jaws and teeth would make the whale's head "bottom-heavy."

The biggest flaw of this theory is that the very buoyancy that allows sperm whales to glide effortlessly on the surface of the water would also require them to struggle when attempting deep dives.

2. *The oil facilitates movement in the water.* The trunk that contains the oil might dispense oil to a particular section of the case to increase the specific gravity of that end. By shifting the oil to one end, the whale can change direction much more easily.

3. *The oil protects whales from the effects of nitrogen.* Nitrogen buildup creates decompression sickness in whales, and sperm whales dive deeper than any other whale. Some theorize that spermaceti oil is capable of filtering out nitrogen from the respiratory and circulatory system. In the past, hunters of sperm whales often found themselves slimed in the worst possible way: Not only did they come away full of oil, but they were beset by other, more serious calamities—severe skin irritations and even temporary blindness. Sea water and oxygen wouldn't cause such a reaction. Perhaps the oil literally carries the nitrogen out of the whale's system.

4. *The oil might be a food source.* Dr. Robert R. Rofen, of the Aquatic Research Institute, wrote *Imponderables* that many aquatic animals store their energy in the form of oil—lipids for future use when their food supply is down.

5. *The oil is used in sound production.* Humpback whales are

DAVID FELDMAN

not the only whales to produce sound. Sperm whales emit high-pitched "wails" and locate objects by sensing how and where their sounds bounce back to them. When on the prowl, there is evidence to suggest that they may incapacitate and stun their prey by producing a sound more piercing than Yoko Ono at her worst. Nobody knows for sure what role the oil may play in production of the scream.

6. *The oil allows whales to dive deeper.* Even though the added buoyancy provided by the spermaceti oil acts to make deep diving more difficult, the case that holds the oil might act as a force pump, drawing in air when necessary and, more importantly, preventing air from escaping when the whale is deep below the surface. The facilitation of oxygen flow between nostrils and lungs is crucial in allowing sperm whales to dive deeper than other whales, but the role of the oil itself in the process is unclear.

7. *The oil provides equilibrium for the whale regardless of what depth it is.* When sperm whales dive, they are hungry. Researchers note that although sperm whales plunge as deep as ten thousand feet, when they resurface, they arrive in the same spot from which they launched. The inescapable conclusion is that the whales are not cruising around but rather descending vertically to the ocean floor and resting there until a promising group of squid or other prey passes overhead.

The natural tendency of the spermaceti-laden whale is to rise to the surface, so adherents of this theory suggest that when sperm whales want to rest on the ocean floor, they fill their nasal passages with water. We are talking about *major* nasal passages here. They are capable of ingesting hundreds of thousands of pounds of water! Since the water is cooler than the sperm oil it now mixes with, it cools and condenses the oil, lowering the buoyancy. Thus, by regulating the amount of water it ingests through its nostrils, the whale can "choose" whether it wants to be buoyant (not ingest water) or to lie on the ocean floor (cram all the water in its nose it can).

All of these theories have some merit, but we must admit that the last is the most inviting, if only because it is the most inclusive.

Submitted by Dan Arick of New York, New York.

Why do women put perfume on their wrists?

We've wondered the same thing. When we pass through the cosmetics counters of department stores, we see women applying perfume to their wrists and then sniffing intently. Why not on their fingers? The back of their hands? Their arms? Their underarms?

What do they know that men don't know? A cursory poll of some females indicated that most of them had no idea why they put perfume on their wrists. But it turns out that there is a method to their madness. Irene L. Malbin, of the Cosmetic, Toiletry, and Fragrance Association, explains:

> Women put perfume on their wrists because there is a pulse point there. Pulse points are located wherever the pulse of the heartbeat is closest to the surface of the skin. The heat generated by the pulse point will intensify a perfume's impact.

Malbin lists other pulse points: behind the ears, the nape of the neck, the bosom, the crook of the elbows, behind the knees, and at the ankles. Obviously, it is easier for a consumer to apply perfume to the wrist than the back of the knee, at least in a department store.

All of this makes perfect sense. But then why don't men apply cologne to *their* wrists? Or do they?

Submitted by Jesse Flores of Henrico, Virginia.

Why do pretzels have their strange shape?

We don't know how every source we read or contacted dated the origin of the pretzel to Italy in A.D. 610, considering that none of them can point to the identity of the inventor or the exact location. But all agree that the pretzel was invented by a monk who used it as a reward for students who recited their catechism properly.

According to the conventional wisdom, the shape was not an accident, and it had nothing to do with expediency in baking. The Italian word for pretzel, *bracciatelli* (variously translated as "small arms" and "folded arms") is the clue: The shape of the pretzel was meant to resemble the arms of a child in prayer. Norma Conley, a self-professed pretzel historian and president of the Pretzel Museum in Philadelphia, told *Imponderables* that in medieval times, people prayed by putting their arms across their chest in a cross shape, placing each hand on the opposite shoulder.

The shape of boys' arms in prayer, and not the letter B, a

knot, or parts of the human body, are what the pretzel was designed to look like. Conley reports that pictures of pretzels can be found in early bibles, sometimes used as page borders.

This said, we would still not be surprised if the monk story was apocryphal. But it's all we have, at present.

Occasionally, rituals around the world take advantage of the unusual shape of the pretzel. A woodcut from the seventeenth century, found in a cathedral in Switzerland, shows the pretzel used as a nuptial knot—a wishbone, of sorts. The bride and groom each pulled on one side of the pretzel; whoever grabbed the larger piece had his or her dreams come true. The two linked arms and ate the pretzel, and the possessor of the short end pretended that the inevitable loss of face involved in losing this contest wouldn't ruin the marriage irreparably.

In parts of Europe, even today, the pretzel is used as a good-luck charm. In Germany, for example, many folks wear a pretzel on a loop around their necks on New Year's Eve. (Try doing that with a pretzel stick!) Supposedly, the pretzel necklace brings them good luck and a long life. If nothing else, it gives them something salty to eat to motivate them to drink more beer—another, less esoteric, German New Year's Eve custom.

Submitted by Jacob Schneider of Norwalk, Ohio.

Why do disposable lighters have two separate fluid chambers, even though the fluid can flow between the two?

One look at Bic's disposable lighter reveals the seemingly needless use of two chambers. When we queried folks at Bic and other lighter manufacturers, representatives calmly and without defensiveness denied that there were two chambers in their lighters.

Not until we heard from Linda Kwong, public relations manager at Bic, did we get the answer: Our eyes deceived us. There *aren't* two chambers, but . . .

The wall of plastic that makes up the fuel reservoir portion of the main body has to be reinforced with a cross rib or web to assure that this containment vessel will exceed the high pressure of the fuel. This cross rib gives the *appearance* of two separate chambers.

Submitted by Joseph P. McGowan of Glenolden, Pennsylvania. Thanks also to Dori Moore of Wheelersburg, Ohio.

In *Do Penguins Have Knees?*, our readers obsessed about bubble gum, but this time around, we seem to have a new junk food obsession: Just what are they putting into those soft drinks of ours?

What ingredient in diet drinks provides the one calorie? Why do some diet drinks have one calorie and some have no calories?

Let's solve the second part of this Imponderable first. Most diet drinks, ones containing aspartame or saccharin, contain less than one calorie per twelve-ounce can but more than one half-calorie. Whether or not the drink gets promoted as "zero calories" or "one calorie," then, usually depends upon how the marketer defines a serving size. Six ounces is the most popular serving size in the soft drink industry. If a twelve-ounce can of diet soda contains .66 of a calorie, then a six-ounce serving would contain .33 of a calorie. Because all figures are rounded off on nutritional labels, this soft drink can be advertised as containing zero calories.

A few soft drinks with mostly artificial sweeteners contain some natural flavorings, such as fruit juice, that contribute a meaningful number of calories (the flavored ginger ales marketed by Canada Dry and Schweppes contain a whopping two

DAVID FELDMAN

calories per six-ounce serving). But for the most part, the contributors to any caloric content in artificially sweetened drinks comes from trace carbohydrates and other elements in flavorings.

So don't blame the sweetener if you binge on one of those fattening one-calorie diet drinks. NutraSweet brand, the most popular artificial sweetener for soft drinks, is made of two amino acids, which are, technically, protein components. So aspartame has the same caloric count, per gram, as the protein in a T-Bone steak—four calories per gram. Fortunately for the dieter, the amount of aspartame in a soft drink doesn't compare to the weight of the protein in a steak. Phyllis Rosenthal, consumer affairs analyst for NutraSweet, explains:

> Since NutraSweet is 200 times sweeter than sugar, only a small amount is needed to sweeten products. Therefore, it contributes negligible calories to a product. A level teaspoon of sugar has 16 calories while the amount of NutraSweet with equivalent sweetness has 0.007 calories.
>
> One 12-ounce carbonated beverage contains approximately 180 mg of NutraSweet, a very small amount, which provides a negligible amount of calories.

Negligible yes. But sometimes enough to push a drink over the precipice into one caloriedom. Of course, then the soft drink company can decide that a serving size should really be three ounces, and the product magically becomes zero calories all over again.

Submitted by Barry Long of Alexandria, Virginia.

Why do diet colas, but not sugared colas, contain phenylalanine? Isn't phenylalanine the same substance found in chocolate?

Relax, Jon. Phenylalanine is one of those two amino acids we referred to above that are used to make aspartame (the other is aspartic acid). You can find phenylalanine in all kinds of foods, including meats, grains, dairy products, and sometimes even chocolate.

If a soda uses sugar as its sweetening agent, it won't contain phenylalanine.

Submitted by Jon. L. Carleen of Chepachet, Rhode Island.

What is brominated vegetable oil, and why is it found only in orange soda?

BVO, as it is known in the trade, is used as a stabilizing agent in beverages. Actually, it is in many other citrus drinks besides orange sodas. BVO consists of a vegetable oil base—usually soybean, but occasionally cottonseed—combined with bromine. You can't taste BVO because it is used in minute amounts.

BVO keeps the flavoring ingredients in sodas from separating from the rest of the drink. It is much less convenient to shake a bottle of carbonated orange soda than it is to shake a carton of orange juice that has been sitting in the refrigerator for a few days. At least, it's more convenient if you are the one who has to clean up the mess from shaking the soft drink.

BVO adds a side benefit, as well, for it is also a clouding agent, lending the liquid a more opaque appearance. Subliminally, the consumer might think of an orange drink as healthier

DAVID FELDMAN

because the opaqueness conjures up an image of actual food, a pulpy, fruit-based rather than a chemical- and flavorings-based beverage.

Submitted by William Rockenstire of Poestenkill, New York.

How do they put the pockets in pita bread?

Who would have ever thought that the pocket is created without human hands intervening? Bakery engineer Simon S. Jackel, director of Plymouth Technical Services, explains:

> Pita bread is placed in the oven as a thin, solid piece of dough. There is no pocket in the dough when it goes into the oven. But the oven temperature is so high, about 900 degrees Fahrenheit, that there is a rapid, explosive expansion of the water in the dough, causing the formation of a pocket by literally ripping the bottom part of the dough piece from the top dough piece. Total baking time at this high temperature is only one and one-half to two minutes.

Submitted by James Frisch of Great Neck, New York.

Why do we wear caps and gowns at graduations? Why are the caps flat and square? What does the color of gowns signify?

The first organized institutions of higher learning appeared in Paris and Bologna in the early twelfth century. In this era, virtually everyone, male and female, old and young, wore long flowing robes that didn't look too different from our graduation gowns of today. Rich people might have worn silk robes with ornamentation while the poor wore plain, coarse wool robes, but the style varied little.

Robes were in vogue until around 1600, when gowns were generally worn only by older and professional men. By the end of the seventeenth century, only legal and other officials wore gowns. But by the time robes for men had become passé, they had long been prescribed for use as academic garb, especially by English universities, and the tradition of wearing gowns at graduation had stuck.

In Roman law, a slave was freed when he was allowed to wear a cap. This symbol of emancipation might have been the inspiration for Oxford adopting the practice of placing a cap on the recipient of a Master's of Art when he graduated. The cap symbolized independence for the former bachelor.

Why was the hat square? Square hats called birettas were already in vogue at the time, but they weren't totally flat like the mortarboard that Oxford established as the standard. In her book *The Story of Caps and Gowns,* published by graduation uniform giant E. R. Moore Company, Helen Walters offers three theories:

1. The shape was derived from the master workman's mortar board.
2. The cap was meant to resemble the quadrangular shape of the English university's campus.
3. The shape symbolized the "squareness" of both the scholar and his books. In those days, we presume, squareness was a positive trait.

Early academic caps sported tufts where we now have tassels. Tassels appeared in the eighteenth century, and appear to be merely cosmetic additions.

Americans were quick to adopt English university customs in graduation garb all the way back to colonial times. Several Ivy League universities and prestigious small colleges used gowns and mortarboards from the start.

Only around 1885 did the practice extend to most colleges. In 1894, a commission was authorized to choose a standard for graduation uniforms. Its conclusions have determined our uniforms for the last hundred years:

Bachelors—wear black gowns with worsted material and long, pointed sleeves.

Masters—wear black silk or black woolen gowns with long, closed sleeves that have an arc of a circle near the bottom and a slit for the arm opening.

Doctors—wear black silk gowns with full, round, open sleeves that are faced with velvet and have three bars of velvet on each sleeve.

All three graduates wear a mortarboard, but only doctors' caps may be velvet, and only doctors and presidents of universities may wear gold tassels.

English universities vary clothing and color schemes from school to school. The United States is one of the only countries to have a standardized code.

In 1911, E. R. Moore introduced the Official High School Cap and Gown. It was gray to differentiate it from the university gown, its sleeves were full and round, and the matching gray cap was the typical Oxford mortarboard with a silk tassel.

Although E. R. Moore's motive might have been commercial, the popularity of caps and gowns for secondary school graduations spread quickly, not only because parents appreciated the pomp and circumstance at a momentous occasion, but for financial reasons. In the early twentieth century, students of affluent families might pay forty or fifty dollars for a graduation outfit when the caps and gowns could be rented for $1.50. The caps and gowns allowed poor students to "compete" with their richer comrades.

Of course, every school soon wanted caps and gowns. Normal schools, and later their descendants, junior colleges, chose blue for the color of their gowns. Some grammar schools even started using caps and gowns—maroon became the most popular color.

Several of the readers who posed this question also asked about the tradition of moving the tassel from left to right to signify graduation. Obviously, the tassel shift symbolizes the graduation itself, but we have been unable to trace its exact origins. We do know that this practice goes in and out of favor. While some schools retain the practice, many, if not most, universities do not, insisting that the tassel remain hanging on the left side of the mortarboard while the commencement speaker drones on and on and on.

Submitted by Andrew Kass of Staten Island, New York. Thanks also to Michael Silverson of Exeter, New Hampshire; Lisa Coates-Shrider of Cincinnati, Ohio; Linda Galvao of Tiverton, Rhode Island; Gina Guerrieri of Shawnee, Oklahoma; and Jamie Hubert of Spring Lake, Michigan.

Why aren't skyscrapers ever made out of brick?

We consulted many architects about this question, and they flooded us with reasons why bricks weren't a particularly desirable material for skyscrapers. In no particular order, here are some of the problems involved:

1. Bricks are more expensive than the alternatives. Not only are they relatively expensive to manufacture, but laying bricks is extremely labor-intensive, which is one of the reasons we see fewer bricks even in ranch style suburban homes than we used to.

2. In order to support a skyscraper, the walls at the base of the building must be extremely thick, wasting valuable space. David Bahlman, of the Society of Architects, indicated that bricks would need to be two and one-half feet deep at the base to support even a six-floor building.

3. Bricks need a substructure of steel beams to support them. According to architectural consultant Bill Stanley of Buellton, California, skyscrapers with steel frames can be covered (or "clad") with brick panels, but "brick is a poor material for cladding because of its weight, and the possibility of coming loose and falling."

4. The size of individual bricks is not large enough aesthetically to fit the scale of a skyscraper.

Notwithstanding this brick bashing, we have a confession to make. The premise of this question is incorrect. There are skyscrapers made of brick. Indeed, one of the first skyscrapers in the world, the Monadnock Building in Chicago, built in 1889, rests mainly on brick. The Monadnock Building is sixteen stories high and is often studied by urban architects.

The design problems inherent in such a tall brick building are elucidated by Lynn S. Beedle, director of the Council on Tall Buildings and Urban Habitat. The bricks make the building so heavy that the walls must be made thicker and thicker on the lower floors, so that the walls at the base are almost six feet thick. You couldn't build a brick building much higher because "there wouldn't be much space left on the ground floor for elevators."

Charles N. Farley, director of the Brick Institute of America, wants *Imponderables* readers to know that brick is being used on newer skyscrapers, too. Most laymen don't realize that the gargantuan Empire State Building contains brick because it is clad with limestone panels. Two recently built New York City skyscrapers, the fifty-three-story World Wide Plaza and the sixty-story Carnegie Hall Tower, both use brick for the exterior skin. Brick remains a feasible exterior for those who can afford it.

Submitted by Herbert Kraut of Forest Hills, New York.

THE FARQUHAR PREPARATORY
ACADEMY TESTS ANOTHER APPLICANT.

Why are nine-volt batteries rectangular?

Most of the best-selling battery configurations (e.g., AA, AAA, C, D) are 1.5 volts. Nine-volt batteries, formerly known as "transistor batteries," contain six 1.5-volt batteries. The 1.5 cells within the casing are cylindrical.

If you were to stack six cylinders in the most economical shape, wouldn't a rectangle be the most natural choice? Just try putting six cylinders into a square or cylindrical casing without wasting space.

Dan Halaburda, marketing manager for Panasonic, told us that the shape of nine-volt batteries goes back to when they were used to power communication devices in which space was at a premium. Today, the most common application for nine-volt batteries is in smoke detectors.

Submitted by Matt Garrett of Augusta, Missouri.

DAVID FELDMAN

Why do most mailboxes say "Approved by the Postmaster General" on them? How do they differ from mailboxes without the approval?

We thought these were simple and innocent questions. But as grizzled veterans of researching postal Imponderables, we should have known better. For the saga of the U.S. mailbox is a long one; in fact, the household mailbox debuted in 1891, when Postmaster General John Wanamaker launched an experiment. Until then, it was the policy of postal carriers to knock on the door of households and hand-deliver mail. Just the seconds waiting for house occupants to come to the door wasted delivery time, so mailboxes were inevitable.

We may think of a mailbox as a rather simple object, but an earlier commission appointed by the postmaster general in 1890 examined 564 prototypes of mailboxes and found them all want-

WHEN DID WILD POODLES ROAM THE EARTH? 105

ing. What the commission was looking for, as the 1891 annual report of the postmaster general stated, was a device

> in which the letter carrier could deposit mail without delay and from which he could also, as he went his rounds upon the same trips, collect mail without delay. Not one of these devices exactly fitted the requirements; for the box must necessarily be inexpensive, neat, proof against the weather, proof against mischiefmakers or thieves, simple enough not to get out of order and not to require time to open, ornamental enough to please the household, big enough to receive papers, and ingenious enough to indicate the presence of mail matter to the passing collector.

The commission later examined another 1,031 designs, and found that "Not one of these was entirely acceptable."

Originally, only rural delivery mailboxes had to be approved by the postmaster general. Imagine the problems of the rural postal carrier with farflung routes. Megaera Harris, research historian at the office of the postmaster general, explains:

> Early rural carriers and the public they served were forced to create their own rules and regulations in the fledgling days of rural mail service. Farmers had been asked to put up their own mailboxes, "buggy high," and within easy reach of the mail carriers, a request with which most of them complied. The resulting mailboxes under these general guidelines were a study in individuality and creativity.

Aware that minimum standards were necessary, the post office department established rules and regulations, effective October 1, 1902, mandating the size, shape, and accessibility of the box. Fourteen manufacturers were approved to build boxes. Each box was to be stenciled with the statement "Approved by the Postmaster General."

In the following ninety years, only mailboxes served by rural carriers were required to have the postmaster's approval, but manufacturers found it a good marketing device to include the approval on all their boxes.

In 1991, the postal regulations widened. Roy Preston, operations officer of the delivery management division, told *Impon-*

derables that "all new [curbside] boxes or replacement boxes must now have the 'Approved' inscription." As old, "grandfathered" mailboxes deteriorate or are replaced for cosmetic reasons, the nonapproved boxes will be a thing of the past.

Preston was kind enough to pass along the rules and regulations to which approved mailboxes must conform, and they are truly scary in their specificity. Boxes are tested for everything from salt spray resistance to flammability to color shade.

Steve Korker, a communications spokesman for the United States Postal System, says that the USPS itself tests mailboxes for manufacturers. Tests include the dreaded "door and flag" test, in which each part is attached to a machine and opened and closed a minimum of 7,500 times. Boxes are dropped on hard surfaces to test their durability, tested for leakage, and exposed to water and high humidity.

So although the postmaster general cannot personally test the flag on each household's mailbox, rest assured that if you have the "Approved by the Postmaster General" inscription, your mailbox is ready to withstand rain, sleet, snow, and the dark of night, and is less likely to complain about these weather conditions than your postal carrier.

Submitted by Scott Kovatch of Dublin, Ohio.

Why does a ball tend to veer toward the ocean when one putts on a golf course?

We were shocked when this truism of the links was denied by the golfing authorities we contacted. Typical was the response of Frank Thomas, technical director of the United States Golf Association:

> I have no evidence that this is the case or that there are any strange forces that could possibly make this happen. If the natural shape of the land is down toward the ocean and the green has a

similar grade, then the ball will tend to veer according to the slope.

We were stymied until we heard from Rand Jerris, at the USGA's museum and library. He called the premise of this Imponderable "one of those great half-truths of life," and indicated that although under certain conditions the ball does tend to veer toward the ocean, "just as often you will find a putt that breaks away from the water." Jerris, however, was our only source to explain the conditions on the golf course that might cause the ball to move in mysterious ways:

1. Drainage. Most greens are constructed with subtle slopes to facilitate drainage in a specific direction. Economically, it makes sense to drain toward natural bodies of water, whether that be an ocean or a lake.

2. Grain of the green. Any golfer knows that putts will tend to break with, and not against, the natural grain of the grass. Jerris notes that grass found in the western United States, such as Bermuda grass, tends to be stronger and thicker than eastern varieties. Since blades of grass tend to grow toward the setting sun to maximize photosynthetic activity, the strong grains of western grass tend to steer putts toward the ocean. Even when the weaker, thinner, bent grass in the East bends toward the West Coast, the effect is imperceptible because the grass has weak grain or no grain at all.

3. Winds. In some shore regions, the dominant winds tend to blow from land toward the sea. According to Jerris, "These winds may also add to the effects of grain, forcing the blades of grass to orient in the direction of the ocean."

So don't blame the tides for your next errant putt. Chances are, your victimizer is the grass beneath your feet, paying you back for all those divots you've dug.

Submitted by John R. Green of Cincinnati, Ohio.

DAVID FELDMAN

Why do dishwashers have two compartments for detergent? And why does only one compartment close?

Our ever cheerful appliance expert, Whirlpool's Carolyn Verweyst, replied to this Imponderable with uncharacteristic testiness: "Consumers frequently ask these questions but never think to consult their use and care manuals supplied with the appliance." Ah, c'mon, Carolyn. Force us to hand-wash our dishes. Refuse to answer our question. But don't condemn us to actually having to read the user's manuals!

An informal survey of moderately intelligent individuals (i.e., we asked a bunch of our friends) indicates that the average dishwasher owner doesn't have the slightest idea how much detergent to put in the dispensers, nor the significance of loading one or both cups.

To save you the agony of user manual ocular bleariness and brain rot, we're here to help. Although there are differences among the dishwashers of different companies, and even among different models from the same manufacturer, a few truisms emerge. Perhaps the most important principle is that you need fill both sections of the dispenser only if you are cleaning heavily soiled dishes or pots and pans—*cycles that require two different wash periods.* The "pots and pans" cycle typically consists of these phases: light wash (using the soap in the uncovered section of the dispenser); rinse-wash (using the covered section); rinse-rinse-dry-off.

In most dishwashers, the "normal" cycle consists of rinse-wash-rinse-rinse-dry-off. Ordinarily, you need fill only one of the two sections with detergent. But make sure you put the detergent in the correct slot. Fill up the covered cup, close it, and a timer within the dishwasher will pop it open automatically at the proper time (after the first rinse cycle). If you put detergent in the uncovered section in a cycle that begins with a rinse, not only are you wasting detergent by washing away the detergent during the first rinse cycle, but you won't have any detergent left to use during the main wash.

A few dishwashers begin their normal cycles with a "light wash" rather than a rinse and do require both sections of the dispenser to be filled with detergent. The only way to be sure, and we say this with *deep* regret, is to consult your use and care manual.

Submitted by Bethany Marcus of Parma, Ohio.

DAVID FELDMAN

Is it true that horses cannot vomit?

WARNING: If you have eaten within the last hour, or contemplate eating within the next hour, we do not recommend perusal of this chapter at the current time.

Equine vomiting is highly unusual but not unheard of. Vomiting is almost impossible because of the acute angle at which a horse's esophagus enters the stomach. In most cases, what might seem to be vomiting is actually regurgitation—the coughing up of food still in the esophagus. A horse's regurgitated food is much more likely to exit through the nose than the mouth (we did warn you!) because the pharynx—the tube connecting the mouth and esophagus—works as a safety valve to prevent exit through the mouth.

Why did nature provide horses with a vomit-proof digestive system? Horses are grazers extraordinaire. They eat almost continuously because of the small size of their stomachs. Their stomach capacity is only about four gallons (compared to forty gallons for a cow)—far less than their daily ration. Thus horses must empty their stomachs while they are eating, through one hundred feet of intestinal tract, to allow them to digest sufficient food.

Vomiting would jeopardize the horse's ability to consume enough grass or hay to provide adequate nutrition. Although we may think of a life of nonstop eating as a pretty nifty one, it would be far less attractive if we knew that disgorging would force us to cut our sleeping hours in order to keep nibbling.

Submitted by L. Love of San Antonio, Texas.

Why does the tax stamp on a pack of cigarettes say "20 *CLASS A* CIGARETTES"?

The grade refers not to the quality of the cigarettes but to their size. Class A cigarettes are the smallest grade—those that weigh not more than three pounds per thousand—and therefore, the class with the smallest excise tax bite.

Submitted by John C. White of El Paso, Texas. Thanks also to Donald Marti, Jr., of New York, New York.

What are the small, light-colored spots on a brown cigarette filter? Do they have any function?

Those spots have one of the most important imaginable functions—to look pretty. Most American cigarettes have either white or brown filter papers. According to Mary Ann Usrey, of R. J. Reynolds, most women prefer white filters. But most men, evidently, find the brown color more macho.

Cigarette companies print the dots with nontoxic ink to simulate the look of cork (in fact, this style is known as a "cork tip"). Winston, Camel, and Marlboro are just three of the brands that feature cork tips, and include them solely because of the delicate aesthetic preferences of their customers.

Submitted by Leroy Thompson II of Leesburg, Virginia.

In movies and television dramas, what is the purpose of boiling water when babies are delivered at home?

Considering the urgency with which characters in movies bark orders to boil water as soon as it becomes evident a woman is going to give birth at home, we assumed there *was* a better reason for the command than to rustle up some tea. But we've never seen the boiled water actually being used on-screen.

Most of the medical authorities we contacted echoed the sentiments of Dr. Steven P. Shelov, professor of pediatrics at the Montefiore Medical Center:

> This is an attempt to make as sterile an environment as possible, though clearly it is far short of inducing any sterility whatsoever. There might be some ability with hotter water to allow for a cleaner, more efficient cleansing of the baby and of the mother postpartum.

Obviously, it can't hurt to sterilize equipment that comes in contact with the mother or baby, such as scissors, cord clamps,

DAVID FELDMAN

white shoelaces (used in lieu of cord clamps), syringes, and tongs (used to lift the other sterile items), or even more importantly, to sterilize other household implements commandeered to act as sterilized medical equipment.

But boiling water isn't confined to emergency deliveries. Midwives have been boiling water for years for planned home deliveries. Most attempt to boil sterile equipment for thirty minutes and then place instruments in a covered dish (syringes are usually wrapped in a sterile cloth).

Dr. William Berman, of the Society for Pediatric Research, indicated that it couldn't hurt to sterilize water for washrags used to cleanse mother and baby, whether they are washcloths or ripped-up bed sheets. Actually, it *could* hurt—if they forget to let the boiled water cool down.

Submitted by Scott Morwitz of Pittsburgh, Pennsylvania. Thanks also to Jil McIntosh of Oshawa, Ontario; and Dr. John Hardin of Greenfield, Indiana.

Why do frogs close their eyes when swallowing?

There is a downside to those big, beautiful frog eyes. While they may attract the admiration of their beady-eyed human counterparts, frog eyes bulge not only on the outside but on the inside of their faces. The underside of their eyeball is covered by a sheet of tissue and protrudes into the mouth cavity. Frogs literally cannot swallow unless they use their eyes to push the food down their stomach. Richard Landesman, zoologist at the University of Vermont, amplifies:

> In order for frogs to swallow, they must be able to push material in the mouth backwards into the esophagus. Humans use their tongue to accomplish this task; however, frogs use their eyes. By depressing their eyes, food can be pushed posteriorly in the

mouth. Frogs also use this same mechanism to breathe, since they lack a diaphragm.

Actually, if we ate what frogs eat, we might close our eyes when swallowing, too.

Submitted by Scott McNeff of Wells, Maine.

Why do the paper bags/sacks in supermarkets have jagged edges where you open them?

Not an earth-shatteringly important Imponderable, perhaps, but we were startled by how little paper bag manufacturers knew about the subject. They couldn't even agree on what to call these edges; depending upon to whom we spoke, the edges were referred to as "serrated," "pinked," "jagged," and "chain cut."

But Brent Dixon, president of the Paper Bag Institute (and, in a naked lust for power, also the majordomo of the Paper Shipping Sack Manufacturers Association), referred us to the only person who knows the real story—George Stahl, who works in sales for Potdevin Machine Company, a large manufacturer of machines that produce paper bags, and has been in the business longer than most of our sources have been alive.

Stahl explains that sack machines are run at a high speed; they produce from four hundred to five hundred sacks per minute. The individual bags are cut from long strips of paper by an anvil-type blade. For technical reasons, if straight edges were desired for the sack's opening, two blades would be necessary, dramatically slowing down the production process.

Although serrated edges might help you open the paper sack faster and more safely, don't for a second presume that your welfare was the reason for the design. The accountants, not the designers, dictate the form of the finished product.

Submitted by Diane Cormier of Bath, Maine.

How and why do hotel amenities (such as turndown service and bathrobes) spread so quickly among different hotel chains?

One of the stranger aspects of our job is the "publicity tour," when we are sent to eleven different cities in eleven days, to flog unremittingly our latest tome upon an innocent public. When we are on our own dime, we tend to stay at motels where the size of the complimentary bath soap slightly exceeds the circumference of a commemorative postage stamp, and the "bath mat" has the texture and width of the paper place mat at Denny's. But for whatever reason, our esteemed publisher sends us to the type of hotels that charge as much for one night's lodging as Motel 6 does for a week's. And since we are pliant, malleable types, we don't complain about being forced to alter our bohemian lifestyle.

On these tours, we have noticed a curious fact. Every year, it seems there is a new "hot" amenity. Two years ago, for example, we noticed that virtually all the hotels we visited now had alarm clocks. In the past, you called the hotel operator if you wanted a wake-up call. We thought perhaps the hotel was saving money by having guests reduce their dependency on operator-assisted wake-up calls. But then last year, those clocks were replaced by clock radios. And when we went up to our room for the first time, the radio, invariably, was on, and tuned to classical music. If the city didn't have a classical music station, the radio played classy elevator music.

We could understand how an individual hotel, or single hotel chain, might decide that the "musical introduction" to the new guest was an elegant touch, but how did many different chains all adopt the practice so quickly? How and why did they all decide simultaneously that guests could not enter their rooms without being greeted by Chopin?

Welcome to the wonderful world of what the lodging industry calls "amenities." In the 1950s and 1960s, patrons of all but the most luxurious hotels were satisfied with a few basic amenities: free soap, a color television, ice, air conditioning, a telephone, and perhaps a swimming pool.

But in the 1980s, when lodging chains overbuilt and the economy turned sour, hotels were faced with severe overcapacity and a true dilemma: how to gain market share without dropping prices? Most decided that the answer was to increase amenities. In most cases, the price differentials among hotels within the same class are small, and business travelers, in particular, are not extremely sensitive to price. As James McCauley, executive director of the International Association of Holiday Inns, told us, the task of the smart hotelier in the 1980s was to attract loyalty among customers by offering amenities that would "impress and attract customers from competitive hotels."

In many cases, the strategy worked. Adding amenities to what were originally budget motels (e.g., Holiday Inns and Ramadas) allowed them to charge more for rooms. Hyatt became identified with their nightly turndown service (including a free mint on the pillow), and Stouffer gained fans for their complimentary coffee and newspaper with wake-up calls. These amenities came at a price to the providers. That little mint on the pillow (along with the labor costs of the turndown service) cost Hyatt more than five million dollars a year.

Still, the list of amenities now offered in hotels is mind-boggling. Some have: business centers; health clubs; two-line telephones; special concierge floors with lounges; in-room movies, VCRs, CD players, safes, coffee makers, and hair dryers; free local telephone calls, breakfast, and airport limousines; shoe polishers; voice mail; and nonsmoking rooms.

How do all these amenities spring up at the same time?

1. Amenities are often pitched to many hotels simultaneously. As Raymond Ellis, of the American Hotel & Motel Association, put it:

> the more effective sales representative is going to be presenting an amenity as the ultimate item or service for attracting the guest, without, of course, indicating that the same article or service has just been sold to three or four other competing properties within the community.

2. Richard Brooks, vice-president of room management at Stouffer Hotels & Resorts, mentioned that outside rating services often act as stimuli to add certain features.

> [AAA, Mobil, and Zagat and other rating services] freely tell us of new amenity items or services they have seen, and often tell us they believe they are appropriate for the ratings we hope to achieve.

3. Spies. The big chains can afford inspectors to scrutinize not only their own units but those of competitors.

4. Trade magazines. The American Hotel & Motel Association was kind enough to send us more information about amenities, just from trade magazines, than we ever imagined. There aren't many secrets in the hotel field.

5. Market research. The biggest hotel chains might employ focus groups or written and telephone surveys. Smaller groups might use guest comment cards (yes, they really *do* read those things) or simply chat with guests about their needs. Richard Brooks indicated that some of Stouffer's most popular amenities, such as two-line telephones, in-room movies, no charge for incoming facsimiles, and complimentary coffee and newspaper with wake-up call, all started with guest requests. Many such guest requests are inspired by seeing the same amenity provided at another hotel, another reason why amenities spread so quickly.

Market research also helps hoteliers avoid costly mistakes. Research shows that the vast majority of patrons expect a swimming pool but fewer than one in five ever use it. One chain contemplated putting color TVs in their bathrooms until research indicated that guests would much prefer a decidedly less costly offering—an ironing board and iron. Any amenity that doesn't add market share is wasteful. In fact, most surveys we perused indicate that low-cost items are among the most popular: in-room coffeemakers, TV remote control, and facial tissues were the favored amenities in one study.

Occasionally, an amenity may be turned into a profit center. The minibar is such an attempt. Contrary to popular opinion, soft drinks and snacks are consumed much more than hard liquor or beer, but the minibars still turn a profit, since they charge more for the same products than vending machines could. One of the secrets of the success of the minibar: For business travelers, the cost is added to the room charge. Coke machines in the hallway don't take company credit cards or give receipts.

Amenity creep is so pervasive that budget hotels have tried to create a backlash. Days Inn based an advertising campaign around the slogan, "We don't have it because you don't want it." At one time, Motel 6 forced you to pump in quarters if you wanted light to emit from the television in your room. The truth is—most patrons "want it," but only if they don't think they are paying for it.

Of course, amenities can also foster goodwill. On our last tour, we encountered our all-time favorite amenity at Chicago's Ambassador East Hotel. As we entered our beautiful room, there above the fireplace, on the mantel, was a spanking new copy of *Do Penguins Have Knees?*, with a request for an autograph from the manager. Guess where we are staying the next time we're in Chicago?

Slash Blade Co. I nc.
Product Development

One Razor, Two Names!

"Mr. Beard" and "Ms. Legs"

OUR ORIGINAL NAME FOR THE LADIES' RAZOR, "MS. ARMPIT," DIDN'T TEST WELL FOR SOME REASON...

Is there any difference between men's and women's razors?

Our examination of this issue, conducted with the naked eye, reveals that the main difference between men's and women's razors, at least the disposable type, is their pigment. Women's razors are usually pink; men's razors are found in more macho colors, like royal blue and yellow.

But the naked eye can deceive. Chats with representatives at Bic, Schick, and Wilkinson indicate that there are at least three significant differences:

1. The most important difference to the consumer is the "shave angle" of the two. A man's razor has a greater angle on the blade, what the razor industry calls "aggressive exposure," for two reasons. Men's beards are tougher than women's leg or underarm hair, and require more effort to be cut and, at least as important, women complain much more than men about nicks and cuts, the inevitable consequence of the aggressive exposure of the men's blades. Women don't particularly like putting hosiery over red splotches, while men seem perfectly content walking around their

122   DAVID FELDMAN

offices in the morning with their faces resembling pepperoni pizzas.

    2. Most women's razors have a greater arc in the head of the razor, so that they can see the skin on the leg more easily as they shave.

    3. Women don't shave as frequently as men, especially in the winter, when most wear pants and long-sleeved blouses. Schick offers a "Personal Touch" razor line for women that features guard bars that contain combs, so that longer hair is set up at the proper angle for shaving.

As far as we can ascertain, all the major manufacturers use the same metallurgy in men's and women's razors.

After enumerating the design features that his company incorporates to differentiate men's and women's razors, Fred Wexler, director of research at Schick, offered a rueful parting observation: Despite all of their design efforts, Schick's research reveals that a solid majority of women use razors designed for men.

Submitted by Kim MacIntosh of Chinacum, Washington.

What are the numbers on the bottom right of my canceled checks? Why aren't those numbers there before the check is canceled?

You are probably vaguely aware of the preprinted numbers running along the bottom left of your personalized checks. The numbers on the far left identify your bank. The numbers to their immediate right are your bank account number. The right half of the bottom of the check is blank.

But when the check is returned with your statement, a mysterious ten-digit number appears. If you look carefully, it doesn't take a rocket scientist to figure out to what the numbers refer—they indicate exactly how much your check is for—down to the penny. Any amount up to $99,999,999.99 can be expressed with these numbers. The fact that most folks are not H. Ross Perot explains why most of these codes start with a bunch of zeros.

You didn't think that banks clerks pore over every check individually and add or subtract from your account with a calculator, did you? These funny numbers on the bottom of your checks are called "MICR" (magnetic ink coding) numbers. Brian Smith, executive vice-president of the United States League of Savings Institutions, explains how the amounts of your check are encoded, as well as a personal Imponderable of ours—does anyone ever read the part of the check where we have to write out in words the dollar value of the check?:

> MICR numbers are keyed in very fast, by clerks reading the items and typing them in via special keyboards on the machine that first processes each check. Writing the dollar amount clearly in numbers at the upper right is vital since nobody ever reads the amount in words, beginning in the middle left, though, legally, that is supposedly the controlling description of the amount of the check. All processing is done by the MICR process after the initial coding.

Why do banks sometimes attach a white piece of paper to the bottom of canceled checks?

The white strip is affixed to the bottom of a check when the MICR process misfires. Sometimes, a scanner can't read the MICR numbers. More often, a clerk mistypes the amount of the check.

John Hall, of the American Banking Association, told *Imponderables* that there is no way for a clerk to erase or overstrike a typing error on a check. Instead, the MICR numbers are encoded on a plain piece of paper, which is placed on the bottom of the check and is read by the same scanners that decode checks without the white appendage.

Submitted by Douglas Watkins, Jr. of Hayward, California.
Thanks also to Joseph P. McGowan of Glenolden, Pennsylvania.

Why do the clearest days seem to follow storms?

Our correspondent wondered whether this phenomenon was an illusion. Perhaps we are so happy to see the storm flee that the next day, without battering winds, threatening clouds, and endless precipitation, seems beautiful in contrast.

No, it isn't an illusion. Meteorologists call this phenomenon "scavenging." The rainwater that soaks your shoes also cleans away haze and pollutants from the atmosphere and sends it to the ground. At the same time, the wind that wrecks your umbrella during the storm diffuses the irritants that are left in the atmosphere, so that neighbors in surrounding areas aren't subjected to those endless days of boring, pollution-free environments.

Of course, where the pollutants end up depends upon the direction of the prevailing winds. If you are living in a community with generally bad air quality, the wind is your friend anyway. Chances are, the wind is carrying in air from a region with superior air quality.

Submitted by Jack Schwager of Goldens Bridge, New York.

Why are paper and plastic drinking cups wider at the top than the bottom?

A reader, Chuck Lyons, writes:

> I have never been able to understand why paper and plastic drinking cups are designed with the wide end at the top. That makes them top-heavy and much easier to tip over. Making them with the wide end on the bottom would make the cups more stable and less likely to tip over, with no disadvantage at all that I can see.

Come to think of it, Chuck's suggestion has been used for eons in the design of bottles. We certainly never found it difficult drinking from a "bottom-heavy" beer bottle. Most glass bottles and many glass or ceramic drinking cups don't taper at the bottom, so why should disposable cups? What are we missing?

Plenty, it turns out, according to every cup producer we spoke to. John S. Carlson, marketing director of James River, put it succinctly:

> The cups are wider at the top so that they can be "nested" in a stack during shipping, storage on the grocery store shelf, and in your cupboard at home. If they weren't tapered slightly, they'd stack like empty soup cans. The current configuration saves space and spills, and is more efficient and cost effective.

In retailing, not only time but *space* is money. Better to get more of your product on the shelf and live with the consequences of an extra customer or two tipping over a cupful of Kool-Aid.

Submitted by Chuck Lyons of Palmyra, New York.

DAVID FELDMAN

Why do steak houses always serve such huge baked potatoes?

The poser of this Imponderable, Gene McBride, advances his own theory to explain the prodigious potatoes we encounter in steak houses. He feels that no home cook would ever buy these elephantine spuds for personal use, so farmers are forced to unload them at bargain basement prices to restaurants, "which is better than using the potatoes for hog feed."

We spoke to restaurateurs, meat marketers, and potato marketers to help confirm Gene's theory, and found only the potato folk eager to speak on the record. Everyone disagreed with our reader, saying that restaurants pay a pretty penny for portly potatoes.

But that doesn't mean that economics don't enter into the equation. Several restaurateurs indicated that a big baked potato adds to the perceived value of a meal, for steak houses, with their macho image, unlike nouvelle cuisine outposts, always would rather send a customer home stuffed to the gills and reaching for the Pepto-Bismol than starving to death and looking for the nearest McDonald's.

Don Odiorne, vice-president of food service at the Idaho Potato Commission, gave us a history of the potato's role in the U.S. steak house and his own theory about the reason for using the huge potatoes:

> Steak houses typically started out serving enormous portions of steaks, bread, and potatoes—steaks so large they wouldn't fit on the plate. Sometimes to accomplish this claim, the plates an operator ordered were smaller in diameter (the standard 12 to 14 inch plate went down to 9 to 11 inches), but it was generally accepted that the cowboy-size western steak was huge and hard to finish eating in one sitting.
>
> This quest for "value" evolved over the years as the cost of food, which had been relatively stable for quite some time, began to rise. Food cost pressures reduced portion sizes or increased the selling prices. Both had negative effects on customer counts. As steaks got smaller, the side dishes, such as potatoes, got larger.
>
> Generally, it is much less expensive to up the size of a potato than to up the size of the meat portion. For example, if an operator serves a 90 count potato (about 9 ounces), and a carton of potatoes cost the restaurant $15.00, the individual serving cost of the potato, not including condiments, would be less than 17 cents. Go up to a 50 count potato (one pound), and the individual cost is 30 cents. Now try and find a cut of steak for 30 cents a pound—it's impossible.

As several restaurateurs told us off the record, the baked potato thus becomes one of the cheapest ways to stuff the customer without increasing costs—but not because the restaurant is paying less per pound for the big potato than the small one. Note that the "bargain" chain steak houses, such as Ponderosa and Bonanza, who don't sell such huge steaks, also downsize their baked potatoes, because their "value" is in their price, not the quantity (or quality) of food.

Still, not all our sources were willing to lay the tradition of the immense Idaho solely on economic preoccupations. To some, the size of the potato is a matter of aesthetics, of poetry, as

DAVID FELDMAN

it were. For example, Meredith Hughes, managing director of the Potato Museum, in Great Falls, Virginia, weighs in with an explanation that is deeper than anything we ever heard on *Kung Fu*:

> You would think that habitués of meat and potato palaces would already know the answer to the question you pose. They enter the gates for the biggest piece of dead animal flesh they can get, and by gum, they get a baker to lie parallel to it in perfect symmetry. Symmetry must be the answer. Balance, the harmony of equals, the yin and yang of it all.

Linda McCashion, director of advertising and public relations for the Potato Board, while acknowledging the perceived "value" added by the hefty potato, also spoke of the "balance to the plate" provided by the vast vegetable. And big potatoes help reinforce the macho image of the steak house. As McCashion puts it, "Real studs eat real spuds."

Submitted by Gene McBride of Winston-Salem, North Carolina.

Since computer paper is longer than it is wide, why are computer monitors wider than they are long?

As Robert Probasco, professor of Computer Sciences at the University of Idaho, puts it, the short answer is: "Monitors (video display tubes) and paper sizes evolved at different times for unrelated technologies, so their recent marriage has been a marriage of convenience." Our personal computer monitors evolved from the round screens of early television; Probasco reminds us that radar screens still retain this efficient shape.

Many of the early microcomputers were designed so that the user could employ a television as the monitor. Early micros had such poor resolution that only forty legible characters per line could be displayed on the screen; now the number has doubled. Still, the monitors aren't long enough to display a whole printed page. The average screen displays about twenty-five lines, whereas a printed single-spaced paper holds about fifty-five lines—hence the need for scrolling up and down when drafting a document on-screen.

But the personal computer configuration is hardly universal in the computer world. For example:

- Newspapers require huge screens capable of displaying an entire page of newsprint. They use monitors that do duplicate the shape of the paper.
- Large work stations often use squarish screens that can display a full page, or more, of information.
- "Page-format" monitors are available for some microcomputers. David Maier, professor in the department of Computer Science and Engineering at the Oregon Graduate Institute of Science & Technology, reports that some monitors alternate between page and standard orientation.
- Many computer printers, especially in business applications, can handle many different sizes and shapes of paper. Many of these papers are wider than they are long—not just mailing labels but wide papers used to print out spread sheets or plans drawn by engineers and architects.

The idea of customizing monitor proportions to specific applications is impractical and could be downright silly. As computer programmer Larry Whitish put it, "Imagine the size of monitor you would need to view a spread sheet that was over six feet long when printed in landscape mode on your printer."

Microcomputer designers found it simpler and less expensive to adapt the monitor to existing technologies. So they appropriated the tubes and circuitry from older VDTs. They used 8½ × 11-inch paper as the standard size so that the paper transport and printing hardware in their printers were compatible with counterparts found in electric typewriters and teletypes. Maier mentions that laser printers borrow much of their optics, hardware, and electronics from small copy machines. They even use the same cartridges, which are made for 8½ × 11-inch paper. This lessens the price of newer technology for both the supplier and the consumer.

As we finished this chapter, we hear a question forming on the lips of an *Imponderables* reader: Why don't monitors have the same format as printers? To forestall the inevitable question, we also found out why these two components couldn't be aligned.

Well, they could, but David Maier explains why they are unlikely to be changed in our lifetimes:

> That would mean making the screen maybe 70 columns wide by 65 lines long to match a page printed in 12 pt. font. Turning a standard PC monitor 90 degrees would give about the right ratio of width to height. However, you would have to shrink the size of characters on the screen and increase the electronic circuitry to handle the greater number of characters. The standard monitor has 80 × 24, or 1920, characters, whereas the page monitor would need 70 × 65, or 4550, characters. It could get hard to read.
>
> However, if all the PC users in the country decided they were only going to buy page-format monitors from now on, the PC manufacturers could provide them in volume at a cost not much greater than what standard monitors cost now. Except.
>
> Except there are now thousands of PC programs that assume a monitor screen has the standard format and whose developers might not be real happy at having to recode them to work with page format.

Submitted by Henry J. Stark of Montgomery, New York.

Why are all calico cats female?

Not quite all. According to Judith Lindley, founder of the Calico Cat Registry International, approximately one male calico is born for every 3,000 females.

The occurrence of male calico cats is theoretically impossible. Ordinarily, male cats have XY sex chromosomes, while females have XX. The X chromosomes carry the genes for coat colors. Therefore, female cats inherit their coat color from both their queens (XX) and their toms (XY). To create a calico (or tortoise-shell) pattern, one of the X chromosomes must carry the black gene and the other the orange gene. If a black male and an orange female mate, the result will be a half-black and half-orange female offspring, a calico. A black female and an orange male will also produce a calico female.

Usually, the male kitten inherits its coat color from the queen alone, since the Y chromosome determines its sex but has nothing to do with its coat color. A male black cat mating with an orange female will produce an orange male; a male orange cat and black female will produce a black male kitten.

Geneticists have discovered that only one of the two X chromosomes in females is functional, which explains why you usually can make a blanket prediction that any male offspring will be the color of the queen. But occasionally, chromosomes misdivide, and a male calico is born with an extra chromosome—two X chromosomes and one Y chromosome. If one of the X chromosomes carries the orange gene and the other the nonorange, a calico will result.

Note that the presence of the extra X chromosome doesn't in itself create the calico. If both chromosomes are coded for orange or black, the offspring will be that color rather than a combination.

Abnormal chromosome counts are unusual but not rare. Most cat cells contain nineteen pairs of chromosomes, but sometimes a mutation will yield one extra chromosome or double or triple the normal number.

Although male calicoes are oddities, the cat experts we consulted indicated that they are normally healthy and have excellent life expectancies. But, unlike their female counterparts, male calicoes do tend to have a common problem—their sexual organs are often malformed, so they are usually sterile.

Submitted by Stacey Shore of West Lafayette, Indiana.

Why do ditto masters come in purple rather than blue ink?

Instant copiers may have supplanted spirit process duplicators (also known as mimeograph duplicators—"Ditto" is actually a trade name of a brand of spirit duplicators) in businesses, but many a handout in schools today is still flecked with the same aromatic purple streaks that we older folks knew and loved as children. For those of you who never made it to the teachers' lounge, a short description of how mimeos are made will help explain why the stains on teachers' hands usually are purple rather than blue or black.

To make copies on a mimeo, one must type, write, or draw on a sheet of white master paper hard enough to make an impression on a sheet of purple backing carbon paper. A negative carbon image is created on the back of the master paper. The master paper is then separated from the carbon and placed on the drum of the duplicating machine. Each time the drum rotates, the machine automatically coats the paper with a small amount of spirit fluid. According to Bill Heyer, the third-generation owner of Chicago's Heyer Company, the spirit fluid dissolves a minute amount of aniline dye found on the carbon sheet and transfers it to the copy sheet each time the drum is rotated, producing a positive image. Heyer reports that this dye is extremely powerful. One thimbleful can turn an entire room blue.

The aniline dye used in spirit duplicators is derived from coal. Don Byczynski of Colonial Carbon Co. of Des Plaines, Illinois, told *Imponderables* that duplicating companies buy the dye in powdered form and mix it with vegetable oils and waxes to arrive at carbon ink.

So why did purple become the industry standard? Carbon companies, of course, wanted the cheapest possible dyes to make their product economical. Although many other solvents were available, alcohol was and still is the cheapest available, so the industry sought to use dyes with the best alcohol solubility. According to Byczynski, the cheapest dye available was crystal violet dye, the lowest-cost color dye with alcohol solubility.

WHEN DID WILD POODLES ROAM THE EARTH?   133

As we learned in *Why Do Dogs Have Wet Noses?*, cash register receipts are purple because the ink lasts longer than other colors. Bill Heyer indicated that the same is true for carbon inks. Other colored dyes (e.g., blue, green, red, and black) are available, but they cost more and would produce fewer copies.

Heyer answered another question we wondered about. Is the carbon in ordinary carbon paper identical to the carbon used in spirit carbons? Surprisingly, the answer is no. The oils and waxes used are identical in both, but carbon paper uses pigments rather than dyes. Carbon paper wouldn't work on duplicating machines because it doesn't have alcohol solubility.

For those of you who worry about kids getting hold of alcohol-laden carbon products—relax. The alcohol is denatured by chemicals so that it is undrinkable.

Submitted by Diana Berliner of Eureka, California.

Why are the interior walls of tunnels usually finished with ceramic tiles? Are they tiled for practical or aesthetic reasons?

Come on. Do you really think tunnel-makers are obsessed with aesthetics? Tiles may look nifty, but they also have many practical advantages.

We heard from officials of the International Bridge, Tunnel & Turnpike Association, the Port Authority of New York and New Jersey, and the chief of the bridge division of the Federal Highway Administration. All hailed ceramic tiles for having two big advantages over other surfaces:

    1. Tiles are easy to clean. Tunnel walls collect dirt the way Madonna collects boys. Walls are subject to fumes, dust, tire particles, exhaust, and, in some locations, salt. Tiles can be cleaned by many means, including detergents, brushes, and high-pressure water jets.

    2. Tiles are durable. As Stanley Gordon, the aforementioned

FHA official, put it, "Finish systems must be resistant to deterioration caused by various kinds of dirt and grime, vehicle emissions, washing, water leakage, temperature changes, sunlight, artificial light, vibration and acids produced by combinations of vehicle emissions and moisture." Tiles perform admirably in this regard.

Gordon mentioned several other qualities that make tiles both practical and economic:

> 3. Reflectance. The more reflective the wall surface, the less money is spent on lighting.
> 4. Adaptability. "The finish [of the wall surface] must accommodate various special conditions at openings, recesses, corners, and sloping grades [of the tunnel], as well as service components such as lights and signs."
> 5. Fire Resistance. Tiles are noncombustible and are likely not to be damaged by small fires.
> 6. Weather Resistance. Fired clay products, tunnel tiles are, for example, frost-resistant.
> 7. Repairability. Nothing is easier to replace, if damaged, than one or more matching tiles.
> 8. Inspectability. It is easy to see if tiles are deteriorating and in need of repair.

What are the alternatives? Gordon elucidates:

> Although many other products, such as porcelain enameled metal, epoxy coated steel, polymer concrete and painted concrete, have been investigated as possible tunnel finishes, the selection of tunnel tile prevails in most cases.

All in all, tunnel tiles are an unqualified success. Unless, perhaps, you are the person responsible for taking care of grout problems.

Submitted by Ann Albano of Ravena, New York. Thanks also to Anthony Masters of San Rafael, California.

DAVID FELDMAN

Why does heat make us sleepy in the afternoon when we're trying to work but restless when we're trying to sleep at night?

Fewer experiences are more physically draining than sitting in an overheated library in the winter (why *are* all libraries overheated in the winter?) trying to work. You can be reading the most fascinating book in the world, (e.g., one of ours), and yet you would kill for a spot on a vacant cot rather than remaining on your hardback chair. So you trudge home, eventually, to your overheated house and try to get a good night's sleep. Yet the very heat that sent your body into a mortal craving for lassitude now turns you into a twisting and turning repository of frustration. You can't fall asleep. Why?

There is no doubt that heat saps us of energy. Many Latin, Asian, and Mediterranean cultures routinely allow their work force to take siestas during the hottest portions of the day, aware both that productivity would slacken during the early P.M. hours without a siesta and that workers are refreshed after an hour or so of sleep.

Yet all of the sleep experts we consulted agreed with the declaration of the Better Sleep Council's Caroline Jones: "Heat is not what makes us sleepy in the afternoon. Researchers have documented a universal dip in energy levels that occurs in the P.M. regardless of the temperature." These daily fluctuations of sleepiness within our body are known as "circadian rhythms." David L. Hopper, president of the American Academy of Somnology, told *Imponderables* that late evening and early afternoon are the "two periods during the twenty-four-hour cycle when sleep is possible or likely to occur under normal conditions."

Some sleep specialists believe that circadian rhythms indicate humans have an inborn predisposition to nap. But somnologists seem to agree that the natural sleepiness most of us feel in the afternoon, when it happens to be hottest outside, has little

WHEN DID WILD POODLES ROAM THE EARTH?   137

or nothing to do with the other very real enervating effects heat has upon us.

Environmental temperatures *do* affect our sleep patterns, though. Most people sleep better in cool environments, which explains why many of us are restless when trying to sleep in hot rooms even when we are exhausted at night. And if the temperature should shift while we are asleep, it can cause us to awaken, as Hopper explains:

> Our body temperature is lowest in the early morning hours and highest in the evening. During deep NREM and REM sleep, we lose our ability to effectively regulate body temperature, so if the outside temperature is too warm or too cold, we must arouse somewhat in order to regulate our body temperature more effectively. During sleep we are not unconscious, so signals are able to get through to arouse us when needed, much as when we awaken from sleep when we need to go to the bathroom.

Submitted by Mark Gilbey of Palo Alto, California. Thanks also to Neal Riemer of Oakland, California.

Why do we feel drowsy after a big meal?

Eating, unlike heat, does directly affect our sleepiness quotient. After we eat a big meal, the blood supply concentrates around the digestive organs and intestinal system, reducing the blood supply for other activities. We tend to slow down metabolically and in our ambitions. ("Sure, why not have a fourteenth cup of coffee? They won't miss us at the office.")

Equally important, during digestion, foods are broken down into many chemicals, including amino acids such as l-tryptophan, which help induce sleep. Serotonins, which constrict the blood vessels, also make us drowsy. Alcohol, too, often produces sleepiness—which may be another reason why so many business lunches end up with fourteen cups of caffeine-loaded coffee.

Submitted by David O'Connor of Willoughby, Ohio. Thanks also to Chaundra L. Carroll of Hialeah, Florida.

Banner: CAREERS in CONDIMENTS Day — Learn about your future as jam, ...lade, preserve

Pennants: FRUIT U / FRUIT U

Speech: EW! · GROSS · WHAT DO I WANNABE WHEN I RIPEN UP?

"Workshop 2-A: Choosing the processing method that's right for you"

What's the difference between jams, jellies, preserves, marmalades, and conserves?

All of these products started as a way to preserve fresh fruit (although they are now used primarily to provide a semblance of flavor on tasteless bread). The preparation of each involves adding sugar or other sweeteners (including other fruit juices) to the fruit to insure flavor preservation, and the removal of water to increase the intensity of taste. And most include additional ingredients found naturally in fruit: citric acid, to impart tartness; and pectin, a natural jelling agent.

The main difference among these foods is texture. Jellies are prepared from strained fruit juices and have a smooth consistency. Jams are made from crushed fruit (conserves, a type of jam, are made from two or more fruits, and often include nuts or raisins). Preserves use whole fruit or pieces of whole fruit. Marmalades use citrus fruit only and include pieces of the peel.

Fruit syrups and toppings, the type used in ice cream parlors, are prepared with the same cooking methods as other preserves. They are usually made from juices or purees of fruit and often contain corn syrup as well as sugar, to provide the runny consistency that insures the topping will topple off even a flat-top ice cream scoop.

Submitted by Pamela Gibson of Kendall Park, New Jersey. Thanks also to Dana Pillsbury, parts unknown (please write with new address); Rich DeWitt of Erie, Pennsylvania; Jeffrey Bradford of Berkeley, California; and Elmo Jones of Burbank, California.

Why don't trees on a slope grow perpendicular to the ground as they do on a level surface?

Trees don't give a darn if they're planted on a steep hill in San Francisco or a level field in Kansas. Either way, they'll still try to reach up toward the sky and seek as much light as possible. Botanist Bruce Kershner told *Imponderables* that

> this strong growth preference is based on the most important of motivations: survival. Scientifically, this is called "phototropism," or the growth of living cells toward the greatest source of light. Light provides trees with the energy and food that enable them to grow in the first place.
>
> There is also another tropism (involuntary movement toward or away from a stimulus) at work—*geotropism*—the movement away from the pull of gravity (roots, unlike the rest of the tree, grow *toward* the gravitational pull). Even on a hill slope, the pull of gravity is directly down, and the greatest source of average light is directly up. In a forest, the source of light is only up.
>
> There are cases where a tree might not grow directly up. First, there are some trees whose trunks grow outward naturally, but whose tops still tend to point upward. Second, trees growing against an overhanging cliff will grow outward on an angle toward the greatest concentration of light (much like a house plant grows toward the window). Third, it is reported that in a few places on

earth with natural geomagnetic distortions (e.g., Oregon Vortex, Gold Hill, Oregon), the trees grow in a contorted fashion. The gravitational force is abnormal but the light source is the same.

John A. Pitcher, of the Hardwood Research Council, adds that trees have developed adaptive mechanisms to react to the sometimes conflicting demands of phototropism and geotropism:

> Trees compensate for the pull of gravity and the slope of the ground by forming a special kind of reaction wood. On a slope, conifer trees grow faster on the downhill side, producing compression wood, so named because the wood is pushing the trunk bole uphill to keep it straight. Hardwoods grow faster on the uphill side, forming tension wood that pulls the trunk uphill to keep it straight.
>
> Why softwoods develop compression wood and hardwoods develop tension wood is one of the unsolved mysteries of the plant world.

We'll leave that unsolved mystery to Robert Stack.

Submitted by Marvin Shapiro of Teaneck, New Jersey. Thanks also to Herbert Kraut of Forest Hills, New York; and Gregory Laugle of Huber Heights, Ohio.

On nutrition labels, why does the total number of grams of fat often far exceed the sum of saturated and polyunsaturated fats?

Foraging through our kitchen cabinet, we lit upon a box of Nabisco Wheat Thins. A consultation with the nutritional panel yielded the following information about the fat content of a half-ounce serving:

DAVID FELDMAN

Fat:	3 grams
Polyunsaturated	*
Saturated	*
* contains less than one gram	

And a look at the label on a Stouffer's Lean Cuisine Oriental Beef with Vegetables and Rice Entree wasn't much more enlightening:

Fat:	9 grams
Polyunsaturated	*
Saturated	2 grams
* contains less than one gram	

We may not have been math whizzes, but even we know that two plus less than one does not equal nine.

What's going on? Sally Jones, food technologist at the USDA's food labeling division, told us that our arithmetic was impeccable but our nutritional IQ was in the dumper. We forgot that there is a third type of fat, monosaturated, which can often, such as in the case of the Lean Cuisine entree, constitute more than half of a product's fat.

Current labeling laws make it optional whether manufacturers list the grams of monosaturated fat, often affectionately known as the "good fat." The government doesn't insist on listing monosaturated levels, since there is some evidence that monos are actually good for us, fighting to raise our levels of HDLs, the "good cholesterol."

When the giant upheaval of American food labels takes place, supposedly in 1993, but presumably later, food manufacturers will only be required to list their products' percentage of saturated fat (i.e., the "bad fat"), the culprit that most consumers are trying to find out about when they consult the nutritional panel in the first place.

Submitted by Solomon Marmor of Portland, Oregon.

Why do ambulances have the emblem of a snake wrapped around a pole painted on them?

For as long as there have been ambulances, manufacturers have sought a symbol so that citizens could recognize the vehicle as an ambulance, even without the wail of the siren. As far back as the nineteenth century, the cross was the most frequently used symbol on ambulances around the world, but it never proved satisfactory, for two reasons. The cross was on the national flags of many countries, causing needless confusion, and the Red Cross Society screamed, pardon the pun, bloody murder whenever the cross was used on anything but military or Red Cross vehicles.

When the National Highway Traffic Safety Administration and the General Services Administration developed new federal specifications for ambulances in 1974, they decided that a new symbol specifically designating an ambulance was needed. The result: two new symbols were affixed to the exteriors of ambu-

DAVID FELDMAN

lances—a six-barred cross and the emblem in question, the "staff of Aesculapius." Aesculapius was the son of Apollo and, in both Roman and Greek mythology, the god of medicine and healing; the snake was Aesculapius's seal.

According to W. J. Buck Benison, national accounts manager for Southern Ambulance Builders, the staff of Aesculapius is a registered trademark of the NHTSA, designated for use only by and for ambulances and emergency medical personnel. But individual ambulance companies are free not to emblazon their vehicles with the staff of Aesculapius if they choose—if they want to risk incurring the wrath of the gods, that is.

Submitted by Gabe Miller of Ann Arbor, Michigan.

What's the difference between "super" and ordinary glues?

The main difference between "super" glues and merely mortal ones is that Super and Krazy glues are fabricated from a man-made polymer called "cyanoacrylate," while most other glues are a combination of natural resins in a solvent solution.

The different ingredients create a different bonding process, too, as Rich Palin, technical adviser to Loctite Corporation, reveals:

> Most adhesives rely on mechanical fastening, meaning they penetrate into the tiny holes and irregularities of the substrate and harden there. Super Glue, on the other hand, creates a polar bond. The adhesive and substrate are attracted to one another like two magnets. Mechanical fastening also occurs with Super Glue, increasing the bond strength.

Borden Glue's John Anderson adds that because super glues don't rely solely on mechanical fastening, they are such better at bonding dissimilar surfaces than conventional glues. Thus, with super glues, the consumer is now able to accomplish many everyday tasks for which regular glue is frustratingly inadequate, such as applying glue to the top of a hardhat so that one can stick to steel girders without any other means of support.

Submitted by Tiffany Wilson (in Mary Helen Freeman's Millbrook Elementary School class) of Aiken, South Carolina.

In what direction are our eyes facing when we are asleep?

Upward, usually. Our eye muscles relax when we are asleep, and the natural tendency, known as Bell's Phenomenon, is for the eyes to roll back above their usual position. Of course, when we experience rapid eye movements during sleep, our eyes dart back and forth.

Submitted by Nadine Sheppard of Fairfield, California.

DAVID FELDMAN

Why do weather thermometers use red chemical instead of the silver mercury found in medical thermometers?

The liquid found in weather thermometers is usually alcohol with red coloring. The main reason why alcohol is preferred over mercury for weather thermometers is that it is much, much cheaper. And alcohol is superior to water because alcohol is far hardier—it won't freeze even at temperatures well below −40 degrees Fahrenheit.

Why the red additive in weather thermometers? So that you can read it more easily. If weather thermometers used a liquid the color of mercury, you'd have to take the thermometer off the wall to be able to read it.

Since the advantages of alcohol are so apparent, why don't medical thermometers, notoriously difficult to read, contain red-colored alcohol instead of dingy mercury? Despite its greater cost, mercury is prized for its greater expansion coefficient—that is, it expands much more than alcohol or water when subjected to small increases in temperature. A weather thermometer might measure temperatures between −30 degrees and 120 degrees

Fahrenheit, a span of 150 degrees, while a medical thermometer might cover only a ten- to twelve-degree range. A doctor might want to know your temperature to the nearest tenth of a degree; if a liquid with a small expansion coefficient were used, you would need a thermometer the length of a baseball bat to attain the proper degree of sensitivity. We don't know about you, but we'll stick with the stick thermometer.

Couldn't the medical thermometer manufacturers color mercury, then? Actually, they could, but don't, for reasons that Michael A. DiBiasi, of Becton Dickinson Consumer Products, explains:

> When you produce medical instruments, the rule of the road states that the fewer additives that you incorporate into any device or component material, the better off you are in gaining approval to market the device, and in avoiding product recalls that may be tied in to those additives. So fever thermometers use mercury in its natural silver-white color, and the glass tube is usually silk-screened with a background color to make it easier to see the mercury level.

Submitted by Herbert Kraut of Forest Hills, New York.

How do they measure the vitamin content of foods?

Some vitamins are present in such small concentrations in food that there are only a few micrograms (millionths of a gram) of the vitamin per hundred grams of food, while other vitamins might constitute ten milligrams per hundred grams of food. The techniques that work to measure the abundant vitamin often won't work to evaluate the presence of the other.

Jacob Exler, nutritionist for the Nutrient Data Research Branch of the Human Nutrition Information Service, told *Im-*

ponderables that there are two types of analytical procedures to measure the vitamin content of foods, chemical and microbiological:

> The chemical procedures measure the actual amount of a vitamin or a derivative of the vitamin, and the microbiological procedures measure the biological activity of the vitamin on some selected organism.

Today, chemical procedures are in vogue. In the past, microbiological studies were more common, and researchers tested not only on bacteria but on live rats. In fact, as late as the 1970s, the FDA used approximately twenty thousand rats a year just to test foods for vitamin D content! Roger E. Coleman, of the National Food Processors Association, explains the theory behind microbiological studies:

> An older, but still very acceptable method for vitamin assay is to measure the amount of microbiological growth a food supports. There are certain bacteria that require an outside source of one or more vitamins to grow. The growth of these bacteria is proportional to the amount of the required vitamin in the food.

But microbiological work is extremely sensitive. If conditions are not perfect, results can be skewed. As an example, an article in *FDA Papers* states that "the organism used for measuring vitamin B12 activity will show a measurable response when dosed with less than one ten-billionth of a gram of the vitamin." Microbiological assays work more effectively than chemical methods for measuring B12 levels (and some other vitamins, such as biotin, B6) because chemical analysis isn't sensitive enough to respond to the minute amounts of the vitamin contained in food.

In a chemical analysis, each vitamin in a given food must be measured separately. There are many chemical procedures to choose from, with catchy names like "gas-liquid chromatography" and "infra-red spectroscopy." Coleman explains a few different types of chemical analysis that are a little more comprehensible:

Each measuring technique is based on a property of the vitamin. For example, riboflavin fluoresces [produces light when exposed to radiant energy] and is measured by a fluorometer or fluorescence detector. Vitamin C combines with a certain purple dye and makes it colorless. By measuring the amount of this dye that is changed from purple to colorless, we can calculate the amount of vitamin C present.

Despite the high-tech names, chemical analysis tends not to be as sensitive as old-fashioned microbiological methods, but it is cheaper and faster—and doesn't necessitate twenty thousand rats a year sacrificing their life for vitamin D.

Submitted by Violet Wright of Hobbes, New Mexico. Thanks also to Todd Grooten of Kalamazoo, Michigan.

Why doesn't the water in fire hydrants freeze during the winter?

It would . . . if the wrong type of fire hydrant were used. In areas that experience cold weather, fire departments use "dry barrel hydrants," with operating valves located below the freezing level of the ground. The fire hydrant itself does not contain any water until the valve is opened.

In temperate climates, "wet barrel hydrants" are often utilized. These hydrants do contain water above ground level. What are the advantages of the wet barrel hydrant that help compensate for the risk of water in the hydrant freezing? We got the answer from the president of fire hydrant maker Hydra-Shield Manufacturing, Henry J. Stehling: "With wet barrel hydrants, each outlet has an operating valve. The wet barrel hydrant will have two or three outlets, each with its own operating valve, providing greater control."

Submitted by Todd Sanders of Holmdel, New Jersey.

Why do baked goods straight from the oven often taste (sickeningly) richer than after they are cooled?

When you ponder this Imponderable for a while, you realize there are only two approaches to the answer: one, the baked item really is different straight from the oven than it is ten or twenty minutes later, or two, that for some reason, the taster perceives the same item differently depending upon when it is consumed. Turns out there are experts who subscribe to each explanation.

Bakery engineer Simon S. Jackel assures us that items really do change in structure after being cooled because of a process called "starch retrogradation." In raw flour, starch exists in a coiled, closed structure. When flour is baked into bread or cakes, the starch uncoils and opens up when exposed to the water in the dough and the high temperature of the oven.

When the product comes out of the oven, it starts to cool down, and the starch begins to revert or "retrograde" to a partially coiled structure. Most importantly for our purposes, when the starch retrogrades, it absorbs some of the flavors and locks them up in the coiled starch so that the taste buds cannot process them. In other words, less flavor is available to the consumer as the product cools. Jackel states that retrogradation continues until the product is stale.

Two other baking experts lay the "blame" for the noxiousness of just-baked products on our noses. Joe Andrews, publicity coordinator for Pillsbury Brands, explains:

> A great deal of taste perception is determined not only by the taste buds, but also by the olfactory senses. . . . When a food is hot, it releases many volatiles that the nose may perceive as sweet. Thus a cake may seem sweeter when it is warm than when it is cold.
>
> The volatiles are perceived by the nose, both by sniffing through the nostrils and by the aromatics released in the mouth

that make their way to the nose via a hole in the back of the mouth, the nasopharynx. We say we "taste" these, but in actuality we are smelling them.

Andrews believes that the "richness" our correspondent complains about may actually be sweetness.

Tom Lehmann, of the American Institute of Baking, also emphasizes the importance of volatiles in taste perception. Many aromatics, including spices, are simply too powerful when hot. Lehmann blames egg whites as particular culprits in making hot bakery items smell vile and taste noxious. Angel food cake, a dessert with a high concentration of egg whites, is particularly lousy hot, Lehmann says, because egg whites are volatiles that are released in heat and have to cool completely in order to avoid producing an unpleasant smell.

Of course, there is nothing mutually exclusive about the retrogradation and volatiles theories. Unlike arguments about genetic versus environmental factors in deviant behavior, or creationism versus evolution, the theories can coexist peacefully and respectfully. After all, bakers are engaged in an important and soul-lifting pursuit; it's hard to get bitter and angry when your life revolves around a task as noble as trying to concoct the perfect doughnut.

Submitted by Connie Kuhn of Beaumont, Texas.

DAVID FELDMAN

Why is gravel often placed on flat roofs?

We were taken aback when Scott Shuler, director of research at the Asphalt Institute, referred to this Imponderable as "oft-asked." But he didn't seem to be kidding, for he had a quick comeback: "Obviously, because it rolls off pitched roofs and there needs to be a place to put all that small gravel."

Shuler put aside his burgeoning stand-up comedy routine long enough to inform us that flat roofs usually consist of aggregate ("there are generally two sources for this stuff: gravel from rivers and stone from quarries are both such materials") embedded in the asphalt mopping. With this technology, often referred to as "built-up roofing," alternating piles of roofing felt and asphalt are placed on the roof to provide a surface. According to Richard A. Boon, director of the Roofing Industry Educational Institute, the gravel is set in a "flood coat" of hot bitumen and is about the size of peas.

What function does the gravel serve?

1. According to William A. Good, executive vice-president of the National Roofing Contractors Association, the gravel helps to protect the roof membrane ("a combination of waterproofing and reinforcing materials" located just above the insulation and below the gravel) from puncture or tear by foot traffic from construction workers, dropped tools, hailstones, or stray meteorites.

2. Gravel provides a lighter, more reflective, color than black asphalt, making the roof more energy-efficient. A side benefit: Gravel lessens the ultraviolet degradation of the roof membrane that would exist if the membrane were exposed directly to the sun.

3. The gravel acts as ballast. In windy conditions, the membrane, which is, in essence, tar paper, can actually lift up and even fly off if left exposed.

4. The gravel provides more secure, less sticky, footing for anyone walking on the roof, increasing the safety not only of maintenance workers but of civilians. (Remember, frisbees and baseballs have a much better chance of landing on a flat roof than a pitched roof.)

5. The gravel acts as a fire retardant.

But gravel's status as the ballast of choice is in jeopardy, according to Boon:

Today, newer technology has allowed for single-layer roofing systems. Larger, ¾"–1½"-diameter stone is used . . . to hold the roofing system in place. The larger stones provide the same protection from sun, traffic, and fire, and the larger size reduces the potential for wind blow-off.

Submitted by Howard Livingston of Arlington, Texas.

There are many miniature dogs. Why aren't there any miniature house cats?

Our correspondent, Elizabeth Frenchman, quite rightly points out that there are legitimate breeds of dogs that resemble ro-

DAVID FELDMAN

dents more than canines. If poodles can be so easily downsized, why can't Siamese or Oriental cats? If dogs can range in size between the pygmyesque Pekingese or a sausage-like Dachshund to a nearly three-foot-high Borzoi or a lineman-shaped Saint Bernard, why is the size variation so small in cats?

According to Enid Bergstrom, editor of *Dog World*, the answer is in the genes. Bergstrom says that dogs are the most genetically variable mammals, the easiest to breed for desired characteristics. The genes of cats, on the other hand, are much less plastic. If you try to mix two different breeds of cats, the tendency is for the offspring to look like an Oriental tabby. Of course, as dog breeder Fred Lanting points out, domestic breeds are miniature cats of sorts, the descendants of the big cats found in zoos.

Helen Cherry, of the Cat Fanciers Federation, told *Imponderables* that felines could be reduced somewhat in size by interbreeding small cats, but she, as well as all of the cat experts we spoke to, insisted that they had never heard of any interest expressed in trying to miniaturize cats. A representative of the American Cat Association remarked that a cat is small enough already.

Cat associations and federations are conservative by nature. Helen Cherry predicted that miniature cats would not be allowed to register or show or be "acknowledged in any way." It isn't easy being small.

Submitted by Elizabeth Frenchman of New York, New York.

What is the meaning of the numbers inside the arrows of the triangle on recyclable plastics? And what do the letters below the triangle mean?

Both the numbers and the letters signify the composition of the plastic used in bottles and other containers. Imagine the problems at recycling centers if workers were forced to judge, by eye, whether a bottle was made out of polypropylene or polyethylene terephthalate, to mention merely two of the hardest to spell plastics.

So the Society of the Plastics Industry, Inc., developed a voluntary coding system for manufacturers to classify plastic containers according to their resin composition. The most common plastics received the lowest numbers. The letters are abbreviations of the dominant resin from which the container is made. If containers are made from more than one material, they are coded by the primary material:

1 = PET, or polyethylene terephthalate, used in plastic soda bottles
2 = HDPE, or high-density polyethylene, used in plastic milk and juice jugs
3 = V, or vinyl
4 = LDPE, or low-density polyethylene
5 = PP, or polypropylene
6 = PS, or polystyrene
7 = Other

The use of the plastic container coding system is voluntary, and the manufacturer does not in any way guarantee that the product will be recyclable or that the resins in the container will be compatible with other containers that have the same code number.

This disclaimer is necessary for several reasons. Virgin materials are manufactured for specific applications; not all polypropylene products, for example, can be blended successfully. In some cases, the intended application for the recycled product might be more demanding than its original use. And plastic, like any other material, can be contaminated by the contents of the container during its original use. We know we have a strong preference not to have the plastic containers recycled at some of the fast food joints where we have eaten.

Submitted by Dave Hanlon of Aurora, Illinois.

DAVID FELDMAN

Why are there no public bathrooms in most supermarkets?

After trying about ten different supermarket chains, we got one on-the-record response—from giant Kroger. Off the record, we got the same response from other stores as we received from Kroger's customer relations representative, Ginger Rawe: "Restrooms have always been available for customers' and employees' use, while not always visible to the public."

What incentive do supermarkets have to make restrooms noticeable or to encourage their use? Shelf space is at a premium, and supermarkets already suffer from very low profit margins. And stores have no desire to encourage noncustomers off the street to use restrooms. Department stores have long made it a policy to locate their bathrooms in the most obscure nooks of their space. You may have to walk past some unopened cartons or some unpackaged meat, but you'll find every supermarket has bathrooms. The next time nature calls, just ask a clerk—assuming you can find one. He or she will know how and where to find relief.

Incidentally, supermarket bathrooms are coming out of the closet, so to speak. With the advent of food superstores and warehouse supermarkets, many chains are trying to keep customers inside the store as long as possible, and floor space isn't quite as tight as in "regular" supermarkets. Some chains are making their bathrooms user-friendly by posting signs so that customers can actually find them. Now if they would just stock the bathrooms with paper towels instead of those infernal hand driers, we'd be content.

Submitted by Michael Reuzenaar of Colorado Springs, Colorado. Thanks also to Jadon Welke of Hebron, Indiana.

Why do babies blink less often than adults?

Babies blink a lot less than adults—many babies blink only once or twice a minute. The purpose of blinking is to spread tears over the surface of the eyes. Adults vary widely in their blink frequency, and such exigencies and circumstances as corneal touching, irritation, drying, foreign matter entering the eye, and emotional distress or excitement can all cause the blinking rate to rise dramatically.

Ophthalmologists we contacted are full of theories but not a definitive answer. James P. McCulley, of the Association of University Professors of Ophthalmology, points out that the nerve structure of the infant's eye is much less well developed than its adult counterpart. Babies don't even manufacture tears during their first month of birth, so they clearly seem immune to the pain of dry eyes that would afflict adults who don't blink more often.

Ophthalmologist Samuel Salamon, of the Cataract Eye Center of Cleveland, Ohio, muses over other possible explanations:

> It is puzzling to us as to why babies' eyes don't simply dry out. Of course, they don't spend that much time with their eyes open and the tiny bit of mucus that the eyes manufacture is usually enough to keep the front surface of the eye, the cornea, moistened sufficiently.
>
> Babies probably do not need to blink as often as adults because their fissures are much smaller. That is, much less of their front eye surface is exposed to the environment both because of the shape of their skulls and because their eyelid openings are very small. Thus, the eyes dry out much more slowly, and need lubrication much less often.

Some ophthalmologists we contacted also speculated that babies' blinking rates may not be caused as much by emotional

DAVID FELDMAN

components as adults' are. Perhaps, but any parent who has had a baby cry for hours for totally unexplained reasons may hesitate to believe that stress isn't a major part of the infant's ecosystem.

Submitted by Julie Ann Jimenez of Houston, Texas.

Why do your eyes hurt when you are tired?

Why do couch potatoes have such a bad reputation? While lying on the sofa perusing an Archie comic book or studying the impact of television violence on children by viewing Bugs Bunny cartoons, they are actually exercising what ophthalmologist James P. McCulley, of the University of Texas Medical School, calls "among the most active muscles in the body."

Actually, your eyes contain three sets of muscle groups:

- Each eye has six *extraocular muscles* attached to the outside of the eyeball, which turn the eyes in all directions. The extraocular muscles must coordinate their movements so that both eyes look in the same direction at the same time.
- The *sphincter and dilatory muscles* open or close the pupils, defining how much light is allowed into the eye.
- The *ciliary muscles* attach to the lens inside the eye. When these muscles contract or relax, they change the shape of the lens, altering its focus.

Concentrated reading or close work provides a workout for these muscle groups strenuous enough to make Richard Simmons proud. Unfortunately, as in all aerobic programs, the saying "no pain, no gain" applies, as Winnipeg, Manitoba optometrist Steven Mintz explains:

> The human eye is designed so that, if perfectly formed, it will form a clear image on the retina (at the back of the eye) of any distant object without having to use any of the muscles. In order to see closer objects clearly, however, each set of muscles has to

work. The extraocular muscles must turn each eye inward; the sphincter muscles must work to make the pupil smaller; and the ciliary muscles must contract to allow the lens to change to a shape that will produce a clearer image.

This minimal muscular effort is significant in itself. However, no human eye is perfectly formed and these imperfections will increase the amount of effort required. For instance, people who are farsighted must exert more than the normal amount of effort on the part of the ciliary muscles. Many people have extraocular muscle imbalances that force them to work harder. Virtually every person, as [he or she] approaches or passes the age of forty, suffers from a stiffening of the lens inside the eye, which forces those ciliary muscles to work even harder. Reading under poor light (either too much or too little) will cause the sphincter and dilatory muscles to work excessively.

Just like doing 100 pushups can cause the arm muscles to become pain[ed], so can the muscular effort . . . described above cause sore eyes. Add to this that after several hours of close work, all of your body's muscles are going to be more fatigued, your level of tolerance or your pain threshold for sore eyes will be less than when you are fresh.

Ophthalmologists we consulted speculated that much of the eye strain attributed to tiredness is in reality caused by dryness. Dr. Ronald Schachar, of the association for the Advancement of Ophthalmology, notes that when one is tired, the blink rate slows down and the eyes are not properly lubricated. Close work also slows down the blink rate. Eye specialists are finding that workers at computer visual display terminals experience decreased blinking. This is one reason most consultants recommend stepping away from VDTs at least once an hour. While most of us are more than happy to rest our muscles after doing a few pushups, we expose our eyes to a marathon just about every day.

Submitted by Martin Nearl of Monsey, New York.

DAVID FELDMAN

Why does after-shave lotion have to sting? What causes the sting, and could it be replaced by a nonsting ingredient?

What's the stinging culprit? Demon alcohol. John Corbett, vice-president of technology at Clairol, elaborates:

> The reason that most after-shave lotions sting is that they contain a relatively high percentage of ethyl alcohol, which, coupled with the fact that the facial skin has been subject to abrasion by the process of shaving, sets up an ideal situation for eliciting the sensation of stinging. The importance of the abrasion contribution can be readily tested by applying after-shave lotion some hours after shaving—no stinging sensation will be observed.

Corbett mentioned that there are nonstinging after-shave balms on the market, but "none have achieved significant popularity." So why do men crave a little pain in the morning? Corbett offers a few possibilities: "Presumably men find the sting of after-shave products an aid to waking up and proof that something is happening—or, maybe, men are masochists at heart."

Irene L. Malbin, vice-president of public affairs at the Cosmetic, Toiletry, and Fragrance Association, told *Imponderables* that after-shave lotions are not merely repackaged colognes or perfumes. Some lotions contain cooling astringent ingredients to heal small nicks and cuts; others moisturize and smooth the skin. Unlike perfumes, the scent is formulated to "perform for a short time."

The alcohol in after-shave lotion that stings you also protects you—it acts as an antiseptic. Cosmetics companies won't brag about this fact in ads, for if they do, the lotion will be classified as a drug. Cosmetics companies avoid the drug classification so that the product will not fall under the regulatory and marketing constraints for pharmaceuticals, which are far more rigorous than for cosmetics.

Submitted by Dr. John Hardin of Greenfield, Indiana.

Why do you often see tires on top of mobile homes in trailer parks?

Our initial research wasn't encouraging. Augie, at Sunset Trailer Park, in San Jose, California, insisted that someone was pulling our leg. He had never heard of putting tires on a trailer and thought it would be a bad idea—if the tire dented the roof, rust, and eventually a hole, would create a major repair job.

We were disappointed when Jane Owens, at Western Trailer Park in San Jose, agreed with Augie that she hadn't seen tires on the roofs of trailers in northern California. But, she added, "They put tires on the roof in Nevada, where it gets windy."

"Oh, no," we thought, "don't tell us that the tires are used to weigh down the trailers to keep them from blowing away during tornadoes?" We were assured not. Kay McKeown, who runs a trailer park in Battle Mountain, Nevada, explained that most mobile homes have tie-downs to keep the trailers in place during severe wind.

The purpose of the tires on the roof, Kay and Jane agreed, is to kill the noise of wind and rain hitting the surface of the aluminum or tin roof. The tires deflect the pinging sound of rain; even better, the weight of the tires keeps the wind from making the roof pop in and out, the most annoying and sleep-destroying sound since the invention of the leaky faucet. One layer of tires does the job effectively, and the tires needn't have new treads or high biases. Of course, some trailers boast shingled roofs— these don't pop in and out, and don't need tires atop them, but they tend to cost more.

We never would have thought of the "prevent the roof popping" answer to this Imponderable, but as ignorant as we were, we still couldn't resist challenging the trailer park mavens about why tires were chosen to kill the sound of falling rain or hail. Surely, the owners could have found a better tool for the purpose —a tire, after all, is almost as much hole as substance. While Jane Owens acknowledged that tires can't cover the whole surface of the roof and are much more successful at solving the popping roof problem, they greatly soften the noise. And, she adds, some people place a tarp or plywood directly over the roof and then place the tires on top. The additional covering not only kills the sound but helps prevent corrosion of the metal roof.

Submitted by Lynne Lichtenstein of Hickory, North Carolina.

Why do cows stick their tongues up their nostrils?

We were tempted to say, "Because they can!" But in our relentless quest for truth we asked several cattle experts about this unsightly habit. Our serious guess was that the tongue was the easiest way to lubricate the dreaded "dry nose" condition that we assumed plagued our bovine friends. Wrong. Cows stick their tongues up their nostrils for two distinct reasons.

Cows have nasolabial glands located in the dermis (just under the epidermis of the skin) that produce a watery secretion that helps keep their noises moist. Cows and other ruminants use these secretions to digest their food, as Michael T. Smith, of the National Cattlemen's Association, explains:

> They frequently thrust their muzzles into the feed and, during rumination, run their tongues into the nostril and over the muzzle, thus bringing the secretion into the mouth. The chemical properties of nasolabial secretions are similar to saliva and aid in the digestive process (e.g., swallowing, enzymatic activity, buffering of the rumen [the cow's first stomach]).

Smith adds that buffalo exhibit the same behavior as their female counterparts.

Cows frequently endure respiratory infections that involve involuntary nasal discharges, sometimes quite heavy. Dr. Harold Amstutz, of the American Association of Bovine Practitioners, told *Imponderables* that these discharges are quite irritating and need to be expelled. But "cows don't have handkerchiefs or fingers." So they use their tongues to remove the irritant instead.

Submitted by Gena Stephenson of Bloomington, Illinois. Thanks also to Irvin Lush of Louisville, Kentucky.

Why don't banks return canceled checks in numerical order?

They could, but it would take one additional step that would ultimately cost the consumer, as well as the banks, more money. Ann Walk, executive director of the National Independent Bank Equipment & Systems Association, explains:

> The average account has only twenty-eight checks per month, and the banks feel that the customer can sort these and save the banks time. If you will notice on your monthly statement, the checks are listed in numerical order for your convenience. This is done automatically by machine and not by hand, as sorting checks would be.

Are the checks placed in your statements in random order? Not really. Banks send bank checks with your statement in the order *they* received them.

Submitted by R. A. Pickett of Danville, Illinois.

What makes cotton shrink more when washed than wool when cleaned?

If we had known how complicated this subject was, we might have tried tackling an easier problem, perhaps solving the unresolved issues in quantum physics or conducting an exhaustive search to find either a scintilla of humor or a decent female role in an Oliver Stone movie.

Trade groups in both the wool and cotton industry sent us literature full of equations and formulas, the likes of which we hadn't seen since we glanced at the textbook for that math class in college that we decided not to take because it was too difficult or, rather, not relevant to solving the social ills of our country. But since we are stuck with the issue at hand, please believe us when we tell you we are *simplifying* our answer.

All the processes that turn cotton into a finished garment (e.g., spinning, weaving or knitting, dyeing, finishing) strain and contract the fabric. Cotton shrinks when this strain is relaxed. Although many factors can contribute to shrinkage, by far the biggest factor is swelling of the yarn when exposed to water.

One might think that swollen yarn would increase the size of the garment, but what happens is that a greater length of yarn, known as warp yarn, is required to interweave the greater diameter of the swollen filling threads if the fibers are to remain in position. But the knitting process doesn't allow enough extra yarn to interweave, so the filling threads are drawn together. This results in a relaxation of the internal strain and shrinkage in length. This shrinkage can occur in the clothes dryer as well

DAVID FELDMAN

as in the washing machine, as anyone who has ever seen an extra-large T-shirt turn into a medium after a prolonged spin can attest. Chemical processes, such as Sanforizing, can eliminate all but about 1 percent of this shrinkage, but the treatment affects the feel and wear characteristics of the cotton.

Despite wool's reputation as a relatively shrink-free material, it is susceptible to the same relaxation of strains problems as cotton, and one more as well: felting shrinkage. Felting shrinkage is why you can't put most wool garments in the washing machine, as the American Wool Council explains:

> Felting shrinkage occurs when wool is subjected to heat, moisture, and friction, the kind of friction that takes place in washing agitation. The microscopic scale-like structures of the wool fiber interlock; the fabric becomes thicker and smaller; it shrinks or felts. This kind of shrinkage is irreversible.

So why doesn't wool shrink when exposed to the heat in dry cleaning? Because as part of the finishing process of making a wool garment, the wool is preshrunk in a process called "fulling" or "milling." Heat, moisture, and friction are applied to the fabric so that it shrinks a specified amount in length and width. Fulling tightens the weave and helps provide the softer texture desired of wool garments. Many chemical processes have been invented to allow treated wool garments to be machine washed and dried.

One advantage of wool over cotton is that shrinkage caused by relaxation of fiber strains can often be reversed. We have been testing this hypothesis by bravely, and without regard to our own welfare, gaining weight over the years. We can conclusively state that our old cotton T-shirts, which once fit perfectly, are not capable of expanding to fit our now ampler frame.

Submitted by John Clark of Pittsburgh, Pennsylvania.

Why are powdered laundry detergents sold in such odd weights?

Call it rigid and boring, but there is something comforting about the sizing of liquid detergents. Most brands, such as the largest-selling liquid detergent in the United States, Tide, manufacture 32-ounce, 64-ounce, 96-ounce, 128-ounce, and 156-ounce sizes. But compare these nice, even sizes (which make sense both as even pound equivalents and as units of quarts and gallons) to Tide's "regular" and "Ultra" powdered detergents. According to Procter & Gamble spokesperson Joe Mastrullo, the company now produces only two sizes of "regular" detergent—in two rather strange sizes: 39 ounces and 136 ounces.

What gives? According to Edna Leurck, of P&G's consumer services,

> When detergents were first introduced, the weight selected was chosen to make the products compatible with those laundry soaps that were in general use. Over the years, increased detergent technology led to changes in the products, which have caused the standard weights to jump around a bit.

The sizes selected are not arbitrary, though. Sheryl B. Zapcic, of Lever Brothers Company, explains that powdered detergents are sold to provide consumers with

> an approximate number of standard dry measured uses. For instance, if a detergent is packaged to provide the consumer with 20 uses and each use measures ½ cup of detergent, the weight of the package is calculated by multiplying 20 times the weight of each ½-cup use. Therefore, the consumer gets an "even" number of washing uses, rather than an "even" number of ounces.

This explains the odd sizes of regular Tide packages we mentioned. The 39-ounce size is meant to clean thirteen loads; the 136-ounce size should handle forty-six loads.

We thought that when concentrated detergents swept the supermarket aisles, their weights might be rounded off like their liquid counterparts, but alas, the tradition of the weird sizing

DAVID FELDMAN

continues. Ultra Tide, the best-selling concentrated powdered detergent, is marketed in five configurations: 23 ounces (ten loads); 42 ounces (eighteen loads); 70 ounces (thirty loads); 98 ounces (forty-two loads); and 198 ounces (eighty-five loads).

If you calculate the weight per load, you will see that the definition of a "load" isn't absolutely precise. But then how many of us are meticulous in measuring the amount of detergent we toss into the washing machine, anyway?

Submitted by Chris Allingham of Sacramento, California.

What are we smelling when it "smells like rain is coming"?

This isn't the type of question that meteorologists study in graduate school or that receives learned exegeses in scholarly journals, but we got several experts to speculate for us. They came down into two camps.

1. *It ain't the rain, it's the humidity.* Biophysicist Joe Doyle blames the humidity, which rises before rainfall. Of course, humidity itself doesn't smell, but it accentuates the smells of all the objects around it. Everything from garbage to grass smells stronger when it gets damp. Doyle believes that the heightened smell of the flora and fauna around us tips us off subliminally to the feeling that it is going to rain. Richard Anthes, of the National Center for Atmospheric Research, points out that many gaseous pollutants also are picked up more by our smell receptors when it is humid.

2. *The ozone did it.* Dr. Keith Seitter, assistant to the executive director of the American Meteorology Association, reminds us that before a thunderstorm, lightning produces ozone, a gas with a distinctive smell. He reports that people who are near lightning recognize the ozone smell (as do those who work with electrical motors, which emit ozone).

Kelly Redmond, meteorologist at the Western Regional Climate Center, in Reno, Nevada, also subscribes to the ozone theory, with one proviso. Ozone emissions are common during thunderstorms in the summer, but not from the rains from stratiform clouds during the cold season. So if it's "smelling like rain" during the winter in Alaska, chances are you are not smelling the ozone at all but the soil, plants, and vegetation you see around you, enhanced by the humidity.

Submitted by Dr. Thomas H. Rich of Melbourne, Victoria, Australia. Thanks also to George Gudz of Prescott, Arizona; Anne Thrall of Pocatello, Idaho; Dr. Allan Wilke of Toledo, Ohio; Matthew Whitfield of Hurdle Mills, North Carolina; Philip Fultz of Twentynine Palms, California; and William Lee of Melville, New York.

Why do unopened jars of mayonnaise, salad dressing, fruit, and many other foods stay fresh indefinitely on the shelf but require refrigeration after being opened?

The three main enemies of freshness in perishable foods are air, heat, and low acidity. Foods such as mayonnaise, salad dressing, and canned fruit all undergo processing to eliminate these hazards. Burton Kallman, director of science and technology for the National Nutritional Foods Association, explains:

> Unopened jars of perishable foods can remain at room temperature because they are sealed with low oxygen levels (sometimes under vacuum), are often sterilized or at least pasteurized, and may contain preservatives which help maintain their freshness.

All three of these foods contain *natural* ingredients that act as preservatives. Roger E. Coleman, senior vice-president of public communications for the National Food Processors Association, differentiates between foods that must be refrigerated immediately and those that can remain unopened on the shelf:

> Products such as marinated vegetables, salad dressings, and fruits, which contain adequate amounts of added acid ingredients such as vinegar and/or lemon juice, will not support the growth of hazardous microorganisms and only need to be refrigerated after opening to prevent them from spoiling. Other products, such as canned meats and vegetables, do not contain acidic ingredients and, thus, can support the growth of hazardous microorganisms. These products must be refrigerated, not only to retard spoilage but to keep them safe to eat after opening.

This last point is particularly important, for many foods that state "Refrigerate after opening" are perfectly safe to store back on the shelf after they are opened. So why the warning? Barbara Preston, executive director of the Association for Dressings and Sauces, writes:

> Most commercial dressings (with the exception of those bought from a refrigerated display case) are perfectly safe stored at room temperature. The words 'Refrigerate After Opening' on the label are intended only to help preserve their taste, aroma, and appearance. They do not relate to spoilage. If an already opened jar of salad dressing is accidentally left out for several hours, don't throw it away. There is no danger of spoiling . . . it just may not taste as fresh.

Submitted by Nancy Schmidt of West New York, New Jersey.

Why are matchbooks assembled so that the sharp side of the staple is on the striking side, risking injury to the fingers?

What piece of legislation in 1978 has affected and changed American life most profoundly? Some would argue it was the Senate's vote to turn the Panama Canal over to the Panamanians. Or Jimmy Carter's signing the Humphrey-Hawkins bill, which attempted to ensure full employment while keeping inflation in check. But some, with great sincerity, will point to the federal regulations enacted requiring the striking strip to be moved to the back of the matchbook.

We all know that the federal bureaucracy gets blamed for imposing too many regulations, but this one actually made some sense. Although matchbooks before 1978 were clearly marked "Close Cover Before Striking," macho types or those in the throes of a nicotine fit often struck the matches without closing the cover; with the striking strip on the front, the exposed matches often came in contact with the heat, or even the flame, of the match, causing burns.

Manufacturers were required to move the strip to the back of the book. Couldn't they simply reverse the staple position on the new books, lessening the chances of staple cuts?

The problem is that the matchbook industry would have had to retrofit all of their existing machinery. So instead of changing the position of the staple, today a machine clinches the staple to ensure it is properly closed. Furthermore, the striker is placed high enough above the staple so that even shaky smokers can avoid hitting the staple. The staple should not penetrate the striking strip at all.

We asked Iain Walton, customer service representative for match manufacturer D.D. Bean & Sons, if they have encountered problems with the staples in post-1978 matchbooks. He replied that there weren't problems with staple cuts, but . . .

> Some people do complain that the staple was responsible for causing flying heads from the matches. In all cases, if the match is struck correctly, the staple is in no way responsible. In fact, the reason this happens is that the match was not struck along the length of the striking strip, as is intended. Instead, it is struck across the width of the striking surface and into the staple.

We have often wondered about this Imponderable ourselves. But we still find it amusing that *staple cuts* are the health hazard smokers worry about.

Submitted by Pete Johnson of Fargo, North Dakota.

Why are paper (book) matches dark on one side and light on the other?

If 1992 seemed like an especially exciting year to you, and you didn't quite understand why, may we suggest the reason. Even if you didn't know it consciously, you were celebrating the hundredth anniversary of the book match. Certainly Iain K. Watson was excited about the August centennial celebration in Jaffrey,

New Hampshire. Even so, he took a little time out to provide us with a precise answer to this Imponderable.

We may take for granted the design of a match book, but manufacturers don't. Who would have thought that the reason for the different colors of matches was . . . aesthetics?

> If you look at a book of matches, you will notice that one side is brown, or "kraft" [the type of strong wrapping paper used in paper shopping bags], while the other is either blue or white. Match stems are manufactured from recycled paper stock, which in its finished form is the ugly brown color of the match backs.
>
> In order to enhance its appearance, in the final stages that this brown paper pulp is being pressed, additional processes are added. In the case of the blue color of the front of the stem stock, blue dye is added to the paper. When this dye is added, the blue coloring only goes partway through the stock. Hence the brown remains the color of the back.
>
> In the case of the white-fronted match sticks, during the final pressing processes of the recycled paper stock, cleaner, whiter recycled paper pulp is added, giving the final layers a whiter appearance than the bulk of the brown recycled board. Generally, the whiter recycled stock is comprised of papers such as white envelopes and white bond papers, whereas the majority of the match stem stock is composed of a mishmash of recycled papers.

We don't know of anyone who ever selected, or for that matter refused, to use book matches (which, after all, are usually given out for free) based on the color of the matches themselves. But match manufacturers hardly want to test the hypothesis. For there are other alternatives, like lighters, lurking around for consumers to use.

Submitted by Rory Sellers of Carmel, California.

How can the blades of electric can openers be sharp enough to cut through metal yet not sharp enough to cut our fingers when touched?

The blade of a can opener is far from dull, but it need not be as sharp as a scalpel to open cans. As Marilyn Myers, of Norelco Consumer Products, put it, "The metal in the opener is made of sturdier stuff than the can it opens."

Just as important, the blade has a lot of help in opening the can. Liz Wentland, of Sunbeam-Oster, explains that pressure is exerted on the blade by the can opener lever to drive it into the can. Once the drive wheel of the can opener pushes the blade through the lid so that the seal is broken, a razor-sharp blade isn't necessary. On an electric can opener, the drive wheel obtains its power from the motor; on hand models, the crank (and human hands) provides the power.

DAVID FELDMAN

Myers adds that can opener blades do occasionally need replacement. Why? "Mainly because they get clogged with goo."

Submitted by Patti Willis of Endicott, New York.

Why do most retail establishments with double doors usually lock one of the two leaves?

In every *Imponderables* book, one chapter becomes an obsession. This time around, we were fixated on solving the double door dilemma, mainly because we face this predicament on a daily basis.

We approach a store. We see double doors in front of us with both leaves closed. Which leaf is locked? Should we try the left or the right? And should we pull? Or should we push? Four possible combinations. Invariably, we succeed. On the fourth try.

We spoke to or received letters from dozens of sources about this Imponderable over the last five years. We heard no consensus and not much sense, either. In despair, we asked trusty researcher Sherry Spitzer to speak to store managers, architects, door manufacturers, and safety inspectors to see if she could make sense out of a confusing assemblage of responses. After many person-hours of work by both of us, all we can report is that while there are many theories to explain why proprietors might lock one leaf of a double door, few of the people who actually *do* lock them could provide a reasonable explanation for their behavior.

Still, we'll share what we've come up with, and pray that an empathic reader will help relieve the pounding sensation in our brain.

First of all, why do stores have double doors in the first place? Local fire codes mandate the minimum width of doors used as exits in public buildings. Double doors are lighter and more practical than single doors to cover a wide area. Electric sliding doors, one possibility, are extremely expensive, while one wide door would sweep over a tremendous area within and outside of the store, posing the threat of accidents and occupying valuable store space. Double doors also allow for easier movement in and out of the store, particularly if customers are trying to enter while others are trying to exit. Double doors also make it possible to move in furniture or other wide objects if the service entrance is impassable.

What explanations did we hear for closing one of the leaves? Here are the most plausible:

1. *Saves energy costs. By opening only one side, stores can retain heat in the winter and air conditioning in the summer.* True, but the savings are minimal, indeed. An individual will not open both sides at once. If a group of people, leaving and/or entering, can't open both leaves at once, they will keep one open much longer than if they were using both to make their transition. Approximately the same amount of heat/air conditioning would be lost.

2. *The wind can kick up when both leaves are open.* Again, not untrue. A good architect can assure that doors will not buckle with gusts, but wind problems are one of the reasons why double doors are often supplied with deadbolts for one leaf. Vestibules also absorb most of the wind tunnel effect that occasionally occurs.

3. *Prevents shoplifting.* Several store managers claimed that this was the main purpose for locking one leaf. But Jack Schultz, of the National Retail Federation, claimed that this argument is ridiculous on its face. The thief has already entered the store—he or she knows full well which door(s) will be open on the way out.

4. *Crowd control/traffic flow.* You must be kidding. Closing leaves causes congestion at the doorways. Control? Maybe. Flow? No. (Besides, we've seen leaves locked in many stores and office buildings without any security or crowd control efforts whatsoever.)

5. *Astragals.* Between 10 and 20 percent of the double doors installed include astragals: metal, rubber, or felt material that cov-

ers the gap between the two leaves of the double door. Astragals help keep the elements, notably dirt, smoke, wind, and precipitation, from entering the store, and help preserve conditioned air inside. Astragals also keep potential criminals from sticking a coat hanger or other wedge in between the doors to force entry.

Obviously, a metal astragal is a far more effective deterrent to thieves than softer materials, but it makes life more difficult for the shopkeeper. According to architect David B. Eagan, of Eagan Associates, the astragal is usually placed on the active door. Why? The door with the astragal has to close last so that the two leaves will close appropriately. (If the leaf with the astragal is closed first, the other leaf won't close all the way.)

If both doors are activated, "coordinating hardware," usually placed at the top of the door, is necessary to make the leaves close harmoniously. But coordinating hardware is very expensive. The path of least resistance (and least strain on the pocketbook) is to lock one leaf and activate the second leaf only when necessary.

While we are always ready to accept any explanation that hinges on saving money or hard work, most stores don't have doors with metal astragals (soft astragals don't require expensive coordinating hardware or one particular leaf to be designated as the active one), so theory number 5 can't explain this universal condition.

Still, we argue that laziness is the dominant motivator in The Case of the Locked Doorleaf. It is easier for store employees to contend with one door than two. Rose Smouse, executive assistant of the National Retail Federation, concurs:

> There is no standard as to why this second double door is locked. It is, best as we can tell, pure convenience. This second door usually has [flush-bolt] locks that go into the top part of the doorjamb and another one that goes into the floor. Some doors have special locks that open them. These second doors are not convenient or easy to open and, therefore, remain locked.

A few off-the-record remarks from store managers and their underlings indicated that the laziness theory has much to commend it.

Judging from our mailbag, most folks wish door policies were more convenient for them, rather than the storekeepers.

National Retail Federation's Jack Schultz, who once operated-department store giant Bloomingdale's, calls closing any of the doors to a retail establishment "the most customer-insulting activity a retail establishment can engage in."

May we include one more, not insignificant point? Closing one leaf may be illegal. Local fire codes ordain the width required of any "means of egress" from an establishment open to the public. If an exit must be six feet wide, can it be counted at that width if one of the two leaves is closed, and the doorway is effectively only three feet wide?

We spoke to Bruce W. Hisley, program chair of the Fire Prevention Technical Program Series at the National Fire Academy, who informed us that although there is no single national standard for such matters, virtually all localities require that doors identified as exits must be open when the building is occupied. The question remains: Does that mean both leaves of the door or only one?

In practice, many stores meet fire codes by installing double doors that the fire department assumes will stay open during business hours. They are committing a code violation by closing one leaf. But until localities hire many more inspectors, we'll all have to play the "guess which door" game a little longer.

> *Submitted by Paul Dunn of Morton, Illinois. Thanks also to Douglas Watkins, Jr., of Hayward, California; Jean Harmon of Silver Spring, Maryland; John V. Dixon of Wilmette, Illinois; Thomas Schoeck of Slingerlands, New York; Nancy Stairs of Revelstoke, British Columbia; Frank P. Burger of Nashville, Tennessee; Nelson T. Sparks of Louisa, Kentucky; and Ralph Kaden of New Haven, Connecticut.*

In large enclosed shopping malls, why is the last door on both sides of the main entrance often closed?

The answer once again is, of course, laziness. Mark Weitzman posed this Imponderable in 1987, and ever since we've sought the solution, we have met with obfuscation worthy of politicians and beauty pageant contestants.

Fire codes mandate wide exits for malls. We've seen many with eight sets of double doors side by side. Barring an emergency, the main entrance/exit is rarely congested. Too often, security personnel at malls find it more convenient to not unlock some doors (usually the doors on the far left and right), so as not to have to lock them up again later. Some mall employees have tried to convince us that outer doors are closed to conserve energy or for security reasons, but the explanations ring hollow for the same reasons as they did in the last entry.

Our friend at the National Fire Academy, Bruce Hisley, told *Imponderables* that when he was a fire marshall, he often found that all but one set of a local mall's doors were locked shortly before closing time, in clear violation of fire codes. A little investigation yielded the discovery that this was the employees' less than subtle method of deterring customers from going into the mall at the last minute. Anyone who has ever entered a restaurant five minutes before the stated closing time and received less than stellar service will comprehend the operative mentality.

Submitted by Mark Weitzman of Boulder, Colorado.

Why are there two red stripes around the thinnest part of bowling pins?

Their sole purpose, according to Al Vanderneck, of the American Bowling Congress, is to look pretty. Part of Vanderneck's job is to check the specifications of bowling equipment, and he reports that without the stripes, the pins "just look funny." The area where the stripes are placed is known as the "neck," and evidently a naked neck on a bowling pin stands out as much as a tieless neck on a tuxedo wearer.

Actually, we almost blew the answer to this Imponderable.

WHEN DID WILD POODLES ROAM THE EARTH?   181

We've thrown a few turkeys in our time, and we always identified the red stripes with AMF pins; the other major manufacturer of bowling pins, Brunswick, used a red crown as an identification mark on its pins. So we assumed that the red stripes were a trademark of AMF's.

AMF's product manager Ron Pominville quickly disabused us of our theory. Brunswick's pins have always had stripes, too, and Brunswick has eliminated the red crown in their current line of pins. A third and growing presence in pindom, Vulcan, also includes stripes on their products.

We haven't been able to confirm two items: Who started the practice of striping the necks of bowling pins? And exactly what is so aesthetically pleasing about these two thin strips of crimson applied to battered, ivory-colored pins?

Submitted by Michael Alden of Rochester Hills, Michigan.
Thanks also to Ken Shafer of Traverse City, Michigan.

Does catnip "work" on big cats like lions and tigers?

Catnip (or *Nepeta cataria*, as scientists so eloquently call it) is a perennial herb that drives many house cats wild with delight. It was probably first noticed as an attractant when big cats swarmed around withered or bruised plants growing in the wild.

A full response to catnip involves four separate actions, usually in this order:

1. Sniffing
2. Licking and chewing with head shaking
3. Chin and cheek rubbing
4. Head-over rolling and body rubbing

The full cycle usually lasts under fifteen minutes. Some cats will also vocalize after the head-over rolling, presumably a response to hallucinations. Although the cats exposed to catnip mimic their behavior when in heat, catnip does not increase sexual interest or activity and doesn't seem to affect cats in heat more perceptibly.

Scientists know quite a bit about how domestic cats react to catnip. Most cats do not begin responding to the plant until they are six to eight weeks of age, and some may not respond until they are three months of age. All of the research provided by the Cornell Feline Health Center indicates that cats' reaction to catnip is independent of sex or neutering status. Susceptibility is inherited as an autosomal dominant trait—about a third of domestic cats have no reaction to catnip.

Two-legged mammals have not been immune to the charms of catnip. Veterinarian Jeff Grognet cites the historical use of catnip by humans; the versatile herb was used to make tea, juice, tincture, poultice, and infusions. Catnip was also smoked and chewed for its reputed therapeutic, hallucinogenic, or euphoria-inducing properties.

Scientists, like our reader, have also been curious about the effect of catnip on other cats, and other types of animals. In the largest study of catnip's effect on a wide range of animals, Dr. N. B. Todd's conclusion was clear: Although a few individual animals of almost every type reacted in some way to catnip, cats responded most often and most intensely.

Out of sixteen lions tested, fourteen had full household cat-type responses. Almost half of twenty-three tigers tested had no response at all, but many had incomplete responses: Some sniffed; fewer licked; only a couple chin-rubbed; and none exhibited head-over rolling. But young tigers had violently strong reactions to catnip. Most leopards, jaguars, and snow leopards had strong, full-cycle reactions to catnip. We know that bobcats and lynx love catnip, for the herb is sold commercially to lure these cats for trapping purposes.

Noncats, such as civets and mongooses, were mostly indifferent to catnip, although a few exhibited sniffing reactions. An

DAVID FELDMAN

earlier study that predates Todd's concluded that dogs, rabbits, mice, rats, guinea pigs, and fowls were indifferent to a powdered form of catnip that seduced domestic cats. Yet many dog owners report that their pets respond to catnip.

For some anecdotal evidence, we contacted several of the largest American zoos to see if they exposed their big cats to catnip. We found cat keepers almost as curious about catnip as the cats themselves.

We spoke to one cat keeper who fed jaguars catnip directly. "They like it," he said. "They get goofy." But the same keeper reported that a snow leopard wasn't interested. Another keeper reported that tigers responded "to some extent."

Rick Barongi, director of the Children's Zoo at the San Diego Zoo, reports that although most pet owners usually spray catnip scent on a favorite toy of their cat, zoo keepers cannot. A jaguar or lion will simply rip apart and then eat the toy, so instead they spray a piece of wood or a log that a big cat can claw or scratch. Barongi shares the belief that all cats respond to catnip to some extent but that younger cats respond more than older cats, and that all cats react more on first exposure to catnip than in subsequent encounters.

After a thrill or two with catnip, the San Diego Zoo keepers have found that big cats are more entertained in the long run by scratch posts, boomer balls, larger cages, or—most expensive, but most satisfying of all—the pleasure of the company of a cage mate.

Submitted by Dave Williams of Ithaca, New York.

Why are there no purple Christmas lights?

We have read marketing studies indicating that purple is one of the least popular colors among consumers. But judging from all the purple stationery we receive from readers, purple is a popular color among women, especially among young women and girls. So it is probably no coincidence that the two correspondents who posed this Imponderable were of the female persuasion.

Some Christmas sets do include magenta lights, but you will never see deep purple lights. The absence is not a matter of taste but of high school physics. Carla M. Fischer, public relations representative of General Electric, explains:

> The reason there are no deep purple lights is because purple light has the shortest wavelength and is not visible to the human eye.
>
> For instance, when you see a red light, it is a result of the transparent material filtering all wavelengths of light except the red. The same is true for the other colors of the spectrum (remember ROY G BIV?) [a mnemonic for the length of wavelengths, representing red, orange, yellow, green, blue, indigo, and violet].
>
> . . . However, when the transparent material is purple, it filters out all other wavelengths of light except purple; since purple light is not visible to the human eye, you would only see black light.

Bill Middlebrook, a lighting applications specialist for Philips Lighting, concurred that purple bulbs emit a dim glow, indeed, while also making other low-output colors, such as green, look washed-out. Middlebrook added that even blue doesn't really do its share of the illumination load and would probably be omitted from Christmas sets if it weren't for its popularity. Philips has found that consumers prefer "the classics": red, green, blue, and yellow. Of these colors, red and yellow provide by far the most illumination.

We asked Middlebrook if Philips conducted research to determine how to arrange the colors in the Christmas set. The answer: They are randomly arranged.

Submitted by Laurie Muscheid of Rocky Point, New York.
Thanks also to Janice Flinn of Kemptville, Ontario.

DAVID FELDMAN

Why do pet rodents drink water out of bottles instead of dishes or bowls?

Because we offer them bottles. Rats or guinea pigs would be more than happy to drink out of bowls or dishes as well. After all, in the wild, rodents have to fend for themselves, gathering water from lakes or ponds if they have easy access. More likely, their search for water will be more labor-intensive, involving extracting moisture from succulent plants or dew drops on greenery, or stumbling upon opportunistic puddles (the natural equivalent of a water dish).

Veterinarian David Moore, of Virginia Tech's Office of Animal Resources, says that the practice of installing water bottles with sipper tubes was developed by researchers to promote the health of laboratory animals. When a rodent soiled the water in a bowl, bacteria grew and caused illness. On the other hand, it is anatomically impossible for a rat to defecate or urinate into a water bottle with a sipper tube.

Rodent owners have adopted the practice not only to safeguard their pets but to avoid the less than pleasant chore of cleaning soiled water bowls. Although dogs occasionally treat the toilet like a water bowl, luckily both dogs and cats can both be trained not to treat their water bowls like a toilet.

Submitted by Karyn Marchegiano of Newark, Delaware.

Why are there holes on the bottom of two- and three-liter soda bottles?

Technically, the holes are not on the bottle but on the bottom of the base cup. (The base cup's function is to keep the bottle from tipping over.) The purpose of the holes is to allow the water that accumulates in the base cup (during the rinsing process at the assembly line) to drain out.

Steve Del Priore, plant manager of the Pepsi-Cola Bottling Company of New York, told *Imponderables* that soda, when first entering the bottle, is at approximately 40 degrees Fahrenheit. The bottle is then placed in a container of warm water so that the soda rises to about 60 degrees Fahrenheit, causing condensation on the bottle, another way for water to seep into the base cup. If no drainage outlet were permitted, foul water might seep out of the base cup every time a consumer poured a drink.

Actually, we may not have holes in base cups to kick around too much longer. Margie Spurlock, manager of consumer affairs for Royal Crown Cola, told us that: "In the near future, base cups may be eliminated from these bottles as technology is in place to produce a one-piece bottle which has a base rigid enough to afford the necessary stability for the tall container."

The main impetus for removing the base cups is environmental. The material used for base cups is not the same as that for the bottle itself, necessitating separating the two plastics at recycling centers, slowing down the process considerably.

Submitted by Carrie Schultz of Hinsdale, Illinois.

Why do drivers wire cardboard to their automobile grills during cold weather?

No, it isn't to keep bugs from slipping under the hood. The cardboard is there to try to keep cold air from entering the engine.

When you drive, some kind of cooling fluid is needed to prevent burning fuel from overheating the car. The fluid is pumped through the engine and then the radiator, where the liquid is cooled by passing outside air over the radiator. The fluid then returns to the engine to remove more heat.

DAVID FELDMAN

To gain efficiency in winter, some of the engine's excess heat is used to warm the interior of the car, by routing some of the engine coolant through the heater's coils and blowing inside air over the warm coils. Two experts we spoke to, one a Federal Highway Administration official who wishes to remain anonymous, and the other, automotive historian Keith Marvin, speculate that the cardboard is probably a makeshift attempt to compensate for the inability of the coolant to get warm enough to operate the heater effectively.

By putting the cardboard over their grills, drivers are blocking air flow to the radiator to decrease the ambient air's cooling effect on the coolant. The theory: If the temperature of the fluid is raised, the heater can better withstand the demands of subzero weather.

Why wire and cardboard? Presumably because they are light, cheap, and easily available materials. But aluminum and twine would do the job, too, or any materials that will shield the grill and can withstand the elements.

Submitted by Mason Jardine of Russell, Manitoba, definitely cardboard-on-the-grill country.

Judges! Try the "Voluminous" COURTROOM ROBE and **NEVER** be caught unprepared again!

HOLDS FOUR LAW BOOKS!

TRICK MOTIONS

FAMOUS TRIALS

TOP 10 TORTS

FUN LAWS

Velcro straps!

Outside: Dignity on the bench

Inside: "Not so fast, counselor!"

Why do judges wear black robes?

American law is derived from English common law. English judges have always worn robes, so it follows logically that American judges would, too. But the road from English garb to American robes has been bumpier than you might expect.

Actually, there wasn't such a profession as judge in England until the last half of the thirteenth century. Until then, high-level clergymen, robe-wearers all, arbitrated disputes and expounded law. But the church eventually forbade its clergy from the practice, and a new job category was born. From the very start, judges, like most important people, wore robes.

Not too long after the first judge donned his robe, Parliament enacted several laws (between 1337 and 1570) dictating just who could wear what kind of robe. Judges' gowns were often elaborate affairs, usually made of silk and fur. (High judges wore ermine; sergeants, lambskin.)

Green was the most popular color for judges' robes at first; later, scarlet gowns and, to a lesser extent, violet gowns, predominated. Black robes did not appear until 1694, when all judges attended the Westminster Abbey funeral of Queen Mary II dressed in black, as a sign of respect for the queen. The mourning period went on for years, and some, but by no means all, lawyers and judges wore black gowns into the next century.

Our founding fathers actually argued over whether our justices of the Supreme Court should wear robes at all. Thomas Jefferson railed against "any needless official apparel," but Alexander Hamilton and Aaron Burr favored them and won the argument. At the first session of the court, Chief Justice Jay wore a robe of black silk with salmon-colored facing. By the early nineteenth century, Supreme Court judges donned black robes of the style worn today.

The solemn costumes of the Supreme Court were not necessarily mimicked by lower courts. Some colonial court judges in the eighteenth century, such as those in Massachusetts, wore gowns and powdered wigs. But in reaction to the Revolutionary War, most trappings of English aristocracy were banished. In fact, the wearing of robes was discontinued in Massachusetts until 1901.

Judges in the West and South tended to be a little less formal. In his book *The Rise of the Legal Profession in America*, Anton-Hermann Chroust described one of the first judges in Indiana as having a judicial costume consisting of "a hunting shirt, leather pantaloons, and a fox skin cap." Most legal scholars believe that the majority of judges in colonial and pre–Civil War times did not wear robes at all.

One reason why so little is known about the dress of judges in early America is that few laws or regulations govern what judges wear. Only Michigan prescribes a dress code ("When acting in his or her official capacity in the courtroom, a judge shall wear a black robe"), and nothing can stop judges from wearing a chartreuse robe if they desire, or none at all.

Still, the vast majority of judges do wear black robes today.

The only reason they aren't wearing more colorful attire is because Queen Mary II died three hundred years ago.

Submitted by Susie T. Kowalski of Middlefield, Ohio. Thanks also to Karen Riddick of Dresden, Tennessee.

Why does the whitewall of a new tire usually have a bluish or greenish tinge?

Isn't there any truth in advertising anymore? Our correspondent wonders why manufacturers don't call them "bluewalls" or "greenwalls."

Ironically, the blue-green stuff on new tires is paint. And it is put there to make sure the whitewall stays white.

Huh? We never said tackling Imponderables was going to be easy, did we? Actually, all will become clear in due time. We heard from General Tire and Goodyear about this subject, but the most complete explanation came from a retired Firestone executive, K. L. Campbell, who wrote a veritable treatise on the subject:

> If black rubber is allowed to be in contact with white sidewall rubber for a few days, the white rubber begins to absorb some of the oils and antioxidant chemicals from the black rubber compound and the result is a permanent brown stain. The longer the black rubber is in contact, the darker the stain. The white rubber compound must be made without any of these oils or antioxidants in order to stay white. Furthermore, it must be protected by barriers so that when it is assembled into a tire, the ordinary black rubber compounds in the rest of the tire are not in contact with it.

Before World War II, manufacturers separated the two by wrapping the white sidewalls with paper at the factory. During the war, whitewalls were not allowed to be manufactured. Once the restriction was lifted, whitewalls became a fad, and tire manufacturers looked for a way to eliminate the expensive paper and concomitant labor expense of unwrapping it.

The answer? The blue or green coating you see on tires now. This paint protects the white rubber from contact with the chemicals in the black rubber. According to Campbell, this paint was always intended to be completely washed off *before* the purchaser took possession of the tires. Bright colors were probably chosen to make it obvious that the paint should be removed to expose the white-as-the-driven-snow rubber underneath.

How do tire dealers (or you) remove the protective paint? Jean Bailey, of General Tire, recommends a good dose of soap and water. Campbell says that even a scrubbing with a stiff brush will usually do the trick. But the way that dealerships solve the problem is by utilizing a steam jet, the type you see at the beginning of most car washes.

Submitted by Lori Videla of Berkeley, Illinois.

Why does inflating tires to the proper pressure help gasoline mileage?

Do you remember, as a child, how hard it was to ride a bicycle with a flat or seriously soft tire? It was harder than trying to pedal a Stairmaster for an hour now, wasn't it?

When you drive an automobile, the same principle applies. The mission of tires is to soften the bumps and bruises you would otherwise experience while negotiating roadways, but a tire that bends too much, whether from underinflation or overloading, is going to take a lot of extra energy to push. Tire pressure can actually affect your gasoline mileage. K. L. Campbell explains:

> About 80% of the energy in the gasoline you buy is used up within your car engine. Of the 20% that is available to move the

car, a small percentage goes into friction losses in the various rotating and moving parts outside the engine. Most of the available energy goes into overcoming wind resistance and in rotating the tires, or in climbing grades.

In order for tires to perform their function of softening the ride of the vehicle, they must deflect under the load of the vehicle and the irregularities encountered on the road. When they deflect, there is internal movement throughout the tire that absorbs energy. The greater the deflection, the more energy the tire consumes as it is rolling.

Tire deflection is increased either by putting more load on the tires (filling up your trunk for a vacation trip or piling a few passengers in the rear seat) or by reducing the pressure in the tires.

When you inflate the tires to the proper pressure, you reduce the rolling resistance. In other words, as Jean Bailey puts it, "It requires much more force or energy to rotate a tire that is underinflated than it does to rotate a tire that is inflated to the proper pressure."

Campbell estimates that by decreasing a typical radial tire pressure of 32 psi (pounds per square inch) to 24 psi, a car traveling at 55 miles per hour would increase fuel consumption by about 2 percent. Perhaps 2 percent does not sound earth-shattering, but to put the matter in perspective, the Department of Energy estimates that if all Americans kept all of their vehicle tires inflated to the manufacturers' recommended pressures, four million gallons of gasoline could be saved *every day.*

One of the reasons why modern radial tires perform much better than their bias-ply predecessors is that radials distribute the deflection around most of the tire, whereas bias plies concentrated the deflection near the road surface. Unfortunately, the byproduct of this technological improvement is that it is difficult to see with the naked eye when a radial is underinflated. A pressure gauge is a necessity.

Don't think that you can get even better mileage if you over-inflate your tires. Once you get above 35 psi, a diminishing effect occurs. Not only do you not increase fuel efficiency, but you will be rewarded with a harsh and potentially wild ride.

Submitted by Linda Seefeldt of Clark, South Dakota.

What do coffee companies do with the caffeine left over from making decaffeinated coffee?

You wouldn't want them to throw away the caffeine, do you? If they flushed caffeine down the drain, it could end up in the ocean, and we wouldn't want to see the effect of a caffeine jolt upon killer sharks. It might be enough to turn a blowfish into a slayfish. If they discarded caffeine in the trash, could the caffeine wake up organic garbage in landfills?

We'll never have to worry about these contingencies, for the decaffeination process used in coffee yields pure caffeine, a marketable commodity. Coffee companies sell caffeine to soft drink companies (who need a little less now that many of them are selling caffeine-free sodas) and pharmaceutical companies.

When coffee companies justify the higher cost of decaf by citing processing costs, they rarely add the information that *they* get reimbursed on the back end for the caffeine they "eliminate."

Submitted by Glenn Eisenstein of New York, New York.

How do they get rid of the remains of dead elephants in zoos?

When an elephant in a zoo dies, a necropsy must be performed. In most cases, the necropsy is conducted by a licensed veterinarian or veterinary pathologist from tissue and blood samples extracted from the carcass.

Most zoos we contacted remove selected organs from the dead elephant, pack them in ice or Formalin, and ship them to various research institutions for reproductive or physiological studies. Typical is the response of San Francisco Zoo's Diane Demee-Benoit. She reports that her zoo has a binder full of requests from universities, zoos, and museums for various animal parts. Forensic labs might need DNA to help identify other creatures. A natural history museum might want skulls or a particular set of bones to perform comparative studies. Zoos make sure that all animal parts are used for research and educational purposes only and are not permitted to sell or donate parts to private individuals.

After organs and other body parts are removed, the least pleasant task is performed—cutting the elephants into smaller pieces, for even elephant *parts* are heavy. The parts are carried by forklifts and cranes and placed on flatbed trailers, dump trucks, or whatever vehicles are available.

Where do the trucks take the remains? That depends upon the zoo. The preference is always for burying animals on the premises. Alan Rooscroft, manager of animals at the San Diego Wild Animal Park, said that out of respect for the animals, their elephants are buried on the grounds of the zoo. But not all zoos have room enough for this "luxury."

Many zoos, such as the San Francisco Zoo, incinerate or cremate elephants. Ed Hansen, president of the American Association of Zoo Keepers, indicated that in areas where such disposal is legal, some elephants are buried in licensed landfills.

Some elephants, particularly those from circuses, meet a more ignoble fate—they are sent to rendering plants. Mark

DAVID FELDMAN

Grunwald, of the Philadelphia Zoo, told *Imponderables* that such boiled elephants end up as an ingredient in soap.

Submitted by Claudia Short of Bowling Green, Ohio. Thanks also to Richard Sassaman of Bar Harbor, Maine; and David Koelle of North Branford, Connecticut.

Why do modern gas pump nozzles have rubber sleeves around them? And what are those red, blue, and green things near the nozzle?

Newfangled gas pumps sport nozzles considerably "pumped up" compared to the puny nozzles of yore. Why is it that as soon as most gas stations became self-service, the pumps became five times as bulky?

The rubber bellows are not there for show. The new nozzles, known as Stage II nozzles, help protect us from harmful fumes emitted by the gas going into our automobiles' tanks. J. Donald Turk, of Mobil Oil's public affairs department, explains:

> These nozzles are part of the vapor recovery system at the service station. The rubber sleeves create a seal between the delivery hose and the car's gas tank so that gasoline vapors are returned to the underground storage tank. From there, the vapors are returned to a gasoline terminal so that no [polluting hydrocarbon] vapors are released to the atmosphere.

And what about those colored doohickeys around the nozzle? According to Mobil Oil's Jim Amanna, those are scuff guards used to protect the car from being scratched by the nozzle.

Submitted by David Kroffe of Los Alamitos, California.

Why do "sea" gulls congregate in parking lots of shopping centers where there is little food or water?

The reason why "sea" is in quotation marks above is that there are many different species of gull, and quite a few of them spend little time near the sea. Several species live inland and survive quite easily.

Nancy Martin, naturalist at the Vermont Institute of Natural Science, told *Imponderables* that ring-billed gulls, the most common inland species, display great affection for fast-food restaurant dumpsters as a feeding site. Ring-billed gulls are happy to leave wide-open landfills to the more aggressive herring and great black-backed gulls.

But even gulls who normally feed at the shore might have reason to visit the local mall parking lot. Little-used areas of parking lots are safe and warm. And don't assume there is nothing to eat or drink there. Humans, whether the intentional bread crumb tossers or the unintentional litterers, leave a veritable smorgasbord for the birds, and gulls can take advantage of pud-

DAVID FELDMAN

dles on the surface of the pavement to take a drink or a quick bath. Martin adds that near the ocean, "hard pavement is good for dropping clams or mussels onto to break them open, although gulls will usually choose an area away from other gulls to carry on this activity."

Tim Dillon, researcher at the Cornell Laboratory of Ornithology, speculates that the open space of a parking lot provides "sea" gulls a terrain "similar to a sandbar or beach where they naturally congregate in large numbers." Just as we may occasionally go to the beach as a break from the dull routine of parking lots and shopping, so might gulls take a spiritual retreat to the natural glories of the shopping center parking lot.

Submitted by Marilyn Chigi of Clarkstown, Michigan. Thanks also to Doc Swan of Palmyra, New Jersey; Annie Bianchetti of East Brunswick, New Jersey; Melanie Jongsma of Lansing, Illinois; and Tim Poirier of Silver Spring, Maryland.

How do they keep air out of light bulbs when they are manufactured? Is a vacuum important for a bulb to function?

As we learned in fire prevention class, oxygen is fire's best friend. If oxygen were inside a light bulb while it operated, the filament would melt as soon as electricity was applied. So at the last stage of manufacture, the air is pumped from the incandescent bulb through a glass exhaust tube that is part of the filament support assembly. Richard Dowhan, GTE's manager of public affairs, told *Imponderables* that the exhaust tube is shortened and sealed so that air cannot reenter and so that the screw base can be installed. Any air that remains is removed with a chemical called a "getter."

An old friend of *Imponderables*, GE Lighting's J. Robert Moody, surprised us by saying that not all bulbs do have a vacuum inside the glass bulb:

The vacuum is not necessary for the operation of the lamp. In fact, if the lamp is 40 or more watts, a fill gas, usually a mixture of nitrogen and argon, is added after the air is pumped out.

Inert gases allow the filament to operate efficiently at higher temperatures, and simultaneously lessen the rate at which the tiny pieces of tungsten evaporate from the filament, yielding a longer bulb life.

Submitted by Mitchell Zimmerman of Palo Alto, California.

Why can't you find English muffins in England?

Probably for the same reason you can't find French dressing in France or Russian dressing in Russia. Or why you're more likely to encounter a New York steak in Kansas City than in New York City. Locales mentioned in food names are more often marketing tools than descriptions of the origins of the product.

At least Samuel Thomas, the inventor of the English muffin, was actually born in England. Thomas emigrated to the United States in 1875 and opened his own bake shop in New York City in 1880. According to Kari Anne Maino, of Best Foods Baking Group, the division of CPC International that markets Thomas' English Muffins, Thomas was probably inspired by the crumpets, scones, and cakelike muffins that were popular in England when he left the country. And he was smart enough to realize that the word "English" would lend his product a certain panache in the United States.

Maino says that her company knows of no "English muffins" that are marketed in England today, but "We have learned that a product very similar to our Thomas' English Muffins did exist in England until about 1920." Why an item would fade in popularity in England while gaining popularity in the United States is anybody's guess. An explanation of the gustatory preferences

DAVID FELDMAN

of the English—a culture that deems baked beans on white toast a splendid meal—would require an exegesis far beyond our mortal powers.

Submitted by Rosemary Bosco of Bronx, New York.

What are those beanbaglike packs found inside electronics boxes that warn, "DO NOT EAT"?

We've always thought that instead of having "DO NOT EAT" plastered on them, a little self-disclosure would help. Why not identify what is inside? (Come to think of it, what is inside regular beanbags?) Most of us don't go around eating beanbags, after all.

It didn't take much digging around to find out that inside those packets is silica gel. Silica is the dioxide of silicon. (Did you know that there is more silicon in nature than any other element except oxygen? You do now.) The "gel" part of the equation is a little more puzzling, since the stuff inside the bag is actually in the form of crystals, but heck, we're not purists.

The sole purpose of the silica gel packet is to absorb moisture (silica gel's most common industrial use is as a drying agent in air conditioning equipment) and help keep your electronic gear in top shape. So that it can fall apart, dependably, the day after your warranty runs out.

Randy Acorcey, of Diversified Electronics Corporation, told *Imponderables* that silica gel isn't used much by American manufacturers. Most often, you will find them inside boxes of goods manufactured in the Far East, because the merchandise is shipped by boat, where it can be exposed to high humidity (and in some cases, water) for weeks.

Submitted by Megan Baynes of Richmond, Virginia. Thanks also to Mary Warneka of Perry, Ohio.

What is the purpose of the sign "THIS DOOR TO REMAIN UNLOCKED DURING BUSINESS HOURS" found atop many doors in retail establishments?

This sign, long present on the West Coast, is spreading throughout the United States. Surprisingly, most of the retail trade associations and architects we consulted didn't understand its purpose. The signs never made much sense to us, since they are often placed aside clearly marked EXIT signs.

The key phrase in the sign, for our purposes, is "business hours." Fire codes specify how many exits are required for each business during operating hours. The required number of exits, and the width of those exits, are based upon the hypothetical stress created by an emergency when the place of business is at maximum occupancy.

But what about when the business is closed and a few employees are working inside? Does a K Mart store have to open every fire exit while a skeleton crew is conducting inventory? Absolutely not. Bruce Hisley, of the National Fire Academy, said that in many localities, doors that are ordinarily used as exits can be locked when only employees are present if the door is marked with these signs. The sign serves as a reminder to store owners and managers to unlock the doors when the store opens.

Mike Fisher, vice-president of sales and marketing at door manufacturer Besam, Inc., told *Imponderables* that these signs are also a reminder to the public to remember their rights. If a door sporting this sign is closed when you are in the store, blow the whistle—unless you are an employee doing inventory, of course.

Submitted by Bryan J. Cooper of Ontario, Oregon. Thanks also to Derek King of Huntington Beach, California.

DAVID FELDMAN

What causes the clicking sound inside a car when you put your turn signal on? Why don't some turn signals make that clicking noise?

The mechanics of the turn signal are simple. Frederick Heiler, public relations manager for Mercedes-Benz of North America, explains the technology:

> The electrical current to make turn signals blink usually comes from a relay—a small box enclosing an electromagnetic switch. Whenever the electromagnet is energized, it mechanically pulls together a pair of contacts, sending a pulse of current to the signal lights and, at the same time, making a clicking sound.

Why do some cars not have clicking turn signals? It's all up to the manufacturer. Most car makers choose to make the clicking noise loud and obvious just in case the driver leaves the turn signal on unintentionally.

What's the big deal if the turn signal is left on too long? If a pedestrian is thinking of jaywalking and sees an oncoming car signaling for a right turn, the pedestrian is lulled into a false sense of security. Oncoming cars and pedestrians often make their decisions about when to proceed based on turn signals, and a little gratuitous clicking is a small price to pay for added safety.

Submitted by Michele Al-Khal of Allentown, Pennsylvania.

Why is there a white paper band around the envelopes in a box of greeting or Christmas cards and not the cards themselves?

Would you be shaken to your core to find out that the band exists for the manufacturer's benefit, not yours? We got this less than startling response from Hallmark spokesperson Barbara Meyer:

The white paper bands are put around our envelopes to speed up the packaging process. It is much more efficient to work with one bundle of envelopes instead of 20 or 21 single ones. The reason a band is not put around the cards is because damage to the cards could occur in this process of banding.

Gibson Greetings doesn't use a band around their envelopes, but Sherry Enzweiler, manager of their Fall Seasons division, says that

many card companies buy envelopes from outside vendors already counted out and banded. They are then placed in the box, precounted and banded, by an assembly line worker.

Submitted by Rev. Ken Vogler of Jeffersonville, Indiana.

Where do computer files and programs go when they are erased?

Not to heaven. Not to hell. Not to Silicon Valley. Not even to Dubuque. For the sad story is that deleted files go nowhere at all. David Maier, professor at the Oregon Graduate Institute of Science & Technology's department of computer science and engineering, elucidates:

> The bits and bytes representing the programs and files on the computer disk are generally unchanged immediately after an erase (or delete) command. What changes is the *directory* on the disk. The directory is a list of the names of all the files and programs on the disk, plus a pointer to the portion of the disk where the contents of the file or program are actually stored. When you issue an erase command, all it generally does is to remove the file or program name from the directory and to record elsewhere that

the storage space on the disk formerly used for the file or program is now "free"—that is, available for reuse.

The mechanism for changing the directory is amazingly simple. Although the deleted files remain on the disk, programmer Larry Whitish told *Imponderables* that the first letter of the file name is deleted and replaced with a symbol that looks like "σ," (ASCII character number 229):

> This signals the computer that the disk space the files occupied is available for use by new files and programs and simply ignores their existence . . .
>
> When new files are copied to or created on a disk, they seek the first available space not being used to begin writing their data. If this space is occupied by a file that has been erased, then kiss your old file goodbye! The old file will be overwritten by the new file.
>
> Erased files and programs can be recovered easily *if they have not been overwritten*. A program like the Norton Utilities can restore these files simply by replacing the symbol "σ" in their name with any letter of the alphabet.

So the "deleted" files are no more erased than the music on an audiotape or television program on videotape that hasn't been recorded over.

Submitted by an anonymous caller on the Jim Eason Show, KGO-AM, San Francisco, California.

When did wild poodles roam the earth?

The thought of wild poodles contending with the forbidding elements of nature makes us shudder. It's hard to imagine a toy poodle surviving torrential rainstorms or blistering droughts in the desert, or slaughtering prey for its dinner (unless its prey was canned dog food). Or even getting its haircut messed up.

For that matter, what animals would make a toy poodle its prey in the wild? We have our doubts that it would be a status symbol for one lion to approach another predator and boast, "Guess what? I bagged myself a poodle today."

If something seems wrong with this picture of poodles in the wild, you're on the right track. We posed our Imponderable to the biology department of UCLA, and received the following response from Nancy Purtill, administrative assistant:

> The general feeling is that, while there is no such thing as a stupid question, this one comes very close. Poodles never did live in the wild, any more than did packs of roving Chihuahuas. The

present breeds of dogs were derived from selective breeding of dogs descended from the original wild dogs.

Sally Kinne, corresponding secretary of the Poodle Club of America, inc., was a little less testy:

> I don't think poodles ever did live in the wild! They evolved long after dogs were domesticated. Although their exact beginnings are unknown, they are in European paintings from the fifteenth century [the works of German artist Albrecht Dürer] on to modern times. It has been a long, LONG time since poodles evolved from dogs that evolved from the wolf.

Bas-reliefs indicate that poodles might date from the time of Christ, but most researchers believe that they were originally bred to be water retrievers much later in Germany. (Their name is a derivation of the German word *pudel* or *pudelin*, meaning "drenched" or "dripping wet." German soldiers probably brought the dogs to France, where they have traditionally been treated more kindly than *Homo sapiens*. Poodles were also used to hunt for truffles, often in tandem with dachshunds. Poodles would locate the truffles and then the low-set dachshunds would dig out the overpriced fungus.

Dog experts agree that all domestic dogs are descendants of wolves, with whom they can and do still mate. One of the reasons it is difficult to trace the history of wild dogs is that it is hard to discriminate, from fossils alone, between dogs and wolves. Most of the sources we contacted believe that domesticated dogs existed over much of Europe and the Middle East by the Mesolithic period of the Stone Age, but estimates have ranged widely—from 10,000 to 25,000 B.C.

Long before there were any "manmade" breeds, wild dogs did roam the earth. How did these dogs, who may date back millions of years, become domesticated? In her book, *The Life, History and Magic of the Dog*, Fernand Mery speculates that when hunting and fishing tribes became sedentary during the Neolithic Age (around 5000 B.C.), the exteriors of inhabited caves were like landfills from hell—full of garbage, animal bones, mollusk and crustacean shells and other debris. But what seemed like waste to humans was an all-you-can-eat buffet table to wild dogs.

Humans, with abundant alternatives, didn't consider dogs as a source of food. Once dogs realized that humans were not going to kill them, they could coexist as friends. Indeed, dogs could even help humans, and not just as companions—their barking signaled danger to their two-legged patrons inside the cave.

This natural interdependence, born first of convenience and later affection, may be unique in the animal kingdom. Mery claims our relationship to dogs is fundamentally different from that of any other pet—all other animals that have been domesticated have, at first, been captured and taken by force:

> The prehistoric dog followed man from afar, just as the domesticated dog has always followed armies on the march. It became accustomed to living nearer and nearer to this being who did not hunt it. Finding with him security and stability, and being able to feed off the remains of man's prey, for a long time it stayed near his dwellings, whether they were caves or huts. One day the dog crossed the threshold. Man did not chase him out. The treaty of alliance had been signed.

Once dogs were allowed "in the house," it became natural to breed dogs to share in other human tasks, such as hunting, fighting, and farming. It's hard to imagine a poofy poodle as a retriever, capturing dead ducks in its mouth, but not nearly as hard as imagining poodles contending with the dinosaurs and pterodactyls on our cover, or fighting marauding packs of roving Chihuahuas.

Submitted by Audrey Randall of Chicago, Illinois.

What does the "Q" in "Q-tips" stand for?

Most users of Q-tips don't realize it, but the "Q" is short for "Qatar." Who would have thought a lone inventor on this tiny peninsula on the Persian Gulf could have invented a product found in virtually every medicine cabinet in the Western world?

Just kidding, folks. But you must admit, "Qatar" is a lot sexier than "Quality"—the word the "Q" in "Q-tips" actually stands for.

Q-tips were invented by a Polish-born American, Leo Gerstenzang, in the 1920s. Gerstenzang noticed that when his wife was giving their baby a bath, she would take a toothpick to spear a wad of cotton. She then used the jerry-built instrument as an applicator to clean the baby. He decided that a readymade cotton swab might be attractive to parents, and he launched the Leo Gerstenzang Infant Novelty Co. to manufacture this and other accessories for baby care.

Although a Q-tip may seem like a simple product, Gerstenzang took several years to eliminate potential problems. He was concerned that the wood not splinter, that an equal amount of cotton was attached to each end, and that the cotton not fall off the applicator.

The unique sliding tray packaging was no accident, either —it insured that an addled parent could open the box and detach a single swab while using only one hand. The boxes were sterilized and sealed with glassine (later cellophane). The entire process was done by machine, so the phrase "untouched by human hands" became a marketing tool to indicate the safety of using Q-tips on sensitive parts of the body.

Gerstenzang wrestled over what he should name his new product, and after years of soul searching, came up with a name that, at the time, probably struck him as inevitable but, in retrospect, wasn't: "Baby Gays." A few years later, in 1926, the name changed to "Q-Tips Baby Gays." Eventually, greater minds decided that perhaps the last two words in the brand name could be discarded.

Ironically, although we may laugh about the dated use of the word "Gays," the elimination of the "Baby" was at least as important. Gerstenzang envisioned the many uses Q-tips could serve for parents—for cleaning not just babies' ears but their nose and mouth, and as an applicator for baby oils and lotions. But the inventor never foresaw Q-tips' use as a glue applicator or as a swab for cleaning tools, fishing poles, furniture, or metal.

Even though Chesebrough-Ponds, which now controls the Q-tips trademark, does nothing to trumpet what the "Q" stands for, the consumer somehow equates the "Q" with "Quality" nonetheless. For despite the best attempts from other brands and generic rivals, Q-tips tramples its competition in the cotton swab market.

Submitted by Dave and Mary Farrokh of Cranford, New Jersey. Thanks also to Douglas Watkins, Jr., of Hayward, California; Patricia Martinez of San Diego, California; Christopher Valeri of East Northport, New York; and Sharon Yeh of Fairborn, Ohio.

Why do deer stand transfixed by the headlights of oncoming cars? Do they have a death wish?

Although no zoologist has ever interviewed a deer, particularly a squashed one, we can assume that no animal has a death wish. In fact, instinct drives all animals to survive. We asked quite a few animal experts about this Imponderable, and we received three different theories, none of which directly contradicts the others.

    1. *The behavior is a fear response.* University of Vermont zoologist Richard Landesman's position was typical:

> Many mammals, including humans, demonstrate a fear response, which initially results in their remaining perfectly still for a few seconds after being frightened. During this time, the hormones of the fear response take over and the

animal or person then decides whether to fight or run away. Unfortunately, many animals remain in place too long and the car hits them.

The self-defeating mechanism of the fear response is perpetuated because, as Landesman puts it, "these animals don't know that they are going to die as a result of standing still and there is no mechanism for them to teach other deer about that fact."

2. *Standing still isn't so much a fear response as a reaction to being blinded.* Deer are more likely to be blinded than other, smaller animals, such as dogs and cats, because they are much taller and vulnerable to the angle of the headlight beams. If you were blinded and heard the rumble of a car approaching at high speed, would you necessarily think it was safer to run than to stand still?

3. *The freeze behavior is an extension of deer's natural response to any danger.* We were bothered by the first two theories insofar as they failed to explain why deer, out of all disproportion to animals of their size, tend to be felled by cars. So we prevailed upon our favorite naturalist, Larry Prussin, who has worked in Yosemite National Park for more than a decade. He reports that deer and squirrels are killed by cars far more than any other animals, and he has a theory to explain why.

What do these two animals have in common? In the wild, they are prey rather than predators. The natural response of prey animals is to freeze when confronted with danger. Ill-equipped to fight with their stalkers, they freeze in order to avoid detection by the predator; they will run away only when they are confident that the predator has sighted them and there is no alternative. Defenseless fawns won't even run when being attacked by cougars or other predators.

The prey's strategy forces the predator to flush them out, while the prey attempts to fade into its natural environment. Hunters similarly need to rouse rabbits, deer, and many birds with noises or sudden movements before the prey will reveal themselves.

Prussin notes that in the last twelve years, to his knowledge only one of the plentiful coyotes in Yosemite National Park has been killed by an automobile, while countless deer have been mowed down. When confronted by automobile headlights, coyotes will also freeze but then, like other predators and scavengers, dart away.

Although deer may not be genetically programmed to respond to react one way or the other to oncoming headlights, their natural predisposition dooms them from the start.

Submitted by Michael Wille of Springhill, Florida. Thanks also to Konstantin Othmer of San Jose, California; and Meghan Walsh of Sherborn, Massachusetts.

If we have heretofore dazzled you with our erudition, it's time to confess our frustrations: ten, to be exact. These are the ten Imponderables we most wanted to answer for this book but could not. Either we couldn't find experts qualified to answer them or we found many experts who couldn't agree on an explanation.

Can you help? We offer a complimentary, autographed copy of the next volume of *Imponderables* to the reader who supplies the best answer, or the first reader who leads to the proof that supplies the answer. And, of course, your efforts will be duly acknowledged and displayed in the book.

We're trying something a little different this time. The first five Frustables deal with the always Imponderable world of gender differences, Frustables many more of you than usual should have an opinion about. We often get questions from men about female psychology, and from women wondering what makes men tick. In this case, you are as expert as any psychologist. Help stamp out Frustability!

FRUSTABLE 1: *Why do women often go to the restroom together? And what are they doing in there for so long?*

It doesn't occur to the average male to turn nature's call into a social occasion. And why do women usually spend so much time once they are in a public bathroom? Are there saunas or video games in women's rooms?

FRUSTABLE 2: *Why do men tend to hog remote controls and switch channels on television sets and radios much more than women?*

Research indicates that women often decide which television show is watched in the home. Yet, give a man a remote control and it is likely you won't be watching any one show for more than fifteen seconds at a time. Why?

FRUSTABLE 3: *Why do some women kick up their legs when kissing?*

And why don't men do it?

FRUSTABLE 4: *Women generally possess more body fat than men. So why do women tend to feel colder than men in the same environment?*

Why do men usually want to open a window before they go to bed while women want to throw on another blanket and turn on the heat?

FRUSTABLE 5: *Why is the average woman a much better dancer than the average man?*

We're not talking about professional dancers, or even serious nightclub amateurs. At any school dance, wedding, or office party, the ineptitude of most males is on display. What accounts for the prancing gender gap?

FRUSTABLE 6: *Why do so many people put their hands up to their chins in portrait photographs?*

We've noticed this pose in author photographs, yearbook pictures, actors' publicity stills, and other types of head shots. Any explanation?

FRUSTABLE 7: *Why do very few restaurants serve celery with mixed green salads?*

Of course, celery is a staple in egg, tuna, and chicken salad. But while celery is a common ingredient in home salads, one rarely encounters celery in restaurant mixed green salads. Celery is cheaper than, say, tomatoes, so why the reluctance of restaurants to use celery?

FRUSTABLE 8: *In English spelling, why does "i" come before "e" except after "c"?*

Where does this arcane rule come from?

FRUSTABLE 9: *What in the world are grocery store managers looking for when they approve personal checks?*

We have been most dissatisfied with the answers we've received from supermarket chains on this topic, so we're hoping that some grocery store checkers, managers, or perspicacious customers can help us with this Frustable. To us, it seems that the manager simply peeks at the check, glances at the customer, and approves the check without really looking for anything in particular. In fact, we've never seen a check rejected.

FRUSTABLE 10: *Why do so many policemen wear mustaches?*

Several policemen have recently sued their department over a regulation that would ban facial hair. The complainants didn't mind a prohibition on beards. But "Don't take away my mustaches!" they insisted. What explains the persistent love affair between cops and upper-lip hair?

Frustables Update

Our Readers Respond to the Frustables First Posed in Do Penguins Have Knees?

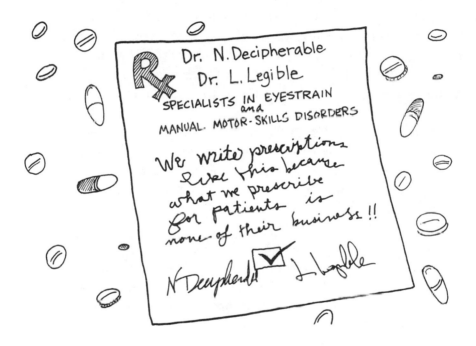

FRUSTABLE 1: *Why do doctors have bad penmanship?*

We were inundated with response to this Frustable. No one disputed the problem. In fact, you were full of anecdotes highlighting the predicament of the poor patient or pharmacist required to read physician chicken scrawlings. Marilyn Brown of Utica, New York, says that she was once given a prescription that three separate pharmacists couldn't read, so she had to traipse back to the doctor:

He eyed it for a short while and inquired, "Who is the patient?" and "What's wrong with her?" With that clue he was able to read the prescription, rewrite it, and call a pharmacy to tell them what it said.

If physicians can't read their own handwriting, we definitely have a problem, one that pharmacists have had to contend with for eons. In fact, Helene Ainspan, the wife of a pharmacist, told us that one of his professional journals had a monthly quiz: Copies of six actual prescriptions were printed; the pharmacists had to decipher them.

Readers were remarkably sympathetic to the plight of doctors. From time to time, we receive queries from readers about why they have to wait so long for doctors to fulfill appointments. Once you get past the waiting room and into an examining room, it seems you have the attention of the doctor for only a short time.

Maybe, our readers infer, doctors really are busy folks. And rushed writing leads to poor handwriting. Brian J. McGrory, a resident in orthopaedic surgery at the prestigious Mayo Clinic, sent us a neatly typed letter. But his signature was illegible; he's going to make a fine doctor:

> Have you ever seen a training surgeon on hospital rounds as he or she tries to keep up with the attending surgeon? Have you ever not had to wait for a doctor during his or her office hours? From medical school to the day of retirement, many doctors are very busy and even harried at times. So even the neatest scribe will become less than perfect when the pressure is on.

Many readers tried to pinpoint the exact time when doctors' penmanship goes bad. A lot of you think it happens during those formative years, medical school. We heard from a retired medical librarian, Aileen Tannenbaum of Irvington, New Jersey:

> Many years ago, I posed this same question to an intern at our hospital. He responded that medical students scribble notes so rapidly in classes that their once legible handwriting deteriorates into an illegible scribble (only decipherable by themselves) . . .

Carrie Schulz, the daughter of a physician, who calls her father's handwriting "despicable," says that he and his doctor friends rationalize their scribbles in the same way.

Another popular theory was that doctors' penmanship is poor because they are constantly writing (e.g., notes on charts, preparation for insurance claims, prescriptions). Cathy Calabrese of Lebanon, Pennsylvania, notes that when she was a bank teller, she often gave customers as many as a hundred traveler's checks to sign at one time: "No matter how carefully the signature was written on the first check, it was a scribbled mess by check number 50 or so." Cathy believes that not only doctors but "a goodly number of executives and other extremely busy people suffer from the illegibility syndrome." As Dr. William Voelker put it:

> It seems from medical school on, there is never enough time to get everything done, and 90 percent plus physicians are constantly rushed and in a hurry. Fast writing is usually illegible writing.

Barth Richards of Naperville, Illinois, and several other readers, pointed to not just the time pressure of physicians but the physical constraints under which they must write: "Doctors are often writing on a clipboard or on a folder held in their hands, instead of at a desk or on a table. These are far from ideal writing conditions."

Several readers noted the repetitive nature of what doctors have to scribble. Dr. Rosanne A. Derango, a dentist in Bartlett, Illinois, argues that since the same medications are prescribed many times a day, the prescriptions become the equivalent of the signature written by a harried executive faced with scores of letters to sign.

The prescriptions of a given doctor might be poorly written, but they are distinctive. Several pharmacists confirmed this. Although a particular physician's writing may be horrible, a pharmacist familiar with that doctor can always decipher it, just as a secretary can usual decode the scribbling of his or her boss.

Don Fallick of Davenport, Washington, hit home with the same point. He points out that anyone, "even authors," will develop bad writing habits if forced to repeat the same thing over and over again. We plead guilty. At autograph sessions, not only does our penmanship deteriorate, but after the fiftieth book or so, we have been known to misspell our own name.

Some readers refuse to concede that doctors' poor penmanship is directly tied to their profession. Three such theories predominated. The most popular, by far, was a sexist (but probably true) syllogism: Most physicians are men. Most men have bad penmanship. Therefore, most physicians have bad penmanship.

The two other theories were a little more bizarre. Our friend Marilyn Brown insists that the higher one's IQ, the worse the penmanship. Since doctors tend to be intelligent, they have poor handwriting. Thanks, Marilyn, for the best-ever alibi for our execrable handwriting.

Dan Butler of Los Alamitos, California, an engineer at a large organization, insists that "the higher you go in an organization, the worse the penmanship. You should see my boss's boss's handwriting."

Rosanne Derango points out that the only physician's writing that most patients ever see is on a prescription. A few readers argued that prescriptions seem illegible not because the penmanship is necessarily poor but because patients cannot interpret the symbols properly. After a few cheap shots ("Hey, if you could make $30 for a five-minute office visit, you wouldn't waste time with trivial things like writing!"), Bill and Mary Ellen Jelen of Akron, Ohio, make a convincing argument:

> Generally, when adults read, they do not focus in at the individual letter level. Rather than sounding words out, our brain recognizes the word and then we "read" the entire word at once.
>
> If you were trying to read handwriting where 20% of the words were in code, it would tend to throw you off. Medical people use lingo that is truly unique. When trying to read a prescription, the patient is facing a whole series of "foreign" words. Besides the drug name, there are all types of codes for when and how to take the drug (e.g., c [with], p [after], prn [as needed]).
>
> Mary Ellen is a nurse. When she was in nursing school, I used to type her papers. I tried to look for spelling and grammati-

DAVID FELDMAN

cal errors, but it was impossible with those medical papers. There were times that I typed a series of words and I had no clue if it was a sentence or not. I couldn't pick out nouns, verbs, anything.

Dentist Rosanne Derango even admitted that occasionally a doctor will intentionally make a prescription hard to read, such as when the medication is a placebo. ("Sometimes we like to keep a little bit of mystery in what we do!")

Obviously, there isn't one single answer to the Frustable at hand, and we're proud of how well our readers coped with the topic. But will we ever solve the problem? Probably not.

Maybe there is a glimmer of hope. Reader Jim Vibber, who has been in the medical device industry for over fifteen years, reports that the American Medical Association is offering a penmanship improvement course for doctors, "with some kind of incentive to take it." What kind of incentives could actually lure physicians to take a continuing education class in what all would concede is a less than fascinating subject? Jim answers:

> I've seen physicians do many things for little premiums, including sitting for an hour filling out a survey. They respond to free pens, golf balls, ice cream—the same sort of "junk" that anybody else might.

> *Submitted by Allen Kahn of New York, New York. Thanks also to Carmel Nelson of West Henrietta, New York.*
>
> *A complimentary book goes to Bill and Mary Ellen Jelen, of Akron, Ohio, who were the first to propose the "demand-side" theory of physician indecipherability.*

FRUSTABLE 2: *Why are salt and pepper the standard condiments on home and restaurant tables? When and where did this custom start?*

Readers didn't get much farther than we did on this subject. Much is known about the history of salt and pepper. Sumerians ate salt-cured meats more than 5,000 years ago. Pepper didn't spread widely into Western cultures until the sixteenth century; indeed, the search for black pepper was one of the prizes that drove explorers such as Columbus around the world.

Salt has become a dominant condiment in almost every culture, not only for its taste but for its preservative qualities. But pepper had to displace other, more popular spices, such as clove and cinnamon, before it became salt's main rival as a condiment.

In her fascinating book *The Rituals of Dinner*, Margaret Visser details the elaborate respect with which costly salt was treated by medieval diners. Separate salt "cellars," often made of precious silver, were placed in front of the lord and

> perhaps each of the highest ranking diners, as an "object of prestige" an indication of status. When the lord sat at what we call the "head" or the host's short end of the table, it became customary to place a standing salt [cellar] as a marker, dividing the lord's intimates grouped at his end of the table from those who were not quite accepted into his inner circle and who sat "below the salt."

We have come a long way from expensive salt dispensers to today's plastic or glass salt and pepper shakers. Visser remarks that even today, the salt shaker is disdained in many formal dining situations.

Matched salt and pepper shakers did not appear until the nineteenth century. Reader Bill Gerk of Burlingame, California, who attacks Frustables with a ferocity that is somewhere between commendable and obsessive-compulsive, believes that the "custom of having salt and pepper as condiments at our home and restaurant tables began no later than the matched salt and pepper sets that first appeared in the nineteenth century." He argues that the need for salt is clear, since saltiness is, along with sweetness, bitterness, and sourness, one of the four basic tastes. Pepper just seems to be the appropriate antidote/complementary spice to saltiness. Not a smoking gun answer, perhaps, but the best we can do for now.

Submitted by Sara VanderFliet of Cedar Grove, New Jersey. Thanks also to John G. Clark of Pittsburgh, Pennsylvania; and Joel Myerson of Helsinki, Finland.

A complimentary book goes to Bill Gerk of Burlingame, California.

FRUSTABLE 3: *Why don't people wear hats as much as they used to?*

Just as the popularity of the undershirt has often been ascribed to Clark Gable's flaunting one in *It Happened One Night*, several readers, as well as many popular press accounts we have encountered, credit Jack Kennedy's bareheaded appearances with dooming the hat. Steve Campion of Tacoma, Washington, makes this point:

> When Lincoln sported a beard, nearly every success-minded politician for fifty years grew whiskers. The president created a fashion. Likewise, when the young, thick-haired Kennedy took office, he rarely donned a hat as all his predecessors had done. His topless style killed the hat fashion.

Clearly, Kennedy intensified the trend, but the hat was already in decline by 1960.

Most of our readers' hypotheses fell in two general camps: those that attributed the fall of the hat to changes in fashion and those that traced the demise of the hat to lifestyle changes.

Fashion Theories

1. *Hairstyles.* Most readers felt that modern hairstyles aren't conducive to wearing hats, and haven't been since the 1950s. Imagine wearing a hat over a beehive. Or Angela Davis wearing a hat over her Afro. Nancy Branson of Safety Harbor, Florida, offers her personal testimony:

> Hairstyles today are not as *flat* as before. I wear fluffier bangs that I don't care to have matted down after I blow-dried them just perfectly. When my hair was all one length, years ago, I *lived* in hats!

Several male readers confessed that when they wore hats, their hair was left with "that helmet look" when they took the hat off. Barbara Zygiel of Alexandria, Virginia, notes that the advent of hairspray also enabled women to "keep a hairdo tidy without confining it under a hat."

Kent State University at Tuscarawas professor Dan Fuller

goes so far as to blame the blow dryer, along with longer hairstyles spearheaded by the Beatles, for hurting hat sales. Fuller points out that although we tend to associate long hair on men with the counterculture, mainstream popular culture figures like Johnny Carson, by the 1970s, were sporting long hair:

> To realize the abrupt shift in attitudes, go back and read how Joe Pepitone was ridiculed in the press for being the first professional athlete to bring a blow dryer into the locker room. It was my wife, however, who first articulated for me the truth that no one who has spent twenty bucks for a hairstyle and has spent many minutes spraying and blowing it dry wants to crush it down and create what she calls "hathead."

2. *Unisex-androgynous fashion.* Our ever-persistent Bill Gerk argues that many fashionable women today have a "tomboy" look, while many trendy men sport an appearance that once would have been called feminine. Gerk believes that both men and women today want to show off their hair, and that traditional hats, which are clearly demarcated as men's or women's apparel, would ruin the androgynous effect.

3. *Informality.* Emil Magovac of Sacramento, California, makes the important point that baseball caps are almost as popular now as fedoras used to be, so we haven't rejected hats *per se.* Magovac mentions watching old films from baseball games in the first half of this century, "where it seemed as if every male in the crowd was in a suit and tie and wearing a fedora." Of course, today neither men nor women usually wear hats for formal occasions, even Easter.

4. *Sunglasses.* We never would have thought of this imaginative suggestion from Vicky Peterson of San Jose, California:

> Prior to the invention of sunglasses, there were very few solutions to the problem of protecting tender eyes and face from the intense glare of the sun. Hats or bonnets with brims were the more practical answer. We now have sunglasses, which do a better job, don't get blown off as often, and don't mess up our hair.

Lifestyle Theories

We have more sympathy with lifestyle theories.

1. *We are now an indoors culture.* Typical of the many readers who emphasized this point was this letter from Judy R. Reis of Bisbee, Arizona:

> There no longer is much reason to wear a hat. In the good old days, people didn't step out of their centrally heated homes into their heated cars and drive to their heated places of work. They lived in poorly heated houses and worked in poorly (or unheated) buildings or outside. And when they traveled, they walked, rode horses, or rode in unheated carriages. Since the head is one of the body's points of greatest heat transfer, wearing a hat made some sense—indoors and out in the winter, to keep the heat in; outdoors in summer to keep the heat out. Hats once had a practical function, although our unceasing efforts to differentiate between the haves and have-nots eventually turned them into fashion statements as well.

Anyone who doubts the practical advantages of hats is advised to visit Chicago in the dead of winter. Somehow, the Windy City's denizens are able to brush off fashion constraints and cover their heads when the wind kicks up.

2. *More women in the workplace.* Catherine Clay, who works for the State of Florida Department of Citrus and has been a valuable source for us in the past, relates a personal story that indicates that hats may not be welcome at work sites for the ever-increasing number of employed women:

> Hats draw attention to the person wearing them, making them stand out in a crowd. Since I like being unique, wearing hats seems only natural. About five years ago, however, my (male) boss told me that I should not wear hats if I wanted to be "accepted" in the South. He said people react negatively to the image of a woman in a hat.
>
> I don't really buy that concept, but I've abided by his

request during the workday. Perhaps hats don't really go well in the work place, and more women work today than ever before.

Once the critical mass of opinion goes against a fashion, it takes true courage to keep it up. Let's be honest: How would we react to a coworker who wears a Nehru jacket to work? Or a polyester pants suit? At most jobs, conformity, rather than fashion statements, is rewarded.

3. *Today's baseball cap, unlike the traditional hat, has become a means of self-expression rather than a signal of one's occupation or status.* Dan Fuller argues that at one time, a working man's hat signaled his occupation and was designed for function rather than aesthetics:

> Newspaper pressmen wore brimless hats made of newspaper to keep ink and lead out of their hair; mechanics wore brimless cloth caps to protect their hair (they worked out of the sun so they needed no brim); truck drivers, service station attendants, and policemen wore the short billed "officer's cap," either with or without the support of internal "points"; cowboys are obvious, but farmers traditionally wore a straw with a medium brim or simply an old dress hat instead of the very wide brim of the Western hat. And so on and on.

Dan is currently working on a long, scholarly article about this very Frustable and has interviewed several hundred farmers, construction workers, and outdoorsmen, and his conclusion is that, unlike most of the hats mentioned above, the cap has distinct advantages:

> The cap is a clear choice over the hat because it doesn't come off in the wind. It can be pulled down tightly, and whether on a tractor, a drill rig, or a golf course, you don't have to worry about chasing down your hat.

Plus, the logos on caps are now a way of projecting an individual identity rather than just one's profession.

4. *The automobile.* As Judy Reis mentioned, the average worker in America used to toil outdoors or take public transportation to reach his or her job. In either case, the worker would be exposed to the elements. Today, the majority of American workers

drive to the job site. Many readers pointed to the automobile as sounding the death knell for hats. Automobiles shielded commuters from the cold, but presented a new problem—a low roof. As Catherine Clay puts it, "Who wants to keep taking a hat on and off?"

You may argue that automobiles were around long before the demise of the hat. True, but they were built differently, as William Debuvitz of Bernardsville, New Jersey, observes:

The modern car has too low a roof to accommodate a hat. But if you look at old photos of earlier cars with drivers (or look at the movie *Bugsy*), you will see that men wore hats when they drove because the car roofs were high enough.

We don't think there is *an* answer to this Frustable, but we think we've pretty much covered all the bases.

Submitted by Kent Hall of Louisville, Kentucky. Thanks also to Douglas Stangler of Redmond, Washington.

A complimentary copy goes to Dan Fuller of New Philadelphia, Ohio, in hope that his own article will plumb new depths in the area of disappearing-hat research.

FRUSTABLE 4: *How and why were the letters B-I-N-G-O selected for the game of the same name?*

As you know, all Frustables start as Imponderables that we research—unsuccessfully. Although we rarely try to answer Imponderables with information gleaned from books, we couldn't find live human beings who could help us solve this problem. We ended up finding many written citations about the origins of Bingo, but they seemed dubious to us.

Several readers found the same books we did, and it points out the problem with "believing everything you read." If Writer A publishes false information, the mistruth is perpetuated if Writer B thinks of Writer A's "facts" as sacrosanct. For this reason, we're always suspicious of the stories of origins of products or enterprises that seem too neat and colorful.

In this case, written sources seem to agree that in December 1929, Edwin Lowe, described as either a toy salesman or a just-laid-off toy salesman, was traveling in Jacksonville, Florida, or Jacksonville, Georgia, or outside Atlanta, Georgia, and stopped at a carnival, where he saw a game called Beano being played. The game was the same as the Bingo we know now but used dried beans for markers. When a winner was called, he or she yelled out "BEANO."

Supposedly, Lowe was observing the game (depending upon the account, either at the carnival or after he tried out the game at home) and heard a young girl, excited at her victory, stutter "B-B-B-I-N-G-O" (depending upon the account, there are three to seven "B's" in her "BINGO"), and a light bulb flashed above Lowe's head. He rechristened the game Bingo and marketed the game within months.

We also know that Lowe consciously marketed the game as a church fund-raiser from its inception, and that he faced an early obstacle when a priest from Wilkes-Barre, Pennsylvania, complained that with the twenty-four-card sets that Lowe initially marketed, one game often produced too many winners to turn a profit for the church. So Lowe employed Carl Lefler, a mathematician at Columbia University, to compose 6,000 different Bingo cards with nonrepeating number groups.

Having suffered through many other shaggy dog stories to explain origins of names, our guess is that Lowe actually changed the name from Beano to Bingo to avoid lawsuits from the gentleman running the carnival game, whose rules he borrowed. Actually, Beano had its roots in similar European games, such as the original Lotto, that date from the sixteenth century. But we'll probably never know the truth for sure, certainly not if half our written sources say that Bingo was born in Florida and the other half in Georgia.

One other little bit of trivia about Edwin Lowe. Several years after his Bingo success, he marketed another game with a nonsense name that would earn him additional millions—Yahtzee. But once again, Lowe did not invent the game. A married couple created the game, which they called "Yacht Game," and asked Lowe to print up a few as gifts. According to Milton Bradley, which acquired the E. S. Lowe Company in 1973,

Lowe liked the game so much he offered to buy all rights. The couple was not interested in receiving royalties, and they readily signed away their rights in exchange for a few copies of the game. Lowe went on to make a huge profit from the game whose name he changed to "Yahtzee," but was never able to remember his benefactors' last name.

Is there any better recipe for success than knowing what products the public will buy but (conveniently) forgetting to acknowledge their inventors?

Submitted by Daniel J. Harkavy of Buffalo, New York.
A complimentary book goes to Ken Giesbers of Seattle, Washington (the first reader to send book excerpts). Thanks also to Richard Miranda of Renton, Washington; and Bill Gerk of Burlingame, California.

FRUSTABLE 5: *Why do they always play Dixieland music at American political rallies when Dixieland isn't particularly burning up the hit parade at the moment?*

We were first asked this question by Jeff Charles, the first radio host who ever interviewed us for an *Imponderables* book. In the last six years, we have spoken to the Republican and Democratic parties, numerous jazz scholars, the New Orleans Jazz Club, and many other sources. No luck.

So we threw out the gauntlet to our readers. While there is no simple answer, you are brimming with ideas.

One point that just about everybody made, including Bruce Walker of San Pedro, California, is that Dixieland is upbeat, happy, American music:

> The music has to be peppy, since they want to fire up the faithful to go out and slave away for Senator Foghorn, not go to sleep or go away crying. It has to be American music, since patriotism is a theme of almost all political campaigns.

Many readers noted that Dixieland has become a tradition at political rallies, and caters to the ever-present nostalgic cravings of Americans.

DAVID FELDMAN

A television programming executive named Paul Klein developed the "least objectionable program" (LOP) theory, which posits that the prudent programmer puts on shows that offend the fewest number of people. Once glued to the set, only an "objectionable" show will drive viewers to change channels. Many *Imponderables* readers believe that the answer to this Frustable lies in LOM—that is, Dixieland is the "least objectionable music." We enjoyed this discussion by Vladimir Kazhin of Towson, Maryland:

> Much music carries with it certain intellectual and emotional baggage, and politics in America today is an attempt to be inoffensive above all else. For example: Classical music is considered too "highbrow," too "arty"; jazz is considered too "earthy," too sensual, as of course, is rock (still the devil's music to some people); country is too "white"; soul too "black"; and new wave music is too "harsh," etc.
>
> I am not saying that there is any truth to these stereotypes, only that they exist, which is enough for most politicians. Dixieland doesn't really have a big following: No one really likes it [on this we'll have to disagree before the hate mail rolls in], but no one dislikes it either. In short, it is a nice, inoffensive, basically pleasant background music.

We received a fascinating letter from Russell Shaw, a journalist from Marietta, Georgia, who has a unique perspective— he covers both political campaigns and the music industry. Russell made all of the points discussed above but also offers a unique argument—that the popularity of Dixieland music at political rallies, despite its lack of radio airplay, might have a partly economic basis. Most music radio stations today employ niche programming, directing music at a particular age and/or demographic group:

> When something is totally noncontroversial, it is likely to be warm and bland—the same frailties that if not present, would foster listener demand and a niche for a musical form like Dixieland on radio.
>
> Yet even this inability to inspire passion has its assets. One of the ways consumers express passion in the entertainment market-

place is to buy records, and attend concerts and clubs featuring their favorite kind of music. Since Dixieland rates low in the passion/demand continuum, there are few full-time opportunities for Dixieland musicians. They, like most of us, are more concerned about the eagle flying than the saints marching.

Hence, Dixieland attracts practitioners who perform almost as a hobby. Not being full-time musicians, they likely will not be union members, and thus come more cheaply than, say, a large orchestra. Dixieland also requires fewer musicians and less in fees. Many of the above principles also apply to the popularity of bluegrass at political events—especially here in the South.

We'd be negligent if we didn't mention that Dixieland was nonexistent during the 1992 Democratic convention in New York City. Clearly, the Clinton/Gore campaign's strategy was to emphasize the ticket's youth and theme of "change" by showcasing the candidates dancing and singing along with the original recordings of Fleetwood Mac's "Don't Stop" and Paul Simon's "You Can Call Me Al." This musical watershed did not go unnoticed. On CNN's "Capital Gang," columnist Robert Novak named the absence of "Happy Days Are Here Again" from the convention as his "Outrage of the Week."

We'd still love to know exactly when and where Dixieland first became associated with political rallies, but then we're used to being frustrated.

> *Submitted by Jeff Charles, formerly of Minneapolis, Minnesota. Where are you now, Jeff?*
>
> *A complimentary book goes to Russell Shaw of Marietta, Georgia.*

FRUSTABLE 6: *Why does eating ice cream make you thirsty?*

Nothing much new to report. All of the reader responses to this question named one or more of the following culprits as the thirst inducer:

1. Salt
2. Sugar

DAVID FELDMAN

3. Butterfat (which is left on the tongue and in the mouth and throat after consuming ice cream). Only drinking eliminates the filmy fat coating.

The answer may lie in any one or all three of these alternatives. Yet one could name foods with greater concentrations of any of these ingredients that don't make you as thirsty. Expert after taste expert we contacted in both sensory studies and the ice cream industry denied that this phenomenon even exists, and refused to single out any or all of the nominees as definitely causing thirst. To which we reply, "Then why do most ice cream parlors, such as Baskin-Robbins, have water fountains in them?"

We were so frustrated divining the truth that a letter from A. A. Spierling of Van Nuys, California, became our favorite discussion about this topic: "Ice cream doesn't make me thirsty —riding buses does. I can consume a quart of fluids after riding two or three buses, going shopping, etc. Going by car doesn't make me thirsty." Good thing they don't let you eat ice cream on the bus. You would have to carry a canteen with you.

Submitted by Kassie Schwan of Brooklyn, New York. Thanks also to Ricky E. Arpin, current address unknown; Lisa Kodish of Albany, New York; and Phil Feldman of Los Angeles, California
A complimentary book goes to A. A. Spierling of Van Nuys, California, for best evasion of this Frustable.

FRUSTABLE 7: *Why are belly dancers so zaftig?*

Our curiosity about this subject stems from our wondering why belly dancers, who spend their professional life manipulating their abdomens, don't seem to have toned abdominal muscles. Professionals we originally contacted disagreed about the reasons why, but we heard from quite a few belly dancers, and they were in unexpected agreement.

As you may have guessed, we receive a lot of unusual mail here at *Imponderables* headquarters. But the first person ever to send us an 8 × 10-inch color glossy was Stasha Rustici of Berkeley, California. By training, Rustici is a social anthropologist, whose interest in folkloric dancing drew her into practicing the ancient art herself. For the last fifteen years, she has been belly dancing professionally, traveling all over the world.

No doubt, her interest in this Frustable was piqued by the fact that although she may have other problems in life, being *zaftig* isn't one of them, as her publicity still makes abundantly clear. She has a unique perspective on the subject, and answers our Frustable in both cultural and technical terms:

> The standards of beauty differ from place to place in this world. Traditionally, in the areas where food is not plentiful, a plump woman is a sign of wealth. She can afford to eat! In these arid desert regions, this maxim holds true. I can't tell you how many times a Middle Eastern person in my audience has told me I'm too skinny. Even Cairo, today, hasn't the selection and availability [of food] that we enjoy in the West. So socioeconomically, plump is pleasing.
>
> Although the lateral oblique muscles are active in this dance form, the rest of the abdomen and the diaphragm are not. In fact, the undulating spine movements, as well as the most ancient move of all, the undulation of the stomach muscles (commonly referred to as the "belly roll") necessitate a supple, yet somewhat flaccid muscle structure. Furthermore, some additional weight reinforces the quality of this dance's earthy movements, a dance whose "center of gravity" is at the hips. As you can see by the publicity photo, I'm not the standard of Middle Eastern plumpness. I can testify that it's harder for me to achieve some movements that my more *zaftig* sisters perform easily. So physiologically, plump is pleasing.

Karen Kuzsel, publisher of *Middle Eastern Dancer*, told *Imponderables* that from the days of the sultans, heavier women were prized by men as status symbols. But another reason why we wouldn't cast Heather Locklear as a belly dancer is that in the Middle East, where dancers are prized for their expressive range, most belly dancers are not spring chickens. Belly dancing is complicated technically, and true artistry doesn't come easily. According to Karen, the most accomplished dancers are usually at least forty years old; even in the ageist United States, most belly dancers are over forty.

DAVID FELDMAN

Honestly, this Frustable was not an attempt to make fun of belly dancers. We've been known to be a little *zaftig* ourselves. And *we* can't execute belly rolls. Yet a few of our belly dancer correspondents were a tad defensive. For example, lapsed belly dancing student Beth Eastman of Richfield, Minnesota, was inspired to deliver a passionate defense of belly dancer physiognomy:

> If belly dancers looked like Arnold Schwarzenegger, their movements would make their skins appear to be lined with live snakes! Yecch! Also, while retaining cuddlability, the strengthening and toning of the muscles beneath and the increased flexibility of the body gives a real boost to the sex life of the dancer. Go for it, girls!

A complimentary book goes to Stasha Rustici of Berkeley, California.

FRUSTABLE 8: *How was hail measured before golf balls were invented?*

This started out as one of those comedian-inspired Imponderables that we detest. Any stand-up comic can get a laugh out of "Why do we drive on parkways and park on driveways?" But we have to answer these rhetorical questions/jokes everyone from Gallagher to Andy Rooney muses about and then discards without pursuing.

Pardon our self-pitying whining—we feel better now—and forgive us for thrusting this very difficult Frustable on our generous readership. But, truth be told, most of our correspondents didn't come up with anything more concrete than we did. Most of you counterpunched with jokes of your own about hail. (Our favorite: Mark Buesing of Peoria, Illinois, reminded us that David Letterman, when he was a weatherman in Indianapolis, once referred to falling hail as "the size of canned hams.")

But two enterprising readers lurched, as John McLaughlin would say, "uncontrollably into the truth." Brad Tucker of Syracuse, New York, happened to be reading *Commerce of the Prai-*

ries, a book by frontiersman Josiah Gregg, who joined a wagon train in 1831. Gregg refers to seeing "hail-stones larger than hen's eggs . . ."

But Dallas Brozik of Huntington, West Virginia, was so inspired by this Frustable that he conducted quite a bit of original research. He found two different citations that manage to avoid what every weathercaster in the world seems to find inevitable —comparing the size of hail to a golf ball:

> The 1880 edition of the *Library of Universal Knowledge . . .* describes hailstones ". . . which may have any size from that of a pea to that of a walnut, or even an orange . . ." The entry goes on to mention an incident when hailstones the size of half a brick were found . . .
>
> The 1940 edition of *Nelson's Encyclopedia . . .* shows a photo of "Hailstones Larger Than Eggs" [of course, golf balls were invented before 1940]. I checked a number of other sources during this period, and most of them refer to the size of hailstones as "one-half to three inches in diameter" or some other measure in inches.
>
> So there is at least part of your answer. If you do not play golf, consider fruits, vegetables, and Euclidian geometry.

Submitted by Donald E. Ullrich of Burlington, Iowa. Thanks also to Edward Hirschfield of Portage, Michigan; and R. W. Stanley of Bossier City, Iowa.

A complimentary book goes to Dallas Brozik of Huntington, West Virginia.

DAVID FELDMAN

Verbose ☆ Studios
"The Fast Talkers"
☆ No one could shut 'em up! ☆
Georgia Glibb
Lew Loquacious
KISS ME QUICK!
I KISS AS FAST AS WE TALK!
She COULD get a word in edgewise! ☆ Mister Mile-a-Minute!

FRUSTABLE 9: *Why did 1930s and 1940s movie actors talk so much faster than actors do today?*

For some reason, this Frustable didn't inspire a great number of responses from readers, but radio talk-show hosts were fond of the topic, and many callers across the country contributed their theories.

Some ascribed the change in speed to technical advances in sound recording. This may explain why early 1930s films often sound fast to our ears. Irv Hyatt, a film buff and collector from Woodbridge, New Jersey, wrote *Imponderables* that many early 1930s movies were recorded with sound on disc rather than on film, which resulted in a higher pitch in the finished recordings:

> These discs were later converted to sound on film, and oft-times to synchronize these it was necessary to adjust these recordings as the negative was being made. Some late 1920s and early 1930s films had scenes that were still shot silent, and some even with hand-cranked cameras left over from the silent era.

But we were referring more to the machine-gun delivery of stars like Humphrey Bogart, Katharine Hepburn, Rosalind Russell, and Jimmy Cagney in classic comedies and dramas. One would think that as the moviegoing audience became more sophisticated, the pace would speed up. Certainly, movies today are visually paced at a hysterical rate compared to movies sixty years ago.

Author Nat Segaloff of Cambridge, Massachusetts, who wrote a popular biography of director William Friedkin, sent us a letter full of possible explanations. He notes that superior recording devices allowed rapid-fire dialogue without hiss and distortion. These technical improvements enabled theater-trained writers to construct scripts and stage actors to perform at a pace to which they were accustomed before live audiences. The theater is a more dialogue-driven medium than film, since the numerous and seamless set and costume changes in movies are impossible to duplicate on a proscenium stage. Most writers for the stage were not trained to allow music or crosscutting to compensate for reams of dialogue.

Segaloff believes that the key to the speed regression was the rise of Method acting, spearheaded by teacher-actor-director Lee Strasberg. Actors like Marlon Brando, Montgomery Clift, Julie Harris, and Kim Hunter, who "went for feeling and truth rather than speed and artifice," changed the pace of delivery. While Marlon Brando searched for his motivation in a scene, Jimmy Cagney would have polished off a page of dialogue. Like their style or not, Method acting rendered the faster cadence of 1930s actors artificial and superficial.

Segaloff suggests that the slower pace of today's dialogue might be a suggestion that contemporary audiences are less, not more, sophisticated. Frank Capra's screwball comedies were paced so quickly because of Capra's conviction that

> people sitting together as an audience comprehend things faster than they do as individuals, and for that reason he directed his actors to speed up their delivery by as much as one-third.

Howard Hawks later introduced overlapping dialogue to increase the sensation of speed. Today, Robert Altman uses the same technique, but without the same commercial success.

Segaloff muses about whether we may return to the "amphetamine school of acting," if only for the crassest commercial reasons:

> Ironically, we may be experiencing an unheralded return to speeded-up dialogue. Some videotape manufacturers are now "compressing" (speeding up) longer movies by as much as eight percent to squeeze them onto shorter, cheaper cassettes. One of the first examples: Walt Disney's 1942 *Fantasia*, which was painstakingly and publicly restored to its original length of 124 minutes, only later to be speeded up to 120 minutes to become the best-selling title in home video history.

The same compression techniques are being used in advertising to cram more words into fifteen or thirty seconds, and in radio, where cutting five seconds from a song allows a station to insert more commercials while still claiming they play more music.

> *Submitted by Bob Hatch of Seattle, Washington.*
> *A complimentary book goes to Nat Segaloff of Cambridge, Massachusetts.*

FRUSTABLE 10: *Why does meat loaf taste the same in all institutions?*

Your response to this Frustable was as inspiring as . . . meatloaf. Not that we have anything to offer.

But don't despair. We've solved some other Frustables that eluded us the first time around. Read on.

The Frustables That Will Not Die

As you have just learned in the "Frustables Update," solving Frustables is, by definition, frustrating. Although we can't demolish every Frustable the first time around, we have just begun to fight. In this section, you'll see the reader contributions from the past year.

Please remember we do not have the space to review all the theories we've already advanced; this section is meant as a supplement, not a substitute, for our discussions in previous books.

Frustables First Posed in *Why Do Clocks Run Clockwise?* and First Discussed in *When Do Fish Sleep?*

FRUSTABLE 1: *Why do you so often see one shoe lying on the side of the road?*

In his column "The Straight Dope," our fellow savant Cecil Adams mused about our devoting seven entire pages to this topic in *When Do Fish Sleep?* Little did he seem to know that we have published more about this subject in every subsequent book. We're afraid that the mysterious appearance of roadway single shoes is one of those problems that will not stay in the closet or just go away if left unattended. To those who may scoff at the frequency of SSS (single-shoe syndrome) or the very real suffering it can inflict, please read these testimonials and see if you can keep from dabbing suddenly moist eyes.

First of all, we cannot ignore the direct correlation between SSS and soaring juvenile delinquency rates. Gabriel Raggiunto, of Lebanon, Pennsylvania, bravely allows us to share secrets from his sordid past:

> When I was in my late teens, I used to play a game with old shoes. My friends and I would go to second-hand clothing stores, yard sales, and our closets to get old worn-out shoes. After gath-

245

ering a dozen or two, we would go on a long drive to throw the shoes out. Score was kept by how many road signs were hit and by the size of the sign. The low scorer would end up buying the drinks. The smaller the sign, the more points were awarded.

As they say, (whoever "they" is), kids can be cruel. But juvenile deviants don't have to be old enough to drive to create SSS, as Dave Moreau of Wappingers Falls, New York, reports:

> The mean kids I knew would grab someone else's sneakers, tie them together, and throw them on to the electric lines. The sneakers would dangle above, so close and yet so far, until the laces eventually weathered (it took almost a year), broke, and the sneaker fell to the street. Of course, this doesn't explain why one sneaker subsequently disappears, but it could help to explain how they got there. This cruel act was not isolated to my neighborhood alone; traveling through adjoining areas, I noticed this same phenomenon at least three other times.

Michael Levin, professor of philosophy at New York City's CUNY, adds that drug dealers often fling tennis shoes atop power lines to mark their territories.

Just as troublesome as our crime rate is our soaring rate of divorce. We have learned from Oprah, Phil, Sally Jessy, and Geraldo that the hallmarks of all successful marriages are respect and communication. But how can one partner withstand the intrusion of SSS into an otherwise happy marriage? Cheryl Thompson of Ludlow Falls, Ohio, faced this heartrending problem:

> One day my husband and I were going fishing, so I grabbed my old, ugly, dirty tennis shoes and threw them in the truck. As we were riding along, my husband reached over and picked one up and said, "I hate these shoes," and chucked it out the window. I grabbed the other one to keep him from littering and never saw the other again.

Can this marriage be saved?

Justin Palmer of Granby, Connecticut, realizes that he who is not part of the solution is part of the problem:

DAVID FELDMAN

While walking home from school late one evening, wearing flexible leather moccasins, I took a shortcut through a grassy field when one of my shoes slid off. I turned around and in the dark patted about only to find what I thought was a new shoe—one of the lost single shoes that everyone comes across!

After considerable time, I abandoned my search, content with my new shoe and acknowledging the loss of the other. Later, under a street lamp, I realized it was the same shoe stuffed with grass and fitting improperly. My negligence, however, could have contributed to the wealth of lost single shoes around the world!

There, there, Justin! Confession is good for the soul. Justin then relates *another* time when he recovered his own lost single shoe, but he's turning that story into a made-for-TV movie.

Justin was kind enough to pass along an entry from *Reader's Digest*'s "Life in These United States," which tells the story of a man who innocently drove his slightly tipsy secretary home after an office party. That night, he and his wife were driving to a restaurant, when he noticed a high-heeled shoe lurking out below the passenger seat. Afraid his wife would misinterpret its significance, he waited until she looked away and flung the shoe out of the car. When they got to the restaurant, his wife squirmed a bit and asked, "Honey, have you seen my other shoe?"

Our guess is that the odds that this story is true are about 100 to 1 against. Still, the story is proof that SSS has achieved urban legend status.

Speaking of legends, Angel Kuo of West Nyack, New York, points out that another book claims to have the answer to SSS: *Faeries*, by Brian Froud and Alan Lee:

> The Irish have their own industrious faerie, the Leprechaun (lep-re-kawn) or one-shoe-maker. He is a solitary cobbler to be found merrily working on a single shoe (never a pair) beneath a dockleaf or under a hedge.

Angel theorizes that leprechauns have emigrated around the world, making single shoes and then tossing them off the sides of the road.

Too fanciful and New Agey for you? Then how about a scientific theory from our new hero, Simonetta A. Rodriguez, of Endicott, New York, who has emerged as the philosopher king of SSS. How does Simonetta explain our phenomenon? Entropy and the second law of thermodynamics, of course. These two scientific principles argue that the universe and the systems within it tend toward greater randomness and increasing disorder over time. Take the floor, Simonetta:

> We normally encounter shoes in pairs only because human life-forms are constantly working to keep them ordered, in pairs. We do not leave the system of shoes to itself; instead, we rigorously enforce extremely artificial pair-bonding in the system. Since we are life-forms, and highly ordered life-forms at that (well, I do know people who are no more ordered than amoeba, but I want to ignore them for the sake of this discussion), we must constantly work like this to prevent disorder, which is the same thing as death for us. We do not even notice our ceaseless efforts to fight entropy. Well, we don't notice most of them—I gave up on a lot of housework I used to do when I was young and dumb, because what's the point? Why fight the universe?
>
> Once some shoes get away from us, the universe does not care about our obsessions. Entropy takes over. The details do not matter: animals, traffic, weather—anything the shoes encounter serves to increase the entropy of the system. If an entire pair of shoes gets away from us, *the very first thing that must go is the pair-bond*, because it was maintained only by extreme and very unnatural efforts . . .
>
> I would be most astonished if I saw a *pair* of shoes by the side of the road, and I never have.

Simonetta must have done *very* well on essay exams.

From this point forward, we now have theoretical, scientific underpinnings for any future foray into SSS studies.

FRUSTABLE 4: *Why do the English drive on the left and most other countries on the right?*

We heard from Stanley Ralph Ross, of Beverly Hills, California, who once had the imposing task of writing the script for the Sound and Light Show at London Bridge in England and later at Lake Havasu City, Arizona. The tremendous research available to him led to some interesting conclusions about this Frustable:

> In the 1600s, London Bridge had many buildings erected on it: homes, stores, etc. . . . Although the width of the bridge was about forty-two feet, the incursion of the buildings made it only twelve feet wide at certain points. The Bridge was the only way one could travel from the city to the country and often had as many as 75,000 people cross it in 24 hours. At that time, there were *no traffic laws whatsoever* and people just pushed past each other.
>
> In 1625, on a hot summer day, a horse drawing a wagon dropped dead of a heart attack in one of the areas only twelve feet wide. This caused the Mother Of All Traffic Jams, and nobody could get through in either direction. Upon hearing of this, the Lord Mayor of London, one John Conyers, decreed that all traffic going *into* the city be on the *upstream* side of the Thames (left) and all traffic going to the country be on the downstream side. And that was the first traffic rule, a totally arbitrary decision by Conyers.

Ross explains that Conyers's fiat was soon extended to the city of London, then to the boroughs of Westminster and Chelsea, to all of England, and then exported overseas.

FRUSTABLE 8: *Why do women in the United States shave their armpits?*

Several readers have taken us to task for not emphasizing the role of advertising in creating the "sudden desire" of women for shaving armpits around 1915. It is true that deodorants were aggressively marketed at this time (ladies' razors were soon to follow) and that women's magazines of the time, ever desirous of pleasing advertisers, chimed in with advice to shave.

But fashion came first. The Mack Sennett Bathing Beauties had an immediate impact on fashion, and many of the first ads for deodorants showed women in "his" bathing suits. Advertisers are responsible for spreading the practice, but probably not for creating it.

FRUSTABLE 9: *Why don't you ever see really tall old people?*

Dr. Daphne Hare, of Buffalo, New York, was kind enough to send us a story summarizing an Ohio study of men who died of natural causes. The conclusions were startling, indicating that each additional inch in height corresponded to a reduction of 1.2 years in life expectancy. A 5'4" man can expect to live almost ten years longer than a six-footer.

According to the *Buffalo News,* an earlier study showed "an average age of death of 82 for men less than 5 feet, 8 inches tall and 73 for those more than 6 feet tall." Is this why H. Ross Perot is always smiling?

Frustables First Posed in *When Do Fish Sleep?* and First Answered in *Why Do Dogs Have Wet Noses?*

FRUSTABLE 3: *How, when, and why did the banana peel become the universal slipping agent in vaudeville and movies?*

In *Do Penguins Have Knees?*, we mentioned that a law student told us about old tort cases involving banana peel slipping, and that Oliver Wendell Holmes actually rendered an opinion on said topic. One enterprising reader, Robert W. Donovan, of Wenham, Massachusetts, went to his attic and dug through old law books to find the cases, and he was successful.

Holmes, when he was the chief justice of the Massachusetts Supreme Judicial Court, rendered a decision in the case of *Goddard* v. *Boston & Maine R.R. Co.* in 1901. Mr. Goddard slipped on a banana peel lying on a railway platform just as he exited the train. Holmes ruled that Goddard could not collect, because the peel "may have been dropped within a minute by one of the persons who was leaving the train."

But not all banana-peel slippers are skinned by the court. Ten years later, in *Anjou* v. *Boston Elevated Railway Co.,* the pratfaller won, as Donovan explains:

The distinction turned on the color of the banana peel. In *Anjou* [the plaintiff, not the pear], the plaintiff slipped on a brown banana peel that had presumably been on the ground for quite awhile. The court ruled that the railway was negligent in failing to keep its station free of ever dangerous banana peels. In *Goddard,* the banana peel was a fresh yellow color, indicating that it had been thrown on the ground shortly before Mr. Goddard had slipped on it.

In this case, the court reasoned that although the railroad owed a duty to its passengers to keep its stations clean, it was not reasonable to expect it to assign a maintenance worker to follow around every passenger who may be inclined to eat a banana and carelessly discard its peel . . .

We will assume that Anjou was not diabolical enough to carry around a mottled banana peel with her—those were more innocent times.

But our most exciting discovery came from film buff Irv Hyatt, who was gracious enough to send us a videotape of the man who might hold the key to the whole banana peel mystery —legendary film producer Hal Roach (who produced Laurel and Hardy, Harold Lloyd, and the "Our Gang" comedies, among many others). When he was presented with his honorary Oscar in 1983, the ninety-two-year-old producer spoke of how the banana peel became the universal slipping agent in movies.

Roach recounted that when he first started working in Hollywood, in 1912, he was paid one dollar a day, plus carfare and lunch. The lunch consisted of two sandwiches and a banana. Every day, after lunch, the prop man would pick up the discarded banana peels and put them away, lest anyone trip over them.

In the famous Mack Sennett comedy shorts of the era, comics took pratfalls on cakes of soaps or puddles of oil. But Hal Roach had a brainstorm. Why not use banana peels? They were available, plentiful, recognizable on-screen, and, best of all, absolutely free for Roach.

Producer and screenwriter Jeffrey J. Silverstein, of Brooklyn, New York, sent us a letter arguing that, from a comedic standpoint, it is strategically essential for the audience to be aware of the identity of the slipping agent before the "slipee" discovers it. Silverstein, having read our chapter about the selection of colors in traffic lights, feels that the fact that yellow is the most visible color from a distance didn't hurt its acceptance among directors:

> Plus, the banana has the additional advantage of giving a natural "accidental" setup. The person eating it doesn't deliberately trip the "slipee"—it is unintentional and therefore funnier.

FRUSTABLE 8: *Why do kids tend to like meat well done (and then prefer it rarer and rarer as they get older)?*

All of the theories we discussed in *Why Do Dogs Have Wet Noses?* and *Do Penguins Have Knees?* were psychological or physiological in nature. But we received a fascinating letter from James D. Kilchenman of Toledo, Ohio, who has spent decades in the restaurant and catering businesses. He believes that the most important influences in preferences for meat doneness are socioeconomic and cultural. The higher the socioeconomic status of a group, the rarer they want their meat. In Kilchenman's catering experience, middle-class white groups invariably order prime rib medium-rare. Working-class black groups tend to order the roast medium-well or sometimes well done. But Kilchenman thinks that class is much more decisive than race: Affluent blacks tend to order meat rarer than less affluent whites.

How can we explain the socioeconomic taste disparity? Kilchenman attributes the difference to exposure to different types of meat. The better the cut of meat, the more essential it is to have it cooked rare. As Kilchenman puts it, no one walks into Wendy's and demands a rare burger. Less affluent people are used to cooking cheaper cuts of meat, cuts that often need to be cooked longer to become tender.

Kilchenman argues that like poor adults, most children have limited exposure to the best cuts of meat. When Mom and Pop take Junior to the restaurant, chances are Junior isn't going to

252   DAVID FELDMAN

order filet mignon for dinner. He'll usually have a hamburger. Kilchenman notes that whenever he has seen children ordering meat rare, they were always from affluent families.

Just as drinkers start with Singapore Slings and end up drinking martinis, or start as children with Kool-Aid and move to sweet white wine and later to dry red wine, so do children start with burnt hot dogs. But with exposure to the "finer things in life," they will end up consuming rare filets as they watch their cholesterol levels rise.

Frustables First Posed in *Why Do Dogs Have Wet Noses?* and First Answered in *Do Penguins Have Knees?*

FRUSTABLE 1: *Does anyone really like fruitcake?*

We heard a disturbing report from Joseph Redman, of Lincoln, Illinois, about nutritional standards in the military:

> In 1968 and 1969 I served two tours in Vietnam as a helicopter ambulance medic. On many occasions we flew around the clock with no regular breaks for hot meals from the mess hall, which meant our option was to eat C-rations. The typical C-ration meal included a main dish of canned meat, sometimes with potatoes; a can of fruit; a can of cheese and crackers or crackers with peanut butter or jelly; and a can of cake.
>
> The three cakes I remember were pound cake (everyone's favorite), a nut-cinnamon cake, and fruitcake. The first two were always in short supply. This left great stacks of round, canned fruitcake available for the taking. When one is hungry, one will eat just about anything.

Our fighting men and women reduced to scavenging for fruitcakes! And they wonder why morale is bad in the military.

FRUSTABLE 3: *We often hear the cliché: "We use only 10 percent of our brains." How was it determined that we use 10 percent and not 5 percent or 15 percent?*

We heard from two professors who found academic studies that could have been the basis for the cliché. Prof. Michael Levin, of the City College of New York, did some calculations based on the work of neurobiologist Harry Jerison. We'll save you the gory details and focus on Levin's conclusions: "The human brain turns out to have about 8.8 billion more neurons than the typical mammal that weighs what a man does. The ratio of 8.8 billion to the total neurons in the brain is about 1/10." But Levin offers even more tantalizing evidence:

> According to Harold Jerison, the relation of brain mass E to body mass P in the typical mammal is given by $E = .12p^{2/3}$. This much brain is assumed to be necessary for housekeeping functions. Anything extra may be assumed to be used for "higher" cognitive functions.
>
> The *ratio* of an animal's actual brain weight to the brain-weight predicted by the equation is what Jerison calls its "encephalization quotient." It tells us how many times larger the animal's brain is than it needs to be for basic housekeeping functions.
>
> The average human male weighs 55,000 grams. Using the above equation, his "expected" brain weight is about 175 grams. The "encephalization quotient" is 7.79—call it 8, or rounding off to the nearest order of magnitude, call it 10. Roughly speaking, we need only 10% of our brains. Of course, what that means is that we need or use only 10% of our brains for the basic functions performed by all mammalian brains. Presumably, the rest is for "higher" functions.

Jerison's early research was conducted in the 1970s, after the birth of our cliché, but this is still fascinating stuff.

Robert P. Vecchio, Franklin D. Schurz Professor of Management at the University of Notre Dame, sent us a copy of some pages from a textbook he read as an undergraduate, *Foundations of Physiological Psychology*, written by Richard F. Thompson.

Could this Frustable have stemmed from a misunderstanding of the physiology of the brain?

> ... Perhaps the greatest source of confounding in the analysis of whole brain tissue is the fact that the majority of cellular elements in brain are not even nerve cells. Ninety percent of the cells in the brain are *glial* cells and only 10 percent are nerve cells . . .glial cells have often been considered as connective tissue, serving the same general kind of supportive function as connective tissue in most organs.

This textbook was reporting on research conducted by J. Nurnberger in 1958 and S. DeRobertis in 1961, well before any of the sources mentioned in *Do Penguins Have Knees?* To be honest, though, more than any insight into this brain stuff, we are dazzled by the fact that Professor Vecchio can remember anything from an old college textbook.

While these scientific studies could, theoretically, have provided the inspiration for the 10% figure, they aren't well enough known or disseminated to have hatched our cliché. So we continued our search for the phrase in popular culture.

We mentioned in *Do Penguins Have Knees?* that friends of ours swore they had read about the "10%" cliche in a Robert Heinlein novel, but James Gleick thinks he's now found the passage, and no numbers are involved. In *Citizen of the Galaxy* (1957), a fictional character says, "He proved that most people go all their lives only half awake." Same idea, but not the nail in the coffin.

That's why we were so excited when we heard from Allan J. Wilke of Toledo, Ohio:

> I've been involved in a Dale Carnegie course these last few months. Required reading includes *How to Stop Worrying and Start Living*. Mr. Carnegie frequently quotes the psychologist William James. On page 146 of this book, there is a paragraph that reads:
> "The renowned William James was speaking of people who had never found themselves when he declared that the average person develops only ten per cent of his or her latent mental abil-

ities. 'Compared to what we ought to be,' he wrote, 'we are only half awake. We are making use of only a small part of our physical and mental resources. Stating the thing broadly, human individuals thus live far within their limits. They possess powers of various sorts which they habitually fail to use.' "

As is his habit, Carnegie doesn't cite where he found this quote. But Carnegie's bestselling book was first published in 1944 and has been taught in courses for nearly fifty years. Who better to spread the word?

Unfortunately, we haven't been able to confirm the James quote, although in his letter to W. Lutoslawski, in 1906, James comes tantalizingly close:

> Most people live, whether physically, intellectually, or morally, in a very restricted circle of their potential being. They *make use* of a very small portion of their possible consciousness, and of their soul's resources in general, much like a man who, out of his whole bodily organism, should get into a habit of using and moving only his little finger. Great emergencies and crises show us how much greater our vital resources are than we had supposed.

Ultimately, it may not matter whether James actually uttered the words ascribed to him—for it is much more likely that Carnegie, and his disciples, spread the word than James, himself.

But perhaps our favorite new pronouncement on this Frustable came from Matthew Cope of Westmount, Quebec:

> Sorry, I don't know who first claimed that we only use 10 percent of our brains. But presumably, whoever it was, there's a 90 percent chance he was wrong!

FRUSTABLE 24: *Where, exactly, did the expression "Blue Plate Special" come from?*

We're hurt. We can't even convince some readers that blue plate specials were actually served on blue plates. Jan Gable, of Cedar City, Utah, insists that "blue" refers not to the color of the plate but to the collars of the workers who purchased inexpensive, complete meals in diners.

DAVID FELDMAN

Allison Berlier demurs. Blue doesn't refer to the plate, she chastises us, but to the food being served!

> During the depression, the most plentiful, and therefore, cheapest meal available, was the locally caught *bluefish* . . .

Honestly, Jan and Allison, there *were* blue *plates*. Many *live* people remember them. Authors even write about them. In fact, reader Jan Saul notes that Mary Higgins Clark, in her book, *Loves Music, Loves to Dance,* was so inspired:

> A blue plate used to be the special of the evening at a cheap restaurant. Seventy-five cents bought you a hunk of meat, a couple of vegetables, a potato. The plate was sectioned to keep the juices from running together. Your grandfather loved that kind of bargain . . .

Robert Klein, of Paramus, New Jersey, has conducted extensive research into the history of this phrase. He sent along a copy of John Egerton's discussion of the blue plate special in *Southern Food.* Egerton notes that restaurants featuring blue-plate specials "came early to the region, and many of the best of them have survived to this day, withstanding the fast-food revolution and other gastronomic upheavals." The typical blue-plate lunch, according to Egerton, consisted of a main dish, three or four vegetables, bread, and a drink, all for one low price. Klein concludes that the blue-plate special probably began in Tennessee or Kentucky during the 1920s.

FRUSTABLE 5: *Why does the traffic in big cities in the United States seem quieter than in big cities in other parts of the world?*

Nityanandan Ashwath, who first posed this Frustable, lurked in the bushes until he read our write-up in *Do Penguins Have Knees?* Now he offers three more reasons why foreign traffic seems noisier:

> 1. Most engines in vehicles on a U.S. street are large gasoline-powered four-stroke automobiles. These are inherently the

quietest type of engine ever invented. Most other places have a high percentage of diesels (buses/trucks), two-strokes (scooters), and small four-strokes (motorcycles) that are all much noisier.

2. The smaller vehicles overseas result in a greater density of exhaust population. That is, an observer on a street corner has more individual sources of sound within a 100-yard radius because bikes and minicars take up less street space per unit.

3. Most U.S. cars have automatic transmissions that limit the rpm buildup of the engine during acceleration. Drivers elsewhere have more opportunity for shrieking starts from a traffic light.

FRUSTABLE 6: *Why do dogs tilt their heads when you talk to them?*

In *Do Penguins Have Knees?*, we heard from readers arguing passionately whether dogs tilt their heads for better vision or better hearing. Reader Fred Lanting wrote with the best discussion reconciling these two viewpoints that we have seen:

> Dogs have a very poor focusing ability because the fovea (focusing depression) in the retina is less developed for that purpose than, say, the fovea of a hawk . . . It's a tradeoff, since dogs have very good night vision and ability to detect motion better than we do. The dog tilts his head for the same reason we do: to get an almost imperceptibly different but significant new perspective—a better 3-D brain image of distance.
>
> The dog uses a *combination* of eyes and ears for this sharpening of the incoming sensory messages. Ears are set apart from each other for a reason: The tiny additional fraction of time it takes sound to reach the second ear tells dogs whence come the sounds. Thus a dog can find you in the dark or behind hiding places if you make a little noise.
>
> He tilts his head even if there's no noise *we* can hear because he wants to get the benefit of not only sight but any sound that *might* be forthcoming. He's trying to get all the sensory input he can because he's very interested in it.

One of our favorite correspondents, David Altom of Jefferson, Missouri, wrote to us about his cockapoo, Midnight, who he owned in the 1970s. Like many dogs, Midnight responded not only to the wail of police sirens outside their home but to the sound of sirens on television:

> Every time the sound of a police siren came on "Kojak," "Baretta," or "McCloud," Midnight would perk up his ears and tilt his head as if trying to understand that sound. His attention was directed to the speaker, not the picture. Once or twice, he went up and sniffed the TV speaker.
>
> Midnight also had two favorite songs: "Sister Golden Hair" by America and "One of These Nights" by the Eagles . . .

"Sister Golden Hair"? I thought dogs were supposed to have *good* hearing?

FRUSTABLE 7: *Why and where did the notion develop that "fat people are jolly"?*

Our 10-percent-of-the-brain expert, Prof. Michael Levin, took us to task for making fun of the validity of somatotypes, developed by William Sheldon about fifty years ago:

> There are three basic somatotypes: mesomorphic (muscular), ectomorphic (skinny), and endomorphic (fat). A good deal of valid research has established a correlation between mesomorphy and extroversion, aggressiveness and a domineering temperament. Criminals tend overwhelmingly to be mesomorphs, or slightly endomorphic mesomorphs.
>
> . . . ectomorphs tend to be introverted, inhibited, and restrained. So, comparatively speaking, endomorphs tend to be "jollier" than either mesomorphs or ectomorphs. They are relatively less inclined to try to dominate others, and are relatively less introspective and reserved. The perception of this is probably the origin of the (correct) stereotype of the jolly fat man. (The writer of this letter is mesomorphic, but has no desire to force his opinions on you.)

Sure, but because we are jolly endomorphs, we'll let you mesomorphic musclemen cram your opinions down our ineffectual throats.

FRUSTABLE 9: *Why does the heart depicted in illustrations look totally different than a real heart?*

In *Do Penguins Have Knees?* we mentioned Desmond Morris's theory that the heart was an idealized representation of the female buttocks. But reader Barth Richards, of Naperville, Illinois, offers a striking amplification of this theory.

During the Middle Ages, many Germanic and Scandinavian people, particularly pagans, used "runes," letters and symbols that had phonetic and often symbolic meanings. Runes were used not only in language but in magical rituals. One rune was our idealized conception of the heart. In the book *Futhark: A Handbook of Rune Magic,* the interpretation of the heart symbol is given as

> (actually an ancient representation of female genitalia and buttocks)—sensuality, eroticism, love. In Old Norse books of magic the sign often appears in spells of love magic; a symbol of sexual intercourse.

Richards theorizes that when Christians tried to subsume pagan culture, they retained the "love" connotation of the heart symbol, while eliminating the sexual components.

> The literal meaning of the symbol was altered to that of a "heart," which fit the Christian belief of the heart being the vessel of the emotions, including love.
> This also meshes nicely with one of the other suggested solutions you printed in *Do Penguins Have Knees?*, which said that the arteries of the systemic arch of many animals closely resemble the shape of the "heart" symbol. This coincidence would surely add to the Christians' sense of justification in referring to the pagan's love symbol as a "heart."

FRUSTABLE 10: *Where do all the missing pens go?*

Reader Jim Kasun claims to have accumulated about 4,400 pounds of them. ("At an average weight of .3 ounce, this translates to approximately 234,600 pens.") Although this doesn't ac-

DAVID FELDMAN

count for every single lost pen, it surely explains the imbalance in Plano, Texas.

Jim believes that while countless pens have fallen out of pockets, as many are misplaced as lost. Look underneath sofa and chair cushions, Jim suggests—pens have a way of migrating deep into the innards of the furniture. Others are buried in overloaded drawers and cabinets.

Jim anticipated what was on our mind after reading his letter: "Why do I spend time doing this? I'm not sure . . . guess I just have a *pen*chant for it." Despite the pun, we can't be too mad at him. After all, he sent us a pen "from the 1980–1985 group. Who knows? Maybe you once owned it."

Letters

Maybe in the future we will publish a book of Letters to Imponderables. *Until that day, we have room to print only a fraction
of the thousands of letters we receive every year. This section is
reserved not for new Imponderables, conjectures about Frustables, or even words of praise, but rather for readers who want
to vent their spleen about what we've written in the past.*

In August 1992, we republished all but the first Imponderables *book in paperback, incorporating many of the suggestions
and corrections of readers. It can sometimes take years to validate objections and change the text on subsequent printings,
but we do so regularly.*

*We appreciate your suggestions and consider every one
carefully. The letters published here are not the only valid criticisms or suggestions we received, just some of the more entertaining ones that we hope will appeal to a wide audience.*

*From now on, maybe we'll need to put an expiration date
on* Imponderables. *In* Do Penguins Have Knees? *we answered
the question, "Why Are There Peanuts in Plain M&Ms?" Guess
what? Hans Fiuczynski, external relations director of M&M/
Mars, writes to tell us that the premise of the Imponderable is
now moot:*

> Historically, M&M/Mars has used the same milk chocolate in
> both M&Ms Plain and Peanut Chocolate Candies. This milk choc-
> olate contained a small amount of finely ground peanuts.
>
> At considerable investment in the plants producing these
> products, the chocolate production has been separated and the
> usage of any peanuts in the chocolate for M&M Plain Chocolate
> Candies eliminated, starting January 1992. However, as a precau-
> tion, we will continue to maintain the declaration of peanuts as an
> ingredient in M&Ms Plain Chocolate Candies. This is to provide
> protection to peanut-sensitive individuals in the event that a small

amount of peanuts may inadvertently appear in M&M's Plain Chocolate Candies.

We're also sad to report that the Imponderable from our first book—"What Is the Purpose of the Red Tear String on Band-Aids?"—won't make sense to kids in the next century. By the end of 1992, Johnson & Johnson will have phased out the tear strings altogether, substituting an adhesive strip.

But M&M/Mars and Johnson & Johnson aren't the only corporations dedicated to reform. Jena Paolilli of Chelmsford, Massachusetts, writes:

> In *Why Do Dogs Have Wet Noses?* you answered the question, "Why is there no expiration date on toothpaste?" by saying that there is none needed. I have found expiration dates on four tubes of toothpaste: two on Colgate for Kids (different sizes), one on Tartar Control Gel Colgate, and one on Colgate's Peak Baking Soda Gel . . .

We called the folks at Colgate, and they corroborated the recent appearance of an expiration date. "Why do you need one now if you didn't a few years ago?" we asked. The consumer affairs representative indicated Colgate probably didn't. The ingredients haven't changed, and it isn't at all dangerous to use toothpaste after the expiration date. But occasionally the flavoring or the fluoride in toothpaste breaks down chemically. The result is usually a watery consistency or a funny taste. In most cases, Colgate advised, the toothpaste is usable for at least a year after the date on the package.

In Why Do Dogs Have Wet Noses? *we stated that, usually, the answer to "What vegetables are used in vegetable oil?" was: soybean oil. But canola oil has made great inroads, as Lauralou Cicierski, of the Canola Council of Canada, was pleased to inform us. Procter & Gamble's Crisco and Puritan Oils now both contain 100 percent canola oil, and other brands' ingredient lists increasingly say "canola oil and/or soybean oil."*

The times, they are a-changin', we guess. And not only in the candy, oil, bandage, and toothpaste industries. It seems like there has been rampant inflation in Social Security numbers, too:

> In your book *When Do Fish Sleep?* you state that the highest numbers assigned as the first three digits of a Social Security number are 575–576 in Hawaii. I don't believe this is true. My wife and I both have SSNs that begin 585. In fact, most of the people I grew up with in Clovis, New Mexico, had 585 numbers.
>
> HAROLD GAINES
> St. Louis, Missouri

You're right. Historically, New Mexico's SSNs start with 525, but when they ran out of numbers, New Mexico, for a while, had the highest number, 585, of the fifty states. But several other states have been assigned bigger numbers since we wrote When Do Fish Sleep? *(Mississippi, 587–588; Florida, 589–595; Arizona, 600–601; and California, 602–626). The highest numbers that the Social Security Administration issues, 700–728, still belong to railroad employees, although new numbers in the 700-series have not been assigned since 1963.*

While we are focusing on geographical grumblings, we heard a chauvinistic chant from Ken Giesbers of Seattle, Washington. He asks us, "How dare you claim East Coast weather is weirder than ours?"

> In *Why Do Dogs Have Wet Noses?* you state: "Of course, the volatility of weather in the East makes the job of a weathercaster considerably dicier than his West Coast counterparts." You should be aware that the West Coast extends northerly past Southern California.
>
> Weather prediction in the Pacific Northwest is considered the hardest in the nation. Having lived in the Portland and Seattle areas all of my life, I was shocked, on a recent trip to Boston, to hear a forecasted high temperature of 82 degrees. In Seattle, no forecaster would ever be so bold. The forecast would be for "a high in the upper seventies to mid-eighties," and it would be wrong as often as right. The proximity of an ocean to the west, inland waterways, and mountain peaks with glacial networks all combine to make prediction very difficult indeed.

Heck, Ken, we think weather forecasting in the Northwest is a snap. "Cool, cloudy, chance of rain and showers" should work, oh, about 355 days of the year. And don't assume the weather forecast of 82 degrees in Boston was correct, either.

Larry Mills of Southfield, Michigan, attributes the presence of the oft-discussed ball on top of a flagpole to weather factors —lightning, in particular:

> The large ball is on top to greatly reduce the electrical tension that might build during electrical storms . . . this is opposite to a lightning rod, which comes to a sharp point to assure that electrical tension that may build at or near a structure will surely strike the rod.

We've never heard this theory before, and we've heard plenty on the topic.

But the flagpole ball Imponderable is a piker compared to all the letters we've received about why ranchers hang their boots on fenceposts, a staple of every Letters section. We are pleased to announce that we received only one new theory in the last year; perhaps we are starting to wean you from this topic. William Papavasilion, a teacher/folklorist from Lancaster, Pennsylvania, writes that in some areas, it was customary for folks to leave unneeded boots outside to be taken for the asking. Nowhere was this policy practiced more than at Boot Hill:

> If a deceased person had a good pair of boots, the undertaker (usually) would place his boots near the entrance of the cemetery. If a person took a kindness to a pair of boots, he simply would take the pair.

Speaking of death, J. Stephen Paul of West Monroe, New York, reports the rare sighting of a bird dying in flight. But he concurs with our analysis of what happens to dead birds: "By the third day, it must have been scavenged or resurrected itself." Paul's son also watched a bird "whop down" in flight. ("Threw a rod, I guess.") If Paul doesn't seem too sentimental about death, it may be because he is a hospital consultant, and he supplied another reason why surgeons wear blue or green uniforms (see Why Do Clocks Run Clockwise?*):*

> When medical personnel are operating, looking at red for a long time, a retinal imprint is established on the eye. When looking away, this appears as a greenish afterimage or "ghost image" wherever they look until it fades out. To counter this bothersome effect, which occurs any time a surgeon or assistant looks away to rest the eyes, the walls and clothing are colored a matching shade to render this effect invisible . . .

Can anyone confirm this theory?

Dead birds weren't the only feathered friends on your minds. Several of you tried to help us out after we confessed in Why Do Dogs Have Wet Noses? *that we didn't know how "turkey" came to mean a show business flop. Terry Pruitt of Gadsden, Alabama, hypothesizes that a bad show is like a turkey trying to fly—it may sputter aloft for a while, but eventually it will flop to the ground. But several readers, Daniel J. Drazen of Berwyn, Illinois, being the first, found citations of this very topic in various books. Drazen located an explanation in Harry and Michael Medved's* Son of Golden Turkey Awards. *According to the Medveds, the colloquialism was coined because vaudeville shows used to conduct Thanksgiving performances but attendance was poor. "Turkey Nights" were dreaded gigs for performers, and mediocre acts got stuck playing them. Such entertainers, without any clout, were called "Turkey Acts" and, eventually, simply "Turkeys." In a recent issue of* Variety, *Jeremy Gerard contended that "turkey" was originally a Broadway term coined to denote a poor show—one that was performed not during bad attendance times but good:*

> . . . "turkey" was coined to denote a show of dubious merit mounted between Thanksgiving and the New Year in order to ride out the seasonal tourist trade regardless of the [critical] pans.

In Why Do Dogs Have Wet Noses? *we tackled a couple of Imponderables about worms. "Are the nineties going to be the Decade of the Larva?" we mused about this obsession. Our joke didn't sit too well with two of our Illinois readers, Neil B. Schanker of Palatine and Craig Cicero of Rockford. As both pointed out, worms are not larvae. They remain the same structurally as they grow. Schanker, by the way, is an assistant professor of biology at William Rainey Harper College. Craig Cicero is not yet a professor—he's thirteen years old.*

While we're on the subject of insects, we have a ticklish issue to discuss. In When Do Fish Sleep? *we quoted an entomologist as saying that crickets "chirp" by rubbing their legs together. In* Do Penguins Have Knees? *we ran an angry letter from another entomologist berating us, insisting that crickets rub the scrapers on their wings to cause the noise. We issued a groveling apology. Several readers have sent us textbooks, most with diagrams, indicating that the noise comes from scrapers on the legs. How can something so simple be in question? The final straw was when our eight-year-old nephew, Michael Feldman, found the following quotation in a book called* Wings, *written by Nick Bantoc: "Crickets chirp by rubbing their wings or legs together." We give up.*

On second thought, we don't give up. How can we rest when we are presented with a new, unsolved mystery by reader Stephen Hostettler of Chico, California?

> I offer further evidence that fish do sleep. Several months ago, I got up to discover one of the swordtails missing from our tank. My wife found him swimming in a teacup on the far side of the double sink. Everything else on the counter and both sides of the sink were dry—proof positive that he was sleepwalking. The event so traumatized the little critter that he hasn't closed both eyes.

How do you know your fish doesn't take naps when you leave the room? Or don't the Hostettlers sleep?

Paul J. Breslin of Tuscaloosa, Alabama, took us to task for our discussion of the role of dalmations in firefighting in Why Do Clocks Run Clockwise? *He thinks we left the impression that the main task of dalmations was to run in front of the coach to clear traffic. Although we did read first-person accounts*

DAVID FELDMAN

*(from the firemen, not the dalmations) of dogs clearing traffic,
we probably did put too much emphasis on this task. Breslin
summarizes their main duties well: "The dalmation's job was to
keep the horses pulling together, to keep them from tangling the
lines, to keep them apart, and to insure they were on the right
lead."*

*Readers' objections to our treatment of animals extends to
animated critters, too. Thaddeus J. Kochanny of Chicago, Illinois, proffers another explanation for why Mickey Mouse has
only four fingers on each hand. He thinks the tradition dates
back to*

> depictions of trolls, leprechauns, meneuni, and other mythical
> "persons" that predate cartoons. In virtually all such carvings, the
> characters have three fingers. I believe this was done to show the
> image was nonhuman. This has nothing to do with the ease of
> drawing.
>
> I collect wood carvings of Anri, an Italian cooperative head-
> quartered in the Italian Alps at Santa Christina, Italy. When the
> carving is a troll or mythic creation, it has three fingers and a
> thumb on each hand. When it is a person, such as a boy eating
> grapes, there are four fingers and a thumb on each hand of the
> figure.

Actually, we mentioned in When Do Fish Sleep? *that Disney
had a habit of giving humans in his cartoons, or at least lead
characters, four fingers and a thumb as well. But every animation expert we've ever consulted concurs with our explanation.*

*While we're on the subject of hands, Dr. Jerry Tennen of
Toronto, Ontario, wants to add another reason why most people
wear wristwatches on their left hand: "If you wear a standard
wristwatch on your right wrist, the stem eventually frays the
cuff on your shirtsleeves. Too bad you didn't consult me first."
Evidently so.*

*Jeff Reese of Mosinee, Wisconsin, wishes we had contacted
him too—before we wrote in* When Do Fish Sleep? *that dollar
bills can't be counted by machines. We overstated the case.
There are machines that count bills, but they are expensive and
can't discriminate among different denominations. The expense*

of the bill-counting machines discourages many vendors from using machines that accept dollar bills.

Now that reader Gabe Raggiunto is too mature to fling single shoes around his neighborhood (see "The Frustables That Will Not Die"), he sits back and reads the paper, luckily for us. He sent us an Associated Press newspaper story that recounts the same origins of the name Dr. Pepper, that we discussed in Do Penguins Have Knees? *But some citizens of Rural Retreat, Virginia, the real Dr. Pepper's home town, think otherwise. The town's mayor (and dentist), Dr. Doug Humphrey, claims that Dr. Pepper himself invented the drink (those medicos always stick together) and that a lovesick Wade Morrison (the hero of our story) stole the formula and sold it in Waco, Texas, as shameless revenge against Dr. Pepper, who would not let Morrison marry his daughter. We'll stick with our version, although we hear that Oliver Stone is trying to option the memoirs of Dr. Humphrey.*

Speaking of conspiracies, readers are still upset about disappearing socks. But have you ever wondered whether this is a problem in France? We guess not:

> At least one person has solved the sock problem to his satisfaction. I have read that Jerry Lewis never wears a pair of socks more than once and that he throws them away after wearing. That means no washing/drying/coupling or worry about the odd sock. He has been criticized for this extravagance by those who feel he should have the socks washed and then given to charity. But Lewis, being the lovable fellow we all know and adore, told the critics to perform a physically impossible act. You see what this sock business can generate in a person.
>
> DANIEL J. TIREN
> *Laurel, Maryland*

We sure do, Daniel. It can drive people to composing horrible puns: Tiren speculates that missing socks have gone into a special, merry resting ground in the sky—the hozone.

We heard from several engineers and technicians who had information to add about why the numbers on tape counters on

DAVID FELDMAN

audio and video tape players don't seem to measure anything. Electronics engineer Kevin Holsinger of Menlo Park, California, explains:

In either a VCR or audio tape player, the tape is moved past the play/record heads when a motor turns the little wheel inside the cassette housing. The unit of measurement on the counter is related to how many times that motor has turned—but each count on the front panel might represent one revolution, five revolutions, one-tenth of a revolution, or whatever else they decide on.

Although manufacturers did not agree on what the counts represent, they did agree on how fast the motors will turn. That doesn't result in a constant tape speed, though, because the reel the tape winds onto is getting larger as tape winds onto it. In one revolution, a reel with a larger diameter will pull more tape onto itself, which means that the tape is passing the read/write heads faster toward the end of the movie than it is at the beginning. You can't see or hear the difference in speed because it was recorded that way, too (and because the change in speed isn't really all that large, since an empty reel's diameter is still around 70% of a full reel). The motors, rather than the tape, run at a constant speed, because it is much less expensive to build things that way.

And while we're speaking of measurement, David Maier of Beaverton, Oregon, offers a simpler explanation (than we did in When Do Fish Sleep?*) for why gas gauges move faster as you empty the fuel tank of an automobile:*

Most gas gauges are hooked to a float that measures the depth of gas. But because tanks don't have straight sides generally, volume doesn't vary linearly with depth. Consider a V-shaped beer glass—each time you drink an "inch" of beer, you are getting a smaller swallow.

Talk of beer always reminds us of baseball. How's that for a smooth segue into a discussion of why females "throw like a girl"? Anita Gertz of Farmington Hills, Michigan, felt we didn't cover all the bases in our discussion of the topic in When Do Fish Sleep? *Her genetics professor at Eastern Michigan University told her that when a person stands with the arms slightly away from the sides and the palms are facing forward,* the angle the bones of the forearm and upper arm make at the elbow (sometimes called the "carrying angle") is fifteen degrees in males and twenty-five degrees in females. Because the angle in males and females is different, so is their throwing ability. The explanation for the larger angle was that it evolved in females because they carried babies and small children much more often than males.

Our exercise physiologists still insist that girls could "throw like boys" if they were trained to do so. But let's not argue. We have more important things to squabble about. Like George Strait's hats ("Why Are There Dents on the Top of Cowboy Hats?" in Do Penguins Have Knees?*). Lee Denham of Warnock Hat Works in Pharr, Texas, sent us a picture of the country and western singer wearing a hat with "dents" (Lee recommends we call these "creases"), and says that all of Strait's hats have creases. We swear that we've seen George in a creaseless hat, but for now we'll concede the point, Lee, and hope we haven't forever tarnished Strait's reputation by implying that he has the same fashion sense as Hoss Cartwright.*

And any discussion of high fashion has to end on this high note: Why do old men wear their pants higher than young men? We shared many theories on this subject in Why Do Clocks Run Clockwise?, *but David Campion, MICP, wants to add two more:*

> Many older men experience deterioration or settling of the bones that comprise the pelvic girdle. It is possible that displacement of the iliac bones (the crests of which form the hips) may render the hips useless as a perch for one's pants.
>
> On close inspection, one will find that old men with high-riding pants are often wearing suspenders. I say "on close inspection" because old men frequently wear sport coats capable of concealing the suspenders. This combination may create the illusion of pants that are intentionally pulled up when, in fact, the underlying cause may simply be a snappy pair of suspenders.

Janyce E. McLean of Beeville, Texas, wrote to complain about our statement that Rinx Records was the first company to produce music specifically for skating rinks. Janyce says that her mother worked for a company called Skatin' Tunes, which

produced organ music for rinks all over the country. The com-
pany was based in Babylon, Long Island, and "was begun some-
time in the early 1940s by Hilliard Du Bois, who also used the
professional name Allan Strow." Can any reader provide more
information about this company?

Several readers, including Dr. John Hardin of Greenfield,
Indiana, who first posed the Imponderable, found it hard to
believe that the green tinge sometimes found on potato chips
was the harmless chlorophyll we claimed it to be in Do Penguins Have Knees? *We've rechecked our sources and are happy*
to reiterate: Relax. Toxins can form on potato chips, but they
reside on the peel. The toxins, glycolalkaloids, develop at the
same time as the chlorophyll, but there is no connection be-
tween the "poison" and the green stuff on potato chips.

In Why Do Dogs Have Wet Noses? *we declared that men's*
nipples were vestigial organs, ones that could conceivably dis-
appear in the distant future. Bill Cohen-Kiraly of Lyndhurst,
Ohio, took us to task for our sloppy, nonpoetic license:

> Evolution does not necessarily rid bodies of things that are
> vestigial unless they offer some disadvantage to the evolutionee
> before he or she can reproduce and raise young to adulthood. So
> as long as nippleless men don't reproduce faster or better than
> nippled men, there is no reason for the nipples to disappear. Be-
> cause of the sexual sensitivity of nipples, the reverse is probably
> true.
>
> But there is a bigger problem with your contention that they
> will disappear from men, however. Evolution is a genetic process
> and the genetic differences between men and women are rela-
> tively minimal, only one part of one chromosome. Many structural
> distinctions are the result of hormonal differences. In short, you
> could not eliminate the nipples on men without eliminating them
> on women because the genes that create them are not gender
> specific.

It's settled. No more government grants for research on male
nipple elimination, then.

Sometimes we hear from correspondents who want to argue
with other letter writers. One young reader from Interlochen,

Michigan, has a bone to pick with SUNY professor Noel W. Smith, who wrote in When Do Fish Sleep? *that the role of pubic and underarm hair was not primarily as a sexual attractant but as a lubricant to facilitate movement of arms and legs. Prof. Smith, meet Ben Randall:*

> If your lubrication theory is correct, why don't young kids get chafed when doing activities? Wouldn't they need "lubrication," too? I'm a mere eighth-grader and even I can see this.
>
> And another thing. Little kids move around a lot more than older, lubricated adults that I've seen.

Kids can be tough. But then so can adults. We recently received this letter from Paul C. Ward of Ligonier, Pennsylvania:

> I am currently reading your book *Do Penguins Have Knees?* with much pleasure and have enjoyed several of your other books. However, one thing bugs me. Why do you almost always answer a question in three hundred words or more when it could be answered in a fraction of that amount? Is this because authors are paid by the word?

Yes.

Do allow us one indulgence. In Do Penguins Have Knees? *we closed with a letter from a woman whose lover read to her from* Why Do Clocks Run Clockwise? *But we found even a better use for Imponderables in bed:*

> Norman Cousins attributed his recoveries to viewing laugh-provoking films. One of your Imponderables recently evoked a far more spectacular response. A friend suffered a stroke with serious sensorimotor deficits and was rendered aphasiac.
>
> During protracted hospital course, responses remained refractory. One afternoon, I was reading aloud from *When Do Fish Sleep?* and burst into laughter. Pausing for breath, into the silence threaded a wavering whisper, my friend's first successful attempt at communication. I bent closer, capturing the long awaited sound, borne aloft like a triumphant banner.
>
> My stricken friend crisply voiced, "Oh, read that again, read

DAVID FELDMAN

that again!," her face ablaze in smiles. All of us are glad your mother had you!

Salli Kamins
Venice, California

Thanks, Salli. You made our year.

And to all of our Imponderable friends, thanks for all of your support. We'll meet you again at the same place, same time, next year.

Acknowledgments

In every Imponderables book, the acknowledgments start with a thanks to my readers. Without your input, I wouldn't have such a wide range of mysteries to explore, answers to Frustables, criticisms that make the books more interesting and more accurate, and praise that often provides the author inspiration to rise from his stupor and trudge on.

If mail has become the lifeblood of the *Imponderables* series, it has also become the bane of my existence. As always, I am sending a personal reply to any reader who encloses a self-addressed stamped envelope, but I am behind, alarmingly behind, in answering correspondence. When I start writing the manuscript for the next book, my letter output dwindles. Please bear with me as I try to catch up, and be assured that I read and appreciate every word of every letter sent to *Imponderables*.

Is it karma or is it just dumb luck that I have the opportunity to work with such wonderful people? My esteem for my editor, Rick Kot, keeps rising as his voice keeps lowering—I have a recurrent nightmare that he will forsake publishing to sing bass for the Temptations. Sheila Gilooly, Rick's assistant, may have her soul in the rarefied world of verse, but she has been of immense help in solving my prosaic problems with great skill and charm. Craig Herman was forced to decide between a career in male modeling and publicity; luckily for me, he eschewed the superficial world of glitter. Andrew Malkin may have flown the HarperCollins coop, but his work in booking my last publicity tour was exceptional.

Imponderables books are produced on an extremely tight deadline, one of the many reasons I'm especially grateful to the production editing/copyediting team that renders my manuscript semicoherent: thank you, Kim Lewis, Maureen Clark, and Janet Byrne. And for her exceptional work on the last two jacket designs, my thanks to Suzanne Noli.

Even the muckety-mucks at HarperCollins have been exceptionally kind and supportive to me, and that starts at the top. Thanks to Bill Shinker, Roz Barrow, Brenda Marsh, Pat Jonas, Zeb Burgess, Karen Mender, Steve Magnuson, Robert Jones, Joe Montebello, Susan Moldow, Clinton Morris, Connie Levinson, Mark Landau, and all my friends in the publicity, special markets, sales, and Harper Audio divisions.

Jim Trupin, the Grand Pooh Bah of literary agents, is a neverending font of curmudgeonly common sense, while Grande Pooh Bette Liz Trupin, on the other hand, is a neverending font of common sense.

Kassie Schwan's illustrations amaze me with their inventiveness and good humor. This book's for you!

And thanks to Sherry Spitzer for her invaluable research assistance and dogged determination to root out Imponderability wherever she finds it.

Who do I run to when I can't moan or vent my insecurities at my publisher (neuroses do not flare only at office hours)? I bother my friends in publishing, of course. Thanks—for the wisdom, as well as the friendship—to Mark Kohut, Susie Russenberger, Barbara Rittenhouse, and James Gleick.

And to my friends and family, who offer both advice about and respite from my work, I thank: Tony Alessandrini; Jesus Arias; Michael Barson; Sherry Barson; Rajat Basu; Ruth Basu; Barbara Bayone; Jeff Bayone; Jean Behrend; Marty Bergen; Brenda Berkman; Cathy Berkman; Sharyn Bishop; Andrew Blees; Carri Blees; Christopher Blees; Jon Blees; Bowling Green State University's Popular Culture Department; Jerry Braithwaite; Annette Brown; Arvin Brown; Herman Brown; Ernie Capobianco; Joann Carney; Lizzie Carnie; Susie Carney; Janice Carr; Lapt Chan; Mary Clifford; Don Cline; Dorrie Cohen; Alvin Cooperman; Marilyn Cooperman; Judith Dahlman; Paul Dahlman; Shelly de Satnick; Charlie Doherty; Laurel Doherty; Joyce Ebert; Pam Elam; Andrew Elliot; Steve Feinberg; Fred Feldman; Gilda Feldman; Michael Feldman; Phil Feldman; Ron Felton; Kris Fister; Mary Flannery; Linda Frank;

Elizabeth Frenchman; Susan Friedland; Michele Gallery; Chris Geist; Jean Geist; Bonnie Gellas; Richard Gertner; Amy Glass; Bea Gordon; Dan Gordon; Emma Gordon; Ken Gordon; Judy Goulding; Chris Graves; Christal Henner; Lorin Henner; Marilu Henner; Melodie Henner; David Hennes; Paula Hennes; Sheila Hennes; Sophie Hennes; Larry Harold; Carl Hess; Mitchell Hofing; Steve Hofman; Bill Hohauser; Uday Ivatury; Terry Johnson; Sarah Jones; Allen Kahn; Mitch Kahn; Joel Kaplan; Dimi Karras; Maria Katinos; Steve Kaufman; Robin Kay; Stewart Kellerman; Harvey Kleinman; Claire Labine; Randy Ladenheim-Gil; Julie Lasher, Debbie Leitner; Marilyn Levin; Vicky Levy; Rob Lieberman; Jared Lilienstein; Pon Hwa Lin; Adam Lupu; Patti Magee; Rusty Magee; everybody at the Manhattan Bridge Club; Phil Martin; Chris McCann; Jeff McQuain; Julie Mears; Phil Mears; Roberta Melendy; Naz Miah; Carol Miller; Honor Mosher; Barbara Musgrave; Phil Neel; Steve Nellisen; Craig Nelson; Millie North; Milt North; Charlie Nurse; Debbie Nye; Tom O'Brien; Pat O'Conner; Joanna Parker; Jeannie Perkins; Merrill Perlman; Joan Pirkle; Larry Prussin; Joe Rowley; Rose Reiter; Brian Rose; Lorraine Rose; Paul Rosenbaum; Carol Rostad; Tim Rostad; Leslie Rugg; Tom Rugg; Gary Saunders; Joan Saunders; Mike Saunders; Norm Saunders; Laura Schisgall; Cindy Shaha; Patricia Sheinwold; Aaron Silverstein; Kathy Smith; Kurtwood Smith; Susan Sherman Smith; Chris Soule; Kitty Srednicki; Stan Sterenberg; Karen Stoddard; Bill Stranger; Kat Stranger; Anne Swanson; Ed Swanson; Mike Szala; Jim Teuscher; Josephine Teuscher; Laura Tolkow; Albert Tom; Maddy Tyree; Alex Varghese; Carol Vellucci; Dan Vellucci; Hattie Washington; Ron Weinstock; Roy Welland; Dennis Whelan; Devin Whelan; Heide Whelan; Lara Whelan; Jon White; Ann Whitney; Carol Williams; Maggie Wittenburg; Karen Wooldridge; Maureen Wylie; Charlotte Zdrok; Vladimir Zdrok; and Debbie Zuckerberg.

We contacted approximately 1,500 experts, corporations, associations, universities, and foundations seeking information to help solve our mysteries. We don't have the space to list everyone who responded, but we want to thank all of the generous people whose information led directly to the solution of the Imponderables in this book:

Randy Acorcey, Diversified Electronic Corporation; Jim Amanna, Mobil Oil Corporation; American Cat Association; Harold Amstutz, American Association of Bovine Practitioners; John Anderson, Borden's Glue; Joe Andrews, Pillsbury Brands; Richard Anthes, National Center for Atmospheric Research; Atlas Casket Company.

David Bahlman, Society of Architectural Historians; Ian Bailey, University of California, Berkeley; Jean Bailey, General Tire; Carol Barfield, United Animal Owners Association; Rick Barongi, San Diego Zoo; Marie Beckey, Perdue Farms; Lynn Beedle, Council on Tall Buildings and Urban Habitat; Denton Belk, Crustacean Society; W. J. "Buck" Benison, Southern Ambulance Builders, Inc.; Maynard Benjamin, Envelope Manufacturers Association of America; Randy Bergman, Colgate-Palmolive; Enid Bergstrom, *Dog World;* Barry Berlin, Goodyear Tire and Rubber Company; William Berman, Society for Pediatric Research; Kathy Biel-Morgan; Bill Biles, Gestetner Corporation; Peter Black, SUNY; Wallace Blanton; Richard Boon, Roofing Industry Educational Institute; J. Gregg Borchelt, Brick Institute of America; G. Bruce Boyer; Kimberly Boyer, Coca-Cola; Ben Brewster, Colonial Brass Company; Roy Brister, Tyson Food, Inc.; Richard M. Brooks, Stouffer Hotels; Lee Brown, Whitehall Products Ltd.; Don Byczynski, Colonial Carbon Co.

K. L. Campbell; John Carolson, Dixie/Marathon, James River Corporation; Jack Castor, San Francisco Zoo; Marc Chernin, Dwelling Managers, Inc.; Helen Cherry, Cat Fanciers Federation; Chesebrough-Ponds, Inc.; Kathryn Cochran, American Hotel and Motel Association; Roger Coleman, National Food Processors Association; Norma Conley, Pretzel Museum; John Corbett, Clairol, Inc.; James Cramer, American Institute of Architects.

Michael D'Asaro; Robert DeChillo, National Coffee Association of USA; Steve Del Priore, Pepsi-Cola Bottling Company of

New York; Diane Demee-Benoit, San Francisco Zoo; Michael DeMent, Hallmark Cards, Inc.; Thomas H. Dent, Cat Fanciers Association; Michael DiBiasi, Becton-Dickinson and Company; Tim Dillon, Cornell Laboratory of Ornithology; Robert J. Dinkin, California State University, Fresno; Brent Dixon, Paper Bag Institute; Richard Dowhan, GTE Products Corporation; Lynn Downey, Levi Strauss & Co.; Joe Doyle; Fred Dunham, Oasis Mobile Homes; William Duval, International Brotherhood of Painters & Allied Trades.

David Eagan, Eagan Associates; Eclair Bake Shoppe; Linda Eggers, Maytag Company; D'Elain Pastries; Raymond Ellis, Hospitality, Lodging and Travel Research; Sherry Enzweiler, Gibson Greetings; Jacob Exler, Human Nutrition Information Service.

Charles Farley, Brick Institute of America; Newton Fassler, Institute of Store Planners; Darryl Felder, University of Louisiana, Lafayette; Carla Fischer, GE Company; Robert Fischer, American Society of Bakery Engineers; Mike Fisher, Besam, Inc.; Hans Fiuczynski, M&M/Mars; Barry Floyd, Philadelphia Fire Code Unit; Edward S. Ford, Grayson Foundation; James B. Ford; Al Fowler, Heyer Company; Matt Fox; Gwendolyn Frost, Cornell Feline Health Center.

Dorothy Garrison, Cooling Towers Institute; Carl Gerster, Mobil Oil Corporation; Lennie Gessler, Professional Bowlers Association of America; Mary Gillespie, Association of Home Appliance Manufacturers; Megan Gillispie, The League of Women Voters; Ellyn Giordano, National Football Foundation and Hall of Fame; Paul Godfrey, Water Resources Research Center; William Good, National Roofing Contractors Association; Danielle Gordon, Kraft General Foods Corporation; Hy Greenblatt, Manufacturers of Illumination Products; Steve Gregg, Coffee Development Group; Mark Grunwald, Philadelphia Zoo.

Robert Habel, Cornell University; Daniel Halaburda, Panasonic Industrial Company; Dianna Hales; John Hall, American Bankers Association; John Haller, Robert Talbott Company; John Hallett, Desert Research Institute; E. E. Halmos, Construction Writers Association; Ed Hansen, American Association of Zoo Keepers; Megaera Harris, Office of the Postmaster General; John Hassett, International Bridge, Tunnel and Turnpike Association; Sylvia Hauser, *Dog World*; Jeanette Hayhurst; Donald Hazlett, Zippo Manufacturing Company; George Headrick, Construction Industry Manufacturers Association; David J. Hensing, American Association of State Highway and Transportation Officials; Jack Herschlag, National Association of Men's Sportswear Buyers; Bill Heyer, Heyer Company; Shari Hiller, Sherwin-Williams Company; Myron Hinrichs, Hasti Friends of the Elephant; Bruce Hisley, National Fire Academy; Sue Holiday, American Greetings; David Hopper, American Academy of Somnology; Tom Horan, American Irish Historical Society; Joe Horrigan, Professional Football Hall of Fame; Meredith Hughes, Potato Museum; Irv Hyatt.

Idaho Potato Commission.

Simon S. Jackel; Rand Jerris, United States Golf Association; William P. Jollie, American Association of Anatomists; Caroline Jones, Better Sleep Council; Chris Jones, Pepsi-Cola Company; Sally Jones, USDA; William Jones, Zippo Manufacturing Company.

Burton Kallman, National Nutritional Foods Association; Jack Katz, SUNY Buffalo Speech and Hearing Clinic; Leon Katz, Port Authority of New York and New Jersey; Kendell Keith, National Grain and Feed Association; Bruce Kershner; Donald Kieffer, National Hay Association; Sally Kinne, Poodle Club of America; Rodger Koppa, Texas Transportation Institute; Steve Korker, United States Postal System; Judith Kraus, FDA; Lucille Kubichek; Anita Kuemmel, Soap and Detergent Association; Karen Kuzsel, *Middle Eastern Dancer*; Linda Kwong, Bic Pen Corporation.

Richard Landesman, University of Vermont; Fred Lanting; Thomas Laronge, Thomas M. Laronge, Inc.; Thomas A. Lehmann, American Institute of Baking; George Lemke, International Brotherhood of Painters and Allied Trades; Joe Lesniak, Door and Hardware Manufacturing Institute; Edna Leurck, Procter & Gamble; Victor Liebe, American Traffic Safety Services Association; Judith Lindley, Calico Cat Registry International; Kick Lorenz, Gibson Greetings; Sally Lorette, Oakland Athletics; Kevin Lowery, Campbell Soup Company; Timothy Lynch, Kenneth Lynch & Sons.

Jane Macdonald-James, International Jelly and Preserve Association and Association for Dressings & Sauces; David Maier, Oregon Graduate Institute of Science and Technology; Kari Anne Maino, Best Foods Baking Group; Irene Malbin, Cosmetic, Toiletry, and Fragrance Association; Marlene Marchut, M&M/Mars; Joanne Marshall, Campbell Soup Company; Nancy Martin, Association of Field Ornithologists; Keith Marvin; Karen Mason, Recreational Vehicle Industry Association; Joe Mastrullo, Procter & Gamble; Doug Matyka, Georgia-Pacific Corporation; Susan Mauro, Pepsi-Cola Company; S. Michael Mazva, Eveready Battery Co.; Linda McCashion, the Potato Board; James P. MaCauley, International Association of Holiday Inns; James P. McCulley, Association of University Professors of Ophthalmology; Kay McKeown; Harry Medved, Screen Actors Guild; Barbara Meyer, Hallmark Cards, Inc.; Jim Meyer, United States Postal Service; Craig Michelson, Pfizer, Inc.; Bill Middlebrook, North American Philips Lighting Corporation; Mary D. Midkiff, American Horse Council; Mark Miller, American Bowling Congress; Stephen Miller, American Optometric Association; Steven Mintz; J. Robert Moody, GE Lighting Business Group; David Moore, Virginia Tech University; E. R. Moore; Randy Morgan, Cincinnati Insectarium; Marilyn Myers, Norelco Consumer Products.

Rosetta Newsome, Institute of Food Technologists; Irene Norman, Goldstein's Funeral Directors, Inc.; Jill Novack, Levi Strauss & Co.

Norman Owen, American International Electric, Inc.; Jane Owens, Western Trailer Park.

Andy Palatka, Business Forms Management Association; Rich Palin, Loctite Corporation; Joseph Pash, Somerset Technologies, Inc.; Wayne Pearson, Plastics Recyling Foundation; Philadelphia Zoo; Susan Pistilli, International Council of Shopping Centers; John A. Pitcher, Hardwood Research Council;

Ron Pominville, AMF Bowling Company; Barbara Preston, Association for Dressings and Sauces; Roy Preston, United States Postal System; Robert C. Probasco; Larry Prussin; Nancy Purtill, UCLA.

Howard Raether, National Funeral Directors Association; Jerry Rafats, National Agriculture Library; Lorraine Ramig, Denver Center for Performing Arts Voice Research Laboratory; Jean C. Raney, American Wool Council; Ginger Rawe, Kroger Company; Oakley Ray, American Feed Industry Association; Kelly Redmond, Western Regional Climate Center; Nan Redmond, Kraft General Foods; Richard Reynells, American Poultry Historical Society; Jim Richards, Cornell Feline Health Center; Chris Rieck, American Banking Association; Nancy Rivera, Greeting Cards Association; Caroline Robicsek, National Association for Plastic Container Recycling; Robin Roche, San Francisco Zoological Society; John Rockwell, National Center for State Courts; John R. Rodenburg, Federated Funeral Directors of America; Robert R. Rofen, Aquatic Research Institute; Alan Rooscroft, San Diego Wild Animal Park; Janet Rosati, Fruit of the Loom; Phyllis Rosenthal, NutraSweet; Kate Ruddon, American College of Obstetricians and Gynecologists.

John Saidla, Cornell Feline Health Center; Samuel Salamon, Cataract Eye Center of Cleveland; San Francisco Zoological Park; Ronald A. Schachar, Association for the Advancement of Ophthalmology; Robert Schmidt, North American Native Fishes Association; Jack Schultz, National Retail Federation; E. H. Scott, J. Hofert Company; Norman Scott, Society for the Study of Amphibians and Reptiles; William Scott, National Highway Traffic Safety Administration; Bert Seaman, B.J. Seamon Company; Keith Seitter, American Meteorological Association; Steven Shelov, Montefiore Medical Center; Hezy Shoshani, Elephant Interest Group; Scott Shuler, Asphalt Institute; Steve Sigman, Zenith Electronics Corporation; Dede Silverston, Eye Information; Harry Skinner, Federal Highway Administration; Brian Smith, U.S. League of Savings Institutions; Gary Smith, Agricultural Extension Service; Michael T. Smith, National Cattlemen's Association; Rose Smouse, National

Retail Federation; J. M. Smucker Company; Bruce V. Snow; Richard Snyder, Asphalt Roofing Manufacturers Association; Society of Plastics Industry; South Brooklyn Casket Company; Mark Spencer, Yellow Freight Systems; Sandra Spiegel, Gibson Greetings Cards; Margie Spurlock, Royal Crown Cola Company; George Stahl, Potdevin Machine Company; Bill Stanley; Elaine Stathopoulos, SUNY Buffalo Speech and Hearing Clinic; Henry Stehlingadam, Hydra-Shield Manufacturing, Inc.; Sunset Trailer Park; Swiss Bakery.

Jeanne Taylor, Milton Bradley Company; Frank Thomas, United States Golf Association; Tire Industry Safety Council; J. Donald Turk, Mobil Oil Corporation; William Turpin, Miles, Inc.

Edwin Uber, Bingo King; Mary Ann Usrey, R. J. Reynolds Tobacco Company.

Al Vanderneck, American Bowling Congress; Carolyn Verweyst, Whirlpool Corporation; James Vondruska, Quaker Oats Company.

Pat Wachtel, Maytag Company; Ann Walk, National Independent Bank Equipment and Systems Association; Iain Walton, D. D. Bean & Sons; Jeanne Washko, Borden, Inc.; Liz Wentland, Oster/Sunbeam; Thomas Werner, New York State Department of Transportation; Fred Wexler, Schick Razors; Larry Whitish, SAC Products; Beth Williams, American Association of Wildlife Veterinarians; Brad Williams, Levi Strauss & Co.; D. L. Woods, Texas A&M; Peter Wulff, *Home Lighting & Accessories*.

Peter Zando, Ebac Systems; Sheryl Zapcic, Lever Brothers Company; Caden Zollo, Specialty Bulb; Mike Zulak, San Francisco Zoological Park.

And to the many sources who, for whatever reason, wished to remain anonymous but still shared your expertise with us, our sincere thanks.

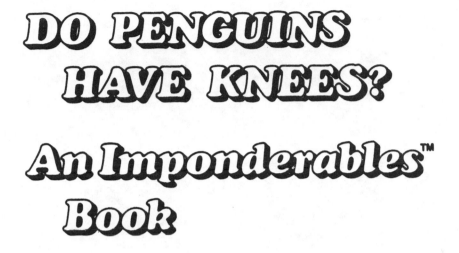

DO PENGUINS HAVE KNEES?

An Imponderables™ Book

For Rick Kot

Contents

CONTENTS

Preface

You may think you've lived a happy life without knowing the answer to why you don't feel a mosquito while it's biting you. Or why the address labels on subscription magazines are usually placed upside-down. Or why the bags on oxygen masks in airplanes don't inflate.

But you're not really happy. Face it. In our everyday life, we're confronted with thousands of mysteries that we cannot solve. So we repress our anxiety (could you imagine a life haunted by the recurring dread of not knowing what function our earlobes serve?). And as those of us who've seen Dr. Joyce Brothers on television know, repression isn't good for you.

So our quest is to eradicate all of these nagging Imponderables. Luckily, we have the best possible collaborators—our readers.

Most of the Imponderables posed in this book were submitted by readers of our first four volumes. In our Frustables section, readers wrestle with the ten most frustrating Imponderables that we weren't able to solve. And in the letters section, readers suggest how our previous efforts may have been ever so slightly less than perfect.

As a token of our appreciation for your help, we offer a free copy of our next book to the first person who sends in an Imponderable or the best solution to a Frustable we use, along with an acknowledgment.

The last page of the book tells you how you can join in our campaign to stamp out Imponderability. We can't guarantee you lifelong happiness if you read *Do Penguins Have Knees?*, but we can assure you you'll know why there are peanuts in plain M&Ms.

Imponderables

Why Don't You Feel or See a Mosquito Bite Until After It Begins to Itch?

We would like to think that the reason we don't feel the mosquito biting us is that Mother Nature is merciful. If we were aware that the mosquito was in the process of sinking its mouth into our flesh, we might panic, especially because a simple mosquito bite takes a lot longer than we suspected.

A female mosquito doesn't believe in a casual "slam bam, thank you, ma'am." On the contrary, mosquitoes will usually rest on all six legs on human skin for at least a minute or so before starting to bite. Mosquitoes are so light and their biting technique so skillful that most humans cannot feel them, even though the insect may be resting on their skin for five minutes or more.

When the mosquito decides to finally make her move and press her lancets into a nice, juicy capillary, the insertion takes about a minute. She lubricates her mouthparts with her own saliva and proceeds to suck the blood for up to three minutes until her stomach is literally about to burst. She withdraws her lancets in a few seconds and flies off to deposit her eggs, assuring the world that the mosquito will not soon make the endangered species list.

A few sensitive souls feel a mosquito's bite immediately. But most of us are aware of itching (or in some cases, pain) only after the mosquito is long gone not because of the bite or the loss of blood but because of the saliva left behind. The mosquito's saliva acts not only as a lubricant in the biting process but as an anesthetic to the bitee. For most people, the saliva is a blessing, since it allows us to be oblivious to the fact that our blood is being sucked by a loathsome insect. Unfortunately, the saliva contains anticoagulant components that cause allergic reactions in many people. This allergic reaction, not the bite itself, is what causes the little lumps and itchy sensations that make us wonder why mosquitoes exist in this otherwise often wonderful world.

Submitted by Alesia Richards of Erie, Pennsylvania.

Why Doesn't Milk in the Refrigerator Ever Taste As Cold As the Water or Soda in the Refrigerator?

Actually, milk *does* get as cold as water or soda. If you are having a particularly boring Saturday night, you might want to stick a thermometer into the liquids to prove this.

Milk at the same temperature as water or soda just doesn't taste as cold to us because milk contains fat solids. We perceive solids as less cold than liquids. Taste experts refer to this phenomenon as "mouth feel."

If the milk/water/soda test wasn't exciting enough for you, run a test in your freezer compartment that will demonstrate the same principle. Put a pint of premium high-butterfat ice cream in the freezer along with a pint of low-fat or nonfat frozen yogurt.

Consume them. We'll bet you two to one that the yogurt will taste colder than the ice cream. For the sake of research, we recently performed this experiment with due rigor, and because we wanted to go out of our way to assure the accuracy of the experiment, we conducted the test on many different flavors of ice cream and yogurt. Oh, the sacrifices we make for our readers!

Submitted by Pat O'Conner of Forest Hills, New York.

Why Are Address Labels on Subscription Magazines Usually Placed Upside-Down?

Our usually reliable sources at the United States Postal Service struck out on this Imponderable, but we were rescued by our friends at Neodata Services. Neodata, the largest fulfillment house in the United States, which we profiled in *Why Do Dogs Have Wet Noses?*, is the company that processes all those subscription forms you send to Boulder, Colorado.

By luck, we rang up Neodata's Biff Bilstein when he was in a meeting with sales executives Mark Earley and Rob Farson. The three share over seventy-five years of experience in the magazine business. "So," we implored, "why are address labels placed upside-down?"

They conferred and answered as one. Even though the folks at the USPS don't seem to know it, the labels are placed upside down to accommodate the postal carrier. All magazines are bound on the left-hand side. Our hypothetical postal carrier, being right-handed, naturally picks up a magazine by the spine with his or her right hand to read the address label—the magazine is thus automatically turned upside down. But the label is now "right side up" and easily read by the postal carrier. Nifty, huh?

Submitted by Geoff Grant of Barrie, Ontario. Thanks also to Beth Jones of West Des Moines, Iowa.

DO PENGUINS HAVE KNEES?

Why Are There Dents on the Top of Cowboy Hats?

Of course, not *all* cowboy hats have dents. How about country and western star George Strait's? Or *Bonanza's* Dan ("Hoss") Blocker's?

Yet the vast majority of cowboy hats do have dents, and no one we spoke to could give us any other explanation than that dents are there "for style." Ralph Beatty, director of the Western/ English Retailers of America, theorizes that early cowboy hats may have acquired dents by wear, and later were intentionally added.

As one, better-to-be-kept-anonymous, western hat marketer put it, "Let's face it. Without the dent, you would look like a dork."

We wonder if he would have said that to Dan Blocker's face.

Submitted by Lisa R. Bell of Atlanta, Georgia.

DAVID FELDMAN

Why Do Grocery Coupons State That They Have a "Cash Value of ⅟₁₀₀ of 1¢"?

We receive a lot of questions not only about everyday life but about the questions we get asked. The most frequently asked question about questions: What is your most frequently asked question?

Imponderables run in cycles. After our first book, *Imponderables,* was published, "Why are buttons on men's shirts and jackets arranged differently from those on women's shirts?" was the most popular question. Then it was "Why is yawning contagious?" Then "Why can't we tickle ourselves?" The all-time champion, though, is "Why do we park on driveways and drive on parkways?" We don't know why people care passionately about this subject, but this is *the* Imponderable that just will not go away. We've discussed the answer in two books, and it is still our second most frequently asked Imponderable.

But the clear champion now is the Imponderable at hand. More than thirty readers have asked this Imponderable in the last two years, and the irony is that the question was one of the original Imponderables we hoped to answer in our first book.

We have spoken to scores of officials in the coupon processing, direct marketing, grocery, and marketing science fields, but nobody could pinpoint the exact reason for the custom or for the particular price of ⅟₁₀₀ of one cent. To make matters worse, we then received a follow-up letter from Kathy Pierce, one of the legions who asked us this question:

> I was reading *The Straight Dope* by Cecil Adams (I'm sorry, I would guess that old Cec' is your arch enemy, but I have to have something besides my Italian textbook to read in between *Imponderables* books). Lo and behold, there was *my* question, right there on page 329.

Kathy proceeded to cite Adams's answer, and we noted that "old Cec'," whom we like to think of as a colleague and pal (at least when there are other people around to hear us think), got just about as far as we had in our research. As usual, he was depressingly accurate.

He noted that some states have laws equating coupons with trading stamps (e.g., S&H Green Stamps). Since consumers pay for the "free" stamps in the form of higher prices for groceries, the jurisdictions forced stamp issuers to redeem the stamps for a cash value. In order to comply with these state laws, which were actually designed to curb abuses among trading stamp issuers, coupon issuers assigned a cash value that nobody in his or her right mind would bother to collect.

We make it a policy to try not to repeat questions or answers we've seen discussed elsewhere (after all, if we know the answer to a question, it's not an Imponderable anymore), but since this is such a popular question, and since we have STARTLING NEW INFORMATION, we are pleased to disclose the true story behind the coupon cash value.

Although some other states treat coupons as scrip, the real driving force behind the practice is the state of Kansas. Ed Dunn, a spokesperson for NCH Promotional Services, told us what prompted these state laws. During the Depression, many stamp issuers would claim that their books of stamps were worth much more than they really were. They would then sell merchandise through catalogs at greatly inflated prices.

This caused problems. Because both the "cash value" and redemption prices (in stamps) were greatly inflated, honest stamp issuers were at a competitive disadvantage, because their own books of stamps didn't seem to be worth much in buying power compared to those of others.

Several states tried to eliminate these injustices by making all books of stamps, *and anything of value that might be used to reduce the price of a product,* have a common value. Obviously, coupons fell into this category.

But Kansas enacted by far the most stringent law. Kansas law overrides the terms and conditions of the coupon for residents of the state and, more important for our purposes, says that *if no cash value is stated on the coupon, the consumer may*

DAVID FELDMAN

cash in the coupon at face value. Obviously, if consumers could take the fifty cents they "save" on their laundry detergent and redeem it for cash, they would. Manufacturers had two choices: make separate coupons for Kansas, or state a cash value on every coupon.

Do folks really try to redeem coupons for the lofty sum of ⅟₁₀₀ of a cent apiece? Not very often (of course, that's why the cash value is set so low). Most companies will probably pay the tariff, but the consumer is stuck with postage costs, which far exceed the refund.

Submitted by Jeff Burger of Phoenix, Arizona. Thanks also to Lisa Lindeberg of Van Nuys, California; Anand S. Raman of Oak Ridge, Tennessee; Larry Doyle of Grand Ledge, Michigan; Jonathan Sabin of Bradenton, Florida; Brian J. Sullivan of Chicago, Illinois; Randy S. Poppert of Willow, Arkansas; Maria Scott of Cincinnati, Ohio; Joe Crandell of Annandale, Virginia; David Grettler of Newark, Delaware; and many others. Special thanks to Kathy Pierce of Boston, Massachusetts.

HOW and Why Did 7UP Get Its Name?

7UP (a.k.a. Seven-Up) was the brainchild of an ex-advertising and merchandising executive, C. L. Grigg. In 1920, Grigg formed the Howdy Company in St. Louis, Missouri, and found success with his first product, Howdy Orange drink.

Intent upon expanding his empire, Grigg spent several years testing eleven different formulas of lemon-flavored soft drinks. In 1929, he introduced Seven-Up, then a caramel-colored beverage.

So where did the "7" and "UP" come from? Despite its identification as a lemon-lime drink, 7UP is actually a blend of seven natural flavors. According to Jim Ball, vice-president of corporate communications for Dr Pepper/Seven-Up Companies,

Inc., all of the early advertisements for the new drink described a product that was uplifting and featured a logo with a winged 7. Long before any caffeine scares, 7UP was promoted as a tonic for our physical and emotional ills:

> Seven-Up energizes—*sets you up*—dispels brain cobwebs and muscular fatigue.

> Seven-Up is as pure as mountain snows . . .

> Fills the mouth [true, but then so does cough syrup]—thrills the taste buds—cools the blood—energizes the muscles—soothes the nerves—and makes your body alive—glad—happy.

7UP's advertising has improved and changed markedly over the years, but its name has proved to be durably effective, even if customers don't have the slightest idea what "Seven-Up" means. Grigg could have chosen much worse. Contemplate sophisticated adults sidling up to a bar and ordering a bourbon and Howdy Lemon-Lime drink.

> *Submitted by Richard Showstack of Newport Beach, California. Thanks also to Roya Naini of Olympia, Washington; Brian and Ingrid Aboff of Beavercreek, Ohio; and Jason M. Holzapfel of Gladstone, Missouri.*

Why Do the Back Wheels of Bicycles Click When You Are Coasting or Back Pedaling?

Has there ever been a child with a bicycle who has not pondered this Imponderable? We got the scoop from Dennis Patterson, director of import purchasing of the Murray Ohio Manufacturing Co.:

> The rear sprocket cluster utilizes a ratchet mechanism that engages during forward pedaling, but allows the rear wheel to rotate independently of the sprocket mechanism. When one

ceases to pedal, the wheel overrides the ratchet and the clicking noise is the ratchets falling off the engagement ramp of the hub.

The ramp is designed to lock engagement if pedaled forward. The ratchet mechanism rides up the reverse slope and falls off the top of the ramp when you are coasting or back pedaling.

Submitted by Harvey Kleinman and Merrill Perlman of New York, New York.

Why Do Male Birds Tend to Be More Colorful Than Females? Is There Any Evolutionary Advantage?

"Sexual dimorphism" is the scientific term used to describe different appearances of male and female members of the same species. Charles Darwin wrestled with this topic in his theory of sexual selection. Darwin argued that some physical attributes of birds evolved solely to act as attractants to the opposite sex. How can you explain the train of the peacock except to say it is the avian equivalent of a Chippendale's dancer's outfit? As Kathleen Etchpare, associate editor of the magazine *Bird Talk,* put it: "As far as an evolutionary advantage goes, the mere number of birds in the world today speaks for itself."

Sure, but there are plenty of cockroaches around today, too, and they have managed to perpetuate themselves quite nicely without benefit of colorful males. Many ornithologists believe that the main purpose of sexual dimorphism is to send a visual message to predators. When females are nesting, they are ill-equipped to fend off the attacks of an enemy. Michele Ball, of the National Audubon Society, says that "It behooves the female to be dully colored so that when she sits in the nest she is less conspicuous to predators."

Conversely, the bright plumage of many male birds illustrates the principle of "the best offense is a good defense." Male birds, without the responsibility of nesting, and generally larger in size than their female counterparts, are better suited to stave off predators. The purpose of their bright coloring might be to warn predators that they will not be easy prey; most ornithologists believe that birds are intelligent enough to register the dimorphic patterns of other birds.

And most animals are as lazy as humans. Given a choice, predators will always choose the easy kill. If a predator can't find a dully colored female and fears the brightly colored male, perhaps the predator will pick on another species.

Submitted by Karen Riddick of Dresden, Tennessee.

DAVID FELDMAN

What Does the USPS Do with Mail It Can't Deliver or Return Because of Lack of a Return Address?

If a piece of mail is improperly addressed and does not contain a return address, it is sent to a dead letter office. Dead letter offices are located in New York, Philadelphia, Atlanta, San Francisco, and St. Paul. There a USPS employee will open the envelope. If no clues to the address of the sender or receiver are found inside, and the enclosures are deemed to have "no significant value," the letter is destroyed immediately.

Frank Brennan, of the USPS media relations division, explains that if the enclosures are deemed to be of some value, the parties involved will have a temporary reprieve:

> This allows time for inquiries and claims to be filed. After 90 days, all items that have not been claimed are auctioned off to the public. Cash or items of monetary value that are found in the mail are placed into a general fund. If it is not claimed after one year,

it is rolled over into a USPS account to be used as the USPS deems necessary.

And of course we can all count on the USPS making the best possible use of any windfalls that come their way.

Submitted by Kathryn Rehrig of Arlington, Texas.

Why Are Baseball Dugouts Built So That They Are Half Below Ground?

If dugouts were built any higher, notes baseball stadium manufacturer Dale K. Elrod, the sight lines in back of the dugout would be blocked. Baseball parks would either have to eliminate choice seats behind the dugout or sell tickets with an obstructed view at a reduced price.

If dugouts were built lower, either the players would not be able to see the game without periscopes or they wouldn't have room to stretch out between innings.

Submitted by Alan Scothon of Dayton, Ohio.

Why Do Trains with More Than One Locomotive Often Have One (or More) of the Locomotives Turned Backwards?

Diesel locomotives work equally well traveling in either direction. Robert L. Krick, deputy associate administrator for technology development at the Federal Railroad Administration, wrote *Imponderables* that

> Locomotives are turned on large turntables, or on "wye" or "loop" tracks. Railroads avoid unnecessary turning of locomotives

because the procedure takes time. The locomotives being turned and the employees turning them could be employed for more constructive purposes.

When locomotives are assembled for a train, if one already faces forward it is selected for the lead position. The others will work equally well headed in either direction; they are usually coupled together without regard for their orientation.

If a group of locomotives is assembled for more than one trip, the cars will often be arranged with the rear locomotive of the group facing the rear. That group of locomotives can then be used on another train going in either direction without any turning or switching.

Using this method, a train can be returned to its original destination on the same track without any turning. Bob Stewart, library assistant at the Association of American Railroads, explains how:

When a train reaches the end of its run and is to return in the direction from which it came, the engineer moves to the cab at the other end. The locomotive can be coupled and switched to a parallel track, run back towards what was the rear of the train and switched back to the original track.

Submitted by Randy W. Gibson of Arlington, Virginia.

Why Is There Steam Coming Up from the Streets of New York?

Historically, of course, the rising steam served the most important purpose of providing menacing atmosphere in *Taxi Driver* and other movies set in New York City. But we still see steam rising out of manhole covers in Manhattan all the time. What causes it?

The biggest source of the steam is New York's utility, Consolidated Edison, which still generates enough steam to service over 2,000 customers in Manhattan. Steam heat is used only in tall buildings and manufacturing plants; the equipment necessary to generate steam power is too large and inefficient for small businesses or modest residential dwellings.

When a small leak occurs in a steam pipe, the vapor must go somewhere. Heat rises and looks for a place to escape: Manhole covers are the most likely egress point for steam. Martin Gitten, Con Edison's assistant director for public information, told *Imponderables* that when a big leak occurs, Con Ed must put tall

DAVID FELDMAN

cones over the manhole covers so that the steam is vented above the level of vehicles. Otherwise, unsuspecting drivers would feel as if they were driving through a large cumulus cloud.

Another source for steam rising out of the streets of New York is excess moisture condensing underground. The excess moisture may emanate from small leaks in city water mains, run-off from heavy rainfalls, or least pleasant to contemplate, sewer backups.

Why do these liquids rise up as steam? Because they come in contact with the scalding hot steam equipment below ground.

Submitted by Chris McCann of New York, New York.

HOW Did They Keep Beer Cold in the Saloons of the Old West?

Just about any way they could. In the nineteenth century, guzzlers didn't drink beer as cold as they do now (the English often imbibed pints of ale warm, for goodness' sake, and still do—as do the Chinese) but even grizzled cowboys preferred their brew cool.

In colder areas of the West, saloons used to gather ice from frozen lakes in the winter. John T. McCabe, technical director of the Master Brewers Association of the Americas, says that the harvest was stored in ice houses, "where the blocks of ice were insulated with sawdust. This method would keep ice for months."

Even where it wasn't cold enough for ice to form, many saloons in the Old West had access to cool mountain streams. Historical consultant William L. Lang wrote *Imponderables* that saloon workers would fill a cistern with this water to store and cool barrels of beer.

And if no cold mountain stream water was available? Phil Katz, of the Beer Institute, says that up until about 1880, many saloons built a root cellar to house beer. Usually built into the side of a hill, root cellars could keep beer below 50 degrees Fahrenheit.

And what if you wanted cold beer at home? According to Lang, "Beer was served in buckets or small pails, and often kids delivered the beer home from the saloons." Consumers in the mid-nineteenth century thought no more of bringing home "take-out beer" than we would think of ordering take-out Chinese food.

Beer expert W. Ray Hyde explains that we needn't feel sorry for the deprivation of Old Westerners before the days of refrigeration. In fact, those might have been the "good old days" of American beer:

> Beer in the Old West wasn't cold in the modern sense of the word—but it was refreshingly cool. Evaporation kept it that way. Beer in those days was packaged in wooden barrels, and the liquid would seep through the porous wood to the outside of the barrel, where it would evaporate. And basic physics explains the cooling effect of evaporation.
>
> Also, it should be noted that beer then was not artificially carbonated. The slight natural carbonation required only that it be cool to be refreshing and tasty. Modern beer, with its artificial carbonation, needs to be very cold to hide the sharp taste of the excess carbon dioxide.

Submitted by Dr. Robert Eufemia of Washington, D.C.

DAVID FELDMAN

What Is the Official Name of the Moon?

Along with our correspondent, we've never known what to call our planet's satellite. Moon? The moon? moon? the moon? Dorothy?

We know that other planets have moons. Do they all have names? How do astronomers distinguish one moon from another?

Whenever we have a problem with matters astronomical, we beg our friends at two terrific magazines—*Astronomy* and *Sky & Telescope*—for help. As usual, they took pity on us.

Astronomy's Robert Burnham, like most senior editors, is picky about word usage:

> The proper name of our sole natural satellite is "the Moon" and therefore . . . it should be capitalized. The 60-odd natural satellites of the other planets, however, are called "moons" (in lower case) because each has been given a proper name, such as Deimos, Amalthea, Hyperion, Miranda, Larissa, or Charon.

DO PENGUINS HAVE KNEES?

Likewise, the proper name for our star is "the Sun" and that for our planet is "Earth" or "the Earth." It's OK, however, to use "earth" in the lower case whenever you use it as a synonym for "dirt" or "ground."

Alan MacRobert, of *Sky & Telescope*, adds that Luna, the Moon's Latin name, is sometimes used in poetry and science fiction, but has never caught on among scientists or the lay public: "Names are used to distinguish things from each other. Since we have only one moon, there's nothing it needs to be distinguished from."

Submitted by A. P. Bahlkow of Sudbury, Massachusetts.

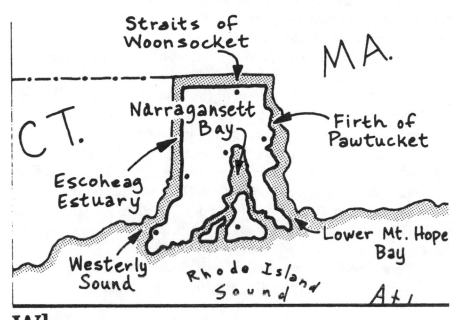

Straits of
Woonsocket

MA.

CT.

Narragansett
Bay

Firth of
Pawtucket

Escoheag
Estuary

Lower Mt. Hope
Bay

Westerly
Sound

Rhode Island
Sound

Atl

Why Is Rhode Island Called an Island When It Obviously Isn't an Island?

Let's get the island problem licked first. No, technically, the whole state isn't an island, but historians are confident that originally "Rhode Island" referred not to the whole territory but to what we now call Aquidneck Island, where Newport is located. Christine Lamar, an archivist for the Rhode Island State Archives, endorses this view.

Why "Rhode"? Lame theories abound. One is that the state was named after a person named Rhodes (although any meaningful details about this person are obscure). Another supposition is that "Rhode Island" was an Anglicization of "Roode Eyelandt," Dutch for "red island." The Dutch explorer Adriaen Block noted the appearance of a reddish island in the area, and maps of the mid-seventeenth century often refer to the area as "Roode Eyelandt."

But all evidence points to the fact that Block was referring not to the landlocked mass of Rhode Island, nor even to the island of Aquidneck, but to an island farther west in the bay. And besides, written references to "Rhode Island" abound long before "Roode Eyelandt."

Most likely, "Rhode Island" was coined by explorer Giovanni da Verrazano, who referred in his diary of his 1524 voyage to an island "about the bigness of the Island of Rhodes," a reference to its Greek counterpart. A century later, Roger Williams referred to "Aqueneck, called by us Rhode Island . . ."

We do know that in 1644, the Court of Providence Plantation officially changed the name of Aquidneck (variously spelled "Aquedneck" and "Aquetheck"—spelling was far from uniform in those days) to "The Isle of Rhodes, or Rhode Island." The entire colony, originally settled in 1636, was known as "Rhode Island and Providence Plantations."

When Rhode Island attained statehood, its name was shortened to Rhode Island, befitting its diminutive size.

Submitted by Tony Alessandrini of Brooklyn, New York. Thanks also to Troy Diggs of Jonesboro, Arkansas.

Why Do Blacktop Roads Get Lighter in Color As They Age?

Our correspondent ponders:

When fresh blacktop roads are laid, they are pure black. Why is it that after a few years, they turn gray? You can notice this when they patch potholes. The filler material is a dark contrast to the surrounding road. Even last year's patched potholes are grayer than the new blacktop patches.

You would think dirt and "worn rubber dust" would make the road blacker, not lighter.

There is only one flaw in your question, Bill. Blacktop isn't pure black, as Amy Steiner, program director of the American

Association of State Highway and Transportation Officials, explains:

> The primary ingredients in "blacktop" are asphalt and stones. Asphalt coats the stones and gives the pavement its black color. As traffic passes over the pavement, the asphalt coating on the surface stones wears off. Since stones are generally lighter in color than asphalt, the road becomes lighter in color.

The other main reason that blacktop lightens in color is oxidation. As the road surface is always exposed to the ambient air, it naturally becomes lighter.

As for what happens to the black tire tread that comes off vehicles, may I suggest you read a stimulating, brilliantly written dissertation on the subject in a wonderful book, *Why Do Clocks Run Clockwise? and Other Imponderables.* The name of the author escapes us at the moment, but we're sure your local bookstore employee will happily lead you to the HarperPerennial book, which, we recollect, is very reasonably priced.

Submitted by Bill Jelen of Akron, Ohio.

Why Must We Push Both the "Record" and "Play" Switches to Record on an Audio Tape Recorder, and Only the "Record" on the VCR?

All of our electronics sources agreed that consumers prefer "one-touch recording" for both audio and video recorders. All agreed that there is no difference in the performance of decks with one-touch or two-touch controls. So why do we have to go the extra step on the audio recorder? Audio recorders predate video recorders, and the history of the audio tape deck gives us our answer. Thomas Mock, director of engineering for the Electronics Industries Association, explains:

> In most earlier audio recorders, the switches were mechanically coupled to the tape drive mechanism. The RECORD button

was designed so that it was not possible to accidentally go into the record mode while playing a tape. In order to record, the RECORD button had to be depressed first, allowing it to sense if the cassette ERASE tab was present. Then it would permit closure of the play button.

Modern recorders, audio as well as VCRs, use servo controls to engage the tape mechanism and sensors to detect if erasure/recording is allowed. With these devices, "one button" recording is possible from the control panel or via an infrared remote or by a preset timer.

William J. Goffi, of the Maxell Corporation, told *Imponderables* that many audio recorder manufacturers have seen the light and are incorporating user-friendly one-touch recording.

Submitted by Richard Stans of Baltimore, Maryland.

HOW Do Bus Drivers Get into a Bus When the Door Handle Is Inside the Bus?

It all depends upon the bus. According to Robin Diamond, communications manager of the American Bus Association, many newer buses have a key lock that will open the door automatically when a key is turned. Mercedes-Benz buses, according to their press information specialist, John Chuhran, have a hydraulic door release that can be activated "by a key located in an inconspicuous place." Most often, the "inconspicuous place" is the front of the bus rather than the door itself.

Instead of a key-activated mechanism, some buses have a handle or air-compression button located in the front of the bus. Others have a toggle switch next to the door that opens it. Along with these high-tech solutions, we heard about some other strategies for bus drivers who may have locked themselves out. Karen E. Finkel, executive director of the National School Transportation Association, was kind enough to supply them:

DAVID FELDMAN

1. Enter through the rear emergency door, which does have a handle.
2. Push the door partially closed, but not enough for the door mechanism to catch, so that the door can be pulled open.
3. Use your hands to pry open the door.

Why do we think that method #3 is used altogether more often than it is supposed to be?

Submitted by Harry C. Wiersdorfer of Hamburg, New York.
Thanks also to Natasha Rogers of Webster, New York.

Why Is the Lowest-Ranked Admiral Called a *Rear* Admiral?

If you think that we are going to joke about the fact that a rear admiral is the lowest-ranked admiral because he tends to sit on his duff all day, you severely underestimate us. Puns are the refuge of the witless.

Dr. Regis A. Courtemanche, professor of history at the C. W. Post campus of Long Island University, wrote to *Imponderables* that the term originally referred to the admirals who commanded English naval fleets in the seventeenth-century Dutch Wars. The fleets were divided into three segments: the vanguard (the ships in front), the center, and the rear. "So," Courtemanche concludes, "the term lies in the fact that the *lowest* ranking admiral controlled the *rear* of the fleet at sea."

Submitted by Peter J. Scott of Glendale, California.

Why Was April 15 Chosen as the Due Date for Taxes?

It wasn't ever thus. In fact, the original filing date for federal taxes, as prescribed in the Revenue Act of 1913, was March 1. A mere five years later, the deadline moved back; until the Internal Revenue Code of 1954 was approved on August 16, 1954, midnight vigils were conducted on *March* 15. Taxpayers who paid on a fiscal year were also given a month's extension in 1954, so that they now filed on the fifteenth day of the fourth month, instead of the third month, after their fiscal year was over. In fact, all federal returns, with the exception of estates and trusts, are now due on April 15, or three and one-half months after the end of the fiscal year.

Were these dates plucked out of thin air? Not really. The IRS wants to process returns as early in the year as possible. In the 1910s, when most tax returns were one page long, it was

DAVID FELDMAN

assumed that after a wage earner totaled his or her income, the return could be filled out in a matter of minutes. Why wait until after March 1? As anyone who now is unfortunate enough to make a so-called living knows, the IRS form isn't quite as simple as it used to be. The 1040 is no easier to decipher than the Dead Sea Scrolls.

Kevin Knopf, of the Department of the Treasury, was kind enough to send us transcripts of the hearings before the House Ways and Means Committee in 1953 pertaining to the revision of the Internal Revenue Service Code. Now we don't necessarily expect the contents of all hearings in the legislature to match the Lincoln-Douglas debates in eloquence and passion, but we were a little surprised to hear the original impetus for the legislation cited by a sponsor of the 1954 IRS revision, the Honorable Charles E. Bennett of Florida, who argued for changing the due date from March 15 to April 15:

> The proposal to change the final return date from March 15 to April 15 was first called to my attention by the Florida Hotel Association. They advised that many taxpayers must cut their winter vacations short to return to their homes and to prepare their tax returns for filing before March 15. They pointed out that changing the deadline to April 15 would help their tourist trade as well as that of other winter tourist areas in the United States such as California, Arizona, Maine, and Vermont.

This is why we changed the tax code? Probably not. A succession of witnesses before the House Ways and Means Committee—everybody from the Georgia Chamber of Commerce to the American Federation of Labor to the American Cotton Manufacturers Institute—argued for moving back the date of tax filing. In descending order of importance, here were their arguments.

> 1. Taxpayers need the extra time to compile their records and fill out the tax forms.
> 2. The IRS needs more time to process returns efficiently. If the date were moved back to April 15, the IRS could rely more on permanent employees rather than hiring temporary help during

the crunch. Perhaps so many taxpayers wouldn't file at the deadline date if they had an extra month.

3. An extension would also ease the task of accountants and other tax preparers.

4. It would make it easier for people who have to estimate their tax payments for the next year to make an accurate assessment.

5. It would allow businesses who have audits at the end of the year time to concentrate on their IRS commitments.

The 1954 bill passed without much opposition. The April 15 date has proved to be workable, but it is no panacea. Any fantasy that most taxpayers wouldn't procrastinate until the last minute was quickly dispelled.

This drives the IRS nuts, because most taxpayers receive refunds. The basis of the free-market economic system is supposed to be that people will act rationally in their economic self-interest. If this were true, taxpayers with refunds would file in January in order to get their money as fast as possible, since the IRS does not pay interest on money owed to the taxpayer.

The IRS would love to find a way to even out its workload from January through April. In reality, most returns are filed either in late January and early February or right before the April 15 deadline. A 1977 internal study by the IRS, investigating changing the filing dates, said that "These peaks are so pronounced that Service Centers frequently have to furlough some temporary employees between the two workload peaks."

Before the code changed in 1954, the IRS experienced the same bimodal pattern—the only difference was that the second influx occurred in mid-March instead of mid-April. If the due date was extended a month, the second peak would probably occur in mid-May.

The IRS has contemplated staggering the due dates for different taxpayers, but the potential problems are huge (e.g., employers would have to customize W-2s for employees; single filers who get married might end up with extra-short or extra-long tax years when they decided to file a joint return; if a change

DAVID FELDMAN

in the tax rate occurs, when does it take effect?; would states and cities conform to a staggered schedule?) and probably not worth the effort. The same study contemplated extending the filing date (while offering financial incentives for filing early) but also concluded that the potential traps outweigh the benefits.

The IRS knows that many taxpayers deliberately overwithhold as a way to enforce savings, even though they will not collect any interest while the government holds their money. These overwithholders, flouting the advice of any sensible accountant, are most unlikely to be tempted to file early because of a possible $10 bonus from the IRS.

Now that the IRS grants an automatic two-month extension on filing to anyone who asks for it, even tax preparers are generally against changing the April 15 deadline. Henry W. Bloch, the president of H&R Block, has penetrated the very soul of his customer, and in 1976 offered this appraisal in the *Kansas City Times:*

> We get people in our office at 10 or 11 the night of April 15 and then they run down to the post office. If you extended that April 15 deadline to June 30, in my opinion, all they're going to do is wait until June 30 instead of April 15. . . . The reason for that is simply the old American habit of putting things off.

Submitted by Richard Miranda of Renton, Washington. Thanks also to Edward Hirschfield of Portage, Michigan.

What's the Difference Between a Lake and a Pond?

"This is an Imponderable?" we hear you muttering beneath your breath as you read the question. "A lake is a big pond."

Sure, you're right. But have you considered exactly what is the dividing line in size between a lake and a pond? And what separates a lake from a sea or a pool? Do you think you know the answer?

Well, if you do, why don't you go into the field of geography or topography or geology? Because the professionals in these fields sure don't have any standard definitions for any of these bodies of water.

As stated in the *National Mapping Division's Topographic Instructions'* "Glossary of Names for Topographic Forms," a lake is "Any standing body of inland water generally of considerable size." The same publication classifies a pond as "a small fresh-water lake." But other government sources indicate that salt-water pools may be called lakes.

And absolutely no one is willing to say what the dividing line in size is between the lake and the pond. In fact, the only absolutely clear-cut distinction between the two is that a lake is always a natural formation; if it is manmade, the body is classified as a pond. Ponds are often created by farmers to provide water for livestock. Some ponds are created to provide feeding and nesting grounds for waterfowl. Hatcheries create stocked ponds to breed fish.

Many communities try to inflate the importance of their small reservoirs by calling them lakes rather than ponds. No one is about to stop them.

Submitted by Jeffrey Chavez of Torrance, California. Thanks also to Ray Kerr of Baldwin, Missouri, and Eugene Bender of Mary, Missouri.

What's the Difference Between an Ocean and a Sea?

The same folks who are having trouble distinguishing between lakes and ponds are struggling with this one, too. Once again, there is general agreement that an ocean is larger than a sea.

The standard definition of an ocean, as stated in the United States Geological Survey's Geographic Names Information Service, is "The great body of salt water that occupies two-thirds of

DAVID FELDMAN

the surface of the earth, or one of its major subdivisions." Notice the weasel words at the end. Is the Red Sea a "major subdivision" of the Indian Ocean? If so, why isn't it the Red Ocean? Or simply referred to as the Indian Ocean?

Most, but by no means all seas are almost totally landlocked and connected to an ocean or a larger sea, but no definition we encountered stated this as a requirement for the classification. Geographical and geological authorities can't even agree on whether a sea must always be saline: the United States Geological Survey's Topographical Instructions say yes; but in their book *Water and Water Use Terminology*, Professors J. O. Veatch and C. R. Humphrys indicate that "sea" is sometimes used interchangeably with "ocean":

> In one place a large body of salt water may be called *lake*, in another a *sea*. The Great Lakes, Lake Superior and others, are fresh water but by legal definition are *seas*.

The nasty truth is that you can get away with calling most places whatever names you want. We often get asked what the difference is between a "street" and an "avenue" or a "boulevard." At one time, there were distinctions among these classifications: A street was a paved path. "Street" was a useful term because it distinguished a street from a road, which was often unpaved. An avenue was, in England, originally a roadway leading from the main road to an estate, and the avenue was always lined with trees. Boulevards were also tree-lined but were much wider thoroughfares than avenues.

Most of these distinctions have been lost in practice over the years. Developers of housing projects have found that using "street" to describe the roadways in their communities makes them sound drab and plebeian. By using "lane," which originally referred to a narrow, usually rural road, they can conjure up Mayberry rather than urban sprawl. By using "boulevard," a potential buyer visualizes Paris rather than Peoria.

For whatever reason, North Americans seem to like lakes more than seas. We are surrounded by oceans to the west and east. By standard definitions, we could certainly refer to Lake

Ontario, which is connected, via the St. Lawrence, to the Atlantic, as the Ontario Sea. But we don't. And no one, other than *Imponderables* readers, evidently, is losing any sleep over it.

Submitted by Don and Marian Boxer of Toronto, Ontario.
Thanks also to June Puchy of Lyndhurst, Ohio.

Why Does the United States Mint Use a Private Firm— UPS—to Ship Its Coin Sets?

Why would anyone, even a governmental agency, want to use the boringly reliable United Parcel Service when it could experience the excitement and sense of danger in using the United States Postal Service to ship its coin sets? By using the USPS, every order's fate could be a potentially unsolved mystery.

Of course, every governmental agency has its own budget to worry about. If a government office feels it can save money or save time by using private industry, it is under no obligation to throw its business to a government agency.

The U.S. Mint actually does use the USPS to ship some coin orders. Francis B. Frere, assistant director of the Mint for sales operations, explained the Department of the Treasury's policy:

> In making the determination as to which service to use, we look at the product we are shipping and the cost involved, taking into consideration value, weight, and distance.
>
> Cost is a concern to us. There are substantial savings to be realized in shipping coins by UPS. On an annual basis, we achieve savings in excess of $1 million by selectively shipping our products by UPS rather than first class mail through the U.S. Postal Service. UPS insures all packages against loss or damage.
>
> The Mint's coin programs are self-supporting. It is our responsibility to manage the coin programs in the most effective and economical manner possible . . .

Submitted by Ray W. Cummings of St. Louis, Missouri.

TECHNICAL MERIT 5.6
ARTISTIC IMPRESSION 5.7
DIZZINESS ACHIEVED

How Do Figure Skaters Keep from Getting Dizzy While Spinning? Is It Possible to Eye a Fixed Point While Spinning So Fast?

Imponderables readers aren't the only ones interested in this question. So are astronauts, who suffer from motion sickness in space. We consulted Carole Shulman, executive director of the Professional Skaters Guild of America, who explained:

> Tests were conducted by NASA several years ago to determine the answer to this very question. Research proved that with a trained skater, the pupils of the eyes do not gyrate back and forth during a spin as they do with an untrained skater. The rapid movement of the eyes catching objects within view is what actually causes dizziness.
>
> The eyes of a trained skater do not focus on a fixed point during a spin but rather they remain in a stabilized position focus-

ing on space between the skater and the next closest object. This gaze is much like that of a daydream.

So how are skaters taught to avoid focusing on objects or people in an arena? Claire O'Neill Dillie, skating coach and motivational consultant, teaches students to see a "blurred constant," an imaginary line running around the rink. The imaginary line may be in the seats or along the barrier of the rink (during layback spins, the imaginary line might be on the ceiling). The crucial consideration is that the skater feels centered. Even when the hands and legs are flailing about, the skater should feel as if his or her shoulders, hips, and head are aligned.

Untrained skaters often feel dizziest not in the middle of the spin but when stopping (the same phenomenon experienced when a tortuous amusement park ride stops and we walk off to less than solid footing). Dillie teaches her students to avoid vertigo by turning their heads in the opposite direction of the spin when stopping.

What surprised us about the answers to this Imponderable is that the strategies used to avoid dizziness are diametrically opposed to those used by ballet dancers, who use a technique called "spotting." Dancers consciously pick out a location or object to focus upon; during each revolution, they center themselves by spotting that object or location. When spotting, dancers turn their head at the very last moment, trailing the movement of the body, whereas skaters keep their head aligned with the rest of their body.

Why won't spotting work for skaters? For the answer, we consulted Ronnie Robertson, an Olympic medalist who has attained a rare distinction: Nobody has ever spun faster on ice than him.

How fast? At his peak, Robertson's spins were as fast as six revolutions per second. He explained to us that spotting simply can't work for skaters because they are spinning too fast to focus visually on anything. At best, skaters are capable of seeing only the "blurred constant" to which Claire O'Neill Dillie was referring, which is as much a mental as a visual feat.

DAVID FELDMAN

Robertson, trained by Gustav Lussi, considered to be the greatest spin coach of all time, was taught to spin with his eyes closed. And so he did. Robertson feels that spinning without vertigo is an act of mental suppression, blocking out the visual cues and rapid movement that can convince your body to feel dizzy.

Robertson explains that the edge of the blade on the ice is so small that a skater's spin is about the closest thing to spinning on a vertical point as humans can do. When his body was aligned properly, Robertson says that he felt calm while spinning at his fastest, just as a top is most stable when attaining its highest speeds.

While we had the greatest spinner of all time on the phone, we couldn't resist asking him a related Imponderable: Why do almost all skating routines, in competitions and skating shows and exhibitions, end with long and fast scratch spins? Until we researched this Imponderable, we had always assumed that the practice started because skaters would have been too dizzy to continue doing anything else after rotating so fast. But Robertson pooh-poohed our theory.

The importance of the spin, to Robertson, is that unlike other spectacular skating moves, spins are sustainable. While triple jumps evoke oohs and aahs from the audience, a skater wants a spirited, prolonged reaction to the finale of his or her program. Spins are ideal because they start slowly and eventually build to a climax so fast that it cannot be appreciated without the aid of slow-motion photography.

Robertson believes that the audience remembers the ending, not the beginning, of programs. If a skater can pry a rousing standing ovation out of an audience, perhaps supposedly sober judges might be influenced by the reaction.

Robertson's trademark was not only a blindingly fast spin but a noteworthy ending. He used his free foot to stop his final spin instantly at the fastest point. Presumably, when he stopped, he opened his eyes to soak in the appreciation of the audience.

Submitted by Barbara Harris Polomé of Austin, Texas. Thanks also to David McConnaughey of Cary, North Carolina.

DO PENGUINS HAVE KNEES?   339

Why Do Straws in Drinks Sometimes Sink and Sometimes Rise to the Surface?

The movement of the straw depends upon the liquid in the glass and the composition of the straw itself. The rapidly rising straw phenomenon is usually seen in glasses containing carbonated soft drinks. Reader Richard Williams, a meteorologist at the National Weather Service, explains the phenomenon:

> ...the rise occurs as carbon dioxide bubbles form on both the outside and inside of the straw. This increases the buoyancy of the straw and it gradually rises out of the liquid.
>
> The gas is under considerable pressure when the drink is first drawn or poured. When that pressure is released the gas forms small bubbles on the sides of the glass and on the straw. As the bubbles grow the straw becomes buoyant enough to "float" higher and higher in the container.

Occasionally, though, a straw will rise in a noncarbonated beverage, and we didn't get a good explanation for this phenomenon until we heard from Roger W. Cappello, president of straw-maker Clear Shield National. We often get asked how our sources react to being confronted with strange questions. The only answer we can give is—it varies. Sure, we like authoritative sources who fawn over us and smother us in data. But we must confess we have a special place in our hearts for folks like Cappello, who make us sweat a little before divulging their secrets. Here is his letter to *Imponderables*, verbatim, skipping only the obvious pleasantries:

> After pondering your question for a while, I decided to toss your letter as I was too busy for this. I later retrieved the letter and decided I would attempt to give you an answer that is slightly technical, mixed with some common sense and some B.S.
>
> First off, I know the action you were referring to had something to do with "specific gravity." Specific gravity, as defined by Webster, is "the rate of the density of a substance to the density

DAVID FELDMAN

of a substance (as pure water) taken as a standard when both densities are obtained by weighing in air."

Straws today are formed from polypropylene, whereas many years ago they were made of polystyrene, before that paper, and before that, wheat shafts.

Assuming water has a specific gravity of 1, polypropylene is .9, and polystyrene is 1.04. A polypropylene straw will float upward in a glass of water, whereas a polystyrene straw will sink. However, a polystyrene straw will float upward in a carbonated drink as the carbonation bubbles attach themselves to the side of the straw, which will help offset the slight specific gravity difference between water and polystyrene. A polypropylene straw will float higher in a carbonated drink for the same reason. If you put a polypropylene straw in gasoline, and please don't try this, it will sink because the specific gravity of gas is lighter than water.

If you lined up ten glasses of different liquids, all filled to the same level, the straws would most likely float at all different levels due to the different specific gravities of the liquids and the attachment of various numbers of bubbles to the straws.

I really wish you hadn't brought this up as I'm going to lunch now. I think I'll order hot coffee so I can ponder the imponderables of my business without distraction.

Good luck.

We can use all that good luck you were wishing us. I'm sure you had a productive lunch, too. Anyone willing to share information with us can eat (and sleep) with a clear conscience, knowing that he has led to the enlightenment of his fellow humans.

Submitted by Merrill Perlman of New York, New York.

Why Is the Tenor Oboe Called an "English Horn" When It Is Neither English Nor a Horn?

Dr. Kristin Thelander, professor of music at the University of Iowa School of Music, among many other experts we contacted, assured us that the "English horn" was, indeed, invented in France. No one knew exactly why or how the instrument got classified as a horn.

But the true mystery is how the credit for this instrument migrated to England. Dr. Margaret Downie Banks, curator of The Shrine to Music Museum and Center for Study of the History of Musical Instruments at the University of South Dakota, told *Imponderables* that the existence of the instrument can be traced back at least to the seventeenth century. According to Banks, in the early eighteenth century the English horn was called the *wald-hautbois* (forest oboe),

DAVID FELDMAN

a name which Baroque composers such as Johann Sebastian Bach and others italianized to *oboe da caccia* (hunting oboe).

About 1760, the name *corni inglesi* (English horn) shows up in scores for music by Haydn and Gluck; but it remains unknown just why the tenor oboe was designated the "English horn."

So what happened between the early eighteenth century and 1760 to change the name of the instrument to the English horn? Some of our experts, such as Alvin Johnson, of the American Musicological Society, and Peggy Sullivan, executive secretary of the Music Educators National Conference, were willing to speculate. They offered an oft-told but possibly apocryphal explanation: that our term is a corruption of *cor anglé*, French for "angled horn." Although they were originally straight, like "regular" oboes, instrument makers started putting angles or curves on English horns in the early eighteenth century when the instrument was used in hunting.

So, the theory goes, the English were fooled by a homonym. (*Anglé* and *anglais* do sound alike in French.) And being good chauvinists, the angled horn metamorphosed into the English horn.

We documented many instances of English words and phrases that were based on mispronunciations or misunderstandings of foreign terms in *Who Put the Butter in Butterfly?* So we'll bite on this theory.

Submitted by Robert C. Probasco of Moscow, Idaho.

Why Are Our Fingers Different Lengths? For Example, Is There a Reason Why the "Pinkie" Is Shorter Than the "Index"?

About the only angry letters we get around here are responses to answers of ours that assume the validity of evolutionary theory. But if you ask an authority, such as Dr. William P. Jollie, chairman of the Anatomy Department at the Medical College of Virginia, about this Imponderable, an evolutionary approach is what you are going to get:

> ... anatomically, fingers are digits (our other digits are toes) and people, like all four-legged vertebrate animals, have digits characteristic both for the large group to which they belong (called a *class:* amphibians, reptiles, mammals) and for a smaller group within the class (called an *order:* rodents, carnivores, primates). So we have five fingers of a length that is characteristic for the hands of primate mammals.

DAVID FELDMAN

Of course, there is variation among different species and even variation among individual members of the same species. Some people have ring fingers noticeably longer than their index fingers; in others, the fingers are the same length. We once knew a woman whose second toe was an inch or more longer than her "big" toe.

But is there any rhyme or reason for the relative size of our digits? Dr. Duane Anderson, of the Dayton Museum of Natural History, was the only source we contacted who emphasized the role of the fingers (and hands) in grabbing objects:

> Pick up a tennis ball and you will see the fingers are all the same length. Length is an adaptation to swinging in trees initially, and then picking things up. An "even hand" would be less versatile. A long little finger, for example, would get smashed more often.

Biologist John Hertner, of Kearney State College, says that two characteristics of the digits of higher vertebrates reflect possible reasons for the unequal lengths. First, there is evidence that we can locomote more effectively with smaller outer toes. Second, over time, many higher vertebrates have a tendency to lose some structures altogether (e.g., horses have lost all but one toe).

Might humans lose a digit or two in the next few hundred million years? Unfortunately, neither the evolutionists nor the creationists will be here to find out.

Submitted by Marisa Peacock of Worcester, Massachusetts.

Why Are Sticks of Margarine and Butter Thicker and Shorter in the Western United States and Longer and Narrower in the East?

Who says we don't tackle important questions in the *Imponderables* books?

We'd love to develop a Freudian analysis to explain this phenomenon. (Are sticks of margarine phallic symbols more threatening to westerners?) Or perhaps a sociological one. (Might the fitness-crazed westerners feel superior to their stubby little western sticks?) But the real answer is a tad more prosaic.

Until recent times, dairies were local or regional in their distribution. For reasons that nobody we contacted could explain, what the industry refers to as the "western-style stick" developed out of local custom. When the behemoth dairy companies attained national distribution, they soon found that it was easier to reconfigure their molds than it was to change consumers' preferences.

So large companies like Breakstone and Land O'Lakes make two different packages, one for the West and the other for the rest of the country. In many cases, the western sticks are packaged four in a row, while the eastern counterparts are placed two by two. This also, of course, makes no particular sense.

Submitted by Alan B. Heppel of West Hollywood, California. Thanks also to Jeff Sconyers of Seattle, Washington, and Connie Krenz of Bloomer, Wisconsin.

Why Do Plastic Milk Cases Contain a Warning That Their "Unauthorized Use Is Illegal and Enforced by Health Department and Penal Codes"?

What do certain firearms, heroin, and milk cartons have in common? Possession of each may be punishable by law. Although the wording above is used in California, many states forbid the unauthorized use of milk cartons.

Why the fuss? To get the answer, we contacted our favorite dairy Imponderables solver, Bruce Snow, recently retired from the Dairylea Cooperative in New York. If you wish to retain your faith in humanity, you may want to skip this explanation:

> For more years than I care to remember, the milk dealers in New York (and other urban areas) lost several million dollars a year on purloined plastic milk cases. Never in the history of man has anything been invented for which so many uses have been found: bookcases; sidewalk flower displays; tool chests; album

storage; toy boxes; transport cases for miscellanea; step stools, etc., *ad infinitum.*

It finally got so bad that milk dealers petitioned their legislators to make possession of a dealer's milk case illegal, subject to a fine. The dealer must have his name on the case, by law.

Theft wasn't all the dealers were contending with. Supermarkets, which daily received thousands of cases around New York, were profligate in their use of plastic cases [which currently cost $2.50 or more] to build displays, cart trash, and carry stuff home. Why not? It didn't cost them anything.

Now, however, the New York State law requires that markets must account for all cases to their milk suppliers. They are required by law to pay $2.00 for every case unaccounted for. Consequently, there is now much stricter control over the cases.

As a final note, it was discovered by some city milk dealers that shipments of new cases were being stolen, sent to plastic recyclers for some amount of money, to reappear as any one of a vast multitude of plastic gewgaws. All in all, it was a very big rathole through which a big piece of milk-generated money (ultimately from consumers) was being lost. The law has not eliminated all theft, but it has sharply reduced the problem.

The great irony, of course, is that the milk carton laws turn the tables on retailers. Supermarkets, often so reluctant to process recycled bottles and cans, now must do the same thing themselves, further proof that recycling efforts seem to work only when strong financial incentives exist.

Submitted by Mitch Hubbard of Rancho Palos Verdes, California. Thanks also to Gregory Reis of Torrance, California.

Why Does Shampoo Lather So Much Better on the Second Application?

Even if our hands and hair are already wet, we can't seem to get a healthy lather on the first try when we shampoo our hair. But

DAVID FELDMAN

after we rinse, the shampoo foams up like crazy. Why is lather more luxuriant the second time around?

Evidently, it's because we have greasy hair, according to Dr. John E. Corbett, vice-president of technology at Clairol:

> In the first shampoo application, the lather is suppressed by the oils in the hair. When the oils are rinsed off [by the first application], the shampoo lathers much better on the second application.

Submitted by Joe Schwartz of Troy, New York.

Why Don't Cigarette Butts Burn? Is There a Particular Barrier Between the Tobacco and the Filter That Prevents the Burn?

Even cigarettes without filters don't burn quickly. If the shredded tobacco is packed tightly enough, not enough oxygen is available to feed the combustion process. The degree of porosity of the paper surrounding the tobacco rod can also regulate the degree of burn.

On a filter cigarette, however, an extra impediment is placed on the combustion process; luckily, it is not asbestos. Mary Ann Usrey, of R. J. Reynolds, explains:

> The filter is attached to the tobacco rod by a special "tipping" paper which is essentially non-porous. This paper acts to extinguish the burning coal by significantly reducing the available oxygen. So, in effect, there *is* a barrier between the tobacco and the filter, but it is *around* the cigarette, not actually between the tobacco and the filter in the interior of the cigarette.

Submitted by Frank H. Anderson of Prince George, Virginia.

What Are You Hearing When You Shake a Light Bulb?

Would you believe the ocean? We didn't think so.

Actually, what you are hearing depends upon whether you are shaking a functional or a burned-out bulb. If you are shaking a newish, functioning bulb, chances are you are hearing the delightful sound of loose tungsten particles left over in the bulb's glass envelope during its manufacturing process.

According to Peter Wulff, editor of *Home Lighting & Accessories*, these loose particles don't affect the bulb's operation or lifespan. Wulff adds that although the tungsten particles aren't left in the bulb deliberately, at one time manufacturers of high-wattage tungsten halogen bulbs did leave such residue: "Occasionally, it was recommended that after use and after the bulb cooled, the bulb should be turned upside down and then shaken to allow the loose particles to clean the inside of the glass."

But today if you hear something jangling around, chances are that you are shaking a burned-out bulb. In fact, this is the

DAVID FELDMAN

way most consumers determine whether a bulb is "dead." Richard H. Dowhan, of GTE Products, told *Imponderables* that in this case you are hearing particles of a broken filament, "the most common type of bulb failure." Barring the rare case of loose tungsten particles inside the bulb, Dowhan says "you should hear nothing when you shake a light bulb that is still capable of lighting."

Submitted by Kari Rosenthal of Bangor, Maine.

Why Do Fluorescent Lights Make a Plinking Noise When You Turn Them On?

We went to Peter Wulff again for our answer. Older fluorescent fixtures used a "preheat system," which featured a bimetallic starter (the small, round, silver piece). Wulff told us that inside the starter is a bimetallic switch which "pings" when energized. Newer fluorescent systems, such as the "preheat" or "rapid start," are rendering the "ping" a relic of our nostalgic past.

Submitted by Van Vandagriff of Ypsilanti, Michigan. Thanks also to Kathleen Russell of Grand Rapids, Michigan; Cuesta Schmidt of West New York, New Jersey; and Walter Hermanns of Racine, Wisconsin.

Why Do Cats Like So Much to Be Scratched Behind the Ears?

Most cats like to be scratched for the same reason that most humans like to be massaged: It feels good. According to veterinarian John E. Saidla, assistant director of the Cornell Feline Health Center,

> Most cats like to have their total bodies rubbed or stroked by humans. A cat's skin is chock full of nerve endings, making your stroking a sensual experience.

But *our* skin is full of nerve endings, and not too many of us start wiggling our legs with delight when we're scratched behind the ears. But then again, unlike cats, we don't tend to have ear mites. Dr. Saidla explains:

> Most cats harbor very few mites, while others have huge infections that are causing serious clinical problems. The mite in the

DAVID FELDMAN

ear canal burrows into the layers of skin lining the ear canal. The cat is allergic, or at least, reacts to the feces and enzymes the mite produces, resulting in pruritus or itching. When the owner rubs the skin behind the ear, it feels good and the cat responds appreciatively.

Submitted by Robert J. Abrams of Boston, Massachusetts.

Why Aren't There Plums in Plum Pudding? And Why Is It Called a Pudding Rather Than a Cake?

Even though it contains flour and is as sweet and rich as any cake, plum pudding cannot be classified as a cake because it contains no leavening and is not baked, but steamed.

Besides flour, plum pudding contains suet, sugar, and spices and is studded with raisins and currants. In early America, both raisins and currants were referred to as "plums" or "plumbs." And presumably because the raisins and currants were the only visually identifiable ingredients in the dessert (which traditionally was served after the pumpkin pie at Thanksgiving), the nickname stuck.

Come to think of it, plum pudding isn't the only weirdly named dessert served at Thanksgiving. We used to ask our parents where the meat was in mincemeat pie.* Give us an honest pumpkin pie any day.

Submitted by Bert Garwood of Grand Forks, North Dakota.

---

* To forestall a flood of letters, may we say on the record that mincemeat pie may or may not have minced meat in it.

What Do the Little Red Letter and Number Stamped on the Back of My Envelope Mean?

When the arm of the United States Postal System's Multi-Position Letter Sort Machine (or, as we close friends like to call it, MPLSM) picks up an envelope, it automatically stamps a letter and number on the back. The letter identifies which MPLSM processes the piece, and the number singles out which console on the machine, and thus which MPLSM operator, handles the piece.

This code has nothing to do with delivering the letter. The code is simply a way for the USPS to identify when a particular machine, or its operator, is malfunctioning. In other words, the A4 on the back of your envelope is the equivalent of the "Inspected by 8" label you sometimes find in the pocket of your new jacket.

Although it is our experience that most of the MPLSM codes are red, a casual glance at our voluminous mail indicates that brown and purple are popular, too. Frank P. Brennan, Jr., general manager of media relations for the USPS, says that each tour or shift has its own color.

Not every letter is processed by a MPLSM; increasingly, the USPS is relying on optical scanners. Scanners may be faster than MPLSMs, but without that red code, they can't be held as accountable as MPLSMs when they screw up, either.

DAVID FELDMAN

Why Do Owners or Handlers Use the Word "Sic" to Instruct a Dog to "Get Him"?

Dog World magazine was kind enough to print our query about this Imponderable in their June 1990 issue. We were soon inundated with letters from dog lovers, the most comprehensive of which came from Fred Lanting, of the German Shepherd Dog Club of America:

> The command "sic" comes from a corruption of the German word *such*, which means to seek or search. It is used by Schutzhund [guardian and protection] and police trainers as well as by people training dogs for tracking. If the command "sic" is issued, it means that the dog is to find the hidden perpetrator or victim. In German, *sic* is pronounced "sook" or "suk," but like many foreign words, the pronunciation has been altered over time by those not familiar with the language.
>
> "Sic" has developed from [what was originally] a command to find a hidden bad guy, who [in training exercises] is usually covered by a box or hiding in an open pyramidal canvas blind. Because in police and Schutzhund training the bad guy is attacked if he tries to hit the dog or run away, the word has become associated with a command to attack.

Lanting's answer brings up another Imponderable: If "sic" is a misspelling of the German word, should it be printed as " 'sic' (*sic*)"?

Submitted by Annie Lloyd of Merced, California.

In Baseball Scoring, Why Is the Letter "K" Chosen to Designate a Strikeout?

Lloyd Johnson, ex–executive director of the Society for American Baseball Research, led us to the earliest written source for this story, *Beadle's Dime Base-Ball Player*, a manual published in 1867 that explained how to set up a baseball club. Included in *Beadle's* are such quaint by-laws as "Any member who shall use profane language, either at a meeting of the club, or during field exercise, shall be fined _____cents."

A chapter on scoring, written by Henry Chadwick, assigns meaning to ten letters:

A for first base
B for second base
C for third base
H for home base
F for catch on the fly
D for catch on the bound
L for foul balls
T for tips
K for struck out
R for run out between bases

Chadwick advocated doubling up these letters to describe more events:

H R for home runs
L F for foul ball on the fly
T F for tip on the fly
T D for tip on the bound

He recognized the difficulty in remembering some of these abbreviations and attempted to explain the logic:

> The above, at first sight, would appear to be a complicated alphabet to remember, but when the key is applied it will be at once seen that a boy could easily impress it on his memory in a few minutes. The explanation is simply this—we use the first

DAVID FELDMAN

letter in the words, Home, Fly, and Tip and the last in Bound, Foul, and Struck, and the first three letters of the alphabet for the first three bases.

We can understand why the last letters in "Bound" and "Foul" were chosen—the first letters of each were already assigned a different meaning—but we can't figure out why "S" couldn't have stood for struck out.

Some baseball sources have indicated that the "S" was already "taken" by the sacrifice, but we have no evidence to confirm that sacrifices were noted in baseball scoring as far back as the 1860s.

Submitted by Darin Marrs of Keller, Texas.

What Are the Skins of Hot Dogs Made Of?

Our correspondent wondered whether hot dog skins are made out of the same animal innards used to case other sausages. We recollect when we sometimes used to need a knife to pierce a hot dog. Don't hot dog skins seem a lot more malleable than they used to be?

Evidently, while we were busy chomping franks down, manufacturers were gradually eliminating hot dog skins. Very few mass-marketed hot dogs have skins at all any more. Thomas L. Ruble, of cold-cut giant Oscar Mayer, explains:

> A cellulose casing is used to give shape to our hot dogs and turkey franks [Oscar Mayer owns Louis Rich] during cooking and smoking, but it is removed before the links are packaged. What may have seemed like a casing to you would have been the exterior part of the link that is firmer than the interior. This texture of the exterior of a link could be compared to the crust on a cake that forms during baking.

Submitted by Ted Goodwin of Orlando, Florida.

DAVID FELDMAN

Why Is Comic Strip Print in Capital Letters?

The cartoonists we contacted, including our illustrious (pun intended) Kassie Schwan, concurred that it is easier to write in all caps. We've been printing since the first grade ourselves and haven't found using small letters too much of a challenge, but cartoonists have to worry about stuff that never worries us. Using all caps, cartoonists can allocate their space requirements more easily. Small letters not only vary in height but a few have a nasty habit of swooping below or above most of the other letters (l's make a's look like midgets; and p's and q's dive below most letters).

More importantly, all caps are easier to read. Mark Johnson, archivist for King Features, reminded us that comic strips are reduced in some newspapers and small print tends to "blob up."

We wish that our books were set in all caps. It would automatically rid us of those pesky capitalization problems. While we're musing . . . we wonder how *Classics Illustrated* would

handle the type if it decided to publish a comics' treatment of
e. e. cummings' poetry?

Submitted by Carl Middleman of St. Louis, Missouri.

Why Are Peanuts Listed Under the Ingredients of "Plain" M&Ms?

We've always felt that "peanut" M&Ms weren't as good as
"plain" ones—that the synergy between Messrs. Goober and
Cocoa just wasn't there. As lovers of chocolate and peanuts and,
come to think of it, hard candy shells, as well, you could have
knocked us over with an M&M when two readers brought it to
our attention that "plain" M&Ms contain peanuts.

We contacted the folks at M&M/MARS to solve this troubling
Imponderable and we heard from Donna Ditmars in the consumer affairs division. She told us that peanuts are finely ground
and added to the chocolate for flavor. The quantity of peanuts in
the candy is so small that "labeling laws do not require that we
list this small amount of peanuts as an ingredient, we do so
voluntarily so that consumers will know that it is in the candy."

Why is listing the peanuts so important? Nuts are the source
of one of the most common food allergies.

FLASH: Just after the publication of the hardcover edition of
Do Penguins Have Knees?, we heard surprising news from the
external relations director of M&M/MARS, Hans S. Fiuczynski.
Starting in January, 1992, the company no longer includes any
peanuts in its plain candies. Even so, this Imponderable will not
become obsolete. M&M/MARS will continue to list peanuts as an
ingredient on the label, just in case a small amount of peanuts
inadvertently appears in the plain candies.

Submitted by Martha Claiborne of Anchorage, Kentucky.
Thanks to Susan Wheeler of Jacksonville, North Carolina.

Why Do the Volume Levels of Different Cable Networks Vary Enormously Compared to Those of Broadcast TV Networks?

Anyone with an itchy hand and a remote control device that can control volume levels knows how often one must adjust the volume control when flipping around stations. Anyone without a volume control on a remote control device has probably walked the equivalent of 892 miles in round trips from the La-Z-Boy to the TV set to keep the Pocket Fisherman commercial from blasting innocent eardrums.

We were confronted with a lot of shilly-shallying about this Imponderable from folks in the cable television industry until we heard from Ned L. Mountain, chairman of the subcommittee on Quality Sound in Cable Television of the National Cable Television Association. Mountain doesn't offer any quick solutions, but he does explain the historical and technological problems involved. He lists three advantages that broadcast stations have over cable outlets in transmitting even audio levels:

> 1. The FCC mandates strict standards for broadcast maximum peak audio levels.
>
> > Most TV stations also employ sophisticated and expensive audio processing equipment to maintain a consistent level for their station. Since they only have one channel to worry about, they can afford it.
>
> 2. At the point where signals originate for a community (called the "head ends"), broadcast stations have personnel to monitor the levels. Most cable head ends don't. Humans can make "subjective audio level control" adjustments as necessary.
>
> 3. Most broadcast stations have converted to stereo; while they did so, they took the opportunity to upgrade their audio facilities. The result: a more uniform sound among broadcast outlets.

Cable operators must also conform to the FCC standard for

peak program levels, but are under numerous handicaps, as Mountain explains:

> A cable operator must attempt to achieve this standard on as many as 30 to 40 channels simultaneously from sources over which he has no control.
>
> The problems start at the sources. Most cable programs are satellite delivered using various technologies where there are no standards, only "understandings." The programmers themselves may or may not use the same type of audio processing as that employed by over-the-air broadcasters.
>
> The cable operator many times compounds this problem by inserting locally generated commercials on these channels. The sound of these may or may not match the network on any given day.
>
> This equipment is automated, and the head end is generally unattended. Without standards or expensive "automatic gain control devices, the levels can and do vary from channel to channel."

Mountain's subcommittee consists of programmers, satellite transmission experts, cable operators, and equipment manufacturers. Their first task is to get the programmers and satellite delivery systems to coordinate the quantification of their audio standards, so that operators at least know how to set levels.

Even though this problem annoys us no end, we can't help being won over by Mountain's sincerity and a hook that is going to compel every reader of this book to buy the *next* volume of *Imponderables*:

> David, I wish there were an easy answer to your question. I can assure your readers, however, that there are significant efforts being expended within our industry to investigate and solve these problems. Perhaps by the time your next issue is in print, we will have made significant inroads and I can give you an update.

We'll be waiting.

Submitted by M. Ian Silbergleid of Northport, New York.

Why Are Men's Shoe Heels Built in Layers?

Rubber is most durable and attractive material for heels, but according to Lloyd E. Brunkhorst, vice-president of research and engineering for Brown Shoe Company,

> A thick rubber heel is often too soft, and the result is instability. Therefore, a heel base made of polyethylene ½" to ¾" thick, with a ½" or so rubber top lift, gives the best performance.

William Kelly, of Brockton Sole and Plastics, echoes Brunkhorst's sentiments, and adds that polyethylene better withstands the moisture to which heels are constantly subjected.

Both sources indicated that the "stacked leather look," which is now in fashion, requires many layers of quarter-inch-thick leather to form the heel. The few shoes that are manufactured with unlayered rubber are considered to be "low class."

Polyethylene heels are cheaper than rubber, which reduces not only the cost of the shoe to the manufacturer and consumer but the cost of repairing the shoe. In many cases, the entire heel need not be replaced when damage occurs. As Brunkhorst mentions, replacement of a top lift rather than a whole heel is much less expensive, and the lifts are more readily available than whole heels.

Submitted by an anonymous caller on "The Ray Briem Show," KABC-AM, Los Angeles, California.

Why Are Horses' Heights Measured to the Shoulder Rather Than to the Top of the Head?

David M. Moore, Virginia Tech University's veterinarian and director of the Office of Animal Resources, compares measuring a horse to trying to measure a squirming child. At least you can back a child up to a wall. If the child's legs, back, and neck are straight, the measurement will be reasonably accurate:

> But with a horse, whose spinal column is parallel to the ground (rather than perpendicular, as with humans), there is no simple way to assure that each horse will hold its head and neck at the same point. Thus, measurements to the top of the head are too variable and of little use.

Dr. Wayne O. Kester, of the American Association of Equine Practitioners, told *Imponderables* that when a horse is standing squarely on all four feet, the top of the withers (the highest point

DAVID FELDMAN

on the backbone above the shoulder) is always the same *fixed* distance above the ground, thus providing a consistent measurement for height. Kester estimates that "head counts" could vary as much as two to six feet.

Submitted by Gavin Sullivan of Littleton, Colorado.

Why Are the Edges on the Long Side of Lasagna Usually Crimped?

Farook Taufiq, vice-president of quality assurance at The Prince Company, had no problem answering this Imponderable:

> The curls at the edge of lasagna strips help retain the sauce and the filling between layers. If the lasagna strips are flat, the sauce and the filling will slip out from between layers while cooking as well as while eating.

Now if someone will only invent a method of keeping lasagna (and its sauce) on our fork while it makes the arduous journey from the plate to our mouths, we would be most appreciative.

Submitted by Sarah Duncan of Mars, Pennsylvania.

What Happens to Your Social Security Number When You Die? How and When, If Ever, Is It Reassigned?

You don't need to be a hall-of-famer to get this number retired. John Clark, regional public affairs officer of the Social Security Administration, explains:

Each number remains as unique as the individual it was first assigned to. When someone dies, we retire the number.

The first number was issued in 1936. The nine-digit system has a capacity for creating nearly one billion possible combinations. A little more than a third of the possible combinations have been issued in the fifty-five years since the first number was issued.

It's comforting to know that you can take *something* with you.

Submitted by Albert Mantei of Crystal, Minnesota.

"I love your cologne... what is it?"

it's **new car**

new car femmes for women...

new car ...men

new car voitures ... old cars

that musky, vinyl-y fragrance everyone **loves!!!**

What Exactly Are We Smelling When We Enjoy the "New-Car Smell"?

You didn't think that only one ingredient could provide such a symphony of smells, did you? No. Detroit endeavors to provide the proper blend of constituents that will provide you with the utmost in olfactory satisfaction. (We won't even talk about the exotic scents of European and Asian cars.) C. R. Cheney, of Chrysler Motors, provided us with the most comprehensive explanation and the most poignant appreciation:

> The smell we all enjoy inside a new vehicle (that "new-car smell") is a combination of aromas generated by fresh primer and paint, and the plastic materials used on instrument panels, around the windows, and on door trim panels. Plus, there are odors given off by carpeting, new fabrics, leather, and vinyl used for soft trim and upholstery. Rubber, adhesives, and sealers also play a part in creating this unique smell that never lasts as long as we would like and seems nearly impossible to duplicate.

Submitted by William Janna of Memphis, Tennessee. Thanks also to Jerry Arvesen of Bloomington, Indiana, and David Nesper of Logansport, Indiana.

DO PENGUINS HAVE KNEES?   367

Why Are Some Cleansers Marked "For Industrial or Commercial Use Only"? How Are They Different from Household Cleansers?

With few exceptions, the chemicals and detergents used in commercial cleansers are no different from those marketed to home consumers, although industrial-strength cleanser is likely to contain much less water than Fantastik or Mr. Clean. Why? The answer has more to do with marketing and sociology than technology.

Until the 1950s, most cleaning was done with soaps (fatty acids and lye) rather than detergents (made from alkaline substances). Unlike detergents, soap didn't need much water to add to its cleaning effectiveness. When using soap, consumers rarely added water.

When synthetic detergents were introduced in the 1950s, most home consumers didn't adjust properly. According to Tom Mancini, of U.S. Polychemical, manufacturers were forced to add water to detergents designed for home use because consumers wouldn't add enough water to the products to make them work effectively. Consumers also enjoyed the convenience of applying cleanser directly to a sponge or dirty surface rather than first diluting the detergent with water.

Of course, consumers have had to pay for the privilege; commercial cleansers are much cheaper than home equivalents, and not just because industry buys cleansers in bulk. When you buy a cleanser in a big plastic package at the supermarket, you are carrying mostly a big package of water, the equivalent of buying a package of ready-to-drink ice tea rather than a jar of iced tea mix.

Industrial users have totally different priorities. They are quite willing to sacrifice a little convenience to save money; by buying a concentrated product, companies can save on unnecessary packaging. Professional cleaners also realize that detergents need to be diluted to work effectively. In almost all cases,

DAVID FELDMAN

"industrial-strength" cleansers can be used in the home if diluted sufficiently.

There is one major difference in the ingredients of home and industrial cleansers. Home consumers care about how their cleansers smell. In most cases, corporate decision makers don't care much about the smell of cleansers (although the janitors, who have to work with the stuff all the time, undoubtedly do); as a result, many household cleansers contain perfume to mask the odor of unpleasant ingredients. Perfume jacks up the price of the product without adding anything to its cleaning ability.

Submitted by Jeffrey Chavez of Torrance, California.

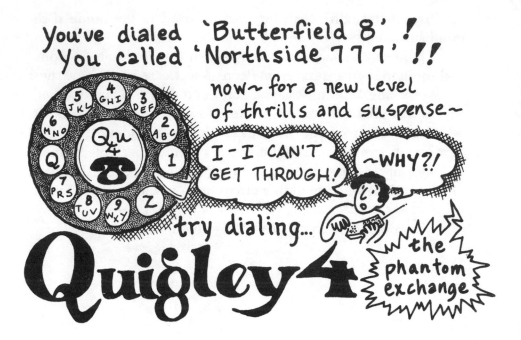

You've dialed `Butterfield 8`! You called `Northside 777`!! now~ for a new level of thrills and suspense~

I—I CAN'T GET THROUGH!

~WHY?!

try dialing... Quigley 4

the phantom exchange

Why Are the Letters "Q" and "Z" Missing from the Telephone Buttons?

The whereabouts of the missing "Q" and Z" are very much on the minds of *Imponderables* readers. In fact, this is easily one of our top ten most frequently asked questions. We have heretofore restrained ourselves from answering it because we've seen the solution bandied about in print already. So we won't call it an Imponderable (we called these questions that have already been in print but just won't go away Unimponderables in *Why do Dogs Have Wet Noses?*), but we will answer it anyway, since it segues neatly into the next Imponderable, a phenomenon less often written about.

Before the days of area codes, operators connected all long distance calls and many toll calls. When the Bell system started manufacturing telephones with dials, users were able to make many of their own local and toll connections. When direct dial-

DAVID FELDMAN

ing was instituted, phone numbers consisted of two letters and five numbers. A number we now call 555-5555 might have then been expressed as KL5-5555. And the phone company provided a nifty mnemonic for each exchange.

So the phone company assigned three letters, in alphabetical order, to each dial number. The number one was skipped because one was assigned as an access code and for internal phone company use (many phone companies used three-digit numbers starting with 1-1 . . . for directory assistance and repair lines); the zero was avoided because it automatically summoned the operator, regardless of subsequent numbers dialed. So there were eight numbers on the dial that needed letters and twenty-six letters available. Eight goes into twenty-six an inconvenient three and one-quarter times. Two of the letters had to be discarded.

Sure, the phone company could have simply dropped the last two letters of the alphabet, but in our opinion they selected well. What letters are less commonly used and more easily discarded than the two letters valuable only to Scrabble players— "Q" and "Z"? "Q" would have been a problematic choice at best. How can you make an effective mnemonic when virtually all words starting with "Q" must be followed by a "U"? If "Q" had its "rightful" place on the number 7, 8 (where "U" is located") would usually have to follow, severely limiting the numbers assignable to the exchange.

"Z," of course, is the last letter and accustomed to suffering the usual indignities of alphabetical order. Maybe the thought of a phone number starting with "ZEbra," "ZInnia," or "ZAire" is overwhelmingly exciting to someone, but for the most part its loss has not been missed.

Submitted by Robert Abrams of Boston, Massachusetts, and a cast of thousands.

Why Is the Middle Digit of North American Area Codes Always a 0 or a 1?

The Bell system introduced three-digit area codes in 1945. Bell was quite aware of the cost savings in direct dialing for long distance calls but also knew that unless it could devise a system to distinguish area codes from the first three digits of ordinary local phone numbers, an operator would have to switch calls.

All ten-digit phone numbers consist of three parts: an area code (the first three numbers); an office code (the next three numbers); and a line number (the last four numbers). We have already explained in the last Imponderable why no office code could start with a 0 or 1. When the Bell system created the area code, it initially extended the "ban" on zeroes and ones to the second digit of the office code as well. By assigning all area codes a second digit of either 0 or 1, automatic switching equipment could differentiate between long distance calls and local or toll calls and route them accordingly. The equipment could also sort calls by the first digit—if the initial digit is a 1, a ten-digit number will follow; while an initial 2–9 means a seven-digit number will follow.

When the area code system was first instituted, all states with only one area code had a 0 as the middle digit; states with more than one area code used 1 for the middle digit of the area code. This practice had to be abandoned when the Bell system ran out of ones as more states needed more than one area code. Now, some populous states have area codes with middle digits of 0.

Because people and telephones have proliferated, the numbering system has had to change several times. The original configuration of office codes yielded a limit of 640 different numbers. To increase the number of office codes available, zeroes and ones have been added to the second digit of office codes, allowing for an eventual expansion of 152 extra office codes.

By the twenty-first century, we would probably run out of

DAVID FELDMAN

area codes if we kept the same numbering method. The phone system is preparing to introduce middle digits other than one or zero in the next century. As long as all long distance calls are preceded by one, it won't be a problem.

Submitted by Carol Oppenheim of Owings Mill, Maryland.
Thanks also to Nicole Donovan of Wenham, Massachusetts.

Why Were Duels Always Fought at Dawn? Or Is This Depiction in Fiction and Movies Not True?

Not true, we're afraid. Historians assured *Imponderables* that duels were fought at any time of the day. But dawn was definitely the preferred time; a duel fought in twilight could turn into more of a crapshoot than a gunshoot.

Doesn't make much sense to us. We might be convinced to get up at dawn to go fishing. But if we knew we had an approximately fifty-fifty chance of dying on a particular day, we'd at least want a decent night's sleep the night before and time for a doughnut or two before we fought.

Historian C. F. "Charley" Eckhardt speculates on this strange predilection of duelists to fight to the death at inconvenient hours:

> Just at sunrise, if the list [the technical term for a dueling ground] was oriented north-south, neither man got the sun-to-the-back advantage. Also, either the local law was still abed or, if there was a regular police force in the area, the day watch and night watch were changing shifts. Fighting at dawn minimized the likelihood of interference by the law, the same reason why many burglaries occur between 3 and 4 P.M. and 11 P.M. to midnight. Most police departments change shifts at 3 P.M., 11 P.M., and 7 A.M.

Submitted by Jan Anthony Verlaan of Pensacola, Florida.

Quaintly Earnest
LIBERAL ARTS COLLEGE
no tuition · no requirements
f. 1968

What Exactly Are the Liberal Arts, and Who Designated Them So?

Our correspondent, Bill Elmendorf, contacted two four-year colleges and one two-year college for the answer to this question. Despite the fact that they were liberal arts colleges, none of the officials he spoke to could answer this question. Evidently, a good liberal arts education doesn't provide you with the answer to what a liberal art is.

Actually, a consultation with an encyclopedia will tell you that the concept of the liberal arts, as developed in the Middle Ages, involved seven subjects: grammar, logic, rhetoric, arithmetic, geometry, music, and astronomy. Why astronomy and not biology? Why rhetoric and not art? For the answers to this question, we have to delve into the history of the liberal arts.

Our expression is derived from the Latin *artes liberalis*, "pertaining to a free man." Liberal arts are contrasted with the "servile" arts, which have practical applications. As educator

DAVID FELDMAN

Tim Fitzgerald wrote *Imponderables,* "the liberal arts were considered 'liberating,' enabling the student to develop his or her potential beyond the mundane, to create, to be fully human, to (in the medieval mindset) believe."

The notion of seven ennobling arts emerged long before the Middle Ages. In Proverbs 9:1, the Bible says, "Wisdom hath builded her house, she hath hewn out her seven pillars." Robert E. Potter, professor of education at the University of Hawaii at Manoa, wrote *Imponderables* a fascinating letter tracing the history of the liberal arts. Before the birth of Christ and into the first century A.D., Roman writers like Cicero and Quintilian discussed the proper curriculum for the orator and public leader. Varro (116–27 B.C.) listed in his *Libri Novem Disciplinarum* the seven liberal arts but also included medicine and architecture.

Potter mentions that in the early Christian era, church elders opposed the classical liberal arts. Perhaps the most stirring condemnation was written in the Apostolic Constitutions in the third century:

> Refrain from all the writings of the heathen for what has thou to do with strange discourses, laws, or false prophets, which in truth turn aside from the faith for those who are weak in understanding? For if thou wilt explore history, thou hast the Books of the Kings; or seekest thou for words of wisdom and eloquence, thou hast the Prophets, Job, and the Book of Proverbs, wherein thou shalt find a more perfect knowledge of all eloquence and wisdom, for they are the voice of the Lord.

Later Christian scholars, including Augustine, embraced the study of the liberal arts.

Potter calls Martianus Capella of Carthage's *The Marriage of Philology and Mercury* the "definitive" work on the liberal arts:

> This fourth-century allegory had nine books. The first two described the wedding of the daughter of Wisdom, a mortal maiden who represented schooling, and Mercury, who, as the inventor of letters, symbolized the arts of Greece. The remaining seven books describe the bridesmaids. Apollo did not admit two

other "bridesmaids," medicine and architecture, "inasmuch as they are concerned with perishable earthly things."

Many people attack the modern liberal arts education, saying that little is taught that pertains to our actual lives now. Little do they know that this lack of "relevance" is precisely what characterized the liberal arts from their inception. In ancient times, servile folks had to sully themselves with practical matters like architecture, engineering, or law. Only the elite freemen could ascend to the lofty plateau of the contemplation of arithmetic.

Today, the meaning of liberal arts is murky, indeed. Art, other hard sciences besides astronomy, foreign languages, philosophy, history, and most social sciences are often included under the umbrella of liberal arts. Just about any school that *doesn't* train you for a particular profession is called a liberal arts institution.

Submitted by Bill Elmendorf of Lebanon, Illinois. Thanks also to Brianna Liu of Minneapolis, Minnesota.

Why Do Birds Tend to Stand on One Foot While Sleeping? Why Do Birds Tend to Bury Their Heads Under Their Wings While Sleeping?

In *When Do Fish Sleep?*, we discussed the amazing locking mechanism of birds' toes that enables them to perch on telephone wires without falling off. In fact, they can perch just as easily while standing on only one leg. Since they can balance as easily on one leg as two, one of the main reasons for perching on one leg (whether or not they are sleeping) is simply to give the other leg a rest.

But birds also seek warmth, and perching on one foot gives them a "leg up" on the situation, as Nancy Martin, naturalist at the Vermont Institute of Natural Science, explains:

DAVID FELDMAN

Since birds' feet are not covered with feathers, they can lose significant amounts of body heat through their feet, especially when standing on ice or in cold water. With their high metabolic rates, birds usually try to conserve as much energy as possible, hence the habit of standing on one leg.

A corollary: Birds also stick their head under their feathers to preserve heat.

Submitted by Lee Dresser of Overland Park, Kansas. Thanks also to Jocelyn Noda of Los Angeles, California.

Why Is a Marshal or Sheriff's Badge Traditionally a Five-Pointed Star but a Deputy's Six-Pointed?

The five-pointed pentacle is the symbol of the United States Marshal's Service. In ancient times, the pentacle was used by sorcerers and believed to impart magical powers. As late as the sixteenth century, soldiers wore pentacles around their necks in the belief that they made them invulnerable to enemy missiles.

But it turns out that even early American lawmen forged a new tradition of forsaking old traditions at the drop of a hat. It just isn't true that sheriffs always wore five-pointed stars and their deputies six-pointed ones. Charles E. Hanson, Jr., director of The Museum of the Fur Trade in Chadron, Nebraska, wrote *Imponderables* that one could despair of trying to find logic to the patterns of badges:

> There seems to be no fixed protocol on five- and six-pointed badges. In America, the five-point star has been preeminent from the beginning. It is the star in the flag, in the insignia of an army general, and on the Medal of Honor. It was obviously the logical choice for the first sheriffs' badges.
>
> When other shapes began to be used for badges, it seemed right that circles, shields, and six-pointed stars would be used for lesser legal representatives than the top lawman.

This didn't hold true indefinitely. Our library has a 1913 supply catalog which offers five-point stars engraved "City Marshal" or "Chief of Police" and six-point stars engraved, "City Marshal," "Sheriff," "Constable," "Detective," etc.

Historian Charley Eckhardt has even developed a theory to explain why the five-point might have been inflated to six points: It was simply too hard to make a five-pointed star.

> The five- and six-pointed star "tradition" seems to be purely a twentieth-century one. I've seen hundreds of badges from the nineteenth century, and they ranged from the traditional policeman's shield to a nine-pointed sunburst. Five- and six-pointed stars predominated, but in no particular order—there was no definite plurality of five points in one group and six points in another. I have noticed, however, that the majority of the *locally* made star-shaped badges produced outside of Texas were six-pointed. There may be a reason for that.
>
> When you cut a circle, if you take six chords equal to the radius of the circle and join them around the diameter, you will find that the chords form a perfect hexagon. If you join alternate points of the hexagon, you get two superimposed equilateral triangles—a six-pointed star. In order to lay out a pentagon within a circle—the basic figure for cutting a five-pointed star—you have to divide the circle into 72-degree arcs. This requires a device to measure angles from the center—or a very fine eye and a lot of trial and error. Since many badges, including many deputy sheriff and marshal badges, were locally made, it would have been much easier for the blacksmith or gunsmith turned badgemaker for a day to make a six-pointed star.

Who says that the shortage of protractors in the Old West didn't have a major influence on American history?

Submitted by Eugene S. Mitchell of Wayne, New Jersey. Thanks also to Christopher Valeri of East Northport, New York.

Foundation Sale!
"Mystery In Lace"

When you put on our girdle...

(you'll never want to peel it off!)

...thousands of delicate lace flowers absorb and hold your excess er~FAT!

$29⁹⁰

When You Wear a Girdle, Where Does the Fat Go?

Depends upon the girdle. And depends upon the woman wearing the girdle.

Ray Tricarico, of Playtex Apparel, told *Imponderables* that most girdles have panels on the front to help contour the stomach. Many provide figure "guidance" for the hips and derriere as well.

"But where does the fat go?" we pleaded. If we cinch a belt too tight, the belly and love handles plop over the belt. If we poke ourselves in the ribs, extra flesh surrounds our fingers. And when Victorian ladies wore corsets, their nineteen-inch waists were achieved only by inflating the hips and midriff with displaced flesh. Mesmerized by our analogies, Tricarico suggested we contact Robert K. Niddrie, vice-president of merchandising at Playtex's technical research and development group. We soon discovered that we had a lot to learn about girdles.

First of all, "girdles" may be the technical name for these

undergarments, but the trade prefers the term "shapewear." Why? Because girdles conjure up an old-fashioned image of undergarments that were confining and uncomfortable. Old girdles had no give in them, so, like too-tight belts, they used to send flesh creeping out from under the elastic bands (usually under the bottom or above the waist).

The purpose of modern shapewear isn't so much to press in the flesh as to distribute it evenly and change the contour of the body. And girdles come in so many variations now. If women have a problem with fat bulging under the legs of the girdle, they can buy a long-leg girdle. If fat is sneaking out the midriff, a high-waist girdle will solve the problem.

Niddrie explains that the flesh is so loose that it can be redistributed without discomfort. Shapewear is made of softer and more giving fabrics. The modern girdle acts more like a back brace or an athletic supporter—providing support can actually feel good.

"Full-figured" women are aware of so-called minimizer bras that work by redistributing tissue over a wider circumference. When the flesh is spread out over a wider surface area, it actually appears to be smaller in bulk. Modern girdles work the same way. You can demonstrate the principle yourself. Instead of poking a fatty part of your body with your finger, press it in gently with your whole hand—there should be much less displacement of flesh.

Niddrie credits DuPont's Lycra with helping to make girdles acceptable to younger women today. So we talked to Susan Habacivch, a marketing specialist at DuPont, who, unremarkably, agreed that adding 15 to 30 percent Lycra to traditional materials has helped make girdles much more comfortable. The "miracle" of Lycra is that it conforms to the body shape of the wearer, enabling foundation garments to even and smooth out flesh without compressing it. The result: no lumps or bumps. Girdles with Lycra don't eliminate the fat but they "share the wealth" with adjoining areas.

Submitted by Cynthia Crossen of Brooklyn, New York.

DAVID FELDMAN

What Do Mosquitoes Do During the Day? And Where Do They Go?

At any hour of the day, somewhere in the world, a mosquito is biting someone. There are so many different species of mosquitoes, and so much variation in the habits among different species, it is hard to generalize. Some mosquitoes, particularly those that live in forests, are diurnal. But most of the mosquitoes in North America are active at night, and classified as either nocturnal or crepuscular (tending to be active at the twilight hours of the morning and/or evening).

Most mosquitoes concentrate all of their activities into a short period of the day or evening, usually in one to two hours. If they bite at night, mosquitoes will usually eat, mate, and lay eggs then, too. Usually, nocturnal and crepuscular female mosquitoes are sedentary, whether they are converting the lipids of blood into eggs or merely waiting to go on a nectar-seeking expedition to provide energy. Although they may take off once or twice a day to find some nectar, a week or more may pass between blood meals.

If the climatic conditions stay constant, mosquitoes tend to stick to the same resting patterns every day. But according to Charles Schaefer, director of the Mosquito Control Research Laboratory at the University of California at Berkeley, the activity pattern of mosquitoes can be radically changed by many factors:

1. Light (Most nocturnal and crepuscular mosquitoes do not like to take flight if they have to confront direct sunlight. Conversely, in homes, some otherwise nocturnal mosquitoes will be active during daylight hours if the house is dark.)

2. Humidity (Most will be relatively inactive when the humidity is low.)

3. Temperature (They don't like to fly in hot weather.)

4. Wind (Mosquitoes are sensitive to wind, and will usually not take flight if the wind is more than 10 mph.)

Where are nocturnal mosquitoes hiding during the day? Most never fly far from their breeding grounds. Most settle into vegetation. Grass is a particular favorite. But others rest on trees; their coloring provides excellent camouflage to protect them against predators.

A common variety of mosquito in North America, the anopheles, often seeks shelter. Homes and barns are favorite targets, but a bridge or tunnel will do in a pinch. Nocturnal or crepuscular mosquitoes are quite content to rest on a wall in a house, until there is too much light in the room. In the wild, shelter-seeking mosquitoes will reside in caves or trees.

We asked Dr. Schaefer, who supplied us with much of the background information for this Imponderable, whether mosquitoes were resting or sleeping during their twenty-two hours or so of inactivity. He replied that no one really knows for sure. We're reserving *When Do Mosquitoes Sleep?* as a possible title for a future volume of *Imponderables*.

Submitted by Jennifer Martz of Perkiomenville, Pennsylvania. Thanks also to Ronald C. Semone of Washington, D.C.

What Does the "CAR-RT SORT" Printed Next to the Address on Envelopes Mean?

Reader Jeff Bennett writes: "CAR-RT SORT is printed on a lot of the letters I receive. Obviously it's got something to do with mail sorting, but what does it stand for?"

Not unlike us, Jeff, it sounds like you've been receiving more than your share of junk mail lately. CAR-RT SORT is short for Carrier Route Presort and is a special class of mail. As the name implies, to qualify for the Carrier Route First-Class Mail rate, mailers must arrange all letters so that they can be given to the appropriate mail carrier without any sorting by the postal system. Each piece must be part of a minimum of ten pieces for that carrier; if there are not ten pieces for a particular carrier route, the mailer must pay the rate for Presorted First-Class Mail. (Presorted First-Class Mail costs more than Carrier Route because it requires only that the mail be arranged in ascending order of ZIP code.)

Don't expect to see CAR-RT SORT on the envelopes of your friends' Christmas cards. Carrier Route Mail must be sent in a single mailing of not less than 500 pieces. And if they really have ten friends serviced by one postal carrier, it would be cheaper for them to hand-deliver the cards.

Submitted by Jeff Bennett of Poland, New York. Thanks also to Matt Menentowski of Spring, Texas.

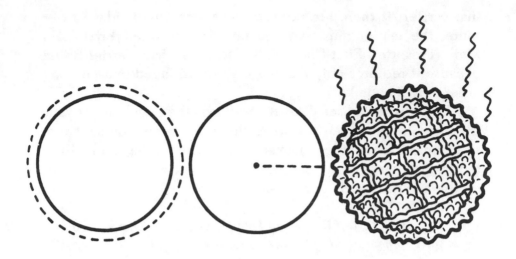

Why Was "pi" Chosen as the Greek Letter to Signify the Ratio of a Circle's Circumference to Its Diameter?

The history of "pi" is so complex and fascinating that whole books have been written about the subject. Still, if you want to make a long story short, it can be boiled down to the explanation provided by Roger Pinkham, a mathematician at the Stevens Institute of Technology in Hoboken, New Jersey:

> There are two Greek words for perimeter, *perimetros* and *periphireia*. The circumference of a circle is its perimeter, and the first letter of the Greek prefix *peri* (meaning "round") used in those two words was chosen.

Mathematicians attempted to calculate the pi ratio before the birth of Christ. But it wasn't the ancient Egyptians or Greek mathematicians who first coined the term. San Antonio math teacher John Veltman sent us documentation indicating that although pi was earlier applied as an abbreviation of "periphery," the first time it was found in print to express the circle ratio was in 1706, when an English writer named William Jones, best known as a translator of Isaac Newton, published *A New Introduction to Mathematics*. "Pi" did not enjoy widespread accep-

DAVID FELDMAN

tance until 1737, when Jones's term was popularized by the great Swiss mathematician Leonhard Euler.

So what did the ancient Greeks call the ratio? They probably did not have a handy abbreviation. Veltman explains:

> It appears that even the Greek mathematicians themselves did not use their letter pi to represent the circle ratio. Several ancient cultures did their math in sentence form with little or no abbreviation or symbolism. It is amazing how much they achieved without such an aid. Archimedes, born about 287 B.C., is said to have determined that the value of pi was between $3\frac{10}{71}$ and $3\frac{1}{7}$ (or in our decimal notation, between 3.14084 and 3.142858).

In the centuries that followed, mathematicians in other countries produced even more precise calculations: Around A.D. 150, Ptolemy of Alexandria weighed in with his value of 3.1416. Around A.D. 480, a Chinese man, Tsu Ch'ung-chih, improved the figure to 3.1415929, correct to the first six numbers after the decimal point.

Why is our mathematical vocabulary a seemingly random hodgepodge of Greek and Latin terminology? Why do we say the Latin-derived "circumference" (originally meaning "to run or move around") rather than the Greek "periphery"? Diane McCulloch, a mathematician at the Mount de Chantal Academy in Wheeling, West Virginia, explains:

> The Greeks were more avid mathematicians than the Romans, who preferred the practical uses and didn't have much time for the analytical aspect of mathematics. Thank goodness the writings of the Greeks were preserved by the Islamic scholars. We have access to the ancient Greek mathematical work because these Islamic scholars established libraries in Spain; when they were eventually driven out of Spain, their books were translated into Latin and then into other European languages, which themselves tended to be derived from Latin.
>
> Therefore, we use the word "triangle" when the Greeks would probably have used the word "trigon," as in "polygon," "octagon," etc.

Submitted by Dennis Kingsley of Goodrich, Michigan.

DO PENGUINS HAVE KNEES?

Why Can't You Buy Macadamia Nuts in Their Shells?

Macadamia nuts do have shells. But selling them in their shells would present a serious marketing problem. Only Superman could eat them. According to the Mauna Loa Macadamia Nut Corporation, the largest producer of macadamias in the world, "It takes 300-pounds-per-square-inch of pressure to break the shell."

After macadamias are harvested, the husks are removed, and then the nuts are dried and cured to reduce their moisture. The drying process helps separate the kernel from the shell; without this separation, it would be impossible to apply the pressure necessary to shatter the shell without pulverizing the contents. The nuts then pass through counter-rotating steel rollers spaced to break the shell without shattering the nutmeat.

Of course, one question remains. Why did Mother Nature bother creating macadamias when humans and animals (even raging rhinos) can't break open the shells to eat them without the aid of heavy machinery?

Submitted by Herbert Kraut of Forest Hills, New York.

If Heat Rises, Why Does Ice Form on the Top of Water in Lakes and Ponds?

Anyone who has ever filled an ice-cube tray with water knows that room temperature water decreases in density when it freezes. We also know that heat rises. And that the sun would hit the top of the water more directly than water at the bottom. All three scientific verities would seem to indicate that ice would form at the bottom, rather than the top, of lakes and ponds. "What gives?" demand *Imponderables* readers.

You may not know, however, what Neal P. Rowell, retired professor of physics at the University of South Alabama, told us:

DAVID FELDMAN

Water is most dense at 4 degrees Centigrade (or 39.2 degrees Fahrenheit). This turns out to be the key to the mystery of the rising ice. One of our favorite scientific researchers, Harold Blake, wrote a fine summary of what turns out to be a highly technical answer:

> As water cools, it gets more dense. It shrinks. It sinks to the bottom of the pond, lake, rain barrel, wheelbarrow, or dog's water dish. But at 4 degrees Centigrade, a few degrees above freezing, the water has reached its maximum density. It now starts to expand as it gets cooler. The water that is between 4 degrees Centigrade and zero Centigrade (the freezing point of water) now starts to rise to the surface. It is lighter, less dense.
>
> Now, more heat has to be lost from the water at freezing to form ice at freezing. This is called the "heat of fusion." During the freezing process, ice crystals form and expand to a larger volume, fusing together as they expand, and using more freezing water to "cement" themselves together. The ice crystals are very much lighter and remain on the surface.
>
> Once the surface is frozen over, heat dissipates from the edges and freezing is progressive from the edges. When the unfrozen core finally freezes, there is tremendous pressure exerted from the expansion, and the ice surface or container sides yield, a common annoyance with water pipes.

Once the top layer of the lake or pond freezes, the water below will rarely reach 0 degrees Centigrade; the ice acts effectively as insulation. By keeping the temperature of the water below the ice between 0 and 4 degrees Centigrade, the ice helps some aquatic life survive in the winter when a lake is frozen over.

The strangest element of this ice Imponderable is that since water at 4 degrees Centigrade is at its maximum density, it always expands when it changes temperature, whether it gets hotter or cooler.

Submitted by Richard T. Mitch of Dunlap, California. Thanks also to Kenneth D. MacDonald of Melrose, Massachusetts; R. Prickett of Stockton, California; Brian Steiner of Charlotte, North Carolina; and John Weisling of Grafton, Wisconsin.

What Happens to the 1,000 or More Prints After Films Have Finished Their Theatrical Runs?

Distribution strategies for films vary dramatically. A "critics' darling," especially a foreign film or a movie without big stars, might be. given a few exclusive runs in media centers like New York City and Los Angeles. The film's distributor prays that word-of-mouth and good reviews will build business so that it can expand to more theaters in those cities and later be distributed throughout the country.

"High-concept" films, particularly comedies and action films whose plot lines can be easily communicated in short television commercials, and films starring "bankable" actors are likely to be given broad releases. By opening the film simultaneously across the country at 1,000 to 2,000 or more theaters, the film studios can amortize the horrendous cost of national advertising. But the cost of duplicating 2,000 prints, while dwarfed by marketing costs, is nevertheless a major expense.

A run-of-the-mill horror film from a major studio, for example, might open in 1,500 theaters simultaneously. The usual pattern for these films is to gross a considerable amount of money the first week and then fall off sharply. A horror film without good word-of-mouth might be gone from most theaters within four weeks. Of course, studios will release the film on videotape within a year, but what will they do with those 1,500 prints?

The first priority is to ship the prints overseas. Most American films are released overseas after the American theatrical run is over. Eventually, those American prints are returned to the United States.

And then they are destroyed and the silver is extracted from the film and sold to precious metals dealers. The studios have little use for 1,500 scratchy prints.

Mark Gill, vice-president of publicity at Columbia Pictures, told *Imponderables* that his company keeps twenty to thirty prints of all its current releases indefinitely. The film studios are

DAVID FELDMAN

aware of all of the movies from the early twentieth century that have been lost due to negligence—some have deteriorated in quality but others are missing simply because nobody bothered keeping a print. With all of the ancillary markets available, including videotape, laser disc, repertory theaters, cable television, and syndicated television, today's movies are unlikely to disappear altogether (though we can think of more than a few that we would like to disappear). But the problem of print deterioration continues.

Submitted by Ken Shafer of Traverse City, Michigan. Thanks also to John DuVall of Fort Pierce, Florida.

Why Is Balsa Wood Classified as a Hardwood When It Is Soft? What Is the Difference Between a Softwood and a Hardwood?

Call us naive. But we thought that maybe there was a slight chance that the main distinction between a softwood and a hardwood was that hardwood was harder than softwood. What fools we are.

Haven't you gotten the lesson yet? LIFE IS NOT FAIR. Our language makes no sense. The center will not hold. Burma Shave.

Anyway, it turns out that the distinction between the two lies in how their seeds are formed on the tree. Softwoods, such as pines, spruce, and fir, are examples of gymnosperms, plants that produce seeds without a covering. John A. Pitcher, director of the Hardwood Research Council, told *Imponderables* that if you pull one of the center scales back away from the stem of a fresh pine cone, you'll see a pair of seeds lying side by side. "They have no covering except the wooden cone."

Hardwoods are a type of angiosperm, a true flowering plant that bears seeds enclosed in capsules, fruits, or husks (e.g., olives, lilies, walnuts). Hardwoods also tend to lose their leaves in temperate climates, whereas softwoods are evergreens; but in tropical climates, many hardwoods retain their leaves.

While it is true that there is a tendency for softwoods to be softer in consistency (and easier to cut for commercial purposes), and for hardwoods to be more compact, and thus tougher and denser in texture, these rules of thumb are not reliable. Pitcher enclosed a booklet listing the specific gravities of the important commercial woods in the U.S. He indicates the irony:

> At 0.16 specific gravity, balsa is the lightest wood listed. At a specific gravity of 1.05, lignumvitae is the heaviest wood known. Both are hardwoods.

DAVID FELDMAN

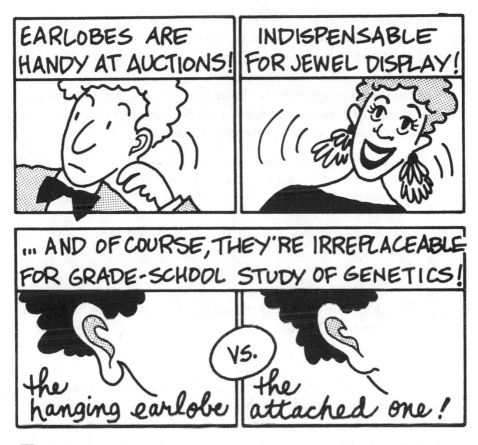

DO Earlobes Serve Any Particular or Discernible Function?

Our authorities answered as one: Yes, earlobes do serve a particular function. They are an ideal place to hang earrings.

Oh sure, there are theories. Ear, nose, and throat specialist Dr. Ben Jenkins of Kingsland, Georgia, remembers reading about a speculation that when our predecessors walked on four feet, our earlobes were larger "and that they fell in[ward] to protect the ear canal." Biologist John F. Hertner recounts another anthropological theory: that earlobes served as "an ornament of interest in sexual selection."

Doctors and biologists we confront with questions like these about seemingly unimportant anatomical features are quick to

DO PENGUINS HAVE KNEES?

shrug their shoulders. They are quite comfortable with the notion that not every organ in our body is essential to our well-being and not every obsolete feature of our anatomy is eliminated as soon as it becomes unnecessary.

Actually, the opposite is closer to the truth. Anatomical features of earlier humankind tend to stick around unless they are an obvious detriment. As Professor Hertner puts it,

> Nature tends to conserve genetic information unless there is selection pressure against a particular feature. Our bodies serve in some respect as museums of our evolutionary heritage.

Submitted by Dianne Love of Seaside Park, New Jersey.

Why Does Butter Get Darker and Harder in the Refrigerator After It Is Opened?

Butter discolors for the same reason that apples or bananas turn dark—oxidation. And although butter doesn't have a peel to protect it from the ravages of air, it does have a snug wrapper surrounding it until it is first used by the consumer. Only after the wrapper is eliminated or loosened does the butter darken.

Why does it get harder? The cold temperature in the refrigerator causes the moisture in the butter to evaporate. Many other foods, such as peanut butter and onion dip, become less plastic when refrigerated because of evaporation of liquid.

Submitted by Mitchell Hofing of New York, New York.

Why Are Dance Studios Usually Located on the Second Floor of Buildings?

Truth be told, the quality of Imponderables we receive on call-in talk shows is usually distinctly inferior to the stuff in our mailbag. But Los Angeles talk-show host Carol Hemingway has an imaginative gang of listeners, and this question was posed to us on her gabfest.

We loved it. This was an Imponderable deeply embedded in our subconscious. We have traveled through small towns with only one two-story commercial building in them. If there was a dance studio in town, it was located in that building. On the second floor.

We recently saw film critic Roger Ebert wax nostalgic about his first date. He asked his friend to a dance at Thelma Lee Ritter's studio in Urbana, Illinois. Unfortunately, the dance was canceled. But not all was lost—Ms. Ritter's second-floor studio was located above the Princess Theater. So Roger and his date went to the movies.

In New York, dance studios are invariably on the second floor as well. Not on the twenty-seventh floor. The second.

The best explanation we could figure out is that rents must obviously be cheaper on higher floors. Dance studios presumably have little walk-in, impulse business. Even folks with happy feet are unlikely, on the spur of the moment, to decide they instantly must have tango lessons. All of our sources indicated that these factors were crucial, but other considerations were important, too.

We heard from Connie Townsend, national secretary of the United States Amateur Ballroom Dancers Association in Baltimore, Maryland, who "reviewed the many studios with which I am familiar and was somewhat surprised to find that, indeed, most are located on second floors." Townsend notes that all the exceptions she could think of were built specifically as dance studios by their owners.

Frank Kiley, a former ballroom dance instructor and former licensee of 1,800 ballrooms nationwide, provides a historical perspective and an architectural answer:

> Previous to 1980, most studio-type ballrooms had to have twelve-foot ceilings to position loudspeakers for maximum effect. Some studios had fourteen- or eighteen-foot-high ceilings for best audio results . . .
>
> Most second-floor buildings in major cities had to use special curtains to subdivide ballroom classes and higher floors tended to have larger windows and smaller pillars in their structural design.

Kiley's reasons were echoed by Vickie Sheer, executive director of the Dance Educators of America, but she added several others as well:

> When I taught for thirty-seven years, my studios were always located on the second floor. My reason was to deter anyone from coming in from street level. If people climbed a flight of stairs, there must be [genuine] interest. Also, the second-floor placement kept out annoying children opening and closing doors and being pests.

In winter, the heat in a building goes up and the cold air does not blow in, as on street level. Usually there is more square footage on a second-floor than a street-level . . .

Kiley, still a major copyright owner in the ballroom industry, notes that dance studios are invading shopping malls, where many have landed on the ground floor.

Submitted by a caller on the Carol Hemingway show, KGIL-AM, Los Angeles, California.

Why Are 25-Watt Light Bulbs More Expensive Than 40-, 60-, 75-, and 100-Watt Bulbs?

The old rule of supply and demand takes effect here. You don't always get what you pay for. Richard H. Dowhan, manager of public affairs for GTE, explains:

> The higher-wattage, 40-, 60-, 75-, and 100-watt light bulbs are manufactured in huge quantity because they are in demand by consumers. The 25-watt light bulb has limited uses, therefore fewer bulbs are manufactured and you don't get the inherent cost advantage of large productions runs.
>
> Secondly, in order to make it worthwhile for the retailer to stock a slow mover, which takes up shelf and storage space for longer periods of time, you increase the profit margin. These two factors result in a higher price.

Submitted by Alan Snyder of Palo Alto, California.

Why Are Water Towers Built So High?

We have passed through small towns and cities where the water tower is by far the highest structure in sight. The name of the city is often emblazoned around the surface of the mighty edifice.

But why are the water towers necessary anyway when most communities have reservoirs? And why are they so tall?

We got our answer from Dr. Paul J. Godfrey, director of the Water Resources Center at the University of Massachusetts at Amherst:

> The task of providing water through a municipal distribution system requires both sufficient volume to meet normal consumption, emergency consumption (such as for fighting major fires), and sufficient pressure to operate household and industrial devices.
>
> The water tower provides, by its volume, a reservoir that can meet short-term needs during periods of high water use, usually in the morning and around dinner time, and allows the various sources of supply, reservoirs, or wells, to catch up during lower demand. The volume chosen for a facility usually assumes that a sufficient volume must be available to meet simultaneous demand during the high consumption period and a major fire. All of these functions do not require a particular water height.
>
> But water pressure is provided by the height of the tower. Water seeks its own level. For example, if we fill a water hose with water and hold each end of the hose at exactly the same level, no water flows out. But if one end of the hose is raised, water flows out of the other end. . . . The more water, and hence weight, above the lower end, the greater the force of water flowing out of the hose. The role of the water tower is to provide an elevated weight of water sufficient to provide adequate pressure at all outlets in the system.

The alternative would be to install electrical pumps to force water out of other reservoirs, but this is an inefficient technology. As Peter Black, president of the American Water Resources, told *Imponderables*, with a pump system "You would have to activate the pump every time anybody wanted any water."

The water tower may be lower tech than an electrical pump, but with the precautions outlined by Dr. Godfrey, it does the job well over any terrain:

DAVID FELDMAN

To create adequate pressure for all parts of a municipality, the water tower must be higher than all the municipality's water taps, sufficiently high to create fire-fighting pressure at all hydrants. In some cities, the municipal supply does not provide enough pressure for tall buildings, so booster pumps and another storage tank on top of the building supplements pressure. [In New York and other big cities, standpipes are placed in front of tall buildings to insure that water can be delivered to the top of the building.]

Water pressure in all areas of the municipality must be carefully controlled. Low pressure will be dangerous in a serious fire and will produce complaints from those who like brisk showers. High pressure will wear out valves and gaskets faster and cause excessive system leakage. Towns with high hills will often have squat water tanks on the highest hill and install pressure regulators to reduce pressure in the valleys. Towns with no hills must compensate by building an artificial hill, the water tower, which is higher than the tallest building.

So those water towers aren't so high just to serve as a monument to the ego of the mayor. The tall water tower ends up saving energy and money. But as Jay H. Lehr, executive director of the Association of Ground Water, explains, even our hero, the water tower, isn't perfect: "Of course, there is no free lunch, as electrical energy is used in pumping the water into the storage tower in the first place."

Submitted by Cheri Klimes of Cedar Rapids, Iowa. Thanks also to George Armbruster of Greenbelt, Maryland; Gary Moore of Denton, Texas; and Jason and Bobby Nystrom of Destrehan, Louisiana.

Why Are Some Watermelon Seeds White and Some Black?

Most of you probably think all watermelons contain black and white seeds. It's time for some serious consciousness raising. And Gary W. Elmstrom, professor of horticulture at the Institute of Food and Agricultural Sciences at the University of Florida, is just the man to do it:

> Different varieties of watermelons have an array of different-colored seeds. Color of mature seed can vary from almost white to black depending upon variety. A watermelon variety named "Congo" has white seeds and "Jubilee" has black seeds. There are also genes for red-colored seeds in watermelons such as in a variety called red-seeded citron. . . . Seed color in watermelons is genetically determined, just as eye color is in humans.

So is one melon bearing both white and black seeds the equivalent of a human with one blue eye and one brown eye? Not quite. Professor Elmstrom explains: "Just as blue-eyed babies turn into brown-eyed children, so do white seeds, barring pollination or fertility problems, end up as black ones."

Submitted by John K. Aldrich of Littleton, Colorado. Thanks also to J. R. Shepard of Plantation, Florida.

What Is the Purpose of the Holes Near the End of Electric Plug Prongs?

Most of our hardware sources knew the answer to this Imponderable, which, judging by our mail, is high in the consciousness of the *spiritus mundi*. Ed Juge, director of market planning for Radio Shack, provided a succinct answer:

The holes near the ends of AC plug prongs are there to mate with spring-loaded pins found in some of the better wall sockets, to help make a good connection, and to keep the plug from falling out of the socket.

Submitted by Venia Stanley of Albuquerque, New Mexico. Thanks also to William C. Stone of Dallas, Texas; George A. Springer of San Jose, California; Barry Cohen of Thousand Oaks, California; Jesse D. Maxenchs of Sunnyvale, California; and Rory Sellers of Carmel, California.

Why Do Paper Mills Smell So Bad?

Rose Marie Kenny, of Hammermill Papers, properly chided us for posing the wrong Imponderable. Paper mills *don't* generate offensive odors, she reminded us. Pulp mills do.

You're right, Ms. Kenny. Excuse us if we were too busy holding our noses to notice that rotten eggs were emanating from a pulp mill, not a producer of finished paper products.

We asked Stephen Smulski, a professor of wood science and technology at the University of Massachusetts at Amherst, to explain how lovely-scented trees turn into foul-smelling pulp:

> Paper is a thin sheet of tangled wood fibers, each of which is like a long, hollow straw with tapering, closed ends, and about ½ inch in length. In the standing tree, wood fibers, which consist mainly of cellulose, are held together by and embedded in an adhesive-like material called lignin.
>
> In order to isolate the individual wood fibers needed for making paper, chips of solid wood are treated with chemicals that

DAVID FELDMAN

selectively dissolve only lignin in a process called pulping. Of the several wood pulping processes, only the kraft sulfate process emits the rotten cabbage smell associated with pulp mills.

In this process, sodium hydroxide (NaOH) and sodium sulfide (Na_2S) are used to dissolve lignin. Though these chemicals are recovered and reused in a closed cycle, and the gases vented from the process scrubbed clean with state-of-the-art pollution control technology, tiny amounts of sulfur still escape into the air.

Unfortunately for all of us, not least the citizens of the towns in which the pulp mill is located, you don't need to be a dog to sniff out the scent of sulfur compounds. Doug Matyka, a public relations manager at Georgia-Pacific's Tissue, Pulp and Bleached Board division, told *Imponderables* these chemicals are "readily noticeable even at levels far below one part per million."

But if a paper company decides to locate a plant in your town, don't despair before you ferret out a few facts. Not all paper plants make their own pulp; many buy their pulp from a pulpmaking facility or from a free-standing mill that makes only pulp.

Also, many papermaking methods don't require these sulfur compounds. The olfactory culprit is the kraft-pulping process ("kraft" derives from the German term meaning "strong"). Kraft paper is best known for making supermarket shopping bags and corrugated cardboard boxes. If the other pulping processes were capable of producing the strength performance of kraft paper at a decent price, don't you think that companies would employ them? After all, even executives of paper companies have to smell the stuff, too.

Lest we seem to be picking on the pulp industry, a few fun facts from our paper sources will help you understand their dilemma:

1. You can't make paper without pulp. According to Kenny, 80 percent of a sheet of paper is made out of pulp.

2. High-tech scrubbers have diminished the odor problem considerably. And more than many other industries, pulp mills conform to EPA air and water pollution standards. The smell of sulfur compounds is more offensive than dangerous.

3. Many other things besides pulp mills produce the smell. Doug Matyka notes that exhaust from vehicles with catalytic converters sometimes smells like mini-pulp mills. And the same smell occurs during natural organic decay. After all, Doug reminds us, the original descriptive phrase "you smell like a rotten egg" comes not from pulp mills but rotten eggs.

Yeah, sure, but it's more fun to pick on heavy industry than a chicken.

Submitted by Barry Long of Alexandria, Virginia.

HOW Are Lane Reflectors Fastened onto the Road So That They Aren't Moved or Crushed?

Most of us, on occasion, have accidentally run over a lane reflector. The little bump is always upsetting. Have we moved the reflector? Have we hurt the reflector? Have we hurt our tires?

Don't worry too much about the reflectors, for you are unlikely to dislodge them. A two-part epoxy cement is used to fasten them to the road surface.

But the nasty little secret of the reflectors' durability is that they are recessed into the road surface to prevent movement and designed in the shape of a two-sided ramp to avoid getting crushed. George E. Jones, highway engineer at the National Highway Institute, told *Imponderables* that

> if you will look closely you will notice a groove about a foot long cut at a downward sloping angle in the pavement. The reflector is then cemented flush with the pavement surface.

Well, not quite flush, and for a good reason. Amy Steiner of the American Association of State Highway and Transportation Officials explains:

DAVID FELDMAN

. . . they do protrude slightly so that they can catch the light emitted from the headlights. Because of this protrusion, they do sustain damage from vehicles driving over them (particularly from snowplow blades). Reflectors require a fair amount of maintenance.

As for your tires, our authorities agree they are safe even if you hit twenty reflectors on the center line of the road. Just make sure you stay in your lane, or more than your tires are in jeopardy.

Submitted by Eric Hartman of Spring Grove, Pennsylvania.

Why Does Nabisco Put the Tiny Picture of Niagara Falls on Its Shredded Wheat Box?

At the beginning of the twentieth century, shredded wheat biscuits were produced at The Palace of Light, a ten-acre site bordering Niagara Falls, New York. According to Michael Falkowitz, director of industry and trade relations for Nabisco Brands, The Palace of Light itself became a tourist mecca and served as the marketing image for the Shredded Wheat Company:

> The plant was decked out in marble tile and glass, and was air conditioned. It was visited by more than one hundred thousand wide-eyed tourists every year. The great falls gave meaning to what was billed as "the cleanliest" product—Shredded Wheat (and Triscuit)—produced in the cleanliest food factory.

DAVID FELDMAN

When the Nabisco Biscuit Company acquired the Shredded Wheat Company in 1928, it didn't mess with packaging that was working just fine. It did mess with The Palace of Light, though. No longer state-of-the-art, the Niagara Falls plant was abandoned by Nabisco before World War II.

Submitted by Sister Anne Joan of Boston, Massachusetts.

Why Do Automobile Batteries Have to Be So Heavy? Why Can't They Be Miniaturized?

Of course, most consumers would prefer car batteries to be AA-size. If a car stalled, a driver could just reach into the glove compartment and pull out a little battery that had been recharged at home.

Automobile manufacturers also want to downsize batteries. Any heavy material, whether it is the steel in the body of a car or the engine and cylinders, interferes with achieving better gasoline mileage.

Battery manufacturers have responded. In some cases batteries are half the size they were twenty years ago. But alas, don't look forward to AA-sized car batteries in the foreseeable future. As Stephen Bomer of the Automotive Battery Charger Manufacturers wrote to *Imponderables*, high-density lead plates are a major component of a battery: "No substitute for lead has been found that can do the job or generate the voltage required."

H. Dale Millay, a staff research engineer for Shell Oil, told *Imponderables* that the greater the surface area of lead in the battery, the easier it is to generate power. Millay claims that we have already paid the price for downsizing batteries: Although modern batteries are good at cold starts, they have low reserve capacities. Translation: They don't last as long as they might under strain.

DO PENGUINS HAVE KNEES?   405

We received our most emphatic endorsement of the heavy battery from John J. Surrette, vice-president of Rolls Battery Engineering:

> The thinner you make the plates in a battery, the lesser the material inside. . . . The heavier the material, the more rugged the batteries are and the longer they will last. When you use thinner plates . . . this lessens the amount of ampere hour capacity. When heavier material is used, like we do in marine and industrial applications, it results in considerably longer life and less exposure [to the elements], which reduces the chance of plates buckling in hard service or the active material shedding from the positive grids.
>   . . . Miniaturized batteries would probably be preferable but would stand little or no abuse or neglect.

Rolls's marketing strategy is to emphasize the *heaviness* of its battery. It boasts a marine battery with ⅛″-thick positive plates (in contrast, some car batteries have plates as thin as .055 inches, which Surrette believes is too fragile to withstand abuse or neglect).

So, Becky, the car battery is one case where you *don't* want to get the lead out.

Submitted by Becky Brown of Iowa City, Iowa.

DAVID FELDMAN

Why Do Automatic Icemakers in Home Freezers Make Crescent-Shaped Pieces Rather Than Cubes?

We cannot be dispassionate about this subject. We hate crescent-shaped cubes. They are so long they get stuck in iced-tea glasses, making it impossible to load enough ice to cool the drink sufficiently. Even in wider glasses, they are too ungainly to stack. And they are too big to pop into one's mouth comfortably.

We contacted the company that pioneered the automatic icemaker for home freezers, the Whirlpool Corporation, and prepared for a battle. What excuse would it trot out to justify banishing the ice cube to oblivion?

Much to our surprise, the manager of Whirlpool's appliance information service, Carolyn Verweyst, disarmed us with her compassion and empathy. She, too, dislikes the crescent-shaped cubes, if only because they make her job harder: She says that Whirlpool gets more complaints about the shape of the ice than anything else about their refrigerator-freezers.

Verweyst and our other appliance sources confirm that there is only one reason why these cubes are crescent-shaped: Any other shape tends to stick to the mold instead of releasing to the ice bin. When first developing the automatic icemaker, Whirlpool experimented with many different shapes but found that any ice with straight edges simply would not release properly.

In fact, Verweyst says that Whirlpool gave an outside think tank a project to come up with a perfect shape for ice molded by an automatic icemaker. Its conclusion: The best shape was a crescent.

Submitted by Emily Sanders and Elizabeth Gaines of Montgomery, Alabama.

What Are Those Computer Scrawls (Similar to Universal Product Codes) Found on the Bottom Right of Envelopes? How Do They Work?

You'd better get used to those scrawls. If the United States Postal Service reaches its goal, every single letter and package sent through them will have bar codes by the year 1995.

The series of vertical lines on the lower-right portion of first-class envelopes is meant for the "eyes" of OCRs, high-speed optical character readers. The Postal Service calls this specific bar code configuration POSTNET, short for Postal Numeric Encoding Technique.

OCRs are now capable of "reading" typewritten or hand-printed addresses and spraying bar codes on an envelope. The bar code readers are considerably less sophisticated and less expensive machines than OCRs (or for that matter, much less expensive than hiring humans over the long haul). By automating the sorting process, the postal service speeds mail delivery and saves more than a buck or two at the same time.

Can a human being interpret the code sprayed by the OCRs? Absolutely, although it's a little tricky. If you look carefully, you will see that all the bars are two heights—either full bars or half-sized. The tall bars represent (binary) ones; the short bars represent (binary) zeros. The bars on the far left and far right, always full bars, are not part of the code, and are there merely to frame the other numbers.

DAVID FELDMAN

All the rest of the bars and half-bars are arranged in groups of five. Each group of five bars represents one of the ZIP code digits, and all numbers are always expressed by two full bars and three half-bars. You can figure out which number the bars represent by noting which of the five positions contain full bars. Here is the code (remember, one equals a full bar; zero equals a half bar):

11000 = 0	01010 = 5
00011 = 1	01100 = 6
00101 = 2	10001 = 7
00110 = 3	10010 = 8
01001 = 4	10100 = 9

These ten combinations can express all possible ZIP codes.

The bar code readers, working from left to right, add the values of the two full bars for each group of five to arrive at the proper ZIP code. Each of the five bar codes always has the same numerical assignment. From left to right, they are 7, 4, 2, 1, and 0. So if one of the digits of the ZIP code is 7, it will be expressed by making the first bar (7) and fifth (0) bar code full. If you add 7 and 0, you get seven (we hope). To express the number 6, the second (4) and third (2) bars in the group would be full height.

Got it? Good, because we have one more feature to confuse you with. After the nine- or five-digit code is sprayed, one other group of five bars is added to the right of the last ZIP code digit —the "correction character." To arrive at this number, add all the digits in the ZIP code. The *Imponderables* post office box, for example, is in the 90024 ZIP area. By adding all the individual digits in the ZIP code, we arrive at the sum of fifteen. To calculate the proper correction character, the bar code reader subtracts this sum from the next highest multiple of ten—in this case, 20. (If the sum were 38, it would be subtracted from 40.) The remainder, five, is expressed as any other five would be in the POSTNET system—with the second and fourth bar being full height.

What is truly remarkable about the POSTNET system is how fast the OCRs can operate, and how they are capable of converting five-digit ZIP codes into the nine-digit ones that the postal system prefers. Reader Harold E. Blake, an expert on OCRs whose expertise was invaluable in writing this entry, summarizes how our letter was processed and sent along its merry way to him in the mellifluously named town of Zephyrhills, Florida:

> This letter went through an OCR at the rate of nine per second. In about one-ninth of a second, the face of the letter was read and reassembled in a computer register. A multimegabyte memory was searched (sort of like an electronic ZIP code directory for the United States) and my post office box number was verified to be identical to the four in the ZIP + 4 (this is not always the case with box numbers). The 33539 was matched with Zephyrhills as a valid association. Then, a signal went from the computer to an A.B. Dick bar code printer, and "spriff," several hundred ink dots got sprayed on this letter as it moved along faster than the eye could track it.
>
> All in 110 milliseconds.

POSTNET codes are now commonly preprinted on business reply and courtesy reply envelopes by mass mailers so that the mail will bypass OCRs altogether and go directly to a bar code sorter. The chance of a misdirected letter is greatly reduced. It might not matter anymore if you "accidentally" put the insert of your utility bill upside-down so that no print shows through the address window. That bar code emblazoned on the return envelope is telling a bar code sorter the nine-digit ZIP code of the utility; chances are, the bill will arrive at its intended destination. Ain't progress grand?

Submitted by George Persico of Thiells, New York. Thanks also to Tom Emig of St. Charles, Missouri; Cynthia J. Gould of Fairhaven, Massachusetts; Harold Fair of Bellwood, Illinois; Bob Peterson, United States Air Force, APO New York; William J. Feole, Alameda, California; Millicent Brinkman of Thornwood, New York; Kristina Castillo of Williamsville, New York; Herman London of Poughkeepsie, New York; Debbie DiAntonio of Malvern, Pennsylvania; and many others.

DAVID FELDMAN

If Water Is Composed of Two Parts Hydrogen and One Part Oxygen, Both Common Elements, Why Can't Droughts Be Eliminated by Combining the Two to Produce Water?

We could produce water by combining oxygen and hydrogen, but at quite a cost financially and, in some cases, environmentally.

Brian Bigley, senior chemist for Systech Environmental Corporation, says that most methods for creating water are impractical merely because "you would need massive amounts of hydrogen and oxygen to produce even a small quantity of water, and amassing each would be expensive." Add to this the cost, of course, the labor and equipment necessary to run a "water plant."

Bigley suggests another possible alternative would be to obtain water as a byproduct of burning methane in an oxygen atmosphere:

Again, it's a terrible waste of energy. Methane is a wonderful fuel, and is better used as such, rather than using our supply to produce H_2O. It would be like giving dollar bills to people for a penny to be used as facial tissue.

The most likely long-term solution to droughts is desalinization. We already have the technology to turn ocean water into drinking water, but it is too expensive now to be commercially feasible. Only when we see water as a valuable and limited natural resource, like oil or gold, are we likely to press on with large-scale desalinization plants. In northern Africa, water for crops, animals, and drinking is not taken for granted.

Submitted by Bill Irvin III of Fremont, California.

Why Does Your Voice Sound Higher and Funny When You Ingest Helium?

The kiddie equivalent of the drunken partygoer putting a lampshade on his head is ingesting helium and speaking like a chipmunk with a caffeine problem. When we saw *L.A. Law*'s stolid Michael Kuzak playing this prank, we were supposed to be smitten with his puckish, fun-loving, childlike side. We were not convinced.

Still, many *Imponderables* readers want to know the answer to this question, so we contacted several chemists and physicists. They replied with unanimity. Perhaps the most complete explanation came from George B. Kauffman:

> Sound is the sensation produced by stimulation of the organs of hearing by vibrations transmitted through the air or other mediums. Low-frequency sound is heard as low pitch and higher frequencies as correspondingly higher pitch. The frequency (pitch) of sound depends on the density of the medium through which the vibrations are transmitted; the less dense the medium,

the greater the rate (frequency) of vibration, and hence, the higher the pitch of the sound.

The densities of gases are directly proportional to their molecular weights. Because the density of helium (mol. wt. 4) is much less than that of air, a mixture of about 78 percent nitrogen (mol. wt. 28) and about 20 percent oxygen (mol. wt. 32), the vocal cords vibrate much faster (at a higher frequency) in helium than in air, and therefore the voice is perceived as having a higher pitch.

The effect is more readily perceived with male voices, which have a lower pitch than female voices. The pitch of the voice [can] be lowered by inhaling a member of the noble (inert) gas family (to which helium belongs) that is heavier than air, such as xenon (mol. wt. 131.29). . . .

Brian Bigley, a chemist at Systech Environmental Corporation, told *Imponderables* that helium mixtures are used to treat asthma and other types of respiratory ailments. Patients with breathing problems can process a helium mixture more easily than normal air, and the muscles of the lungs don't have to work as hard as they do to inhale the same volume of oxygen.

Submitted by Jim Albert of Cary, North Carolina. Thanks also to James Wheaton of Plattsburg AFB, New York; Nancy Sampson of West Milford, New Jersey; Karen Riddick of Dresden, Tennessee; Loren A. Larson of Altamonte Springs, Florida; and Teresa Bankhead of Culpepper, Virginia.

Why Is the French Horn Designed for Left-Handers?

We hope that this Imponderable wasn't submitted by two left-handers who learned the instrument because they were inspired by the idea that an instrument was finally designed specifically for them. If so, Messrs. Corcoran and Zitzman are in for a rude awakening.

If we have learned anything in our years toiling in the mine-fields of Imponderability, it is that *nothing* is designed for left-handers except products created exclusively for lefties that cost twice as much as right- (in both senses of the word) handed products.

In case the premise of the Imponderable is confusing, the French horn is the brass wind instrument with a coiled tube—it looks a little like a brass circle with plumbing in the middle and a flaring bell connected to it. The player sticks his or her right hand into the bell itself and hits the three valves with the left hand. So the question before the house is: Why isn't the process reversed, with the difficult fingering done by the right hand?

You've probably figured it out already. The original instrument had no valves. Dr. Kristin Thelander, professor of music at the University of Iowa School of Music and a member of the International Horn Society, elaborates:

> In the period 1750–1840, horns had no valves, so the playing technique was entirely different from our modern technique. The instruments were built with interchangeable crooks which placed the horn in the appropriate key for the music being played, and pitches lying outside of the natural harmonic series were obtained by varying degrees of hand stopping in the bell of the horn.
>
> It was the right hand which did this manipulation in the bell of the horn, probably because the majority of people are right-handed [another theory is that earlier hunting horns were designed to be blown while on horseback. The rider would hold the instrument with the left hand and hold the reins with the right hand].
>
> Even when the valves were added to the instrument, a lot of

DAVID FELDMAN

hand technique was still used, so the valves were added to the left-hand side.

On the modern French horn, this hand technique is no longer necessary. But so many generations grew up with the old configuration that the hand position remains the same. Inertia triumphs again, even though it would probably make sense for right-handers to use their right hands on the valves. But fair is fair: Lefties have had to contend with all the rest of the right-dominant instruments for centuries.

Most of our sources took us to task for referring to the instrument as the "French horn." In a rare case of our language actually getting simpler, the members of the International Horn Society voted in 1971 to change the name of the instrument from the "French Horn" to the "horn."

Why? Because the creators of the instrument never referred to it as the "French horn," any more than French diners order "French" dressing on their salads or "French" fries with their steak. As we mentioned earlier, the horn was the direct descendant of the hunting horn, which was very popular in France during the sixteenth and seventeenth centuries. The English, the same folks who screwed us up with the *cor anglais* or English horn started referring to the instrument as the "French horn" as early as the late seventeenth century, and the name stuck. Americans, proper lemmings, followed the English misnomer.

Submitted by Edward Corcoran of South Windsor, Connecticut. Thanks also to Manfred S. Zitzman of Wyomissing, Pennsylvania.

Why Do Milk Cartons Indicate "Open Other End" on One Side of the Spout and "To Open" on the Other When Both Sides Look Identical?

In our first book, *Imponderables*, we discussed why milk cartons are so difficult to open and close. To make a long story short, the answer: The current milk carton is extremely cheap to manufacture, and customers don't complain about the problem enough to motivate milk suppliers to change the packaging.

But three readers have written recently to ask about another milk carton conundrum that has always perplexed us. The top of the milk carton looks so symmetrical, it hardly *seems* to matter where you form the spout.

Alas, it does matter. Milk companies buy the paperboard for milk cartons unformed. Machines at the milk distributor form the paperboard into the familiar carton shape, seal the bottoms, fill the cartons with milk, and then seal the top. Bruce V. Snow, recently retired from the Dairylea Cooperative, explains:

> The machine is adjusted so that only one side of the gable (the "open this side" end) is sealed; when you pull the gable sides, the spout is exposed and opens. If you pull back the gable sides on the other end of the top, then squeeze the sides, nothing happens. The gable on that side stays sealed.

Why does it stay sealed? The secret, according to Dellwood dairy's Barbara Begany, is an ingredient called abhesive, "applied to the 'pour spout,' which makes it easier to open. Abhesive also prevents solid bonding of paper to paper as occurs on the 'open other end' side."

Submitted by Grayce Sine of Chico, California. Thanks also to Alice Conway of Highwood, Illinois, and Jeffrey Chavez of Torrance, California.

DAVID FELDMAN

Why Do We Feel Warm or Hot When We Blush?

We blush—usually due to an emotional response such as embarrassment (we, for example, often blush after reading a passage from our books)—because the blood vessels in the skin have dilated. More blood flows to the surface of the body, where the affected areas turn red.

We tend to associate blushing with the face, but blood is sent to the neck and upper torso as well. According to John Hertner, professor of biology at Nebraska's Kearney State College,

> This increased flow carries body core heat to the surface, where it is perceived by the nerve receptors. In reality, though, the warmth is perceived by the brain in response to the information supplied by the receptors located in the skin.

Because of the link between the receptors and the brain, we feel warmth precisely where our skin turns red.

Submitted by Steve Tilki of Derby, Connecticut.

During a Hernia Exam, Why Does the Physician Say, "Turn Your Head and Cough"? Why is the Cough Necessary? Is the Head Turn Necessary?

Although a doctor may ask you to cough when listening to your lungs, the dreaded "Turn your head and cough" is heard when the physician is checking for hernias, weaknesses or gaps in the structure of what should be a firm body wall.

According to Dr. Frank Davidoff, of the American College of Physicians, these gaps are most frequently found in the inguinal area in men, "the area where the tube (duct) that connects each testicle to the structures inside the body passes through the body wall." Some men are born with fairly large gaps to begin with. The danger, Davidoff says, is that

> Repeated increases in the pressure inside the abdomen, as from repeated and chronic coughing, lifting heavy weights, etc., can push abdominal contents into the gap, stretching a slightly enlarged opening into an even bigger one, and leading ultimately to a permanent bulge in contents out through the hernia opening.
>
> Inguinal hernias are obvious and can be disfiguring when they are large and contain a sizable amount of abdominal contents, such as pads of fat or loops of intestine. However, hernias are actually more dangerous when they are small, because a loop of bowel is likely to get pinched, hence obstructed, if caught in a small hernia opening, while a large hernia opening tends to allow a loop of bowel to slide freely in and out of the hernia "sac" without getting caught or twisted.
>
> Doctors are therefore particularly concerned about detecting inguinal hernias when they are small, exactly the situation in

which they have not been obvious to the patient. A small inguinal hernia may not bulge at all when the pressure inside the abdomen is normal. Most small hernias would go undetected unless the patient increased the pressure inside the abdomen, thus causing the hernia sac to bulge outward, where it can be felt by the doctor's examining finger pushed up into the scrotum.

And the fastest, simplest way for the patient to increase the intra-abdominal pressure is to cough, since coughing pushes up the diaphragm, squeezes the lungs, and forces air out past the vocal cords. By forcing all the abdominal muscles to contract together, coughing creates the necessary increase in pressure.

If the physician can't feel a bulge beneath the examining finger during the cough, he or she assumes the patient is hernia-free.

And why do you have to turn your head when coughing? Dr. E. Wilson Griffin III, a family physician at the Jonesville Family Medical Center, in Jonesville, North Carolina, provided the most concise answer: "So that the patient doesn't cough his yucky germs all over the doctor."

Submitted by Jeffrey Chavez of Torrance, California. Thanks also to J. S. Hubar of Pittsburgh, Pennsylvania.

Why Is the "R" Trademark Symbol on Pepsi Labels Placed After the Second "P" in "Pepsi" Rather Than After the Words "Pepsi" or "Cola"?

We spoke to Chris Jones, Pepsi's charming manager of public affairs, who is by now used to our less than earth-shatteringly important questions. She told us that, legally speaking, the company could have put the registered mark wherever it wanted to.

But the company wanted to place the mark in the "Pepsi" rather than the "Cola." It seems that Pepsi has a competitor in the cola wars—its name escapes us at the moment—so they wanted to draw attention to the "P-word" rather than the "C-word."

DO PENGUINS HAVE KNEES?

Jones says that graphic designers felt that the mark after the second "p" looked better than placing it after the "i" in Pepsi: It made the design more symmetrical and didn't butt up against the hyphen after Pepsi.

Submitted by Tom Cunnifer of Greeley, Colorado.

Why Do Magazine and Newspaper Editors Force You to Skip Pages to Continue an Article at the Back of the Magazine/Newspaper?

We answered the question of why page numbers are missing from magazines in *Why Do Dogs Have Wet Noses?*. Now, from our correspondent Karin Norris: "It has always annoyed me to have to hold my place and search for the remainder of the article, hoping the page numbers will be there."

We hear you, Karin. In fact, one of the great pleasures of reading *The New Yorker* is the certainty that there will be no such jumps. We had always assumed that the purpose of jumps was to force you to go to the back of the book, thus making advertisements in nonprime areas of the paper or magazine more appealing to potential clients. Chats with publishers in both the newspaper and magazine field have convinced us that other factors are more important.

A newspaper's front page is crucial to newsstand sales. Editors want readers to feel that if they scan the front page, they can get a sense of the truly important stories of the day. If there were no jumps in newspapers, articles would have to be radically shortened or else the number of stories on the front page would have to be drastically curtailed.

Less obviously, magazine editors want what Robert E. Kenyon, Jr., executive director of the American Society of Magazine Editors, calls "a well-defined central section." Let's face it. Most magazines and newspapers are filled with ads, but with the pos-

DAVID FELDMAN

sible exception of fashion and hobbyist magazines, readers are usually far more interested in articles. Magazine editors want to concentrate their top editorial features in one section to give at least the impression that the magazine exists as a vehicle for information rather than advertising. J. J. Hanson, chairman and CEO of The Hanson Publishing Group, argues that sometimes jumps are necessary:

> An article that the editor feels is too long to position entirely in a prime location will jump to the back of the book, thus permitting the editor to insert another important feature within the main feature or news "well." Many publishers try very hard to avoid jumps.
>
> The unhappiest version of a jump is one where an article jumps more than once so that instead of completing the article after the first jump, the reader reads on for a while and then has to jump again. That's almost unforgivable.

Hanson adds that another common reason for jumps in magazines, as opposed to newspapers, is color imposition:

> Most magazines do not run four-color or even two-color throughout the entire issue. Often the editor wants to position the major art treatment of his features or news items within that four-color section. In order to get as many articles as possible in that section, the editor sometimes chooses to jump the remaining portions of the story to a black and white signature.

Of course, advertising does play more than a little role in the creation of jumps. Most publications will sell clients just about any size ad they want. If an advertiser wants an odd-sized ad, one that can't be combined with other ads to create a full page of ads, editorial content is needed. It is much easier to fill these holes with the back end of jumps than to create special features to fill space. *The New Yorker* plugs these gaps with illustrations and funny clippings sent in by readers, which, truth be told, may be read more assiduously than their five-part book-length treatments on the history of beets.

Submitted by Karin Norris of Salinas, California.

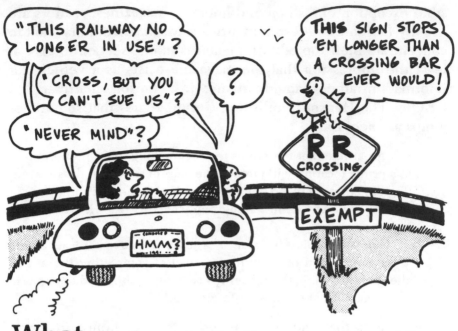

What Does the EXEMPT Sign Next to Some Railroad Crossing Signs Mean?

EXEMPT signs are not intended for drivers of private cars, but rather for drivers of passengers for hire, school buses carrying children, or vehicles carrying flammable or dangerous materials. Ordinarily, these vehicles must stop not more than fifty feet or less than fifteen feet from the tracks of a railroad crossing, and their drivers are supposed to listen for signs of an approaching train, look in each direction along the tracks, and then proceed only if it is apparent no train is near.

But an exception to this federal regulation is granted to

> an industrial or spur line railroad grade crossing marked with a sign reading "EXEMPT." Such EXEMPT signs shall be erected only by or with the consent of the appropriate state or local authority.

According to the signage bible, the *Manual on Uniform Traffic Control Devices*, an EXEMPT sign informs the relevant

DAVID FELDMAN

drivers that "a stop is not required at certain designated grade crossings, except when a train, locomotive, or other railroad equipment is approaching or occupying the crossing or the driver's view of the sign is blocked."

Robert L. Krick, of the Federal Railroad Administration, told *Imponderables* that some states do not permit the use of EXEMPT signs or may attach additional meanings to them. And Krick makes it clear that an EXEMPT sign does not relieve any driver from the responsibility of determining that no train is approaching before entering a crossing. Krick emphasizes the motto of the FRA's Operation Lifesaver: "Trains Can't Stop; You Can."

Submitted by Tisha Land of South Portland, Maine.

In *Why Do Clocks Run Clockwise?*, we answered a myriad of questions about M&Ms. What food product seems to mystify North America today? Bubble gum, evidently.

What Flavor Is Bubble Gum Supposed to Be?

"No particular flavor," said a representative from Bubble Yum about its "regular" flavor.

"Fruit flavor—sort of a tutti frutti," responded an executive from Topps.

We hadn't encountered so much secrecy about ingredients since we pried the identity of the fruit flavors in Juicy Fruit gum from the recalcitrant folks at Wrigley.

In *When Do Fish Sleep?*, we discussed how bubble gum was invented by Walter Diemer, a cost accountant with the Fleer Corporation. Bruce C. Wittmaier, a relative of Mr. Diemer's, was the only source who would reply to our bubble gum question. And luckily, Wittmaier obtained his information directly from

Mr. Diemer. The main flavors in the original bubble gum: wintergreen, vanilla, and cassia.

Submitted by John Geesy of Phoenix, Arizona.

What Makes Bubble Gum Blow Better Bubbles Than Regular Chewing Gum?

All chewing gums consist of gum base, some form of sugar (or sorbitol in sugarless gums), softeners, and flavoring. The key to producing good bubbles is the proper gum base. As a representative of Amurol Products Company put it, "Gum base is the part that puts the 'chew' in chewing gum and the 'bubble' into bubble gum." Until recently, the gum base consisted mostly of tree resin; now, most manufacturers use polyvinyl acetate, a synthetic resin.

In order to produce a substantial bubble, the gum must be strong enough to withstand the pressure of the tongue and the formation of an air pocket but also flexible enough to stretch evenly as it expands. The secret ingredient in bubble gum is a class of ingredients called "plasticizers," a synthetic gum base that stretches farther than plain resin. Plasticizers guarantee sufficient elasticity to insure that little kids can pop bubbles big enough to plaster pink crud all over their chins and eyes simultaneously.

Submitted by Karin Norris of Salinas, California.

Why Does Bazooka Joe Wear an Eye Patch?

Rest easily. Bazooka Joe has 20-20 vision and no eye deformity. But ever since he was introduced in 1953, Joe has donned an eye patch to give himself a little bit of that Hathaway Man panache.

And before you ask—Herman has always hidden behind his turtleneck, but he does have a perfectly functional neck.

Submitted by Christopher Valeri of East Northport, Rhode Island.

What Is the White Stuff on Baseball Card Bubble Gum and Why Is It There?

The white stuff is powdered sugar. And according to Bill O'Connor, of Topps, it is sprinkled on gum to keep it from sticking to other pieces of gum during the manufacturing process.

Both before and after "baseball" gum is cut to its final size, it is placed in stacks in a magazine. The powdered sugar prevents the pieces from clumping together. Bazooka brand gum, also made by Topps, doesn't need the powdered sugar because it isn't stacked in the same way.

Card gum contains less water than conventional bubble gum, but in humid conditions it absorbs moisture. The powdered sugar also prevents the wrapper from sticking to the gum on hot, sticky days.

Why Are Baseball Card Wrappers Covered with Wax?

Wax wrap allows the cards and gum to be sealed with heat, an economical, quick, and safe method to secure the integrity of the packaging. But most bubble gum manufacturers are switching to poly-wraps because new equipment is faster and poly creates a more airtight seal. Now that baseball cards can be worth as much as objets d'art, it seems appropriate that the waxy texture of the wrappers will be eradicated.

Submitted by Kim Chase of Crestline, California.

Why Do Some Binoculars Have an Adjustment Only for the Right Eyepiece?

Militant left-handers swear to us that we live in a right-handers' world. But their argument doesn't hold up too well when it comes to binoculars; this is one case where the lefties have priority over those right-dominant types.

Binoculars can be focused in two ways. The "individual focus binocular" provides diopter scales for each eyepiece and spiral-type adjustments so that you can fix each eyepiece.

But our Imponderable refers to the "central focusing system," which has a focusing wheel in between the barrels of the two eyepieces. According to Bill Shoenleber, of Edmund Scientific Co.,

> This model is equipped with an individual diopter focus on *one* of the eyepieces (usually the right one). The center focus is used

DAVID FELDMAN

until the image seen by the left eye is clear. Then the diopter adjustment is used to adjust the focus for the right eye. Once corrected for your own individual diopter difference between eyes, it is then necessary only to use the center focus itself to get equally clear images for both eyes.

Bushnell and many other companies do make binoculars with the individual focus on the left, but for unknown reasons this configuration has never sold as well.

Submitted by Owen Elliott of Juno Beach, Florida.

Why Do Scabs Always Itch So Much?

Scabs don't itch, Ruth. People do.

Honest. Scabs are just crusts of dried blood and fiber that cover a wound. It's the wound that itches.

In *Imponderables*, we discussed how the itching sensation is sent through the same neural pathways as pain signals. In fact, most scientists and doctors believe that, as dermatologist Jerome S. Litt describes it, "An itch is a minuscule pain." Litt explains why the wound itches:

> In the healing process, some of the nerve fibers that mediate both pain and itch become irritated and inflamed. This process leads to the small pain (itch) we encounter. . . . Were these scabs deeper, we would then experience frank pain.

What happens during the recovery period to irritate nerve fibers? Wounds repair themselves and shrink in size, partly because of the elasticity of the skin, but partly because the scab pulls on the wound.

Less frequently, itching can be caused by infections or small cracks in the scab as it dries. Dermatologist Samuel T. Selden, of Chesapeake, Virginia, treats wounds with moist dressings, allowing the wound to heal without scabbing, and reports that he has not heard any complaints from patients about itching.

Submitted by Ruth Gudz of Prescott, Arizona. Thanks also to Tricia Roland of St. Louis, Missouri.

What Is the Purpose of the Holes on the Sides of Men's Hats? Decoration? Ventilation? A Receptacle for Feathers? Or?

Clothing historian and writer G. Bruce Boyer is emphatic: "The holes in the sides of men's hats are specifically and exclusively for ventilation."

Every hat manufacturer we spoke to agreed with Mr. Boyer. Feathers are usually placed in the hat band, not the holes. Nobody thought that the holes added much to the look of the hat.

So we went back to the poser of this Imponderable, proud of our newfound knowledge. And then he gave us a discomfiting response. If the holes are for ventilation, why does the sweat band inside of his hat cover the holes from the inside?

Hmmm.

Submitted by Ron Weinstock of New York, New York.

How Do They Peel and Clean Baby Shrimp?

Increasingly, by machine. The Laitram Corporation, based in New Orleans, Louisiana, dominates the field of automatic shrimp processing. With four separate stations, Laitram machines can process hundreds of pounds of shrimp per hour.

1. The high-capacity shrimp peeler can peel between 500 and 900 pounds of shells-on shrimp per hour, with or without heads.

2. The cleaner detaches unwanted gristle and waste appendages and then sends the shrimp on a flume ride to clean the crustaceans.

3. The waste separator segregates the waste material detached in the last step.

4. The deveiner deveins the shrimp.

These machines are neither sleek nor pretty—one peeler weighs more than two tons—but they save money. Machines also can grade shrimp and separate them by size, and they work just as easily on baby shrimp as jumbos.

How Do Football Officials Measure First Down Yardage with Chains, Especially When They Go on Field to Confirm First Downs?

In professional football, careers and millions of dollars can rest on a matter of inches. We've never quite figured out how football officials can spot the ball accurately when a running back dives atop a group of ten hulking linemen, let alone how the chain crew retains the proper spot on the sidelines and then carries the chain back out to the field without losing its bearings. Is the aura of pinpoint measurement merely a ruse?

Not really. The answer to this Imponderable focuses on the importance of an inexpensive metal clip. The National Football League's Art McNally explains:

> If at the start of a series the ball was placed on the 23-yard line in the middle of the field, the head linesman would back up

DAVID FELDMAN

to the sideline and, after sighting the line of the ball, would indicate to a member of the chain crew that he wanted the back end of the down markers to be set at the 23-yard line. Obviously, a second member of the chain crew would stretch the forward stake to the 33-yard line.

Before the next down is run, one of the members of the chain crew would take a special clip and place that on the chain at the back end of the 25-yard line. In other words, the clip is placed on the five-yard marker that is closest to the original location of the ball.

When a measurement is about to be made, the head linesman picks up the chain from the 25-yard line and the men holding the front end of the stakes all proceed onto the field. The head linesman places the clip on the back end of the 25-yard line. The front stake is extended to its maximum and the referee makes the decision as to whether or not the ball has extended beyond the forward stake.

Thus the chain crew, when it runs onto the field, doesn't have to find the exact spot near the 23-yard line where the ball was originally spotted, but merely the 25-yard line. The clip "finds" the spot near the 23-yard line.

Submitted by Dennis Stucky of San Diego, California.

How Did Dr Pepper Get Its Name? Was There Ever a Real Dr. Pepper?

Yes, there was a real one, although he had a period after the "r" in "Dr". Dr. Charles Pepper owned a drug store in Rural Retreat, Virginia, and employed a young pharmacist named Wade Morrison.

Unfortunately for Wade, Dr. Pepper wasn't too happy when a romance blossomed between the young pharmacist and his attractive daughter. Pepper nixed the relationship, and the dejected Morrison moved to Waco, Texas, and opened Morrison's Old Corner Drug Store.

Morrison hired Charles Alderton, a young English pharmacist, whose duties included tending the store's soda fountain. Alderton noted the waning interest of his customers in the usual fruit-flavored soft drinks and decided to blend several fruit flavors himself. Alderton finally hit upon a concoction that satisfied Morrison and his taste buds.

Word of mouth spread about Alderton's new creation, and in 1885, what we now know as Dr Pepper became a popular item at the Corner Drug Store. But what would they call the new drink? The Dr Pepper Company supplied the answer:

> Morrison never forgot his thwarted romance and often spoke fondly of Dr. Pepper's daughter. Patrons of his soda fountain heard of the affair, and one of them jokingly suggested naming their new fountain drink after the Virginia doctor, thinking it would gain his favor. The new drink became known as Dr Pepper. It gained such widespread favor that other soda fountain operators in Waco began buying the syrup from Morrison and serving it.

Even certified Peppers might not realize that Dr Pepper is the oldest major soft-drink brand and was introduced to a national constituency at the 1904 World's Fair Exposition in St. Louis, a conclave which was to junk food what Woodstock was to the musical counterculture. (The St. Louis Fair also featured the debut of the ice cream cone, as well as hamburgers and hot dogs served in buns.)

Morrison made a fortune and in that sense wreaked some revenge on the real Dr. Pepper, but he never regained the attentions of Miss Pepper. Alderton, the actual originator of the drink, was content to mix pharmaceutical compounds, and was never involved in the operation of the Dr Pepper Company.

Submitted by Barth Richards of Naperville, Illinois. Thanks also to Kevin Hogan of Hartland, Michigan, and Josh Gibson of Silver Spring, Maryland.

DAVID FELDMAN

Why Is the Home Plate in Baseball Such a Weird Shape?

Until 1900, home plate was square like all the other bases. But in 1900, the current five-sided plate was introduced to aid umpires in calling balls and strikes. Umpires found it easier to spot the location of the ball when the plate was elongated. If you ask most players, it hasn't helped much.

Submitted by Bill Lachapell of Trenton, Michigan. Thanks also to Michael Gempe of Elmhurst, Illinois, and John H. McElroy of Haines City, Florida.

Why Do Hospital Gowns Tie at the Back?

It's bad enough being laid up in the hospital. Why do patients have to undergo the indignity of having their backsides exposed to all? This is a fashion statement that even sick people don't want to make.

We realize that hospital gowns aren't the first priority of hospital administrators, that items like nursing staffs, research budgets, and surgical care justifiably occupy much of their time. But while hospitals pursue the impossible dream of serving edible food, the eradication of the back-tied gown is possible right now.

The original justification for the back closure of hospital gowns was that this configuration enabled health care workers to change the gowns of the bedridden without disturbing the patients. If the gown tied in the front, the patients would have to be picked up (or lift themselves up) to remove the garment.

Perhaps it is growing concern for "patient modesty" (buzz words in the "patient apparel" industry), or perhaps it is jock-

DAVID FELDMAN

eying for competitive advantage among hospitals, especially private, for-profit hospitals, but many health-care administrators are starting to recognize the existence of alternatives to the back-tied gown. Scott Hlavaty, director of patient/surgical product management of uniform giant Angelica, told *Imponderables* that ties on the sides provide a maximum of patient modesty while requiring no more patient inconvenience to remove.

Angelica and other companies manufacture gowns for patients that minimize patient exposure and inconvenience when procedures are performed. Hlavaty explains:

> There are specialized gowns with "I.V. sleeves" that allow the gown to be removed by unsnapping the sleeves so that the I.V. tubes do not have to be removed from the patient in order to change a gown. Also, with the advent of pacemakers and heart monitors, "telemetry pockets" have been placed in the center of gowns. These pockets have openings in the back to allow for the pass through of the monitoring device so that these do not have to be disconnected either.

Some nurses we spoke to commented that gowns with back closures make it more convenient to give shots (in the backside, of course). But many patients prefer to wear their own pajamas, and nurses always manage to administer the shot.

Even if a patient were so incapacitated that a back closure was deemed best, many improvements have been made in hospital uniforms to prevent patients from exposing themselves to roommates and passersby. Back-closure gowns wouldn't be such a problem if the closures were made secure. Uniforms are now available with metal or plastic grippers, as well as velcro. And just as important, gowns are available with a "full overlap back," which provides enough material to overlap more like a bathrobe than a traditional hospital gown. At least with a full overlap gown, you have a shot at covering your rump if the closure unfastens.

Sure, these improvements in gown design cost a little more. But in times when a day in the hospital costs more than the weekly salary of the average person, who cares about a few more cents? After all, how can you encourage postsurgical patients to take a stroll around the hospital corridors when they're more concerned about being the objects of peeping Toms than they are about aches and pains?

Submitted by Diane M. Rhodes of Herndon, Virginia.

What's the Difference Between White Chocolate and Brown Chocolate?

One big difference seems to be that white chocolate doesn't exist. We were shocked to consult five dictionaries and find that none of them has a listing for "white chocolate." And the Food and Drug Administration, which regulates all the ingredients, properties, and definitions of chocolate, also does not recognize the existence of white chocolate.

Therefore, we may conclude that white chocolate is not a form of chocolate at all. Charlotte H. Connelly, manager of consumer affairs for Whitman's Chocolates, wrote *Imponderables* that because there is no legal definition of white chocolate, manufacturers are "not restricted to the type or the amount of ingredients that are incorporated in the 'white chocolate' recipe."

In practice, however, there is only one difference between white and brown chocolate—brown chocolate contains cocoa powder. Richard T. O'Connell, president of the Chocolate Manufacturers Association of the United States of America, explains:

> The cocoa bean from whence chocolate comes is ground into a substance called chocolate liquor (nonalcoholic) and when placed under hydraulic pressure, it splits into two parts, one of cocoa butter and the other cocoa powder. In normal "brown" chocolate, the chocolate liquor is usually mixed with additional cocoa butter to get that "melt-in-your-mouth" flavor. In "white" chocolate (which is not a chocolate), cocoa butter is usually mixed with

DAVID FELDMAN

sugar. Cocoa butter is light tan in color and, therefore, the term "white" is given to it.

Submitted by Vivian Delduca of Berkeley Heights, New Jersey. Thanks also to Fay Gitman of Pottsville, Pennsylvania.

Why Aren't Large-Type Books as Big as They Used to Be?

Twenty-five years ago, it was easy to spot the large-print books in bookstores—they were the ones that had to be housed in oversized bookshelves. And if you bought a few copies, you needed a dolly to haul them away.

No more. In the past, publishers simply enlarged the "regular" book until the print was big enough for the visually impaired to read. Now, most publishers reset the type and keep the size of the pages identical to those of its "small-print" companion.

Obviously, if the print is bigger and the book size is the same, either the margins must be reduced or the page count must increase. In most cases, book designers can't steal enough white space to avoid increasing the page count of the large-print book. But in order to keep them from getting too bulky and expensive, large-print manufacturers use thinner paper that is sufficiently opaque so that the print doesn't bleed over to the other side of the page.

What Causes the Green-Tinged Potato Chips We Sometimes Find? Are They Safe to Eat?

Potatoes are supposed to grow underground. But occasionally a spud becomes a little more ambitious and sticks its head out. Nature punishes the potato by giving it a nasty sunburn.

But why do potatoes turn green rather than red? No, it's not out of envy. The green color is chlorophyll, the natural consequence of a growing plant being exposed to light. According to Beverly Holmes, a public relations representative of Frito-Lay, chip producers try to eliminate the greenies. But a few elude them:

> We store our potatoes in dark rooms and have "pickers" on our production lines who attempt to eliminate [green] chips as they move along on the conveyers because of their undesirable appearance. However, a few chips can make their way through the production process.

Is it harmful to eat a green-tinged chip? Not at all. Chlorophyll stains are as harmless as the green beer or green bagels peddled on St. Patrick's day, and chlorophyll contains no artificial ingredients.

Submitted by Dr. John Hardin of Greenfield, Indiana. Thanks also to Ed Hirschfield of Portage, Michigan.

Why Are Tortilla Chips So Much More Expensive Than Potato Chips?

In the supermarket, potatoes are more expensive than corn. And potato chips are less expensive than corn tortilla chips. Doesn't anything make sense anymore?

Faced with our whining, snack food representatives remain unbowed. Expense of raw food supplies isn't the only determinant of food costs, they explained with patience and a tinge of exasperation. It's the processing of tortilla chips that makes them more expensive.

Even before it is cooked, the corn must be soaked for hours prior to processing. And then the fun begins. Al Rickard, director of communication for the Snack Food Association, explains:

> To make a tortilla chip, a snack manufacturer must cook the corn, grind it into a corn flour, mix it into the proper consistency, and send it through a large machine that rolls the dough into large sheets and cuts out the tortilla chips. The chips are then baked and fried before moving to the seasoning and packaging operations.
>
> By contrast, potato chips are made by simply washing, peeling, and slicing potatoes, which then move through a continuous fryer before moving out to the seasoning and packaging operation. Tortilla chip manufacturing requires more equipment and more labor, so the final cost is higher.

Frito-Lay's Beverly Holmes mentions that tortilla chips vary more in price than potato chips. Frito-Lay's Doritos brand is priced higher than potato chips, but in many markets, "restaurant-style" tortilla chips have been introduced.

> Restaurant-style tortilla chips are often sold in large, clear bags. They tend to be larger in size and are made with less salt, oil, and seasoning since these chips tend to be eaten with dips and sauces.

Submitted by John Morgan of Brooklyn, New York.

Does the Moon Have Any Effect on Lakes or Ponds? If Not, Why Does It Only Seem to Affect Oceans' Tides? Why Don't Lakes Have Tides?

If there is any radio show that we fear appearing on, it's Ira Fistel's radio show in Los Angeles. Fistel, a lawyer by training, has an encyclopedic knowledge of history, railroad lore, sports, radio, and just about every other subject his audience questions him about, and is as likely as we are to answer an Imponderable from a caller. Fistel can make a "Jeopardy!" Tournament of Champions winner look like a know-nothing.

So when we received this Imponderable on his show and we proceeded to stare at each other and shrug our shoulders (not particularly compelling radio, we might add), we knew this was a true Imponderable. We vowed to find an answer for the next book (and then go back on Fistel's show and gloat about it).

Robert Burnham, senior editor of *Astronomy*, was generous enough to send a fascinating explanation:

> Even the biggest lakes are too small to have tides. Ponds or lakes (even large ones like the Great Lakes) have no tides because these bodies of water are raised all at once, along with the land underneath the lake, by the gravitational pull of the Moon. (The

DAVID FELDMAN

solid Earth swells a maximum of about eighteen inches under the Moon's tidal pull, but the effect is imperceptible because we have nothing that isn't also moving by which to gauge the uplift.)

In addition, ponds and lakes are not openly connected to a larger supply of water located elsewhere on the globe, which could supply extra water to them to make a tidal bulge. The seas, on the other hand, have tides because the water in them can flow freely throughout the world's ocean basins . . .

On the side of Earth nearest the Moon, the Moon's gravity pulls sea water away from the planet, thus raising a bulge called high tide. At the same time on the other side of the planet, the Moon's gravity is pulling *Earth* away from the *water*, thus creating a second high-tide bulge.

Low tides occur in between because these are the regions from which water has drained to flow into the two high-tide bulges. (The Sun exerts a tidal effect of its own, but only 46 percent as strong as the Moon's.)

Some landlocked portions of the ocean—the Mediterranean or the Baltic—can mimic the tideless behavior of a lake, although for different reasons. The Mediterranean Sea, for example, has a tidal range measuring just a couple of inches because it is a basin with only a small inlet (the Strait of Gibraltar) connecting it to the global ocean. The Gibraltar Strait is both narrow and shallow, which prevents the rapid twice-a-day flow of immense volumes of water necessary to create a pronounced tide. Thus the rise and fall of the tide in the Atlantic attempts to fill or drain the Med, but the tidal bulge always moves on before very much water can pour in or out past Gibraltar.

Alan MacRobert, of *Sky & Telescope,* summarizes that a body of water needs a large area to slosh around in before tidal effects are substantial, and he provides a simple analogy:

Imagine a tray full of dirt dotted with thimbles of water, representing a land mass with lakes. You could tilt it slightly and nothing much would happen. Now imagine a tray full of water—an ocean. If you tilted it just a little, water would sloop out over your hands.

Submitted by a caller on the Ira Fistel show, KABC-AM, Los Angeles, California.

DO PENGUINS HAVE KNEES? 443

~AND YOUR CELESTIAL SECURITY NUMBER IS ~?

REGISTRAR

Why Do the Backs of Social Security Cards Say "Do Not Laminate" When We Are Expected to Keep the Cards for Our Entire Lives?

The main purpose of the social security card seems to be to prove that we exist. And laminating a card hampers the ability of the government to ascertain whether a card has been tampered with or counterfeited. If your card doesn't pass muster, you don't exist, so we're talking about important stuff here.

John Clark, officer of the Social Security Administration, told *Imponderables* that the social security card incorporates several security features to foil would-be card defacers:

- The [card] stock contains a blue tint marbleized random pattern. Any attempt to erase or remove data is easily detectable because the tint is erasable.
- Planchets (small multi-colored discs) are randomly placed on the paper stock and can be seen with the naked eye.
- Intaglio printing of the type used in U.S. currency is used for

DAVID FELDMAN

some printing on the card and provides a raised effect that can be felt.

"A laminated card hampers the ability of the government to utilize these security features," Clark summarizes.

Sure, the Social Security Administration would love us to keep the same social security card until we die, but it is used to doling out replacements for lost or damaged cards.

And there's good news to report. Sure, the government won't let you laminate your social security card, but it will replace it for free. Trish Butler, associate commissioner for public affairs for the Social Security Administration, asked us to remind *Imponderables* readers that "there is *never* a charge for any service we provide."

Now if only the IRS would adopt the same policy, we'd be happy campers.

Submitted by Kristi Nelson of Vancouver, Washington. Thanks also to April Pedersen of Edmond, Oklahoma.

Why Are Nonsweet Wines Called "Dry"?

"Sweet" makes sense. Sweet wines *do* have more sugar in them than dry ones. The main purpose of the sugar is to combat the acidity of the tannic and other acids found in wine.

Consumers may disagree sharply about how much sugar they prefer in wines, but can't we all agree that "dry" wine is just as wet as sweet wine?

Surprisingly, few of our wine experts could make any sense of "dry" either, but two theories emerged. Spirits expert W. Ray Hyde argues that the terminology stems from both the sensory experience of tasting and more than a little marketing savvy:

Sugar stimulates the saliva glands and leaves the mouth wet. Acids, on the other hand, have an astringent quality that leaves the mouth feeling dry. Winemakers know that the consumer prefers a "sweet" wine to a "wet" wine and a "dry" wine to an "acidic" wine.

But Irving Smith Kogan, of the Champagne News and Information Bureau, wrote *Imponderables* about an intriguing linguistic theory:

> . . . the explanation is in the French language. *"Sec"* is a synonym of lean, and means *peu charnu* (without flesh), without softness or mellowness. This image appears in the English expression "bone-dry." *"Sec"* also means neat, as in undiluted, pure, bare, raw (*"brut"* in French), i.e., unsweetened.
>
> The issue of "dry" versus "sweet" is not the same for Champagne as for still wines. In the case of Champagne, the wine was originally labeled *"doux"* which is the French word for sweet. But in the mid-nineteenth century a Champagne-maker named Louise Pommery decided to make a less-sweet blend and called it *"demi-sec"* (half-dry), which is still quite sweet but less so than the *doux*.
>
> Since her day, Champagnes have been blended progressively dryer (i.e., less and less sweet). So, today we have a range of Champagnes in ascending order of dryness, demi-sec, sec, extra-dry, brut, and extra-brut. The doux is no longer commercially available.

Kogan adds that the above etymology of "dry" does not apply to still wines, for which "dry" simply means not sweet. Notice our current bias for dry champagne. Now the "driest" champagne you can buy is half-bone-dry.

Submitted by Bob Weisblut of Wheaton, Maryland.

Why Do the Rear Windows of Taxicabs (and Some Other Cars) Not Go Down All the Way?

Although we associate this Imponderable with cabs, everyone we spoke to in the taxi industry assured us that they didn't modify the back windows of their fleet cars. Nor was the movement of back seat windows of any concern when considering which models to buy (although it can be of great concern to passengers —when is the last time you've ridden in an air-conditioned cab?). They provide the rear windows for their fares that Detroit (or Japan) provides them.

So the real question is why auto manufacturers don't design their back windows to go down all the way. C. R. Cheney, of Chrysler's Engineering Information Services department, wrote to us about this decision:

> With the advent of automotive air conditioning, the need for this feature disappeared, since it was no longer necessary to pro-

mote maximum flow-through ventilation in this way (at one time, windshields could be opened, too). We can also probably make a good case for improved safety in vehicles with a fixed rear window because this area can no longer be a path of entry for exhaust fumes, insects that could distract the driver, noise, etc.

Of course, occupants of a car are as worried about what might go *out* of a car as what might traipse in. Max E. Rumbaugh, Jr., vice-president of the Society of Automotive Engineers, wrote that

> Some engineers in the past have been known to limit the downward movement of rear windows in the belief that customers want protection that prohibits young children from climbing out of a wide open rear window while a vehicle is moving down a highway.

And all things being equal, why wouldn't manufacturers design a rear window so that customers could put the window down as far as they want? Rumbaugh explains:

> . . . some engineers may be faced with constraints caused by the design and manufacture of a smaller car. In smaller cars, the location of the rear wheel dictates the shape of the rear door. This shape can force a restriction on the downward movement of a full-size rear window.

> *Submitted by Joanne Walker of Ashland, Massachusetts. Thanks also to David A. Kroffe of Los Alamitos, California; Stephanie Suits of San Jose, California; and Renee Tribitt of Minot, North Dakota.*

What Is the Two-Tone Signal at the Start of Many Rented Videotapes?

Yes, it has a purpose other than to puncture your eardrums. Or at least that's what several videotape experts have claimed, anyway.

DAVID FELDMAN

William J. Goffi, of Maxell Corporation, told *Imponderables* that the tone

> is used to facilitate the recording and loading process of video-tapes. As the videotapes are duplicated on high-speed duplicators, the tone "tells" the machine to either stop or start the duplicating process. As the tape is loaded into the shells, the tone again "tells" the loader where the tape starts and ends.

Not all professional duplication is done on high-speed machines. Some production houses duplicate in real time, with one "master" machine supplying the material for dozens of "slave" copying machines. According to Panasonic's public relations manager, Mark Johnson, the two-tone signal is also used to set the audio levels for the slave machines.

All we know is that the two-tone signal sure doesn't help us set the proper volume level on our television. Nothing can sell us on the idea of a remote that can set volume levels more than a trip up to the TV set to turn down the shrieking blast of the two-tone frequency (which only a dog could love). Inevitably, we follow up with a weary trek, fifteen seconds later, to turn up the sound so that our witty comedy doesn't turn out to be an unintentional mime show.

Submitted by Cary Chapman of Homeland, California.

How Was 911 Chosen as the Uniform Emergency Telephone Number?

Old-timers like us will remember when the codes for telephone services were not uniform from city to city. In one town, "information" could be found at 411; in another, at 113. The Bell system needed to change this haphazard approach for two reasons. Making numbers uniform throughout the country would promote ease of use of their services. And reclaiming the 1 as an access code paved the way for direct dialing of long-distance calls.

Most of AT&T Bell's service codes end in 11. 211, 311, 411, 511, 611, 711, and 811 were already assigned when pressure accumulated to create a uniform, national number for emergencies. According to Barbara Sweeney, researcher at AT&T Library Network Archives, all the numbers up to 911 had already been assigned. So 911 become the emergency number by default.

Think of how sophisticated the automated routers of the phone system are. When you dial 411 for directory assistance, each digit is crucial in routing the call properly. The first digit, 4, tells the equipment that you are not trying to obtain an operator ("0") or make a long-distance call. The second and third digits, 11, could be used in an area code as well as an office code, so the equipment has to be programmed to recognize 211, 311, 411, 511, 611, 711, 811, and 911 as separate service codes and not "wait" for you to dial extra digits before connecting you with the disconnected recording that will tell you the phone number of Acme Pizza.

Submitted by Karen Riddick of Dresden, Tennessee.

DAVID FELDMAN

Why Do Birds Bother Flying Back North After Migrating to the South?

Why bother flying so many miles south, to more pleasant and warmer climes, only to then turn around and trudge back to the only seasonably hospitable northeastern United States? Come to think of it, are we talking about birds here or half the population of Miami?

We're not sure what motivates humans to migrate, but we do have a good idea of what motivates birds to bother flying back north again. Of course, birds probably don't sit around (even with one leg tucked up in their feathers) thinking about why they migrate; undoubtedly, hormonal changes caused by natural breeding cycles trigger the migration patterns. After speaking to several bird experts, we found a consensus on the following reasons why birds fly back to the North:

1. *Food.* Birds fly back north to nest. Baby birds, like baby humans, are ravenous eaters and not shy about demanding food.

As Todd Culver of the Laboratory of Ornithology at Cornell University put it, "The most likely reason they return is the super abundant supply of insects available to feed their young." The more food the parents can raise, the healthier the offspring will be and the lower the babies' mortality rate.

2. *Longer daylight hours.* The higher the latitude, the longer period of daylight parents have to find food and feed it to their babies. Some birds find food sources solely by using their vision; they cannot forage with any effectiveness in the dark.

3. *Less competition for food and nesting sites.* If all birds converged in the southern latitudes when nesting, it would be as easy to find a peaceful nest and plentiful food sources as it would be to find a quiet, pleasant, little motel room in Fort Lauderdale during spring break.

4. *Safety.* Birds are more vulnerable to predators when nesting. In most cases, there are fewer mammal predators in the North than in the South. Why? Many mammals, who don't migrate, can't live in the North because of the cold weather.

5. *Improved weather.* Some birds migrate south primarily to flee cold weather in the North. If they time it right, birds come back just when the weather turns pleasant in the spring, just like those humans in Florida.

Submitted by Michael S. Littman of Piscataway, New Jersey. Thanks also to Jack Weber of Modesto, California; Lori Tomlinson of Newmarket, Ontario; and Saxon Swearingen of La Porte, Texas.

DAVID FELDMAN

Why Are the Oceans Salty? What Keeps the Oceans at the Same Level of Saltiness?

Most of the salt in the ocean is there because of the processes of dissolving and leaching from the solid earth over hundreds of millions of years, according to Dr. Eugene C. LaFond, president of LaFond Oceanic Consultants. Rivers take the salt out of rocks and carry them into oceans; these eroded rocks supply the largest portion of salt in the ocean.

But other natural phenomena contribute to the mineral load in the oceans. Salty volcanic rock washes into them. Volcanos also release salty "juvenile water," water that has never existed before in the form of liquid. Fresh basalt flows up from a giant rift that runs through all the oceans' basins.

With all of these processes dumping salt into the oceans, one might think that the seas would get saturated with sodium chloride, for oceans, like any other body of water, keep evaporating. Ocean spray is continuously released into the air; and the recycled rain fills the rivers, which aids in the leaching of salt from rocks.

Yet, according to the Sea Secrets Information Services of the International Oceanographic Foundation at the University of Miami, the concentration of salts in the ocean has not changed for quite a while—about, oh, 1.5 billion years or so. So how do oceans rid themselves of some of the salt?

First of all, sodium chloride is extremely soluble, so it doesn't tend to get concentrated in certain sections of the ocean. The surface area of the oceans is so large (particularly since all the major oceans are interconnected) that the salt is relatively evenly distributed. Second, some of the ions in the salt leave with the sea spray. Third, some of the salt disappears as adsorbates, in the form of gas liquids sticking to particulate matter that sinks below the surface of the ocean. The fourth and most dramatic way sodium chloride is removed from the ocean is by the large accumulations left in salt flats on ocean coasts, where the water is shallow enough to evaporate.

It has taken so long for the salt to accumulate in the oceans that the amount of salt added and subtracted at any particular time is relatively small. While the amount of other minerals in the ocean has changed dramatically, the level of salt in the ocean, approximately 3.5 percent, remains constant.

Submitted by Merilee Roy of Bradford, Massachusetts. Thanks also to Nicole Chastrette of New York, New York; Bob and Elaine Juhre of Kettle Falls, Washington; John H. Herman of Beaverton, Oregon; Matthew Anderson of Forked River, New Jersey; and Cindy Raymond of Vincentown, New Jersey.

DAVID FELDMAN

How Do 3-D Movies and 3-D Glasses Work?

3-D movies are a variation of the stereovision systems (e.g., Viewmasters) that we see used in tourist trinkets and children's toys. These devices present two different views a few inches apart from the viewpoint of the human eyes. The left image is presented only to the left eye and the right image is sent directly to the right eye.

But the technology for a 3-D film is more complicated, because the filmmaker must invent some way to keep the left eye from seeing what only the right eye is supposed to view, even though both images are being projected on the screen simultaneously. The history of the technology was reviewed for us by David A. Gibson, of the Photo Equipment Museum of Eastman Kodak Company:

> The first system was invented in the 1890s, and the images are called anaglyphs. The left-eye image was projected with a red colored filter over the projector lens and a blue-green filter [was

put] over the lens of the projector for the right-eye image. Glasses with the same color filters were used in viewing the images—the red filter for the left eye transmitted the light from the left-image projector, and blocked the light from the right-image projector. This system has also been used to print such things as stereo comic books and has been used experimentally with stereo images broadcast on color television.

The only problem with this technology is that it works best with monochrome images. The red and blue-green tints of the glasses add unwanted and unsubtle coloration to a color 3-D film.

The solution, Gibson is generous enough to admit, came from rival Polaroid, which developed, appropriately enough, a polarization method specifically for 3-D films. The Polaroid technology beams

> the angle of polarization for one eye at right angles to that for the other eye, so that one image is transmitted while the other eye is blocked. This is the system used for the 3-D movies made in the 1950s.

Submitted by Don Borchert of Lomita, California.

What Use Is the Appendix to Us? What Use Are Our Tonsils to Us?

The fact that this Imponderable was first posed to us by a medical doctor indicates that the answer is far from obvious. We asked Dr. Liberato John DiDio this question, and he called the appendix the "tonsils of the intestines." We wondered if this meant merely that the appendix is the organ in the stomach most likely to be extracted by a surgeon. What good are organs like tonsils and the appendix and gall bladder when we don't seem to miss them at all once they've been extracted?

Actually, tonsils and the appendix do have much in common. They are both lymphoid organs that manufacture white

DAVID FELDMAN

blood cells. William P. Jollie, professor and chairman of the Department of Anatomy at the Medical College of Virginia at Virginia Commonwealth University, explains the potential importance of the appendix:

> One type of white blood cell is the lymphocyte; it produces antibodies, proteins that distinguish between our own body proteins and foreign proteins, called antigens. Antibodies, produced by lymphocytes, deactivate antigens.
>
> Lymphocytes come in two types: B-lymphocytes and T-lymphocytes. T-lymphocytes originate in the thymus. There is some evidence to suggest that B-lymphocytes originate in the appendix, although there is also evidence that bone marrow serves this purpose.

If our appendix is so important in fighting infections, how can we sustain its loss? Luckily, other organs, such as the spleen, also manufacture sufficient white blood cells to take up the slack.

Some doctors, including Dr. DiDio, even suggest that the purpose of the appendix (and the tonsils) might be to serve as a lightning rod and actually attract infections. By doing so, the theory goes, infections are localized in one spot that isn't critically important to the functioning of the body. This lightning-rod theory is supported, of course, by the sheer numbers of people who encounter problems with appendix and tonsils compared to surrounding organs.

Accounts vary on whether patients with extracted tonsils and/or appendix are any worse off than those lugging them around. It seems that medical opinion on whether it is proper to extract tonsils for mild cases of tonsillitis in children varies as much and as often as hemlines on women's skirts. Patients in the throes of an appendicitis attack do not have the luxury of contemplation.

Submitted by Dr. Emil S. Dickstein of Youngstown, Ohio.
Thanks also to Lily Whelan of Providence, Rhode Island, and George Hill of Brockville, Ontario.

Where Does the Moisture Go When Wisps of Clouds Disappear in Front of Your Eyes?

A few facts about clouds will give us the tools to answer this question:

1. A warm volume of air at saturation (i.e., 100 percent relative humidity), given the same barometric pressure, will hold more water vapor than a cold volume of air. For example, at 86 degrees Fahrenheit, seven times as much water vapor can be retained as at 32 degrees Fahrenheit.

2. Therefore, when a volume of air cools, its relative humidity increases until it reaches 100 percent relative humidity. This point is called the dew point temperature.

3. When air at dew point temperature is cooled even further, a visible cloud results (and ultimately, precipitation).

4. Therefore, the disappearance of a cloud is caused by the opposite of #3. Raymond E. Falconer, of the Atmospheric Sciences Research Center, explains:

> As a volume of air moves downward from lower to higher barometric pressure, it becomes warmer and drier, with lower relative humidity. This causes the cloud to evaporate.
>
> When we see clouds, the air has been rising and cooling with condensation of the invisible water vapor into visible cloud as the air reaches the temperature of the dew point. When a cloud encounters drier air, the cloud droplets evaporate into the drier air, which can hold more water vapor.
>
> When air is forced up over a mountain, it is cooled, and in the process a cloud may form over the higher elevations. However, as the air descends on the lee side of the mountain, the air warms up and dries out, causing the cloud to dissipate. Such a cloud formation is called an orographic cloud.

Submitted by Rev. David Scott of Rochester, New York.

DAVID FELDMAN

Why Is Frozen Orange Juice Just About the Only Frozen Product That Is Cheaper Than Its Fresh Counterpart?

Our correspondents reasoned, logically enough, that since both fresh and frozen orange juice are squeezed from oranges, and since the frozen juice must be concentrated, the extra processing involved would make the frozen style more expensive to produce and thus costlier at the retail level. But according to economists at the Florida Department of Citrus, it just ain't so.

Although the prices of fresh fruit, chilled juice, and frozen concentrate are similar at the wholesale level (within two cents of the fresh fruit equivalent per pound), they depart radically at the retail level. In the period of 1987–1988, frozen concentrated orange juice cost 24.6 cents per fresh pound equivalent; chilled juice was 35 cents per fresh pound equivalent; and the fruit itself a comparatively hefty 58.5 cents per pound. Why the discrepancy?

In the immortal words of real estate brokers across the world, the answer is: location, location, location. Chilled juice (and the fresh fruit itself, for that matter) would cost less than frozen if it didn't need to be shipped long distances. But it does. The conclusion, as Catherine A. Clay, information specialist at the Florida Department of Citrus, elucidates, is clearly that the costs at the retail level are due to distribution rather than processing costs.

> One 90-pound box of oranges will make about 45 pounds of juice. Concentrating that juice by removing the water will reduce the weight by at least two-thirds, so the amount of frozen concentrate in one box would be about 15 pounds.
>
> So you can ship three times as much frozen concentrated juice in one truck than you can chilled juice, and twice as much chilled juice as fresh oranges. In the space in which one 90-pound box of oranges is shipped, you could ship six times as much frozen concentrated orange juice.

In addition, fresh fruit can begin to decay or be damaged during transit to the retailer. So while the retailer may have paid for the entire truckload, he may have to discard decayed or damaged fruit. Yet his cost for that load remains the same regardless of how much actual fruit he sells.

Frozen concentrated juice does not spoil, so there is no loss. The higher price for fresh fruit would compensate the retail buyer for the cost of the lost fruit.

Clay didn't add that many juice distributors who use strictly Florida oranges for their chilled juice use cheaper, non-American orange juice for their concentrated product. Why don't they use the cheaper oranges for their chilled juices? Location. Location. Location. It would be too expensive to ship the heavier, naturally water-laden fruits thousands of miles.

Submitted by Eugene Hokanson of Bellevue, Washington.
Thanks also to Herbert Kraut of Forest Hills, New York.

DAVID FELDMAN

MAGAZINES: LIGHT READING, FOLLOWED BY **HEAVY CLEANING**!

How Are the Subscription Insert Cards Placed in Magazines? What Keeps Them from Falling Out As the Magazine Is Sent Through the Postal System?

Fewer things are more annoying to us than receiving a magazine we put our soft-earned bucks down to subscribe to, and being rewarded for our loyalty by being showered with cards entreating us to subscribe to the very magazine we've just shelled out for.

Why is it necessary to have to clean a magazine of foreign matter before you read the darn thing? Because the cards work. Publishers know that readers hate them; but the response rate to a card, particularly one that allows a free-postage response, attracts more subscribers than a discreet ad in the body of the magazine.

Those pesky little inserts that fall out are called "blow-in cards" in the magazine biz. We thought "blow-out" cards might be a more descriptive moniker until we learned the derivation of the term from Bob Nichter, of the Fulfillment Management Association.

Originally, blow-in cards were literally blown into the magazine by a fan on the printer assembly line. Now, blow-ins are placed mechanically by an insertion machine after the magazine is bound. Nothing special is needed to keep the cards inside the magazine; they are placed close enough to the binding so that they won't fall out unless the pages are riffled.

Why do many periodicals place two or more blow-in cards in one magazine? It's not an accident. Most magazines find that two blow-in cards attract a greater subscription rate than one. Any more, and reader ire starts to overshadow the slight financial gains.

Submitted by Curtis Kelly of Chicago, Illinois.

Why Do We Put Thermometers Under Our Tongues? Would It Make Any Difference If We Put Them Above Our Tongues If Our Mouths Were Closed?

Anyone who has ever seen a child fidgeting, desperately struggling to keep a thermometer under the tongue, has probably wondered why this practice started. Why do physicians want to take our temperature in the most inconvenient places?

No, there is nothing intrinsically important about the temperature under the tongue or, for that matter, in your rectum. The goal is to determine the "core temperature," the temperature of the interior of the body.

The rectum and tongue are the most accessible areas of the body that are at core temperature. Occasionally the armpit will be used, but the armpit is more exposed to the ambient air, and tends to give colder readings. Of course, drinking a hot beverage, as many schoolchildren have learned, is effective in shooting one's temperature up. But barring tricks, the area under the

DAVID FELDMAN

tongue, full of blood vessels, is almost as accurate as the rectal area, and a lot more pleasant place to use.

So what are the advantages of putting the thermometer *under* the tongue as opposed to over it? Let us count the ways:

1. *Accuracy*. Placing the thermometer under the tongue insulates the area from outside influence, such as air and food. As Dr. E. Wilson Griffin III told *Imponderables*, "Moving air would evaporate moisture in the mouth and on the thermometer and falsely lower the temperature. It is important to have the thermometer under the tongue rather than just banging around loose inside the mouth, because a mercury thermometer responds most accurately to the temperature of liquids or solids in direct contact with it. . . ."

2. *Speed*. The soft tissues and blood vessels of the tongue are ideal resting spots for a thermometer. Dr. Frank Davidoff, of the American College of Physicians, points out that compared to the skin of the armpit, which is thick, horny, and nonvascular, the "soft, unprotected tissues under the tongue wrap tightly around the thermometer, improving the speed and completeness of heat transfer."

3. *Comfort*. Although you may not believe it, keeping the thermometer above the tongue would not be as comfortable. The hard thermometer, instead of being embraced by the soft tissue below the tongue, would inevitably scrape against the much harder tissues of the hard palate (the roof of your mouth). Something would have to give—and it wouldn't be the thermometer.

Davidoff concedes that in a pinch, placing the thermometer above the tongue might not be a total disaster:

In principle, you could get a reasonably accurate temperature reading with a thermometer above your tongue *if* you hadn't recently been mouth breathing or hadn't recently eaten or drunk anything, *if* you held the thermometer reasonably firmly between your tongue and the roof of your mouth, and *if* you kept it there long enough.

Do Penguins Have Knees?

They sure do, although they are discreetly hidden underneath their feathers. Anatomically, all birds' legs are pretty much alike, although the dimensions of individual bones vary a great deal among species.

Penguins, like other birds, have legs divided into three segments. The upper segment, the equivalent of our thigh, and the middle segment, the equivalent of our shinbone, or the drumstick of a chicken, are both quite short in penguins.

When we see flamingos, or other birds with long legs, they appear to possess a knee turned backwards, but these are not the equivalent of a human knee. Penguins, flamingos, and other birds do have knees, with patellas (knee caps) that bend and function much like their human counterparts.

We spoke to Dr. Don Bruning, curator of ornithology at the New York Zoological Park (better known as the Bronx Zoo), who told us that the backwards joint that we perceive as a knee in flamingos actually separates the bird equivalent of the ankle from the bones of the upper foot. The area below the backwards joint is not the lower leg but the upper areas of the foot. In other words, penguins (and other birds) stand on their toes, like ballet dancers.

Penguins are birds, of course, but their element is water rather than sky. Penguins may waddle on land, but their legs help make them swimming machines. Penguins use their wings as propellers in the water, and their elongated feet act as rudders.

So rest assured. Even if you can't see them, penguins have legs (with knees). And they know how to use them.

Submitted by John Vineyard of Plano, Texas. Thanks also to Ruth Vineyard of Plano, Texas.

DAVID FELDMAN

How Do They Make Hot Dog Buns That Are Partially Sliced?

Now that we solved the Imponderable of why there are ten hot dogs in a package and only eight hot dog buns in a package (see *Why Do Clocks Run Clockwise?*), we can tackle a few less challenging bread Imponderables without guilt.

Barbara K. Rose, manager of consumer affairs at Continental Baking Company (the folks who bring us Wonder Bread and Twinkies), answered this question with ease:

> The hot dog buns are removed from the baking pans and placed on a conveyer-type system. These buns slide past circular blades that are mounted on rotating vertical shafts. Two buns are allowed between each blade: the bun on the right is sliced on the right side; the bun on the left is sliced by a blade on the left. These blades are set to slice only a specific distance into the bun and will not slice through. The tops of the buns hold them together.

Submitted by Laurie Hutler of Boulder Creek, California.
Thanks also to Robert Chell of Harrisonburg, Virginia, and Deb Graham of Mt. Vernon, Washington.

How Do They Fork Split English Muffins? What Causes the Ridges in English Muffins?

English muffins also run past circular blades, actually two blades, which slice only one-quarter inch or so into the muffin. But each muffin is also "forked," passed through two spinning wheels with Roman spear points. These spears penetrate into the muffin anywhere from one to one and one-half inch, depending upon the baker's preference.

Tom Lehmann, director of baking assistance at the American Institute of Baking, told *Imponderables* that the initial one-quarter-inch slice of the outer edges of the muffin yields a smooth consistency. The forking doesn't sever the muffin into two separate pieces but does produce the perforations by which they slice the muffin and the ridges, nooks, and crannies that provide the rough texture for which English muffins are famous.

Continental Baking's Barbara Rose reports that her company found that fork splitting didn't work on their Raisin Rounds, which are sliced all the way through the muffin: "Raisin Rounds must be sliced because the raisins will accumulate on the fork splitting machinery causing several mechanical breakdowns and halting production."

Submitted by Donna Burks of Gilroy, California. Thanks also to Ruth Mascari of Monkton, Maryland.

DAVID FELDMAN

Why Do Cat Hairs Tend to Stick to Our Clothes More Than Those of Dogs or Other Pets?

A cat's hair is the most electrostatic of all pet hairs, which may be the main reason why cat hairs stick to clothes. But the physiology of cat hair also contributes to kitty cling. Dr. John Saidla, assistant director of the Cornell Feline Health Center, explains:

> The hair coat in the cat consists of three different types of hair: primary or guard hairs within the outer coat: awn hairs (intermediate-sized hairs forming part of the primary coat); and secondary hairs (downy hair found in the undercoat).
>
> The guard hairs are slender and taper towards the tip. The cuticles on these hairs have microscopically small barbs that are very rough. This is the main reason cat hairs stick to clothing, and it is this hair that is found most commonly on clothing.
>
> The awn hairs have broken or cracked cuticles that are rough and would aid in their clinging, also. The secondary hairs are very

thin and are wavy or evenly crimped. These hairs are caught and held in more roughly textured clothing.

Submitted by an anonymous caller on Owen Spann's nationally syndicated radio show.

Why Are You Never Supposed to Touch a Halogen Light Bulb with Your Fingers?

Conventional light bulbs use soda-lime glass, which is perfectly functional. But tungsten-halogen bulbs are made of much more durable quartz glass because they must withstand much higher temperatures, a minimum of 250 degrees Centigrade.

Rubin Rivera, of Philips Lighting, told *Imponderables* that quartz halogen lamps must not be touched with the fingers because the natural oils from the skin, in combination with the high temperatures reached by the bulbs when illuminated, will cause the crystalline structure of the bulb glass to change.

Caden Zollo, product manager of The Specialty Bulb Co., adds that contact with human oils can cause the glass to crack and leak. Air can then get into the filament and, in extreme conditions, can cause the bulb not only to leak but to explode.

To avoid this "explosive" situation, some halogen lamps come with a separate outer bulb so that the lamps can be touched. If your hands have come in contact with the bulb, or you need to clean the bulb, wiping it with denatured alcohol will reverse the effect of your greasy hands.

Submitted by Gail Lee of Dallas, Texas.

Why Is There an "H" Inside of the "C" in the Hockey Uniform of the Montreal Canadiens?

The "H" stands for hockey. When the team was founded in 1909, it was known as "Club Canadien" and its sweaters sported a big white "C." This tradition lasted all of one year, when the club switched to a red uniform with a green maple leaf and a Gothic "C." Not content to rest on its fashion statement, the team changed its look again, adopting a blue, white, and red "barber pole" symbol featuring the letters "CAC," which stood for Club Athlétique Canadien.

In 1917, the Club Athlétique Canadien folded, but owner George Kennedy replaced the "A" inside the large "C" with the letter "H," to signify "hockey." The letters then stood for "Club de Hockey Canadien," the official name of the team for more than seventy years.

Submitted by Bob Tatu of Conshohocken, Pennsylvania.

Why Don't Radio Shack Stores Use Cash Registers?

Have you ever noticed that most of the time when you make a purchase at Radio Shack, salespeople ask you for your address? Clearly, the Tandy Corporation likes to compile as much information about its business as possible, and no figures are of more interest than how their individual stores are faring in sales and inventory control.

Befitting a retail business that specializes in high technology, cash registers don't impart enough information to satisfy the Tandy Corporation. Ed Juge, Radio Shack's director of market planning, explains:

> Radio Shack does not use cash registers. They're decades-old technology. Every company-owned Radio Shack store is

equipped with state-of-the-art electronic point-of-sale terminals, which are really "diskless" Tandy 1000 SX computers, tied to a multi-user Tandy computer in the office area.

These POS systems assure correct pricing and inventory counting of every item sold, along with a lot of other information that helps us run our business more efficiently. Every evening by 7:00 P.M., we can tell you exactly how many of any one of our 3000 + line items were sold that day in our 5,000 stores across the country.

Each individual store transmits sales data, every day, to Fort Worth [Tandy's corporate headquarters]. As that is being done, our Fort Worth computer can update the individual stores' files with new prices, or newly available product information, as well as sending them important information bulletins.

The system assures that every customer is getting the benefit of every sale price in effect on the date of purchase [we assume this up-to-the-minute price accuracy applies to price rises, as well], even if the sale price somehow escaped notice by our employees. Sales are written up about three times as quickly, and with the error rate reduced by a factor of one hundred to one over previous methods.

Don French, chief engineer for Radio Shack, adds that in many cases salespeople are away from the counter helping customers, making it relatively easy to have money stolen: "Keeping the money in a drawer makes it a little harder for this to happen."

Submitted by Doc Swan of Palmyra, New Jersey.

　　　　　　　　　　　DAVID FELDMAN

HOW Do They Decide Where to Put Thumbnotches in Dictionaries?

A frustrated David S. Clark wrote to us:

> When I updated my *New World Dictionary* a year or two ago I thought I'd bought a defective copy. The thumb indexes didn't match with the first page of the letter indicated. When I later bought a *Merriam-Webster's* and found the same situation, I concluded it must be a cheaper way to thumb index. Is there some other reason?

A good question, David, and you were right in concluding that saving money had a lot to do with the new indexing system. Maybe not too many other people have lost sleep over this issue, but dictionary publishers have.

Some form of visual indexing is necessary to make a dictionary user-friendly. But thumbnotches are expensive to install. Most unabridged dictionaries contain thumbnotches at the beginning of each alphabet entry, but this is impossible in thinner collegiate dictionaries, where twenty-six thumbnotches would bleed into each other. Furthermore, thumbnotching at the beginning of each letter is expensive.

Merriam-Webster Inc. found an elegant solution that has been widely imitated. John M. Morse, manager of editorial operations and planning, explains:

> For a good many years, thumbnotches in our dictionaries have referenced two letters of the alphabet each; for example, in the *Ninth Collegiate* there is one notch for *L* and *M*. In the past, this *LM* tab would have been placed at the beginning of the letter *L*, but in 1978 (during the life of the eighth edition) we changed over to an automatic thumbnotching system which places the tab somewhere close to the middle of the pages devoted to the referenced letters. In part this was done to control the costs of thumbnotching and so the price of the dictionary, but it is not really a disadvantage to the dictionary user.
>
> When a user goes to the dictionary to find a word beginning with *L* or *M*, we have no way of knowing which word is being sought, but we do know it will fall within the roughly 120 pages on which words beginning with *L* and *M* appear. Under the old system, one could find the tab and still be 100 pages or more away from the desired word. With the tab nearly in the middle of those pages, one is never more than, say, 70 pages away.
>
> It is true that this is a break with tradition and it is also true that we have received perhaps several hundred letters from users who feel uncomfortable with the new system, but we think most people become used to the arrangement quite quickly. We have sold millions of dictionaries indexed in this way, and other publishers have since followed our lead, so that now it is fair to say that most thumb-indexed desk dictionaries sold in this country use this indexing system.

Submitted by David S. Clark of Northridge, California.

What Is the Purpose of the Button You Press to Unlock the Key from the Ignition on Some Cars? If It Is a Worthwhile Mechanism, Why Isn't It on All Cars?

The purpose of the ignition locking mechanism is to comply with the Federal Motor Vehicle Safety standard that mandates that the key that deactivates the engine also lock the steering column. But foiling a car thief poses safety risks. If you accidentally pulled out the key while the car was in motion, you had better pray for sparse traffic and rubber guard rails on the road: You wouldn't be able to steer.

To avoid inadvertent key withdrawal and the resultant steering column locking, the standard mandates that a separate action (other than turning the key) be required to pull the key out of the ignition. If the car's gear shift selector is mounted on the column, the movement to the park position is considered a "separate action."

But if the shift is mounted on the floor or console, another motion is required. Thomas J. Carr, director of safety and international technical affairs for the Motor Vehicle Manufacturers Association of the United States, told *Imponderables* that most manufacturers comply by using an unlock button, but others require the key to be pushed in toward the column to release it for withdrawal.

Submitted by William C. Nielsen of Rolling Hills Estate, California.

How Did Kodak Get Its Name? Is It True That the Name Comes from the Sound of the Shutter?

Standard Oil of New Jersey was roundly criticized when it changed its name to Exxon, a word chosen for its euphony and uniqueness rather than any obvious meaning or associations. The name change was deplored by editorialists for confirming the soullessness of the post–World War II era.

But George Eastman trademarked "Kodak" in 1888. And the word didn't mean a darn thing.

The Eastman Kodak Company gets asked this question so often that they have prepared a pamphlet on the subject. Yes, they have heard the rumor that Kodak was the onomatopoeic description of the shutter closing, but the truth, although more prosaic, is fascinating nonetheless. As Eastman Kodak describes it, "George Eastman invented it out of thin air!" In several letters, Eastman described the less than scientific process that led to the creation of one of the most famous trademarks of the United States:

> I devised the name myself. . . . The letter "K" had been a favorite with me—it seems a strong, incisive sort of letter. . . . It became a question of trying out a great number of combinations of letters that made words starting and ending with "K." The word "Kodak" is the result.

> . . . it was a purely arbitrary combination of letters, not derived in whole or part from any existing word, arrived at after considerable search for a word that would answer all the requirements for a trademark name. . . . it must be short; incapable of being misspelled so as to destroy its identity; must have a vigorous and distinctive personality; and must meet the requirements of the various foreign trademark laws.

The last point is important. One can't receive a trademark if the proposed name is merely an existing word (or words) found in the dictionary that accurately describes the item. As Eastman wrote in 1906, "There is, you know, a commercial value in having a peculiar name."

Submitted by John M. Clark of Levittown, New York.

DAVID FELDMAN

Why Are There Ridges (Often Painted Black) on the Sides of Most School Buses?

Those ridges are called "rub rails," and their main purpose is to add strength to the sides of the vehicle. According to John Chuhran, of Mercedes-Benz of North America: "If they were flat, the sides of buses would have more of a tendency to flex."

Rub rails have an additional benefit. Pete James, regional director of the National Association for Pupil Transportation, told *Imponderables* that rub rails also help maintain the structural integrity of the bus when it is broadsided. The rub rails help prevent the crashing vehicle from penetrating farther into the bus.

Why are the rub rails painted black? No, they are not racing stripes. The answer is murky indeed. Although there is a national standard mandating that school buses be painted "national school bus chrome yellow," some states require that both the rub rails and bumpers be painted a contrasting color to "stand out" from the yellow. In most cases, this color is black. Different sources attribute the choice of black to everything from aesthetics to hiding marks on the school bus to differentiating the rub rails from the main panel of the bus to making the school bus look different than other buses.

Pete James feels that the black stripes actually detract from the instantaneously recognizable look of school bus yellow. Karen E. Finkel, executive director of the National School Transportation Association, notes that several states specify that their buses may not be painted black. Yet Kentucky specifies that "the area between the window rub rail and the seat rub rail be painted black so that the white letters for the school district name will show up better." In matters of color choice, states' rights still prevail.

Submitted by Jens P. Aarnaes of Schaumburg, Illinois.

Why Do All the Armed Forces Start Marching with the Left Foot? Is There Any Practical Reason? Is This Custom the Same All Over the World?

Bottom line: We can only answer the third question with any confidence. As far as we can ascertain, soldiers all over the world step off on the left foot.

We contacted many of our trusty military sources about why the practice spread. They collectively shrugged their shoulders.

Imponderables has been besieged by questions about the origins of left/right customs (e.g., why we drive on the right side of the road, why the hot water faucet is on the left, why military medals are worn on the left) and found that usually the practices stem from a technical advantage.

What possible advantage could there be in starting a march with the left foot? We received a fascinating speculation on the subject by Robert S. Robe, Jr., president of The Scipio Society of Naval and Military History, which may not be definitive but is certainly more sensible and interesting than anything else we've heard about the subject.

> When warfare was institutionalized in prebiblical times so that trained armies could fight one another on a battlefield, the evolution of infantry tactics in close formation required regimented marching in order to effectively move bodies of heavy and light infantry into contact with an enemy.
>
> I am hypothesizing that some long forgotten martinet discovered by accident or otherwise that a soldier advancing at close quarters into an enemy sword or spear line could, by stepping off on his foot in unison with his fellows, maintain better balance and sword contact to his front, assuming always that the thrusting or cutting weapon was wielded from the *right* hand and the shield from the left. The shield would also protect the left leg forward in close-quarter fighting.

Robe's explanation echoes the usual explanation of why we mount horses from the left. The horse itself couldn't care less

DAVID FELDMAN

from what side its rider mounts it. But in ancient times, when riders wore swords slung along the left side of the body (so that the swords could be unsheathed by the right hand), riders found it much easier to retain their groin if they mounted on the left.

Submitted by John Williams of North Hollywood, California. Thanks also to Ann Czompo of Cortland, New York, and Sylvia Antovino of Rochester, New York.

Why Do Rabbits Wiggle Their Noses All the Time?

Rabbits don't wiggle their noses *all* the time, but enough to make one wonder if they have a cocaine habit or a bad allergy. Little did we suspect that this charming idiosyncrasy is a key to the workings of the rabbit's respiratory system. There are at least four reasons why rabbits' noses twitch away.

1. The movement activates the sebaceous gland (located on the mucus membranes) and creates moisture to keep the membranes dampened and strong. Furthermore, like other animals (including, ahem, dogs with wet noses), rabbits can smell better off of a wet surface.

2. Frequent wiggling expands the nasal orifices, or nares, so that the rabbit can inhale more air. Like dogs with wet noses, domestic rabbits can't perspire. According to Dr. T. E. Reed, of the American Rabbit Breeders Association, nose wiggling actually helps rabbits cool themselves off on hot days:

> The only method of cooling themselves is by expiring the super heated air from the respiratory tract to the environment and through the convection of heat from the ears. . . . The inhalation . . . of a voluminous amount of air is extremely important.
>
> The normal respiratory rate in the domestic rabbit is approximately 120 breaths per minute. However, during extremely hot weather, it is not uncommon for the respiratory rate to approach 300 to 350 breaths per minute.

The nares [control] the amount of air rabbits can inhale. In order to increase the volume of air that is inhaled, the rabbit will twitch its nose by activating the various types of muscles surrounding each of the nostrils to increase the orifice size.

3. When a rabbit's whiskers are touched, the muscles surrounding the nostrils expand and contract in order to sharpen the animal's olfactory abilities.

4. If a rabbit continuously wiggling its nose appears to be nervous, T. E. Reed reminds us that it might be:

When a rabbit is calm and unattended, each of the nostrils usually will remain in a stationary position. However, if the rabbit gets excited, the rabbit's pulse rate and respiratory rate increase and there is a nervous intervention to the nose that causes a constriction and relaxation of the paranasal muscle—the "wiggle" that most lay individuals observe.

Although some readers have speculated that the "wiggle" is caused by the continual growth of the incisor teeth, each of the rabbit experts we spoke to disputed the claim.

Submitted by Garnett Budd of Eldorado, Ontario. Thanks also to Jason Gonzales of Albuquerque, New Mexico.

Why Are There Legless Ducks in the Crest of Cadillacs?

Jil McIntosh, who writes for several automotive magazines and owns a 1947 Cadillac, told us that two rumors abound about the ducks on the Cadillac crest: that the six ducks signify the original founders of the Cadillac company; and that each duck stands for one of the six cylinders.

These rumors are wrong on all counts. Cadillac was founded by one person, a Civil War riflemaker, Henry Leland, in 1902. After selling the company to General Motors, Leland proceeded to introduce the Lincoln, which later became Cadillac's main luxury rival.

McIntosh laughs off the cylinder theory:

> The first Cadillacs were one-cylinder, and then four-cylinder. In 1915, Cadillac brought out their first V-8 engines. . . . No six-cylinder engine was ever used until the Cimarron of the mid-1980s (and I hope some Caddy stylist rots in hell for *that* one!). So the cylinder theory is out; and since Leland was the main brain, the partnership theory is out. The crest is actually a coat of arms.

But not just anybody's coat of arms. The Cadillac is named after Antoine de la Mothe Cadillac, the French explorer who founded the city of Detroit in 1701. McIntosh told *Imponderables* that "the Cadillac coat of arms crest is a version of Cadillac's family crest, which had been in his family for 400 years prior to his birth."

Those aren't ducks in the crest—they are merlettes, heraldic adaptations of the martin (a kind of swallow). The merlettes on the Cadillac crest have no beaks or legs. When merlettes appear in threes, they refer to the Holy Trinity.

The Cadillac division receives many queries about the birds, and has even explained why the merlettes are missing legs:

> The merlettes were granted to knights by the ancient School of Heralds, together with the "fess" [the wide, dark horizontal band separating the two upper birds from the one on the bottom of the quarterling], for valiant conduct in the Crusades. The birds shown in black against a gold background in this section of the Cadillac arms denote wisdom, riches, and cleverness of mind, ideal qualities for the adventurous and zealous Christian knight.
>
> Of the merlette, Guillaume, an ancient historian, says: "This bird is given for a difference, to younger brothers to put them in mind that in order to raise themselves they are to look to the wings of virtue and merit, and not to the legs, having but little land to set their feet on."

The Cadillac crest has graced every Cadillac ever built,

often in several places. The crest has changed cosmetically from time to time—it has been lengthened or thinned, adorned with laurel leaves, etc. But the heraldic design has remained the same.

We hope we have answered the Imponderable once posed by Chico Marx: Viaduct(s)?

What Is the Technical Definition of a Sunset or Sunrise? How Is It Determined at What Time the Sun Sets or Rises? Why Is There Natural Light Before Sunrise and After Sunset?

The definitions are easy. A sunrise is defined as occurring when the top of the sun appears on a sea-level horizon. A sunset occurs when the top of the sun goes just below the sea-level horizon.

But how do scientists determine the times? No, they do not send meteorologists out on a ladder and have them crane their necks. No observation is involved at all—just math. By crunching the numbers based on the orbit of the Earth around the Sun, the sunrise and sunset times can be calculated long in advance.

Richard Williams, a meteorologist at the National Weather Service, explains that published times are only approximations of what we observe with our naked eyes:

> The time of sunrise and sunset varies with day of the year, latitude, and longitude. The published sunrise and sunset times are calculated without regard to surrounding terrain. That is, all computations are made for a sea-level horizon, even in mountainous areas. Thus the actual time of sunrise at a particular location may vary considerably from the "official" times.
>
> When we observe sunset, the Sun has already gone below the horizon. The Earth's atmosphere "bends" the Sun's rays and delays the sunset by about three minutes. Likewise with sunrise, the sun makes its first appearance before it would on a planet with no

DAVID FELDMAN

atmosphere. We actually get five to ten minutes of extra sunlight due to this effect.

Submitted by a caller on the Larry Mantle show, Pasadena, California.

Why Is Pubic Hair Curly?

In *Why Do Clocks Run Clockwise?*, we discussed why we have pubic hair. But you weren't satisfied. So we will continue our nonstop exploration of what seems to be an insatiable North American interest in body hair.

If you want to know the anatomical reason why pubic hair is curly, we can help you. Dr. Joseph P. Bark, diplomate of the American Board of Dermatology, explains:

> Pubic hair is curly because it is genetically made in a flat shape rather than in a round shape. Perfectly round hair, such as the hair seen on the scalps of Native Americans, is straight and has no tendency to curl. However, ribbonlike hair on the scalps of blacks is clearly seen to curl because it is oval in construction. The same is true with pubic hair. . . .

But answering what function curly pubic hair serves is a much trickier proposition. Some, such as Samuel T. Selden, a Chesapeake, Virginia, dermatologist, speculate that pubic hair might be curly because if it grew out straight and stiff, it might rub against adjacent areas and cause discomfort. (Dermatologist Jerome Z. Litt, of Pepper Pike, Ohio, who has been confronted with the question of why pubic and axillary hair doesn't grow as fast as scalp hair, facetiously suggests that "not only wouldn't it look sporty in the shower room, but we'd all be tripping over it.")

Before we get carried away with our theories, though, we might keep in mind a salient fact—not all pubic hair is curly.

Early in puberty, it is soft and straight. And Selden points out that if this book were published in Japan or China, this Imponderable likely would never have been posed. The pubic hair of Orientals tends to be sparser and much straighter than that of whites or blacks.

Submitted by Suzanne Saldi of West Berlin, New Jersey.

Why Are There Tiny Holes in the Ceiling of My Car?

For the same reason there are tiny holes in the ceiling of many schools and offices. They help kill noise. Chrysler's C. R. Cheney explains:

> The headliners in some automobiles and trucks have small perforations in them to help improve their sound-absorbing qualities. The perforated surface of the headliner is usually a vinyl or hardboard material and it is applied over a layer of foam. The holes serve to admit sound from inside the vehicle and allow it to be damped by the foam layer to promote a quieter environment for passengers.

> To some, the patterns made by the tiny perforations were also pleasing to the eye, so perhaps the perforations served double duty.

Let's not stretch it, C.R.

Submitted by Garland Lyn of Windsor, Connecticut.

DO PENGUINS HAVE KNEES? 483

What Does the "YKK" Emblazoned on My Zipper Mean?

It means that you are the proud possessor of a zipper made by YKK Inc. (That *is* why you bought that pair of pants, isn't it?) Now perhaps YKK's emblem is a little less picturesque than an alligator or a polo player, but then, who except *Imponderables* readers busy themselves by reading their zippers, anyway? And the subdued logo hasn't seem to hurt YKK's business; Izod and Ralph Lauren would kill for the 75+ percent share of their market that YKK commands.

YKK, the largest zipper manufacturer in the world, stands for Yoshida Kogyo Kabushikikaisha (now you know why they call themselves YKK). Yoshida is the last name of the founder of the company, Tadao Yoshida. In English, YKK is translated as Yoshida Industries Inc.

Submitted by Juli Haugen of West Boothbay Harbor, Maine. Thanks also to Gwen Shen of San Francisco, California; M. Sullivan of Miami, Florida; Becky Wrenn of Palo Alto, California; Tisha Land of South Portland, Maine; Anne Daubendiek of Rochester, New York; Chris Engeland of Ottawa, Ontario; and many others.

Why Do VCR Manuals Advise You to Disconnect the Machine During Storms?

If lightning strikes your home and your antenna or AC power line is not properly grounded, you can find yourself with a busted VCR. William J. Goffi, of the Maxell Corporation, explains:

> . . . the electrical surge will find its way through your home's wiring and into your VCR, and consequently cause much damage to your unit. This is true, however, for any electrical appliance you

DAVID FELDMAN

have. A surge of lightning can blow out your television monitor, your stereo, etc.

Purchasing a surge protector will protect your investments.

As Mark Johnson, a spokesperson for Panasonic, points out, an electrical surge can blow out an electrical appliance even if it is off, which is why the manual recommends disconnecting the plug.

Another potential threat to a connected appliance is a sudden surge of power from the local electric power utility. Surge protectors will also usually solve this problem.

Submitted by Richie, a caller on the Dan Rodricks show, Baltimore, Maryland.

In Baseball, Why Is the Pitcher's Mound Located 60′6″ from Home Plate?

The answer comes from Bill Deane, senior research associate of the National Baseball Hall of Fame:

> The pitcher's box was originally positioned 45 feet from home plate. It was moved back to 50 feet in 1881. After overhand pitching was legalized, it was moved back to 60′6″ in 1893.

Why was the mound moved back? For the same reason that fences are moved in—teams were not generating enough offense. Morris Eckhouse, executive director of the Society for American Baseball Research, told *Imponderables* that around the turn of the century, batters were having a hard time making contact with the ball.

But what cosmic inspiration led to the choice of 60′6″ as the proper distance? Deane says there is evidence indicating that "the unusual distance resulted from a misread architectural drawing that specified 60′0″."

Submitted by Kathy Cripe of South Bend, Indiana.

DO PENGUINS HAVE KNEES?   485

Why Does Grease Turn White When It Cools?

You finish frying some chicken. You reach for the used coffee can to discard the hot oil. You open the lid of the coffee can and the congealed grease is thick, not thin, and not the yellowish-gold color of the frying oil you put in before, but whitish, the color of glazed doughnut frosting. Why is the fat more transparent when it is an oil than when it is grease?

When the oil cools, it changes its physical state, just as transparent water changes into more opaque ice when it freezes. Bill DeBuvitz, a longtime *Imponderables* reader and, more to the point, an associate professor of physics at Middlesex County College in New Jersey, explains:

> When the grease cools, it changes from a liquid to a solid. Because of its molecular structure, it cannot quite form a crystalline structure. Instead, it forms "amorphous regions" and "partial crystals." These irregular areas scatter white light and make the grease appear cloudy.
>
> If grease were to solidify into a pure crystal, it would be much clearer, maybe like glass. Incidentally, paraffins like candle wax behave just like grease: They are clear in the liquid form and cloudy in the solid form.

Submitted by Eric Schmidt of Fairview Park, Ohio.

Why Is the Skin Around Our Finger Knuckles Wrinkled When the Skin Covering Our Knees Is Not?

We received this Imponderable about three years ago, in a stack of letters from Judith Bambenek's South St. Paul High School class. No doubt, her students were bludgeoned into writing us, but we were nevertheless impressed by the quality of the ques-

DAVID FELDMAN

tions. By now, we're sure that Chris Dahlke is on the way to becoming a Rhodes Scholar.

Dr. Harry Arnold, Jr., a distinguished dermatologist from the land of Rice-A-Roni, was happy to solve the Imponderable troubling the youth of South St. Paul:

> In extension, the knuckles need enough skin to permit flexing the joint roughly through 100 degrees, so there is excess skin when the joint is fully extended.
>
> The knees require much less skin but there is wrinkling there too, over a much larger area, so it is less obvious. Even with the extra skin, we get "white-knuckled" when the joints in the knee are fully flexed.

We're sometimes amazed at the lengths to which our sources will extend themselves for the sake of science and the vanquishing of Imponderability. In the case of Chesapeake, Virginia, dermatologist Samuel T. Selden, it included disrobing. Selden has a speculative but fascinating anthropological theory to explain the knee-finger disparity:

> I had to take off my shoes and socks to check, but interestingly, the skin over the knuckles of our toes is not very wrinkled either. The skin over our elbows is corrugated, but not to the degree that the skin over the finger knuckles is wrinkled.
>
> My theory for the wrinkling is that our ancestors, the apes, walked on their fingers, as we probably did prior to becoming upright beasts. The wrinkles are most apparent over the middle knuckles, the proximal interphalangeal joints, where apes place most of their weight when walking. Some individuals, through heredity, have thickened skin in this area known as "knuckle pads," and they are probably even more of a throwback to their ape ancestors.

We're sure they'll be thrilled to hear that.

Submitted by Chris Dahlke of South St. Paul, Minnesota.
Special thanks to Chris's teacher, Judith Bambenek.

Where Does All of the Old Extra Oil in Your Car's Engine Lurk After an Oil Change?

Our befuddled correspondent, Victor Berman, elaborates:

> Just before you change your oil you can check the dipstick. The oil level is "full." You then drain the oil and change the filter, put in the recommended amount of oil, and check the dipstick. The level is "full."
>
> Now you go to dispose of the old oil from the crank case and the filter and, lo and behold, there is less than five quarts. More like three to three and one-half quarts. I know that even after turning over the filter and letting it drain there is some oil left in the filter, but not one and one-half quarts. Is my car's engine storing an extra quart and a half every time I change the oil?

We were intrigued with this mystery, so we contacted several auto manufacturers, who had no explanation for the case of the missing oil. So we persisted, engaging in two long conversations with oil specialists: H. Dale Millay, a research engineer for Shell Oil, and Dan Arcy, a technical service representative for Pennzoil Products Company. After much soul-searching, all of us decided we still had an Imponderable, bordering on a Frustable, on our hands.

Some questions don't yield one simple answer. So the experts ventured several possible explanations:

> 1. If the oil change is conducted while the engine is cold, the oil will be thicker and tend to sit on the motor's surface and coat internal surfaces. Even hot oil will wet the internal surfaces and result in some oil loss.
>
> 2. The amount of oil unleashed depends to a great extent upon the location of the plug on the drain. Dan Arcy points out that Ford, for example, manufactures several models with two drain plugs—one needs to pull both plugs to get rid of all the oil.
>
> 3. In some cases, the slant of the car may inhibit or promote freer flow of oil out of the drain. Any flat reservoir has to be tipped over to spill out all of the contents.

DAVID FELDMAN

4. Are you sure you drained the oil filter adequately? Millay thinks the oil filter, which is built to hold up to two quarts of oil, is the most likely hiding place for most of the missing oil.

5. Oil will continue to drizzle out of the plug a long time, often an hour or more. This doesn't explain the loss of a quart and one-half, but then every drip counts when trying to solve this Imponderable.

6. A significant amount of oil may be left on your oil pan. Not a quart, perhaps, but a half-pint or so may be underestimated if spread around a pan with a large circumference.

7. Not to challenge your dipstick-reading acuity, Victor, but our experts wanted to ask you if you are sure you were really checking the oil directly before changing it. All engines are designed to consume some oil when operating.

8. How about a mundane reason? A leak? Arcy relayed an astonishing maxim of the industry: The loss of one drop of oil every fifty-five feet is equivalent to the consumption of one quart of oil in 500 miles. Of course, the leak theory doesn't explain why the oil shortfall occurs only when changing the oil.

Any readers have a solution to this greasy Imponderable?

Submitted by Victor Berman of East Hartford, Connecticut.

Why Do Fish Float Upside-Down When They Die?

Imponderables cannot be held responsible for the consequences if you read this answer within thirty minutes of starting or finishing a meal. With this proviso, we yield the floor to Doug Olander, director of special projects for the International Game Fish Association:

> Fish float upside-down when they die because internal decomposition releases gases that collect in the gut cavity. Anyone who's ever cleaned a fish knows the meat is on top (dorsally) and the thin stomach wall on the bottom (ventrally). So as gases accumulate, the dense muscle mass of the top of the fish is positioned down and the gas-filled stomach up.
>
> Fishes with swim bladders already have gas inside, which tends to make them at least neutrally buoyant. Benthic fishes, lacking swim bladders (flatfishes, for example) would *not* float upon death.

490   DAVID FELDMAN

Deepwater fishes float high atop the surface when pulled rapidly upward, a common angling experience, because the gas trapped inside their swim bladder expands at the reduced pressure of the surface.

Dr. Robert Rofen, of the Aquatic Research Institute, adds that since so much of a fish's body weight is concentrated along the bone structure of the back and skull, it is not uncommon to find dead fish floating with heads down.

Submitted by Melissa Hall of Bartlett, Illinois.

Why Do Some Companies Use Mail-In Refunds Rather Than Coupons?

Applying our usual paranoid logic, we always assumed that more people will redeem coupons at a grocery store than will bother tearing off proofs of purchase and mailing in forms to receive a refund. Therefore, a mail-in refund's purpose in life was to seduce you into buying eight cans of tuna but then being too lazy to ever send in the proofs of purchase and cash register receipt to receive the rebate.

We remember once soaking pineapple cans in hot water, trying to peel labels off to send as proofs of purchase, and wondering: "Is this why we were put on earth? There must be a better way." But there is logic in marketers' refund nonsense.

F. Kent Mitchel, chairman of the Marketing Science Institute, confirmed our conspiracy theory:

Mail-in refunds are generally less expensive largely because of lower usage by the public, yet they protect existing brands about as well as coupons in a competitive situation.

What does Mitchel mean by "protect"? In many cases, coupons are used to promote items that consumers consider as commodities, with insubstantial differences in quality, and where brand loyalty may not withstand a pricing differential. Pepsico and Coca-Cola wage perpetual price wars in the stores and through coupons. A similar skirmish invades the detergent and coffee aisles. Coupons and mail-in refunds, then, are often used to "protect" one brand against price cuts by competing brands.

In many cases, the cash reward for mail-in refunds is higher than those for coupons, but the lower redemption rates make mail-ins cheaper in the long run. As Robert A. Grayson, publisher of *The Journal of Consumer Marketing*, told *Imponderables*, "the promotion looks as big but doesn't cost as much," particularly if consumers purchase the goods and neglect to ever send for the rebate.

But cost isn't the primary consideration in implementing a mail-in rather than a coupon campaign. The choice is really a strategic decision dictated by whom the marketer is trying to attract. Thomas L. Ruble, consumer response manager of the Louis Rich Company, explains:

> Coupons are used to stimulate new business—to encourage first-time buyers. Mail-in refunds, on the other hand, encourage continuity among the established customer base. Mail-ins also encourage established customers to purchase multiple packages.

Mail-in refunds are also most effective for products, including foods, sold outside of grocery stores. Supermarkets are geared for the paperwork involved in processing coupons. But a family-run hardware or camera store might not know how to receive compensation for the refund on a package of batteries or be willing to put up with the nuisance of doing so.

One other crucial point. By making you fill out personal information for the refund, the marketer now has in its possession your name and address. Most companies retain this information in databases, and then can ply you with direct-mail campaigns.

DAVID FELDMAN

Why Do Grocery Coupons Have Expiration Dates?

Why are some grocery coupons effective for only a few weeks? Why would the marketer spend so much money, not only in redeeming coupons but in placing them in newspapers, only to invalidate the coupons so quickly?

Usually, the expiration date is added for the same reason a deadline was placed on when your term paper in school was due: Marketers, like teachers, know that you need a cattle prod and the threat of a deadly weapon to motivate you to act in the "right" way.

Occasionally, a company might want to spur sales, either because the brand is in danger of losing its shelf space if sales don't improve or because the company (or a particular executive) needs to demonstrate sales growth in a short period. As we have already said, coupons can be used as a preemptive price-cutting strike against new (or old but gaining) competition.

But another, more important financial consideration plagues food marketers, one that threatened the financial stability of the airlines after frequent flier programs were instituted. F. Kent Mitchel, chairman of the Marketing Science Institute, explains:

> Expiration dates reduce the liability of the float. Only a small percentage of coupons are ever redeemed and a company budgets to cover the expected redemption. There are literally billions of coupons floating around at any time and if all the coupons that a company issued were redeemed, it would be an enormous unanticipated expense and could quite possibly bankrupt even a large company.
>
> To avoid this unsavory possibility, coupons are rendered valueless after a certain time by using expiration dates. It has been my experience that most major manufacturers will redeem coupons beyond their expiration dates if presented with the proper proof of purchase.

Maybe. But will the supermarkets redeem them?

Submitted by Linda Harris of Holbrook, Maine.

DO PENGUINS HAVE KNEES? 493

Why Do Only Female Mosquitoes Eat Human Blood? What Do Male Mosquitoes Eat?

No, the mosquito menfolk aren't out eating steak and potatoes. Actually, the main food of both male and female mosquitoes is nectar from flowers. The nectar is converted to glycogen, a fuel potent enough to provide their muscles with energy to fly within minutes of consuming the nectar. Mosquitoes also possess an organ, known as the fat-body, that is capable of storing sugar for conversion to flight fuel.

Male mosquitoes can exist quite happily on a diet of only nectar, and nature makes certain that they are content—males don't have a biting mouth part capable of piercing the skin of a human. But females have been anatomically equipped to bite because they have an important job to do: lay eggs. In some species, female mosquitoes are not capable of laying any eggs unless they eat a nutritional supplement of some tasty, fresh blood. Their organs convert the lipids in blood into iron and protein that can greatly increase their fecundity.

A mosquito that would lay five or ten eggs without the supplement can lay as many as 200 with a dash of Type O. Although we don't miss the blood sucked out of us, this is quite a feast for the mosquito; many times, she consumes more than her own body weight in blood.

But let's not take it personally. Some studies have indicated that given a choice, mosquitoes prefer the blood of cows to humans, and in the jungle are just as likely to try to bite a monkey or a bird as a human.

Submitted by Carolyn Imbert of Yuba City, California.

DAVID FELDMAN

If the Third Prong on an Electrical Plug Is for Grounding and Shock Protection, Why Don't All Plugs Have Three Prongs?

In the good old days, electrical plugs had two prongs and the receptacles were ungrounded. If you happened to use the wrong side of the circuit, it could be a shocking experience. So a simple and effective idea was developed: add a third prong. Don French, chief engineer for Radio Shack, explains the principle:

> If any short circuit developed in the wiring or device being powered, then instead of shocking the next person who touched the device, the third prong, being grounded, would carry the current until a fuse would blow. Now it is common to find three-pronged plugs on most portable and stationary appliances.

Meanwhile, however, other engineers were working on "double insulated" prongs that do not require a third prong for protection. Although the third prong was rendered unnecessary, most old receptacles weren't wide enough to receive the fatter prongs—another example of incompatible technologies that benefited the manufacturers (think of all the consumers who had to refit receptacles and buy new extension cords to hold double insulated prongs) and bankrupted the consumer.

Submitted by Ronald C. Semone of Washington, D.C. Thanks also to Terry L. Stibal of Belleville, Illinois; David A. Kroffe of Los Alamitos, California; Margaret K. Schwallie of Kalamazoo, Michigan; Kurt Dershem of Holland, Michigan; Layton Taylor of Yankton, Michigan; and Robert King of Newbury Park, California.

Why Does Menthol Feel Cool to the Taste and Cool to the Skin?

Of course, the temperature of menthol shaving cream isn't any lower than that of musk shaving cream. So clearly, something funny is going on. R. J. Reynolds's public relations representative, Mary Ann Usrey, explains the physiological shenanigans:

> The interior of the mouth contains many thermoreceptors that respond to cooling. These thermoreceptors may be compared to the receptors for the sensations of "sweet," "salty," "bitter," etc.
>
> In other words, individual receptors respond to specific types of stimulation. For example, a person's perception that sugar is sweet is initiated when the receptors in the mouth for "sweet" are stimulated. Menthol feels cools to the taste because menthol stimulates the thermoreceptors that respond normally to cooling.
>
> Menthol has the ability to "trick" those thermoreceptors into responding. The brain receives the message that what is being experienced is "cool."
>
> Although not as easy to stimulate by menthol as those in the mouth, the skin also contains those types of thermoreceptors, which is why menthol shaving cream or shaving lotion feels cool to the skin.

Submitted by Allan J. Wilke of Cedar Rapids, Iowa.

Why Do Bridges Freeze Before Nearby Roads?

Asphalt, used in most roads, retains heat better than bridge decks, which are usually made out of concrete slabs. But the most important reason has more to do with elementary physics. Stanley Gordon, chief of the Bridge Division of the Federal Highway Administration, explains:

> A bridge deck will freeze before a roadway pavement because it is exposed to the environment from both the top and the bottom sides. In contrast, a roadway pavement is only exposed to the environment from the top side.

In other words, the earth itself provides insulation to roads. Any heat that accumulates in the bridge during the day will be released as the ambient temperature drops. As Amy Steiner, program director for the American Association of State Highway and

Transportation Officials, put it, "Bridge decks can release only heat absorbed by the deck itself and obviously do not benefit from the heat retained by the soil."

Submitted by Roger Mullis of Eureka, California.

Chew ...it won't lose its flavor you-know-where!

Why Can't They Make the Flavor in Chewing Gum Last Longer?

Call us paranoid, but we always suspected that gum manufacturers attended trade seminars on such subjects as "The Enemy: Long-Lasting Flavor," "How to Make Sure Your Customers' Chewing Gum Loses Its Flavor on the Bedpost Overnight," and "How to Make Your Gum Tasteless Before Your Sucker Customer Has Thrown Away the Wrapper." Emboldened by such rhetoric, the gum makers see dollar signs floating above their eyes and produce gum whose flavor lasts less time than a Zsa Zsa Gabor marriage. Naive consumers are then confronted with the imperative of plopping another stick of gum into their mouths to receive the flavor jolt they received all of, maybe, three minutes ago.

But industry folks insist that the conspiracy theory just isn't true. In fact, Bill O'Connor, director of administration at the Topps Company, told *Imponderables* that if a company could create a gum that retained flavor longer, it would hammer this competitive advantage home in advertisements. Wrigley's has done just that with its Extra gum, which uses "encapsulation," little flavor pockets that require more mouth action than conventional gum to draw out its flavor. In essence, Wrigley created a time-release gum.

But even encapsulation doesn't beat the two main enemies of flavor retention in chewing gum:

1. The saliva generated from chewing literally drags the flavoring (and sugar) out of the gum.
2. The mouth gets fatigued and sensitized to any flavor eventually.

O'Connor suggests that if you put aside a "used" piece of gum, eat a saltine to cleanse the palate, and then plop the gum back into your mouth, it will taste flavorful again.

May we suggest an alternative: plopping a new stick of gum in your mouth.

What Is the Purpose of the Plastic Bags in Airline Oxygen Masks When They Don't Inflate?

We're always amazed when we find out that an airplane has been evacuated successfully during an emergency landing. The airlines try to do a good job briefing passengers on the safety requirements before takeoff. But a quick scan of the passengers will indicate that the seasoned fliers are already napping or deeply engrossed in the scintillating inflight magazine, while the less experienced tend to be hanging on every word, in a panic, trying to conjure in their minds how they can convert their seat cushion into a flotation device.

We tend to combine the worst aspects of both types of passengers. We attempt to read our newspaper, having heard the announcement 80 million times, but we're actually trying to suppress our fear that there aren't *really* oxygen masks up there that are going to drop down during an emergency.

All white-knucklers are familiar with the proviso in the safety demonstrations of oxygen masks: "Although the bag won't inflate, oxygen is still flowing . . ." or the variant, "Although the bag will not *fully* inflate . . ." Several sharp *Imponderables* readers have wondered: If the bag doesn't inflate, why does it have to be there? Our image of an oxygen bag comes from *Ben Casey*, where resuscitators inflated, deflated, and reflated as violently as a fad dieter.

But the bag does serve a purpose. Honest. The mask used by airlines is called a "phased-dilution" mask. As you inhale, you are breathing in a mixture of ambient air and oxygen. Compressed oxygen is quite expensive, and particularly at low altitudes, you actually need very little pure oxygen even if the cabin is depressurized.

A nasty little secret is that a bizarre cost-saving device, the "oxygen mask" used in safety demonstrations, is not the real thing (if you look carefully, on most airlines, the mask will be marked "DEMO") and isn't even an exact replica. The real oxygen mask contains three valves that are the key to regulating your breathing in an emergency. The first, interior, valve pumps in pure oxygen. When the oxygen is depleted, the valve closes and the second, exterior valve opens and brings in ambient air (thus the term "phased-dilution"). The third, external valve, with a spring device, opens only to allow you to vent your exhalation.

According to oxygen equipment expert David DiPasquale, an engineer and administrative and technical consultant and major domo at DiPasquale & Associates, the normal cabin pressure is set to simulate the atmosphere of approximately 8,000 feet. The oxygen system automatically adjusts to different altitudes, varying the flow of oxygen. The higher the altitude, the higher percentage of oxygen (to ambient air) and the faster the flow rate of oxygen is required. During decompression, a plane may suddenly find itself at an atmosphere equivalent to the ambient air at 35,000 feet or higher.

The bottom line is that there is no reason on earth why the plastic bag should inflate dramatically. The oxygen bag itself might hold about a liter and one-half of gas. At 18,000 feet, the system might pump in about one liter per minute; at 40,000 feet, about three liters per minute. But unlike the *Ben Casey* resuscitator, only a small percentage of this gas is inhaled in any one breath.

At higher altitudes, the bag will noticeably inflate, both because the flow rate of oxygen is much higher and because the bag has a natural tendency to expand when air pressure is lower. As Richard E. Livingston, of the Airline Passengers Association of North America, put it:

> Since oxygen, like other gases, expands at higher altitudes, maximum inflation will be obvious at high altitude. Conversely, gases are more compressed at low altitudes, so little or no bag inflation will be evident at lower altitudes.

Submitted by Charles Myers of Ronkonkoma, New York. Thanks also to Mick Luce of Portland, Oregon, and Stanley Fenvessy of New York, New York. Special thanks to Jim Cannon of Lenexa, Kansas.

Frustables

The 10 Most Wanted OR Imponderables

We don't claim to be infallible. In fact, most of the time, we are experts in fallibility. Too often for our satisfaction, readers confront us with fascinating Imponderables that we cannot answer. These Imponderables tend to fall into two groups: mysteries that totally baffle the experts we consult; or mysteries that every expert has an opinion on, but for which there is no consensus.

Either way, our inability to answer these questions makes us frustrated. So, we throw Frustables (short for "frustrating Imponderables") out to you in the fervent hope that you can do better than we can. It's amazing how often you can, as demonstrated in the Frustables Update section that follows.

To lure you into sharing your wisdom, we offer a complimentary, autographed copy of our next volume of *Imponderables* to the first person who can lead to the proof that solves any of these Frustables. And of course, your contribution will be displayed and acknowledged in the book.

But don't get smug until you see the new Frustables. Solving these will not be easy.

FRUSTABLE 1: *Why Do Doctors Have Bad Penmanship?*

Even physicians we contacted agreed that the stereotype is, more often than not, true. You wouldn't believe how many theories we've heard to explain/deplore/rationalize/excuse this phenomenon. We have been able to confirm that no medical school in the United States offers a specific course on bad penmanship. So is there any other explanation?

FRUSTABLE 2: *Why Are Salt and Pepper the Standard Condiments on Home and Restaurant Tables? When and Where Did This Custom Start?*

We look upon salt and pepper on the table as being as inevitable as the plate and silverware. But it didn't have to be that way.

FRUSTABLE 3: *Why Don't People Wear Hats as Much as They Used to?*

The comeback of the hat has been bandied about as much as the return of big bands. But it never seems to happen. We have millions of theories about this but no consensus has emerged. Have any *Imponderables* readers given up wearing hats? If so, why?

FRUSTABLE 4: *How and Why Were the Letters B-I-N-G-O Selected for the Game of the Same Name?*

Before bingo, many similar games existed with different names.

FRUSTABLE 5: *Why Do They Always Play Dixieland Music at Political Rallies When Dixieland Isn't Particularly Burning Up the Hit Parade at the Moment?*

Do political consultants hire Dixieland bands because that's what politicians have always done? Is Dixieland the least objectionable musical form? If so, why don't you hear it more often on the radio?

FRUSTABLE 6: *Why Does Eating Ice Cream Make You Thirsty?*

Most of the taste experts and ice cream makers we've contacted deny that the premise of this question is true. But we've received the question several times and experienced the sensation ourselves. We even had a friend who loved malts and would drink one and then order an iced tea to quench his thirst.

FRUSTABLE 7: *Why Are Belly Dancers So Zaftig?*

By Western standards, belly dancers are rather fleshy around the midriff, surprising in artists who are constantly exercising this region. Experts we've contacted differ violently on this subject.

DAVID FELDMAN

Some say that the muscles contracted to belly dance are not those that would make the belly look Sheena Eastonish. Some say that standards of beauty in the Middle East are different and that most dancers deliberately keep some flesh. And others denied the premise. What do you think?

FRUSTABLE 8: *How Was Hail Measured Before Golf Balls Were Invented?*

Okay, we admit we're being facetious here, but we would be interested if any readers have heard hail compared to *anything* besides a ball (golf balls and baseballs are about all we ever hear) by local weathercasters.

FRUSTABLE 9: *Why Did 1930s and 1940s Movie Actors Talk So Much Faster Than They Do Today?*

Compare a Katharine Hepburn–Cary Grant comedy or a Bogie–Bacall melodrama with their contemporary counterparts, and they sound like a 45-rpm record playing at 78. What accounts for the huge change? We've heard tons of theories about this Frustable, too. But what are yours?

FRUSTABLE 10: *Why Does Meat Loaf Taste the Same in All Institutions?*

We admit that this is a personal obsession of ours. Ever since we noticed that meat loaf tasted the same in every school we ever attended, we've sampled the meat loaf any time we've been forced to eat at a cafeteria in an institution such as a federal building, hospital, or college. Does the government circulate a special *Marquis de Sade Cookbook?* Not all meat loaf tastes the same, but somehow the meat loaf at an elementary school in Los Angeles tastes the same as the meat loaf at a courtroom cafeteria in New York. Why does it?

Frustables Update

FRUSTABLE 1: *Does Anyone Really Like Fruitcake?*

As expected, we received more mail about fruitcake than all the other Frustables in *Why Do Dogs Have Wet Noses?* combined. When we posed this Frustable, we suspected that there wasn't one definitive answer to explain such a complex phenomenon as the perpetuation of this foodstuff, especially as a gift, that nobody seems to like. We were right.

Reader Bill Gerk, of Burlingame, California, was kind enough to point out that one of our favorite writers, Calvin Trillin, devoted a whole magazine column to this subject. Trillin claimed that "nobody in the history of the United States has ever bought a fruitcake for himself." Trillin was besieged with letters from readers claiming they had bought fruitcakes, "although the receipts are never enclosed."

Like Trillin, we can't offer proofs of purchase, but we certainly heard from fruitcake lovers. Scores of readers, including Lilet Quijano of Livermore, California, Edmund DeWan of Urbana, Illinois, Anne Wingate of Salt Lake City, Utah, and Betty Begley of Cambria, California, offered to accept the unwanted fruitcakes of *Imponderables* readers. We'd include the full addresses of these folks, but fear lawsuits if the offers were simply a sick joke.

Several fruitcake-loving readers tried to ingratiate themselves by claiming that the silent majority would grow to love fruitcake *if they only tried a good one.* Claire Manning of Brooklyn, New York, not only admits to liking fruitcake ("a noble, beloved, memory-evoking little piece of heaven") but to perpetrating said dessert on innocent friends and family:

> Consider yourself among the underprivileged for this omission in your poor life. I not only adore fruitcake but I *make* it every year at the winter holiday season and do occasionally give it as a gift. So far, I haven't *received* any . . . are they trying to tell me something?

Fruitcake can bring people together. Robert Tanner, of Naples, Florida, reports that he and his wife both love fruitcake. We are genuinely happy that they found each other but we must raise a sobering question: Should such a couple have children? Is the preference for fruitcake a hereditary trait? From the evidence of our mailbag, we think so.

Dorothy Lant, of Concord, New Hampshire, reports that her entire family likes fruitcake. Bisbee, Arizona's Judy R. Reis notes that her daughters do, her sisters do, and her parents do. Her son doesn't, but he only likes things with ketchup on them.

But fruitcake worship can cause family problems. Kim Anderson, of Alma, Arkansas, reports that because "My mom, my sister, my grandma, and my aunt like it, we always have fruitcake at Christmas, much to the dismay of me and the rest of the family members." But Kim's suffering is nothing compared to the shame of Melanie Morton, of Branford, Connecticut:

> Yes, there are people who like fruitcake. I believe this is an indication of mental imbalance. I offer as an example my father. He is overly fond of the stuff. In fact, he is not content to wait to be gifted with it. He actually goes out *in search of fruitcake!* As if

this is not enough, he hates chocolate. He's not allergic, mind you, he merely detests this wonderful creation.

Yes, fruitcake can wrench families apart.

So if the love of fruitcake is an unnatural preference, who is conspiring to foist this Milli Vanilli of foods upon us? Fred Steinberg, of Newton, New Jersey, thinks it is the evil of free enterprise. Fred once had a business professor who told the story of the marketing of the electric knife. Market research indicated from the start that consumers wouldn't actually use the appliance once they owned it. Still, they proceeded with the introduction of the product because it was a perfect present,

> a present for "kids" to give to their mom for Mother's Day, for people to give as shower gifts. An electric knife is not inexpensive, not expensive, and appears to be useful. That's why they were manufactured, bought by consumers, and now lie dormant in some remote drawer . . .

In other words, Steinberg's theory is that enterprising bakers have created a food designed to be given away rather than eaten. When you think of it this way, fruitcake is the ultimate diet food, since it is never actually consumed.

Some readers thought that fruitcake was a foreign conspiracy, with the English cited as the usual culprits. Given their reputation for fine cuisine, we are inclined to believe that the English invented fruitcake. Jennifer Beres, of Norwalk, Connecticut, actually sent us a sample of her mother's homemade fruitcake, which, even in the spirit of scientific investigation, we did not have the fortitude to sample. Jennifer veritably gushes with praise for the English art:

> My mother is British born and professes the fruitcake's existence originates in English tradition. Perhaps the reason that no one likes fruitcake is that the creation of a fruitcake is an art not to be duplicated in commercial factories by swiftly moving assembly lines. In order for a fruitcake to be made in the true English tradition, it must be meticulously and lovingly prepared by an experienced and appreciative fruitcake lover.

. . . After the fruitcake itself has been made, it is covered with a layer of marzipan, followed by a light and fluffy white icing of egg whites and confectioners sugar, which hardens to resemble snow. The cake is then decorated with Christmas scenes, using miniature wooden sleighs, plastic Santas, and the like.

Presumably, the diner can discriminate between the taste and texture of the cake and the plastic Santa.

But it is too easy to blame the English for what is now a worldwide problem. We are more concerned about the tight connection between fruitcake and alcohol. Timothy Taormino, of Baltimore, Maryland, admits to liking fruitcake, but is open-minded enough to concede that "when it's bad, it's *BAD!*" What he may not realize is that all fruitcakes might taste bad if it weren't for the demon alcohol:

> I know of a recipe from Ireland that replaces the usual brandy or whiskey with Guinness Extra Stout. My girlfriend made it for a pot-luck dinner and it was quite a hit (especially when served with an Irish whiskey hard sauce).

Why do we get the feeling that dessert, or for that matter, the appetizer, was preceded by a few cocktails?

Similarly, Jack Adams, of Valencia, California, reports that the only fruitcake he ever liked was his grandmother's, and even this affection deserves a demurral:

> She bought a fruitcake from the store and would put a shot glass of whiskey in the center hole of the fruitcake. After a few weeks of this the cake became so saturated you didn't care what else was in it.
>
> Anyway, please don't publish my address. I've already got a shot glass and whiskey. That's all I need.

Jack seems to have the right idea. If you want to drink whiskey, cut out the middleman (i.e., fruitcake) and admit what you really want to consume. If you don't, you may end up like Nancy Schmidt, who not only admits to liking fruitcake but

> so loving its distinctive flavor that I purchase surplus loaves at the

holidays to stock up so I can savor my favorite sweet yearlong.

Whew, now that I've publicly confessed to my fruitcake fetish, I'll either live a lauded life at the hands of other secret indulgers or, more likely, soon have uninvited guests in funny little white coats pounding at my front door.

Don't put yourself down, Nancy. Admitting your problem is the first step in solving it.

Honestly, now, despite the naysaying of the apologists, the sympathizers, and the fetishists, fruitcake truly is awful stuff. If people really do like fruitcake, why can't it compete on the open market? If anyone would ever order it, restaurants would offer fruitcake as a dessert. If fruitcake is so visually inviting and festive, why don't cafeterias ever offer it to lure customers? Wouldn't someone at Christmas dinner eat it (besides the baker of the cake, of course)?

We do not doubt the sincerity of the many readers who've had the courage to admit their dubious preference. We can only hope that greater minds than ours can someday finally figure out whether the preference is hereditary or environmental, mental or physical, spiritual or demonic. Until then, our mailbox is open to your theories, suggestions, and sordid confessions.

Submitted by Sheila Payne of Falmouth, Massachusetts.

A complimentary book goes to Nancy Schmidt of West New York, New Jersey, who perhaps will spend her holiday period reading instead of roaming the streets in search of surplus fruitcake; and to Melanie Morton, of Branford, Connecticut, in the fervent hope that reading this chapter together will help heal her family from the wrenching tragedy of fruitcake friction.

FRUSTABLE 2: *Why Does the Stroking of Index Fingers Against Each Other Mean "Tsk-Tsk"?*

We still don't have a definite answer to this Frustable, but two readers, Marsha Bruno of Norwich, Connecticut, and David

Schachow of West Hill, Ontario, came up with the identical theory. Although neither claims to have any evidence to prove the contention, it makes sense to us. Since David was the first to write, we'll quote him:

> The two index fingers are generally the two that are used in making the sign of the cross (and the same fingers we use to cross our fingers for good luck, or make the sign of the cross to ward off vampires and relatives).
>
> But why the stroking? Perhaps this is an evolved form of the whole cross (both fingers) being waved at or pushed toward the naughty-doer.

In other words, the "tsk-tsk" stroke is emblematic of pushing evil away.

Can anyone come up with anything better?

Submitted by Jim Hayden of Salem, Oregon. Thanks also to Mr. and Mrs. William H. McCollum of Oakdale, Minnesota.

FRUSTABLE 3: *We Often Hear the Cliché: "We Only Use 10 Percent of Our Brains." How Was It Determined That We Use 10 Percent and Not 5 Percent or 15 Percent?*

A few readers found written references to this cliché, but they have had no more luck than we did in tracking down its origins. Jeff White of Etobicoke, Ontario, and Albert J. Menaster of Los Angeles, California, both remembered that Richard Restak's 1984 book, *The Brain*, based on the PBS television series, mentioned the 10 percent theory. Menaster summarizes the contents:

> Restak says that the claim is probably based on studies showing large portions of the brain being damaged without any observable effects. ... His conclusion is that since no one knows the number of neurons in the brain, it is simply impossible to determine how much of the brain is actually being used, and thus the 10 percent figure is without any basis and is unsupported by anything. I should add that I have read extensively on the subject of the brain, and I have never seen any scientific discussion of the 10 percent figure, which certainly supports Restak's position.

DAVID FELDMAN

Restak goes on to note that the destruction of even a small portion of certain areas of the brain, such as the visual area, "can have a devastating effect."

One of the studies that Restak refers to obliquely is psychoneurologist Karl Lashley's, who removed portions of the cerebral cortex of rats without ruining their memory of how to run mazes. Reader Jeffrey McLean of Sterling Heights, Michigan, drew our attention to Carl Sagan's *The Dragons of Eden,* which discusses this issue. Sagan warns readers that just because we cannot see any behavioral change in a rat doesn't mean that there isn't a profound change when humans lose a portion of their brains:

> There is a popular contention that half or more of the brain is unused. From an evolutionary point of view this would be quite extraordinary: why should it have evolved if it had no function?

Sagan suggests that it is likely that the removal of a significant part of the brain does have a significant effect, even if we aren't currently capable of measuring or quantifying the change.

So, at least two popular science books testify to the existence of the cliché, but we are no closer to an answer to the genesis of the belief. Two friends swear that they remember reading about the 10 percent theory in a novel by Robert Heinlein, but we haven't been able to track it down yet.

Frustable 3 from *Why Do Dogs Have Wet Noses?* is still open for business.

Submitted by David Fuller of East Hartford, Connecticut.
Thanks also to Ray Jackendoff of Waltham, Massachusetts, and
Jeff White of Etobicoke, Ontario.

FRUSTABLE 4: *Where, Exactly, Did the Expression "Blue Plate Special" Come From?*

Reader Marty Flower provided us with a hot tip. She suggested we call the Homer Laughlin China Company, in Newell, West Virginia, the largest and one of the oldest suppliers of café and hotel china in the United States.

We called them and found to our consternation that although

they sell blue plates, they didn't start the practice, and didn't know the origin of "blue plate specials."

We were forlorn until we heard from Roger Bosley, of Arvada, Colorado, who sent along a reprint from a book (*A History of Man's Progress*) from and about Pioneer Village in Minden, Nebraska. This book claims that the now familiar blue willow pattern of china was inspired by a Chinese legend about a poor coolie, named Chang, who fell in love with Li Chi, the daughter of a mandarin, while playing under a willow tree. The mandarin forbade the relationship, and the willow tree drooped in sorrow over the broken romance.

The Chinese depicted the story on blue dishes, some of which were brought back to the West by Marco Polo. According to the book, written by Harold Ward, "restaurants serve their leading course on a blue willow plate and call it a 'Blue Plate' special—in tribute to this legend." Unfortunately we couldn't find any evidence connecting the "special" to the blue willow pattern.

We heard from a couple of people who encountered blue plate specials. Nazelle Trembly, of Ocean Grove, New Jersey, remembers that the plates had three-way partitions to keep sauces from running into one another. Trembly theorizes that these plates were exported from China, probably first used at sea, and then later shipped to port towns like New York, Boston, and San Francisco.

But Oree C. Weller, of Bellevue, Washington, is our only correspondent who ever washed a blue plate special. He believes that Americans imported this china from Japan!

> During the 1930's, Japan exported a lot of dishes, cups, and saucers in a hideous pattern. Cafés all over, especially the South, bought these dishes because they were cheap and the cafés could tolerate the high incidence of breakage by low-paid ($.10 per hour) dishwashers like me.
>
> The cafés served a fixed price, fixed menu lunch every day and soon customers began saying as they sat down for lunch: "What's on the blue plate for lunch today?" And hence the name stuck.

DAVID FELDMAN

Perhaps we're no closer to knowing exactly where the expression comes from, but at least we have some tantalizing theories.

A complimentary book goes to Oree C. Weller of Bellevue, Washington.

FRUSTABLE 5: *Why Does the Traffic in Big Cities in the United States Seem Quieter Than in Big Cities in Other Parts of the World?*

All of our mail echoed the same sentiment: Traffic seems quieter in the U.S. because it *is* quieter. The hero, it seems, is the catalytic converter. Typical of the responses was the letter of Toledo, Ohio's David G. Conroy:

> Traffic in Europe seems louder because it is louder. The reason—emission standards. Since 1972, all cars made in America and those imported to America must have catalytic converters built into the mufflers. Not only do these little marvels clean up auto exhausts, but they also make cars quieter. If you disagree, simply take the shielding off the converter on your car and see how much noisier it becomes.

But other factors are involved, too, best summarized by reader Jerry Arvesen of Bloomington, Indiana:

> Our federal emissions laws are more stringent than most other countries'. Only recently are European countries requiring unleaded gasoline and the technology that reduces emissions, pollution, and consequently, noise.
>
> A better-running, state-of-the-art vehicle is much quieter than a carbon-belching monster. This is especially true when comparing the United States with countries from behind the Iron Curtain, whose technology in automobiles is the equivalent of the cars we were producing in the 1950s and 1960s.
>
> Also, the traffic laws of the United States are both enforced by police and obeyed by drivers much more than they are in European countries. This would naturally lead to less noise from horns honking, the sound of fender benders, drivers yelling at each other, and the like. I once read that in Italy, traffic lights are

a guideline. A green light there means to go without reservation; a red light means go, but look first.

Our cities and states are more modern and therefore laid out much more efficiently for vehicular traffic than they are in the older European cities that are centuries old and originally designed with narrow, twisting streets barely wide enough for horses and one-way traffic to pass through.

Submitted by Nityanandan Ashwath of Richmond Heights, Ohio.

A complimentary book goes to Jerry Arvesen of Bloomington, Indiana. Thanks also to David Schachow of West Hill, Ontario, and Ron Gulli of Tuscon, Arizona.

DAVID FELDMAN

FRUSTABLE 6: *Why Do Dogs Tilt Their Heads When You Talk to Them?*

We assumed that this would be the easiest of the ten Frustables to answer. We're still amazed that not one of the thirty or so dog experts we've contacted would venture an opinion on the issue.

Imponderables readers, however, have no such compunctions. Readers were split among three camps: those that thought the tilting had to do with the dog trying to hear better; those who thought the dog was trying to sharpen his vision; and the doggy anthropologists who are confident that the tilting is a sign of (pick one) aggression or friendliness.

Devotees of the last camp often compared dogs' tilting behavior to that of wolves, who are also known to tilt their head. Typical of the anthropology camp is the response of Marty Flowers, of Weirton, West Virginia:

> Dogs tilt their heads when you talk to them to let you know they are listening to you. They don't want to just stare at you, because that's a sign of aggression in the animal world, but if they look away it might seem that they are not paying attention to you. So they look at you but tilt their heads to show that it doesn't

mean aggression. Dogs don't growl and attack you with their heads tilted to one side.

We wouldn't know. We'd be too busy hightailing it away from the dog.

The eye-camp was best represented by Jim Vibber, of Tustin, California:

> Dogs aren't the only animals that tilt their heads when listening to humans talk, and I think this may relate to the answer.
>
> We humans often forget that most other animals do not perceive the world as we do. Binocular, 3-D vision probably should head the list of differences. Most animals (including dogs, birds, cattle, and fish) have one eye on each side of the head, and each eye sees half the world with little overlap in the fields of vision. We find it disconcerting to watch a chameleon looking at its surroundings, as each eye gawks around independently of the other like some clown doing cross-eye tricks. But we think it nothing unusual to watch a cockatoo turn its head sideways to get a close look at something. The same can be seen with goldfish and parakeets whenever you do something that gets their attention.
>
> Dogs and cats have eyes a little more forward on the head than, say, sheep or elephants, but not so far forward as people. They turn their heads sideways, but also frequently perform the more subtle movement of tilting the head at an angle while keeping the nose mostly pointed in the same direction. I've also seen this tilting movement in movies, such as when a wolf is looking at something, but I have no idea how much of this is in response to off-camera coaching by the animal trainer.
>
> This *may* be a way of looking at something tall, such as a human being or a tree. Has anyone checked whether dogs respond differently according to whether one is standing, sitting, or lying down?

Not to our knowledge. Before we write the next volume of *Imponderables,* we'll consult some more veterinary ophthalmologists and check out your theory, Jim.

One point that several dog experts emphasized to us is that dogs' hearing is so good that it is highly unlikely that they are tilting their heads in order to hear us. Still, we're most sympathetic with the simpler but not unreasonable ear-theory proponents, led by Susan Scott, of Baltimore, Maryland: "Wouldn't you tilt your head if everyone around you were speaking gibberish?"

We haven't given up yet. We're going to nail this Frustable eventually.

Submitted by Mark Seifred and Denise Meade-Seifred of Memphis, Tennessee.

A complimentary book goes to Jim Vibber, who certainly has the best rap, even if we're not sure we believe it.

FRUSTABLE 7: *Why and Where Did the Notion Develop That "Fat People Are Jolly"?*

We didn't get much mail on this subject, but most of the letters we did receive were choice.

Rick DeWitt, of Erie, Pennsylvania, sent us a reprint of an essay written by Eric Berne (author of *Games People Play*) called "Can People Be Judged by Their Appearance?," which first appeared in his book *Mind in Action*. Berne argues that the three main body types (endomorph, mesomorph, and ectomorph) each yield specific personality characteristics.

According to Berne, the round, soft, thick build characteristic of the viscerotonic endomorph is usually possessed by someone who likes to "take in food, and affection, and approval as well. Going to a banquet with people who like him is his idea of a fine time." Berne's depiction of the endomorph is a catalog of stereotypes about the jolly fat person ("The short, jolly, thickset, red-faced politician with a cigar in his mouth, who always looks as though he were about to have a stroke, is the best example of this type.") with no evidence whatsoever to corroborate his conclusions.

Berne, a psychiatrist, notes that most people do not fall clearly into one body type, but claims that if someone does, he or she tends to display behavior characteristic of that body type

DO PENGUINS HAVE KNEES?   521

("If he is a viscerotonic, he will often want to go to a party where he can eat and drink and be in good company at a time when he might be better off attending to business . . ."). We're not sure Berne's discussion really answers our Frustable, but it surely demonstrates how pervasive the image of the fat, jolly person is.

We're more sympathetic with the homegrown theory of Kim Anderson, of Alma, Arkansas: "The excess fat under the skin of their faces hides wrinkles and stress lines so they appear to always be happy." This makes more sense to us than Berne.

But Melinda S. Mayfield, of Kansas City, Missouri, took us at our word about digging into the history of the fat/jolly notion:

> In ancient and medieval times, the physiologists believed that the four chief fluids or "cardinal humours" of the human body, blood, phlegm, choler (yellow bile), and melancholy (black bile), decided a person's physical and mental qualities and disposition by the dominance of one over the others. In the case of the humour blood, it created a temperament, or "complexion," called *sanguine*. A sanguine person was characterized by a ruddy countenance, a courageous, cheerful, amorous disposition, and an obese body.
>
> Even in William Shakespeare's day, people believed in the four temperaments, a fact evident in his plays. (Ever notice how the comic, happy people in them, such as Falstaff and Juliet's nurse, are fat? Well, now you know the reason.) In modern times, we no longer follow the theory of the four humours, but we do still follow Shakespeare's plays, and the idea of the florid-faced, jolly, roly-poly person has lived on.

Sounds pretty convincing to us.

A complimentary book goes to Melinda S. Mayfield of Kansas City, Missouri.

FRUSTABLE 8: *Why Do Pigs Have Curly Tails?*

We spoke to many zoologists, veterinarians, and swine breeders about this topic and struck out, so we thought we would throw the question to readers. Lo and behold, your response was exactly the same as that of the "experts."

We heard from reader Nena Hackett, who used to raise pigs. She claims, as do the swine authorities we spoke to, that you can gauge the healthiness of the pig by the curl of its tail: "The tighter the tail, the less likely it will have parasites. If the tail is loose or just 'hanging around,' the pig will be sick every time." As Richard Landesman, associate professor of zoology at the University of Vermont, put it: "There seems to be only one good reason for the curl in a pig's tail, and that is to call the vet when it straightens out. More than likely, the trait for a curly tail is just part of the pig's genetic repertoire."

Maybe the uncurled tail is like the popout thermometer on a store-bought turkey. When you see it, it's nature's way of warning you to spring into action.

Submitted by Jill Clark of West Lafayette, Indiana. Thanks also to Colleen Crozier of Anchorage, Alaska, and George Hill of Brockville, Ontario.

A complimentary book goes to Nena Hackett of Harvey in the Hills, Florida.

FRUSTABLE 9: *Why Does the Heart Depicted in Illustrations Look Totally Different Than a Real Heart?*

Before we get too carried away with wild theories, our illustrious illustrator, Kassie Schwan, gently indicated that the "symbolic" heart doesn't look *that* unlike a real heart. The two upper lobes look a lot like real atria, and the "real" heart does taper at the bottom, although not as drastically as the heart we see on Valentine's Day cards and playing cards. From her point of view, the "symbolic" heart is much easier to draw than a "real" one.

So is our stereotyped heart merely the result of lazy efforts of mediocre artists? Anthropologist Desmond Morris, always quotable, if speculative, suggests in *Bodywatching* that the form of the symbolic heart might actually have been based on the shape of the female buttocks.

A startling theory? Not compared to the discovery of New York City broadcast designer Laura Tolkow, who was looking through a book of Egyptian hieroglyphics and stumbled across several upside-down stylized hearts depicted alongside a bird and a pyramid. Laura was shocked that our stylized conception of the heart dated back to ancient times, until she read the translation of the meaning of the upside-down hearts—they weren't hearts at all, but rather human testicles (right side up!).

So now we have our Valentine shape signifying the human heart, the female buttocks, and the testicles. Any other possible explanations?

We didn't think so until we heard from reader Howard Steyn, of Morristown, New Jersey, who claims that he was taught the answer to this Frustable in his seventh-grade science class! His teacher said that the reason for our stylized heart is the vessel structure surrounding the heart. Howard sent a diagram of the circulatory system of a frog, with a series of arteries, called the systemic arch, that looks *exactly* like the Valentine heart.

We immediately called up our favorite biologist, Professor John Hertner of Kearney State College in Nebraska, to talk to him about this breakthrough in Frustability. On very short notice, John conducted some comparative embryology and reported that indeed, most vertebrates, including humans, have a structural equivalent to the frog's systemic arch, although not necessarily the "perfect" heart.

Hertner made an important point that lends even more credence to Steyn's theory. In earlier days, the Catholic Church frowned on pathological or gross anatomical work on human bodies. Most European scientists conducting research on humans were thus not able to gain access to human cadavers. Many experiments were conducted on amphibians and rodents. There is a chance, in other words, that the systemic arch of a frog, or some other animal, was considered to be part of the heart, and perhaps even an assumption that the human heart looked like the frog's.

Submitted by Kathy Cripe of South Bend, Indiana.

A complimentary book goes to Howard Steyn of Morristown, New Jersey. Special thanks to John Hertner for help beyond the call of duty.

FRUSTABLE 10: *Where Do All the Missing Pens Go?*

This question was inspired by our observation that everyone we have talked to thinks that they are a "net" loser of pens. So where do they all accumulate?

Evidently, a lot of them end up in Highland Park, Illinois:

> Most pens are probably lost through holes in pockets. I see lots of them lying on the ground, and pick up any that seem in good shape. I admit it! If you can prove that I have one of *your* pens, I would be happy to return it to you.
>
> Most of the rest of missing pens are probably borrowed temporarily, and not returned, accidentally.

This last thought was echoed by Bill Gerk, of Burlingame, California, who was the smoothest operator we heard from. With folks like Bill around, we know why banks chain their pens:

> I can't account for all of the missing pens. Just a few of them. Whenever I need to write a check in public or sign for a withdrawal, I ask the clerk or cashier, "May I borrow a pen?" After using the pen, I ask, "Did you give me this pen?" Usually the clerk or cashier will say, "Yes." I'll smile, say "Thank you," and start to put the pen into my pocket.
>
> But then I start to return it. About one out of ten times I hear, "That's O.K. You can keep it. We have a lot more." At first I did this for laughs, but if some choose to take me seriously, I settle for the pen, even if I don't get a laugh along with it.
>
> There are probably a few other similar, shameless, joking customers. Those who do this nefarious trick contribute to the disappearing pool of pens you're concerned about. By the way, if the pen you have been lent (given) doesn't write too well or you don't like the color, you may want to ask for another one before you sign anything.

We were surprised at how few readers sent theories about this Frustable. Our guess is that most readers, like us, are still losing pens and don't know why. Those of you in the state of Pennsylvania, however, are in serious jeopardy. We got a long, chatty letter from Philip M. Cohen, from West Chester, Penn-

DAVID FELDMAN

sylvania, that ended with these two chilling sentences: "Oh, one other thing. I have your pens." Aha!

Submitted by Damon Hunzeker of Boise, Idaho. Thanks also to Barry Long of Alexandria, Virginia.

A complimentary book goes to Bill Gerk of Burlingame, California. After all, if we didn't give him a book, he'd probably ask if he could borrow one. Then he'd ask if we gave him the book . . . Well, you get the idea.

The Frustables That Will Not Die

By their nature, Frustables aren't easy to solve. Even the crack *Imponderables* readers can't answer definitively some of our metaphysical quandaries. So we've promised you that we would keep you up to date on new contributions and discoveries in our search to take the Frust out of Frustables. This has become especially important since we've been putting out a new book of *Imponderables* each year, for it means that the readers of the paperback editions haven't had a chance to contribute to our forum. Here, then, are some of the best new ideas about old Frustables.

Frustables First Posed in *Why Do Clocks Run Clockwise?*

FRUSTABLE 1: *Why Do You So Often See One Shoe Lying on the Side of the Road?*

We have devoted more space to this topic than any other we have written about. We have received more mail about this subject than anything else we have ever written about. In *When Do Fish Sleep?*, we listed scores of theories to explain the phenomenon. Many of these theories assume that people deliberately throw shoes on the road. But until now, something was pointedly missing: an eyewitness account of a deliberate one-shoe toss.

We are no longer deprived. We heard from Joseph Metzelaar of Masonville, New York:

> I was reminded of an incident that happened to me while riding in a car driven by a woman wearing high heels. Her right foot repeatedly became wedged under the brake pedal, so out of sheer frustration she threw the right shoe out the window . . .

But don't get smug, readers. Cars aren't responsible for all one-shoe citings. And an alarming trend is evident. IT'S

SPREADING! We don't get too many letters from Sierra Leone, but we did get one from Peace Corps volunteer Jay D. Dillahunt, who is working in Freetown, Sierra Leone, West Africa:

> While walking down a bush path near my village, I spotted a single shoe lying in the path. There is no way it was tossed out of a car or bus window, because drivers of cars and buses have better sense than to drive down bush paths.

More proof that there is no escape from Imponderability.

FRUSTABLE 2: *Why Are Buttons on Men's Shirts and Jackets Arranged Differently from Those on Women's Shirts?*

Most readers seemed satisfied with the explanations we provided. But we heard from Tereen Flannigan of Livonia, Michigan, who said that she heard in school that during the Industrial Revolution, different taxes were imposed on the importation of men's and women's clothing in several European countries. Ingenious importers had the manufacturers change the button configuration to guarantee preferential tax treatment.

We haven't been able to confirm any of this. Does anyone else know more about this angle?

FRUSTABLE 9: *Why Don't You Ever See Really Tall Old People?*

Daphne Hare of Buffalo, New York, passed along a clipping from *Men's Health* magazine, with the results of an Ohio study that provides some pertinent data. In this study, men lost 1.2 years of life for every extra inch of height. That's right. A 6'0" man can expect to live six years less than a man of 5'7".

A previous study indicated even more dramatic height effects. Men who stood less than 5'8" lived to an average age of 82; those over six feet tall lived to the unripe age of 73.

FRUSTABLE 10: *Why Do Only Older Men Seem to Have Hairy Ears?*

We're glad we put the word "Seem" in the question, for some younger men do have hairy ears. In fact, we heard from a middle-aged man who can so testify—Albert Jeliner of Mauwatosa, Wisconsin:

> I have had extremely hairy ears since I was in my late teens and early twenties. Back in those days it was long, blond fuzz and as the years have passed it has gotten more and more coarse. I am now 51. Since I was 22, I have had to have my ears trimmed each time I went to the barber.
>
> I don't know how you got into this "hairy" situation; but I inherited mine.

In *When Do Fish Sleep?*, we mentioned that all of the endocrinologists we spoke to begged off this question, claiming geneticists would have the answer (the geneticists, of course, sent us to the endocrinologists). But we heard from one endocrinologist, Dr. Clayton Reynolds of Lancaster, California, who claims the answer does lie within his field:

> The explanation for the hair growth in the ear canals of men is that these are the so-called androgenic zones. The hair follicles in the ear canals have receptors that are acted upon by the male hormones, or androgens.
>
> The hair of the human body can be divided into three categories: *nonsexual hair* (such as that on the arms and legs), which is not dependent upon the gender of the individual; *ambisexual hair*, which grows during adolescence in the same areas in the body in males and females (such as the axillary and pubic hair); and thirdly, *male sexual hair*, which grows on the face and chest and between the umbilicus and the pubic area.
>
> Not so well known is the fact that the male sexual hair occurs also in the other androgenic zones, the ear canals.

But why would this hair tend to sprout as we get older? We heard from University of Texas medical student John Chaconas, of Corpus Christi:

There are two types of hair on the body, *vellus* and *terminal*. Vellus is present on the parts of the body usually considered hairless, such as the forehead, eyelids, and eardrums. Terminal hair is present on our heads and arms.

Sometimes, as we age, vellus hair follicles are differentiated (transformed) into terminal follicles, and give rise to terminal hair. This transformation usually does not occur at an early age—therefore only older man have hairy ears.

Frustables First Posed in *When Do Fish Sleep?*

FRUSTABLE 3: *How, When, and Why Did the Banana Become the Universal Slipping Agent in Vaudeville and Movies?*

In *Why Do Dogs Have Wet Noses?*, we announced that we had made no progress at all in answering this Frustable. We're now a little, and we stress the word "little," further along in our quest. Most of our mail assumes that the banana's role as a slipping agent came from burlesque itself. Peter Womut of Portland, Oregon, makes an intelligent stab:

> I believe the connection is with the three comedians in a burlesque show and their title of top, second, and third bananas. Perhaps they became known by these names because of slips on banana peels, or perhaps banana peels became the symbol because of their names. Perhaps the solution is in the lyrics to the song, "If You Want to Be a Top Banana," from the musical *Top Banana*.

After an appearance on "CBS This Morning," when we mentioned our frustration about solving this mystery, we received a call from an excited law student who promised to but never did send us information about some cases he was studying in torts class. Lo and behold, the Supreme Court, and Oliver Wendell Holmes himself, rendered several decisions on personal injury cases involving folks slipping on banana peels on the street.

DAVID FELDMAN

Why were there banana peels on the street? The law student cited the same reason that Les Aldridge, of Milltown, New Jersey, wrote to us about:

> My wife reports that her grandfather used to say that when he was young, people would often use banana peels (the soft inner part) to shine their shoes. If they got some of it on the bottom of the shoe and fell, they would say that they had "slipped on a banana peel."
>
> The banana peel makes an easily recognizable prop for the stage to give comedians the occasion for humorous pratfalls. They needed some slipping agent—an egg might do it but it would be too messy. Perhaps the banana peel suggested itself as the agent due to the shoe shining association mentioned above.

Shannon Arledge, of Livingston, Louisiana, adds an even stranger use for the lowly banana peel: "In olden times, banana peels were often used on boat docks as a way of sliding the boats down to the water. However funny, slipping on those peels was a common occurrence." We'll try to track down the Supreme Court cases on banana peels for our next opus.

FRUSTABLE 6: *Why Do So Many People Save National Geographics and Then Never Look at Them Again?*

We thought we had covered all the possible answers to this Frustable in *Why Do Dogs Have Wet Noses?*, but a letter from Laurie Poindexter, of Fowler, Indiana, made us realize we had been negligent:

> My mother used *National Geographics* as booster seats for all of us during childhood, so we could easily reach the table at mealtimes. Once we had all grown sufficiently, we sold them at yard sales.
>
> Now that she has grandchildren, she is subscribing to *Smithsonian*, which has equal thickness but a wider base for more secure stackability and bottom comfort.

Yes, but do they come with lap restraints and air bags?

But we shouldn't joke about this matter. Mark Arend of Beaver Dam, Wisconsin, was kind enough to send us an article by George H. Kaub, published in the *Journal of Irreproducible Results*. This ground-breaking article, entitled, *"National Geographic,* The Doomsday Machine," succinctly states the problem:

> Since no copies have been discarded or destroyed since the beginning of publication it can be readily seen that the accumulated aggregate weight is a figure that not only boggles the mind but is imminently approaching the disaster point. That point will be the time when the geologic substructure of the country can no longer support the incredible load and subsidence will occur.

Kaub concludes that the entire country will fall below the sea and "total inundation will occur" unless drastic measures are taken. *National Geographic,* he is quite sure, is responsible for many of the so-called natural calamities of our time—including activity on the San Andreas fault.

Kaub's article is a clarion call, warning us that unless the publication of *National Geographic* is terminated, the North American continent is doomed.

FRUSTABLE 8: *Why Do Kids Tend to Like Meat Well Done (and Then Prefer It Rarer and Rarer As They Get Older)?*

Several readers have written in to add a third possible answer to the two we tentatively suggested. Most persuasive was Babette Hills of Aurora, Colorado: "I asked my two boys why they don't like their meat rare and their answers were just what I had observed: Rare meat is harder to chew." Rare meat, still containing more natural juices and fats than a well-done piece, is chewier. Hills argues that "baby" teeth are not equipped to do the necessary damage to a piece of rare meat with ease or comfort. This also explains why children often like to have their meat cut into small pieces.

Hills assumes that as soon as chewing the meat is no longer a problem, most kids will start preferring rarer meat, which is more flavorful. Her theory would be confirmed, she says, if people with missing teeth or dentures like their meat more well done than those not dentally challenged.

FRUSTABLE 10: *Why Are So Many Restaurants, Especially Diners and Coffee Shops, Obsessed with Mating Ketchup Bottles at the End of the Day?*

We thought we answered this Frustable definitively. But then we received a startling new reason for this seemingly silly obsession: Ketchup mating saves lives. Waitress Mary A. Taft of Deming, Washington, explains:

> As a waitress, I had often asked myself, "What is the object of this tedious chore?" One day, I finally got my answer when a bottle of ketchup exploded when the lid was taken off.
>
> My boss informed me that to prevent explosions of this kind, the bottles low in ketchup must be poured on top of the bottles more full of ketchup. Otherwise, some ketchup can end up perpetually on the bottom of the bottle instead of on someone's burger.
>
> If the ketchup stays on the bottom long enough, it can ferment, causing a buildup of gas that can create the explosion.

Of course, this explosive effect can better be cited as a reason to eliminate the practice of mating altogether. But we won't hold our breath until restaurateurs change their practice.

We receive thousands of letters every year. Most of them pose Imponderables, try to answer Frustables, or ply us with undeserved praise. But this section is reserved for those letters that take us to task or have something significant to add to our statements in previous books.

Many of you have written with valid objections to parts of our answers in previous books. As much as it pains us to make a mistake, we appreciate your input. Unfortunately, it can take months or even years to validate these objections. We have made several changes in later printings of our books because of your letters. The letters we include here are not the only accurate comments, just some of the most entertaining.

In Why Do Dogs Have Wet Noses?, we discussed why there is no Boeing 717. We heard from a pioneer of the Boeing Company, who told us that the version we related was a little sanitized:

> I was assigned to the group that prepared the detail specifications for the various airplane models. We put together a Boeing Model 717 detail specification and used it in preliminary configuration negotiations with United Airlines.
>
> William Patterson, who started his aviation career as William E. Boeing's administrative assistant in the 1930s, was president of United Airlines at the time. He was very pro-Douglas Aircraft, and had stated that he would never buy a Boeing Model 707 and that "Model 717 was too close to 707."
>
> We obliged him by changing the name to "Boeing Model 720" and he (and many other airlines around the world) bought it. That's the only gap in the "7–7 Series." All we had to do to the specification was change the title page. When we sold the 720 to UAL, no engineering drawings had been released, so other than my small wages, the change cost Boeing nothing. End of story.
>
> OREE C. WELLER
> Bellevue, Washington

In Imponderables, we discussed why cashews aren't sold in their shells. We blew the answer. We indicated that cashews are actually seeds and that they don't have hard shells. Well, the cashews we eat are seeds, but M. J. Navarro of Latrobe, Penn-

sylvania, humbled us by sending some unshelled cashews that proved our discussion erroneous. He added: "The shell is too hard for people to have any chance at the seed itself. The shell must be thoroughly roasted to get to the seed and the seed must be roasted to make it edible."

True enough. And there are other reasons why cashews are not sold unshelled in stores. We heard from a reader who spent more than a little time with cashew shells during his childhood:

> The mature shell is thick and leathery and contains a corrosive brownish black oil that causes blisters on skin. . . . The juice of the apple causes indelible stains on clothes . . .
>
> It would be uneconomical to import cashews in their shells, and that is why they are not sold this way . . .
>
> As a child, I grew up with cashew trees all around, played with thousands of unshelled cashews (a game similar to marbles), raided the cashew grove near my high school, and watched moonshine cashew liquor being made as well as sold and consumed.
>
> DINESH NETTAR
Edison, New Jersey

And a special apology to Daniel Pittman of LaSalle, Illinois, who defended our discussion of cashews to his merciless friends.

In Why Do Dogs Have Wet Noses?, *we discussed why a new order of checks starts with the number 101 rather than 1. Walter Nadel of Pembroke, Massachusetts, provides a technical reason why starting with 101 saves checkmakers some money:*

> When checks are printed, the first sheet through is at the bottom of the hopper, and the last sheet through is at the top. This requires backward-functioning numbering machines, which are set to start at the ending number and finish with the starting number. The order of checks can then be completed and shipped in the proper numerical sequence ready for use by the customer.
>
> As the order is printed, and the numbers recede, they would read 102, 101, 100, 099, 098, etc., unless the press is stopped and the superfluous zero is manually depressed after 100. Again, at the

point of 12, 11, 10, 09, the press would have to be stopped again to eliminate the second superfluous zero.

By encouraging the use of starting check orders with 101, the printer has saved the need to stop the press twice, a saving in time and efficiency, not to mention money.

WALTER NADEL
Pembroke, Massachusetts

Many readers were not satisfied with the explanation pro-vided in Why Do Clocks Run Clockwise? *about why IIII, and not IV, is used to signify the number four on clocks. We heard from Alden Foltz of Port Huron, Michigan, who collects ancient coins. Foltz assures us that all of his Roman coins used "IIII" to signify the number four. If coins don't reflect the proper way to express four, what would? asks Foltz.*

Further corroboration comes from Bruce Umbarger, who, like many readers, wondered how our explanation resolved the dilemma of how 9 would be expressed in Roman numerals in ancient times. Bruce consulted a book called Number Words and Number Symbols, *by Kurt Menninger, which clearly shows "IIII" used to express 4 from as early as circa 130 B.C. He also enclosed two multiplication tables from thirteenth-century mo-nastic manuscripts: They also expressed 4 as "IIII." "How can the habit of 'IIII' on clocks be traced to illiterate peasants when a copy of a sixteenth-century astrolabe [a device used to tell the time by observing the stars or sun] clearly shows a four ren-dered as 'IIII'?"*

So why might the IIII have been changed, eventually, to IV? Reader Tom Woosnan of Hillsborough, California, sent us an excerpt of Isaac Asimov's Asimov on Numbers *that provides one possible explanation:*

[IV] . . . are the first letters of IVPITER, the chief of the Roman gods, and the Romans may have had a delicacy about writing even the beginning of the name. Even today, on clock faces bearing Roman numerals, "four" is represented as IIII and never IV. This is not because the clock face does not accept the subtractive prin-ciple, for "nine" is represented as IX and never as VIIII.

An alternate explanation is that the expression of Roman numerals was not standardized throughout the Roman Empire, let alone throughout Europe.

Speaking of clocks, we heard from someone who was presented with a copy of Why Do Clocks Run Clockwise? *for his eighty-third birthday:*

> The title struck a tender chord with me, for I was asked to reset a friend's wall clock last fall, when folks were going from daylight savings time to the daylight wasting time.
> I had pulled the clock's cord from the wall outlet to make the change. When I returned the connection in the wall's electric outlet, the clock was running backwards!
> I pulled the cord from the outlet, turned the male fitting of the cord over, and plugged it in again. It ran forward, properly.
> Why? God only knows. And he won't tell.
>
> VERNE O. PHELPS
> *Edina, Minnesota*

For some reason, we tend to make exactly one really *stupid mistake in each book. In* Imponderables, *it was the cashew question, but in* When Do Fish Sleep?, *it was this one:*

> For shame, young man . . . Crickets do not produce chirps by rubbing their legs together. They have on each front wing a sharp edge, the scraper, and a file-like ridge, the file. They chirp by elevating the front wings and moving them so that the scraper of one wing rubs on the file of the other wing, giving a pulse, the chirp, generally on the closing stroke.
> On a big male cricket, the scraper and the file can often be seen by the naked eye. You can take the wings of a cricket in your fingers and make the chirp sound yourself.
>
> CLIFFORD DENNIS
> PH.D. ENTOMOLOGY
> *Prairie du Chien, Wisconsin*

In Why Do Clocks Run Clockwise?, *we discussed why dogs circle around before lying down. Although we stand by our answer, several readers wrote to us with an additional possible reason: to determine which way the wind is blowing. In this way, they can sleep with noses into the wind, in order to be warned of a predator approaching. Being on the "right" side of the wind may also help them hear predators.*

In Imponderables, *we discussed who is criminally responsible when an elevator is illegally overloaded. One reader indicates that the answer might be . . . a restaurant:*

> A few years back, I was in a building in Washington, D.C., with passenger elevators that might be accurately described as cozy. The building had an Italian restaurant on the ground floor, and as I arrived, four secretaries from an upstairs office were just getting on the elevator to go back to work, having had lunch together downstairs.
>
> Every time they tried, though, the same thing happened: the doors would close, but as soon as they pressed the button for their floor, the doors would open again. They became rather angry at me, thinking I was doing something to keep the elevator from working properly.
>
> I finally suggested that it appeared to me that they had overloaded the car and that it would probably work if one of them got out. One did leave the elevator, and the other three women were able to return to their floor immediately.
>
> What amused me, though the women were rather embarrassed about it, was that the four were able to ride down together for their lunch, but their group weight gain during the meal was enough to trip the overload protection.
>
> DALE NEIBURG
> *Laurel, Maryland*

On to a less weighty subject, we heard from Terri Davis, of Newark, Delaware . . .

> Reading your book *Why Do Clocks Run Clockwise?*, I came across the question, "Why do so many mass mailers use return envelopes with windows?" The answer was interesting and reminded me of something I saw at work last year that answered a question I never thought to ask: What happens to the paper that gets punched out of envelopes to provide the window?
>
> Scott Paper, Inc. uses a great deal of recycled fiber during the manufacturing process of its many products—so much so that it

buys scraps from many other companies . . . Can you imagine the sight of 125 cubic feet of compressed envelope windows heading down to a watery grave? There were literally tons more of these windows waiting on the incoming barge to be turned into toilet paper, napkins, tissues, etc.

We're happy that at least one company is making good use of scrap paper. After all, in Why Do Clocks Run Clockwise?, *we already chastised doughnut stores for having clerks picking up doughnuts with tissues and then stuffing the same tissues, germs and all, into the bag the customer takes home. Jack Schwager of Goldens Bridge, New York, mounts a passionate defense of the practice:*

> Germs are not the only issue. If they were, then indeed it would make no sense to put the tissue in the bag. Let me suggest a simple experiment, which would make it clear to anyone why it would be desirable to leave the doughnut wrapped in a tissue.
>
> Wait for a hot, humid summer day. Go into Dunkin' Donuts and order a dozen doughnuts. Make sure they all have icing and that the attendant uses a bag instead of a box. Now go into an unairconditioned car (preferably black in color) and drive around, taking care of several errands before returning home. Upon returning home, separate the doughnuts, giving the one with chocolate icing to the anxious child who loves chocolate but hates strawberry, and the strawberry one to his brother, who hates chocolate.
>
> What? You can't neatly separate the doughnuts, which have by now turned into a congealed blob? Hmmmm.

Hmmm, indeed. It has been our experience that the tissues do absolutely no good in keeping the frosting separated, since they aren't large enough to surround the doughnuts and the tissues are far from surgically inserted to minimize friction between icings. We won't even go into the dreaded powdered sugar crisis, in which every doughnut in the bag becomes sprinkled with the white stuff whether you like it or not. If the stores really wanted to make sure the doughnuts did not mate, they could certainly make a form-fitting tissue for them, a little baggie that covered the pastries, or provide a box with dividers.

DAVID FELDMAN

Readers are still fuming about the purpose of the balls on top of flagpoles. Everyone seems totally sure of the purpose, but we've gotten about ten different explanations. We've received a few letters like this one, from Heather Muir of Phoenix, Arizona:

In the military, the ball on the top of the flagpole is referred to as a "truck." The "truck" contains a gold bullet, a silver bullet, and a match. Buried at the base of the flagpole is a 50mm shell. The bullets and the shells are essentially memorials, in remembrance of the various wars the United States has been engaged in. The match, however, is stored in the "truck" for one purpose—to burn the flag in case the post is overrun by enemy troops, thus preventing the desecration of our national symbol.

Two problems with this explanation. First, the representatives of the armed services we spoke to say that it isn't true. And second, if your post is being overrun, would you really have time to take off the truck and retrieve a match? Wouldn't matches be more readily available elsewhere?

We heard from Elsie McManigal of Hercules, California, who said that before World War I, when most flagpoles were made of wood, balls were inserted to prevent water damage to the open grain on the top of the flagpole.

Betsy Kimak of Boulder, Colorado, took us to task for our discussion of why two horses in an open field always seem to stand head to tail. She notes that horses, and other ungulates, use posture to indicate who is the dominant animal:

With only two horses alone in a field, one will always be dominant and aggressive, depending on size, strength, and sex.

Two different postures are applicable here. The first is initiated by the submissive horse, who faces away from the dominant one to announce that it is not a threat and has no intentions of fighting or challenging the dominant horse. The second posture is initiated by the dominant horse and is called the "dominance pursuit march." The dominant horse crowds in behind the second horse and initiates a march head-to-tail, in which the recipient horse must accept submissiveness or face an aggressive confrontation.

We heard from Bill Beauman, research manager at Ever-pure, Inc., who wanted to add to our discussion in When Do Fish Sleep? *about why some ice cubes come out cloudy and others come out clear.*

At home, using still (not moving) water in an ice cube tray in the freezer, air entrapment may be a minor cause of cloudiness, but the most common explanation is that the salts and other minerals in nearly all water supplies are gradually forced to the center of the cube by the freezing of the "pure" water around the sides. As the concentration rises and exceeds the minerals' natural limits of solubility, they precipitate as particles and make an ugly, cloudy center. When the ice melts, the minerals make sediment in the glass.

Commercial cube-type icemakers recirculate water from a sump to cascade over freezing plates. Both dissolved and particulate impurities are readily rinsed away, and only the relatively pure water freezes. Such equipment routinely makes ice which, when melted, contains only about 5 percent of the minerals originally present in the water [so this is why ice cubes often don't taste like the water they are made out of!]. . . . Such machines always make clear ice, unless there isn't enough refrigerant to make the plates cold enough.

What is an Imponderables *book without a ketchup controversy? We heard from the president of The Throop Group, William M. Throop, who questioned Heinz's explanation for the necessity of the neck band on their bottles (they said it was a way to keep the foil cap snug against its cork and sealing wax prior to the introduction of the screw-on cap in 1888).*

Sealing wax sticks quite well to bare glass. The real reason for the neck band is that air left in the bottle allowed a black ring of oxidized material to form. The neck band was designed to hide this black ring. Although it did not detract from the product quality, the ring was unsightly.

In 1952, the company for which we worked (Chain Belt Co., now Rexnord Inc.) developed a product called a Deaerator. This removed the air pocket from the bottle when filling and eliminated this black layer at the top of the bottle. The neck band was retained as a signature of Heinz ketchup. However, all other brands of ketchup used similar neck bands prior to deaerating for the same purpose.

Speaking of packaging, we are amazed that we actually heard from someone who defended milk cartons (we wrote about why they were difficult to open and impossible to close in Imponderables):

> Your assertion that paper milk cartons are "difficult to open . . . and close" goes far beyond reality. After a few initial experiments years ago, I found opening and closing such paper containers rather simple.
>
> One need only place the side to be opened facing one, insert a thumb on either side of the rooflike structure under the eaves, twist one's hands forward and upward, steadying the container with the fingers until the roof portion pushed by the thumbs becomes detached from the roof peak and pressed forward by the thumbs until nearly flush against the carton top. Then hold the carton with one hand while using the other thumb and one or two fingers to pinch back the edges of the eaves the thumbs have just pushed back, and bring them forward, which forms an opening from which to pour the milk.
>
> To close, merely reverse the process. The whole operation should take three to five seconds by the third attempt. No problem!
>
> JERROLD E. MARKHAM
> *Hansville, Washington*

We rest our case.

Jerrold, do you by any chance know Jan Harrington of New York, New York? If not, we think you have the potential for a wonderful friendship based on mutual proclivities. In Why Do Clocks Run Clockwise?, *we whined that Coca-Cola from two- or three-liter bottles just doesn't taste as good as from smaller containers. Jan Harrington agrees with us that large bottles have too large an air capacity, but Jan, unlike us, does something about it:*

> I never buy the three-liter (they don't fit in the refrigerator door and never cost less per liter than the two-liter bottles), but I

have a solution for the two-liter bottles. They are flexible. Once opened, I squeeze the plastic so that the liquid fills the entire volume of the container and keep squeezing more and more air out before closing the cap each time I pour a later drink. I find this preserves the flavor much better than leaving the bottle as a bottle shape.

Try it yourself (if you have small hands you can press the bottle against your chest using one arm until the Coca-Cola has just filled the bottle, then screw the cap on tightly). The bottle will retain the squozen shape. Eventually, you have a plastic bottle that looks as if run over by a car tire.

Heaven knows what Jan does with toothpaste tubes. We prefer just whining about the Coke problem.

Speaking of liquids, we have another theory about why the cold water that comes from the bathroom faucet seems colder than the cold water from the kitchen faucet:

Most kitchen faucets are equipped with water-saving aerators, which decrease the percentage of water in the stream; the stream from the kitchen faucet is actually part water *and* part air at room temperature and therefore can not be as cold as the stream from the bathroom faucet. Even kitchen water that is dispensed into a glass has been slightly warmed by this phenomenon.

Furthermore, the body parts that encounter water in the bathroom (face and body) are far more unaccustomed and sensitive to cold than the parts that encounter water in the kitchen (usually only hands).

TONY ACQUAVIVA
Towson, Maryland

O.K., but the original impetus for the question was that several readers went to the bathroom to get drinking water because it was colder. And we have experienced the same phenomenon in kitchen faucets without aerators.

Speaking of the kitchen, Rice Krispies are often eaten there:

In *When Do Fish Sleep?*, you told us how Rice Krispies go Snap! Crackle! and Pop! Now could you explain why in French

DAVID FELDMAN

they go Cric! Crac! Croc!? And in Japanese, they go Pitchi! Patchi! Putchi!?

M. PICARD
Montreal, Quebec

No, M. Picard, we can't.

Speaking of complex carbohydrates, Ivan Pfalser of Caney, Kansas, took us to task for not including another reason why silos are round in When Do Fish Sleep?:

> It's the same reason that water towers, grain elevators, gas tanks, and barrels are all round. A circle is the most efficient configuration to carry the stress produced by an internal load. . . . If a square or straight-sided silo is used, the internal pressure tries to bend the side into a hoop shape, inducing a momentary bending . . . which can cause overstressing in the corners and can cause them to tear apart.

Speaking of tearing apart, the issue of "Where are the missing socks?" is evidently ripping apart the fiber of the Western world. We received letters from smug individuals who pin their socks together when they throw them in their laundry hamper and claimed they never lose a sock. In our opinion, they are merely shrugging off the challenging and character-building exercise of trying to preserve the sanctity of sock coupling. We were a little ironic in our treatment of this issue in Why Do Dogs Have Wet Noses?. *So we'll let an expert, Sam Warden of Portland, Oregon, who describes himself as a "multifarious mechanic and not-bad-housekeeper-for-a-guy," provide pretty much the same answer we do when confronted with this question by investigative reporters and talk-show callers:*

> Yes, Virginia. Socks do abscond in the wash. I have watched plumbers pull socks out of blocked laundry drains; I have done so myself. I have retrieved them in midflight from my laundry sink, and found them (not surprisingly) inside jammed washing machine pumps. Every plumber and repairman wherever washing machines are used must know about this.
>
> The great majority of fugitives are children's sizes and short-length sheer stockings. (Handkerchiefs jump ship, too; they just

DO PENGUINS HAVE KNEES?   549

aren't kept in pairs.) The cheaper models of washing machines and front loaders seem to be the main offenders.

And may we add the other major culprit. We have found many a sock clinging fervently to the drums of dryers.

And in reference to clinging of the static variety, several readers wrote to us about an additional reason why television sets are measured diagonally (we discussed this Imponderable in Why Do Dogs Have Wet Noses? *):*

> The early TV picture tubes were all circular, so that the size of the tube was the diameter of the circle. A rectangle was masked on the front; thus, the diameter of the tube became the diagonal of the picture. In order to make the picture as large as possible, the corners of the picture were curved.
>
> When the first rectangular tubes were produced, they were measured on the diagonal, since this was equivalent to the diameter of the round tubes that they were meant to replace.
>
> Roy V. Hughson
Stamford, Connecticut

Speaking of technological devices throwing off light, Douglas S. Pisik of Marietta, Georgia, read our discussion in Why Do Clocks Run Clockwise? *and says that he learned in driver education (and you know how reliable driver education teachers are) why the red light is on top of a traffic signal—if you are coming over a hill, you will see the red light first. This won't help you pass a driver's test, but it makes a little sense.*

We don't usually discuss letters about our word book, Who Put the Butter in Butterfly?, *in these pages, but we couldn't resist sharing the information we were seeking about the origin of our favorite English euphemism for sex, "discussing Uganda":*

> "Discussing Uganda" was popularized in England following an incident at Heathrow Airport when the (female) Ugandan ambassador was caught using the restroom for uses other than those for which it was intended [how's *that* for a euphemism].
>
> *Private Eye*, a British magazine dedicated to humorously exposing such stories, ran this piece and then continued to discuss

similar incidents using the euphemism, "discussing Ugandan relations," helping the magazine avoid many potential lawsuits from those who were exposed.

MARTIN BISHOP
Marina del Rey, California

And what would a letter column be without the "mother of all Imponderables," which we first discussed in Why Do Clocks Run Clockwise? *and then have discussed in every subsequent* Imponderables *book:* Why do some ranchers hang old boots on fenceposts?

Since we first wrote about the subject, it has become en vogue *among the literary set. Lance Tock of Brooklyn Park, Minnesota, sent us an excerpt from a book called* Farm, *written by Grant Heilman, that endorses one of the theories we've mentioned—that boots were put on top of fences to prevent rainfall from rotting post ends. We received a copy of a newsletter called* Nebraska Veterinary Views *that includes a regular column by Dr. Larry Williams entitled "Old Boots & Fence Posts." He was shocked to find that only half of a group of forty Nebraskans he had spoken to had seen old boots on fenceposts, "let alone wonder[ing] about the[ir] meaning. They claim to be Cornhuskers, but can they be 'real' Nebraskans until they have seen and held in reverence old boots and fence posts?"*

Paul Kotter of Lebanon, New Hampshire, informed us that in Tony Hillerman's novel Talking God, *page 28 contains the sentence, "An old boot was jammed atop the post, signaling that someone would be at home." We don't buy this theory, because the boots observed in Kansas and Nebraska, anyway, stay on the posts all the time.*

Duane Woerman, who lives in Kearney, Nebraska, near the epicenter of boot-fencepost activity, has strong opinions:

In Nebraska, the shoe is placed upside-down so that the cowboy's *souls* [get it?] will go to heaven. The toes of the boots are always pointed towards the house. In a snowstorm, the cowboys can always find their way home by following the direction in which the toes are pointed.

If it's that bad a storm, the cowboys may end up at someone else's home, but we get the point. At least a poet with the same answer admits that there are many possible explanations. Roger Hill of Vandalia, Ohio, sent us a poem called "Roadside Riddle" by Faye Tanner Cool, who writes about the boots along the prairie highways near her home of Fleming, Colorado. The last five lines of the poem:

> The local folk
> offer up two dozen explanations,
> but the one to ponder on:
> as reward for miles of walking
> those soles face heaven.

Veterinarian Lucy Hirsch of Smithville, Missouri, suggests that shoes and boots are put on metal fenceposts for a most practical reason: "Metal fenceposts known as 'T' posts are sharp. Many horses have impaled themselves on them. Boots and shoes on top can protect the horses from the sharp points." *But they do things differently in South Carolina. Amanda Stanley writes to inform us that we are wrong to be worrying about the fenceposts. We should be worrying about the boots:*

> In South Carolina, ranchers hang them to dry the leather in the sun after a big rain. After the leather has dried, they grease them down with mink oil. When old boots get hard, they leak water; after they are dried, the mink oil will stop the leaks. The smell of the boots will keep crows out of the fields.
> . . . I hope this answer will get this Imponderable out of the Frustables section.

It's way too late for that.

Finally, we have always feared that Imponderables *might be soporific. We never dared dream they could be used as aphrodisiacs. We received a letter from a woman from Burbank, California, whose name we'll keep anonymous, which begins in the following way:* "Every night, my lover reads to me from Why Do Clocks Run Clockwise?." *Now there is a basis for a wonderful relationship.*

Acknowledgments

The best part of my job, even better than cashing my paychecks, is hearing from you. Not only do readers supply most of the Imponderables, but your encouragement and support have kept me going at times when I've wanted to pack it in. More than anyone, you deserve my gratitude.

I've tried to express my thanks by responding personally to readers who enclose a self-addressed stamped envelope, and I will continue to do so. But I can't promise I'll be prompt in my response. *Imponderables* receives thousands of letters a year now, so if I'm on deadline or on the road promoting the books, I fall behind in my correspondence. I apologize for the delay but hope you agree that the alternative (form letters) just wouldn't be as satisfying for you or me. Rest assured that I treasure and read every letter I receive.

This is my fifth book at HarperCollins, and luckily for me, my fifth with Rick Kot as editor. Since the last book, Rick has been promoted once again—and he has no relatives in upper management to explain this inexorable rise, either. Rick's assistant, Sheila Gillooly, has been a godsend, dispatching problems with unfailing intelligence and good humor. My publicist, Craig Herman, has been responsible for thrusting *Imponderables* onto the airwaves and his assistant, Andrew Malkin, has been an able and enthusiastic co-conspirator. And the production editing/copy editing team of Kim Lewis, Maureen Clark, and Janet Byrne helped make this book at least semicomprehensible.

Thanks to the many movers and shakers at HarperCollins who have allowed me to concentrate on the writing while they worried about the flogging: publisher Bill Shinker; Roz Barrow; sales honchos Brenda Marsh, Pat Jonas, Zeb Burgess, and all the HC sales reps; marketing mavens Steve Magnuson and Robert Jones; special marketing titans Connie Levinson and Mark Landau (and all my other pals in special markets); and primo publicist Karen Mender. And thanks to all the folks at HarperCollins with less lofty titles, who have been so kind and supportive when they didn't have to be.

Jim Trupin, wise beyond his years, as he will be only too glad to inform you, is a terrific agent and friend, as is his wife and partner, Elizabeth.

If Kassie Schwan wrote as well as I drew, she'd be unreadable. So you will understand why I so appreciate her cartoons; if you knew Kassie, you'd certainly understand why I prize her so much as a friend.

Lest I be accused of Dorian Grayish tendencies, a team of thugs lugged me in front of a camera to finally change the photograph on the back cover. I wouldn't have sat still in front of a camera for a minute without the gentle coaxing and sensitivity of photographer supreme, Joann Carney. Thanks to Fran Hackett and Peter Fenimore, of the New York Aquarium in Coney Island, for introducing me to Klousseau, the very special penguin featured on the cover. James Gorman, author of *The Total Penguin,* was kind enough to lead me to the folks who would allow me the privilege of spending an hour with Klousseau and his feathered colleagues.

Several of my personal friends just happen to work in publishing, and have been invaluable sources of support and counsel and, more often than I would like to admit, passive and helpless recipients of my endless whining. Thank you Mark Kohut, Susie Russenberger, Barbara Rittenhouse, and James Gleick.

And then there are my friends and family, who see me disappear for months at a time during deadline sieges or publicity tours. Thanks for putting up with me to: Tony Alessandrini; Michael Barson; Sherry Barson; Rajat Basu; Ruth Basu; Jeff Bayone; Jean Behrend; Brenda Berkman; Cathy Berkman; Sharyn Bishop; Carri Blees; Christopher Blees; Jon Blees; everyone at Bowling Green State University's Popular Culture Department; Jerry Braithwaite; Annette Brown; Arvin Brown; Herman Brown; Joann Carney; Lizzie Carney; Susie Carney; Janice Carr; Lapt Chan; Mary Clifford; Don Cline; Alvin Cooperman;

DAVID FELDMAN

Marilyn Cooperman; Judith Dahlman; Paul Dahlman; Shelly de Satnick; Charlie Doherty; Laurel Doherty; Joyce Ebert; Pam Elam; Andrew Elliot; Steve Feinberg; Fred Feldman; Gilda Feldman; Michael Feldman; Phil Feldman; Ron Felton; Phyllis Fineman; Kris Fister; Mary Flannery; Linda Frank; Elizabeth Frenchman; Susan Friedland; Michele Gallery; Chris Geist; Jean Geist; Bonnie Gellas; Richard Gertner; Amy Glass; Bea Gordon; Dan Gordon; Ken Gordon; Judy Goulding; Chris Graves; Adam Henner; Christal Henner; Lorin Henner; Marilu Henner; Melodie Henner; David Hennes; Paula Hennes; Sheila Hennes; Sophie Hennes; Larry Harold; Carl Hess; Mitchell Hofing; Steve Hofman; Bill Hohauser; Uday Ivatury; Terry Johnson; Sarah Jones; Allen Kahn; Mitch Kahn; Joel Kaplan; Dimi Karras; Maria Katinos; Stewart Kellerman; Harvey Kleinman; Claire Labine; Randy Ladenheim-Gil; Debbie Leitner; Marilyn Levin; Vicky Levy; Jared Lilienstein; Pattie Magee; Jack Mahoney; everyone at the Manhattan Bridge Club; Phil Martin; Chris McCann; Jeff McQuain; Julie Mears; Phil Mears; Carol Miller; Barbara Morrow; Honor Mosher; Phil Neel; Steve Nellisen; Craig Nelson; Millie North; Milt North; Charlie Nurse; Debbie Nye; Tom O'Brien; Pat O'Conner; Joanna Parker; Jeannie Perkins; Merrill Perlman; Joan Pirkle; Larry Prussin; Joe Rowley; Rose Reiter; Brian Rose; Lorraine Rose; Paul Rosenbaum; Carol Rostad; Tim Rostad; Leslie Rugg; Tom Rugg; Gary Saunders; Joan Saunders; Mike Saunders; Norm Saunders; Laura Schisgal; Cindy Shaha; Patricia Sheinwold; Kathy Smith; Kurtwood Smith; Susan Sherman Smith; Chris Soule; Kitty Srednicki; Karen Stoddard; Bill Stranger; Kat Stranger; Anne Swanson; Ed Swanson; Mike Szala; Jim Teuscher; Josephine Teuscher; Laura Tolkow; Carol Vellucci; Dan Vellucci; Hattie Washington; Ron Weinstock; Roy Welland; Dennis Whelan; Devin Whelan; Heide Whelan; Lara Whelan; Jon White; Ann Whitney; Carol Williams; Maggie Wittenburg; Karen Wooldridge; Maureen Wylie; Charlotte Zdrok; Vladimir Zdrok; and Debbie Zuckerberg.

The *Imponderables* books wouldn't be possible without the cooperation of experts in every subject from acting to zoology.

For this book, we contacted nearly 1,500 corporations, educational institutions, foundations, trade associations, and miscellaneous experts to find answers to our readers' Imponderables. Usually, there is nothing to gain for these sources other than the psychic benefit of sharing their knowledge. The following generous people, although not the only ones to supply help, gave us information that led directly to the solution of the Imponderables in this book:

Dr. Robert D. Altman, A & A Veterinary Hospital; American Academy of Dermatology; Dr. Duane Anderson, Central States Anthropological Society; Scott Anderson, Anheuser-Busch; Dan Arcy, Pennzoil Products; Dr. Harry Arnold; Sandi Atkinson.

Jim Ball, Dr Pepper/Seven-Up Companies; Michele Ball, National Audubon Society; Dr. Margaret Downie Banks, American Musical Instrument Society; Dr. Joseph Bark; J. P. Barnett, South Bend Replicas; Bausch & Lomb, Inc.; Ralph Beatty, Western/English Retailers of America; Barbara Begany, Dellwood Milk; Prof. George Bergman, University of California; Brian Bigley; Biff Bilstein, Neodata Services; Michelle Bing, United Fresh Fruit & Vegetable Association; Peter Black, American Water Resources Association; Harold Blake; Prof. Dee Boersma, University of Washington; Stephen Bomer, Automotive Battery Charger Manufacturers; G. Bruce Boyer; Frank Brennan, United States Postal Service; Dr. Donald Bruning, New York Zoological Park; Lloyd Brunkhorst, Brown Shoe Company; Robert Burnham; Trish Butler, Social Security Administration.

Jim Cannon; Roger W. Cappello, Clear Shield National; Thomas J. Carr, Motor Vehicle Manufacturers Association; Louis T. Cerny, American Railway Engineers Association; C. R. Cheney, Chrysler Motors; John Chuhran, Mercedes-Benz of North America; John Clark, Social Security Administration; Catherine Clay, Florida Department of Citrus; Prof. Richard Colwell, Council for Research in Music Education; Charlotte Connelly, Whitman's Chocolates; John Corbett, Clairol, Inc.; Capt. Kenneth L. Coskey, Navy Historical Foundation; Dr. Regis Courtemanche, C. W. Post; Brian Cudahy, Urban Mass Transportation

Administration; Todd Culver, Cornell University Laboratory of Ornithology; Fred A. Curry.

Dr. Frank Davidoff, American College of Physicians; Bill Deane, Hall of Fame Museum; William Debuvitz; Roger De-Camp, National Food Processors Association; Richard Decker, International Conference of Symphony and Opera Musicians; Thomas H. Dent, Cat Fanciers Association; Robin Diamond, American Bus Association; Dr. Liberato DiDio, International Federation of Associations of Anatomists; Claire O'Neill Dillie; David DiPasquale, DiPasquale & Associates; Donna Ditmars, M&M/Mars; Sara Dornacker, United Airlines; Richard H. Dowhan, GTE Products Corporation; Ed Dunn, Cramer-Krasselt; Steven Duquette, National Cartoonists Society.

Mark Earley, Neodata Services; Charley Eckhardt; Morris Eckhouse, SABR; Prof. Gary Elmstrom, University of Florida; Dale Elrod, Jack K. Elrod Co.; Kathleen Etchpare, *Bird Talk*.

Raymond Falconer, SUNY at Albany; Michael Falkowitz, Nabisco Brands; Rob Farson, Neodata Services; Peter Fenimore, New York Aquarium; Stanley Fenvessy, Fenvessy Consulting; Karen Finkel, National School Transportation Association; Tim Fitzgerald; George Flower; Carol Frasier, Montana Historical Society; Eileen Frech, Thomas English Muffins; Don French, Radio Shack; Francis Frere, United States Mint.

Stan S. Garber, Selmer Co.; R. Bruce Gebhardt, North American Native Fishes Association; David A. Gibson, Eastman Kodak Company; Mark Gill, Columbia Pictures Entertainment; Mary Gillespie, Association of Home Appliances; Martin Gitten, Consolidated Edison; Dr. Paul Godfrey, Water Resources Research Center; William Goffi, Maxell Corporation of America; Tamara Goldman, *Food & Beverage Marketing*; Stanley Gordon, Federal Highway Administration; Robert Grayson, Grayson Associates; Dr. E. Wilson Griffin III, Jonesville Family Medical Center; David Guidry, Ushio America.

Susan Habacivch, DuPont; Fran Hackett, New York Aquarium; Brian Hannan, Urban Mass Transportation; Charles E. Hanson, Museum Association of the American Frontier; Joseph

Hanson, Hanson Publishing Group; Larry Hart, Talon Inc.; Sylvia Hauser, *Dog World;* Jeanette Hayhurst; Peter Heide, Association of Manufacturers of Confectionary and Chocolate; Prof. John Hertner, Kearney State College; Dr. James Riley Hill, Clemson University; Ruth Hill, Internal Revenue Service; Scott Hlavaty, Angelica Uniform Group; Dick Hofacker, AT&T Bell Laboratories; Beverly Holmes, Frito-Lay, Inc.; W. Ray Hyde.

Pete James, National Association of Pupil Transportation; Dr. Ben H. Jenkins; Alvin H. Johnson, American Musicological Society; Lloyd Johnson, SABR; Mark Johnson, Matsushita Electric Corporation of America; Dr. William P. Jollie, American Association of Anatomists; Chris Jones, Pepsico; George E. Jones, National Highway Institute; Ed Juge, Radio Shack.

Phil Katz, Beer Institute; Prof. George Kauffman, California State University, Fresno; William Kelly, Brockton Sole and Plastics; Rose Marie Kenny, Hammerhill Papers; Robert E. Kenyon, American Society of Magazine Editors; Dr. Wayne O. Kester, American Association of Equine Practitioners; Frank Kiley; Jula Kinnaird, National Pasta Association; Klousseau, New York Aquarium; Kevin Knopf, Department of the Treasury; Irving Smith Kogan, Champagne Association; Robert L. Krick, Federal Railroad Administration; Lucille Kubichek.

Dr. Eugene LaFond, International Association for Physical Sciences of the Ocean; Christine Lamar, Rhode Island Secretary of State's Office; Prof. Richard Landesman, University of Vermont; William L. Lang, Columbia-Wren; Fred Lanting; Michael Lauria; Carol Lawler, Land O' Lakes, Inc.; Thomas A. Lehmann, American Institute of Baking; Dr. Jay Lehr, Association of Ground Water Science and Engineering; Dr. Jerome Z. Litt; Richard Livingston, Airline Passengers Association.

David MacKenzie, University of Northern Colorado; Alan MacRobert, *Sky & Telescope;* Tom Mancini, U. S. Polychemical Corporation; Nancy Martin, Association of Field Ornithologists; John Matter, National Ballroom and Entertainment Association; Doug Matyka, Georgia-Pacific Corporation; Mauna Loa Macadamia Nut Company; Karen E. McAliley, United States Postal System; John T. McCabe, Master Brewers Association of the

Americas; Diane McCulloch, Mount de Chantal Academy; Larry McFather, International Brotherhood of Locomotive Engineers; Jil McIntosh; Dr. Jim McKean, Iowa State University; Art McNally, National Football League; Mary Medin, "How to with Pete"; Jim Meyer, United States Postal System; Jerry Miles, American Baseball Coaches Association; H. Dale Millay, Shell Development Company; F. Kent Mitchel, Marketing Science Institute, Thomas Mock, Electronic Industries Association; Nevin B. Montgomery, National Frozen Food Association; Dr. David Moore, Virginia Tech University; Jeffrey Mora, Urban Mass Transportation Office; John M. Morse, Merriam-Webster, Inc.; Claude Mouton, Montreal Canadiens.

National Mapping Division, Department of Interior; Niagara Straw Company; Robert Nichter, Fulfillment Management Association; Robert Niddrie, Playtex Apparel.

Richard T. O'Connell, Chocolate Manufacturers of the USA; Bill O'Connor, Topps Chewing Gum; Doug Olander, International Game Fish Association; Karen Orme, *Footwear Forum*.

Dennis Patterson, Murray Bicycle Company; Bill Paul, *School Bus Fleet*; Roger Payne, Department of Interior; Roger S. Pinkham, Stevens Institute of Technology; John A. Pitcher, Hardwood Research Council; Joseph Pocius, National Turkey Federation; Prof. Anthony Potter, University of Hawaii at Manoa.

Dr. T. E. Reed, American Rabbit Breeders Association; Prof. Billy Rhodes, Poole Agricultural Center; Al Rickard, Snack Food Association; Robert S. Robe Jr., Scipio Society of Naval and Military History; Ronnie Robertson; Dr. Robert R. Rofen, Aquatic Research Institute; Barbara Rose, Continental Baking; Prof. Neal Rowell, University of South Alabama; Thomas Ruble; Tom and Leslie Rugg; Oscar Mayer Foods; Max Rumbaugh, SAE.

Dr. John Saidla, Cornell Feline Health Center; Kim Sakamoto, California Melon Research Board; Norman Savig, University of Northern Colorado; Dr. Charles Schaefer, University of California at Berkeley; Robert Schmidt, North American Native Fishes Association; Kassie Schwan; Dr. Samuel Selden; Vickie Sheer, Dance Educators of America; Bill Shoenleber, Edmund

Scientific Company; Carole Shulman, Professional Skaters' Guild of America; F. G. Walton Smith, International Oceanographic Foundation; Prof. Stephen Smulski, University of Massachusetts; Bruce V. Snow; Charles Spiegel; Cherie Spies; Continental Baking; Amy Steiner, American Association of State Highway and Traffic Officials; Bob Stewart, Association of American Railroads; David Stivers, Nabisco Brands; Lisa Stormer; Amurol Products Company; Peggy Sullivan, Music Educators National Conference; John J. Surrette, Rolls Battery Engineering; Barbara Sweeney, AT&T Library Network Archives.

Farook Taufiq, Prince Company; Dr. Kristin Thelander, University of Iowa; Susan Tildesley, Headwear Institute of America; Fran Toth, Cadillac Motor Car Division; Constance Townsend, U. S. Amateur Ballroom Dancers Association; Jim Trdinich, National League; Ray Tricarico, Playtex International.

Mary Ann Usrey, R. J. Reynolds Tobacco Company.

John Veltman; Carolyn Verweyst, Whirlpool Corporation.

A. R. Ward, Railroadians of America; Pat Weissman, American Association of Railroad Superintendents; Richard Williams; Bruce Wittmaier; Peter Wulff, *Home Lighting & Accessories*.

YKK Inc.

Caden Zollo, The Specialty Bulb Company, Inc.

HOW DOES ASPIRIN FIND A HEADACHE?

An Imponderables® Book

For Michele Gallery

Contents

CONTENTS

Preface

We break down Imponderables into two categories. Type A Imponderables are the mysteries of everyday life that have always driven us nuts. Like why do lion tamers use kitchen chairs to fend off wild animals? Or why don't disc jockeys identify the titles and artists of the songs they play anymore?

Type B Imponderables are just as perplexing. These are mysteries we had never contemplated until our readers brought them to our attention. Believe us, we had never worried before about why the Muppets are left-handed, or why the Three Musketeers didn't carry muskets. But once we heard the questions, we *had* to find out the answers.

The readers of our last six *Imponderables* books have supplied us with scads of great Type A and Type B Imponderables. If we are stumped by a particularly challenging Imponderable, we convert it into a Frustable (short for Frustrating Imponderables) and ask readers to help bail us out. And in the Letters section, we let you enumerate our multifarious shortcomings.

We implore you to help us in our quest to stump out all types of Imponderability, wherever they should lurk. If you are the first to submit an Imponderable we use in a book or provide the best solution to a Frustable, we offer you a grateful acknowledgment and a complimentary autographed copy of that book.

Want to contribute to this noble pursuit? See the last page to find out how you can join in. Don't be afraid. We're not carrying kitchen chairs.

Imponderables

Roaches In Your Car ?!
Park It in a Kill 'Em ROACH GARAGE!!
OH NO!
NEW
Choose from CAPE COD or RAISED RANCH!
Roaches may hitch a ride...
...but it's a DEAD END street!

Why Don't We Ever See Cockroaches in Our Usually Crumb-Filled Cars?

Our correspondent, Manny Costa, wonders why an automobile, laden with assorted crumbs, wouldn't be a buffet paradise for our little scampering friends. Mary H. Ross, professor of entomology at Virginia Polytechnic Institute, isn't willing to state unequivocally that cockroaches are never found in cars, but she agrees it is rare. And she offers two main reasons why.

For one, cars may get too cold. Cockroaches dislike the cold and would refuse to stay in the car. Secondly, water is essential for cockroaches' survival and reproduction.

Richard Kramer, director of research, education, and technical resources at the National Pest Control Association, told us that while cockroaches require food every seven to ten days, they must take in water every three days. Perhaps a cockroach might be attracted to a stretch limousine with a leaky wet bar, but most of us don't drive limos.

If you really want to entice cockroaches into your automobile,

Kramer suggests scattering your empty beverage cans alongside your array of crumbs—you may be able to "support a cockroach infestation for a limited period of time."

Submitted by Manny Costa of Warwick, Rhode Island.

Why Does Barbie Have Realistic Nylon Hair While Ken Is Stuck with Plastic Hair or Painted Hair?

Poor Mattel is being attacked from all sides. Many feminists have criticized Barbie for setting up unrealistic expectations among girls about what their bodies should look like. Mattel answers, understandably, that Barbie was created to be a fashion doll, a model-mannequin suitable for hanging a variety of clothes upon. Of course, girls fantasize about themselves *as* Barbie, and this identification with the doll is precisely what the critics are worried about.

As if these complaints weren't enough for Mattel to worry about, here come six female *Imponderables* readers accusing the company of reverse discrimination. "What's the deal with Ken's hair?" they all wondered.

Informal chats with a gaggle of Barbie enthusiasts, both young and middle-aged, yielded the information that most girls are indifferent to Ken. To these fans, "Barbie doll" connotes visions of loveliness, while "Ken doll" evokes the image of the sterile figure atop wedding cakes.

Mattel's research indicates that there isn't much demand among girls for more realistic hair for Ken. Lisa McKendall, manager of marketing communications for Mattel, provides an explanation:

> In general, the most popular play pattern with fashion dolls among young girls is styling the hair. That is why long, combable hair is such an important feature of fashion dolls. Since the Ken doll's hair is short, there is much less to style and play with, so having "realistic" hair has not been as important.

Needless to say, "Ken hair" is much cheaper for Mattel to produce, particularly because painted hair doesn't have to be "rooted" to the top of the doll's head.

The choice of hairstyles for the Barbie lines is not taken casually. Meryl Friedman, vice-president of marketing for Barbie consumer products, told *Imponderables* that the length and texture of dolls' hair depends upon which "segment," or line of Barbies, Mattel is conceptualizing. Friedman reports that the best-selling doll in the history of Mattel is the "Totally Hair Barbie" line. The Barbie in the Totally Hair line is ten and one-half inches long—and the doll is only eleven and one half inches tall. In this particular segment, even Ken has combable, if short hair, as McKendall explains:

> . . . the Ken doll *does* have realistic-looking hair and actually comes with styling gel to create many different looks. A special fiber for the hair called Kankelon is produced specifically for us in Japan.

Friedman reports that in 1994, a Ken will be produced with longer hair.

Who says the men's liberation movement hasn't achieved anything?

Submitted by Dona Gray of Whiting, Indiana. Thanks also to Laura and Jenny Dunklee of Sutter Creek, California; Jessica Barmann of Kansas City, Missouri; Rebecca Capowski of Great Falls, Montana; and Nicole McKinley of Rochelle, Illinois.

On the U.S. Penny, Why Is the "o" in the "UNITED STATES oF AMERICA" on the Reverse Side in Lower Case?

Believe it or not, that little "o" is an artistic statement. According to Brenda F. Gatling, chief, executive secretariat of the United States Mint, the designer of the reverse side of the one-cent piece, Frank Gasparra, simply preferred the look of the little "o" alongside the big "F." And this eccentricity is not an anomaly; the Franklin half-dollar and several commemoratives contain the same, puny "o." .

Submitted by Jennifer Godwin of Tyrone, Georgia.

BONG-BONG! CAPTAIN PRICE TO THE SPORTING GOODS DEPARTMENT!

BONG!

ARE WE FLYING THROUGH MACY'S?!

What Do All the Chime Signals on Airlines Mean? Are They Uniform from Airline to Airline?

We might not be white-knuckle fliers anymore, but let's put it this way: We're closer to a pale pink than a full-bodied red. So we're not too happy when we find ourselves sitting next to fearful fliers. Why is our fate in life always to be seated alongside a middle-aged passenger taking his or her first flight? Invariably, our rowmates quake when they hear the landing gear go up. And more than one has reacted to the chime signals as if they were a death knell; one skittish woman knocked our Diet Coke off our tray when she heard the chimes. She assumed that the three-chime signal must signify that our flight was doomed. Actually, all that happened of consequence was that our pristine white shirt soon resembled the coat of a dalmatian.

But we always have been curious about the meaning of these chime codes, so we contacted the three largest airlines in the United States—American, United, and Delta—to ask if they would decode the mystery. We were surprised at how forthcoming they were. Nevertheless, for the first time in the history of *Imponderables*, we are going to withhold some of the information our sources willingly

DAVID FELDMAN

provided, for two reasons. First, airline chime-signals vary not only from airline to airline but from plane to plane within companies, and today's signals are subject to change in the future. Second, every airline *does* have a code to signify a true emergency, and the airlines aren't particularly excited about the idea of passengers decoding such a signal before the cockpit crew has communicated with flight attendants. Airlines are justifiably concerned about readers confusing emergency signals with innocuous ones and confusing one company's codes with another's. We agree.

Michael Lauria, an experienced pilot at United Airlines, told *Imponderables* that he has never had to activate an emergency chime signal. He is much more likely to sound one chime, to indicate that the cockpit wishes to speak to the first-class cabin attendant or (two chimes) to the coach flight attendants. Even if Lauria's passengers are enduring particularly nasty turbulence, chances are that the cry for help from the cockpit, expressed by the chimes, is more likely to be for a coffee or a soda than for draconian safety measures.

The number of chimes is not the only way of differentiating signals. Some United planes emit different tone frequencies: a lower-tone chime is heard for a passenger call than for a crew call, and a "bing bong" indicates a call from one flight attendant to another.

American Airlines uses different chime configurations to inform attendants when they should prepare for landing, remain seated with seat belts fastened, and call the cockpit crew. Although American does have a designated emergency signal, like other airlines' it is rarely used.

Delta Airlines features an array of different chime signals, which specify events during a flight. For example, when the "fasten seat belt" signs are turned off, a double high-low chime marks the event. These chimes also tell the flight attendants what elevation the plane has attained. Even during uneventful flights, there are periods of "sterile cockpits," when attendants are not supposed to disturb the cockpit crew except in an emergency. Sterile cockpits occur during takeoff and landing, and even though domestic airlines no longer allow smoking anywhere on the plane, some airlines still use the turning off "no smoking" sign as the marker for when the pilots can be contacted freely.

On most Delta planes, each phone station has a select tone, so that on a widebody plane, the flight attendant can recognize who is calling, and the flight crew can call any one or all of the flight attendant stations at one time. Alison Johnson, manager of aircraft interiors for Delta, told *Imponderables* that during an emergency, it is important for the flight crew to be able to speak to flight attendants without causing panic among passengers. Obviously, if the entire staff is briefed, a game plan can be established before informing passengers about a potential problem.

Submitted by Gabe Wiener of New York, New York. Thanks also to Dr. Richard Presnell of Augusta, Georgia.

DAVID FELDMAN

Are Lions Really Afraid of Kitchen Chairs?

Give us a bazooka, a ten-foot pole, forty bodyguards, and excellent life insurance and hospitalization policies, and we might consider going into the ring with a lion.

Come to think of it, we think we'll still pass on it. But how in the h°@# did professional animal trainers choose such inappropriate tools as a whip and a kitchen chair? Why would a kitchen chair tame a lion? It doesn't even scare us!

At one time, animal trainers did use more forceful weapons against big cats. In his book *Here Comes the Circus,* author Peter Verney reports that the foremost trainer of the 1830s and 1840s, Isaac Van Amburgh, used heavy iron bars. Other trainers employed red-hot irons, goads, and even water hoses to control unmanageable beasts.

As far as we could ascertain, the considerably calmer instrument of the kitchen chair was introduced by the most famous lion tamer of the twentieth century, Clyde Beatty, who trained lions from 1920 until the late 1960s (when, ironically, he died of a car accident). His successor at the Clyde Beatty Circus, David Hoover, has strong feelings about the psychology of lions. Hoover believes that each lion has a totally different set of fears and motivations. For example, one lion he trained had a perverse fear of bass horns, while another went crazy when the circus's peanut roaster was operating.

Hoover believes that the only way for a human to control a lion is to gain psychological dominance over the animal—what he calls a "mental bluff." He also feels it important that the lion believe it couldn't harm the trainer. When he sustained injuries in the ring, Hoover always finished the act

> because the animal is operating under the assumption that he can't hurt you. If you leave the cage after the animal has injured you, then the animal knows he's injured you. You can't handle that animal anymore.

Hoover favored a blank cartridge gun over a whip. The purpose of the blanks was simply to disrupt the animal's concentration:

> They have a one-track mind. A blank cartridge goes off, and if you holler a command that the animal is familiar with, the animal will execute the command because he loses his original train of thought.

But what about the chair?

> The chair works the same way. The chair has four points of interest (the four legs). The animal is charging with the idea to tear the trainer apart. You put the chair up in his face. [When he sees the four legs of the chair] he loses his chain of thought, and he takes his wrath out on the chair and forgets he's after the trainer.

Ron Whitfield, lion tamer at Marine World Africa USA, told *Imponderables* that the chair is used more for theatrical reasons than for defense. If the instrument of the lion tamer is used as a tool of distraction rather than aggression, it makes sense to use flimsy props. Lions can be trained to bounce, swat at the chair—even to knock the chair out of the hands of the trainer. Ron assured us that if the lion wanted to attack, the chair would not offer any real protection.

Whitfield, who has trained lions for twenty-two years, has never used a chair. (He uses a stick and a crop whip.) The whip, he believes, is used as an extension of the hand of the trainer—to cue lions, who are lazy by nature. If they are sitting idly when they are supposed to be per-

DAVID FELDMAN

forming, a snap near them or a touch on their behinds will provide "motivation" to perform. And the whip provides negative reinforcement. Like a child, the lion learns that certain behaviors will induce a sting on the behind and will alter its behavior accordingly.

Even if lions have been performing in acts for years, they are still wild animals. Gary Priest, animal behavior specialist at the San Diego Zoo, reminds us that much of the behavior of even a "tamed" lion is instinctual and automatic. Like Hoover, Priest emphasizes the necessity for trainers to demonstrate a lack of fear of the animal. Without intervention of some kind, lions would revert to the appetitive cycle (crouching, eyes squinting, ears pinned back, lowering into a crouch, and springing) characteristic of lions on the hunt.

If trainers run or show fear, Priest explains, lions will think of them as prey. But if you approach the lion before it snares you, the appetitive cycle is disrupted. In the wild, no prey *would* approach a lion, so the cat is not genetically encoded to respond to this aggressiveness. (Indeed, Priest told us that if you ever encounter a lion in the wild, especially one that is starting to crouch, do *not* run away. Instead, run *toward* the lion, yelling "bugga bugga bugga," or some such profundity. Says Priest: "This will probably save your life," as the lion usually retreats when confronted.)

Priest thinks that the whip and chair are a good combination, with the noise from the whip a particularly good distraction and the chair allowing the trainer to approach the lion and still have some distance and (minimal) protection.

The one part of this Imponderable we would have loved to unravel is how and why Clyde Beatty thought of the idea of using a kitchen chair in the first place. Did he have a scare with a cat one day when the chair was the only object handy? Was he sitting on a chair when a lion attacked? Or did he just want an excuse to drag his favorite kitchen chair around the world with him?

Submitted by Steven Sorrentino of West Long Branch, New Jersey.

Why Is Pistachio Ice Cream Colored Green?

We first were asked this question in 1988 but decided not to answer it because we thought the answer was obvious: Pistachio nuts *are* green (sort of). Sure, you have to liberate the nutmeats from their ivory or red-colored shells (please don't ask us why pistachios are dyed red—see *Imponderables* for the thrilling answer), and then detach the thin, reddish-brown husk. Underneath its wrappers, though, is a yellowish nut with an obvious green tinge.

But this question seems to be on the minds of North Americans everywhere, and we are the last to deprive our readers of the knowledge that can set them free. We first contacted Ed Marks, an ice cream expert and historian, who told us that the first reference he could find to green pistachio ice cream was in *The Standard Manual for Soda and Other Beverages* (1897), by A. Emil Hiss. The directions state: "Color green with a suitable delicate color."

Why was green chosen? Marks has his ideas:

> The use of color in ice cream and other food items is predicated on two things: to make the food appealing to the eye and to generally make a processed item appear more closely to its natural state. One would presume that the use of green serves either or both of these purposes. I always associated green with the color of the pistachio nutmeat, although the truth is that the term "yellow-green" is a more apt description. Perhaps the early ice cream makers made a subjective decision that green was more appropriate than yellow.

Donald Buckley, executive director of the National Ice Cream Retailers Association, echoed Marks's sentiments and added that the color green had relatively little competition in early ice cream fountains. Yellow was already "taken" by vanilla. The average person probably associates the color green most closely with mint, not then popular as an ice cream flavor. (Now, green is a popular color in mint chocolate chip ice cream.)

Kathie Bellamy, of Baskin-Robbins, indicated that consumers are very conscious of whether the color of an ice cream simulates the "pub-

DAVID FELDMAN

lic perception of pistachio." Note that most commercial pistachio ice creams, including Baskin-Robbins', are invariably a pale green, and that considerable research is conducted on "color appeal." After all, with inexpensive food colorings, pistachio could just as easily be colored chartreuse, if the public would buy it.

Submitted by Lynda Frank of Omaha, Nebraska. Thanks also to Morgan Little of Austin, Texas; Bob Muenchow of Meriden, Connecticut; and many others.

Why Are Graves Six Feet Deep and Who Determined They Should Be That Deep?

Graves haven't always been that deep. Richard Santore, executive director of the Associated Funeral Directors International, told *Imponderables* that during the time of the Black Plague in Europe, bodies were not buried properly or as deep as they are today. These slovenly practices resulted in rather unpleasant side effects. As soil around the bodies eroded, body parts became exposed, which explains the origins of the slang term "bone yard" for a cemetery. Beside the grossness content, decomposing flesh on the surface of the earth did nothing to help the continent's health problems.

England, according to Santore, was the first to mandate the six-foot-under rule, with the idea that husband and wife could be buried atop each other, leaving a safe cushion of two feet of soil above the buried body, "the assumption being that if each casket was two feet high, you would allow two feet for the husband, two feet for the wife, and two feet of soil above the last burial." At last, there were no bones in the bone yard to be found.

DAVID FELDMAN

The six-foot rule also puts coffins out of reach of most predators and the frost line. Of course, caskets could be buried even deeper, but that would be unlikely to be popular with gravediggers, as Dan Flory, president of the Cincinnati College of Mortuary Science, explains:

> Six feet is a reasonable distance for the gravedigger [to shovel] and is usually not deep enough to get into serious water or rock trouble.

Submitted by Patricia Arnold of Sun Lakes, Arizona. Thanks also to Deone Pearcy of Tehachapi, California.

Why Doesn't Ham Change Color When Cooked, Like Other Meats?

Let's answer your Imponderable with a question. Why isn't ham the same color as a pork chop, a rather pallid gray?

The answer, of course, is that ham is cured and sometimes smoked. The curing (and the smoking, when used) changes the color of the meat. You don't cook a ham; you reheat it. According to Anne Tantum, of the American Association of Meat Processors, without curing, ham would look much like a pork chop, with perhaps a slightly pinker hue.

Curing was used originally to preserve meat before the days of refrigerators and freezers. The earliest curing was probably done with only salt. But salt-curing alone yields a dry, hard product, with an excessively salty taste.

Today, several other ingredients are added in the curing process, with two being significant. Sugar or other sweeteners are added primarily for flavor but also to retain some of the moisture of the meat that salt would otherwise absorb. Sugar also plays a minor role in fighting bacteria.

For our purposes, the more important second ingredient is nitrites and/or nitrates. Sodium nitrate is commonly injected into the ham, where it turns into nitrite. Nitrite is important in fighting botulism and other microorganisms that spoil meat or render it rancid. Nitrites also lend the dominant taste we associate with cured meat (bacon wouldn't taste like bacon without nitrites).

Unfortunately, for all the good nitrite does in keeping ham and other meats from spoiling, a controversy has arisen about its possible dark side. When nitrites break down, nitrous acid forms. Combined with secondary amines (an ammonia derivative combining hydrogen and carbon atoms), nitrous acid creates nitrosamines, known carcinogens. The debate about whether nitrosamines develop normally during the curing process is still swirling.

But nitrite was used to cure pork even before these health benefits and dangers were known, because it has always been valued as an effective way to color the meat. Nitrites stabilize the color of the muscle tissues that contain the pink pigment we associate with ham, as do some of the other salts (sodium erythorbate and/or sodium ascorbate) that help hasten the curing process.

Most curing today is done by a machine, which automatically injects a pickle cure of (in descending order of weight) water, salt, sweetener, phosphate, sodium erythorbate, sodium nitrate, and sodium nitrite. Usually, multiple needles are stuck in the ham; the more sophisticated machines can inject even bone-in hams. After this injection hams are placed in a cover pickle, where they sit for anywhere between a few days and a week. Hams that sit in cover pickle sport rosier hues than those that are sent directly to be cooked.

Hams are smoked at very low temperatures, under 200 degrees Fahrenheit, usually for five to six hours. Some cooked hams ("boiled ham" is a misnomer, as few hams are ever placed in water hotter than 170 degrees Fahrenheit) are cooked unsmoked in tanks of water and tend to be duller in color. These hams are usually sold as sandwich meat.

One of the reasons why hams are beloved by amateur cooks is that, like (cured) hot dogs, they are near impossible to undercook or overcook. More than a few Thanksgiving turkeys have turned into turkey jerky because cooks didn't know when to take the bird out of the oven. Luckily, hams are precooked for us. We might have to pay for the privilege, but it is hard for even noncooks to ruin their texture or tarnish their pinkish color.

Submitted by Dena Conn of Chicago, Illinois.

Why Does Warm Milk Serve as an Effective Sleep-Inducer for Many People?

Scientists haven't been able to verify it, but there is some evidence to support the idea that milk actually might induce sleep. Milk contains tryptophan, an amino acid, which is the precursor of a brain transmitter, serotonin, which we know has sedative qualities.

Recently, L-tryptophan supplements, which had gained popularity as a sleeping aid, were banned by the Food and Drug Administration because they caused severe reactions in some users, including eosinophilia, an increase in the number of white blood cells. Earlier research confirmed that L-tryptophan did help many people get to sleep faster than a placebo.

But does cow's milk contain enough tryptophan to induce sleepiness? This has yet to be proven. Representatives of the dairy industry, who might be the first to claim such a benefit for milk, are reluctant to do so and are openly skeptical about its sleep-inducing qualities. Jean Naras, a media relations specialist at the American Dairy Association, although dubious about the sedative effects of milk, cited research that indicated it might take a dose as high as a half-gallon to provide any sleep benefits. And with this quantity of milk intake, your bladder might argue with your brain about whether you really want to sleep through the night.

And does warm milk promote sleep any better than cold milk? It does if you believe it does, but none of the experts we consulted could provide a single logical reason why it should.

Submitted by R.W. Stanley of Bossier City, Louisiana.

Why Doesn't Glue Get Stuck in the Bottle?

There are two basic reasons:

1. In order for glue to set and solidify, it must dry out. Latex and water-based glues harden by losing water, either by absorption into a porous substrate (the surface to be bonded) or by evaporation into the air. The glue bottle, at least if it is capped tightly, seals in moisture.

2. Different glues are formulated to adhere to particular substrates. If the glue does not have a chemical adhesion to the substrate, it will not stick. For example, John Anderson, technical manager for Elmer's Laboratory (makers of Elmer's Glue-All), told us that the Elmer's bottle, made of polyethylene, does not provide a good chemical adhesion for the glue.

Even when the cap is left off, and the glue does lose water, the adhesion is still spotty. We can see this effect with the cap of many glue bottles. In most cases, dried glue can and does cake onto the tip after repeated uses. But Anderson points out that the adhesion is "tenuous," and one can easily clean the top while still wet and remove the glue completely. Likewise, if you poured Elmer's on a drinking glass, it might adhere a little, but you could easily wipe it off with a cloth or paper towel, because the glue cannot easily penetrate the "gluee."

Submitted by Jeff Openden of Northridge, California.

Why Don't People in Old Photographs Ever Seem to Smile?

Sometimes, the more you delve into an Imponderable, the murkier it becomes. We asked about twenty experts in photography and photographic history, and the early responses were fairly consistent: The subjects in old photographs weren't all depressed; the slowness of the exposure time was the culprit. In some cases, the exposure time in early daguerreotypes was up to ten minutes. Typical was the answer of Frank Calandra, secretary/treasurer of the Photographic Historical Society:

> Nineteenth-century photographic materials were nowhere near as light-sensitive as today's films. This meant that instead of the fractional second exposure times we take for granted, the pioneer photographers needed several minutes to properly set an image on a sensitized plate. While this was fine for landscapes, buildings and other still-lifes, portraits called for many tricks to help subjects hold perfectly still while the shutter was open. (The first cameras had no shutter. A cap was placed over the lens and the photographer would remove it to begin the exposure and replace it when time was up.)

Holding a smile for that length of time can be uncomfortable; that's why you see the same somber look on early portraits. That's what a relaxed face looks like.

If that's so, Frank, we'll look jittery, anytime.

Of course, the problem with trying to hold a smile for a long period of time isn't only that it is difficult. The problem is that the smile looks phony. Photographer Wilton Wong told *Imponderables* that even today,

> A good portraitist will *not* ask subjects to smile and have them hold it even for more than a few seconds, as the smile starts looking forced. With the long exposures of old, the smiles would look phony and detract from the photo. Look at yourself in the mirror with a thirty-second smile on your face!

The stationary of the Photographic Historical Association depicts a head clamp, which, although it looks like an instrument of torture, was used during the early days of photography to prevent a subject's head from moving while being photographed. In order to avoid blurring, subjects were forced to fix their gaze during the entire session. Iron braces were also utilized to keep the neck and trunks of subjects from moving. According to photographer Dennis Stacey,

> Sometimes all three brace methods were used, and in the case of young children, a sash was employed to tie them to the fixture where they sat to assist in holding them motionless.

In his book *The History of Photography from 1839 to the Present,* Beaumont Newhall recounts many anecdotes about the hardships caused by long exposure times. American inventor Samuel Morse, who was sent an early prototype by Daguerre (the French artist who pioneered photography), sat his wife and daughter down "from ten to twenty minutes" for each photograph. Newhall also describes the travails of an anonymous "victim," who suffered through an excruciating single shot:

> . . . he sat for eight minutes, with the strong sunlight shining on his face and tears trickling down his cheeks while the operator promenaded the room with watch in hand, calling out the time every five seconds, till the fountains of his eyes were dry.

We were satisfied with this technological explanation for unsmiling subjects until we heard from some dissenters. Perhaps the most vehement is Grant Romer, director of education at the George Eastman House's International Museum of Photography. Romer told us that the details of the daguerreotype process were announced to the public on August 19, 1839, and that only immediately after this announcement were exposures this long. By 1845, exposure time was down to six seconds. Yes, Romer admits, often photographers did utilize longer exposure times, but the technology was already in place to dramatically shorten the statuelike posing of subjects.

So could we find alternative explanations for the moroseness of early photographic subjects? We sure could. Here are some of the more plausible theories:

1. *Photographs were once serious business.* Joe Struble, assistant archivist at the George Eastman House, told us that the opportunity to have a photographic portrait was thought of as a once-in-a-lifetime opportunity. And it isn't as if the Victorian era was one where goofiness was prized. Roy McJunkin, curator of the California Museum of Photography at the University of California, Berkeley, feels that the serious expressions embody a "Victorian notion of dignity—a cultural inclination to be seen as a serious, hardworking individual." Photographer John Cahill told us that even in the 1990s, it is not unusual for a European or Middle Eastern subject to thank him for taking even a casual snapshot.

2. *Early subjects were imitating the subjects of portrait painters.* Daguerre was himself a painter, and early photographers saw themselves as fine artists. Jim Schreier, a military historian, notes that subjects in this era did not smile in paintings. John Hunisak, professor of art history at Middlebury College, who concurs with Schreier, adds that early photographs of landscapes also tried to mimic still-life paintings.

3. *"Technology and social history are intimately interwoven."* This comment, by Roy McJunkin, indicates his strong feeling that George Eastman's invention of roll film, and the candid camera (which could be carried under a shirt or in a purse), both before the end of the nineteenth century, eventually forced the dour expressions of early photographic subjects to turn into smiles. The conventions of the early portrait pictures were changed forever once families owned their own cameras.

In the 1850s, according to McJunkin, the average person might have sat for a photographic portrait a few times in his or her life. With roll film, it became possible for someone oblivious to the techniques of photography to shoot pictures in informal settings and without great expense.

4. *Early photographs were consciously intended for posterity.* When asked why people didn't smile in old photographs, Grant Romer responded, "Because they didn't want to." Romer was not being facetious. Photographic sessions were "serious business" not only because of their rarity and expense but because the photographs were meant to create documents to record oneself for posterity. Rather, he emphasizes that until the invention of the candid camera, photographers might have asked subjects to assume a pleasant expression, but the baring of teeth or grinning was not considered the proper way to record one's countenance for future generations.

5. *Who wants to bare bad teeth?* Romer does not discount the poor dental condition of the citizenry as a solid reason to keep the mouth closed. As Tampa, Florida, photographer Kevin Newsome put it:

> Baking soda was the toothpaste of the elite. Just imagine what the middle class used, if anything at all.

6. *Historical and psychological explanations.* As compelling as all of these theories are, we still feel there are psychological, historical, and sociological implications to the expressions of the subjects in old photographs. In "The Photography of History," a fascinating article in *After Image,* Michael Lesy discusses the severe economic depression that began in 1836 and lasted six years. Photography was brought to the United States in the thick of it. Lesy observes that early American photographers were not seen as craftsmen or artists but as mesmerists and phrenologists (belief in both was rampant):

> The daguerreotypists were called "professor" and were believed to practice a character magic that trapped light and used the dark to reveal the truth of a soul that shone through a face. These men may have been opportunists, but they moved through a population that lived in the midst of a commercial, political, and spiritual crisis that lasted a generation that ended with carnage and assassination. The craft they practiced and the pictures they made

were the result not only of the conventional rationalism of an applied technology, but of irrational needs that must be understood psychologically.

In other words, this was not a period when photographers enticed subjects to yell "cheese," or put a devil sign over the heads of other subjects.

By the time George Eastman introduced the roll camera, Victorian morality was waning. People who bought hand cameras, for the most part, were not the generation that suffered through the privations of the Civil War. At the turn of the century, there was a new middle class, eager to buy "cutting edge" technology.

As a benchmark, Roy McJunkin asks us to look at photographs of Queen Victoria and President McKinley and compare them with the visage of Teddy Roosevelt, a deft politician who consciously smiled for the camera: "He was the first media president—he understood what a photo opportunity was and took advantage of it." The politics of joy was born, and with it a new conviction that even the average working stiff had a right not specified in the Constitution—not only to the pursuit of happiness but to happiness itself.

We have one confession to make. Our research has indicated that smiles in old photographs, while uncommon, did exist. Dennis Stacey told us that more than a few existing Victorian photographs show the sitter "grinning or smiling, usually with the mouth closed." Grant Romer has an 1854 daguerreotype at the Eastman House of a woman standing on her head in a chair, smiling.

Romer admits that she was clearly defying the conventions of the period. But then, a little smile made Mona Lisa daring in her day, too.

Submitted by Ken Shafer of Traverse City, Michigan. Thanks also to Donna Yavelak of Norcross, Georgia; Rick Kaufhold of Dayton, Ohio; Sally Esposito of Las Vegas, Nevada; and Bart Hoss of Kansas City, Missouri.

Why Did Men Thrust Their Right Hand into Their Jackets in Old Photographs?

Most of the photo historians we contacted discounted what we considered to be the most likely answer: These subjects were merely imitating Napoleon and what came to be known as the Napoleonic pose. Maggie Kannan, of the department of photographs at the Metropolitan Museum of Art, and other experts we contacted felt that many of the reasons mentioned in the Imponderable above were more likely.

Just as subjects couldn't easily maintain a sincere smile during long exposure times, so was trying to keep their hands still a challenge. Frank Calandra wrote us:

> The hand was placed in the jacket or a pocket or resting on a fixed object so that the subject wouldn't move it [or his other hand] and cause a blurred image. Try holding your hands at your sides motionless for fifteen minutes or so—it's not easy.

Grant Romer adds that this gesture not only solved the problem of blurring and what to do with the subject's hands while striking a pose but forced the subject to hold his body in a more elegant manner.

Still, if these technical concerns were the only problem, why not thrust both hands into the jacket? Or pose the hands in front of the subject, with fingers intertwined? John Husinak assured us that this particular piece of body language was part of a trend that was bigger and more wide-ranging than simply an imitation of Napoleon.

Early portrait photographers understood the significance of particular gestures to the point where they were codified in many journals and manuals about photography. Some specific examples are cited in an article by William E. Parker in *After Image*, an analysis of the work of early photographer Everett A. Scholfield. Parker cites some specific examples: Two men shaking hands or touching each other's shoulders "connoted familial relationship or particular comradeship"; if a subject's head was tilted up with the eyes open or down with eyes closed, the photographer meant "to suggest speculative or contemplative moods."

Harry Amdur, of the American Photographic Historical Society, told us that early photographers tried to be "painterly" because they wanted to gain respect as fine artists. Any survey of the portrait paintings of the early and mid-nineteenth century indicates that the "hand-in-jacket" pose was a common one for many prominent men besides Napoleon.

Another boon to the Napoleonic pose was the invention of the *carte de visite*, a photographic calling card. Developed in France in the 1850s, small portraits were mounted on a card about the size of today's business card. Royalty and many affluent commoners had their visages immortalized on *cartes*. In France, prominent figures actually sold their *cartes*—ordinary citizens collected what became the baseball cards of their era. *Cartes de visite* invaded the United States within years.

These photos were far from candid shots. Indeed, Roy McJunkin told *Imponderables* that *carte de visite* studios in the United States used theatrical sets, and that subjects invariably dressed in their Sunday best. The hand-in-jacket pose was only one of many staged poses, including holding a letter or bible, holding a gun as if the subject were shooting, or pointing to an unseen (and usually nonexistent) point or object.

Some of the pretensions of this period were downright silly—silly enough to inspire Lewis Carroll to write a parody of the whole enterprise. In Carroll's poem, actually a parody of Longfellow's *Hiawatha*, Hiawatha is transformed into a harried, frustrated portrait photographer:

> From his shoulder Hiawatha
> Took the camera of rosewood,
> Made of sliding, folding rosewood;
> Neatly put it all together,
> In its case it lay compactly,
> Folded into nearly nothing;
> But he opened out the hinges,
> Pushed and pulled the joints and hinges,
> Till it looked all squares and oblongs,
> Like a complicated figure
> In the second book of Euclid,
> > This he perched upon a tri-pod—
> > Crouched beneath its dusty cover—

Stretched his hand enforcing silence—
Mystic, awful was the process,
    All the family in order
Sat before him for their pictures:
Each in turn, as he was taken,
Volunteered his own suggestions.
    First the governor, the father:
He suggested velvet curtains
Looped about a messy Pillar;
And the corner of a table.
He would hold a scroll of something
Hold it firmly in his left hand;
He would keep his right hand buried
(Like Napoleon) in his waistcoat;
He would contemplate the distance
With a look of pensive meaning,
As of ducks that die in tempests.
Grand, heroic was the notion:
Yet, the picture failed entirely:
Failed, because he moved a little,
Moved because he couldn't help it!

Who would have ever thought of Lewis Carroll summarizing the answers to an Imponderable, while simultaneously contemplating the plight of a Sears portrait photographer?

Submitted by Donald McGurk of West Springfield, Massachusetts. Thanks also to Wendy Gessel of Hudson, Ohio, and Geoff Rizzie of Cypress, California.

DAVID FELDMAN

Why Are Carpenter's Pencils Square?

Two reasons. Carl Reichenbach, product manager at pencil giant Dixon-Ticonderoga, told *Imponderables* that the square shape enables carpenters to draw thin or thick lines more easily than with conventional pencils.

But a more pressing point: If we drop a pencil from our desk, it's not a big deal to lean over and pick it up from the floor. However, what if we happen to drop a pencil from a beam on the thirty-fourth floor of a construction site? Or the roof of a home? As Ellen B. Carson of Empire Berol USA put it, "The carpenters' pencils are produced in a square shape so they won't roll off building materials."

Submitted by Nate Woodward of Seattle, Washington.

Why Don't Windshield Wipers in Buses Work in Tandem Like Auto Wipers?

Hearing that two *Imponderables* readers were obsessed with this question made us feel less lonely. We've always wondered whether we were the only ones bugged by the infernal racket and displeasing look of two huge, awkward, asymmetrical windshield wipers churning away on rainy trips.

The answer turns out to be simple, if technical. Most automobiles use one motor to power two windshield wipers. With bigger windshields and blades, the two bus wipers are driven by separate, independent motors, so the movement of the two blades is not coordinated.

Isn't there any way to get the two wipers to work together? Sure, for a cost, as Karen Finkel, executive director of the National School Transportation Association, explains:

> A larger motor to accommodate the larger blade and windshield could be developed. However, there isn't a reason to synchronize the wipers so it hasn't been done.

Hmmm. Not driving us nuts, we guess, isn't reason enough to change the status quo.

Submitted by P.M. Cook of Lake Stephens, Washington. Thanks also to Karyn Heckman of Greenville, Pennsylvania.

Why Were Athos, Porthos, and Aramis Called the Three Musketeers When They Fought with Swords Rather Than Muskets?

The Three Swordsmen sounds like a decent enough title for a book, if not an inspiring name for a candy bar, so why did Dumas choose *The Three Musketeers*? Dumas based his novel on *Memoirs of Monsieur D'Artagnan,* a fictionalized account of "Captain-Lieutenant of the First Company of the King's Musketeers." Yes, there really was a company of musketeers in France in the seventeenth century.

Formed in 1622, the company's main function was to serve as bodyguard for the King (Louis XIII) during peacetime. During wars, the musketeers were dispatched to fight in the infantry or cavalry; but at the palace, they were the *corps d'élite.* Although they were young (mostly seventeen to twenty years of age), all had prior experience in the military and were of aristocratic ancestry.

According to Dumas translator Lord Sudley, when the musketeers were formed, they "had just been armed with the new flintlock, muzzle-loading muskets," a precursor to modern rifles. Unfortunately, the musket, although powerful enough to pierce any armor of its day, was also extremely cumbersome. As long as eight feet, and the weight of two bowling balls, they were too unwieldy to be carried by horsemen. The musket was so awkward that it could not be shot accurately while resting on the shoulder, so musketeers used a fork rest to steady the weapon. Eventually, the "musketeers" were rendered musketless and relied on newfangled pistols and trusty old swords.

Just think of how muskets would have slowed down the derring-do of the three amigos. It's not easy, for example, to slash a sword-brandishing villain while dangling from a chandelier, if one has a musket on one's back.

Submitted by John Bigus of Orion, Illinois.

Why Don't Public Schools Teach First Aid and CPR Techniques?

Wouldn't our world be a safer place if every high school required students to take a class in life-saving techniques? Reader Charles Myers sure thought so, so we tried to find out why CPR isn't a part of schoolroom curriculums in most communities. Considering the violence in our schools, the argument needn't be made that such training would only be usable in the "outside world." In fact, this issue recently has become a hot topic among educators, particularly because of concerns about the response times of fire, paramedic, police, and other emergency medical services in many communities.

All of the health officials we contacted felt that CPR and first aid training in public schools could be valuable, but they provided a litany of reasons why we shouldn't expect to see it in the near future. Why not?

1. *Money.* Most school systems are riddled with financial problems. CPR training is labor-intensive. While a normal classroom might have a ratio of twenty-five or thirty students per teacher, CPR requires a six-to-one or eight-to-one ratio. And training teachers to learn and then teach CPR costs money.

2. *Liability problems.* "America," says Bill Powell, prehospital emergency training coordinator for Booth Memorial Medical Center in Flushing, New York, "is the land of the suing." What if a student botches a rescue operation? Would the school be legally and financially liable for poor training?

3. *No one should be forced to administer CPR.* Several of our sources indicated that although it is an admirable goal to have every student learn first aid techniques, in practice it might not be a good idea to force those who don't desire to learn or who are incapable of administering them properly. Georgeanne Del Canto, director of health services for the Brooklyn, New York, Board of Education, told *Imponderables* that good intentions notwithstanding, asking every student to learn first aid would be a little like asking every schoolkid to go out for the wrestling team: Too many students would be insufficiently strong, energetic, or limber to apply CPR adequately, and more than a few would be too squeamish.

If we required all students to learn CPR, we would be forcing them to learn a technique that they would not be obligated to use outside of school. In most states, Bill Powell told us, lay citizens are under no legal obligation to act as a Good Samaritan (in most states, physicians do have such an duty), even in life-threatening situations.

4. *Motivation of students.* Powell isn't too sanguine about the desire of students to learn CPR properly. Why should they pay any more attention to first aid training than they do to math or history? Most non-health professional students in CPR courses are people who are friends or family of someone who they fear is at risk; few learn CPR out of sheer altruism or an abstract academic interest.

5. *Time.* CPR certifications must be renewed every two years, not so much because first aid techniques change but because most students, thankfully, never get a chance to apply their lessons in real life. Constant retraining of students might be another financial and labor drain on schools, although this problem could be ameliorated by introducing the subject in the junior year of high school, thus saddling colleges with the task of recertification.

6. *Training of trainers.* "A little knowledge is a dangerous thing," emphasizes Ira Schwartz, project director of the New York State Regents Advisory Committee on Community Involvement. Schwartz and others we talked to thought that finding a ready supply of teachers qualified to

teach CPR, or training nonqualified teachers to do so, was a major hurdle.

7. *Competition.* CPR isn't the only health item clamoring to be included in public school curriculums. Although she joined in the chorus of educators who thought that universal CPR training would be a noble idea, Arlene Sheffield, director of the school health demonstration program for the New York State Education Department, told us that many educators believe that teaching students about bulimia, anorexia nervosa, and child abuse has a higher priority. Sheffield's program, for example, focuses on eliminating drug abuse among students, a subject of more pressing importance to students, educators, and parents than CPR. As Sheffield puts it,

> The pool of money and time available for schooling in any given subject is finite and CPR and first aid have a lot of healthy competition.

CPR training is not totally abandoned in our public schools. Many schools offer kids training on an elective basis; community groups and hospitals offer low-cost courses. And a few public school systems, such as Seattle's, find the time, money, and training resources to offer all students CPR courses.

Charles Myers was not alone in wondering if some of that time he (and, let us admit, we) wasted in school might have been better spent learning a skill that could save others' lives. When we asked Emmanuel M. Goldman, former publisher of *Curriculum Review*, this Imponderable, he echoed our sentiments exactly:

> As to why CPR isn't taught, at least in high school: It beats me. Probably because it is such a logical, desirable, and useful skill.

Submitted by Charles Myers of Ronkonkoma, New York.

Why Do Peanuts in the Shell Usually Grow in Pairs?

Botany 101. A peanut is not a nut but a legume, closer biologically to a pea or a bean than a walnut or pecan. Each ovary of the plant usually releases one seed per pod, and all normal shells contain more than one ovary.

But not all peanut shells contain two seeds. We are most familiar with Virginia peanuts, which usually contain two but occasionally sprout mutants that feature one, three, or four. Valencia and Spanish peanuts boast three to five seeds per shell.

Traditionally, breeders have chosen to develop two-seeded pods for a practical reason: Two-seeders are much easier to shell. According to Charles Simpson, of Texas A & M's Texas Agricultural Experiment Station, there is little taste difference among the varieties of peanuts, but the three-seed peanuts are quite difficult to shell, requiring tremendous pressure to open without damaging the legume. We do know that patrons of baseball games wouldn't abide the lack of immediate gratification. They'd much rather plop two peanuts than three into their mouths, at least if it means less toil and more beer consumption.

Submitted by Thad Seaver, A Company, 127 FSB.

Why Are Children Taught How to Print Before They Learn Cursive Handwriting?

While most of us were taught how to print in kindergarten and learned how to write in late second or third grade, this wasn't always the case. Until the early 1920s, children were taught only cursive handwriting in school. Margaret Wise imported the idea of starting kids with manuscript writing (or printing) from England in 1921, and her method has become nearly universal in North America ever since.

DAVID FELDMAN

Wise used two arguments to promote the radical change: With limited motor skills, it was easier for small children to make print legible; and print, looking more like typeset letters than cursive writing, would enable children to learn to read faster and more easily. Subsequent experimental research has confirmed that Wise's suppositions were correct.

In the seventy years since Wise revolutionized kindergarten penmanship, other reasons for teaching children printing have been advanced: Print is easier for teachers and students to read; students learn print more quickly and easily than cursive writing; and despite protestations from some, children can print as fast as they can write. While adults tend to write faster than they can print, experiments have indicated that this is only true because most adults rarely print; those who print as a matter of course are just as fast as cursive writers.

We have pored over many academic discussions about children's writing and haven't found anyone strenuously objecting to teaching children how to print first. What surprised us, though, is the lack of reasoned justification for weaning children from printing and, just after they have mastered the technique, teaching them cursive writing. After reviewing the literature on the subject, Walter Koenke, in an article in *The Reading Teacher*, boiled the rationales down to two—tradition and parental pressure:

> Since printing can be produced as speedily as cursive handwriting while being as legible and since it is obvious that the adult world generally accepts printing, it seems that the tradition rather than research calls for the transition from some form of printing to cursive handwriting.

A litany of justifications for cursive writing has been advanced, but none of them holds up. If print is easier to read and write, why do we need to learn cursive script? Why do we need to teach children duplicate letter forms when there is hard evidence that the transitionary period temporarily retards students' reading and compositional ability? (One study indicated that for each semester's delay in introducing cursive handwriting, students' compositional skill improved.)

In a wonderful article, "Curse You, Cursive Writing," the University of Northern Iowa's Professor Sharon Arthur Moore argues passionately that there is no need to teach children cursive writing and rebuts most of the arguments that its proponents claim. It is not true, as conventional wisdom might have it, that cursive writing is harder to forge than manuscript print, nor is it true that only cursive writing can be a valid signature on legal documents (X can still mark the spot).

Moore feels that parental pressure and a belief that cursive is somehow more "grown up" or prestigious than print permeates our society and leads to an unnecessary emphasis on cursive style:

> From the time they enter school, children want to learn to "write"; near the end of second or the beginning of third grade, the wish comes true. The writing done to that point must not be very highly valued, or why would there be such a rush to learn to do "the real thing"? . . . perceptions are so much more powerful than reality at times that it may not even occur to people to question the value of cursive writing.

Why, she argues persuasively, do business and legal forms ask us to "please print carefully"? The answer, of course, is that even adults print more legibly than they write cursively. If cursive is superior, why aren't cursive typefaces for typewriters and computer printers more popular? Why aren't books published in cursive?

Moore, like us, can't understand the justification for teaching kids how to write, and then changing that method in two years for no pedagogical purpose. She endorses the notion of teaching cursive writing as an elective in eighth or ninth grade.

Several handwriting styles have been advanced to try to bridge the gap between manuscript and cursive styles—most prominently, the "D'Nealian Manuscript," which teaches children to slant letters from the very beginning and involves much less lifting of the pencil than standard printing. Proponents of the D'Nealian method claim that their style requires fewer jerky movements that may prove difficult and time-consuming for five- and six-year-olds and eases the transition from manuscript to cursive by teaching kids how to "slant" right away. And the D'Nealian method also cuts down the reversal of letters that typifies children's printing. It is far less likely that a child, using D'Nealian, will misspell "dad" as "bab," because the "b" and "d" look considerably different. In standard manuscript, the child is taught to

DAVID FELDMAN

create a "b" by making a straight vertical line and then drawing a circle next to it. But in D'Nealian, the pencil is never picked up: the straight but slanted vertical line is drawn, but the "circle" starts at the bottom of the line, and the pencil is brought around and up to form what they call the "tummy" of the "b."

We'll leave it to the theorists to debate whether the D'Nealian, or more obscure methods, are superior to the standard "circle stick" style of manuscript. But we wish we could have found a clearer reason why it's necessary to change from that style into cursive writing—ever. We couldn't argue the cause more eloquently than Janice-Carol Yasgur, an urban elementary schoolteacher:

> Just as kids begin to get competent in printing their thoughts, we come along and teach them cursive—and what a curse it is! Now they devote more of their energy to joining all the letters together than to thinking about what they're trying to communicate, so that it's a total loss: It's impossible to make out their scribbles; but even if you can, it's impossible to figure out what they're trying to say. It's a plot to keep elementary schoolteachers in a state of permanent distress.

Submitted by Erin Driedger of Osgoode, Ontario.

Why Do Most Women's Hairbrushes Have Long Handles When Men's Hairbrushes Have Short Handles or No Handles at All?

Why are men deprived of the graceful, long handles on women's hairbrushes? According to the experts we contacted, the answer seems to be that the longer the hair of the user is, the longer the handle of the brush should be. Carmen Miller, product manager of Vidal Sassoon brushes and combs division, explains:

> Traditionally, men have used what is referred to as a "Club" brush—a wide-based brush with densely packed bristles and a shorter length handle. This brush is best used for smoothing hair, not texturizing or detangling, as most women's brushes are used for. Since men usually have closely cropped hair, they need to use a brush closer to the scalp to effectively smooth their hair.

This response, of course, begs the question of whether Annie Lennox and Sinead O'Connor use long- or short-handled brushes. Or imagine the plight of Daniel Day Lewis, in *Last of the Mohicans*, ferreting the burrs out of his hair with a handleless brush. Fabio could use a long handle too.

Miller indicates that the shape of the man's hand, as well as the shortness of his hair, is a consideration in handle length:

> The [short] handle was designed to allow a man's hand to closely grip the brush and thus better control its smoothing action. In addition, the shorter handle style is usually a wider or thicker handle, which fits a man's larger hand more comfortably and provides a stronger brush that won't break easily.

The Fuller Brush Company's laboratory manager, Bill Dayton, suggests another theory that explains why men's hairbrushes have gotten shorter and shorter over the centuries (many older men's brushes were indistinguishable from women's): "Men's brushes were designed to conserve space in military duffel bags and dop kits."

Submitted by Anne Taylor Spence of Washington, D.C.

Why Do Some Ladybugs Have Spots and Others Have None?

Ladybugs, beloved by children and politically correct animal lovers, have a great public relations person. In reality, they are just a type of beetle. There are somewhere between three thousand and four thousand species of ladybugs in the world.

Their colorings and markings vary so much that most entomologists have concluded that nothing in particular separates a ladybug with spots from a spotless individual. You can't tell the sex or gender of a ladybug from its markings. One individual ladybug from a given species might have spots; others of the same species, from the same region, might not.

The variations of coloring are almost endless. Ladybugs' bodies might be red with black markings, or orange with blue markings. Some have only two spots, while the Thirteen Spotted Lady Beetle, appropriately enough, sports thirteen. Why has nature provided them with such a seemingly random succession of markings?

Most entomologists believe that spots are there for defensive purposes. Robin Roche, keeper and entomologist at the Insect Zoo in San Francisco, told *Imponderables* that in nature, red and black (two of the most common colors for ladybugs' spots) are warning colorations. Other creatures, especially birds and rodents, learn that animals with certain colors sting or taste less than delectable. Even animals that don't emit toxins might mimic the appearance of spotted animals that do. Many ladybugs actually do make a lurking predator's life most unpleasant: Some spray blood, while others spray a poisonous fluid.

Although no one can be sure, most entomologists lend credence to the theory that regional spotting variations occur because the ladybugs' spots simulate the appearance of a more venomous animal. But others aren't so sure and wonder why, if the markings are so important to their defense, other individual ladybugs in the same region aren't born with a similar defense mechanism. Lynn S. Kimsey, director of the Bohart Museum of Entomology at the University of California, Davis, suggests that some variations in spotting might be due to temperature differences, "or it may be a genetic component of a population, much like the coloration of domestic dogs (e.g., dalmatians versus Labrador retrievers).

Submitted by Angel Vecchio of Fresno, California. Thanks also to Ashley Watts of Caledonia, Ontario.

Why Does a Loud Bang or Opening and Closing the Oven Door Sometimes Make Soufflés and Cakes Fall in the Oven?

Tom Lehmann, bakery assistance director at the American Institute of Baking, told *Imponderables* that while a cake is being baked, the batter rises to a point slightly higher than its fully baked height. The baking powder in the batter produces gas that causes the leavening effect. "At a time when the batter is at its maximum height, but has not 'set' due to starch gelatinization and protein coagulation, the batter is very unstable." The cake is at its most fragile and delicate because, according to bakery consultant Dr. Simon S. Jackel, "the air cells holding the entrapped gases are very thin and weak."

Not all cakes will crash if confronted with a loud noise. But most will fall during this vulnerable time during the cooking process, and soufflés are always in danger. Joe Andrews, publicity coordinator for Pillsbury Brands, explains:

> The basic structure of a soufflé is developed by egg proteins, which are whipped into a foam and then set by baking. When whipping of the

egg whites occurs, large pockets of air are trapped by the albumen, and in the process, this protein is partially denatured. The denaturation (or setting) continues (along with the expansion of the air bubbles) when the proteins are heated in the oven. If the oven is opened while this expansion is taking place, the air pressure change and temperature change can cause the whole structure to collapse.

The most common bang, of course, is the opening and closing of the oven door. Anyone near a loudspeaker at a rock concert knows that sound vibrations can be felt; a soufflé or cake can be pummeled by a nearby noise. Although cakes are usually hardier than soufflés, Andrews indicates the same problems that afflict soufflés also make cakes fall,

> especially if the primary source of leavening for the cake is beaten egg whites (e.g., angel food or chiffon cakes). Layer cakes contain more flour and the structure is formed as much by starch gelatinization as egg denaturation, so they would not be as susceptible to falling when the door is opened—unless the door is opened too early in the baking process (during the first twenty minutes) before the cake structure has set.

Only when the internal temperature of the cake reaches a range of 160 to 180 degrees Fahrenheit is the cake out of the woods, because, as Jackel puts it, "the liquid batter is now converted to a solid cake structure."

Submitted by Sherry Grenier of Amos, Quebec.

The famous "Angel Food Cake" portal at Gateaux Cathedral.

Why Do Angel Food Cakes Have to Be Turned Upside-Down While Cooling?

As we just learned, angel food cakes are structurally delicate when baking, but once they've achieved a solid state, why in the heck do we have to turn them on their heads? We headed back to our trusty experts for their counsel. Tom Lehmann responded:

> Angel food cakes are really nothing more than an expanded egg white foam with sugar added for sweetness, and flour added to stabilize the foam and prevent it from collapsing during baking and cooling. Due to their inherent weakness, angel food cakes would collapse during baking and cooling if it weren't for two things. First, an angel food cake pan is never greased. This allows the batter to grip the pan sides for added support. The cakes are then stuck tightly enough to the pan after baking to allow them to be inverted without the cake falling out of the pan. By inverting the pan, we prevent the cake from further settling during cooling and obtain a light, tender finished cake.

Dr. Jackel notes that inverting the cake is absolutely essential for achieving an evenness of consistency:

> Although the top of the angel food cake has lost moisture in the oven during baking, and formed a dry skin, the bottom of the cake has retained some of the moisture and is slightly soft and sticky, because the bottom of the pan is not designed to release moisture as the cake bakes. When the cake is cooled, it is turned over so that the sticky, moist bottom of the cake has a chance to lose the extra moisture to the atmosphere and form a skin. The top has already formed the skin in the oven and therefore is already dry and firm.

Submitted by Gregg Hoover of Pueblo, Colorado.

Why Have Auto Manufacturers Moved the Brights/Dimmer Switch from the Floorboard to the Stalk of the Steering Column?

We have fond memories of cross-country trips in which we were so bored during barren stretches that we would amuse ourselves by clicking the dimmer control on the floorboard, even though our lights weren't on. This may not compete with square dancing or coin collecting as a pastime, but it was some solace as we fantasized about the next odometer check or Stuckey's we might encounter.

Alas, our old diversion has now faded into nostalgia. In the 1970s, Detroit followed the lead of European and Japanese automakers and mounted brightness controls on a stalk of the steering column. At first we wondered whether this change was mandated by regulation, but we quickly learned there was no such requirement. An expert at the National Highway Traffic Safety Administration who prefers to remain anonymous informed us that the Department of Transportation only cares that there be a control to turn the high beams on and off, and that a (blue) light alerts the driver that the brights are on. (Red lights are reserved for warning indicators, such as overheating, oil shortages, etc.)

DAVID FELDMAN

From the government's standpoint, the location of the control is not a safety issue, so the dimmer switch could be mounted on the ceiling and require a head butt to engage. So why did the automakers bother changing? We received five different explanations:

1. The move allowed auto manufacturers to put all the electrical features in the steering column instead of isolating one electrical element far away on the floor. This is why light, windshield wiper, and cruise controls have joined the horn and directional signals on the steering columns of most cars. Furthermore, as pointed out by Vann Wilber, director of safety and international technical affairs for the American Automobile Manufacturers Association, the floors of cars tend to get wet in the winter, and the water can seep into the electrical system, a potential safety hazard.

2. Consumers seem to prefer it. Wilber told *Imponderables* that the Big Three American automakers conducted human factors research indicating that drivers can identify hand-operated controls more quickly and easily than floor-mounted counterparts. Obviously, if the controls are adjacent to the steering wheel, the driver's hands are close to the beam control. Now that automobiles are often laden with as many gewgaws as jet instrument panels, the visibility of controls has become increasingly important. According to a member of the Society of Automotive Engineers' Lighting Committee, well-labeled stalk controls forestall drivers from looking around the dashboard, feeling around with their feet, or even worse, looking on the ground for the right pedal to depress, when they should be looking at the road.

Notwithstanding this reasoning, we must argue that markings on the stalk are of little use if the interior of the car is dark. Although one eventually becomes accustomed to the location of controls on one's own cars, it is disconcerting to rent an automobile and find oneself turning on the windshield wipers when one meant to cut off the high beams. Locating the old controls at worst required a one-time foot grope—knowing that there were no other controls on the floor made us less queasy about searching for it.

3. For people driving with standard transmissions, who must constantly use the left foot for the clutch, floor-mounted controls were often a nuisance and potentially even a safety hazard.

4. Mounting the brightness control on the steering stalk has enabled manufacturers to allow drivers to put on the high beams even when their lights

were not previously on. This feature makes it possible for drivers to alert the car in front of them to move over so that they can pass.

5. Because of the increase in international travel and alliances between American and foreign automakers, it makes sense to standardize as many features of automobiles as possible, particularly safety features.

We can't stop progress, we guess. But we're not happy about this particular change. If you are depressed about your car's barren floorboards, you may perk up a little when you find out that the issue of dimmer controls has inspired a joke among folks in the auto industry:

> General Motors is circulating a new service bulletin regarding cars with high beams on the stalk. G.M. is going back to the floor-mounted switch because too many_____(fill in favorite oppressed group) were getting their feet tangled in the steering wheel when they tried to turn on their brights.

And then again, maybe you won't perk up after hearing the joke.

Submitted by David Letterman, somewhere in Connecticut.

Why Is an Ineligible College Athlete Called a "Redshirt"? And Why Do Colleges Redshirt Players?

We were surprised at how difficult it was to obtain hard information about the history of redshirting. But every football source we contacted told us to contact Pat Harmon, legendary Cincinnati sportswriter and currently historian of the College Football of Fame. Harmon was kind enough to write us about the origins of this colorful term:

> At the University of Alabama many years ago, the coaching staff had recruited a large number of new students who were football players. Some of them were mature enough to work in the regular format—four years of college, four years of football.

DAVID FELDMAN

But if the coaches had an overabundance of player-candidates at one position—say tackle or end—they would decide to hold some of the newcomers back a year.

These students would go to class for five years. *They would practice football for five years but play only four.*

For that first year, when they practiced every day but were not used in games, they needed an identification so the coaches could spot them quickly. They were given red shirts [to separate them from the varsity playing squad].

The practice of developing five-year players spread to other schools, and so did the use of red shirts. Thus a player who was held out for a year was called a redshirt.

The redshirted player lives in a twilight zone best described by writer Douglas Looney in a 1982 *Sports Illustrated* article:

> The redshirt gets to practice like the other players, gets chewed out like the other players, goes to sleep in meetings like the other players, and takes his lumps like the other players, except he doesn't get to play in games. Which is to say, he gets everything football has to offer but the fun.

College football researcher Ray Schmidt told *Imponderables* that in practice, many coaches and other players actually *do* take it a little easier on redshirted freshmen. After all, why should coaches "waste" their time trying to perfect a play with athletes who will never implement it?

The National Collegiate Athletic Association (NCAA) has had a long love-hate relationship with redshirting. The NCAA first legally adopted the practice in 1961 on behalf of a DePaul basketball player who did not play his freshman year. Because of technical regulations then in place, the player was free to play during the college season but ineligible during postseason competition.

Unfortunately, the redshirt rule was abused. Although technically legal, murmurs of discontent among coaches was heard when the head football coach of the University of Washington, Ray James, who had a particularly talented group of upperclassmen, redshirted twenty-one of his twenty-three freshmen in 1978. As Bob Carroll of the Pro Football Researchers Association told *Imponderables*, eventually "coaches started stashing players away simply to preserve their eligibility."

Of course, if the coaches' redshirting strategy works, the academic sophomore/football freshman starts off his actual intercollegiate play bigger, faster, and smarter than he would if he played right away. But redshirting can backfire. If he does not impress the coaching staff, he risks losing a scholarship for the next four years; if successful the freshman increases his potential marketability in the pros and could dominate his nonredshirted college competitors.

Submitted by Dr. John Nushy of Torrance, California.

If You Dig a Hole and Try to Plug the Hole with the Very Dirt You've Removed, Why Do You Never Have Enough Dirt to Refill the Hole?

After speaking to several agronomists, we can say one thing with certainty: Don't use the word "dirt" casually among soil experts. As Dr. Lee P. Grant of the University of Maryland's Agricultural Engineering Department remonstrated us, dirt is what one gets on one's clothes or sweeps off the floor. Francis D. Hole, professor emeritus of soil science and geography at the University of Wisconsin-Madison, was a little less gentle:

> What would you do if you were some fine, life-giving soil who is twenty thousand years the senior of the digger, and you were operated on by this fugitive human being with a blunt surgical instrument (but without a soil surgeon's license), and if you were addressed as so much "dirt," to boot? I am suggesting that a self-respecting soil would flee the spot and not be all there for you to manipulate back into the hole.

So there's the answer: The soil is offended by you calling it dirt, Loren, and has flown the scene of your crime against it.

We promised Grant and Hole we would treat soil with all the respect it was due, and temporarily suppress the use of the "d" word, if they would answer our question. They provided several explanations for why you might run out of soil when refilling a hole:

DAVID FELDMAN

1. *Not saving all the soil.* Dr. Hole reported one instance, where in their excitement about their work, a team of soil scientists forgot to lay down the traditional canvas to collect the collected soil: "We had lost a lot of the soil in the forest floor, among dead branches and leaves."

2. *You changed the soil structure when you dug up the dirt.* Grant explains:

> Soil is composed of organic and inorganic material as well as air spaces and microorganisms. Soil has a structure which includes, among other things, pores (or air spaces) through which water and plant roots pass. Within the soil are worm, mole, and other tunnels and/or air spaces. All of this structure is destroyed during the digging process.

Hole confirms that stomping on the hole you are refilling can also compact the soil, removing pores and openings, resulting in plugging the hole too tight:

> It sounds like a case of poor surgery to me. You treated the patient (the soil) badly by pounding the wound that you made in the first place.

3. *Soil often dries during the digging/handling/moving.* Grant reports that the water in soil sometimes causes the soil to take up more space than it does when dry.

Both of our experts stressed that the scenario outlined by our correspondent is not always true. Sometimes, you may have *leftover* soil after refilling, as Dr. Hole explains:

> It is risky to say that "you never have enough soil to refill." Because sometimes you have too much soil. If you saved all your diggings on a canvas and put it all back, there could be so much soil that it would mound up, looking like a brown morning coffee cake where the hole had been.
>
> . . . you loosened the soil a lot when you dug it out. When you put the soil back, there were lots of gaps and pore spaces that weren't there before. It might take a year for the soil to settle back into its former state of togetherness. A steady, light rain might speed the process a little bit.

Submitted by Loren A. Larson of Orlando, Florida.

Why Was Twenty-one Chosen as the Age of Majority?

Has there ever existed a teenager who has not wailed, loudly and frequently, "Why do I have to wait until I'm twenty-one until I can (fill in the blank)?" To a kid with raging hormones, the number seems totally arbitrary.

And of course, the age *is* arbitrary. Now that some states have lowered the drinking age to eighteen ("If we are old enough to fight in Vietnam, we're old enough to vote and drink ourselves silly," went the argument), the number twenty-one seems downright capricious. How did this tradition begin?

Michael de L. Landon, professor of history at the University of Mississippi, provided us with the proper ammunition to blame the appropriate party: the British.

> Of course, twenty-one is approximately the age when both young men and women complete their full physical growth. More specifically, in medieval times in western Europe, young men of noble and knightly families normally left their homes to enter into service in the household of

DAVID FELDMAN

someone of equal or higher rank (as compared to their parents) around the age of nine to eleven. Until fourteen, they served as pages, mostly under the supervision of the ladies of the household. From fourteen to twenty-one, they served as (e)squires attached to adult knights who, in return for having their horses attended to, their armor polished, etc., were supposed to train them in the knightly arts.

By the thirteenth century, twenty-one was customary age for a young man to be knighted. Likewise, among middle-class families in the towns and cities, a boy would normally be apprenticed at adolescence (i.e., around fourteen) to a "master" to learn a trade or craft. The customary apprenticeship period was seven years, until the age of twenty-one.

We wonder whether today's teenagers would exchange the right to drink at an earlier age for the right to leave home and work for up to twelve years before the age of twenty-one.

The English age of majority was by no means universal, even in Europe. Professor de L. Landon points out that in Roman law, children were "infants" until the age of seven; "pupils" until the age of puberty (girls, twelve; boys, fourteen); and minors until marriage for girls or age twenty-five for boys.

Submitted by Scott Wallace of Marion, Iowa. Thanks also to John Anthony Anella of South Bend, Indiana; and Joey Maraia of Nacogdoches, Texas.

Why Don't Disc Jockeys Identify the Titles and Artists of the Songs They Play?

We have a nifty secret for curing the morning blahs—sleep through them. Yes, we admit it: We're night people. We sleep until noon, run the shower, and flip the radio on to WHTZ, better known as Z100 in the New York City metropolitan area, and listen to the midday jock, Human Numan. Z100 is what the radio trade calls a CHR (Contemporary Hits Radio) station, a modern mutation of the old Top 40 format. Z100 has a small playlist of current songs.

Human's a terrific disc jockey. He's not full of himself. Doesn't reach for laughs. But we have one big complaint: He rarely, if ever, identifies songs. As we're writing this chapter, we've heard the new New Order single played at least twenty-five times on his show but have yet to hear the title identified.

Fate threw us into Human's lap one day, and we got to talk to him about this Imponderable. DJs have two options in identifying a song: introducing it before they play it, or "frontselling"; or playing the song and announcing the name of the recording artist and/or song afterward, or "backselling." The first thing that Human wanted to let *Imponderables* readers know is that the vast majority of DJs, especially in major urban markets, have little artistic control over what they play and what they say on the air. In a letter, Human discussed the pressures and constraints of a DJ in his kind of format and used a fifteen-minute segment of his show to demonstrate:

> Think of the DJs in the Top 100 markets as actors or football players. The coach designs the plays and the playwright gives the actor his lines: It's the same for the American DJ.
>
> The program director (PD) is the second most powerful person at a radio station, behind the general manager (GM). The PD hires the DJs and has the power to fire them, promote them, and has complete control over their shows.
>
> The PD creates a structure for the DJ's show called a *format clock*. This is a paper clock that has no hour hand because it is used every hour. On this clock, for example, it says where the one is: SEGUE, to proceed without pause (radio language for "shut up, just play the next song"). A DJ can never talk where the PD has indicated SEGUE on his routine clock.
>
> Then between the 1 and 2 on the clock, somewhere about seven minutes past the top of the hour, the PD might indicate LINER. This element means that the DJ has been given a 3" by 5" card with the "lines" he should ad lib or read verbatim, depending upon how strict the PD is. The LINER is a very important sell, one that the station must convey without any DJ clutter. The liner should not be diffused with additional information, such as a backsell of the previous record.
>
> The next element marked on the clock, at perhaps twelve minutes past, might say "BACKSELL/FRONTSELL NEW MUSIC—OPEN

SET." This element indicates that every hour at this point, the third or fourth record in the hour will be a brand new song that the PD wants to identify to the listener. Aha! The DJ may now ID the song. But notice he or she may ID only when indicated by the clock. Here my format clock also said "OPEN SET." This is the time when a DJ is free to express himself or herself (as long as the DJ remembered to sell the NEW MUSIC in this case!).

I'm just the tailback running up the left side, running a play the coach has called. I try to put my own spin on it, and dodge the tackles, but it is somebody on the sidelines calling the play.

PDs love to use a private Batphone setup in virtually every studio in every radio station. It's called the HOTLINE. If you don't follow the format, guess who's calling?

So if it's the PD calling the shots, why don't PDs instruct DJs to identify more songs? We talked to scores of disc jockeys and PDs and found absolutely no consensus about the wisdom of frequent song identification. Here are some of the most important reasons for lack of IDs, followed by the rebuttal case for more IDs.

1. *Research shows that listeners want more music and less talk.* Jay Gilbert, afternoon drive DJ on WEBN, Cincinnati, one of the first Album-Oriented Rock stations, told us that every research survey he has ever seen has indicated that most listeners want DJs to shut up and play more music. Originally, the relative lack of commercials and DJ chatter on FM helped the fledgling band win over AM listeners.

Sure, says Cleveland radio personality Danny Wright, who is generally against overdoing IDs, every poll he has seen in his twenty years in broadcasting indicates that listeners hate jocks who talk too much. But then who are the most popular people on the air? According to Wright, "the folks with the oral trots"—Rush Limbaugh, Howard Stern, Rick Dees, Scott Shannon, etc. Wright believes that if a jock has nothing to say, he is better off just playing music, but that audiences love patter if it is entertaining.

2. *IDs slow down the show.* In order to speed up the pace of the show and to provide the illusion of more music being played, stations will do everything from playing records at a higher than normal speed to instructing DJs to talk over the music. To many PDs, back announcing, in particular, is just dead air, particularly when the time could be devoted to more jingles promoting the call letters of the station.

Of course, the five or ten seconds devoted to identifying a song could be spent playing more music, but then perhaps a radio show should be more than a jukebox with commercials. Al Brock, a PD and on-air personality at WKLX, an oldies station in Rochester, New York, told *Imponderables* that identifying a song is a way of connecting the DJs with the music, showing listeners that the jocks are interested in and committed to the music. PDs who are for frequent IDs see them as part of the music programming, while anti-ID PDs see them as part of the talk. Brock feels strongly enough about the issue to try to frontsell or backsell every song on the station (which can't always be done, because of time constraints).

3. *Why tell audiences what they already know?* A classical music station usually IDs every selection it plays, because the audience might not be able to recognize a particular piece or the conductor and orchestra. But does a DJ really have to tell an audience "That was Whitney Houston and 'I Will Always Love You'?"

The answer of the pro-ID side is, "Yes, you do." Al Brock informed us that most people know some songs by titles and other by artists but that few can remember both. For example, after the Righteous Brothers' "Unchained Melody" was rereleased during the popular run of the movie *Ghost,* the song was not only played on oldies stations (it never stopped being played there) but promoted as if it were a new song on many CHR and AC (Adult Contemporary) stations. Yet listeners constantly called to ask the name of the song or the group who sang it. Another DJ told us that every time he plays Paul Stookey's "The Wedding Song" (the title is not part of the lyrics), even if he front- or backsells it, he gets calls asking, "What song was that?"

Obviously, the need for IDs depends upon the format of the station and the familiarity of a given song. Virtually every PD and DJ we spoke to identified a brand new song, one that the station has been playing for two to four weeks. (These songs are called "currents.") All agreed that the songs least needed to be ID'd are songs that are no longer current but are still popular and haven't left the playlist. These are known as "recurrents" and are usually played less than "currents" but more than oldies. Some PDs argue that oldies don't require IDs because they are so familiar, but even this strategy has pitfalls, for oldies stations are trying to attract younger listeners, including people who might not have been *alive* when a song was recorded.

DAVID FELDMAN

4. *IDs create clutter.* An old broadcasting bromide is that each music set on a radio show should stress one thought. Considering that there are many elements in a radio show—music, talk, promos, ads, weather, contests, jingles—IDs can cause more confusion than enlightenment. Steve Warren, a veteran New York radio personality now heading his own programming consulting company, MOR Media, reminded us that for most of the audience, radio is a secondary medium. Most listeners are doing other things, such as driving cars, sewing, or taking a shower, while listening to the radio. Overloading any format with too much information can backfire.

Even pro-ID programmers realize that, for example, during morning drive shows, when information about weather and traffic may be paramount and commercials are most frequent, backselling may not be prudent. They often fine-tune their volume of ID's by daypart.

5. *IDs slow the momentum of the show.* One of the tenets of CHR radio is "always move forward." The name of the ratings game in radio is to keep listeners as long as possible. Unlike television, where viewers generally have some loyalty to particular shows and are likely to stick with them for the half-hour or hour, PDs are acutely aware that listeners in automobiles have push-buttons that can "eject" their station the moment they hear an unwanted song or one too many commercials. This is one reason why many stations start a new song before the DJ talks over it—subliminally, this tells the listener, "Don't worry, there is no advertisement coming up."

One of the main strategies for keeping us tuned in longer is to promote what is coming up next. As Danny Wright puts it,

> Never talk about last night or a movie you saw last week or what you just played. Billboard the next few tunes and events to keep listeners sticking around.

PDs employing this strategy often frontsell. Before a commercial break, a jock might say, "Coming up, the new Eric Clapton, Whitney Houston, and an oldie by the Beatles." The hope is that the listener will stay glued to the station if she likes one or more of the songs.

Of course this strategy can backfire too. If a listener would rather hear fingernails on a blackboard than Whitney Houston, he may desert the station, even if he was mildly curious about the identity of the Beatles oldie.

Many of the "more music, less talk" stations feature "music sweeps," in which five or more songs are played in a row without commercial interruption. Frontselling eight songs at a time is tedious, and backselling is deadly. Some stations solve the problem by frontselling only one or two songs and doing the same on the back end. Some feature what Al Brock calls "segue assists," in which the jock IDs the song before or after every record.

> 6. *Selling records isn't a radio station's job.* We spoke to several radio programmers who echoed this sentiment. The trade association of the recording industry, the Recording Industry Association of America (RIAA), launched a campaign to promote IDs, plastering stickers on DJ record copies saying, "When You Play It, Say It," the "It" meaning title and artist. In 1988, the RIAA released a study of over one thousand radio listeners, between the ages of twelve and forty-nine, indicating that about two thirds of the respondents would like more information about the records they heard on radio. Listeners between twenty-five and forty-nine years old were particularly vehement, and several programmers we spoke to revealed that the lack of IDs has surpassed "too much talk, not enough music" as the number one complaint of listeners.

Increasingly, radio stations are conducting "outcall" research, telephoning listeners and asking them about their musical preferences. This type of research is of little value if respondents don't know the titles and artists of the songs played on the stations. One PD we consulted, who wished to remain anonymous, indicated that his policy of heavy backselling had nothing to do with helping record companies:

> We try to backsell as much as possible for two reasons. First, it answers the listeners' primary question: What was that we just heard? Second, it helps us with our research. How are we supposed to ask listeners to call in our request line if they don't know what they've heard on our station?

Consultant Steve Warren suggests that there *are* alternate ways of supplying listeners with information about titles and artists, including manned request lines and listener hotlines (in which an employee answers questions about the music, the station, contests, etc.). Warren indicated that at times it doesn't hurt to have calls come in directly to the DJ—it's a good way for jocks to stay in touch with their fans.

Disc jockeys have so many chores to perform besides listening to music that many are understandably not excited about IDs; after all, their time on the air is extremely limited. So, we guess we can't be too hard on our very Human Numan for not frontselling or backselling every song. After all, he estimates that on his average three-hour shift, he speaks on-air for a grand total of *seven minutes*.

Submitted by the guy in the shower, New York, New York.

Whistling Dove Orchestra

Winged Symphony

Why Do Pigeons Make a Whistling Sound When They Take Off in Flight?

Those aren't pigeons' voices but rather their wings you are hearing. Bob Phillips, of the American Racing Pigeon Union, told *Imponderables* that we are hearing the sound of air passing through feathers that are spread wide for acceleration, beating faster for lift, and spread wide for takeoff. Although we tend to associate this kind of high-frequency noise with hummingbirds, many birds produce similar tones, not unlike the sound of the wind whistling through the branches of trees.

Submitted by Martin C. Farfsing of Redwood City, California.

To prove the wholesome, family orientation of our readership, we can point to a surprising cluster of Imponderable obsessions about the subject of milk. Perhaps not the sexiest topic, but certainly among the most nutritious.

What's the Difference Between Skim and Nonfat Milk? And How Do They Skim the Fat from Whole Milk?

Don't believe it if anyone tells you there is any difference whatsoever. By law, skim milk and nonfat are the same: containing less than 0.5 milkfat content. (The milk solids that are *not* fat must equal or exceed 8.25 percent.) In practice, all the fat possible is eliminated from the product.

Any nonfat (or lowfat) milk that is shipped interstate must contain added vitamin A. Most of the vitamin A content in milk is contained in the milkfat. Most manufacturers add enough to equal the amount of vitamin found naturally in whole milk.

How do they separate the fat from whole milk? Our favorite dairy consultant Bruce Snow, explains:

> When milk comes from old Bossy, it contains somewhere between 3 to 4 percent butterfat content (sometimes a percentage point more from cows like Guernseys and Jerseys). To obtain true skim milk, a machine called a "separator" is used. It whirls the milk around, and because the fluid and the butterfat content have different weights, centrifugal force separates the two ingredients into skim milk and cream. The cream is used to make butter, ice cream, whipped cream, etc.

Submitted by Herbert Kraut of Forest Hills, New York.

Why Does Some Lowfat Milk Contain One Percent Fat and Other Lowfat Milk Contain Two Percent Fat?

As we just learned, most cows naturally produce milk containing from 3 to 5 percent butterfat. In most states, "whole" milk is defined as milk with at least 3.25 percent butterfat. Lowfat milk, then, is any milk that falls between .5 percent (skim or nonfat) and 3.5 percent (whole).

In practice, 1 and 2 percent milks are the most popular types of lowfat milk. In fact, we've never seen 3 percent milk, probably because that one half a percent would not reduce the calorie count enough to appeal to dieters.

Many consumers were sick of looking at what looked like water residue on the bottom of their cereal bowls; lowfat has been steadily gained market share for the last thirty years, stealing customers from both former skim milk and whole milk drinkers. In fact, lowfat milks outsell "whole" milk in most parts of the country. Two percent seems to be winning the cash register battle against 1 percent, but not without a

DAVID FELDMAN

cost to the waistline; that extra percent of fat adds about thirty calories to each cup of 2 percent lowfat milk.

Submitted by Herbert Kraut of Forest Hills, New York.

Why Do Plastic Gallon Milk Containers Have the Counter-Sunk Dips on Their Sides?

According to Michelle Mueckenhoff, technical services manager of the Dairy Council of Wisconsin, and every other dairy expert we bored with this question, those dips are there to provide structural support and strength to the container. And nothing more.

Submitted by Daniell Bull of Alexandria, Virginia.

Why Aren't "Green Cards" Green?

We've never been ones to make cheap, easy jokes about our federal government. Sure, there is excess and incompetence in any large conglomeration of workers. We were confident that there was a perfectly brilliant strategy behind naming what are most often blue cards "green cards."

So we contacted the Immigration and Naturalization Service and were lucky enough to come in contact with Elizabeth A. Berrio, chief of the INS Historical Reference Library, who specially prepared a document to share with *Imponderables* readers. And we're happy to conclude that there is a totally logical reason why green cards aren't green. Well, would you believe semilogical?

> What we know as a "green card" came in a variety of different colors at different times in its history. We still refer to them as "green cards"

for the same reason dismissal notices are called "pink slips," sensational-
ized news is called "yellow journalism," and intended distractions are
called "red herrings." In each case, an idea was originally associated with
an actual item of the respective color. A Lawful Permanent Resident
(LPR) alien living in the United States may carry a card that is not green,
but refers to it as a "green card." The alien does so because the card
bestows benefits, and those benefits came into being *at a time when the
card was actually green.*

The green card is formally known as the Alien Registration Receipt
Card, form I-151 or I-551. The first receipt cards were form AR-3 and
were printed on white paper.

This receipt proved that a noncitizen of the United States did register, but it didn't indicate whether the alien was legal or illegal. After
World War II, when a new wave of immigration began, the INS started
issuing different documents to indicate whether an alien was a visitor, a
temporary resident, or a permanent resident.

This method . . . helped to identify the immigration status of each alien.
Thus, the small, green I-151 had immediate value in identifying its holder
as a LPR, entitled to live and work indefinitely in the United States. As
early as 1947, LPRs protested delays in processing their I-151s, complain-
ing that employers would not hire them until they could prove their permanent resident status.

In 1951, the green cards became even more valuable:

regulations allowed those holding AR-3 cards to have them replaced with
a new form I-151 (the green card) . . . only aliens with legal status could
have their AR-3 replaced with an I-151. Aliens who applied for replacement cards but could not prove their legal admission into the United
States, and for whom the INS had no record of legal admission, did not
qualify for LPR status and might even be subject to prosecution for violation of U.S. immigration laws.

By 1951, then, the green Alien Registration Receipt Card Form I-
151 represented security to its holder. It indicated the right to perma-
nently live and work in the United States and instantly communicated
that right to law enforcement officials. As a result of the card's cumbersome official title, aliens, immigration attorneys, and enforcement officers
came to refer to it by its color. The term "green card" designated not only

DAVID FELDMAN

the document itself, but *also the official status* desired by so many legal nonimmigrants (students, tourists, temporary workers) and undocumented (illegal) aliens. The status became so desirable that counterfeit form I-151s became a serious problem.

To combat document fraud, the INS issued nineteen different designs of the I-151 between its introduction in the 1940s and its complete revision in 1977. One alteration to the design in 1964 was to change the color of the card to blue. The 1964 edition was a pale blue. After 1965, it was a dark blue. Regardless of color, the I-151 still carried with it the benefits indicated by the term "green card," and those who wanted, obtained, issued, or inspected I-151s continued to refer to it by that name.

The INS has not given up on foiling counterfeiters. In 1977, it issued a machine-readable receipt card and keeps experimenting with new colors, including such unlikely choices as pink and pink-and-blue. But Berrio is resigned: "Despite these changes in form number, design, and color, the INS document which represents an alien's right to live and work in the United States will probably always be known as a "green card."

Submitted by Eileen Joyce of Texarkana, Texas.

TODAY I AM A GOAT!

~ BUT ≥SNIFF≤ THERE'LL ≥SOB≤ ALWAYS BE SOME KID IN YOU~

Billy has his Bar Kidvah

When Do Kids Turn into Goats?

When they have their bar mitzvah?

But seriously, folks, though it may have been submitted by a "kid" in Mary Helen Freeman's Aiken, South Carolina, Millbrook Elementary School class, this Imponderable was sufficient to stump most of the goat authorities we contacted. For example, John Howland, secretary-treasurer of the American Goat Society, was modest enough to admit he wasn't sure of the answer and was kind enough to write to several other experts. They couldn't reach a definitive consensus: Some argued for four months; others for six months; and some maintained that kids didn't turn into goats until they were old and large enough to breed.

Rowland then consulted the text *Raising Milk Goats the Modern Way*, by Jerry Belanger:

> Mr. Belanger said that kids are ready to breed when they are about seven months old and weigh about seventy-five to eighty pounds. In his glossary, he says: "Kid: a goat under one year of age."

Bonnie Kempe, secretary of Alpines International, concurred with Rowland that definitions of "kid" vary from expert to expert, but she did offer what she thought was the most popular definition:

> Baby goats are called "kids" the first year of their life. The second year they are called "yearlings," and after age two either "does" or "bucks."

Still, some veterinarians we spoke to felt that once a goat can breed and bear offspring, it is inappropriate to call mama or papa a kid.

Submitted by Ivy Moore of Aiken, South Carolina.

Why Do Baked Hams Usually Have a Checkerboard Pattern Along the Top?

Most of the time, the checkerboard pattern is created by the cook scoring the top of the ham for purely decorative reasons. Unlike the brittle skin of a turkey, it is quite easy to cut superficial slices in ham, and many cooks find the pattern visually pleasing.

Chances are, though, that scoring of ham was originally initiated for more practical reasons. According to pork experts at the National Live Stock & Meat Board,

> . . . this process probably began with the old-style hams that had more fat. The scoring, or slicing, of the surface may have been done as a way to allow the fat to drain during cooking. Hams today are much leaner, so the scoring may be done simply for visual reasons.
>
> Since the hams are so lean, it is important not to score too deep. This will cause the natural juices to run out and make the ham very dry.

Robin Kline, director of consumer affairs at the Pork Information Bureau of the National Pork Producers Council, concurs with the "decorative" theory and adds that many other decorations are used routinely to embellish the cooked ham:

> One might also stud the top of the ham with cloves. You've probably seen pineapple rings, maraschino cherries, and pecan halves. Different strokes . . .

Occasionally you will buy a ham with a checkerboard pattern already emblazoned in the animal. These are the imprints of the netting used to hold and shape the meat during curing. The nets may be made of rubber-elastic, plastics, or natural fibers. According to Anne Tantum, of the American Association of Meat Processors, nettings (also known as "stockings") are used particularly often in the curing of boneless hams, which tend to bulge if left to cure without "undergarments."

Ham stockings come in many configurations, but most often the resultant patterns are square, rectangular, or diamond-shaped. And although these designs were probably the last thing on the minds of the ham processors, net-created patterns save the cook the not particularly time-consuming task of scoring the ham to create a little ocular razzle-dazzle.

Submitted by Wayne Rhodes of Deerfield, Illinois.

What Is the Emblem on the Pittsburgh Steelers' Helmets? And Is There Any Particular Reason Why the Pittsburgh Steelers Are the Only NFL Team to Have Their Logo on Only One Side of Their Helmets?

We thought this Imponderable might be a little obscure to include here, but when we found out that the Pittsburgh Steelers public relations department developed a form letter expressly to answer it, we realized that football fans must be burning to know all about the Steelers' helmet emblem. So here's the form letter:

> The emblem, called a steelmark, was adopted in 1963 and is the symbol of the Iron and Steel Institute. There is not a special reason as to why the emblem is only on the right side. That is the way the logo was originally applied to the helmet, and it has never been changed.

So many NFL teams redo their helmet design at the drop of a hat, so to speak, that our guess is that in 1963, the Steelers were not alone in their single-sided emblem configuration.

Submitted by Sue Makowski of Depew, New York. Thanks also to Thomas Ciampaglia of Lyndhurst, New York.

Why Did the Rabbit Die When a Pregnant Woman Took the "Rabbit Test"?

Ever since we were babes (as in "babes in the woods," not as in "hot babes," of course), popular culture, especially bad jokes, has informed us that "the rabbit died" meant "pregnant." But we always wondered why a rabbit had to die in order to diagnose a pregnancy. So we were gratified when this Imponderable was sent in by a reader who happens to be a physician. If he didn't know, maybe we weren't so dim-witted for not knowing ourselves.

At its height of popularity, the rabbit test would be administered to women after they missed two consecutive menstrual periods. A small sample of urine was injected into a female rabbit. But why urine? Why a rabbit?

Urine has been used to diagnose pregnancies as far back as the fourteenth century B.C. by the Egyptians. They poured urine on separate bags of barley and wheat. If either grain germinated, the woman

HOW DOES ASPIRIN FIND A HEADACHE? **643**

was pregnant. They believed that if the wheat germinated, it would be a boy; the barley, a girl. There were probably a lot of unused cribs and miscolored baby clothing in ancient Egypt.

The early Greek physicians also dabbled in urine analysis for the detection of pregnancy. In his book *Obstetric and Gynecologic Milestones,* Dr. Harold Speert notes that urine analysis was a particular favorite of medieval English quacks, often called "piss-prophets," who claimed to diagnose just about any malady from indigestion to heartache. Reaction against these charlatans was so strong that urinary diagnosis was rejected during most of the eighteenth and nineteenth centuries by reputable physicians.

But in 1928, two German gynecologic endocrinologists, Selmar Ascheim and Bernhard Zondek, announced a urinary test that could be replicated easily throughout the world. They injected urine into five infant mice. Ascheim and Zondek explained why they needed five mice:

> Five infantile mice are used for each urine examination. The urine must be tested on several mice because an animal may die from the injection, but more important because not all animals react alike.... *The pregnancy reaction is positive if it is positive in only one animal and negative in the others.*

The A–Z test, as it has become known, is still the basis for all urine-based pregnancy exams, including the rabbit test.

So why the switch from mice to rabbits? Dr. T.E. Reed, of the American Rabbit Breeder's Association, explained the advantages of rabbits, and we promise to get through this discussion with no cheap "breeding like rabbits" jokes.

Most mammals have "heat" cycles, when females are receptive to the male. These cycles are physiologically based and are accompanied by changes in hormonal levels. The ovary is affected by the estrogenic hormone, the animal ovulates, and then is receptive to the male for breeding.

But the domestic rabbit is different, as Reed explains:

> The rabbit does not ovulate until it has been mated with the buck. The rabbit then ovulates ten hours later and the sperm that was deposited during the copulation process will fertilize the ovum.

DAVID FELDMAN

The uniqueness of domestic rabbits' physiology of reproduction is what allowed the pregnancy tests for humans to be utilized. Virgin does were used in the "rabbit test." Because researchers used does that had not been mated, the ovaries of the animal had never produced follicles from the ovaries.

Rabbit tests proved to be faster and more reliable than the original A–Z test.

But why did a pregnant woman's urine kill the rabbits? Ah, the nasty little secret: The test itself did not kill the rabbits, as Reed explains:

> The rabbit does not die of natural causes. The rabbit is euthanized after a specific amount of time [usually forty-eight hours after the first injection] has passed after being inoculated and the ovaries observed by the diagnostician. When the woman is pregnant, the follicles, which look like blisters on the ovary, would be present. If the woman was not pregnant, the ovary would be smooth as in virgin does.

The inventor of the rabbit test, Maurice Harold Friedman, injected the rabbits three times a day for two days, but later practitioners simplified the procedure to one injection and a twenty-four-hour waiting period. Through trial and error, researchers later found that it was not necessary to kill the rabbit at all, and one rabbit was used for several tests, after allowing the ovaries to regress after a positive result.

Although the theory behind the rabbit test was perfectly sound, one problem in reliability persisted: The rabbits chosen weren't always virgins, resulting in false positives. More sophisticated tests were developed without needing animals at all. But even modern laboratories, like the home pregnancy kits, measure the same hormone levels that Friedman, Ascheim and Zondek, and maybe even the piss-prophets and ancient Egyptians predicted pregnancy by.

Submitted by Dr. Ray Watson of Shively, Kentucky.

Why Is It That What Looks to Us Like a Half-Moon Is Called a Quarter-Moon by Astronomers?

An intriguing Imponderable, we thought, at least until Robert Burnham, editor of *Astronomy*, batted it away with the comment, "Aw, c'mon, you picked an *easy* one this time!"

Much to our surprise, when astronomers throw lunar fractions around, they are referring to the orbiting cycle of the Moon, not its appearance to us. *Sky & Telescope*'s associate editor, Alan M. MacRobert, explains:

> The Moon is *half* lit when it is a quarter of the way around its orbit. The count begins when the moon is in the vicinity of the sun (at "new Moon" phase). "First quarter" is when the Moon has traveled one-quarter of the way around the sky from there. The Moon is full when it is halfway around the sky, and at "third quarter" or "last quarter" when it's three-quarters of the way around its orbit.

Robert Burnham adds that "quarter-Moons" and "half-Moons" aren't the only commonly misnamed lunar apparitions. Laymen often call the crescent moon hanging low in the evening sky a "New Moon," but Burnham points out that at this point, the moon is far from new: "In fact, by then the crescent Moon is some three or four days past the actual moment of New Moon, which is the instant when the center of the Moon passes between the Earth and Sun."

Submitted by Susan Peters of Escondido, California. Thanks to Gil Gross, of New York, New York.

What's the Deal with the Grades of Architectural and Art Pencils? What Do "H," "HB," "F," "B," and "E" Stand For?

Here's the code: "H" stands for Hardness and "B" stands for "Black." With pencils, "hard" means a pencil that yields a lighter image. "Soft" pencils provide darker images. In this case, "black" means soft.

From hardest to softest, these are the grades: 9H, 8H, 7H, 6H, 5H, 4H, 3H, 2H, H, HB, F, B, 2B, 3B, 4B, 5B, 6B.

HB is the equivalent of the "regular" number 2 pencil. The grade "F" is a grade between "HB" (hard and black) and "B." Ellen Carson, of pencil manufacturer Empire Berol USA, told us that "F" was originally introduced for taking shorthand, because it was "hard enough to withstand extended use without resharpening and black enough so as to ensure that the shorthand was subsequently legible."

The "E" grades are used to designate the hardness of Filmograph leads. According to Carson, these leads are produced for plastic film and used in technical drawing. Filmograph leads contain no graphite and are based upon polymers and carbon black: "They are used in order to prevent the written or drawn line from being smudged when the drawing is being handled." E1 is the softest grade and E4 the hardest.

Submitted by Myron Kozman of Webster Groves, Missouri. Thanks also to Carol McDaniel of Castro Valley, California, and Roslyn J. Dy of Charleston, West Virginia.

How Do Hermit Crabs "Relieve Themselves" When in the Shell Without Getting Filthy? Or Do They Get Filthy?

The last few chapters have been altogether too pleasant. We don't want you to get complacent; it's time for a real gross-out now.

We often hear the bromide about the perfection of Mother Nature—that everything is part of her plan. But she had some strange plans in mind when she created the hermit crab. A "hermit crab" is not a particular species or family of crab; the term refers to various crabs that have soft abdomens and live in the empty shells of mollusks. The vision of a crab living in a vacated snail shell isn't too appetizing to begin with; but combine it with the crustacean's questionable bathroom habits, and we are stuck with one unpleasant visual image.

We asked one of our favorite crustacean experts, Dr. Darryl Felder, chairman of the biology department at the University of Louisiana, Lafayette, to explain our Imponderable. Even this expert couldn't remain totally clinical:

> Their urine is passed from pores at the base of the antennae, near the base of the eyes (as in all crabs, shrimp, and lobsters). The fecal material is passed from the posterior end deep within the shell and moved as a string-like fecal strand out the aperture of the shell. You too would be a "hermit" if you did such things in your home.

Not content to render an expert opinion on such a weighty subject alone, Dr. Felder was kind enough to pass along our query to Dr. Rafael Lemaitre, a research zoologist at the National Museum of Natural History at the Smithsonian Institution. Dr. Lemaitre concurred with all of Dr. Felder's conclusions but was kind enough to provide even more repellent details:

> . . . many worms, amphipods [crustaceans with one set of feet for jumping or walking and a separate set for swimming], and other animals are frequently found inside shells inhabited by hermits. It is quite possible that some of these "associates" help in the recycling of the hermit's wastes.

DAVID FELDMAN

Lemaitre adds that the hermit crab can, by itself, create the currents necessary to flush the wastes out of its system. And if its plumbing fails, and it gets too grubby for the crustacean, it can always do what is most characteristic of a hermit crab: Ditch the shell it's living in and find more pristine accommodations elsewhere.

Submitted by Elaine Coyne of Brick, New Jersey.

Why Does Getting a Hair in Our Mouth Make Us Gag?

Our correspondent, Ilona Savastano, was passionate in her need for an answer to this burning Imponderable:

> How are we able to swallow just about any type of food, at times very large mouthfuls of it, with no problem, and yet we nearly gag to death if we get a tiny little hair in our mouth? I feel even one piece of fur in our mouth doesn't quite bring the same "yucky" reaction.

We flew your question by our dental experts, who are used to patients gagging (sometimes even *before* they receive their bill).

Their first reaction was to emphasize the sensitivity of the mouth. Dentist Ike House, of Haughton, Louisiana, amplifies:

> Our mouths are the most sensitive parts of our bodies, especially at birth and in childhood. Children use their mouths for food (nursing), comfort (thumb-sucking or pacifier), pleasure (witness the random exploration of children with their hands in their mouths), and exploration (children put a foreign object in their mouths to determine what it is). Because of our pattern of oral stimulation and exploration from an early age, the mouth is very sensitive.

DAVID FELDMAN

Now that we have established how sensitive our mouths are, we might ask whether there is anything particularly nasty about the hair itself that might cause particular problems if found in the mouth. Yes, indeed, insist our experts. Dentist Barnet Orenstein, of the New York University David B. Kriser Dental Center, explains:

> Physically, a hair has two sharp ends capable of stimulating the very sensitive mucous membrane lining the oral cavity. Furthermore, the fine diameter and convoluted shape of a hair enable it to adhere to the mucosa. Dislodgement with the tip of the tongue is virtually impossible.

The gag reflex isn't necessarily more likely to occur when the mouth is full than when it contains one lonely hair. We can be tickled more easily by the light touch of a feather on the neck than by a hard rubbing of a bulkier object.

But the main culprit in hair-gagging is well above the throat. All of our dental experts think that the main cause of hair-gagging is psychological

Dr. House reports that he has often been able to decrease or eliminate a patient's gag reflex simply by talking to him or her about the problem. And he opines that the nature of a foreign body determines our reaction to it:

> For example, spaghetti would not feel much different in our mouth than worms (assuming you had some GREAT sauce, and the worms were already dead and not wiggling around) but most people would choke at the thought. Hair is perceived as being dirty by most folks, witness the displeasure people have with finding a hair in their food. During lovemaking, however, touching your partner's hair with your mouth might be enjoyable.

So buck up, Ilona. Sure, you may not be able to control your gag on a single strand of hair, but blame the messenger, not the message. Gagging can be good for you, as Dr. Orenstein explains:

> The gag reflex is one of the many defense mechanisms nature has so miraculously endowed us with. Even infants will react violently to tickling of the soft palate. If it were not for this mechanism, many of us would expire by having the airway shut off by some foreign body lodged in our throat.

Submitted by Ilona M. Savastano of Cleveland, Ohio. Thanks also to Herbert Biern of Reston, Virginia.

Why Does Pasta Create Foam When Boiling?

Pasta is made from durum wheat, a particularly hard wheat. More precisely, pasta is created from durum wheat *semolina*, fine particles derived from the much coarser durum. The extraction of the semolina is largely responsible for the foaming of pasta when cooking, as Farook Taufiq, vice-president of quality assurance at Prince Company, explains:

> Durum wheat semolina consists of carbohydrates (starches) and protein. In the process of grinding wheat to extract semolina, some starch links are broken.
>
> When pasta is put in boiling water, these broken starch links swell up, taking in tiny air bubbles, along with water. These air bubbles come to the surface of the boiling water and appear as foam. So the foam is a combination of starch molecules, water, and air.

Submitted by Sam Rosenthall of Amherst, Massachusetts.

Why Do Many Elderly People, Especially Those Missing Teeth, Constantly Display a Chewing Motion?

Dr. John Rutkauskas, of the American Society for Geriatric Dentistry, consulted with two of his geriatric dentistry colleagues, Dr. Saul Kamen and Dr. Barry Ceridan, and told *Imponderables* that this chewing motion is found almost exclusively in people who have lost teeth. On rare occasions, certain tranquilizers or antidepressants (in the phenothiazine family) may cause a side effect called tardive dyskinesia, an inability to control what are ordinarily voluntary movements. These movements are as likely to involve the nose as the mouth or jaws, though.

In most cases, Rutkauskas believes that the chewing motion is a neuromuscular response to the lack of teeth: an attempt by the oral cavity to achieve some form of equilibrium. In particular, these sufferers can't position their upper and lower jaws properly. With a full set of ivories, the teeth act as a stop to keep the jaws in place.

Of course, most people who lose teeth attempt to remedy the problem by wearing dentures. And most people adapt well. But Ike House, a Louisiana dentist and *Imponderables* reader (we're sure he is prouder of the first qualification), told us that a significant number of elderly people have lost the ability to wear dentures at all because of an excessive loss of bone:

> They can close their mouth much fuller than they would with teeth present, resulting in the "nose touching skin" appearance of many elderly folks. Since the normal "rest position" of about 2–3 mm between the upper and lower natural or artificial teeth is not able to be referenced, they may be constantly searching for this position.

Many elderly people who wear dentures feel that the prostheses just don't feel normal. And restlessness leads to "chewing in the air," as House amplifies:

> If you had two objects in your hands, such as two pecans or two coins, you would probably manipulate them in some way. When not using

a pen or pencil, for example, but holding it passively, we usually move it in our hand. It may be that folks wearing dentures constantly manipulate them in some way just because objects being held but not used are often moved by unconscious habit.

I have a great-uncle who lets his upper teeth fall down between words and pushes them back up against his palate. This is a most disconcerting habit to his family! I know some elderly patients cannot tolerate dentures in their mouths unless they are eating because they can't leave them alone.

Barnet B. Orenstein, an associate clinical professor of dentistry at New York University's College of Dentistry, told *Imponderables* that the tongue is often the culprit in creating the chewing motion:

> Elderly people often display a constant chewing motion because, having lost their lower teeth, their tongue is no longer confined to the space within the dental arch. The tongue spreads out and actually increases in size. What appears to be a chewing motion is actually a subconscious effort to find a place for the tongue.

The last time we were at the *Imponderables* staff's official dentist, Phil Klein, of Brooklyn Heights, we asked him to wrestle with this mystery while he mauled our molars (and we pondered whether we could deduct the office visit from our income tax as a research as well as medical expense). Much to our relief, Dr. Klein concurred with the theories stated above but raised the possibility of a few others, including rare neurological conditions and grinding of teeth to the point where the lower and upper jaws can't mesh comfortably.

Klein also mentioned that problems with salivation, and particularly dryness, is a constant problem for numerous elderly people, and many with this problem move their mouth and jaw in response to this dryness.

And then he told us we had no cavities.

Submitted by Dennis Kingsley of Goodrich, Michigan.

Note to IRS: We deducted our trip to Dr. Klein as a medical expense.

DAVID FELDMAN

Do Butterflies (and Other Insects) Sneeze or Cough? If So, Do They Do So Loud Enough for Humans to Hear?

All of the entomologists we contacted were sure about this Imponderable. Butterflies and other insects don't sneeze or cough. It's particularly difficult for them to sneeze, as they don't possess true noses.

So then how do insects breathe? Leslie Saul, Insect Zoo director at the San Francisco Zoo, explains:

> Butterflies and other insects breathe through holes in the sides of their bodies called spiracles. Spiracles are provided with valvelike devices that keep out dust and water. Some insects, such as some flies, june beetles, lubber grasshoppers, and notably the Madagascar hissing cockroaches, make sounds for communication purposes by forcing air out through the spiracles. Hence they hiss.

Karen Yoder, certification manager of the Entomological Society of America, concurs with Saul and adds that it isn't possible to hear insects breathing with the naked ear, either:

> In my days of insect appreciation, I have never heard the expiration of air from an insect. . . . Certainly, it could be possible to hear the transpiration in insects with the aid of an amplifier, but not with the naked ear.

But one needn't be wearing a stethoscope to hear the aforementioned hissing cockroach, better known to entomologists as *Gromphadorhina portentosa*. Our trusted informant, Randy Morgan, head keeper at Cincinnati's Insectarium, wrote an article for *Backyard Bugwatching*, a favorite magazine of our family's to pass around at barbecues, in which he chronicles the decibel-producing potential of these two- to three-inch cockroaches.

The Madagascar hissing cockroaches produce the hiss by contracting their abdomens and pushing the air out of constricted spiracles: The noise can be heard from several feet away. Whereas most cockroaches deter predators by running away, flying away, or producing unpleasant secretions, not so the *Gromphadorhina portentosa:* "Their secretive nature and ability to hiss seem to be their primary defense against enemies." Morgan cites an example of a lemur, eager to dine on our poor cockroach. But the hiss convinces the lemur it might have a rattlesnake or other dangerous critter on its hands: "In the leaves, a hissing cockroach continued feeding, unaware it had just narrowly escaped being eaten." Even if the cockroach wasn't aware of its near demise, the lemur's flight wasn't a coincidence. The hiss is a voluntary reflex, generally used only when a cockroach is in danger from predators or competing for mates.

Submitted by Marti Miller of Flagstaff, Arizona. Thanks also to Russell Shaw of Marietta, Georgia.

What Is the Liquid That Forms on Top of Yogurt? Is It Water or Does It Have Nutrients? Should It Be Drained or Stirred Back into the Yogurt?

That liquidy stuff is whey, the very stuff that Little Miss Muffet ate on a tuffet. When the bacteria that forms yogurt grows sufficiently, the milk coagulates. The proteins squeeze together and form curds, pushing out the watery whey.

Whey may be watery, but it isn't water. Whey contains sugar, minerals, some protein, and lactose. Don't waste it. Mix it back in with the rest of the yogurt. You'll be a better person (nutritionally, anyway) for it.

Submitted by Emanuel Kelmenson of Jericho, New York.

Why Do Most Yogurts Come with the Fruit on the Bottom? Why Not on the Top? Or Prestirred?

We had no idea that this topic so consumed yogurt lovers. But our dairy consultants indicated that yogurt lovers have strong feelings about where to put the fruit in their yogurt containers. Dairy expert Bruce Snow told us that there is no difference in the contents of fruit-on-the-bottom yogurts versus prestirred varieties, but added:

> Many people like the idea of stirring the cup and doing their own mixing. Some claim that they like to see just how much fruit is really in the cup! Other people couldn't be bothered and much prefer to have the premixed product.
>
> But if you notice, almost everyone stirs even the premixed yogurt to some extent. As the French say, *"Chacun à son goût!"*

Kent Sorrells, director of research and development at California dairy giant Altadena, marvels at the variety of preferences of yogurt eaters. Some prefer the prestirred varieties because they tend to have a slightly softer consistency. Others feel cheated if they can't stir the yogurt themselves. And some yogurtphiles, Sorrell notices, like to keep the fruit on the bottom, dipping in when desired. They alternate spoonfuls of pure yogurt with doses of fruit and yogurt, not unlike those of us who pick apart Oreos like biology students dissecting butterflies or who eat all the cake before devouring the frosting.

But not everyone eats yogurt straight out of the cup, Sorrell reminds us. Many folks like to eat yogurt out of a bowl. They tip the container upside-down into a bowl, and end up with what looks like a fruit sundae, with the topping where Nature intended it to be—on top.

Why don't yogurt makers try putting fruit on the top? The heavy fruit would sink anyway, and unevenly at that.

Submitted by Darcy Gordon of Los Altos, California.

Why Do You Need to Supply Oxygen to a Tropical Tank When Fish Are Quite Capable of Surviving Without Extra Oxygen in Lakes and Oceans? Why Do You See Oxygen Tanks More in Saltwater Aquariums Than Freshwater?

Robert Schmidt, of the North American Native Fishes Association, answers the first part of this Imponderable succinctly:

> You have to provide oxygen to any tank that has more fish (thus higher oxygen demand) than the plants and algae in that atmosphere can supply.

Most natural bodies of water are replete with oxygen-producing plants—by comparison, the plant life in a home tank is like a sprig of parsley next to a piece of halibut in a restaurant.

Oceans tend to have a richer and more abundant plant life than freshwater environments, but the absence of sufficient flora is not the only reason why saltwater aquaria require oxygen tanks, as Dr. Robert Rofen, of the Aquatic Research Institute, explains:

DAVID FELDMAN

Salt water tanks need more aeration than fresh water aquaria to keep their inhabitants alive because the oxygen level is lower in salt water. With the added salt molecules present, there is less room around the H_2O molecules for oxygen O_2 molecules to be present. Salt water absorbs less O_2 than does fresh water.

Submitted by Rudy, a caller on the Lee Fowler radio show, West Palm Beach, Florida.

What Happens to Criminals' Firearms Confiscated by Police During Arrests?

Somehow, we doubted that the police give criminals a claim check for their unlicensed Saturday night specials. The image of a hardened convict, just released from a federal penitentiary after ten years of hard time for armed robbery, being issued a new suit, twenty dollars, and his old, trusty semiautomatic didn't ring true.

So we conducted a survey of about ten police departments all over the United States to find out how the authorities contend with newfound criminal firearms. We discovered quickly that policies about confiscated guns are up to each jurisdiction and that their strategies vary wildly.

The first priority of all police departments is to hold firearms in case they will be needed as evidence in a trial. Corporal Joseph McQue, of the Philadelphia Police Department's Public Affairs Office, told *Imponderables* that guns are first taken to the ballistics unit, where they are checked for fireability. In order to prosecute someone under the Uniform Firearm Act, the weapon must be fireable. (Toting a nonfireable weapon may also be a lesser offense.)

Whether or not ballistics checks the weapon, most jurisdictions place guns in a property unit until the case comes to trial. In many areas, if the defendant is found guilty and the gun was taken to the courtroom as evidence, the firearm is taken back to the property unit until a judge rules upon its disposition. In most of the jurisdictions we surveyed, if the defendant is found guilty, the judge releases the gun to the police department.

And what do the police departments do with the weapons? Just about everything you can imagine:

1. Most commonly, police departments destroy confiscated weapons, and the preferred method seems to be melting. Firearms gathered by the Chicago, New York City, and Philadelphia police are usually melted and sold for scrap, although McQue added that in Philadelphia the melted metal is used to make manhole covers and sewer inlets. Pawnshop owners everywhere must heave a weary sigh when they ponder over the notion that guns worth five thousand dollars are melted alongside pieces of junk.

Some localities, such as Denver, prefer to crush guns and sell the flattened firearms for scrap. A few jurisdictions, such as Miami, sometimes merely disassemble firearms and trash them. This procedure is far superior to a method of disposal that Miami has long ago discarded: tossing unwanted guns in the ocean.

2. Some police departments use the guns that they confiscate. Most firearms confiscated from criminals are of low quality, but better pieces are often given to undercover police officers. In Louisiana, the Code of Criminal Procedure mandates that a court order will be issued to either destroy a weapon or to use it in the department. Police officer Christopher Landry told *Imponderables* how he obtained his duty gun:

> My duty weapon is now a Glock 17 (9mm), thanks to some juvenile delinquent unknown to me. Now that my department has approved .40 caliber for duty use, I'm going to call the judge again to put my name on the list [to obtain confiscated guns]. This judge has no problem with releasing weapons for duty use, but the full automatics get destroyed.

3. Some police departments sell confiscated guns, often at auctions, but the practice is becoming less common. According to several police officials we spoke to, selling firearms creates bad publicity; opens up potential liability problems; and perhaps worst of all puts more guns out on the streets.

An official at the Justice Department who wishes to remain anonymous told us that about ten years ago, when a certain jurisdiction decided

DAVID FELDMAN

to adopt a different model for its entire force, it sold all its guns back to the manufacturer.

And Officer Angelo Bitses, of the Miami Police Department Public Information Office, told us that on rare occasions, confiscated guns might be sold to another police department.

4. A few guns are donated to museums or are used for other police training.

5. John Kearney, a Chicago sculptor, provides perhaps the most uplifting use for confiscated guns. A friend of the artist was killed on his birthday by a neighbor who collected guns. Kearney was also deeply affected by the assassination of John F. Kennedy and Martin Luther King and joined the growing gun control movement. In the late 1960s, he created an outdoor sculpture, using seventy-five melted handguns, called "Hammer Your Swords into Plowshares."

This large piece is now owned by The Committee to End Handgun Abuse in Illinois. Every year, Kearney creates an original sculpture out of a gun used in a capital crime in the Chicago area, and the artwork is given to a politician or other notable who has worked to institute handgun control. Some of the recipients include: John Anderson, Sarah Brady, Pete McCloskey, and Dianne Feinstein.

Submitted by Christopher Stamler of Woodbridge, Virginia.

Why Is There a Worm on the Bottom of Some Tequila Bottles?

Because worms aren't good swimmers?

Those worms are a marketing concept designed to demonstrate that you've bought the real stuff. In order to research this topic with the rigorousness it deserves, we recently undertook a worm-hunting expedition to our local liquor store but found no tequila bottles with worms. We had heard about the worm-filled tequila bottles for years but had never found one ourselves.

So we beseeched one of our favorite liquor authorities, W. Ray Hyde, to help us. As usual, he knew the answer immediately.

We couldn't find worms in tequila bottles because they are included only in bottles of mescal, as he explains:

> Tequila and mescal are related beverages. Both are distinctive products of Mexico. While mescal is any distillate from the fermented juice of any variety of the plant *Agave Tequiliana Weber* (also known as

DAVID FELDMAN

maquey), tequila is distilled from the fermented juice of only one variety of this plant and only in one restricted area of Mexico. Therefore, all tequila is [technically] mescal but not all mescal is tequila.

The worm is placed in bottles of mescal as an assurance that the beverage is genuine since the worm used lives only in the *Agave Tequiliana Weber* plant.

The worm is found only in the agave cactus in Oaxaca province. Natives of Oaxaca consider the worm a delicacy and believe that the agave possesses aphrodisiac powers.

Lynne Strang, of the Distilled Spirits Council of the United States, adds that the United States Food and Drug Administration approved the practice of allowing the worm in imported bottles of mescal and tequila in the late 1970s. Although actual worms were once the rule, most are now replicas, made of plastic or rubber.

Submitted by Suzanne Bustamante of Buena Park, California. Thanks also to Teresa Rais of Decatur, Georgia; Dianna Love of Seaside Park, New Jersey; Richard T. Rowe of Sparta, Wisconsin; Dana Patton of Olive Branch, Mississippi; Tim Langridge of Clinton Township, Michigan; Mary J. Davis of El Cajon, California; and Aaron Edelman of Jamesburg, New Jersey.

Do Fish Pee?

You don't see them swimming in your toilet, do you? Yes, of course, fish urinate.

But not all fish pee in the same way. Freshwater fish must rid themselves of the water that is constantly accumulating in their bodies through osmosis. According to Glenda Kelley, biologist for the International Game Fish Association, the kidneys of freshwater fish must produce copious amounts of dilute urine to prevent their tissues from becoming waterlogged.

Compared to their freshwater counterparts, marine fish, who *lose* water through osmosis, produce little urine. For those readers who have asked us if fish drink water, the surprising answer is that saltwater fish do, because they need to replenish the water lost through osmosis, as Kelley explains:

> This loss of water is compensated for largely by drinking large amounts of sea water, but the extra salt presents a problem. They rid themselves of this surplus by actively excreting salts, mainly through their gills.

DAVID FELDMAN

Dr Robert R. Rofen, of the Aquatic Research Institute, told *Imponderables* that fish are able to excrete liquids through their gills and skin as well, "the counterpart to humans' sweating through their skin."

Submitted by Billie Faron of Genoa, Ohio.

Why Are Screen Door Handles and Knobs Located Higher than Their "Regular" Counterparts?

The height of door knobs and handles has become so standardized that we can usually find, say, a bathroom door knob in an unfamiliar hotel room, with the room pitch black. That's why it is so disconcerting to reach for the handle of a screen door and find that we are hitting the screen itself. Why aren't they the same height as "regular" hardware on doors?

According to Joe Lesniak, of the Door and Hardware Institute, screen doors are usually adjacent to another conventional (or sliding) door, which has its own fixtures. If the hardware on the screen door were at the same height as that on the conventional door, the fittings would conflict. This is also the reason why the door knobs in connecting hotel rooms are deliberately placed at "mismatching" heights.

So the height of screen (or storm) door handles is an afterthought. Most manufacturers choose to go higher with their screen-door fittings, but a minority go lower—anything to avoid a direct confrontation with the dreaded door knobs and handles of conventional doors.

Submitted by Lora B. Odom of Carmel, Indiana.

Why Aren't Automobiles Designed So That the Headlamps Shut Off Automatically When the Ignition Key Is Removed?

We venture to speculate that the three correspondents who submitted this question were motivated by a common experience: leaving the headlamps on inadvertently while running out of a just-parked car. Nothing makes one think more about headlamp design than having to buy a new battery.

Alas, the most common explanation for why headlamps stay on even when the ignition is shut off is that consumers want to be able to mark their vehicles' presence at night, particularly in emergency situations. Some drivers may also want to use headlamps, on occasion, as a giant flashlight, to illuminate a dark area in front of them. Still, we don't understand why these operation couldn't be performed by turning the auxiliary switch and turning the lights on manually. We came to the conclusion that an obvious reason why headlamps don't switch off automatically is simply because that's the way it has always been done.

Increasingly, automakers are listening to consumers' concerns on the matter. Richard Van Iderstine, of the National Highway Traffic Safety Administration, wrote *Imponderables* that there is no law governing the relationship between ignition and headlamp status but that many manufacturers are experimenting with delayed turn-off options for headlamps,

> allowing people to get out and see their way into their home at night. Others automatically turn the headlamp off . . . but leave the parking and tail lamps on to conserve the battery.

Vann H. Wilber, director of the safety and international department of the American Automobile Manufacturers Association, the organization that represents the Big Three Detroit automakers, told us that the current experiments with cutting headlamps automatically when the ignition is turned off are part of a long tradition of rolling out "limited introductions" of convenience features to selected models. If consumers prefer the change, automatic headlamp shutoff will join the illustrious list of now standard features that were once introduced only in limited introductions: automatic transmissions; power steering and brakes; radios; and air conditioning.

Submitted by Ed Leonardo of Arlington, Virginia. Thanks also to Jim Lyles II of Shreveport, Louisiana; Richard Tiede, Jr. of Mansfield, Georgia; and Christopher Doody of Shortsville, New York.

Why Do Many Blind People Wear Dark Glasses?

If David Letterman and Mr. Blackwell can do it, so can the Braille Institute: put out a top ten list, that is. Every year, the Braille Institute issues a list of the ten most unusual questions it receives. We are proud to report that this Imponderable made number nine on the 1993 list (edging out number ten: "Do blind babies smile?").

In our previous research on blindness, several authorities

emphasized that the majority of legally blind people do have some vision. The Braille Institute's answer to this question stresses the same point:

> Not everyone who is legally blind is totally blind. More than 75 percent of people who are legally blind have some residual vision. Blindness is the absence of sight, not necessarily the absence of light.

Alberta Orr, of the American Foundation for the Blind, adds, "Many visually impaired persons are extremely sensitive to bright light and glare and wear sunglasses to reduce the amount of light on the retina."

Some blind persons wear dark glasses for cosmetic purposes, because they are self-conscious about the physical appearance of their eyes. Increasingly, blind people are forgoing dark glasses, but we tend to associate dark glasses with blind people because so many of the high-visibility blind celebrities, such as Stevie Wonder, George Shearing, and Ray Charles, usually wear them. Even this is starting to change—the last time we saw José Feliciano perform on television, he was shadeless, despite the glare of the spotlights.

Submitted by Amy Kelly of Cleburne, Texas. Thanks also to Jim Wright, of New Orleans, Louisiana.

Why Do Many Fast Food Restaurants and Convenience Stores Have Vertical Rulers Alongside Their Main Entranceways?

On an episode of "The Simpsons," Marge was found shoplifting at the local convenience store. Her arrest was made considerably simpler when she passed the vertical measuring scale mounted along the exit doorway. It isn't often, even in a cartoon, that a suspect can be positively ID'd as an eight-foot woman, with a considerable percentage of that height consisting of bright blue hair.

Police officers we have spoken to over the years have regaled us with stories about how often witnesses supply them with unreliable descriptions of suspects. In particular, frightened witnesses tend to overestimate the height (and weight) of criminals. The ruler is an attempt to remedy flawed guesstimates.

We weren't able to locate any convenience store or fast food chain that installs measuring scales in all of its branches; obviously, scales tend to show up in urban, high-crime areas. Some chains, like Wendy's, never use scales. But Kim Bartley, director of marketing at White Castle, says that any White Castle store that wants one can install it; employees at those locations are instructed to view criminals leaving and observe their height as the miscreants take flight. Many White Castles, like convenience stores, are open at all hours, and more vulnerable to late-night stickups than their fast food competitors.

Submitted by Don Marti, Jr., of New York, New York. Thanks also to Viva Reinhardt and family of Sarasota, Florida.

What Does "100% Virgin Acrylic" Mean?

Acrylonitrile, the chemical substance from which acrylic fibers are derived, was first developed in Germany in 1893, but commercial production didn't begin until Du pont released Orlon in 1950. Monsanto, Dow Chemical, and American Cyanamid followed, all with their own trade names. Acrylic proved to be a durably popular wool substitute—it can be dyed more easily than wool, can be laundered easily, and is almost as versatile—and like wool, acrylics can be found in carpets as well as garments.

Our correspondent, Shirley Keller, was baffled by the meaning of the oft-found "virgin acrylic" label on many knit labels:

> Does this mean that the product comes from: a) the first polymerization of the Acryl; b) that the fiber was not previously woven; or c) is it a marketing scam to raise the price of the garment, a la "French" Dry Cleaning?

The answer is b. According to Bob Smith, of Cytec, the division of American Cyanamid that manufactures the product, "100% virgin acrylic" means that the material comes directly from the manufacturer and was never used before. Occasionally, acrylic fibers are reprocessed; just as with humans, acrylic fibers can be virgins only once.

The "100%" part of the label is a tad misleading. To be legally classified as acrylic, the fiber only has to be 85 percent acrylonitrile (by weight). According to Roscoe Wallace, chemical engineer for Monsanto, the other 15 percent may be comprised of other fibers, some of which may more easily allow dyeing or change the texture of the finished garment.

Actually, even our acrylic marketers were willing to concede that there is a bit of answer c in "100% virgin acrylic" labels. Sure, Monsanto's Larry Wallace was willing to concede, 100% virgin acrylic has no additives, it is not reworked after manufacturing, and was never reclaimed or redissolved. But even non-100% virgin acrylic must meet the same specifications as its more innocent brethren.

Submitted by Shirley Keller of Great Neck, New York.

Do Snakes Sneeze?

Norman J. Scott, Jr., zoologist and past-president of the Society for the Study of Amphibians and Reptiles, told *Imponderables,* "As far as I know, snakes don't sneeze with their mouths shut, but they do clear fluid from their throat with an explosive blast of air from the lungs."

Snakes don't sneeze very often, though. In fact, a few herpetologists we contacted denied that snakes sneeze at all. But John E. Simmons, of the American Society of Ichthyologists and Herpetologists Information Committee, insisted otherwise:

> Snakes sneeze for the same reason as other vertebrates—to clear their respiratory passages. Snakes rarely sneeze, however, and people who keep them in captivity know that sneezing in snakes is usually a sign of respiratory illness resulting in fluid in the air passage.

Submitted by Sue Scott of Baltimore, Maryland. Thanks also to June Puchy of Lyndhurst, Ohio.

Why Do Cookbooks Often Recommend Beating Egg Whites in a Copper Bowl?

We don't know whether any cookbook writers have received kickbacks from copper bowl manufacturers, but this advice always struck us as unnecessary and fussy. But then again, our cakes compare unfavorably to the offerings of school cafeterias.

We consulted our pals at the American Egg Board and United Egg Producers, and we learned there really *is* something to this copper bowl theory. The copper in the bowl reacts to a protein (the conalbumin, to be precise) in the egg whites, and helps stabilize the eggs and may actually increase their volume when whipped. Cream of tartar combines with egg whites in a similar fashion, working to keep the whites from separating from yolks. One reason why some cooks prefer to stabilize the whites with cream of tartar rather than the "no-cost" copper bowl is that if you leave the egg whites in the bowl for too long (sometimes, for as little as five minutes), the whites will turn pink.

Cooking is an art rather than a science, and we seem to see the prescription for the copper bowl less often these days. Kay Engelhardt, test kitchen supervisor for the American Egg Board, waxes philosophical:

> Perception of the copper bowl's merits varies considerably among various experts. The Strong Armed swear by it. The punier among us are willing to settle for an electric mixer and a bit of cream of tartar.

Submitted by Merilyn Trocino of Bellingham, Washington.

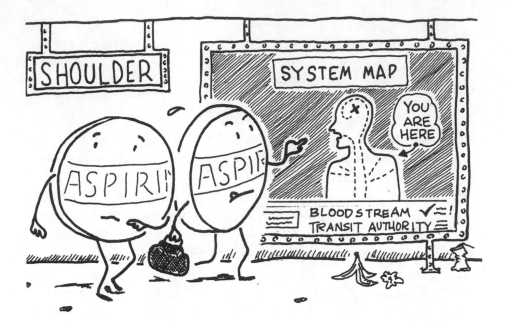

HOW Does Aspirin Find a Headache?

When we get a minor headache, we pop two aspirin and *voilà*, the pain diminishes within a matter of minutes. How did those little pills find exactly what ailed us instead of, say, our little right toe or our left hip?

We always assumed that the aspirin dissolved, entered our bloodstream, and quickly found its way to our brain. The chemicals then persuaded the brain to block out any feelings of pain in the body. Right? Wrong.

Willow bark, which provided the salicylic acid from which aspirin was originally synthesized, had been used as a pain remedy ever since the Greeks discovered its therapeutic power nearly 2,500 years ago. Bayer was the first company to market Aspirin commercially in 1899 ("Aspirin" was originally a trade name of Bayer's for the salicylic acid derivative, acetylsalicylic acid, or ASA). The value of this new drug was quickly apparent, but researchers had little idea how aspirin allevi-

DAVID FELDMAN

ated pain until the 1970s. In their fascinating book *The Aspirin Wars,* Charles C. Mann and Mark L. Plummer describe the basic dilemma:

> Aspirin was a hard problem. . . . It relieves pain but, mysteriously, is not an anesthetic. . . . And it soothes inflamed joints but leaves normal joints untouched. "How does aspirin "know" . . . whether pain is already present, or which joints are inflamed? Researchers didn't have a clue. They didn't even know whether aspirin acts peripherally, at the site of an injury, or centrally, blocking the ability of the brain and central nervous system to feel pain.

The breakthrough came more than seventy years after the introduction of the best-selling pharmaceutical in the world, when researcher John Vane discovered that aspirin inhibited the synthesis of prostaglandins, fatty acids manufactured by virtually every cell in the human body. They resemble hormones, insofar as they secrete into the bloodstream, but unlike most hormones, they tend to stay near their point of manufacture. Prostaglandins serve many biological functions, but the particular ones that cause headache pain, usually known as PGE 2, increase the sensitivity of pain receptors.

So the function of prostaglandins seems to be to produce discomfort, inflammation, fever, and irritation in areas of the body that are not functioning normally, thus serving as an internal warning system. According to Harold Davis, consumer safety officer with the Food and Drug Administration, prostaglandins dilate blood vessels, which can also produce headaches.

The discovery of the role of prostaglandins in producing pain explains why aspirin works only on malfunctioning cells and tissues; if aspirin can stop the production of prostaglandins, pain will not be felt in the first place. Still, aspirin doesn't cure diseases; it can alleviate the symptoms of arthritis, for example, but it doesn't stop the progress of the condition.

In all fairness, scientists still don't know exactly what causes headaches, nor all the ways in which aspirin works to relieve pain. Unlike morphine and other mind-altering drugs, aspirin works peripherally. The key to the success of any peripheral painkiller is in reaching the pain receptors near the irritation or inflammation, not simply in reaching sufficient concentrations in the bloodstream. In the case of aspirin, the ASA is connected to the bloodstream; the bloodstream's connected to the prostaglandins; the prostaglandins are connected to the receptors; and the receptors are connected to the headache.

Submitted by Debra Allen of Wichita Falls, Texas. We know we have received this question many times over the last five years, but we cannot find our records. If you previously submitted this question (postmarked before June 1, 1993), please let us know, and we'll include your name in future printings. Our apologies for this mistake.

Is Goofy Married? If Not, Where Did Television's Goofy, Jr., Come From?

Do you really expect Disney to give old Goof a child out of wedlock? We are pleased to announce that Goofy is, or possibly only was, married to a lovable mate named Mrs. Goofy.

Mrs. Goofy first appeared in a short, "Fathers Are People," but was far from salient; in fact, she can be seen only fleetingly. Although she was a Donna Reed-like suburban housewife, she had her husband well trained: Goofy's response to just about everything she ever said was, "Yes, dear."

Junior, with a red nose at the end of his snout and a mop of red hair on his head, was featured more often and prominently than his mother, but as Disney's Rose Motzko told *Imponderables*, "Goofy, Jr.'s main function was to allow his father to burst with pride while allowing his father not to live up to [minimal] expectations." Junior understood that his father was not a brain surgeon but tried hard not to let his father know.

On the current cartoon series *Goof Troop*, Junior is called "Max." Goofy is a single father, and Goofy's mother is never discussed. But come to think of it, most of the "family" TV sitcoms with live actors feature single parents, too: Max has plenty of company.

Submitted by Tai Palmgren of Davis, California.

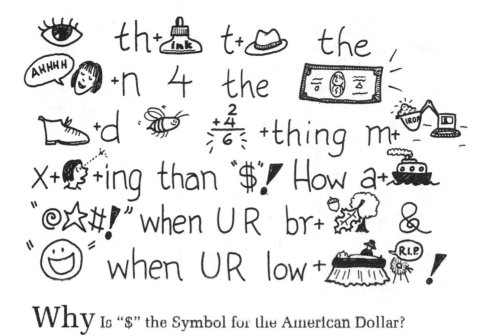

Why Is "$" the Symbol for the American Dollar?

We remember reading a numismatics book thirty years ago that stated the $ was derived from a stylized version of an "S" superimposed on a "U." We never understood this explanation, because we could never see the "U" in the dollar sign. A professor of the history of mathematics at the University of California, Dr. Cajori, spent decades researching this Imponderable in the 1910s and 1920s. He concluded:

> The American dollar sign, popularly supposed to be derived from the letters U and S, is, instead a lineal descendant of the Spanish abbreviation "ps" for "pesos."

Cajori pored through hundreds of early colonial manuscripts and could find no proof of the "US" theory.

So, the official position of the Department of Treasury is that the "S" gradually came to be written over the "P" in the "pesos" abbreviation,

> developing a close equivalent of the $ mark, which eventually evolved [into our current mark]. The $ was widely used before the adoption of the United States dollar in 1785.

Indeed, as we discussed in *Why Do Clocks Run Clockwise?*, Spanish and Mexican coins were the main currency in many parts of the United States in the eighteenth and much of the nineteenth centuries. We're still not sure if the $ looks any more like a P and an S than a U and an S, but at least the abbreviation of "pesos" makes more sense than a shortening of "United States."

Submitted by Ed Booth of Chico, California. Thanks also to Ken Shafer of Traverse City, Michigan; Josh Siegel of Fountain Valley, California; and Barry Kaminsky of Brooklyn, New York.

DAVID FELDMAN

What Do Paper Manufacturers Do with the "Holes" Punched Out of Looseleaf Paper? Do They Recycle Them?

You can bet your bippy that manufacturers recycle the liberated hole punches. But they differ in how they recycle. Forest products giant International Paper, for example, boils more than 90 percent of its paper byproducts to power the very plant that manufacturers looseleaf paper, according to IP representative Michael Goodwin.

But Mead's strategy is more common. Mary Potter, Mead consumer relations representative, told us:

> "Hole punches," as well as other types of paper trim or waste, are baled and sold for scrap. It is and has always been recycled (for approximately 100 years), usually winding up in chipboard, boxes, etc.

Indeed, when we asked this Imponderable of Fort Howard, its consumer affairs coordinator responded, "Nearly all Fort Howard products [mostly toilet paper, facial tissue, paper towels, and napkins] are made from 100% recycled paper fiber."

Bet you never considered that the missing dots in your notebook paper made their way into your toilet paper.

Submitted by Wendy Rath of Sandy, Utah. Thanks also to Alvin Polanco of Philadelphia, Pennsylvania.

Why Do We Bury the Dead with Heads Toward the West Facing East?

The following passage appears in Matthew 24: "For as the lightning cometh out of the east, and shineth even unto the west; so shall also the coming of the Son of man be."

Interpreting this as an indication that when Jesus is resurrected he will appear in the east, early Christians buried the deceased with the feet nearest the east and head towards the west (but facing east) so that the dead could best see and then hurry to rise up to meet Him. Dan Flory, president of the Cincinnati College of Mortuary Sciences, wrote *Imponderables* that this custom inspired the phrase "the wind of the dead man's feet" to describe an east wind.

The practice, both in Europe and North America, has steadily declined over time, but our informal observation is that the older the gravesite, the more likely the headstones will be situated in the western portion of the plot. In fact, burying the dead with this east-west orientation predates Christianity. Pagan societies, being sun worshipers, lay their deceased down to face the sunrise or sunset, depending upon the particular religion.

Submitted by Joseph Centko, Jr., of Streator, Illinois.

Why Do Birds Usually Take Flight Against the Wind?

Nancy Martin, naturalist at the Vermont Institute of Natural Science, points out that, given the constraints of runway design, airplane pilots prefer to take off against the wind as well. And for the same reason: It facilitates lift because of increased air speed. Martin elaborates:

> Birds' wings are structured like an airfoil and so work best with air flowing from front to back. Also, feathers are arranged to overlap like shingles to aid in smooth air flow—taking off with the wind ruffling up the feathers from behind creates a lot of useless turbulence.

Janet Hinshaw, librarian at the Wilson Ornithological Society at the University of Michigan, adds that birds with disproportionately heavy bodies for the size of their wings would probably take off against the wind more consistently—they can use all the lift they can get.

Submitted by Arpi Calioglu of Northridge, California.

Why Do Geese Honk Furiously While Migrating? Doesn't Honking Squander Their Energy on Long Flights?

Unlike humans, geese and other migrating birds don't have car radios and Stuckey's to keep them occupied on long trips. Honking allows geese to maintain communication during long flights. Most importantly, it helps them to avoid midair collisions. As Todd Culver, education specialist at the Cornell Laboratory of Ornithology, succinctly states, "Honking is cheap compared to crashing."

Culver adds that the call and response of birds is the main reason for flying in "V-formation." *Imponderables* has no desire to enter this raging debate, which we get asked about frequently. But our province is questions that aren't so well traveled. We have read theories about the etiology of V-formations ranging from greater aerodynamics to superior defense against predators and from facilitation of vision to Culver's theory about better auditory communication.

Janet Hinshaw, of the Wilson Ornithological Society, assures us that honking doesn't sap geese of vital energy: "They honk while exhaling, which they obviously have to do anyway."

Submitted by Steve Acheson of New Berlin, Wisconsin.

DAVID FELDMAN

Dress Salmon

Dress Heathcliff

Dress Haggis

HERE BE SOME OF THE MORE OBSCURE CLAN TARTANS!

Dress Single Malt

Why Do Scotsmen Wear Kilts? And Why Didn't Men in Surrounding Areas Wear Kilts?

Entire books have been written about the history of the kilt, so the first part of this question is hardly imponderable. Our reader's focus is on why this strange garment was a mainstay in the Highlands of Scotland and not in the rest of Scotland or surrounding countries.

Although we are most likely today to see a Scot in a kilt, inside or outside Scotland, only in a parade or on a formal occasion, its initial popularity was based on practical rather than ceremonial or aesthetic considerations. Although the contemporary kilt resembles a skirt, early kilts covered not only the waist to knee region of the body but the upper torso as well. Essentially, the earliest kilts were huge blankets, which were wrapped around the body several times and draped over the shoulder. This one garment served as blanket, sleeping bag, cloak, and trousers.

The geography of the Highlands of Scotland was no doubt responsible for the kilt's longevity. The Highlands are mountainous and damp, with innumerable streams and rivers. Anyone traversing the countryside in long pants and shoes would quickly be wearing wet long pants and wet shoes. The kilt saved the wearer from continually rolling up his pants. By rearranging the kilt, he could shield himself from the cold and wind. Perhaps most importantly, shepherds could leave their home base for months at a time wearing one garment and no "extra" clothes. As kilts were constructed out of elements easily obtainable in the Highlands (wool from the omnipresent sheep, and the plaid prints from native vegetable dyes), even the poorest of Highlanders could afford one. And the poor wore the kilt the most: According to Steward MacBreachan, a Scottish historian, performer, and demonstrator of Highland games and ancient Scottish culture, the kilt was of special importance to those who had to spend most or all of the day outdoors. More affluent Highlanders could switch from kilts to pants once they returned home from a day's work.

We had a long talk with Philip Smith, Ph.D., one of thirteen fellows of the Scottish Tartan Society worldwide and an author of several books about Scotland. He informed us that kilts, or their equivalents, were worn in many parts of Europe in the ancient world. The Scottish kilt is not too different from the garb of the ancient Romans and the Portuguese.

Smith feels that the widespread use of the horse in other countries eventually led to the abandonment of kiltlike clothing. For rather obvious anatomical reasons, kilts and horse riding are, let us say, an uncomfortable fit for men.

After an unsuccessful Jacobean uprising in 1745, the English Prohibition Act of 1746 (more commonly known as the "Dress Act") banned the wearing of both the kilt and any tartan material by anyone except the Highlands regiment. Ironically, the prohibition is probably responsible for our current association of Scotsmen with kilts. Scotsmen kept their kilts during the ban and wore them surreptitiously at closed gatherings. Along with the tartan, which identifies the clan of the wearer, the kilt became a symbol of Scottish pride.

As Scotsmen needed the blanketlike garment less and less for practical reasons in the nineteenth and twentieth centuries, the kilt, if anything, gained in significance as a way for Scotland to carve its psychic independence from England. If proof of this were necessary, we need only point to the wearing of kilts in ceremonial occasions by Scotsmen from the south, who never wore them in the eighteenth century.

Submitted by Yvonne Martino of La Verne, California.

DAVID FELDMAN

Why Are the Muppets Left-Handed?

Our sharp-eyed correspondent, Jena Mori, first noticed that all the Muppet musicians seem to be left-handed, and then realized that just about all of the Muppets' complicated movements were done with their left hands. We went to the folks at Jim Henson Productions for the answer to Jena's conundrum and were lucky enough to get an expert answer right from the frog's mouth, so to speak.

Steve Whitmire has been a Muppet performer for fifteen years, and currently "is" Kermit The Frog. Steve performs Wembley Fraggle and Sprocket the Dog from "Fraggle Rock," as well as Rizzo the Rat, Bean Bunny, and numerous lesser-known Muppets. He also performs Robbie and B.P. Richfield on "Dinosaurs" and has worked on all of the Muppet movies.

Since we don't often have the opportunity to speak with Muppet performers, we imposed on Steve to answer in interview form.

IMPONDERABLES: Steve, why are Muppets left-handed?

STEVE: Because most puppeteers are right-handed.

IMPONDERABLES: Huh?

STEVE: Imagine standing with your right hand in the air. You are wearing a hand puppet that fits down to approximately your elbow. Now imagine that a television camera is raised to six feet off the floor and is pointing at everything above your head. You are watching what the camera sees on a television monitor on the floor in front of you. Your right hand is in the head of the character. If you want to move the puppet's arms, you reach up in front of your face and grasp one or both of the two wire rods that hang from the puppet's wrists. You have to make sure that your head is low enough to clear the camera frame, so you'll probably have to shift your weight to your left as you duck your head to the left.

IMPONDERABLES: Why do you duck to your left instead of your right?

STEVE: The right hand is stretching as high to the right as possible because that is most comfortable. When the right hand stretches up, the left side automatically hunches down a bit. It's easier for me to duck my head to the left; otherwise, I'd be ducking my head under my right arm.

HOW DOES ASPIRIN FIND A HEADACHE?

IMPONDERABLES: If your right hand is controlling the head of the puppet, how are you controlling its arms?

STEVE: You reach up in front of your face and grasp one or both of the two wire rods that hang from the puppet's wrists. You'd be able to have general control of both arms with your left hand. If you needed to do some bit of action that is more specific, you'd likely use the puppet's left arm.

IMPONDERABLES: Aha, we're now at the crux of our Imponderable. But since you are controlling both of the puppet's arms with *your* left hand, why does it matter which of the *puppet*'s hands you control?

STEVE: Right-handed people tend to have more dexterity and stamina in their right hand and arm, so it goes into the head of the puppet. It is an ergonomic choice more than anything. If the puppeteer is right-handed, it is the more coordinated arm and hand, and it is usually best for it to be in the head. The left arm of the puppeteer is just below the puppet's left arm, so making the left hand of the puppet its dominant hand seems like the natural choice.

IMPONDERABLES: You are implying that a Muppet performer concentrates much more on the head of a character than its arms.

STEVE: The attention of the audience is generally focused on the puppet's face and, more specifically, its eyes. That's part of the appeal of the Muppets—they seem to be looking at whatever they are focused on, whether it is a prop, another character, or the home audience via the camera. The arms are somewhat secondary, although if they are performed badly, say, with arms dangling, they can attract unwanted attention.

Eye contact, and life within the face, is always the first priority in bringing our characters to life: simple head moves and gestures, accurate lip sync, etc., mimic human or animal movement. We keep all of the movement of the characters to the minimum needed to give them the life we want. There shouldn't be any movement without a purpose.

IMPONDERABLES: But some of the Muppets' movements seem awfully complicated. How can you control intricate movements with your "wrong" (i.e., left) hand manipulating two rods?

STEVE: If there is specific action that requires precision that would draw our attention away from the head for too long, we will often have another puppeteer handle the right, and occasionally both, hands.

IMPONDERABLES: Couldn't it get tricky having two people manipulate the same puppet?

DAVID FELDMAN

STEVE: It can. Having one performer manipulating the head and left hand and another the right hand of the puppet can help. This method allows the puppeteer on the head to do any action with the left hand if it needs to come in contact with the face, or the puppet's right hand.

However, when Jim Henson did the Swedish Chef, he worked only the head, and it was usually Frank Oz in *both* hands. One reason for this was that the Chef's hands were actually human hands and needed to match. Another reason was that Jim and Frank loved to do difficult and silly things like that. Frank's goal was to break the china on the back wall each time they did a bit and the Chef threw something over his shoulder during his opening song. We would all take bets. I think he only did it [successfully] once or twice.

IMPONDERABLES: So this answers the question reader Robin R. Bolan asked about why some Muppets don't seem to have wires: The answer is that sometimes they don't.

STEVE: Right. These types of puppets are good for handling props because the puppeteer can simply pick things up. In this case, a second puppeteer *always* does the right hand of the character, because the lead performer is completely tied up with the head and left hand.

IMPONDERABLES: Sounds like it's easier to be green than a Muppet performer.

STEVE: I always liken what we do to being an air traffic controller, because there is so much to concentrate on while we are performing. Not only are we manipulating the puppet's mouth, body movements, and arms, we are doing the voice, remembering dialogue, watching a television screen (we never look at the puppet—only the screen), and tripping over cables, set pieces, and five other puppeteers who are doing the same thing we are.

It's a wonder we ever get anything done considering how truly complex it really is. Fortunately, and for good reason, the audience only sees what goes on up there above us.

Submitted by Jena Mori of Los Angeles, California. Thanks also to Robin R. Bolan of McLean, Virginia.

HOW DOES ASPIRIN FIND A HEADACHE?

Why Do We Have a Delayed Reaction to Sunburn? Why Is Sunburn Often More Evident Twenty-four Hours After We've Been Out in the Sun?

It's happened to most of you. You leave the house for the beach. You forget the sunscreen. Oh well, you think, *I won't stay out in the sun too long.*

You *do* stay out in the sun too long, but you're surprised that you haven't burned too badly. Still, you feel a heaviness on your skin. That night, you start feeling a burning sensation.

The next morning, you wake up and go into the bathroom. You look in the mirror. George Hamilton is staring back at you. Don't you hate when that happens?

Despite our association of sunburn and tanning with fun in the sun, sunburn is, to quote U.S. Army dermatologist Col. John R. Cook, nothing more than "an injury to the skin caused by exposure to ultravio-

DAVID FELDMAN

let radiation." The sun's ultraviolet rays, ranging in length from 200 to 400 nanometers, invisible to the naked eye, are also responsible for skin cancer. Luckily for us, much of the damaging effects of the sun is filtered by our ozone layer.

Actually, some of us do redden quickly after exposure to the sun, but Samuel T. Selden, Chesapeake, Virginia, dermatologist, told us that this

> initial "blush" is primarily due to the heat, with blood going through the skin in an effort to radiate the heat to the outside, reducing the core temperature.

This initial reaction is not the burn itself. In most cases, the peak burn is reached fifteen to twenty-four hours after exposure. A whole series of events causes the erythema (reddening) of the skin, after a prolonged exposure to the sun:

> 1. In an attempt to repair damaged cells, vessels widen in order to rush blood to the surface of the skin. As biophysicist Joe Doyle puts it, "The redness we see is not actually the burn, but rather the blood that has come to repair the cells that have burned." This process, called vasodilation, is prompted by the release of one or more chemicals, such as kinins, setotonins, and histamines.
> 2. Capillaries break down and slowly leak blood.
> 3. Exposure to the sun stimulates the skin to manufacture more melanin, the pigment that makes us appear darker (darker-skinned people, in general, can better withstand exposure to the sun, and are more likely to tan than burn).
> 4. Prostaglandins, fatty acid compounds, are released after cells are damaged by the sun, and play some role in the delay of sunburns, but researchers don't know yet exactly how this works.

All four of these processes take time and explain the delayed appearance of sunburn. The rate at which an individual will tan is dependent upon the skin type (the amount of melanin already in the skin), the wavelength of the ultraviolet rays, the volume of time in the sun, and the time of day. (If you are tanning at any time other than office hours—9:00 A.M. to 5:00 P.M.—you are unlikely to burn.)

Even after erythema occurs, your body attempts to heal you. Peeling, for example, can be an important defense mechanism, as Dr. Selden explains:

> The peeling that takes place as the sunburn progresses is the skin's effort to thicken up in preparation for further sun exposure. The skin thickens and darkens with each sun exposure, but some individuals, lacking the ability to tan, suffer sunburns with each sun exposure.

One dermatologist, Joseph P. Bark, of Lexington, Kentucky, told us that the delayed burning effect is responsible for much of the severe skin damage he sees in his practice. Sunbathers think that if they haven't burned yet, they can continue sitting in the sun, but there is no way to gauge how much damage one has incurred simply by examining the color or extent of the erythema. To Bark, this is like saying there is no fire when we detect smoke, but no flames. Long before sunburns appear, a doctor can find cell damage by examining samples through a microscope.

Submitted by Launi Rountry of Brockton, Massachusetts.

Why Do Hockey Goalies Sometimes Bang Their Sticks on the Ice While the Puck Is on the Other End of the Rink?

No, they are not practicing how to bang on an opponent's head—the answer is far more benign.

In most sports, such as baseball, football, and basketball, play is stopped when substitutions are made. But ice hockey allows unlimited substitution *while the game is in progress,* one of the features that makes hockey such a fast-paced game.

It is the goalie's job to be a dispatcher, announcing to his teammates when traffic patterns are changing on the ice. For example, a minor penalty involves the offender serving two minutes in the penalty box. Some goalies bang the ice to signal to teammates that they are now at even strength.

But according to Herb Hammond, eastern regional scout for the New York Rangers, the banging is most commonly used by goalies whose teams are on a power play (a one-man advantage):

> It is his way of signaling to his teammates on the ice that the penalty is over and that they are no longer on the power play. Because the players are working hard and cannot see the scoreboard, the goalie is instructed by his coach to bang the stick on the ice to give them a signal they can hear.

Submitted by Daniell Bull of Alexandria, Virginia.

What Is the Substance That Resembles Red Paint Often Found on Circulated U.S. Coins? And Why Do Quarters Receive the Red Treatment More Often Than Other Coins?

The substance that resembles red paint probably *is* red paint. Or fingernail polish. Or red lacquer. Or the red dye from a marking pen.

Why is it there? According to Brenda F. Gatling, chief, executive secretariat of the United States Mint, the coins usually are deliberately "defaced" by interest groups for "special promotions, often to show the effect upon a local economy of a particular employer." Other times, political or special interest groups will mark coins to indicate their economic clout. Why quarters? As the largest and most valuable coin in heavy circulation, the marking is most visible and most likely to be noticed.

Some businesses—the most common culprits are bars and restaurants—mark quarters. Employees are then allowed to take "red quarters" out of the cash register and plunk them into jukeboxes. When the coins are emptied from the jukebox, the red quarters are retrieved, put back into the register, and the day's income reconciled.

Submitted by Bill O'Donnell of Eminence, Missouri. Thanks also to Thomas Frick of Los Angeles, California, and Michael Kinch of Corvallis, Oregon.

Why Are So Many Farm Plots Now Circular Instead of Squarish?

Our peripatetic correspondent Bonnie Gellas first noted this Imponderable while on frequent airplane trips. The neat checkerboard patterns of farm plots that she remembered from earlier days have transformed themselves into pie-plots. Are there hordes of agricultural exterior decorators convincing farmers that round is hip and rectangular is square?

We're afraid the answer is considerably more prosaic. The round farm plots are the result of modern irrigation technology—specifically, "center pivot irrigation" systems. Dale Vanderholm, associate dean for agricultural research at the University of Nebraska, Lincoln, told *Imponderables* that one of the problems with squarish plots was the expense required to water them. They required lateral movement systems, in which one huge pipe the length (or width) of the land traveled back and forth in order to irrigate the entire field.

DAVID FELDMAN

Center pivot systems, on the other hand, require only one water source, at the center of each plot. Pipes must still move, but they travel only the relatively short distance around the "pivots." According to Lee Grant, of the University of Maryland's Agricultural Engineering Department:

> The traveling system moves on "tractors," spaced at intervals along the irrigation pipe. The "tractors" are supported by pairs of tractor type tires arranged one in front of the other. Motors driven by the flowing water turn the tires to pivot the irrigation pipe around the field.

We asked Vanderholm what farmers did with the "corners" of the circle, the small portions of land outside the reach of the spray. Usually farmers plant crops that don't require irrigation or don't farm that area. If they want to spend the money, they can also buy auxiliary arms, which can water areas beyond the reach of the center pivot.

According to Vanderholm, center pivot systems are most popular in the high plains states, just where you would likely be looking out the window on cross-country flights, bored out of your mind, craving sensory input, and seeking any alternative to the airplane food, movie, or seatmate.

Submitted by Bonnie Gellas of New York, New York. Thanks also to Gloria Klinesmith of Waukegan, Illinois.

Why Are Virginia, Massachusetts, Pennsylvania, and Kentucky Called "Commonwealths" Instead of "States"? What's the Difference Between a Commonwealth and a State?

These four states chose to call themselves commonwealths, yet trying to find a reason why they did so is a futile exercise. By all accounts, the word "state" preceded "commonwealth." Etymologists argue over whether the term predated medieval Europe, but all agree that the concept of "state" was well established by then. Most social scientists define "state" as any discrete political unit that has a fixed territory and a government with legal or political sovereignty over it. Theoretically, though, a "state," in its abstract form, could be taken over by a military dictator and retain its "stateness."

The notion of a commonwealth can be traced directly to the social philosophers of the seventeenth century, particularly Thomas Hobbes of England. He argued that the government should work for the "common weal" (or welfare) of the governed. These Hobbesian principles were articulated by John Winthrop, the first governor of the Massachusetts Bay colony, in 1637:

> the essential form of a common weale or body politic, such as this, is the consent of a certaine companie of people to cohabitate together under one government for their mutual safety and welfare.

All the historians we contacted thought that the four states called themselves "commonwealths" to emphasize their freedom from the monarchy in England and the republican nature of the government, while also indicating there was no evidence that they consciously tried to separate themselves from the other colonies that deemed themselves "states." Indeed, looking over the constitutions of the four commonwealths, we see that the crafters of the documents often used "commonwealth" and "state" interchangeably. For example, while the constitution of Virginia refers in several places to "the people of the Commonwealth" and "government for this Commonwealth," it also declares that "this State shall ever remain a member of the United States of America."

The Massachusetts Constitution, in the "Frame of Government" section, indicates its purpose:

> The people inhabiting the territory formerly called the province of Massachusetts Bay do hereby solemnly and mutually agree with each other to form themselves into a free, sovereign, and independent body-politic or State, by the name of the commonwealth of Massachusetts.

DAVID FELDMAN

Of course, as far as the federal government is concerned, commonwealths are just like any other states, with all the privileges, rights, and taxes due thereto.

Submitted by Randall S. Varner of Mechanicsburg, Pennsylvania. Thanks also to Rick DeWitt of Erie, Pennsylvania, and William Lee of Melville, New York.

How Do Engineers Decide Where to Put Curves on Highways?

We don't expect to jolt any of you by announcing that the shortest distance between two points is a straight line. So one might think that it would be cheapest, most efficient, and most convenient to decide where a highway starts and where it ends, and then construct a straight roadway and link the two. But *one* would be wrong.

Sometimes it costs more to build in a straight line. For example, if a mountain happens to lie right in the middle of a proposed route, a consultation with engineers will reveal quickly that it is cheaper to direct the highway around the mountain than it is to level the natural formation.

If housing or commercial buildings are in the path of the "straight line," then it may be cheaper to lay extra cement and reduce the cost of buying out the more expensive land. Community opposition has killed more than one proposed highway, but evacuating dwellers and leveling buildings is not only a public relations disaster—it can be an economic one. As communities protest, delays create cost overruns.

Increasingly, environmental factors determine the curvature of a highway. Joan C. Peyrebrune, technical projects manager for the Institute of Transportation Engineers, told *Imponderables* that while highway officials have always been concerned about the impact of new highways upon existing houses and businesses, they are now equally aware of how highways might affect wetlands, parklands, wildlife habitats, etc.

If topography, economics, or community pressure necessitates curves in the highway, engineers are first concerned about safety. Peyrebrune notes that many studies have been conducted about the relationship between the radius of curvature and what speeds can be navigated safely on roadways. The American Association of State Highway and Traffic Officials publishes tables that determine the proper speed limits for given radii of curvature and slopes of highways.

Thomas Deen, executive director of the Transportation Research Board of the National Research Council, provided us with a "philosophy of curvature" that echoed our other sources:

> The alignment should consist of long, gentle curves with straight tangent sections for passing on two-lane roads. The design speed of the highway is the limiting factor on the minimum radius of curvature, but the alignment should if at all possible incorporate flat, long curves with the smallest central angle. The alignment should be consistent and not incorporate short, sharp curves with long, straight tangent sections. The choice of highway alignment is made to facilitate the motoring public's trip from one location to another in a safe, efficient, and pleasing manner.

Properly designed curvature doesn't render a highway less safe than a straight roadway. In fact, Peyrebrune indicates that "curvature of highways is preferred to long, straight stretches by most motorists," who can be lulled into obliviousness by the dullness of a straight route.

We have learned quite a bit about how to construct highways in the last few hundred years—it wasn't always a science. Thomas Werner, director of the traffic engineering and safety division of the New York State Department of Transportation, explained to us how one city wound up with its "distinctive" asymmetrical street structure:

> In colonial Boston, cattle once roamed the city. Where they trampled the grass and wore a path, colonialists used the trail to transport goods from one point to another. These cow paths soon became the basis of the city's street network.

Evidently, colonial cows didn't walk in a straight line, either.

Submitted by Rory Sellers of Carmel, California.

DAVID FELDMAN

The great prima ballerina Bragonova entertains her biggest fans...

Why Are There So Many Different Types of Wine Glasses? Would Champagne Really Taste Worse If Drunk Out of a Burgundy Glass?

We have always been a tad suspicious about the pretensions of wine connoisseurs, and we, too, have wondered whether the "flute" glass for champagne truly enhances the taste of the bubbly wine. We were shocked when we found out that Riedel, the Austrian specialist in glassware for wines, now sells twenty-three different glass types—each is designed to be used with one particular variety of wine.

To help answer this Imponderable, we contacted Pat McKelvey, librarian of the Wine Institute in San Francisco, California. She told us that appropriate glassware meets three criteria:

1) It is thin and clear, to best show off the beauty of the wine.

2) Its shape is best suited to enhance and accentuate the natural bouquet of the wine.

3) Perhaps most importantly, the shape of the rim should direct the wine onto the appropriate portion of the tongue.

Our tongues are full of taste buds—four distinctive types. The buds at the tip of the tongue are most sensitive to sweetness; the buds at the edges are most sensitive to salt (which is why we put salt on the edges of tequila glasses); the buds at the sides of the tongue are most sensitive to acidity; and the buds at the back of the tongue are most sensitive to bitterness. Until recently, most glassmaking technology has focused on designing the appropriate shape and size of the bowl of the glass. The deep, narrow champagne flute was designed to conserve and accentuate the bubbles; the wide burgundy glass, tapered at the top, attempted to catch and release the fruity aroma, while letting in as little ambient air as possible that might dissipate the wine's character.

But even if the bouquet were enhanced by the shape of the glass, it meant little if the wine didn't *taste* better; this is why the emphasis, increasingly, is on "rim technology." In a young burgundy, for example, the high acid level can sometimes overcome the desired fruity taste. The solution, in this case, was to flare the rim so that the wine hit the tip of the tongue, which detects the sweetness of the grapes.

Some wines tend to become unbalanced, with the acid/fruit quotient at one extreme or the other. This is one reason why wine lovers swirl the filled glass. A cabernet Sauvignon glass is wide, so that swirling will blend the flavors more easily. The mouth of the glass is narrow, so that when you drink from it, the liquid hits the middle of the tongue. The proper cabernet Sauvignon glass is designed to hit all four types of taste buds each time you take a swallow.

Riedel has changed the shape of the classic German Riesling glasses. Riesling used to be sweeter, so glasses were designed to direct the wine to the sides of the mouth, where the buds would detect acids more acutely. But now that vintners have made German Rieslings more dry by introducing more acids into the wine, Riedel's glass has an out-turned rim, in order to guide the wine directly to the tip of the tongue, where the wine's sweetness will be perceived first.

Riedel tests the efficacy of its designs by conducting blind taste testings, in which the same wine is poured into many different glass configurations. If the "right" glass is not preferred, then Riedel knows it's time to go back to the drawing boards.

Of course, if your preference is for wine that comes in screw-top bottles, disregard the foregoing.

Submitted by Adrienne Ting of Laguna Hills, California.

Why Do Soft Breads Get Hard When They Get Stale While Hard Starches Like Crackers Get Softer When Stale?

Staling bread is a perfect example of reversion to the mean. Bakery consultant Simon Jackel told *Imponderables* that the typical soft bread contains 32 to 38 percent moisture. If the bread is left unwrapped and exposed to the elements, it will become hard when it lessens to about 14 percent moisture.

Why does the bread get stale and lose the moisture? Although food technologists don't fully understand all the causes, a process called "retrogradation" occurs, in which internal changes take place in the starch structure. Although bread items are formulated to have a softer crumb portion than crust area, during retrogradation some of the crumb moisture migrates to the crust, which results in the softening of the crust and a hardening of the crumb.

Tom Lehmann, of the American Institute of Baking, adds that as the bread retrogrades, "a portion of the starch in the flour undergoes a gradual change, known as "crystallization," which results in a gradual firming of the bread. Some of the edible ingredients in the dough, such as enzymes and monoglycerides, act to slow up the rate of retrogradation, but the process is inevitable and will occur quickly if the bread is unwrapped and exposed to air.

Hard starches, such as crackers, are crisp because they are baked with an extremely low moisture level, usually 2 to 5 percent. When they soften, their internal structure doesn't change like staling hard breads. As they are exposed to the ambient air, crackers absorb the air's moisture. According to Jackel, hard crackers will be perceived as soft once the moisture level reaches 9 percent.

Submitted by Robert Prots of Waverly, Ohio. Thanks also to Jim Clair of Philadelphia, Pennsylvania.

Why do Hardcover Books Have Exposed, Checkered Cloth as Part of Their Bindings (on Top and Bottom)?

We are ashamed, almost morose, about the fact that we have spent nearly forty years of our lives reading books and never noticed the checkered cloths until reader Valerie Y. Grollman came into our lives. After we received Ms. Grollman's letter, we fondled many books in our collection and discovered that just about all our hardbound books did, indeed, have this embellishment on top and bottom.

We contacted several publishing authorities and received a fascinating historical explanation from Gerald W. Lange, a master printer associated with Los Angeles's Bieler Press. His remarks were so interesting that, with his permission, we are quoting them at length:

> The "cloth" you refer to is the "headband," which was originally a cord or cloth tape with colored thread or string tightly wound around it. The headband was an integral part of the binding structure in early forms of the "codex" book. The codex has been with us for nearly two thousand years and is the physical form of the book we are all familiar with today. (The primary ancestral form of the book prior to the codex was the papyrus roll.)
>
> In early examples of the codex, the thread winding around the cord actually pierced through into the folded "signatures" [grouping of pages] of the book's "text block" [the finished, sewn gathering of the signatures] and the cord itself was tied to the edges of the binding's casing at the head (upper) and tail (lower) of the spine, and as such, provided a great deal of structural strength to the binding.

Some historians have suggested that a later and more cosmetic function of the headband was to hide from view the internal casing material of the binding's spine. Early Western books were part and parcel of a pervasive religious world view and any visually displeasing structural imperfections were hidden or disguised with decoration. Long after original intent, of course, traditional practices remain in place.

With the development of commercial bookbinding production during the Industrial Revolution, the headband became less structurally important and was merely attached to the edges of the text block, rather than sewn into it. Today the headband serves a purely decorative purpose, and is now more often a thin strip of colored or patterned cloth glued to the edge of the spine. There are still a few fine craft hand binders who will take the time to provide headbands in the "old fashioned" way.

Lange mentions that a second theory has been advanced to explain the origins of the headband: It might have served as a buffer to support the spine material "at its vulnerable edges." We tend to pull books from a shelf by yanking on the top of the spine and pulling the spine backwards, which places obvious stress upon the cover. Lange dismisses this theory as the original reason for the headband, since the codex book, for more than one thousand years of its existence, was designed to lie flat, not upright. Bookshelves didn't exist, and most books were too heavy and cumbersome to stand upright.

Stephen P. Snyder, executive vice-president of the Book Manufacturers Institute, concurs with Lange's historical assessment and adds that headbands have sometimes served the purpose of hiding glue that has seeped out of the adhesive bindings of books. When the headband is applied mechanically, as they are in most commercial books today, the bands are fed from a big spool. With the spiraling cost of hardcovers, it is nice to know that one step on the assembly line is there merely to apply some thread to make your book a little prettier.

Submitted by Valerie Y. Grollman of North Brunswick, New Jersey.

Will Super Glue Stick to Teflon?

We were wary of contacting Loctite and Teflon about this almost meta-physical Imponderable, for it would be like prying a confession from the immovable object (Teflon) and the unstoppable force (Super Glue) that one of their reputations was seriously exaggerated. But we are worldly wise in such matters. After all, we had already cracked the centuries-old conundrum about "If nothing sticks to Teflon, how do they get Teflon to stick to the pan?" in *Why Do Clocks Run Clockwise?* We were ready for a new challenge.

So first we contacted Du Pont, the chemical giant that markets Teflon, a registered trademark for polytetrafluoroethylene (which, for obvious reasons, we'll call ptfe). As we expected, Kenneth Leavell, research supervisor for Du Pont's Teflon/Silverstone division, took a hard line. He firmly holds the conviction that Super Glue won't stick to Teflon, at least "not very well and certainly not reliably." Here are some of the reasons why not:

1. The combination of fluorine and carbon in ptfe forms one of the strongest bonds in the chemical world and one of the most stable.

2. The fluorine atoms around the carbon-fluorine bond are inert, so they form an "impenetrable shield" around the chain of carbon atoms, keeping other chemicals from entering. As Leavell puts it,

> Adhesives need to chemically or physically bond to the sub-strate to which they are applied. Ptfe contains no chemical sites for other substances to bond with.

3. As we just learned with glue bottles, adhesives need to wet the substrate directly or creep into porous areas in the substrate. But the low surface energy of ptfe prevents wetting and bonding. Leavell compares it to trying to get oil and water to stick together.

And then he lays down the gauntlet:

> Super Glue is "super" because of its speed of cure and relatively strong bonds. As an adhesive for ptfe, it's no better than epoxies, polyurethanes, etc., would be.

So, the immovable object claims near invincibility. How would the unstoppable force react? We contacted Loctite's Richard Palin, technical service adviser. And he folded like a newly cleaned shirt. Yes, Palin admitted, Teflon lacks the cracks necessary for Super Glue to enter in order to bond properly; there would be nowhere for the glue to get into the pan. Yes, he confessed, the critical surface tension is too low for the adhesive to wet the surface. Yes, he broke down in sobs, Super Glue would probably just bead up if applied to a Teflon pan.

Just kidding, actually. Palin didn't seem upset at all about Super Glue's inability to stick to Teflon. By all accounts, there doesn't seem to be much demand for the task.

Submitted by Bill O'Donnell of Eminence, Missouri.

Why Do Many Women's Fingernails Turn Yellow After Repeated Use of Nail Polish?

Chances are, the culprit is one of two types of ingredients contained in all nail polish:

1. *Nitrous cellulose.* Nitrous cellulose is wood pulp treated with acids; it provides the hardness necessary to make polish stay on your nail plate. As a senior chemist from a major cosmetics company told us: When the moisture from polish dries, all you are left with is nitrous cellulose and pigment.

When nitrous cellulose breaks down, nitric acid forms. Nitric acid attacks the proteins in the nail and turns the nail yellow. The yellowing occurs only on the top layers of the nail plate and will eventually fade away if more acids aren't applied.

2. *Preservatives.* Tolulene-sulfonimide and formaldehyde are part of the base coat of nail polishes and are used as preservatives. According to dermatologist Jerome Litt, of Beachwood, Ohio, formaldehyde resin can turn keratin (the tough, fibrous protein that is the principal constituent in nails) yellow.

But don't assume that yellow nails are necessarily caused by the chemicals in nail-care products (or other, noncosmetic chemicals, such as inks, shoe polishes, and dyes, which can also stain nails yellow). Many heavy smokers, for example, have yellow nails. Even the ingredients in some orally administered pharmaceuticals can stain nails.

Physicians often examine fingernails to help determine the general health of patients, for many illnesses are betrayed by yellowing. The most common noncosmetics cause of yellowed nails is a yeast or other type of fungus infection underneath the nail plate. But many other, more serious illnesses can occasionally be diagnosed when a physician spots yellow nails, including diseases of the lymphatic system, thyroid, chronic respiratory disease, diabetes, and certain liver and kidney diseases.

Other maladies are tipped off by different-colored nails. If the normal Caucasian nail looks pink, because of the ample blood supply to the nail bed underneath the nail plate, it can turn white when a person is anemic, and blue if the patient is suffering from heart or lung disease and insufficient oxygen is sent to the nail bed.

Now that we've scared you sufficiently, we'll remind you that nail polish is much more likely to cause the discoloration than the illnesses we've chronicled above.

Submitted by Barbara Forsberg of Ballston Spa, New York.

Why Are Most Corrugated Boxes from Japan Yellow?

Unless it is bleached, the color of a box will be the color of its main material source—the wood that is turned into pulp fiber. In Japan (and China), the most plentiful source of fiber is straw, which has a yellow color, whereas North America's main source for pulp is tannish trees.

Robert H. Gray, vice-president of the corrugated division of Old Dominion Box Company, told *Imponderables* that demand for paper is so great that most countries turn to local fiber sources that can be "easily grown and harvested in volume." Corrugated boxes often contain recycled fibers besides wood, and Japanese boxes tend to have a higher percentage of recycled material in their pulp, both for ecological reasons and because straw fibers are weaker than wood fibers and bond less effectively.

As a result, the natural shade of Japanese boxes is more variable than our reliably colored kraft tan boxes. We don't know whether the yellowish tinge of straw is what motivated Japanese boxmakers to dye their boxes yellow, but that is indeed what they do, as James F. Nolan, vice-president of the Fibre Box Association, explains:

> The paper used in Asia for corrugated boxes is primarily recycled—with highly mixed sources of waste paper. In order to provide a uniform color for good print quality, the paper for the outer sheet of the corrugated board must be dyed.

Not that American boxes are beyond dye jobs. Although tan boxes are not dyed, liner-board white boxes are, according to Jim Boldt, of corrugated container giant Great Northern.

One glimpse of what undyed paper might look like was supplied by Karl Torjussen, of Westvaco. He asked us if we could think of the color of the cardboard backing on legal pads. "Sure," we responded, "sort of a dishwater gray."

That gray is the *natural,* undyed color of newsprint that has *not* been de-inked. No one cares too much what the back of a legal pad looks like, but we might find a stack of gray boxes utterly depressing—which is why, if boxes are made out of mostly recycled material, we dye them white and Asians dye them yellow.

Submitted by Kirk Baird of Noblesville, Indiana.

Why Are Covered Bridges Covered?

We have driven by stretches of rivers where, it seemed, about every third bridge we passed was a covered bridge. Why is one covered when the next two are topless?

The most obvious advantage to a covered bridge is that it blocks "the elements," particularly snow. Accumulated snow can render a bridge impassable, and it is true that covered bridges are found most often in cold climates. Of course, one could argue that engineers should design covers for all roadways. But as we learned in *Do Penguins Have Knees?* (ah, but have we retained it?), bridges remain frozen long after adjacent road surfaces, primarily because bridge surfaces are exposed to the elements from all sides, the bottom as well as the top.

But then some folks believe that covered wooden bridges were originally constructed to ease the fears of horses, who were skittish about crossing bridges, particularly if they saw torrents of water gushing below. The fact that covered bridges resembled wooden barns supposedly also allayed the horses' anxiety.

DAVID FELDMAN

This question is reminiscent of one of our chestnut-Imponderables: Why do ranchers hang boots upside-down on fenceposts? The most likely answer is the same for both: to save wood from rotting. Alternate cycles of rain and sun play havoc on the wood. According to Stanley Gordon, of the Federal Highway Administration's Bridge Division, an uncovered wooden bridge might last twenty years, while a covered bridge can last a century or longer.

Submitted by Gary L. Horn of Sacramento, California. Thanks also to Matthew Huang of Rancho Palos Verdes, California.

HOW Do Waiters and Waitresses Get Their Tip Money When the Gratuity Is Placed on a Credit Card?

Let's look at the life cycle of a credit card transaction at a restaurant:

1. You get the bill. You pull out your trusty credit card and hand it to the waiter.

2. In most restaurants, the waiter or other employee must authorize the charge. In all but small restaurants, this authorization is now done electronically, and increasingly, a "record of charge" is printed out automatically displaying the food, liquor, and tax charges. Some restaurants still use the old-fashioned "chit," in which the amounts must be entered by pen.

3. Conveniently (for the wait staff, anyway), a gaping space is left for "gratuity," and the total amount of the bill is left empty.

4. The waiter also puts his name or ID code on the record of charge (this is the strange, unidentifiable number often put in a box toward the bottom of credit card chits).

5. If the charge has been approved, the waiter brings the paperwork back to the customer.

This is the point at which many diners have no idea what to do. For some reason, the myth persists that waiters do not want you to charge their gratuity. Walter Sanders, director of corporate affairs for

Citicorp Diners Club (Citicorp bought Diners Club in 1980), phrased the dilemma so charmingly that we are allowing him a blatant plug:

> My dad is one of those people so concerned about waiters and waitresses getting their tips that even when he charges a meal (on the Diners Club Card, of course) he still painstakingly digs for a *cash* tip, which he leaves under the coffee saucer.
>
> Well, your readers—and my dad—can now rest assured that waitpeople everywhere get their full tips, in cash, even when those tips are put on the Diners Club Card.

6. Let's assume the customer does pay the gratuity using a credit card. When the restaurant closes, the night's proceeds are tabulated, and the waiter is paid on the spot, in cash (some restaurants pay on a weekly basis). The ID number of the waiter is used to identify his share of the gratuity money (although some restaurants pool tips). According to Melissa A. Bertelsen, of First Data Resources,

> most merchants have Electronic Data Capture devices that will allow the merchant to enter the amount of the ticket and tip. The device will then break out the tip by waiter number and total his amount in tips for the evening.

7. Most credit card companies pay the merchant's bank, electronically, the total amount charged, often within twenty-four hours. This quick transfer of money is one of the reasons why restaurateurs are willing to pay the "discount fee" that allows the credit card companies to make money. While it may take six weeks for the credit card company to be paid for the restaurant bill by the consumer, the restaurant is paid within a day or two. Thus the credit card issuer has to "eat" the float—the "free" use of the value of the charge—that the consumer has been granted.

The negative float of credit card issuers, especially those, like American Express, that do not impose (high) finance charges for late payments by consumers, is one of their major costs of business. Nobody, especially you, is going to get rich by not having to pay a bill of fifty dollars for forty-five days, but imagine the impact of a financial institution contending with twenty million consumers receiving an interest-free loan for that period. Premium cards, such as American Express, try to regain the revenue lost in finance charges by pricing their cards higher than Visa or Mastercard, and by charging merchants a higher-percentage fee.

If there is any reason why waiters might prefer cash, it might have to do with three letters—IRS. Obviously, tips put on credit cards leave a paper trail; increasingly, the IRS is trying to find ways to chase after undeclared income from workers who derive most of their money from tips.

Submitted by Maria Scott of Cincinnati, Ohio.

Why Do Beacons on Police Cars Flash Blue and Red Lights? Why Are the Blue Lights on the Passenger's Side and the Red Lights on the Driver's Side?

Police work is serious business. We've always wondered why officers in fast pursuit of bad guys flash two-tone signals from their beacons. We called many big-city police departments to find out who their color consultant was.

We quickly discovered that there is no national law specifying the colors on police car beacons. Yet in practice, the choices are few. A law enforcement information specialist at the National Criminal Justice Reference Library who wished to remain anonymous told *Imponderables* that at the time when red and blue lights were chosen for most police department beacons, high-intensity lights were not in use. So there was a practical advantage to using two colors—blue was easier to see during the day, and red was more clearly discerned at night.

From time to time, there have been attempts to make yellow (the easiest color to observe from long distances) the official color of beacons throughout the United States, but the expense and effort of defying tradition and passing the legislation have killed such attempts. A federal regulation would cause disruptions in states like Pennsylvania, which have laws designating the color of beacons (in this case, blue and red for police). And opponents argue that yellow flashing lights would be confused with construction or street lights.

HOW DOES ASPIRIN FIND A HEADACHE?   **709**

Blue was probably chosen initially for its long association with police (e.g., blue lights in front of police stations, blue uniforms), and because of its high daylight visibility. And red has long been a symbol of warning and danger, and a signal to stop. Police departments in Los Angeles, Dallas, Detroit, Philadelphia, and Salt Lake City all use the red and blue beacons. Chicago and the Virginia State Police, on the other hand, have switched from red and blue to all-blue beacons.

Several of the police officers we contacted argued that blue is the most effective color for beacons because no other emergency service uses it (both firefighters and ambulances use red beacons, and most construction and emergency transport cars employ yellow or amber). According to Bill Dwyer, of beacon manufacturer Federal Signal Corporation, big-city police departments, in particular, tend to prefer blue beacons, because the color distinguishes them from the many other emergency vehicles. And no other emergency vehicle features a two-colored beacon.

Why is the red light on the driver's side? We received the same answer from everyone, but Officer Romero, of the Los Angeles Police Department, put it best:

> The reason that the red light is over the driver's seat is so that the driver being pursued can better see it. People are conditioned to stop for a red light; this is the most efficient way to signal the driver of a car in front of you to stop.

A passenger in the offending car cannot see the red nearly as well as the blue light. The LAPD uses an amber light on the rear of the car, which is activated by an on-off switch. We are also conditioned to think of a yellow light as a caution light; in this case, cars behind the police vehicle are being cautioned by the amber lights to slow down because police activity is taking place.

Police departments are constantly experimenting with color possibilities. The Virginia State Police experimented with blue lights for four years with equipment from six manufacturers before adopting them. Maryland tried a multicolor approach: Different colors hooked to switches controlled inside the car, with the intention of color-coding specific activities. In hot pursuit of a car, all-red might be appropriate;

for a routine traffic ticket, red and blue might do the trick. And yellow would be the perfect understated fashion statement for lurking around a bend on a highway speed trap. But the state decided such color tactics were altogether too subtle and abandoned the idea.

Submitted by Ronald Lindow of Pittsburgh, Pennsylvania. Thanks also to Jim Wright of New Orleans, Louisiana, and Sean O'Melveny of Littleton, Colorado.

Why Is It So Hard to Find Single-Serving Cartons of Skim or Lowfat Milk? Why Is It So Hard to Find Single-Serving Cartons of Whole-Milk Chocolate Milk?

Obviously, milk distributors *do* make single-serving sizes of lowfat milk and skim milk. They can be found in schools and institutions throughout the country. As Paul E. Hand, secretary and general manager of the Atlantic Dairy Cooperative reminded us, single-serving cartons of lowfat milk are a staple at McDonald's, Burger King, and many other fast food establishments. Hand added that many school lunch programs do include prepackaged chocolate whole milk in one-cup cartons.

So why can't you find them in the supermarket? In some cases, you can. But grocery stores want to stock a limited number of container sizes and prefer selling big containers to small ones to maximize profits. (Note the demise of the seven-ounce soda bottle while three-liter containers proliferate on supermarket shelves.)

Dairy distributors realize economies of scale by saving on packaging costs (obviously, four single-serving packages of milk are required to provide the milk in one quart container). Milk is a staple in most households, one used on a daily basis; Hand reports that there simply isn't sufficient demand for single-serving cartons. If consumers bought them or demanded them in sufficient quantity, they'd be on the shelves.

Prepackaged chocolate milk, an insignificant category two decades ago, while steadily gaining in market share, is still a stepchild to unflavored milks. In most cases, supermarkets don't want to stock more than one type of chocolate milk. For example, Hershey, the closest to a national brand in this category, licenses local dairies to produce its brand of chocolate milk. Individual dairies can choose whether to use 2 percent or whole milk. According to Hershey Foods' Carl Andrews, most local dairies will base their decision on whether to use whole or lowfat milk by assessing which type of unflavored milk sells better in their region.

You live in southern California, Mitch, where 2 percent milk dwarfs the sale of whole milk. In many parts of the East coast of the United States, you'd have a hard time finding single-serving cartons of lowfat chocolate milk.

Submitted by Mitch Hubbard of Rancho Palos Verdes, California.

What Happens to the Ink When Newspapers Are Recycled?

Before used newsprint can be recycled, it must be cleaned of contaminants, and ink is the most plentiful contaminant. The newsprint must be de-inked.

Although synthetic inks are gaining market share, most newspapers still use oil-based inks. To clean the newspaper, the newsprint is chopped up and boiled in water with some additional chemicals until it turns into a slurry. As the fibers rub against each other, the ink rises to the surface, along with other nuisances, such as paper clips and staples. A slightly different, more complicated procedure is used to clean most newsprint with polymer-based inks.

Theodore Lustig, a professor at West Virginia University's Perley Isaac Reed School of Journalism, and printing ink columnist for *Graphic Arts Monthly*, stresses that current technology is far from perfect:

You should be aware that it is impossible to remove *all* ink from the slurry prior to recycling it into new paper. Since microparticles of ink remain, this would leave the paper rather gray if used without further processing. It is often subjected to bleaching or is mixed with virgin fibers to increase the finished recycled paper's overall brightness, a requisite for readability contrast.

More and more states are requiring publishers to use a higher proportion of recycled paper. As recyclers extract more ink from more newsprint, it may save trees in the forest, but it results in another ecological problem: what to do with unwanted ink. Although we may think of ink as a benign substance, the EPA thinks otherwise, as Lustig explains:

> The ink residue is collected and concentrated (i.e., the water is removed) into a sludge for disposition. However, since there are trace elements of heavy metals (lead, cadmium, chrome, arsenic, etc.) in this residue, this sludge is considered by EPA and other agencies to be a hazardous waste and has to be disposed of in accordance with current environmental laws.

In the past, sludge was dumped in landfills. Today, many options are exercised. According to Tonda F. Rush, president and CEO of the National Newspaper Association, some mills burn the waste, while others sell it to be converted to organic fertilizer.

Recycled newsprint can feel differently to the touch than virgin stock. Lustig explains that paper cannot be recycled infinitely. Three or four times is a maximum:

> Eventually, the fibers lose their ability to bind together, resulting in a paper that is structurally weak and unable to withstand the tensile pressures put to it on high-speed web presses.

Submitted by Ted Winston of Burbank, California. Thanks also to Meadow D'Arcy of Oakland, California.

Why Do Lizards Sleep with One Eye Open?

We imagine that Sarah Robertson, who lives in Nevada, has had ample opportunity to observe lizards sleeping, but our experts beg to differ with this Imponderable's premise. Professor Joseph C. Mitchell, secretary of the Herpetologists League, says that it is rare for lizards to sleep with one eye closed. Norman J. Scott, Jr., zoologist in lizard country (New Mexico), says, "Every lizard that I caught sleeping had both eyes closed. They may partially or totally open one or both eyes if they are disturbed."

So is our questioner hallucinating? Not necessarily. Chameleons are distinguished not only by their ability to change color but by their knack for moving each eye independently. John E. Simmons, of the American Society of Ichthyologists and Herpetologists, thinks that a shifty chameleon might have been trying to snare our Sarah:

> It is not uncommon for a chameleon to sit motionless for long periods of time with one eye closed and one open, but it is not sleeping when it does this, it is awake and watching for prey items and predators with the open eye.

Simmons also mentions that some lizards have a transparent membrane that closes over the eye to protect it. And according to Richard Landesman, a zoologist at the University of Vermont, some lizards have a pattern of scales and coloration on their eyelids that might fool predators into thinking their eyelids are closed. These lizards might also look like they have one eye closed but are actually capable of seeing with both eyes. Illusions that trick us into thinking they have an eye closed might be used to fool their potential predators as well.

Submitted by Sarah Robertson of Sun Valley, Nevada.

If Grapes Are Both Green and Purple, Why Are Grape Jellies Always Purple?

If you read our first book of Imponderables (entitled, appropriately enough, *Imponderables*), you know how they make white wine out of black grapes. But for those of you who aren't yet fully literate, we'll reiterate: The juice from grapes of any color is a wan, whitish or yellowish hue. White wine is the color of that juice. Red wine combines the juice of the grape along with its skin. The color of the skin, not the juice, gives red wine its characteristic shade.

If you want to prove this premise, go out to your local supermarket or produce store and crush a few red and green grapes into empty containers—you'll be surprised at how similar the colors of the liquids are. But throw grapes with skin into a blender or food processor, and you'll have a very different color. One more suggestion: We recommend using seedless grapes.

Ever since 1918, when Welch's started marketing grapelade, a precursor of the jellies soon to follow, the company used Concord grapes exclusively. By the time the company pioneered the mass distribution of jelly, it was already established in the juice business: Welch's introduced grape juice in 1869, using the same dark Concord grapes. James Weidman III, vice-president of corporate communications for Welch's, told us that the characteristic color of Welch's grape jelly comes from the purple skin of the Concord grape, although the pulp of the Concord grape is white: "Because the basic ingredient in grape jelly is juice, the jelly is therefore purple."

Megan Haugood, account manager at the California Table Grape Commission, told us that consumers now expect and demand the purple color established by Welch's and would be uncomfortable with the appearance of a green grape jelly, even assuming a jelly could be made from green grapes that tasted as good. So all of Welch's competitors adopted the same bright color for their grape jellies.

We asked Sandy Davenport, of the International Jelly and Preserve Association, whether her organization was aware of any green

DAVID FELDMAN

jellies in the marketplace. She started looking through her six-hundred-page directory, finding marketers of rhubarb jelly, partridge berry jelly, California plum jelly, and, of course, kiwifruit jelly. But no green grape jellies in sight. Most of the experts we consulted felt that green grapes are considerably blander in taste and would be unlikely to gain a foothold in the marketplace, even if youngsters could tolerate the idea of eating peanut butter and green jelly sandwiches.

Submitted by Jeff Thomsen of Naperville, Illinois.

Why Didn't Fire Trucks Have Roofs Until Long After Cars and Trucks Had Roofs?

The first fire wagons in America were not motorized. They weren't even horse-drawn. They were drawn by humans. Bruce Hisley, instructor at the National Fire Academy, told *Imponderables* that verifiable records of human-drawn fire engines show that they were in use as late as 1840. Horse-drawn open carriages were then the rule until motorized coaches were introduced in 1912.

By today's standards, the early motorized fire trucks were far from state of the art. Not only were they topless, but they lacked windshields. Early designers didn't realize the environmental impact of greater speeds upon fire crews, especially the driver. Although drivers soon put on goggles to help fight off the wind, rain, and snow to which they were exposed, the addition of windshields was a major advance for safety and driver comfort. So was another afterthought: doors on the sides of the cab.

Of course, it was the rule for the crew to stand on the outside of the truck during runs, exposing them to further unsafe conditions. Although roofs and closed cabs were introduced in the late 1920s or early 1930s, many firefighters continued to ride on the outside. As David Cerull, of the Fire Collectors Club, puts it: "When it comes to change in the fire service, the attitude that prevails is: 'If we did not have them before, why should we have them now?'"

Fire departments did have some legitimate arguments against the covered cabs. Martin F. Henry, assistant vice-president of the National Fire Protection Association, told *Imponderables* that many fire departments, upon receiving covers for their fire trucks, promptly removed them. Why?

> The thinking at the time was that the open cab provided an ability to see the fire building in an unrestricted fashion. Ladder companies, it was thought, would have a better opportunity to know where to place the aerial if they could see the building from the cab.

This objection was particularly strong in urban areas. Cerull points out that when approaching a fire in a highrise, the company could see the upper floors and roofs more easily. Eventually, the "sun roof" solved this problem.

The other complaint about early roofs was that the roofs themselves were fire hazards. Arthur Douglas, of fire equipment manufacturer Lowell Corporation, told us that many of the roofs were protected by weatherproofing, sometimes wood covered with a treated fabric. "Both of these materials were, of course, flammable, thus a high risk on a firefighting unit." The metal roof obviously solved this argument against the closed cab.

So why didn't the changeover occur more quickly? One reason, besides sure inertia, opines Henry, is that the life span of fire trucks is twenty to twenty-five years. Many departments were loath to abandon functioning apparatus. And although many firefighters enjoyed riding the tail-board, statistics accumulated, to no one's surprise, proving that the outside of a truck moving at forty miles per hour wasn't the best place to be during an accident.

But perhaps the precipitating factor in closing cabs is a sadder commentary on our culture than a disregard for safety, as Martin Henry explains:

> Open cabs came to an abrupt halt in major metropolitan areas when it became fashionable to hurl objects at firefighters. All riding positions were quickly enclosed.

Submitted by Scott Douglas Burke of Charlestown, Maryland.

DAVID FELDMAN

Why Are There So Few Brazil Nuts in Mixed Nuts Assortments?

We contacted a slew of nut authorities and quickly realized that the ratio of various nuts in an assortment is *serious business*. The industry rule of thumb is that there is never less than 2 percent by weight of any type of nut in a mixed-nut assortment, but how do they arrive at the proper proportion? Focus groups, of course. Nut marketers attract roving hordes off the street, sit them down at a table, and find out what people's deepest fears, needs, and fantasies about mixed nut assortments truly are.

And here's why Brazil nuts get the shaft:

1. *People don't like them that much.* If Brazil nuts were popular, you'd see the big nut companies, like Planters, selling whole jars of Brazil nuts. They don't because an insufficient number of consumers would buy them. As one nut expert so accurately put it: "Generally, the last nut remaining in the nut bowl after favorites have been picked by consumers

in the Brazil nut." A representative of Planters Peanuts who preferred to remain anonymous assured us that cashews, pecans, and almonds are all preferred over Brazil nuts.

2. *People don't like the color of Brazil nuts.* Walter Payne, of Blue Diamond, wrote *Imponderables* that it is difficult and quite expensive to take the skin off (i.e., blanch) Brazil nuts. Consumers prefer lighter colored nuts, which limits the distribution ratio of the Brazil nuts. Payne notes that in assortments offering blanched Brazil nuts, "the Brazil population in the mix is much higher."

3. *Brazil nuts are too big.* If you put more of them in an assortment, they would physically dominate the mix.

4. *Brazil nuts are expensive.* We contacted the Peanut Factory, a Rome, Georgia, marketer of many mixed assortments. The folks at the Factory assured us that when determining a ratio of nuts in a mix, there is always a balance between popularity and price. Brazil nuts, imported from Brazil, Peru, or Bolivia, are just too expensive to justify increasing their proportion. If consumers wanted more Brazil nuts, they would complain. But no one we contacted showed the slightest indication that they've ever been confronted with angry consumers demanding more Brazil nuts.

We don't know why you asked this question, Michele, but we hope you are satisfied. If you aren't, I'm sure you derive pleasure from being invited to many parties, where your main role is to eat all the Brazil nuts left by more conventional partygoers.

Submitted by Michele Baerri of Leonie, New Jersey.

Stop the Presses. Days before we submitted this manuscript, we heard from Kimberly J. Cutchins, president of the National Peanut Council:

> As the National Peanut Council, we do not represent other nuts. However, I did call one of our members, Planters, to get a response to this question. A pound of peanuts costs between 35 cents and 70 cents, depending on the size and variety. Brazil nuts cost approximately $1.25 per pound. Although the difference in price of the nuts is significant, it is not the reason there are so few Brazil nuts in mixed nut assortments.

DAVID FELDMAN

According to Planters, it is consumer preference that determines the ratio of nuts.

So far, Cutchins merely confirms our research. But then she dropped the bombshell:

Just recently, Planters has increased the number of Brazil nuts in their assortment to reflect consumer demand.

There you are, Michele. An unprecedented boomlet for Brazil nuts has changed the equation. Can filberts be far behind?

CHOOSE A DOOR AND **WIN** A DREAM KITCHEN, AN EXCITING TRIP TO EUROPE, **OR** GERMS TO AN EMBARRASSING DISEASE!

Why Do American Doors Have Round Door Knobs, While Many Other Countries Use Handles?

Our correspondents wonder why the knob is virtually ubiquitous when it is much more inconvenient than the handle. Anyone who has ever arrived home carrying three sacks of groceries, with an eight-year-old child and a dog in tow, quickly grasps the notion that it would be far easier to pull down a lever with a loose elbow than to grasp a knob tightly and twist.

All of the hardware sources we contacted indicated that the primary reason knobs are more popular in the United States is simply because customers prefer their looks. Richard Hudnut, product standards coordinator for the Builders Hardware Manufacturers Association, told us that knobs are also easier to manufacture and thus usually cheaper for the consumer.

Joe Lesniak, technical director of the Door and Hardware Institute, says that handles (or "levers," as they are known in the trade) are making a comeback, for at least two reasons. Just as tastes in hem-

DAVID FELDMAN

lines vary for no discernible reason, so do preferences for door finishings. As this book is being written, short skirts and door handles are in vogue. But more importantly, the soon to be enforced Americans with Disabilities Act and the Fair Housing Act are going to change Americans' knob habit indefinitely. This legislation mandates that doors in buildings other than one- and two-family dwellings must contain handles and pulls that are easy to activate with one hand and that don't need to be tightly held.

Submitted by Dainis Bisenieks of Philadelphia, Pennsylvania. Thanks also to George Marchelos of 291st BSB.

Why Do Starving Children Have Bloated Stomachs?

How often have we seen pictures of young children, near death from starvation, with emaciated faces and bloated stomachs? The image is haunting and yet ironic: Why do these children, desperately in need of food, have such protruding abdomens?

Bloated abdomens are a symptom of protein calorie malnutrition (PCM). Many of these youths are starving from a generally inadequate calorie consumption and concomitant insufficient protein. But others are suffering from "kwashiorkor," a condition in which children who consume a proper amount of calories are not eating enough protein. Kwashiorkor is most common among many of the rice-based cultures in the third world, where traditional sources of protein (meat, fish, legumes) are uncommon or too costly for the average citizen.

Insufficient protein consumption can lead to severe problems—it produces the lack of energy reflected in the passive, affectless expression of these PCM children. PCM can affect every organ in the body, but it is particularly devastating to the pancreas, liver, blood, and lymphatic system.

A healthy person's blood vessels leak a little fluid, which collects outside of the vessels. Ordinarily, the lymphatic vessels remove this liquid. But when the lymphatic system malfunctions, as it does in PCM children, the fluid builds up in the skin, causing a condition known as edema.

In these children, a particular type of fluid accumulation, ascites (the fluid buildup in the abdominal cavity), accounts for much of the bloated stomach. A little fluid in the abdominal cavity is a desirable condition, because the fluid helps cushion organs. Ascites in isolation may not be dangerous, but they are often a symptom of liver damage. Don Schwartz, a pediatrician at Philadelphia's Children Hospital, told *Imponderables* that membranes often weaken during protein calorie malnutrition, which only adds to the leakage of body fluids into the abdominal cavity.

Dysfunctional livers often swell. The liver is one of the largest organs in the body and usually constitutes 2 to 3 percent of one's entire body weight. According to Dr. Schwartz, an enlarged liver can contribute to a swollen belly.

Of course, not only small children are subject to this condition. Bloated stomachs are common in any individuals suffering malnutrition, and are most often seen in Western countries among sick people who have experienced sudden weight loss. Hospitals are alert to the problem of PCM among adults—one estimate concluded that about 25 percent of hospitalized *adults* in the United States have some form of PCM.

Submitted by Candace Adler of La Junta, Colorado.

Why Do Most Buses and Trucks Keep Their Engines Idling Rather Than Shutting Them Off While Waiting for Passengers or Cargo?

During the first big gas crisis, public service announcements on radio and television urged us not to leave engines idling unnecessarily. Why don't buses and trucks live by the standards we mundane auto drivers do?

DAVID FELDMAN

The key to the answer is the fuel used in the bus or truck. If you observe carefully, you'll notice that the "idlers" are diesel-powered vehicles. We always thought that bus drivers were leaving engines idle out of laziness, but Morris Adams, of Thomas Built Buses, set us straight:

> These diesel-powered engines require a certain level of heat to operate most efficiently. It is cheaper to leave them running than cold starting. Diesel fuel will last almost twice as long as gasoline when used *under the same atmospheric conditions.*

Idling can also be a safety issue. Most buses, and many big trucks, operate with air brakes. Air brakes can't operate effectively until sufficient air pressure has built up, a process that can take about ten minutes.

And one issue pertains specifically to school or public buses—comfort. Karen E. Finkel, executive director of the National School Transportation Association, explains:

> [Bus riders] want and expect comfort—air conditioning in the summer and heat in the winter. Buses have a massive amount of air space that takes a longer period of time to heat or cool than an individual's automobile.

Submitted by Alka Bramhandkar of Vestal, New York. Thanks also to Brian Dunne of Indianapolis, Indiana.

Why Does One Sometimes Find Sand in the Pockets of New Blue Jeans?

Conceivably, you might have picked up a pair of jeans returned by a previous customer who went to the beach, but that is highly unlikely. We aren't gamblers by nature, but we would be willing to wager a small sum that the jeans in question were stonewashed.

Stonewashed jeans are softened by rubbing against pumice stones during washing. Dori Wofford, a marketing specialist at jeans behemoth Levi Strauss & Co., explains how mighty stones can turn into sand:

> Pumice is a soft white stone that is placed in huge washers along with jeans to be "stonewashed." Pumice stones used in the stonewashing process sometimes disintegrate into tiny particles (or sand) that end up in the pockets of stonewashed jeans.

Obviously, pockets are the one portion of the jeans most susceptible to trapping loose pumice. Any other sand would tend to get rinsed away with the wash water.

Submitted by Lisa R. Bell of Atlanta, Georgia.

DAVID FELDMAN

Why Do So Many Recreational Vehicle Owners Put Cardboard or Plywood Square Covers over Their Wheels?

The ultraviolet rays from direct sunlight oxidizes the rubber in tires rapidly, leading to premature cracking and drying. Bill Baker, media relations manager for the Recreation Vehicle Industry Association, told us that "there are vinyl covers manufactured and sold to meet this need." We have seen many a custom-cover, emblazoned with family names, mottoes, and mascots, as we passed RVs on the highway. But enterprising and frugal RV owners have found a solution that not only recycles forest products but, not coincidentally, saves them a few bucks.

Submitted by Howard Helman of Manhattan Beach, California.

Why Are Most People Buried Without Shoes?

Personally, we can't imagine an eternal life with uncomfortable shoes. This funeral tradition has always made sense to us; we don't even like to wear shoes when we are awake.

Richard A. Santore, executive director of the Associated Funeral Directors International, reminded us that for those buried in half-open caskets, the shoes (or lack therof) wouldn't be visible and are thus unnecessary. And he added devilishly, aware of the precarious logic behind his assertion, "Now you may ask why we are buried with underwear—I don't know!" We have yet to meet a funeral director without a wicked sense of humor. Comes in handy in the profession, we'd guess.

Several members of the funeral profession claimed that nearly as many folks are buried with shoes as without these days. Indeed, one of the "options" bereaved families are given, when arranging the ceremony, is "burial slippers."

Dr. Dan Flory, president of the Cincinnati College of Mortuary Science, told us that some people believe that a dead person can rest better and "the spirit will not wander if shoes are omitted." But his other theory ties in specifically to the comfort we feel in repressing the finality of death:

> Being without shoes is also a typical sleeping position, and many people like to think of death as a kind of sleep.

We agree with the thesis. But then, following this logic, wouldn't we be buried in pajamas?

Submitted by Harold Fair of Bellwood, Illinois. Thanks also to N. Dale Talkington of Yukon, Ohio, and Deone Pearcy of Tehachapi, California.

DAVID FELDMAN

Typical NEW YORK Resident:

- CHEWS 2 PACKS OF GUM DAILY
- HAS NEVER BEEN TO STATUE OF LIBERTY
- CALLS THE AVENUE OF THE AMERICAS "SIXTH AVENUE"
- CAN RIDE SUBWAY STANDING UP WITHOUT HOLDING ON
- HAS NEVER EATEN A NEW YORK STRIP STEAK

~NEVAH EV'N HOIDA IT!

What Is a "New York Steak"? Is It a Cut of Meat? Is It a Part of the Cow? And Why Can't You Find "New York Steaks" in New York?

Reader Douglas Watkins, Jr., posed this Imponderable four years ago and has waited patiently while we've been researching it ever since. We've contacted about twenty meat experts and have come to the conclusion that Douglas might decide, after having read this chapter, that the wait wasn't worth it.

One of our first conversations on the topic was with Merle Ellis, a combination butcher-media star, who wrote an excellent book, *Cutting-up in the Kitchen*, which, among other things, rigorously defines all of the cuts of a cow. Ellis places the New York steak in the short loin, between the rib and the sirloin of the cow, in the middle of the back. The short loin contains a high percentage of fat and very little muscle. As a result, the most expensive cuts of meat come from this 10 percent of edible beef: filet mignon, porterhouse, tournedos, T-bones, and, alas, the New York steak. But what part of the short loin constitutes the New York steak?

On this question, we're afraid, the National Association of Hotel and Restaurant Meat Purveyors, the American Meat Institute, the National Live Stock & Meat Board, and the numerous restaurateurs and butchers we spoke to cannot agree. Merle Ellis votes for the top loin muscle of the tenderloin; others vote for the center of the loin. Indeed, the *New York Times*'s Molly O'Neill was inspired by this dilemma and wrote a whole story about it in the January 2, 1991, article "In Search of New York Steak? Ask Anywhere but New York." She eventually came to the same conclusion that we have: "There is no part of a cow with New York stamped on it, nor any particular cut of beef that is peculiarly 'New York.'"

Several of our sources, including Dr. Stuart Ensor, of the National Live Stock & Meat Board, suggested that "New York" does not refer to a particular type of cut but is merely a promotional adjective. New York equals "the best." This helps explain the last part of our Imponderable: why New York steaks are rarely called "New York steaks" in New York! Alas, the grass is always greener on the other side. While New York steaks might have allure in the West, New Yorkers conjure the Midwest as the true home of the stockyards and therefore the best beef. As Ellis so eloquently put it in *Cutting-up in the Kitchen:*

> The top loin muscle becomes a New York Strip in Kansas City and Kansas City strip in New York City. . . . On your side of the street it could be almost anything: Shell Steak, Hotel Steak, Sirloin Club Steak, Boneless Club Steak or Charlie's Gourmet Special. Whatever it's called, it too will be most definitely on the expensive side.

Submitted by Douglas Watkins, Jr., of Hayward, California.

Why Are Some Aluminum Cans—Even Different Cans of the Same Product—Harder to Crush Than Others?

Let's get one issue out of the way immediately. Even the largest beverage producers (or "fillers," as they are known in the canning industry) don't make their own cans. A company like Coca-Cola has many different suppliers. And these canners may have many plants designed to produce cans of slightly different composition and dimensions.

Jeff Solomon-Hess, executive editor of *Recycling Today,* reminds us that not all beverage cans are made of aluminum only:

> Manufacturers commonly produce two types of beverage cans today: all aluminum and bi-metal. The all aluminum can crushes slightly easier because of its thinner construction. The bi-metal can consist of a steel body and an aluminum top. While steel technology allows for much thinner construction than in the past, the steel cans remain slightly thicker and harder to crush.

William B. Frank, of the Alcoa Technical Center, points out that the "trained consumer" can differentiate between the two types of cans:

> The steel can has a matte finish on the bottom and a "stiff" sidewall; the aluminum can is shiny on the bottom and is less stiff after opening. A sure way to distinguish a steel can from an aluminum can is to see whether a small magnet will stick to the body or bottom of the can. Ferromagnetism is used to separate steel cans from aluminum cans in recycling of UBCs [used beverage cans].

We don't mean to imply that all aluminum cans are created equally. Indeed, off the top of his head, E.J. Westerman, manager of can technology at Kaiser Aluminum, listed five reasons why all-aluminum cans might vary in crushability:

> 1) There are small differences in diameters of cans (e.g., Coors-type cans are 2 9/16", while most other American cans are 2 11/16").

2) Fillers give aluminum producers different requirements for alloy strength and composition.

3) Aluminum producers vary the wall thicknesses of the cans from about 0.0039" to approximately 0.0042".

4) Cans can vary in "wall thickness gradation" at the neck and base of the can, which can affect the point at which "column buckling" begins when a can is crushed.

5) The end or lid diameter and thickness can have a great impact upon crushability, particularly if the can is not crushed in the axial direction.

Solomon-Hess feels that the role of the crusher cannot be underestimated:

> Most people place the can on end and step on it. If you step on it with a rubber sole shoe (such as a sneaker), your foot sometimes forms an airtight seal. This results in the inside air pressure of the can making it more rigid, and again, harder to crush. Tilting your foot slightly and allowing the air to escape or laying the can on its side makes it crush much easier.

And don't forget the condition of the can itself. We have found ourselves, often unconsciously, squeezing or popping aluminum cans. As soon as you mess with the structural integrity of the container, it becomes much easier to crush. Solomon-Hess even offers an experiment that you can do at home (children under eighteen, please ask your parents for permission); for reasons too obvious to explain, this experiment may best be conducted outdoors:

> If you put a couple of small dents in the can, it requires much less pressure to crush, so people who routinely "pop" the sides of cans as they drink from them find the empty cans easier to crush. For a dramatic example, try this experiment.
>
> Take an empty soda can and place it upright on a hard floor (concrete works best) and ask someone who weighs under 150 pounds to very carefully place his or her full weight on the can with one foot and balance there. Most cans will support such a weight. Now take two pencils and simultaneously tap opposite sides of the can with a firm motion. The

resulting dimples cause the can to quickly collapse by creating weak spots in the can's structure. The effect is the same as scoring a sheet of glass in order to break it cleanly.

Not quite the same—you don't need a sponge to clean up after breaking a sheet of glass.

Submitted by Roy L. Youngblood of Oceanside, California.

Why Are Pigs Roasted with an Apple in Their Mouth?

Is this the first reference book in history to devote three chapters to the appearance of cooked pork products? Maybe so, but we follow the lead of our readers, and pig pulchritude seems to be very much on your minds.

Unfortunately, we have not gotten to first base in answering how this practice originated. But the same pork experts who guided us before are quick to assure us that if an apple was put in the suckling pig's mouth before roasting, it would quickly turn to a texture more like apple sauce than apples. The pristine apple is put in the pig's mouth after it is removed from the spit.

So the apple is purely a decorative item, perhaps inserted out of a sense of loss of the aforementioned checkerboard pattern on hams. Tonya Parravano, of the National Live Stock & Meat Board, told *Imponderables* that most recipes

> suggest placing a small block of wood in the pig's mouth before roasting to brace it so an apple can be inserted later. Cranberries or cherries are often used in the eye sockets and some like to give the pig a collar of cranberries, parsley, or flowers.

The poor pig, whose very name conjures up filth and sweat in common parlance, is subjected to even greater indignities before it is consumed.

Submitted by Christine Whitsett of Marion, Alabama.

Why Do Many Streets and Sidewalks Glitter? Is There a Secret Glittery Ingredient?

Two main ingredients create the glittering appearance of our concrete and asphalt roadway surfaces: natural rocks and glass. When it comes to asphalt and concrete, the contents are always hybrids, mixes of stones, sand, petroleum derivatives, and "fillers," ingredients that aren't necessary for the integrity of the pavement but provide bulk—the construction equivalent of Hamburger Helper.

Sand, glass, silicon, and many natural stones, such as quartz, all glitter. According to Jim Wright, of the New York State Department of Transportation, glass is included in roadways as a way of recycling used byproducts. Other fillers, such as used tires, are thrown in to the mix as a way of keeping solid waste dumps from looking like canyons exclusively devoted to showcasing beaten-down, giant chocolate doughnut lookalikes.

Construction engineers are sensitive to the aesthetics of streets and sidewalks. Billy Higgins, director of congressional relations at the American Association of State Highway and Transportation Officials, told *Imponderables* that glass is often used primarily to make surfaces more attractive. For example, Higgins says that concrete sidewalks routinely are smoothed down with a rotary blade to allow the shiny surfaces to show off to best effect.

Portland cement, a mix made primarily of limestone and clay, becomes a particularly glittery surface when it bonds with sand and other filler agents to become concrete. Portland cement concrete becomes shinier and shinier as it is used, as Thomas Deen, executive director of the Transportation Research Board of the National Research Council, explains:

> Some of the aggregate used in portland cement concrete is like a natural mirror; that is, it reflects light. In theory, all aggregate in concrete is completely coated with cement. However, the aggregate on the very top surface of the street or sidewalk will lose part of that coating due to the weathering and vehicular or pedestrian traffic. Once exposed, the light from the sun, headlights, street lights, or other sources bounces off the tiny surfaces of the aggregate, causing the streets and sidewalks to glitter.

Submitted by Sherry Spitzer of San Francisco, California.

DAVID FELDMAN

Why Hasn't Beer Been Marketed in Plastic Bottles Like Soft Drinks?

Now that the marketing of soda pop in glass bottles has pretty much gone the way of the dodo bird, we contacted several beer experts to find out why the beer industry hasn't followed suit. The reasons are many; let us count the ways:

1. Most beer sold in North America is pasteurized. According to Ron Siebel, president of beer technology giant J.E. Siebel Sons, plastic bottles cannot withstand the heat during the pasteurization process. Plastics have gained in strength, but the type of plastic bottle necessary to endure pasteurization would be quite expensive.

John T. McCabe, technical director of the Master Brewers Association of the Americas, told *Imponderables* that in the United Kingdom, where most beer is not pasteurized, a few breweries are marketing beer in plastic bottles. Siebel indicated that he would not be surprised if an American brewer of nonpasteurized (bottled) "draft" beer doesn't try plastic packaging eventually.

2. Breweries want as long a shelf life as possible for their beers. According to Siebel and McCabe, carbon dioxide can diffuse through plastic and escape into the air, while oxygen can penetrate the bottle, resulting in a flat beverage. Glass is much less porous than plastic.

3. Sunlight can harm beer. Siebel indicates that beer exposed to the sun can develop a "skunky" taste and smell; this is why many beers are sold in dark and semi-opaque bottles.

4. Appearance. We have no market research to support this theory, but we wouldn't guess that beer would be the most delectable looking beverage to the consumer roving the supermarket or liquor store aisle.

One might think that breweries would kill to package their product like soft drinks. Could you imagine the happy faces of beer executives as they watched consumers lugging home three-liter plastic bottles of suds?

Submitted by John Lind of Ayer, Massachusetts.

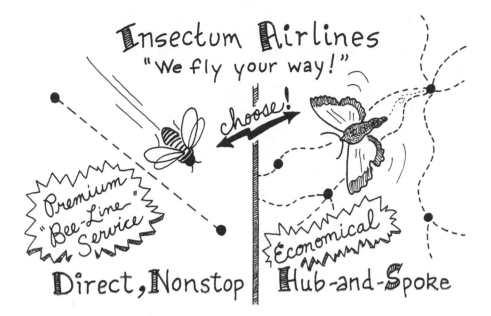

Insectum Airlines
"We fly your way!"

choose!

Premium "Bee-Line" Service

Economical

Direct, Nonstop | Hub-and-Spoke

Why Do Some Insects Fly in a Straight Line While Others Tend to Zigzag?

As entomologist Randy Morgan of the Cincinnati Insectarium puts it, "Flight behavior is an optimization of the need to avoid predators while searching for food and mates." Gee, if Morgan just eliminated the word "flight" and changed the word "predators" to "creditors," he'd be describing *our* lives.

Notwithstanding the cheap joke, Morgan describes the problems of evaluating the flight patterns of insects. An insect might zigzag because it is trying to avoid an enemy or because it doesn't have an accurate sighting of a potential food source. A predatory insect might be flying in a straight line because it is unafraid of other predators or because it is trying to "make time" when migrating; the same insect in search of food might zigzag if its target wasn't yet selected.

Leslie Saul, Insect Zoo director at the San Francisco Zoological Society, wrote *Imponderables* that the observable flying patterns of different insects can vary dramatically:

> Flight paths are usually determined by visual, auditory, or olfactory stimulation. For example, bees and butterflies orient to the color and size of flowers; dragonflies orient to their prey items; moths orient to a wind carrying a specific smell, usually a "pheromone."

Submitted by Dallas Brozik of Huntington, West Virginia.

DAVID FELDMAN

What's the Difference Between "French" and "Italian" Bread?

Not a whole lot, it turns out. But there are enough differences in ingredients to account for the subtle differences in taste and, particularly, texture.

Baking consultant Simon Jackel kindly wrote us a primer on the subject:

> French and Italian breads are made from the same basic ingredients: flour; water; salt; and yeast. Both use "strong" flours. And they both develop crisp crusts in the oven due to the injection of live steam.
>
> But there the similarity ends, because "French" breads, but not "Italian," also incorporate small amounts of shortening and sugar in the

formulation. The effect of these additional ingredients is to allow the French dough to expand more and become larger in volume, lighter in consistency, and more finely textured in the interior. In contrast, Italian breads are denser and less finely structured in the interior.

The shape of the loaf may tip off the nationality of the bread. Sometimes, "Italian" bread is formed in a football-like shape, as opposed to the sleeker "French." And sometimes "Italian" bread is topped with sesame seeds, an embellishment that would probably make the French pop their berets.

Submitted by Todd Kirchmar of Brooklyn, New York.

Why Have So Many Pigeons in Big Cities Lost Their Toes?

The three main dangers to pigeons' toes are illnesses, predators, and accidents. Pigeons are susceptible to two diseases that can lead to loss of toes: avian pox, a virus that first shrivels their toes to the point where they fall off, and eventually leads to death; and fungal infections, the price that pigeons pay for roaming around in such dirty environments.

Nonflying predators often attack roosting pigeons, and the toes and lower leg are the most vulnerable part of pigeons' anatomy. Steve Busits, of the American Homing Pigeon Fanciers, told *Imponderables* that "Rats or whatever mammal lives in their habitat will grab the first appendage available."

Accidents will happen, too. Busits says that toes are lost in tight spaces, namely "any cracks or crevices that their toes can become stuck in." Bob Phillips, of the American Racing Pigeon Union, adds that toes get lost while pigeons are in flight, with television antennas and utility wires being the main culprits.

Submitted by Nancy Metrick of New York, New York. Thanks also to Jeanna Gallo of Hagerstown, Maryland.

How Do Highway Officials Decide Where to Put a "Slippery When Wet" Sign?

The holy grail of signage policy is the *Manual on Uniform Traffic Control Devices,* a Federal Highway Administration publication that is followed by state jurisdictions as well. In other *Imponderables* books, we've regaled you with complex descriptions of how the MUTCD specifies exactly where, how, and why certain traffic signs should be posted.

But the MUTCD passage on "Slippery When Wet" signs is remarkably vague by comparison:

> The Slippery When Wet sign is intended for use to warn of a condition where the highway surface is extraordinarily slippery when wet.
>
> It should be located in advance of the beginning of the slippery section and at appropriate intervals on long sections of such pavement.

Without specific instructions, state highway agencies have to decide where to place signs.

So how do they decide what roadways are slippery?

1. According to Harry Skinner, chief of the traffic engineering division of the Federal Highway Administration's Office of Traffic Operations,

> Highway surface will become extraordinarily slippery if the aggregate or rock in the pavement becomes polished and cannot drain off all water with which it comes in contact.

Obviously, all surfaces are more slippery when wet than when dry, and a roadway shouldn't be slapped with a "Slippery" sign merely because it becomes slick when ice accumulates. In fact, specific "Icy Pavement" signs are available to warn about these conditions. Sometimes, "Slippery" signs are erected precisely because the roadway looks innocuous; one state document we read indicated that a "Slippery When Wet" sign should be placed where "skid resistance is significantly below that normally associated with the particular type of pavement, or where there is evidence of unusual wet pavement."

2. Bridges tend to be more slippery than adjacent pavements and may warrant a sign.

3. If a roadway is suspected of being slippery, engineers can do a technical analysis, determining the "coefficient of friction."

4. But the most common motivation for placing a "Slippery When Wet" sign is a little more depressing, as Joan C. Peyrebrune, technical projects manager of the Institute of Transportation Engineers, explains:

> Generally, signs are placed at locations where an accident analysis indicates that a significant number of accidents caused by slippery conditions has occurred. The number of accidents that warrant a "Slippery When Wet" sign varies for each state.

This strategy reminds us of an old cartoon we found in a sick joke book: As an automobile pileup of epic proportions turns an intersection into a scrap-strewn catastrophe, an expressionless policeman mounts a ladder to place an "out of order" sign over a failing traffic light.

The intent of the "Slippery When Wet" sign is no different from the "Falling Rock" sign we talked about in *When Did Wild Poodles Roam the Earth?* The hope is that the driver, fearing impending doom, will slow down a tad. And maybe now that you know that these notices serve as markers for misguided drivers who once veered off the road, the signs will do their jobs even more effectively.

Submitted by Herbert Kraut of Forest Hills, New York.

Can One Spider Get Caught in the Web of Another Spider? Would It Be Able to Navigate with the Skill of the Spinner?

Yes, spiders get caught in the webs of other spiders frequently. And it isn't usually a pleasant experience for them. Theoretically, they might well be able to navigate another spider's web skillfully, but they are rarely given the choice. Spiders attack other spiders, and, if anything, spiders from the same species are more likely to attack each other than spiders of other species.

Most commonly, a spider will grasp and bite its intended victim and inject venom. Karen Yoder, of the Entomological Society of America, explains, "Paralysis from the bite causes them to be unable to defend themselves and eventually they succumb to or become a meal!"

Different species tend to use specialized strategies to capture their prey. Yoder cites the example of the Mimetidae, or pirate spiders:

They prey exclusively on other spiders. The invading pirate spider attacks other spiders by luring the owner of the web by tugging at some of the threads. The spider then bites one of the victim's extremities, sucks the spider at the bite, and ingests it whole.

The cryptic jumping spider will capture other salticids or jumping spiders and tackle large orb weavers in their webs. This is called web robbery.

Other spiders will capture prey by grasping, biting, and then wrapping the victim with silk. Leslie Saul, Insect Zoo director of the San Francisco Zoo, cites other examples:

Others use webbing to alert them of the presence of prey. Others still have sticky strands such as the spiders in the family Araneidae. Araneidae spiders have catching threads with glue droplets. The catching threads of Uloborid spiders are made of a very fine mesh ("hackel band"). *Dinopis* throws a rectangular catching web over its prey item and the prey becomes entangled in the hackle threads.

Saul summarizes by quoting Rainer F. Foelix, author of *Biology of Spiders*: "The main enemies of spiders are spiders themselves."

Not all spiders attack their own. According to Saul, there are about twenty species of social spiders that live together peacefully in colonies.

Submitted by Dallas Brozik of Huntington, West Virginia.

Over the years, we have received many Imponderables about McDonald's but have found answers elusive. Now, with the help of Patricia Milroy, customer satisfaction department representative, we can finally unburden you of some of your obsessions.

To Exactly What Is McDonald's Referring When Its Signs Say "Over 95 Billion Served"?

This Imponderable has provoked more than one argument among our peers. We're proud to finally settle the controversy. No, "95 billion" does not refer to customers served, sandwiches served, food items served, or even hamburgers served.

The number pertains to the number of *beef patties* served. A hamburger counts as one patty. A Big Mac counts as two. A quarter-pounder with cheese counts as one. A double cheeseburger counts as two. Got it? The practice undoubtedly started when McDonald's served no other sandwiches besides (single-patty) hamburgers and cheeseburgers.

By the time you read this, McDonald's will have "turned over" the sign and added another digit. Expectations are that the corporation will have sold 100 billion beef patties before the end of 1993.

Submitted by Jena Mori of Los Angeles, California.

Why Are McDonald's Straws Wider in Circumference Than Other Restaurant or Store-Bought Straws?

McDonald's has test-marketed numerous sizes and materials for their straws. Milroy says:

> After working with our suppliers and testing them with our customers, we've found that the present size of our straws is preferred by the majority of our customers.

One of the readers who posed this question guessed the key to the wider circumference of McDonald's straws—many, many milkshakes get sold at the Golden Arches. Any fan knows of the frustration of trying to suck up a thick glop of milkshake through a narrow straw: liquid gridlock. Sure, Mickey D's might give us more straw than we need for Coca-Cola, iced tea, or milk, but when we choose milkshakes, the bigger the better.

Submitted by Melanie Dawn Parr of Baltimore, Maryland. Thanks also to Sandra Baker of Nicholasville, Kentucky.

Why Are the Burgers Upside-Down When You Unfold the Wrapper of a McDonald's Hamburger?

For the same reason you put a gift upside down before you wrap it. As Milroy puts it:

> To provide a neat appearance, a hamburger is placed upside-down on its wrapper, then the ends of the wrapper are brought together on the bottom side of the hamburger. The hamburger is placed right side up in the transfer bin for sale.

If the burger was placed on the wrapper upright, the "loose ends" of the wrapping paper would land atop the finished product, giving it an unkempt appearance and threatening the unraveling of the paper. Using the preferred method, the loose ends of the wrapping paper end up on the bottom of the wrapped burger as it is put in the bin for sale, allowing gravity and the weight of the burger to hold the loose ends in place.

Submitted by Renate Dickey of Macon, Georgia.

What, Exactly, Is the McDonald's Character "The Grimace" Supposed to Be?

Milroy reported that Imponderables readers are not alone; this is among the most asked questions of the corporation. What does this say about our culture?

We're not here to judge, however, so we are proud to announce the official position of McDonald's on the exact description of The Grimace: "He is a big fuzzy purple fellow and Ronald's special pal." That's it. Regardless of our prodding, our cajoling, our penetrating interrogation, our rare paroxysms of hostility, this was the most we could prod out of our golden-arched pals. But we are assured that this is as much as Ronald McDonald himself knows about his fuzzy purple friend.

Submitted by Michael Weinbeyer of Upper Saint Clair, Pennsylvania. Thanks also to Joe Pickell of Pittsburgh, Pennsylvania; Samuel Paul Ontallomo of Upper Saint Clair, Pennsylvania; Nicole Cretelle of San Diego, California; Ruth Homrighaus of Gambier, Ohio; and Liam Palmer and Jonathan Franz of Corbett, Oregon.

What Did Barney Rubble Do for a Living?

We have received this Imponderable often but never tried to answer it because we thought of it as a trivia question rather than an Imponderable. But as we tried to research the mystery of Barney's profession, we found that even self-professed "Flintstones" fanatics couldn't agree on the answer.

And we are not the only ones besieged. By accident, we called Hanna-Barbera before the animation house's opening hours. Before we could ask the question, the security guard said, "I know why you're calling. You want to know what Barney Rubble did for a living. He worked at the quarry. But why don't you call back after opening hours?" The security guard remarked that he gets many calls from inebriated "Flintstones" fans in the middle of the night, pleading for Barney's vocation before they nod off for the evening.

We did call back, and spoke to Carol Keis, of Hanna-Barbera public relations, who told us that this Imponderable is indeed the company's most frequently asked question of all Flintstone trivia. She confirmed that the most commonly accepted answer is that Barney worked at Fred's employer, Bedrock Quarry & Gravel:

> However, out of 166 half-hours from 1960–1966, there were episodic changes from time to time. Barney has also been seen as a repossessor, he's done top secret work, and he's been a geological engineer.
>
> As for the manner in which Barney's occupation was revealed, it was never concretely established (no pun intended) [sure]. It revealed itself according to the occupation set up for each episode.

Most startling of all, Barney actually played Fred's boss at the quarry in one episode. Sure, the lack of continuity is distressing. But then we suspend our disbelief enough to swallow that Wile E. Coyote can recover right after the Road Runner drops a safe on Coyote's head from atop a mountain peak, too.

Hanna-Barbera does not have official archives, so Keis couldn't assure us that she hadn't neglected one of Barney Rubble's jobs. Can anyone remember any more?

Submitted by Rob Burnett of New York, New York.

For any other readers who submitted this Imponderable, please write so that your name can be included for future editions.

DAVID FELDMAN

Why Do We Wave Polaroid Prints in the Air After They Come Out of the Camera?

Imponderables often has to ask anthropologists, anatomists, physiologists, or geneticists questions about bodily quirks or anachronisms. Why do we have patches of hair between our knuckles? Why do we have an appendix? What good are earlobes? More often than not, experts shrug their shoulders and reply that at one time in our evolution these features might have served some purpose, but their function is now lost in obscurity. Humans have many such vestigial anatomical remnants.

Likewise, some human activities that now seem meaningless might have served some purpose in an earlier era. To wit: gratuitous hand flapping. We have all seen someone inadvertently consume something that was too hot to put in the mouth. What is the universal cure for a scorched throat? Invariably we see the victim waving a hand violently up and down in front of an opened mouth.

HOW DOES ASPIRIN FIND A HEADACHE?

How can flapping your limbs possibly solve the problem of a 900-degree pizza hitting the roof of your mouth? It can't, of course. We can only surmise that in the paleolithic period, perhaps a now-extinct flying insect was preternaturally attracted to burning mouth flesh, and that this waving of hands served as a deterrent.

Other examples of unproductive flapping are not confined to empty hands, however. As our astute field observer, Christine Schomer, points out, millions of amateur photographers can be seen flapping just-issued Polaroid prints with the enthusiasm of Chubby Checker demonstrating The Fly, a dance whose moves might have been inspired by instant photographers waiting for their pictures to develop.

We contacted the folks at Polaroid to ask if there is any method to the seeming madness of flappers. Bob Alter, in the Public Affairs and Community Relations department at Polaroid, told us that flapping undeveloped prints doesn't serve any useful function whatsoever. In fact, if the prints are waved too vigorously, the picture will bend.

But unlike earlobes or finger hair, at least the Polaroid flapping can be explained. Many years ago, Polaroid prints used to come out of the camera in a two-part sandwich, with the positive print sticking to the negative. The two parts were peeled apart. Often, a little polymer, the agent used to transfer the negative to the positive print, stuck to the positive print.

Photographers often waved the print in order to dry off the tacky polymer, in the mistaken belief that the photograph would develop sooner. Now Polaroid uses "integral film," so that the print comes out of the rollers in a self-contained unit. The transfer from negative to positive occurs inside the unit, so that the exposed print isn't moist. Flapping the print around does nothing except kill time until the photo is developed.

So Polaroid flapping is a perfect example of vestigial behavior, an activity that once had some justification and now has none. When will this characteristic be bred out of us? Is Polaroid flapping motivated by genetic or environmental causes? Nature or nurture? Stay tuned.

Submitted by Christine Schomer of New York, New York.

DAVID FELDMAN

Frustables

The 10 Most Wanted OR Imponderables

Impressed with our perspicacity in the Imponderables section? Whenever we get full of ourselves, gloating about how we stumbled upon the solution to a knotty Imponderable, our darker side whispers, "Frustables. Frustables. Frustables."

Ah, Frustables (short for "Frustrating Imponderables"), the ten Imponderables we most wanted to answer for this book but could not. In most cases, we contacted experts who came to no useful consensus, or we suspect our sources are not delving into the Imponderable with the depth it deserves.

So we leave it to you. Can you help? We offer a complimentary autographed copy of our next volume of *Imponderables* to the reader who supplies the best answer to each, or the first reader who leads us to the proof that supplies the answer. And of course, your contribution will be printed and acknowledged in the book. Remember, only you can prevent Frustability.

FRUSTABLE 1: *Why do we close our eyes when we kiss?*

Interested in any and all theories, as well as any amusing anecdotes about this subject.

FRUSTABLE 2: *Why do women "of a certain age" usually start wearing their hair shorter?*

The hairdressers and beauty consultants we spoke to, for the most part, felt there was no good reason for women to wear their hair shorter as they got older. Why has ever-shortened hair become a traditional fashion statement of mature women? Or is this custom merely a way to avoid the inconvenience of dealing with long hair?

FRUSTABLE 3: *Why do the clasps of necklaces and bracelets tend to migrate from the back toward the front?*

Can this phenomenon be explained by some weird, unwritten rule of physics? Does the slight extra weight of the clasp affect its ability to stay put on the wrist or neck? We have received this complaint from several women and so far have heard no good explanation.

FRUSTABLE 4: *Why is it customary to include the full address of the recipient of a business letter before the salutation?*

Presumably, the recipient of a letter knows his or her address. When a letter is prepared for a window envelope, this practice saves the sender the time and aggravation of addressing an envelope. But isn't it a waste of time and space otherwise?

FRUSTABLE 5: *Why do most women like shopping more than men?*

Yes, we *know* this is a gross generalization. But it is fair to say that far more women were "born to shop" than men. We thought men were supposed to be the hunter-gatherers. Why do women seem to derive far more psychic benefits from shopping than men?

FRUSTABLE 6: *How and why did the association between wearing eyeglasses and nerdiness and/or greater intelligence begin?*

Was the original assumption that people needed glasses because they wore out their eyes reading books? Were glasses considered to be signs of physical weakness? This is one stereotype that never made much sense to us.

FRUSTABLE 7: *Why and where did the tradition of tearing down football goalposts begin?*

We're confident that the practice started during the days of early American college football, but our usually reliable college football experts can't pinpoint either where it started or whether it began as a demonstration of joy at a victory or a riot after a defeat.

FRUSTABLE 8: *Why do artists, models, and bohemians wear black clothing?*

In almost any metropolitan area in the Western world, black seems to be a uniform of hipness. Sure, we know that "black makes you look thinner," "everybody looks good in black," "black goes with everything," etc. But why would folks who wouldn't think twice about dyeing their hair purple or inserting earrings through any possible bodily protuberance find black eternally chic?

FRUSTABLE 9: *Why is the best restaurant coffee better than home-brewed coffee?*

We expect to hear complaints about the premise of this question. Yes, there is plenty of pitiful coffee served in restaurants and cafés, but several readers have asked why they can't make coffee at home that competes with the best restaurant coffee, especially when they are often using more expensive coffee beans than the restaurant.

FRUSTABLE 10: *Why don't women spit more?*

Yes, we know we are culturally conditioned to consider spitting to be the domain of uncouth males. We realize that males of yore smoked cigars and chewed tobacco that stimulated saliva production. But most of the tobacco-abstaining, ultracouth males we've spoken to commonly feel the urge to spit.

Yet many women deny they ever have such a need. Can there be a physiological explanation? Are women suppressing a desire to spit?

Can you help us? We have great expectorations about this Frustable!

DAVID FELDMAN

Frustables Update

Our Readers Respond to the Frustables First Posed in
When Did Wild Poodles Roam the Earth?

FRUSTABLE 1: ***Why do women often go to the restroom together? And what are they doing in there for so long?***

Since we are in the rare position of having read several hundred people, mostly female, describe their restroom habits in graphic detail, and since we are about to embark on a dissection of such habits in detail worthy of a Ph.D. in anthropology, it is only fair we share with women what a men's room is like: a morgue.

About the only place where one can observe the average man more uptight is in an elevator. Even if a male should happen to saunter into a bathroom with a friend, any vocal interplay between them is strictly prohibited (unless approved in writing by Major League Baseball, of course). Men glide over to the urinals, unzip, and look straight ahead with a steadiness of gaze that a marine drill sergeant would envy. They go about their business with the seriousness and speed of someone paying by the hour. By our casual observation, an embarrassing percentage wash their hands as they make a beeline for the exit door. Average time in restroom? Fifteen seconds. Maybe we're exaggerating a tad, but you get the idea.

No wonder, then, that men are amazed that women will troop off together to the bathroom, just as the dinner table is engrossed in a fascinating conversation about the relative merits of the Tampa Bay Buccaneers and the Phoenix Cardinals, or about whether the family auto requires 10–40 or 10–50 motor oil. As their dinner curdles, the men wonder what happened to the women. Have they been spirited into UFOs? Having a Tupperware party? Having a sauna? Here's what we heard:

Safety

We were surprised how many women echoed the sentiments of Lin Sherfy of Nevada, Iowa:

> Practically from birth, Mommy tells her little girl how dangerous public restrooms are. They are dirty, they are filled with strange, unspecified diseases, and they teem with evil strangers who must never be spoken to. One of the most popular urban legends, after all, deals with the little girl who was drugged by an evil woman in a department-store restroom, her hair dyed. Her mother "just happened to catch a glimpse of her shoes as she was carried out the door and rescued her!"
>
> Consciously or subconsciously, a woman feels vulnerable with half her clothes down around her ankles and only half a door between her and whomever walks into the restroom. If there's another woman around, most women will issue a general invitation and a group will go together to watch out for each other. Besides, it's nice to have someone to hold the stall door shut since the lock has almost always been removed, and to pass you a Kleenex when, as usual, there isn't any toilet paper.

DAVID FELDMAN

Meryl Silverstein of Brooklyn, New York, also mentioned that women are conditioned to fear restrooms from an early age:

> Despite many people insisting that things are worse "now" than they were "then," when I was in elementary school, girls were never permitted to leave the classroom singly, certainly not to go to the bathroom. Presumably a would-be mugger or child molester would be deterred by two little girls. The college I attended had signs on the restroom doors advising women, "Never enter a bathroom alone." Old habits die hard.

Several women mentioned that they fear not only physical attacks but unwanted attention from lecherous men en route to the bathroom. We received a particularly biting primer on the subject from Nancy Tropkoff of Brunswick, Ohio, who even included suggested dialogue to assist, as she so delicately puts it, "moron-evaders":

> Why would you want to go alone if you could be molested by some moron? [If you run into a jerk], your companion can say, "Let's go, I gotta go real bad!" In especially urgent times, "Mrphh-gag-gag . . . I don't feel so good" is also effective. On the way back from the bathroom, friends can also be a human shield ("No, I haven't seen her.") If a woman is somewhere with husband and kids, she will enlist children ("I know you have to go. At least *try* to go!").

To Kill Time

High on the list of most women's pet peeves are the long lines to get into restrooms. Diane Larson of Lakeville, Minnesota, summed up the thoughts of many women when she said that having a companion along is preferable so "that you have someone to talk to during the interminable wait to get into a stall."

Hair/Make-Up

This may surprise our male readers, but beauty makeovers do not occur only in salons and on afternoon TV talk shows—actually, the epicenter of fashion and cosmetics is not Paris or New York City but your local women's room. For men, a toilet is a toilet. For women, evidently a toilet is a toilette, or more precisely, a continuing education course in toilette, as Lin Sherfy explains:

> Any group of more than two women invariably includes one who's recently read one of those "How To Make Lipstick Stay On" magazine articles, and often she's also read that "everyone ought to use a lipstick brush." So there stand her companions, waiting patiently because it would be rude to walk out and leave a friend alone in that evil place, while she gets out her lipstick brush, unscrews brush and lipstick, loads the brush, carefully paints her lips, blots, powders the blotted lipstick, picks her brush up off the floor where it rolled, washes it, dries it, loads the brush, paints over the powdered lipstick, blots . . . and then, she takes her comb and brush and spritzes spray. . . "

You get the idea.

Sharon Brandon of Indianapolis, Indiana, wrote:

> Women are (wrongly) conditioned by our culture to place a heavy emphasis on their appearance. Therefore they feel a need to make sure they still look "all right" at some point in the evening.

All the respondents who mentioned this point added that men are "easy graders" in this department. As Kelli Zimmerman of Milwaukee, Wisconsin, put it,

> My date isn't going to tell me that something doesn't look right. My girlfriend will.

Some women use their companions for positive feedback, too, such as Joan Cartan-Hansen of Boise, Idaho:

> Women seem to need confirmation that they look okay. After fixing your face in the bathroom mirror, it is nice to turn to your companion for a quick approval.

Female Bonding

We heard from many fans of Deborah Tannen's bestseller, *You Just Don't Understand*. Tannen posits that while men are task-oriented in word as well as deed, what she calls "rapport talk" is extremely important to women. Mary Roush of Wilmington, Delaware, explains:

DAVID FELDMAN

Where better to have conversational intimacy than in a women-only restroom? . . . You have to go to the restroom together to help form a relationship or otherwise miss an alliance-building, affiliative opportunity. The task (going to the restroom) is simply the secondary vehicle for the primary work [of women] in life: relationship maintenance.

One reader, Charles T. Galloway of Bolton, Ontario, compares mass restroom migration to earlier, seemingly anachronistic rituals:

There are certain subjects that both males and females seem to regard as appropriate for discussion when the other sex is absent but unsuitable when they are present. The ladies' trip to the washroom takes the place of the old Victorian habit of the ladies withdrawing from the dining room to "leave the gentlemen to their cigars" so that these conversations can take place. What the ladies are doing in there so long is engaging in "girl talk."

David Ryback, a psychologist in Atlanta, Georgia, finds that "girl talk" is not only a way for women to increase intimacy but also serves to defuse what could turn into conflicts and turn them into ego-boosters:

Women will often go to the restroom together precisely when they are in the company of men who take a dominant role in the discussion of the group. . . . The men are airing their opinions, controlling the direction of conversation and, for the most part, dismissing the women's contributions. The simple outlet for the building frustration on the women's part is to take leave of the men's company temporarily without challenging their pompous position. It may come at a time when one of the women truly needs to use the restroom. What better occasion for the other women to take leave of a frustrating, possibly boring, situation without the slightest hint of confrontation!

Once in the restroom, the women now have an opportunity to regain their sense of self-esteem. They can do this by having a brief discussion of their own choosing. If they feel particularly put down by their male counterparts, they can restore the balance by sharing their opinions of the men awaiting their return. No wonder we men start fidgeting after a while. And then we wonder why the women look so radiant and self-satisfied when they return.

Nothing we heard from our readers contradicted Dr. Ryback's observations. Indeed, Karen Pierce of Springfield, Virginia, eerily echoed his words, and added, "I've had better discussions fixing my make-up than I've ever had talking to my boyfriends."

Men, on the other hand, aren't too likely to bond in restrooms; one reader, Bob Kowalski of Detroit, Michigan, thinks the reason might relate to Darwinesque theories:

> Men, probably harking back to their caveman hunter days, prefer to respond to nature's call alone. You don't want a prospective enemy too close at hand when you have your, uh, guard down!

Facilitating Conversations Outside of the Restroom

Readers brought up two points we had never considered. Diane Larson notes that since women seem to use the restroom much more often than men,

> it's better to have one lull in the conversation while several women go to the restroom at once. Otherwise, the table is constantly having to play catch-up because someone is always missing part of the conversation.

And Jennifer Talarico of Bethel Park, Pennsylvania, uses her group defections during double-dates to force the deserted males to bond:

> When we are in the restroom for extended amounts of time, the topic of conversation is undoubtedly the men we are with. And we know that the men back at the table are discussing us as well. Sometimes the purpose of our escape is so that the men can get to know one another, especially when we girls have been friends for a while and the guys have just recently met.

Conspiracy Theories

Several respondents have already suggested that the conversation regarding the abandoned males might be less than laudatory. This was very much on the minds of many of the males who wrote, including Wayland Kwock of Aiea, Hawaii:

As to why women go to the restroom in packs . . . it has to do with make-up. . . . The alternative, that they are making fun of their dates, is just unthinkable.

Sorry to do this, Wayland, but please meet Linda Lassman of Winnipeg, Manitoba:

> . . . another reason women leave together is because they often think the things men say are *really* stupid, but they don't want to cause hurt feelings or arguments by saying so. Going to the restroom in groups allows them to talk about things that actually interest them, to discuss the same topics and have their opinions listened to, and to laugh at the men they're with without worrying about how the men will feel.

If we are indeed engaged in a war of the sexes, perhaps the paranoid musings of Ted Baxter might contain the true answer. Several readers, including Mark La Chance of Pleasanton, California, remember the "Mary Tyler Moore Show" news anchor's answer to this Frustable:

> He believed that there was a women's plot to take over the world, and that their secret meetings were held in the ladies' rooms so that men wouldn't hear. I have to admit that after my history of disastrous and humiliating relationships, the idea of gender-guerrilla warfare rings true to me.

Sorry things haven't been working out, Mark, but by the time you finish this discussion, you will have delved as deeply into the female psyche as is genderly possible. Perhaps you will now be able to plumb the psyches of a woman as deftly as Richard Gere's *American Gigolo*.

And What Are They Doing in There for So Long?

Many of the explanations mimicked the discussions above. Several women cataloged the checklist of make-up and grooming that must be undertaken before any restroom exit. But more moaned about clothing problems. Diane Larson is typical:

> I defy any man to don pantyhose, a girdle, a slip, a tight skirt and high heels and then go to the restroom in record time after squeezing

into a tiny cubicle barely big enough to sit down in without your knees hitting the door.

And one type of apparel not to buy for women with weak bladders was mentioned by Joan Cartan-Hansen: "Woe to the woman who wears a one-piece jumpsuit and practically has to do a striptease to answer's nature's call."

Most of all, women wailed about the dearth of stalls in women's bathrooms. Nothing makes men prouder about their gender than cruising into a men's room at a ball game or concert while women stand glumly in long lines. Just in case men haven't noticed it, women wanted to point out that their anatomy is slightly different from men's. Even if women had more stalls in their restrooms and fewer make-up, grooming, clothing, and conversational distractions, it would still take longer for them to urinate than men. Several readers sent us graphic descriptions; Sharon Brandon was more discreet:

> Men have more plentiful "opportunities," shall we say, in their restroom, while women are often limited to a small number of closed, private stalls. I hope I don't have to go into grade school health class review to explain any other possible time-consuming differences to you between men and women.

No, thanks.

Another reader made it clear that even if a particular gaggle of women entering a restroom is childless, women with children can drastically affect restroom timing. Among the factors that Judy R. Reis of Bisbee, Arizona, cited in prolonging restroom visits are the following: "helping the kids go potty," "waiting for the women ahead of them to get done helping the kids go potty," and "relinquishing their places in line to the women whose kids can't wait to go potty." Obviously, some of the kids in the women's room are boys, not girls.

Most of the female respondents to this question were feeling a little sorry for themselves. But we know that all types of facilities are provided for women that are not given to men. At times, women's rooms look more like Ethan Allen showrooms, with all sorts of paraphernalia. Rosemarie Gee of Ridgefield, Washington, reminisced with

DAVID FELDMAN

us about the restrooms in the library at her alma mater, Brigham Young University. They provided couches and chairs, so a woman could eat lunch there, the only place besides a small room in the basement where one could sit, eat, and study at the same time. Some women's rooms even had beds! Rosemarie also mentions that many women's rooms contain full-length mirrors and chairs by the mirrors, to assist in undertaking all the tasks that make women take so long in there in the first place.

But even stripped of all fineries, Gee insists that a woman's task in the restroom is far more arduous than a man's, and she supplied us with a handy comparison chart to see how a man and a woman's trip to the restroom is likely to compare (your results might differ):

Men	Women
Open door or enter doorway	Open door or enter doorway
Step to urinal	Choose a stall
	Open door—maneuver in cramped quarters
	Hang up purse/coat
	Flush to ensure fresh water
	Wipe off seat
	Put on seat cover
Unzip	Unzip and pull down pants or lift up dress and pull down nylons.
Do business	Do business
	Use toilet paper
Flush (optional)	Flush
	Realign clothing
	Gather personal possessions
	Open door in cramped area
	Set personals on counter
Wash hands (optional)	Wash hands (likely)
Dry hands (conceivable)	Dry hands (optional)
	Gather stuff
Leave	Leave (eventually)

Obviously, if all the talking/make-up/child care/grooming behavior occurs as well, it is a wonder women ever emerge from the restroom at

HOW DOES ASPIRIN FIND A HEADACHE?

all. But faced with the thrilling prospect of rejoining their waiting specimens of male hunkitude, they always seem to come out
eventually.

Submitted by Ray Bauschke of Winnipeg, Manitoba. Thanks also to
Douglas Watkins, Jr., of Hayward, California; Edward T. Coglio of
Pittsburgh, Pennsylvania; Ish Narula of Upper Darby, Pennsylvania; John
Heggestad of Fairfax, Virginia; Bruce Kershner of Williamsville, New
York; T. Wenzel of Charleston, West Virginia; and Alice Conway of
Highwood, Illinois.

A complimentary book goes to Rosemarie Gee of Ridgefield, Washington.
Thanks to the scores of readers who duplicated sentiments expressed
above.

DAVID FELDMAN

FRUSTABLE 2: *Why do men tend to hog remote controls and switch channels on television sets and radios much more than women?*

Right after the publication of *When Did Wild Poodles Roam the Earth?*, *Consumer Reports* published the findings of a survey conducted among their readers about remote control usage (thanks to one of our favorite correspondents, Kenneth Giesbers of Seattle, Washington, who called this to our attention). Their study indicated that men are more than twice as likely to hog the TV remote (38 percent to 15 percent). And not only do men "channel surf" more often than females (85 percent to 60 percent); they are less likely to complain about their mate's surfing (66 percent to 43 percent).

Although the Frustable, as posed, refers to channel switching on radios as well, we received little response to radio station hopping. In fact, Jennifer Talarico, of Bethel Park, Pennsylvania, while concurring that men switch car radio channels far more often than women, did not agree that they exhibited this behavior at home. What accounts for the discrepancy? "At home, a man is too busy watching all three hundred channels on television to be preoccupied with the radio."

How can we account for this male obsession? More than a few folks had a simple explanation, most eloquently stated by Donald Wiese of Anaheim, California: "Maybe men are simply jerks!"

Certainly a plausible theory, Donald. Indeed, most of the conjectures were not ones that would deepen men's self-esteem. About the sunniest possible explanation that we received was that men are obsessed with gadgets and will play with them regardless of whether it advances any particular goal. Most correspondents, though, found far darker reasons for hogging remotes:

1. Men Need to Dominate and Control

"The remote control gives the man power. Plain and simple," responds Kelli Zimmerman of Milwaukee, Wisconsin. Lauren Goldfarb of Huntington, New York, issues a call to arms:

> The male gender tends to dominate more than the female. Like it or not, the reality is that this world is still run by men. So you ladies at home, take control and refuse to give up the remote. It may be well worth it in the end.

So the battle of the sexes is waged not in boardrooms but in living rooms. Concurring with this sentiment is Kathy Smith of New Bern, North Carolina:

> My husband is a "remote controlaholic" because he can't control *me*—it's a displacement behavior that gives him a feeling of accomplishment and superiority.

2. Men Are Hunters

Jerry Seinfeld has postulated that channel surfing is a modern equivalent of hunting for men. Lauren Goldfarb concurs:

> In the cave days, men were hunters while women nurtured the family. The action of flipping the channels on the remote control is similar to the hunt. A man with a remote control in hand is a man with power, hunting for something exciting and interesting.

3. Men Require Instant Gratification

"Perform on command or I'm off," says David Ohde of Weaverville, California, is the watchword of most men. Lane Chaffin of Temple, Texas, adds that because men watch so many sporting events, where dead time is clearly demarcated, this tendency is exaggerated.

4. Men Are Promiscuous

Why do men require instant gratification? Because they are used to insisting upon control/dominance, according to the readers mentioned above. But Lauren Goldfarb is back with a theory on this subject, too:

> Most men don't like to commit or get attached to just one show, which is not all that different from a typical teenage boy. A girl dreams of her wedding day while a guy dreams of how many women he will "have." Why just have one when you can have them all?

Several readers indicated that women are much more willing to commit, in time and emotion, to one program. Who would have thought that remote control hogging could be directly traced to a fear of intimacy?

5. Men Are Mice

Men are animals, insists Karen Flanery, of Casper, Wyoming, and act like any other creature that scientists have investigated:

> Remote controls are a prime illustration of the response-reward theory advocated by early psychiatrists. Mice, simians, canines, and felines soon learn to press a lever that will give them a reward (say, a piece of cheese). If the response is intermittently rewarded, the drive to press buttons intensifies.

Men didn't receive much sympathy from our female readers, but we did receive a poignant note from Ruth M. Johnson of Tacoma, Washington, which testifies to the primal connection among males, channel surfing, and the beloved remote control:

This is purely a matter of control. The remote control device is an ideal way to drive a female out of her mind.

My husband died of Lou Gehrig's disease in 1991 and the remote control was the last thing he was able to operate. At the end, he had to have a holder on his palm, which held a pencil to enable him to punch the buttons, but he never failed to change the station the minute I became engrossed in a program or to skim the channels so fast my eyes would glaze.

It was the only thing he could do for himself, so I let him carry on. The television has been on exactly three times since he left me for a better place.

Submitted by Patricia M. Delehanty of Poughkeepsie, New York.

A complimentary book goes to Lauren Goldfarb of Huntington, New York.

FRUSTABLE 3: *Why do some women kick their legs up when kissing?*

Some of you believed that leg-kicking kissers are merely imitating the lovers in romantic, old movies. But this begs the question. Then why did the heroines in old movies kick their legs up?

Most of you were prosaic. You thought it had to do with a simple, anatomical truism: Women tend to be shorter than men. Bob Kowalski of Detroit, Michigan, had a typical response;

> Maybe women kicking a leg up while kissing has something to do with most women having to reach up to kiss their love! Most men, being taller, kiss down. The leg up may be an automatic balancing response, and they are probably unaware that they even do it.

Of course, kicking doesn't bring them straight up; it also moves women forward, as Kelli Zimmerman explains:

> Women stand on the tiptoe of one leg while lifting the other so that they can lean forward. Why we don't just ask the tall men to bend down a little bit is beyond me.

Maybe, Kelli, the reason is that the leg kicking facilitates more than just lip clinching, as David Ryback postulates:

DAVID FELDMAN

> Women . . . can get their upper bodies closer to the men of their
> desire by standing on tiptoe and kicking up one leg behind them. If you
> find this hard to believe, try standing close to a wall. Then lift one leg
> behind you. You'll find yourself "hugging" the wall.

We just did. Thanks, David, that's the closest we've come to an intimate
relationship in months.

Although all of these explanations make some sense, we have a
nagging suspicion there is more to the issue. Lane Chaffin of Temple,
Texas, is the only reader who indicated that height is not the only factor
in leg kicking. He has never seen a short man kick up his leg when kissing a taller woman,

> probably because it would make the man feel weak and the (taller)
> woman would feel uncomfortable because she would be in a physically
> awkward position. Maybe the leg kicking started as a woman's exhibition
> of trust in her male companion.

Could be. Our informal survey indicates that leg kicking occurs only in
public places (a classic place: airports, when loved ones greet one
another). And leg kicking is clearly a romantic gesture: If it were merely
a convenience to compensate for height differences, why don't daughters kick up their legs when kissing their fathers good night? Or little
kids when kissing their taller grandparents?

We wouldn't be surprised if the reason why we find leg kicking
in public places is that the gesture is used by the woman, usually sub-
consciously, as a marker, to stake a claim that "this man is mine"—
to the world and to other women in particular. Outlandish? Not really.
When we see couples strolling down the street, with the man putting
his arm over the shoulder of his companion, it is a way of telling the
world, "She's taken." Yet in the privacy of their own home, husbands
and wives seldom walk hand in hand from the dining room to the
kitchen to do the dishes after a meal or while taking the garbage
outside.

Anyone have any better theories?

*Submitted by Jerrod Larson of South Bend, Indiana. Thanks also to
Rosemary Lambert of Kanata, Ontario.*

HOW DOES ASPIRIN FIND A HEADACHE?   771

FRUSTABLE 4: *Women generally possess more body fat than men? So why do women tend to feel colder than men in the same environment?*

Many readers tackled this Frustable, but we were most impressed with the arguments of two professors, especially because their two discussions complement each other. Dallas Brozik, chair of the department of finance and business law at Marshall University, theorizes why the extra fat might make a woman feel cooler rather than hotter than men in the same room:

> The reason that women may feel chilled even with an extra layer of body fat has to do with the body's attempt to maintain a central core temperature. As the body tries to maintain 98.6 degrees Fahrenheit, the blood system is used to transfer inner heat to the skin, where it can be radiated away. Heat transfer can only be accomplished through a temperature gradient across a boundary, and the additional layer of fat makes it more difficult for women to rid themselves of excess heat.
>
> At this point the body has two mechanisms it can employ to rid itself of the excess heat. First, it could raise the core temperature to establish the proper temperature gradient with the ambient external temperature. But the body is trying *not* to heat up, so this mechanism is self-defeating. The second mechanism is to sweat so as to bring evaporative cooling into play. The extra layer of fat makes women sweat a little more than men under the same conditions. And when this sweat is evaporated, the nerve cells in the skin feel the chilling effect; hence, women will tend to feel colder than men under similar conditions.

But other physiological forces are at work, deftly explained by Richard Landesman, of the department of zoology at the University of Vermont:

> Body temperature is the result of metabolism, and, at rest, the bulk of the heat to warm the body is produced by the liver, heart, brain, endocrine organs, and skeletal muscle. The latter is responsible for about 30 percent of heat production at rest. During exercise, the heat produced by the muscles contributes significantly to body temperature.
>
> There are two temperature regions of the body: the core, whose temperature remains relatively constant; and the shell or surface, whose temperature tends to vary with physical and environmental changes.

DAVID FELDMAN

There are many mechanisms to raise and lower the temperature of the body: for example, shivering raises the temperature and sweating lowers the temperature. Another way to conserve heat is for the blood vessels in the skin to vasoconstrict, thereby shunting the warm blood to the core of the body. One obvious symptom of vasoconstriction is for the skin to feel cold. Now with that preamble, the answer to the Frustable . . .

> 1. As a general rule, men have more muscle mass than do women; therefore, men can maintain their body temperature at rest without feeling as cold as women.
> 2. Women do have more subcutaneous fat compared to men. This layer serves to give the women body shape as well as to provide a layer of insulation. When it is cool, the blood vessels in the skin vasoconstrict, shunting the warm blood into the core of the body. The skin now feels cool. The layer of insulating fat, while conserving the heat in the core of the body, contributes to the skin remaining cool.

Submitted by David Held of Somerset, New Jersey. Thanks also to Bruce Kershner of Williamsville, New York.

Complimentary books go to Dallas Brozik of Huntington, West Virginia, and Richard Landesman of Burlington, Vermont.

FRUSTABLE 5: *Why is the average woman a much better dancer than the average man?*

Fred Astaire, Mikhail Baryshnikov, and Gregory Hines aren't exactly chopped liver in the dance department, so we know that men *can* dance well. The conundrum is why the average man doesn't.

Our readers came up with five possible explanations:

1. Girls Practice Dancing More Than Boys

This was by far the most popular theory among *Imponderables* readers. Jody Jamieson Dobbs's response was typical:

Women start at an early age dancing with their moms, sisters, and friends—they don't need male partners. Men wouldn't be caught dead dancing with each other. So females get to practice from a very early age and, let's face it, practice makes perfect. (I'm an excellent dancer and my husband is an excellent hunter and fisherman.)

Ah, the typical American family: the wife is graceful, while the husband is proficient at protein-gathering.

But why don't boys dance together . . .

2. Dancing Is for Sissies

Western culture has deeply conflicting feelings about male dancers. On the one hand, fictional depictions of ballroom dancers, ranging from Fred Astaire to John Travolta to Gene Kelly to Patrick Swayze, invariably portray the male as virile and extremely attractive to women. Yet the general attitude of the average boy has not changed much since Robert Coulson of Hartford City, Indiana, was avoiding the dance floor:

> I can't speak for the current generation, but when I was a boy, dancing was considered "sissy." I went to a rural school, and I don't think any male ever learned to dance while I was there. From TV reports, boys today seem willing to learn the more athletic dances, such as break-dancing, but I suspect that ballroom dancing is still considered beneath contempt.

Curiously, though, dancing has often been considered a macho pursuit among diverse working-class subcultures, ranging from the Italians depicted in *Saturday Night Fever,* the spiritual descendants of the kids who danced on "American Bandstand" in the 1950s, to the African-Americans in inner cities, where break-dancing and hip-hop cultures emerged.

Another correspondent, Joseph M. Novak of Pittsburgh, Pennsylvania, argues that from the earliest ages, boys are touted toward what society deems gender-specific physical activities emphasizing strength and power, such as football and wrestling. Girls, on the other hand, are encouraged to develop grace and beauty, in sports

DAVID FELDMAN

such as gymnastics and arts such as ballet. Novak even argues that the musculature of the two genders might play a factor: "Who do you think is a better dancer, Arnold [Schwarzenegger] or Maria [Shriver]?"

We're betting on Maria. But we're still concerned that we haven't pinned down why dancing is considered a feminine form. Some readers feel the answer is . . .

3. Dancing Is an Emotional Expression, and Men Don't Like to Express Their Emotions

Cheryl Stevens's response speaks for several readers:

> Dance is an emotional expression, like any art. Men are not (or were not) encouraged to express their emotions, especially with potential spectators around. Maybe as men are allowed to be more sensitive, they'll become better dancers.

Cheryl, we're betting that big bands will come back before men become more sensitive. But we like your point about spectators. Men tend to open up emotionally to a few selected intimate friends, whereas women are more likely to share emotions with acquaintances; therefore, men might be more reluctant to express their emotions (and thus their vulnerability) in public, even through dance.

Still, why would men have no problem expressing emotion in writing or music but stumble upon dance? Perhaps the answer is that while we don't tend to read the average Joe's prose or listen to an amateur's musical stabs, we are constantly subjected, whether at wedding parties or at discos, to the prancing of amateur dancers, many of whom are coerced onto dance floors by their dates or mates. After all, there are plenty of spectacularly graceful *professional* male dancers; maybe the average man would be just as reticent about playing the oboe or reciting his poetry in public.

4. Men Don't Like to Dance, So They Don't Do It Well

This may not be the most profound explanation, but it makes some sense. For all the reasons stated above, many men don't like to dance. LaNue Parnell-Reynolds of Warren, Arkansas, thinks this insight unlocks the Frustable:

> You need to watch some *country* dancing! Men are good at what they enjoy. More women than men like ballroom-type dancing.

5. Dancing Seduces Men More Easily than Women

We have no idea if Robin Pearce's theory is correct, but it was the only answer we received that ties together the many threads we've discussed in a way that, well, might bag her an "A" in an anthropology course:

> Dancing, like brightly colored clothing and makeup, is a way of visually displaying one's self to potential mates. Since men are visually oriented, women take greater pains to make themselves attractive [to men], and this includes dancing well; gay men are usually excellent dancers for the same reason [they are also trying to attract men].
>
> Your average straight white American male subconsciously feels that dancing well, like being too concerned with one's appearance, is not masculine. However, heterosexual men in cultures where visual display is considered appropriate for the male (i.e., Latin, Mediterranean, and black men) both dance well and dress colorfully.

Robin is obviously generalizing about gender and various ethnic and national types, but her notion is fascinating. After all, choreographers and lyricists constantly cast dance as a metaphor for sex. And although it is hard to conjure up any woman being enticed by the fellow performing a lumbering lambada at the disco, it is hard to argue with Pearce that the ultimate, if often subconscious, goal of much social dancing is seduction.

While most men are attracted *by* the dancing of potential mates, it doesn't necessarily follow that most men are attractive *when they dance*. Maybe the maladroit average male is showing rare good sense in being a wallflower—better not to attract a mate than to lose any chance by flailing around on the dance floor.

Submitted by Judith Dahlman of New York, New York.

A complimentary copy goes to Robin Pearce of Kansas City, Missouri.

DAVID FELDMAN

FRUSTABLE 6: *Why do so many people put their hands up to their chins in photographs?*

"Because the photographer tells them to!" answers Rosemary Gee of Ridgefield, Washington. She's right, in a sense. We doubt if many portrait subjects spontaneously thrust their hands into their chins upon hearing "cheese." As Bill Jelen of Akron, Ohio puts it:

> It is a conspiracy by all of the professional photographers. Have you ever seen anyone posed this way in an amateur photograph? No!

We can testify to the existence of hand-in-face commands by professional photographers. We didn't spontaneously place our fingers on our forehead when the picture on the back cover was shot. We were asked to do so.

Still, we need to plumb deeper. Even if only professional photographs seem to feature this pose, why do these photographers request it? We spoke to many professional photographers and received quite a bit of response from readers, too. As usual, with Frustables, answers were all over the map; but they fell into five major categories:

1. Look Ma, No or Two Hands

We received this unusual theory from James P. Gage of Washington Island, Wisconsin:

> Many portraits were requested by immigrants to send to relatives in the "old country." Should the fingers not be shown, the relatives would assume the immigrant had lost some or all of the digits in transit or at work. Even in the 1960s, when I worked as an apprentice at a portrait studio, "Show their fingers!" was the request of the boss.

Finger-posing can exhibit good news as well as bad. Gail Lee Dunson of Dallas, Texas, points out that "in a wedding or graduation portrait, the pose is used so that the 'portraitee' can show off the new ring."

2. A Cheap Form of Plastic Surgery

The most popular theory among readers is that the pose is used to cover a myriad of physical defects in the subject: wrinkles in the neck; a weak chin; a double chin; acne or other blemishes; a scar; or even bad teeth.

Of course, no subject is going to look great if the image is blurred. Curtis Krause of Vernon, Connecticut, offers a theory similar to that mentioned earlier in this book during our discussion of why people didn't smile in old photographs:

> Many old photographs contain blurs caused by movement during exposure. Exposures were originally rather lengthy. . . . It may be that the hands on the chins helped to steady the head and avoid blurring. As film speeds increased, this pose would have become less necessary, but might have been continued as part of the style.

Ultimately, the more important reason why the hand-to-chin pose might make the subject look better was expressed by John C. White of El Paso, Texas:

> People posing for photo sessions often feel awkward and don't know what to do with their hands. Photographers have learned to resolve this problem with the hand-to-chin pose. It may be a bit hackneyed but it sure beats the Napoleonic pose.

3. Spruces Up the Image

Many readers ("Dobie Gillis" fans?) mentioned that the hand-in-chin pose reminds them of Rodin's *The Thinker*. To them, the pose conjures in the viewer the notion that the subject is an intellectual, of a philosophical and cerebral nature.

Gene Lester of the American Society of Camera Collectors notes that hands can enhance the subjects in other ways:

> Hands are very expressive and the way people hold them or use them shows a bit more of their character. Hands can help express deep thought, puzzlement, even humor, depending upon how the subject uses them.

Reader Joanna Parker of Miami, Florida, corroborates and expands upon Lester's thesis. If you want to show the potential power of this pose, suggests Parker, watch actors:

DAVID FELDMAN

If you watch truly adept actors, you will find that they consider the body to be three spheres, balanced one atop the other. When you want to express power, you use all your arm and hand gestures in the middle sphere. You punch from there, poke your fingers into the other guy's chest from there, tell people "no!" with a slicing gesture of the open hand from there, etc.

If the actor wants to exude sex, he works with his arms/hands in the lower sphere. All gestures originate from and work in this area.

The top sphere projects intelligence, thoughtfulness, and intimacy. Watch good actors who are playing professors. Chances are that when they are on camera, they are fiddling with their glasses, moving their hair off of their foreheads, using a pipe by gesturing with it held close to their faces, etc.

In still photography, perhaps the placing of the hands under the chin enhances this expression of intimacy with the viewer of the photo. It lends the photo a feeling of sincerity.

4. Improves the Composition

Several readers and professional photographers noted that a head floating in space looks funny in a photograph. The hand-in-chin pose anchors the head, but it also makes the composition look more natural, at least according to photographer Mike Brint, who notes that in nature, larger objects usually support smaller ones. He speculates that the originator of the pose might have thought that a head shot featuring a thin neck supporting the head looked funny, like an ice cream cone.

Why might the hand-in-chin pose create a superior composition? Photographer Bill O'Donnell supplies an explanation:

> The most common explanation is that the vertical or diagonal line formed by the arm will tend to "lead" the viewer's eye to the face. A simple face-front picture looks rather static and may be unflattering; the hand-in-chin pose makes the subject appear more relaxed and life-like. There's a reason why mug shots and driver's license photos look like they do—no hands, no relaxed pose, no suggestion of possible movement.

Chandra L. Morgan-Henley of Cleveland, Ohio, is also a proponent of the "composition theory" and notes that good photographers

> compose photographs in their minds before clicking the shutter. . . . What might otherwise be a poorly composed and boring portrait can, with the addition of a carefully placed hand, strike exactly the right balance for visual interest.
>
> Please note that I said *can* in the above sentence, because poorly trained (and untrained) photographers often copy techniques that they have seen, with results that are less than pleasing. Incidentally, my father and two brothers are all portrait photographers, and I studied retouching before deciding my talents lay elsewhere—such as in writing letters to authors.

Good idea, Chandra, there's a great future in the lucrative and expanding field of writing letters to authors.

5. It Sells, Stupid

The chin-in-hand pose was met mostly by derision by the professional photographers we contacted. Yet many noted that the pose is consistently popular with subjects. And if subjects want a pose, even if photographers disdain it? In this case, presumably, the customer is always right.

Typical, if slightly more emotional than most, was the reaction of professional Wilton Wong of Belmont, California:

> I get nauseated every time I encounter a senior photo on someone's wall or desk, with the senior shown with the hand up to the chin or side of head. It is obviously so phony, since one can tell that absolutely no weight of the head is resting on the hand (since that would cause facial distortion). . . . As for why this is done, I'll speculate that it is merely the result of a photographer who shoots "by formula" as learned in a workshop ("Now remember, pose #147 is great for seniors!") and relies on cliche poses rather than being a real artist and coming up with innovative ways of making the photo interesting.

Over the last five years, we've harassed Joann Carney, the talented photographer who managed to keep the *Imponderables* author photo down to only a minor sales deterrent. "Why did you suggest the hand-on-forehead pose for this photo?" we prodded.

Believe it or not, Carney didn't know herself. She mentioned that amateur subjects are often nervous and that movement distracts them from focusing on the mechanics of the shoot; she noted that some people come alive when using their hands; and she muttered something about the composition being more interesting. Maybe, in a burst of psychic energy rarely encountered, she anticipated the appropriateness of this pose for the title of this book.

Submitted by Alice Conway of Highwood, Illinois.

A complimentary book goes to Joanna Parker of Miami, Florida.

FRUSTABLE 7: *Why do very few restaurants serve celery with mixed green salads?*

It's green. It's crunchy. It's low in calories. It's in tuna and chicken salad. Can you think of another vegetable, besides lettuce, more qualified to belong in a mixed green salad than celery?

But a glance at just about any mixed green salad will reveal a lack of celery. What's going on? Mark Watson of Cary, North Carolina, formerly responsible for the preparation of the salad bar at the Chapel Hill Country Club restaurant, weighs in with three important reasons:

> First, every competent restaurateur knows that "people eat with their eyes." Many of the ingredients in any item served in a restaurant are there as much for visual appeal as for flavor. Since celery is the same color as the lettuce base, it fails to improve visual appeal. On the other hand, tomatoes, carrots, and onions (white or purple) provide contrast. I cannot overemphasize the importance of visual presentation in the restaurant business. I have seen time and again that a good meal, poorly presented, will generate complaints, while a mediocre meal, presented colorfully and artistically, will bring raving compliments.

Second, the preparation of celery is relatively labor-intensive. It must be washed, and the widely flared white base must be cut off because it tends to be too fibrous and ugly. The leafy tops and often the narrow branches are removed, and then any damage spots on the stalk are excised. Finally, it is usually chopped into fairly narrow slices.

Third, the one superior attribute that celery does have disappears quickly in storage: that crispy crunchiness. Another maxim in the food industry is that food should have "good mouth feel." Celery provides a satisfying crunch that consumers (correctly) associate with freshness. Leftover chopped celery tends to turn brown and become rubbery rather quickly compared to other vegetables; this increases food waste. Restaurants used to solve this problem by storing celery (and lettuce and sliced potatoes) in a container of water mixed with a powdered vegetable preservation product that contained sulfites. To the best of my knowledge, this process has been widely abandoned, because the FDA discovered an annoying drawback to the practice. People all over the country were eating sulfite-treated salad vegetables, keeling over, and plummeting into life-threatening allergic anaphylactic shock!

Ronald J. Moore of Ecorse, Michigan, a professional chef for more than thirty years, backs up Watson's complaint about the quick spoilage of celery. Restaurant personnel don't appreciate having to prepare celery for dinner just hours before customers enter:

> If salad is kept from, say, 2:00 P.M. to 9:00 P.M., it is fine without celery. If it contains chopped celery, seven hours will have turned it from mixed green salad into mixed brown garbage.

Even before it oxidizes, celery tends to be dirty. Travel writer Judy Colbert reports that her food service friends tell her that celery is full of bacteria and is particularly difficult to clean properly. Another complaint that Judy and Ronald Moore mention is that celery is stringy and tends to get caught between teeth. Moore reports that older customers complain that celery gets trapped in their dentures.

Sure, celery adds crunchiness to a salad, but reader Cheryl Stevens notes that the cabbage and lettuce in a mixed green salad also

DAVID FELDMAN

provide snap. Tuna and chicken salad, on the other hand, "squishy in consistency," require celery for texture.

Finally, Ronald Moore contributes what could be a decisive factor in the demand-side of the missing celery equation: "An amazing number of people absolutely hate the taste of celery."

Submitted by Malcolm Boreham of Staten Island, New York. Thanks also to Launie Rountry of Brockton, Massachusetts.

A complimentary book goes to Mark Watson of Cary, North Carolina.

FRUSTABLE 8: *In English spelling, why does "i" come before "e" except after "c"?*

We're afraid that as of now this Frustable is frustrating our readers as well as us. But we have just begun to fight.

Store Managers' 5804 Guide...

IS THIS A 'GOOD' ADDRESS IN TOWN?

TIGHT LOOP ON 'L' MEANS WRITER FEARS JOB IS IN JEOPARDY

JANE Q. SPENDTHRIFT
61 Forger's Alley
Kiting, MO. 00100

July 16 19 94

Fisher Market

42·70

70/100 //////DOLLARS

PAY TO THE ORDER OF

Fourty-Two and

RUPTCY ~ BANK

groceries

Jane Q Spendthrift

MEMO

WHEN IN DOUBT, CHECK SPELLING

EUROPEAN "7" DE-NOTES EXPENSIVE TASTE

POOR RIP MEANS CHARGE CARD USED AS ID IS ALREADY MAXED OUT

...to a risky check! $

FRUSTABLE 9: *What in the world are grocery store managers looking for when they approve personal checks?*

When we first posed this Frustable, we wrote:

> We have been most dissatisfied with the answers we've received from supermarket chains on this topic, so we're hoping that some grocery store checkers, managers, or perspicacious customers can help us with this Frustable. To us, it seems that the manager simply peeks at the check, glances at the customer, and approves the check without looking for anything in particular. In fact, we've never seen a check rejected.

We've never dealt with a question pertaining to a particular profession that has generated so much mail. If supermarket chains were reluctant to discuss this issue with us, current and former grocery store checkers and managers were not reticent at all. We received dozens of letters from readers in the trade, including a magnum opus from Stephen H. Cook of North Providence, Rhode Island, who has spent twenty-three years in the personal credit and retail computer systems business and has done research on the machines that provide electronic approval of personal checks.

Cook confirms that grocery store managers are often negligent in their duties but notes that they must be on the lookout for four types of bad checks:

1) bad checks deliberately written by persons who know it's illegal

2) checks written by persons who don't know how to do a good job of using a checking account (the careless and disorganized)

3) bad checks from people without overdraft protection on their checking account, who know they can't cover the check at the moment but are hoping that a recent or planned future deposit will clear before the check does

4) bad checks from those who have made a recent deposit but have erred in assuming when the check will clear (these folks also have no overdraft protection)

According to Cook,

Most bad checks fall into categories two and three. All checks in category four and some checks in categories two and three may be made good by being presented again to the bank. But checks in category one are totally worthless and represent the biggest risk to the retailer.

Although the store fears the bad-check artist most, some of the problem items that a manager scans a check for are just as likely to arise not only with the other three types but with customers whose checks are valid. For the protection of the store, managers may look for all of these red flags:

- Is the check signed?
- Does the written amount on the check match the numerical amount?
- Are the address and phone number of the customer printed on the check? (Many grocery stores will not accept starter checks or checks without imprinted addresses; at the very least, they will insist upon other identification, such as a driver's license or credit card, confirming the address of the shopper. In this case, a credit card not only corroborates identification but serves as a credit check.)

- Is the customer on a bad check list published by a consumer credit clearinghouse or by the grocery store (chain) itself?
- Does the name signed match the name imprinted? Former store manager John Schaninger of Easton, Pennsylvania, reports, "I once had an assistant manager who did not check this; when I received the bad check back from the bank, the signature read, "I Beat You."
- Is the check made out to my store?
- Has the check been tampered with? Per C. Clarke, night manager of a Hy-Vee Food Store in Spencer, Iowa, reports he recently saw a check with a "void" clearly etched but (mostly) erased.
- Is the date correct? Let's use this seemingly innocent item as an example. Joseph S. Blake, Jr., a store manager, wrote to us about all of the potential problems inherent in an incorrectly dated check:

> If a check is postdated, it is legally considered a promissory note and not a check. If it is returned, the person who wrote it merely has to say, "I asked him if he could hold it until the date on the check and he said it would be okay." Although I would never agree to such a condition, the bank endorsements would clearly show that I deposited it before the date on the front. I would be screwed.
>
> I note that the year is correct, particularly during the first couple of months of the new year. A check that is dated more than six months ago is considered "stale dated" and cannot be collected as a cash item. . . .
>
> While I may have just thought that it was a confused little old lady that inadvertently wrote May 10 when it was really April 10, I find out later that she has done the same thing all over seven states. She has thousands of dollars of judgments against her, but no one can ever collect, since her only real asset is her checkbook for an account that never has more than five dollars in it.

All of these eight red flags are cut and dried; there is no particular reason why a checker wouldn't be qualified to verify them. But some verifications require a little more skill to examine. Blake named the three most important:

- Is it a genuine ID? Anyone can obtain a fake ID for a nominal amount. Many of them are horribly executed, but some can fool an inexperienced checker.

- Does the photo ID or description on a driver's license match the person trying to cash the check? As Blake puts it,

> If someone were to break into your car or home, he could easily end up with your checkbook as well as several pieces of your identification. It would be less likely that the ID would match your height, weight, hair color, and other features. If the check were stolen from someone, my only recourse is against the person who wrote the check, not the person who had it stolen from him.

- Is the check writer signing the check in the manager's presence? Some managers insist on seeing the customer sign the check in front of them (in our experience, this is not the case), and Blake offers a reason we would have never thought of, naifs that we are:

> Here's a popular scam from a few years ago that still happens from time to time. Suppose that you and I were in the business of writing bad checks together. Before I entered the store, I would have you sign my name of one of my checks. I would then go into the store with my checkbook with the check that you had signed, pick up all the big-ticket items that I could load in my cart, then proceed to the checkout counter. I would have my own identification, and my own checkbook where you had signed my name on the check, and would complete the sale.
>
> What could be more perfect? Unless the clerk or manager noticed that the signature on my ID and the check were not the same? We could do this in a couple of dozen places, preferably on a weekend. I would then wait and call the bank on Monday morning and notify them that my checkbook and wallet had been lost or stolen, or even wait until I started to receive overdraft protection before I "realized" it.
>
> An examination of the signatures would reveal that they were not mine—and they wouldn't be. The checks would all be returned to wherever they came from, and the merchants would be stuck. This is the reason why many places installed cameras that take a picture of the person writing the check.

Obviously, a bright and inexperienced cashier could be trained to perform all of these check-verification functions now usually undertaken by the store manager. We understand why supermarkets might

HOW DOES ASPIRIN FIND A HEADACHE?

want to lay responsibility on more experienced personnel, but isn't the practice a horrendous waste of time? Maybe there isn't a logical reason why the manager has to approve each check personally. Certainly, Russell Shaw, a journalist who writes frequently for *Supermarket News*, the largest publication covering supermarket management, has a jaundiced view of the check approval process:

> There's an insidious reason why supervisors approve checks, and this is where corporate culture fits in. Unlike some more progressive and newer industries, supermarkets have never been known as places to empower their hourly workers (read, cashiers). If you listen to a cashier paging a manager on the PA system, the manager will always be referred to by a surname ("Mr. Smith, register 8"), even though supervisor Smith's $18,000 a year salary and high-school education might pale next to the $100,000 salary and MBA of an executive at a nearby office park where the secretaries call him by his first name.
>
> Some of these attitudes are due to a caste system driven by low pay and low skill levels fostered by the tight profit margins of supermarkets. Many hire young and inexperienced cashiers, and management doesn't trust seventeen-year-old cashiers.
>
> As this feudal system affects the supervisors' relations with cashiers, it affects relations with their supervisors as well. In many cases, supervisors approve checks because there is little else for them to do. Virtually all the product-buying decisions are made at the regional or district-manager level. In some supermarkets, supervisors have little responsibility other than scheduling of workers. This gives them something else to do.
>
> It's a fact, Dave, that when a line is held up while a supervisor is paged for check approval, customers get annoyed. Yet this fact seems to be ignored by the by-the-book types who write thick policy manuals yet are oblivious to customer convenience.

This inconvenience is what prompted this Frustable in the first place. If customers are going to be subjected to a long delay while the manager ambles over to the checkout line, at least the inspection of the check shouldn't be so cursory.

Of course, the upper management of supermarket chains could argue that the identification amassed by a supervisor can be vitally important. Lawyer Jim Wright of Decatur, Georgia, informs us that the gathering of backup verification (e.g., social security number, driver's license number) grants the grocer immunity from civil or criminal liability for false arrest or malicious prosecution if the store prosecutes someone:

> In short, by obtaining verification, the manager is covering his butt should the check be bad and a warrant taken out. Quite frequently, when someone is arrested for writing a bad check, the accused claims that some other family member wrote the check without permission. The checking account holder than countersues the retailer for false arrest. If the verification of identity is written on the face of the check, the grocer is granted immunity from all liability for bringing the bad check warrant. He's not looking to reject your check; he's looking to protect himself.

A fascinating thesis, but one that wasn't mentioned by a single retailer.

In fact, we must confess that we have personally approached many grocery store cashiers and managers about this topic. When we ask what they are looking for when they take a passing glimpse at ours and others' checks, the answer is usually, "We're looking at the check number." Typical was the response of Fran Burns of Moneta, Virginia:

> Many banks print the month and year the account was opened on the check. If that isn't printed, we take note of the check number. Presumably, a low check number is a newly opened account. On a recently opened account, we generally will do some additional checkup on the customer.

The "low-number" theory was by far the most popular explanation from our readers, as well. We heard from some employees whose stores use 150 (or 49 checks past the usual 101 first number of checks), 300, and 500 as the demarcation line for additional security, whether it is more identification, calling the bank, or, in some cases, refusing to cash low-numbered checks or starting checks. Still, as we have discussed before, most banks allow new customers to start checking accounts with any number they want on their first checks (many businesses don't want to broadcast the fact that they are starting a new enterprise, and we'd be surprised if cunning bad-check passers would either).

Stephen H. Cook chronicles a cagier strategy:

> Most bad-check crooks have to move fast for their schemes to work consistently. This forces them to use checks with low numbers. The first rule for retail store managers is to be suspicious of low check numbers. Managers are supposed to engage in conversation with anyone presenting such a check, starting with questions along the line of, "New in town? Tell me about your apartment or house? Have you met your new neighbors yet?"
>
> The grocery store manager is then supposed to point where the cleaning and related household supplies aisle is. If the shopper is legitimately new in town and is unfamiliar with the store, this apparent friendliness on the part of the store manager is very welcome, and is good business practice for the retailer. If the person is a crook, all of this attention from the store manager should force a decision to take the bad checks elsewhere.

Sounds like Cook is implying that every grocery store manager is a would-be Columbo, making criminals squirm. And several of our readers were sure that this thesis explains why the examination of the proffered checks is often so cursory. Lane Chaffin of Temple, Texas, wrote:

> The whole rigmarole is to make a would-be bad check writer "sweat it out." If the check writer feels he may be turned down or possibly even recognized as a previous violator, he may change his mind.

Cook confirms that part of a manager's job is to "size up" check writers, and that certain profiles persist that can lead to prejudicial judgments. According to Cook, the best risks for personal checks include:

> 1) clean-cut parents shopping with children
> 2) clean-cut father shopping with children
> 3) well-dressed, well-groomed woman (especially if shopping in the evening after work and before dinner)
> 4) male coming in after work, still wearing a necktie, who is buying a few items
> 5) any clean-cut person who is making a large purchase and who is able to present enough cash to cover most of it, but needs to write a check only for the discrepancy

According to Cook, these are the worst risks:

1) single males buying staples

2) harried, "thirty-something" women, especially if overweight, unattractive, or shopping with children

3) married males buying staples, who present little cash and no credit cards

4) any shopper using food stamps

Says Burns, this list represents the following prejudices:

1) Single males are notorious for being sloppy and disorganized about household habits, including the proper maintenance of a checking account.

2) Unattractive divorced women with children have trouble making ends meet.

3) Suspicion of any married man doing the family grocery shopping by himself.

4) Any person using food stamps is too poor to properly maintain a good checking account.

Some of these prejudices may have enough basis in fact to perpetuate themselves, some are just based on outmoded traditions about who does the grocery shopping.

Grocery store managers are supposed to be suspicious of personal checks because grocery shopping has traditionally been a cash-only business. As a result, grocery stores get more bad checks than other types of retailers from people who are *not* crooks.

In conclusion, the answer to our Frustable is: Grocery store managers can be looking at about twenty-five different things when they give your check the once-over. But if they approve it as quickly and as superficially as most seem to do, either they are not doing their job right or you live in Mayberry R.F.D., or some other place where store managers actually know customers by name and by sight.

Submitted by Chuck Jeffries of Greensboro, North Carolina.

A complimentary book goes to Stephen H. Cook of North Providence, Rhode Island, and to Joseph S. Blake, Jr., of Ottawa, Kansas. Thanks also to the scores of readers who made the same points as our grocery experts but whom we did not have space to quote.

HOW DOES ASPIRIN FIND A HEADACHE?

FRUSTABLE 10: *Why do so many policemen wear mustaches?*

For some reason, civilians were reluctant to speculate about this issue, but we heard from quite a few policemen and friends and relatives of cops. We were surprised that so many responses echoed that of Scott Miles of Santa Monica, California:

> My best friend, Tim, is a police officer. Like many of his fellow officers, Tim has what some would call a "baby face." His features are very soft and his looks lead people to assume, initially, that he is a good-natured, easygoing guy.
>
> In Tim's case, this impression is true, but it is not a very good image for a police officer who needs to command authority. Tim grew a mustache to harden his look, to make him look a little older and tougher.

Of course, some prefer to look older for personal reasons. A few officers repeated the sentiment of Eric Crane of Texarkana, Texas: "My wife won't let me shave mine off because I would look like I'm sixteen years old."

Many readers and police officers mentioned that in our culture, mustaches mean macho. We are left with a chicken/egg problem: Do cops grow mustaches because they are already macho? Or do they appear more macho because they wear a mustache? Clifford Smith, an officer in Anne Arundel County, Maryland, notes that mustaches date back to the very first "cops" in Robert Peel's London service, and that "staches" have always been associated with military and paramilitary men.

Although a young officer might want to project machismo, we're guessing that other factors are more important. Most of the military and police officers we've met, despite the visual image they project, want to express their individuality as persons. Confronted with strict controls over what they can wear and how they can look, a mustache becomes a way to stand out from the crowd. Many cops concurred, among them Ohio police officer Mike Foley:

> We have to have short hair and no beard. The *only* allowance for any "style" is a mustache. Most cops (after a few years) want to look like something other than a boy scout, so they grow one. Plus, it keeps the bosses mad when you don't trim it.

DAVID FELDMAN

Foley's combination of humor and mild rebellion was typical of almost all of the letters we received from police officers. Noncop Bob Kowalski of Detroit, Michigan, aptly summarizes the feelings of many police officers who wrote us:

> Perhaps policemen would not be so keen to have mustaches if police departments weren't so keen on banning them! The old forbidden fruit . . .

And we were moved by this note from the policeman's bulletin board on Prodigy Service. Leo Martin raises a point we had not considered—some cops might tire of looking like cops:

> I am a cop out in northern California, and I've had hair growing from my lip up to my nose for most of my life. It started in the Marine Corps, where the only facial hair you could have was a "stache."
>
> Most police departments have the same policy. I think growing a mustache makes us feel and look more like regular people and less like cops.

We're faced with a paradox. Cops grow mustaches to express their individuality, yet so many cops wear them that it defeats the purpose. This irony was not lost on our favorite self-examination, from admitted baby face Steven J. Schmidt of Covington, Kentucky:

> As a mustache wearer for eighteen of my nineteen years as a policeman, I have some insight into the question. The obvious answer to this Frustable is, "Because they can." Although police departments aren't as paramilitary as they used to be, most policemen cannot wear beards or grow their hair long. A mustache, therefore, becomes a symbol of their individuality.
>
> I know that makes about as much sense as all the people in the 1960s who grew their hair long to demonstrate their "individuality," but there it is. You might notice that a lot of retired policemen and discharged servicemen grow their hair long or grow a beard right after leaving "uniformed" service "just because they can." Once the novelty wears off, they revert to what's comfortable for them.

Schmidt reports that once he turned forty, "I didn't need the mustache to look older anymore. In fact, I cut it off to look younger."

As we mentioned, the cops we heard from demonstrated quite a sense of humor. Here are some of the, er, more unusual solutions to this Frustable:

> I have a "stache" just because it gives me something to do while I drive around for eight hours. You can twist it and pull it for eight hours and you smoke fewer cigarettes. Sounds silly but it works for me. (Bill Pador, Jr., New Jersey)

> I like to make my partner feel like I'm one of *him*. You may not realize that I'm referring to my partner, Max, who is a horse, and also has hair around his lips. (Christopher Landry, New Orleans, Louisiana)

> Now that you mention it, my mustache probably came from off the top of my head. (Greg Wilson, Delaware)

> I guess it was so my kids could pull it when it was time to get up for work. (Alan Levine, Philadelphia)

And, last but not least,

> You can lick the doughnut powder off a mustache for hours after the last coffee break—and it still tastes good. I usually cut mine off in summer because if I don't, everyone knows I've been eating ice cream. Also, a "stache" may act as the last air filter in the air we sometimes have to breathe—I go home and hose it out. Lastly, if a catfish can have one, so can I. (William Howe, IV, Prodigy Service)

Submitted by Steve Propes of Long Beach, California. Thanks also to Laura Arvidson of Westville, Indiana, and Brad Huddleston of Bakersfield, California.

A complimentary book goes to Steven J. Schmidt of Covington, Kentucky. Thanks to all the officers from the Police Topic on the Prodigy Service.

DAVID FELDMAN

The Frustables That Will Not Die

Imponderables readers don't give up. Even though we have partially flushed out the frustration posed by the Frustables in other books, readers want to leave no stone unturned. Your most recent contributions to the demolition of past Frustables are presented here.

Please remember we do not have the space to review all the theories we've already advanced; this section is meant as a supplement, not a substitute, for our discussions in previous books.

Frustables First Posed in *Why Do Clocks Run Clockwise?* and First Discussed in *When Do Fish Sleep?*

FRUSTABLE 1: *Why do you so often see one shoe lying on the side of the road?*

In the past, we've heard from mostly urban SSS (single-shoe syndrome) theorists. But there has been a recent rash of sightings in more bucolic settings, like this one from Donald Mueggenborg of Lemont, Illinois:

> We marathon canoe racers often get our feet wet. One year, it became fashionable to tie our wet shoes to the rear thwart when transporting canoes. The shoes not only dried out but became sort of a sign of fellowship. Often, one shoe would become untied and fall off.
>
> Is there any good way to use one tennis shoe?

Sure, if you are Alyssa Constantine, of New York City. Alyssa lives in a woodsy area of Queens, where hikes and field trips are often conducted by nearby schools, with

> ... students carry bulging backpacks, heavy sleeping bags, and a tote full of life's necessities. Every forty minutes or so, the teacher allows students to take off their shoes and pamper their aching feet.

Every day, I come out and collect forgotten, mateless shoes, lost in the sea of jackets, totes, sleeping bags, etc. I now have at least one hundred different shoes in my basement.

One hundred shoes in the basement? Whatever happened to collecting dolls? Or stamps? We still don't think Alyssa's stash is sufficient to explain the widespread sightings of single shoes on the road. Perhaps the answer could lie in perverse camp counselors? We heard this startling testimony from Mary Beth MacIsaac, from beautiful Cape Breton Island, Nova Scotia:

When I was nine (that was only two years ago), I went to Brownie camp. They had a contest among the cabin mothers to see who could kick off their shoes the farthest. Many of them lost the shoe that they had kicked off. If every Brownie and scout camp did that every year, you can just imagine how many shoes that is.

The mind shudders.

But American citizen Regina Earl thinks that the SSS conspiracy is broader than infiltrating scout camps. Regina has recently come back from a stint in Japan, where she saw an ominous shoe commercial, featuring Charlie Sheen, of all people:

Charlie Sheen is shown lying in the center of a long, deserted road holding one shoe, while a girl drives away in a red convertible holding the other. I know this doesn't provide any answers, but it shows Frustables jumping international borders.

That's okay, Regina. We must confront the scope of a problem before we can solve it. In this spirit, Wayland Kwock of Aiea, Hawaii, was brave enough to share a harrowing article found in the November 1992 *Scientific American,* announcing that on May 27, 1990, a freighter dumped five shipping containers containing eighty thousand Nike shoes into the waters of the Pacific Northwest.

Several scientists decided that the accident afforded them a unique opportunity to study ocean drift. At last report, some of the shoes are heading for Japan (sorry, too late to retrieve them, Regina). Amazingly enough, none of the scientists tracked how many Nikes ended up, singly, on the side of a road.

DAVID FELDMAN

FRUSTABLE 2: *Why are buttons on men's shirts and jackets arranged differently from those on women's shirts?*

We are still receiving loads of mail on this button Frustable. Most people debate the relative merits of what we've already published. But we did receive one new theory this year from Terri Longwell of Richland, Washington:

> Unless I was lied to at a young age, I learned the answer to this question as a sophomore in my high school American history class. The answer dates back to the garment sweat shops in the days before unions. The "piece workers" were paid more for sewing women's garments than for men's. . . . To separate the men's blouses from the women's blouses, which in those days were similar, the buttons were sewn on opposite sides. . . . The employees who were favored by management got the better, more high-paying pieces, which were the women's blouses.

Terri, we think you were probably "lied to." In what era were women's blouses indistinguishable from men's shirts? Weren't the collars totally different?

FRUSTABLE 4: *Why do the English drive on the left and most other countries on the right?*

Readers can't stop debating this Frustable, either. We have nothing new to say, other than that we despair of ever getting a definitive answer. If you want to become more informed, if perhaps more confused, you might want to read a whole book on the subject: *The Rule of the Road: An International Guide to History and Practice,* written by Peter Kincaid (Greenwood Press, 1986). Thanks to reader John P. Hersh of Concord, Massachusetts, for recommending it.

FRUSTABLE 6: *Why do so many people save National Geographics and then never look at them again?*

Mike Teige of Seattle, Washington, tipped us off to the latest literary take on this (literally) weighty subject. In his 1992 book *Clutter Control,* cleaning expert Jeff Campbell devotes an entire chapter to the topic of controlling rampant National Geographic proliferation. Campbell's chapter heading, "They seem to be everywhere," echoes the sentiment that inspired this Frustable:

> As of September 1991 there were approximately 3.784 *billion* copies of *National Geographic* in print, and just about every one of them is still in somebody's garage.

Unfortunately, Campbell provides many more tips about how to get rid of the magazines than theories about why we didn't throw them away in the first place. Still, if Campbell can inspire enough people to get off their duffs and recycle *National Geographic,* we could at least eradicate the intellectual clutter created by this Frustable.

FRUSTABLE 7: *Why do people, especially kids, tend to stick their tongues out when concentrating?*

Reader James D. Kilchenman of Toledo, Ohio, was kind enough to pass on the information that in his recent book, *Babywatching,* anthropologist Desmond Morris weighed in on our debate about this Frustable. Morris notes that children, when rejecting food (either solid, a bottle, or mother's breast), stick out their tongues to push away the food source.

Morris believes that sticking out the tongue is a universal rejection signal, even when used unconsciously. When an adult is concentrating on a difficult task and sticks out the tongue,

DAVID FELDMAN

the tongue is behaving just as it did when, in infancy, it rejected an insistent parent offering food. The message now, as then, is the same, namely: "please leave me in peace."

While we think that the physiological theory presented in *Why Do Dogs Have Wet Noses?* is compelling, Morris's explanation also makes some sense. But we were also taken aback by a letter from reader Mark McGrew of Bucyrus, Ohio, who offers an alternative:

> Human kids are not the only kids to stick out their tongues when they are trying to concentrate. In the Jane Goodall documentary "People of the Forest," you can see a young chimpanzee trying to twirl around, which he can do well only after he begins sticking out his tongue. Perhaps we simply inherited the practice from them.

**Frustables First Posed in *Why Do Dogs Have Wet Noses?*
and First Discussed in *Do Penguins Have Knees?***

FRUSTABLE 1: *Does anyone really like fruitcake?*

We'd like to think that we have been duly modest in boasting about
attempts to edify our readers. After all, we're not dealing with
metaphysics here. Still, every once in a while, we receive a letter that
lets us know we have made a profound difference in someone's life. We
received a moving letter from Howie Saaristo of Norfolk,
Massachusetts, indicating that our modest efforts have changed his life
unalterably for the better:

> For years I ordered and gave away more than a dozen fruitcakes at
> Christmas. Then I read that you asserted that most people do not like
> fruitcake. I was completely astonished! I like fruitcake so much that such
> a thought had never occurred to me.
>
> After some thought, I decided that I had better ascertain the truth.
> I called each one of my former recipients and told them what I had read
> and pleaded with each to tell me the truth.
>
> Out of the lot, it turned out that I was the only one who really liked
> the stuff. The others just suffered in silence. I put a stop to giving them
> away. What a shame they don't know what they are missing!

After such a great start, Howie, we're worried about that last sentence.
We suggest a local twelve-step program.

According to Julia Ecklar of Monroeville, Pennsylvania, the
answer to whether anyone really likes fruitcake is: "Yes, but only when
the fruitcake aficionado has a physical problem." Julia can think of only
two possible reasons for her father's strange predilection: One, he loves
rum, particularly hot buttered rum. Many fruitcakes contain rum,
which, as Ecklar so felicitously puts it, supplies the cake with "its
strong, odious flavor." But we're more concerned with her second
explanation:

> My father has no sense of smell. As far as I know, he never did, and
> it has certainly affected his ability to taste. . . . This lack of taste discrimi-
> nation might also have contributed to his liking of fruitcake.

We're a little upset at the Ecklar extended family for taking advantage of his handicap, for Ecklar reports:

> When I was a kid, all our relatives knew that giving fruitcake to my father would just make his holiday; all our friends knew that they could dispose of unwanted fruitcakes by giving them to us.

Christopher K. Degnan of Whitefield, New Hampshire, theorizes that the reason fruitcake is so unpalatable is that most cakes withhold *the* crucial ingredient: pork. Christopher shared with us a recipe contained in a book called *Vermont Cooking*. The recipe for two loaves includes the usual nuts, molasses, raisins, fruits, eggs, and sugar, as well as "one cup of chopped pork (all fat)." The mind reels.

FRUSTABLE 4: *Where, exactly, did the expression "blue plate special" come from?*

Several correspondents were aghast at the readers quoted in *When Did Wild Poodles Roam the Earth?* who doubted that blue plates were ever actually used in restaurants. Our favorite was Dave Rutherford of Holcomb, New York, who sent us a color snapshot of a classic diner, the Miss Albany Diner in Albany, New York. Right next to the name on the sign above the door was another sign: "Blue Plate Specials." Dave reports that specials advertised on the sign "were and continue to be served on blue plates." Judy Stuart of DeLand, Florida, enclosed an article about the blue willow plates we wrote about in our initial discussion of this topic in *Do Penguins Have Knees?* But Judy has more concrete evidence that blue plates were used in restaurants: Her husband, Dick, worked in diners in the late 1930s and early 1940s and served many a meal on blue plates.

Indeed, we heard from several readers who collect blue willow china. We particularly enjoyed a long discussion by Pat Kaniarz of Harbor Springs, Michigan. Kaniarz confirms that the earliest blue and white china was imported, appropriately enough, from China, and was all hand painted.

With the advent of the Industrial Revolution, English potters figured out how to transfer print designs stolen from uncopyrighted Chinese design. Eventually, the English mass-produced willow patterns in a myriad of colors, but blue and white was always the most popular.

Most blue plate specials were served on divided dishes called "grill plates." According to Kaniarz:

> Those grill plates, once so inexpensive that restaurants let low-paid dishwashers handle them, now are offered in antique shops at twenty to thirty dollars each. Lots of restaurants used blue willow, although not all confined their use to the grill plates.
>
> The restaurant ware is very collectible. Some of us who are hooked on blue willow (we have a newsletter called "The Willow Word" that is subtitled "The Newspaper for People Addicted to Willow-Pattern China") collect only the restaurant ware. Because it was made for heavy use, a lot of it has survived in pretty good condition.

In the three books since *Why Do Dogs Have Wet Noses?*, we have pieced together the origin of the blue plate special, but our initial target still eludes us. We still haven't found *the* restaurant that initiated or inspired the expression.

FRUSTABLE 7: *Why and where did the notion develop that fat people are jolly?*

In *Do Penguins Have Knees?*, we mentioned Shakespeare's Falstaff, the archetypical fat-jolly person. But reader Judith Goldish of Lakewood, California, reminded us of another of the Bard's pronouncements, from Julius Caesar:

> Let me have men about me that are fat;
> Sleek-headed men and such as sleep o' nights.
> Yond Cassius has a lean and hungry look;
> He thinks too much: such men are dangerous.

FRUSTABLE 8: *Why do pigs have curly tails?*

Buhnne Tramutola of Annandale, New Jersey, an ex–pig raiser, confirmed what we have written before—that a curly tail is an indicator of healthiness and happiness, just like a dog's wagging tail. If the pig's tail was not curly, we would check into its health or living conditions.

Old news. But Tramutola has something new to contribute. Pigs' tails were once used to grease pancake griddles. According to an unidentified book he sent, a pig's tail "would last for weeks if kept cold. But mostly the extra fat was used in soap making." That would be enough to curl our tails.

FRUSTABLE 9: *Why does the heart depicted in illustrations look totally different from a real heart?*

We thought we exhausted the possibilities in this question. But we were wrong. In *Do Penguins Have Knees?*, we mentioned Desmond Morris's theory that our Valentine's heart is an idealized version of the female buttocks; reader Kierstyn Piotrowski of Parsippany, New Jersey, with the help of Kassie Schwan, presents a similar, ingenious theory:

> If you put the profile of a man and woman in a "kissing position" (excluding the inevitable turning of heads to avoid nose bumping), it looks roughly like this.

Jerry Tucker of Burton, Michigan, claims that the secret to this Frustable has been unlocked for centuries by fellow Native Americans:

> Take a walk in the woods. Any bush or shrub that has a leaf shaped like the Valentine heart has medicinal qualities especially beneficial to the human heart.
>
> We have for centuries identified medically beneficial shrubs and bushes by the shapes of their leaves. This particular shape was adopted by white people to represent their concepts of love, romance, etc.

We're not sure, though, how this theory accounts for the spread of the "leaf-shaped" heart to non–Native Americans. Tucker presented us with some leads to confirm his theory, and we'll report back if we find out more.

FRUSTABLE 10: *Where do all the missing pens go?*

Two readers have taken us to task for our secular-humanist explanations for the disappearance of pens. The answer, they insist, lies in felonious felines. To wit: Here is the sworn testimony of Rainham D.M.H. Rowe of Jacksonville, Florida:

> One morning I was faced with the task of finding my wedding rings, after I had left them on the kitchen counter the night before. I happen to have three cats, two of which are notorious for climbing on the counter, where they know they aren't supposed to be, to find things to play with.
>
> One cat in particular loves the little rings that come off milk jugs. I figured this cat must have seen my rings and thought they were milk jug rings and knocked them off the counter to play with.
>
> I began my search by shining a flashlight into every crevice in the kitchen, to no avail. I then pulled out the appliances. Under the range I found a handful of magnetic ABCs, about ten milk jug rings, and lo and behold, *five pens*. There was a similar sight under my refrigerator.
>
> I eventually found my rings under the computer desk, and found *another handful of pens,* piles of paper that had fallen out of the back drawer, and a toy car. So if *Imponderables* fans have cats, perhaps their pens are being used as nocturnal entertainment.

DAVID FELDMAN

Rainham, you won't convince Janet Sappington of Hope Mills, North Carolina, otherwise. In her cats' "hidey holes," she has found numerous pens, as well as pen caps, coins, lighters, socks (oh, that's where the missing socks are!), and once, a whole shirt.

Frustables First Posed in *Do Penguins Have Knees?* and First Discussed in *When Did Wild Poodles Roam the Earth?*

FRUSTABLE 1: *Why do doctors have bad penmanship?*

We thought we exhausted this topic in *Poodles,* but two readers raised points that we never considered. David A. Crowder of Miami, Florida, stresses that penmanship is not stressed or valued highly in schools, particularly for boys:

> As a child, I got excellent grades in all subjects but penmanship. My parents, who would have hit the ceiling had I gotten less than a B in any other subject, would shrug at a D in penmanship—after all, their son was going to be a doctor!
>
> With no pressure to perform in this subject, and no apparent benefit otherwise, I would never put much effort into it.

We doubt if penmanship is highly prized in medical school, either. But Crowder feels that there may be neurological reasons why doctors might tend to have poor penmanship:

> As Betty Edwards points out in her seminal book *Drawing on the Right Side of the Brain,* "you can regard your handwriting as a form of expressive drawing." That is, there is an artistic form to handwriting, an indication of, among other things, artistic ability and perception. Since good artwork is predominately right-brain activity, it is not surprising that any sort of scientist or technician, whose life, work, experience, and study involve mainly left-brain activity, would be deficient in a right-brain function (after all, who can be good at everything?).

Crowder indicates that he never became a doctor but that his "lousy handwriting" led directly to his career in computers. We can testify though, after seeing David's signature, that he would have made a *fine* physician.

In *When Did Wild Poodles Roam the Earth?*, we mentioned that on occasion physicians might deliberately attempt to obscure their handwriting for relatively benign reasons. But Rose Marie Centofanti of Chicago, Illinois, offers a far darker scenario:

DAVID FELDMAN

I am a member of a profession called "health information manager." Part of our professional responsibilities entails the legalities of medical records.

The documentation in a medical search is primarily the responsibility of physicians. If a case is brought before a jury in a court of law, the medical record may be subpoenaed as evidence. The physicians will also be subpoenaed and have to read aloud their documentation as testimony in court.

Because their penmanship is illegible in most cases, they can state they've written just about anything.

FRUSTABLE 3: *Why don't people wear hats as much as they used to?*

Several readers wanted to add another motivator for uncovered pates, at least for females: the Catholic church. Typical were the remarks of Vega Soghomomian of Maple Grove, Minnesota, who wrote:

> In the Catholic church, females were *required* to wear a head cover. (We would not want to offend God!) If a woman forgot her hat, she wore a hanky or even a piece of tissue paper on her head. With the women's movement, the Catholic church removed the rule and women went out and bared their heads to the world.

FRUSTABLE 4: *How and why were the letters B-I-N-G-O selected for the game of the same name?*

Not too much to report here, other than a fascinating theory by Rick Biddle, president and general manager of WOWL-TV, an NBC affiliate in Florence, At The Shoals, Alabama. Biddle was once responsible for producing, directing, and starring in a television bingo show, and heard from a bingo supplier that the expression in question is an acronym:

> Think of what it would be like if you filled all the numbers on your bingo card. At the same time, three or four other people filled in the numbers on their cards and you all jumped up simultaneously yelling, "I've placed all the little balls in the holes with corresponding numbers and have won the game!"

Rather than going through this rather lengthy dissertation, the word bingo is derived from, "*Balls In Numbers Game Over.*"

We know for a fact that the original bingo markers were not balls, but beans and seeds, which makes this theory less than likely to be true.

FRUSTABLE 8: *How did they measure hail before golf balls were invented?*

We received, pardon the expression, a flood of letters about this Frustable in the past year. Most were variations on the analogies to edibles (e.g., peas, eggs, walnuts) we discussed in *Poodles.* But four different readers directed us to what might be the first written reference to the size of hail in the Western canon, Revelation 16 verse 21: "And great hail from heaven fell upon men, each stone about the weight of a talent."

According to reader L. Ray Black of Arcadia, Florida, the talent was the largest of the Hebrew units of weight. Two Davids from Keizer, Oregon, Messrs. Engle and Volkov, indicated that the talent fluctuated over time from fifty to one hundred pounds. Reader Dale Gilbert of Chillicothe, Ohio, adds that the Bible indicates that hailstones provoked men to blaspheme God, "for the plague thereof was exceeding great."

Now that *Imponderables* books are being published overseas, we are starting to hear reports from far-flung ponderers. Emmanuelle Pingault reports that in France, hailstones in weather reports are invariably, if unsurprisingly, compared to foodstuffs.

> A small hailstone may be compared to a nut (in French, *noisette*), while a larger one will be "as large as a walnut" (*gros comme une noix*). But the more frequent set of comparisons, regularly heard in weather reports, is as follows: as large as a pigeon's egg; as large as a hen's egg; and larger than a hen's egg.

Emmanuelle wonders how many of us have actually ever seen a pigeon egg. We now know why Imponderables are universal—the seeming nonexistence of baby pigeons was one of the original inspirations for our first book, *Imponderables.*

But all the other efforts of readers pale before the research undertaken by reader Chip Howe of Washington, D.C., who conducted a

DAVID FELDMAN

Nexis database search of newspaper weather reports and proved conclusively that we sorely overestimated the ubiquity of "golf ball" analogies to the size of hail. We're proud to announce that literary imagination is not dead. Here are the categories and some of the quotes that Chip found in newspapers over the last six years:

• *Sports:* softball-sized; tennis ball-sized; baseball-sized; golf ball-sized, of course; marble-sized; and ping pong ball-sized.

• *Food:* grapefruit-sized; orange-sized; lime-sized; cherry-sized; egg-sized; walnut-sized; "hail the size of Spanish olives"; bean-sized; pea-sized; butterbean-sized; ice cube–sized; and our personal favorite, dry roasted peanut-sized hail, from Georgia, the peanut state.

• *Money:* Chip could almost start a coin collection. He found references to every current denomination of American coinage except the silver-dollar.

• *Body Parts:* "Hail the size of babies' toes" and this scary report from Canada: ". . . after a torrential thunderstorm had pelted Edmonton with fist-sized hail stones."

• *Two-for-one:* pea- to marble-sized hail and quarter to tennis ball-sized hail.

• *Nature's Own:* acorn-sized hail; pellet-sized hail; pebble-sized hail; mothball-sized hail; and a contribution from Bulgaria (snowball-sized hail), a country that must have more uniformity of snowball size than we do in North America.

FRUSTABLE 10: *Why does meat loaf taste the same in all institutions?*

When we first posed this Frustable in *Do Penguins Have Knees?*, we mused: "Does the government circulate a special Marquis de Sade Cookbook?" One reader, Carl Bittenbender of Staunton, Virginia, answers "yes":

> Many institutions of all kinds, college, military, hospitals, etc., use the armed forces menu cards, which give recipes for cooking hundreds of meals at a time. The cards give formulas for figuring the amounts of ingredients needed for large recipes. This accounts for the bland, tasteless quality of many of the recipes, as they are designed to be eaten by people who do not have a choice.

Reader George E. Jackson, Jr., of Mantua, Ohio, notes that the federal government supplies many institutions with surplus food and that they are

> extremely picky about their suppliers meeting stringent specifications. . . . As an example of what I mean: the military recipe for fruitcake is eight pages in length. Perhaps if you contacted the Government Printing Office, you might be able to get their recipes for meat loaf and fruitcake.

Sorry. We'd rather write the IRS, asking them to please audit us.

Of course, the government has its civilian culinary counterparts in the large institutional catering companies, such as Marriott and ARA. As Mike Tricarico, Jr., of Dubuque, Iowa, puts it:

> The meat loaf you had last month for lunch at a hospital in New York was very possibly made by the same company, following the same recipe, as the meat loaf that you ate yesterday at an IBM cafeteria in southern California. Marriott also serves food on airlines, so it is even possible that you had the very same meat loaf on board flight 123 from New York to southern California. Hopefully, this entree was not followed by fruitcake!

Is it our fate for fruitcake to follow us everywhere? We're talking meat loaf, now.

Only one reader was willing to plumb the ineffable essence of meat loaf. And that savior is Wayland Kwock of Aiea, Hawaii:

> It boggles the mind that nobody would be brave enough to expose the meat loaf conspiracy. Closer inspection would probably show that meat loaf is served on Friday, the end of the week. The day to get rid of all the "extra" food, the dregs, the leftovers. All of this goodness is unceremoniously included in the meatloaf.
>
> So why does it taste the same? Mathematics, specifically probability, provides the answer. If an infinite number of monkeys . . . No, that's not quite right. If an infinite number of institutions served an infinite variety of food, the amounts and types of leftovers would tend to form a Gaussian distribution. This means that there may be meat loafs out there that taste better (not better—different), but they are outside one, if not two, standard deviations. All other meat loafs contain an average amount of a generic sampling of foods and thus, on average, taste the same.

We don't understand a word that Wayland says here, but we smell greatness. Or is that fruitcake we smell?

LETTERS

Imponderables readers have continued to flood our post office box with thousands of letters in the past year. We appreciate all your new Imponderables and solutions to Frustables. And we wouldn't be human if your words of praise didn't put a spring in our step. But this section is reserved for those of you who have a bone to pick with us: Some of you want to add to what we've discussed; others want to disagree with what we thought were words of wisdom.

Please remember we can publish only a fraction of the terrific letters we receive. Many of you have submitted corrections or suggestions that we will be researching; we will check out your concerns even if we don't publish your letter. Because of the mechanics of publishing, it can sometimes take years to validate objections and change the text on subsequent printings, but we do so regularly. The letters contained here are chosen for their entertainment value and the merit of their argument. Let the bashing begin!

Is it Clintonomics? The coming millennium? We don't know why, but Imponderables readers were particularly testy this year. Sometimes for good reason. Several readers, such as Jon A. Kapecki of Rochester, New York, took us to task for our discussion of peanut M&Ms:

> Nuts may indeed be "the source of one of the most common food allergies," as you assert on page 56 of *Do Penguins Have Knees?* However, peanuts—the subject of discussion—are not nuts, but legumes, specifically members of the pea family.
>
> This is no pedantic distinction. People who are allergic to nuts are usually not allergic to peanuts and vice versa, and a failure to observe such distinctions can have fatal consequences.
>
> That said, I enjoyed the book.

Gee, Jon, that's a little like saying other than being mass murderers, we have a pleasant personality. But you are right. Peanuts are not technically nuts, and we should have been more careful in our terminology. Violent allergic reactions both to peanuts and other nuts are common, but someone who reacts to pecans or walnuts may suffer no adverse effect from consuming peanuts.

Speaking of getting sick, two more faithful readers and correspondents, Rabbi Joseph Braver of Baltimore, Maryland, and Fred Lanting of Union Grove, Alabama, wrote to complain that our dis-

cussion of the snake emblem found on ambulances in When Did Wild Poodles Roam the Earth? *was woefully incomplete. For the associations of the snake and the pole have Jewish and Christian as well as Roman and Greek significance. In Numbers 21, the wandering Israelites were afflicted by snakes sent by God to punish them for speaking against Him. Moses interceded on behalf of his suffering followers:*

> Then the Lord said to Moses, "Make a seraph figure and mount it on a standard. And if anyone who is bitten looks at it, he shall recover." Moses made a copper serpent and mounted it on a standard; and when anyone was bitten by a serpent, he would look at the copper serpent and recover.

Fred Lanting points out that the snake and staff symbolism continues in the New Testament and asserts that "the Greek myths were corruptions of the stories of Israel's experiences with this Old Testament healing.

While we're on the subject of vehicles, readers are still trying to figure out where the old oil lurks in automobiles after oil changes. In Do Penguins Have Knees? *we could account for much but not all of the disappearing oil. We heard from Dan Kiser of Elmira, New York, a student studying automotive technology. If you combine Dan's account with our previous discussion, we think this Imponderable is finally nailed:*

> Assuming that the engine is warm and that it does indeed have five quarts of oil, here is where the oil "lurks." Most all engines are made out of cast iron and manufactured by a process where cast iron is poured into a sand mold. This process creates a rough texture on the surface of the engine block. Oil will cling to this surface because of the rough texture of the block. Oil will settle mainly in the lifter galley (located directly under the intake manifold). It will also accumulate on the top surfaces of the cylinder heads.
>
> The crankshaft and connecting rods in your engine ride on a thin film of oil between two bearing halves. If oil was not present here all of the time, your engine would self-destruct due to lack of lubrication. There is about .003 clearance between these bearing halves and the crank or rods. This oil will not drain out during an oil change.

Oil will also stay inside the oil pump and oil pump pickup during an oil change. The lifters in an engine operate the pushrods, which in turn open the valves. These lifters (one for each valve, sixteen in a V-8 engine) are of the hydraulic type: They are filled with oil during their lifetime. This oil will not drain during an oil change, either.

If you were to drain the oil out of your engine and then put the drain plug back in, you would have to wait several weeks before any of the oil in the aforementioned spots drained into the pan. . . .

I have had the opportunity to rebuild several engines. In each case, the oil was drained and the engine was allowed to sit for several weeks. By the time I started to disassemble the engine, residual oil had drained into the pan, resulting in about three-quarters of a quart of oil on my garage floor when I pulled the oil pan off.

Oil wasn't the only liquid on your minds over the past year. Many of you are concerned about water, in particular, bodies of water. In Do Penguins Do Knees? *we discussed the difficulties in differentiating a lake from a pond. Several readers insisted there was a distinction. Typical was this letter from Bill O'Donnell of Eminence, Missouri:*

As an ecosystem, a pond is defined as a body of water of such a depth that light can penetrate all the way to the bottom, allowing rooted submergent vegetation to grow across the entire bottom. Lakes are deeper, so that rooted plants cannot draw at the deepest parts. They also have differences in temperature, called thermoclines, which ponds usually lack. Of course, many true ponds are called lakes and vice versa, but as you said, people can get away with calling most things anything they want.

Exactly, Bill. We're talking apples and oranges. We were discussing geographical definitions, and you are speaking of biological ones.

More liquids? In When Did Wild Poodles Roam the Earth? *we discussed what we are smelling when it "smells like rain." Ron Smith of Winnipeg, Manitoba, wants to supplement our explanation:*

Just before a storm, the barometric pressure decreases. Rising air reduces surface pressure and produces condensation, quite often resulting in cloud formation and frequently precipitation. The reduced surface pressure causes slight gas release from the soil resulting in a fresh or "earthy" smell.

A fellow Canadian, Gilles Fournier of Calgary, Alberta, wanted us to know that in local folklore, the "H" in the "C" of the Montreal Canadiens stands not for "hockey" but for "habitants":

> In the English media, the Montreal Canadiens are often affectionately called "the Habs." Most people believe that Habs is short for "habitants," the French word often used to mean "farmer" in Quebec. What do farmers have to do with hockey? Many of the Canadiens wunderkinder came and still come from the rural areas of the Belle Province . . . so from Habitants, to Habs, to . . . the H in the C!

In Why Do Dogs Have Wet Noses?, *we discussed why there is no channel 1 on televisions. Gilles wanted to add:*

> the FCC (and its Canadian counterpart, the CRTC) gave it back to radio buffs because channel 1 was a poor TV performer, riddled with ghost images. That frequency was just too prone to interference from other radio frequencies.

Most of your complaints this year have been about our discussions of technology. We can always count on a few correspondents to offer constructive criticisms about our explanations of gadgets and widgets. One of our more irrepressible contributors is William Sommerwerck of Bellevue, Washington:

> When Did Wild Poodles Roam the Earth? states that 9-volt "transistor" batteries are rectangular because they take the shape of six stacked cylindrical cells.
> This is absolutely, utterly, completely, and *totally* wrong, wrong, Wrong, *Wrong*, WRONG!!!
> The cells in a 9-volt battery are rectangular. They look like little sardine cans, but (as a friend said) without the key. If your so-called "expert" had ever bothered to open one, he or she would have seen this.

But how do you really *feel about our discussion, Bill? You motivated us to call back several battery companies, and all we can tell you is that if the cells of 9-volt batteries are rectangular, the technical staffs at Eveready, Duracell, and Panasonic don't know about it. Eveready's 9-volt alkaline battery, for example, contains six quad-A cells, which are now being marketed separately as E-96 batteries and are used primarily in penlight flashlights and laser pointers. Perhaps, William, you are thinking about less popular carbon-zinc batteries, which often contain rectangular or "cake" cells stacked atop one another inside the case.*

Believe us, William Sommerwerck isn't our only correspondent with a bee in his bonnet. By far the angriest and most vociferous mail we received this year came from the eight readers who violently objected to a letter we published in Poodles *about why tape counters on audio and video tape players don't seem to measure anything. We quoted an electronics engineer who claimed that tapes didn't run at a constant speed. Thank you, Stan Sieger, Michael Javernick, Dallas Brozik, Nils J. Dahl, Jr., Charles Kluepfel, Jim Tanenbaum, and Bruce Hyman for setting us straight; but we'll quote the letter from John B. Dinius, of West Hartford, Connecticut, because his explanation is simple enough for even us technoramuses:*

All audio tape recorders (with the possible exception of some really cheap models that would be considered toys) move the tape past the heads at a constant speed, by using a capstan and pinch roller. The function of the takeup reel is not to control the speed of the tape but merely to collect the tape after it passes the capstan/pinch roller device. This constant tape speed is evidenced by the fact that technical specifications for tape recorders always express the tape speed in terms of inches per second (e.g., cassette tapes play at 1-7/8 inches per second).

Your correspondent suggests that the tape passes the read/write heads of a VCR faster towards the end of a movie because the effective diameter of the takeup reel has been increased by the tape that has been collected. In fact, you can observe (by noting the number on the counter every fifteen minutes while the tape is running) that the tape counter runs more and more slowly as the movie progresses. This indicates that the takeup reel has to turn more and more slowly in order to collect the tape, which is moving past the heads at a constant speed.

As far as the original question is concerned, the reason [why tape counter numbers seem arbitrary] is that they measure revolutions of the takeup reel, which don't bear a constant relationship to the things that people really care about (i.e., how many minutes into the tape they are, and how much time is left on the tape). Note that if the reel actually ran at a constant speed, as your correspondent suggested, then the number of revolutions would be proportional to the elapsed time of the tape, and people could use the counter numbers fairly well, by realizing that a certain number of revolutions represented one minute of tape.

As Dinius mentions later in his letter, fortunately for us, most VCRs now use time counters, which measure information much more important to the average consumer. Our next angriest group of correspondents challenged the comments of a source in When Did Poodles Roam the Earth? *who discussed why trees on a slope don't grow perpendicular to the ground. Our first correspondent is Stanley Sieger of Pasadena, California:*

> Hardly one of his sentences is without error *or worse.* He attributes "motivation" to trees, claims that light provides trees with food (rather than just the energy to "digest" the food they absorb), claims that in a forest the source of light is "up," etc.
>
> But worse, oh so much worse, is his confusing geomagnetism with gravitation and claiming that there are places of "abnormal" gravity on this planet. Wrong!

The original reference was to the Oregon Vortex in Gold Mill, Oregon, where our source said that "it is reported" that trees grow in a contorted fashion because of abnormal gravitational forces. Scot Morris joins Sieger in (justifiably) abusing us for allowing these statements to go uncriticized. Morris, a regular contributor to Games *magazine, personally conducted an investigation of the Oregon Vortex, published in the December 1987 edition of* Omni, *and proved that this place where balls that appeared to roll uphill was clearly an illusion.*

Another reader, David A. Crowder of Miami, Florida, has a bone to pick with another one of our sources, who in Do Penguins Have Knees? *claimed that surge protectors can protect your VCR from damage during lightning storms:*

> A surge suppressor will only protect against minor power surges and spikes such as commonly occur in any electrical line. . . . Lightning, though, is far more powerful than anything any surge suppressor or line stabilizer is capable of handling. A lightning strike will simply blow the surge suppressor as it fries your VCR or computer.

While we're on the subject of things technological, Howard L. Helman of Manhattan Beach, California, rightfully comments that our discussion of "Where do computer files and programs go when they are erased?" was correct for MS-DOS machines but not necessarily for other operating systems:

> As far as I know, MS-DOS is the only system that uses the signa character to mark the deletion. Other systems usually have a flag in the directory to mark the entry free.

While we're speaking of computers, we heard from Harold Gaines of St. Louis, Missouri:

> I must comment on your response to the question, "Since computer paper is longer than it is wide, why are computer monitors wider than they are long?" Your answer is fine, except that an important fact was overlooked. The reason virtually all computer displays are eighty characters wide (especially terminals on multiuse systems) is because the first popular highspeed input devices for computers were card readers. The now almost obsolete IBM Hollerith card held exactly eighty characters. The first monitors were used as an adjunct to the card readers; the most obvious format was a width of eighty characters (one card per line). . . .
>
> As for the number of lines, I am sure that this was chosen for hard ware reasons. However, the twenty-four-line standard is a multiple of eight, as is eighty, and computer people *love* eights.

In When Did Wild Poodles Roam the Earth? *we quoted an official of the American Banking Association who stated that the little pieces of white paper attached to the bottom of our checks were inserted when a typist made a mistake, and that these MICR numbers cannot be erased. The answer was correct as far as it goes, but reader Jeff Reese of Mosinee, Wisconsin, works for a company that sells a solvent that does erase those little numbers on the bottom of the check. He also adds that some banks use small stickers in lieu of a strip that runs along the bottom of the entire check.*

We told you in Poodles *that many drivers in cold climates wire cardboard to their grills to keep cold air from entering the engine. But one reader, Bruce Hyman of Short Hills, New Jersey, added some "lore" on the subject:*

Years ago, cars did not have thermostats in the radiator system, and the only way to keep the coolant warm enough (an oxymoron, of sorts) was to restrict the air flow to the radiator. Early cars sometimes had a pullchain from the radiator grill (which at that time was a set of venetian blind–type slats) into the passenger compartment, letting the driver control the amount of air to the radiator, and hence the engine water temperature.

At this point, these [makeshift equivalents of] "radiator blinds" are totally useless as long as the car has a functioning 180 degree Fahrenheit or hotter thermostat, because the thermostat controls the water temperature. Thermostats are placed in a housing with three hose connections: from the engine; to the radiator; and back to the engine. If the radiator gets too much cooling air, the thermostat simply closes down, and the water recirculates back to the engine through the "bypass" hose.

In When Do Fish Sleep? *we analyzed why most cameras are black. Freelance photographer Grace B. Weinstein of Los Angeles, California, adds two more reasons:*

Most cameras are black, with chrome trim, the chrome trim giving it a "classier" appearance. As a camera with chrome trim gets older and used more often, the chrome tends to wear off, while the black part stays black. It would take a pretty penny to have the worn chrome rechromed, but the black part can be refinished easily with matte paint. Another reason for a camera being all black is that chrome parts would catch the light and bring attention to the camera. A photographer who is working under cover would not like to bring attention to his camera because of the reflective catch lights in the chrome, which would act as a mirror that catches the light.

But not all our readers were concerned with technological Imponderables. Scott McDougall of Boise, Idaho, wanted to add another reason why dance studios are so often located on the second floor, a weighty question we tangled with in Do Penguins Have Knees?

As you noted in your answer, dance studios are most often located in commercial buildings, which usually have a concrete floor on the main level. Concrete is hard and nonresilient. Older commercial buildings of the type that typically house dance studios will have wood joists

DAVID FELDMAN

supporting a wood or wood composite floor beginning on the second level; this type of floor is gentler on the legs and provides more spring. That's the reason given when a dance company once rented space from me.

Speaking of movement, we received a long letter from Rick Ballard of East Lansing, Michigan, who says that he logs about 35,000 miles per year. He wanted to add to our discussion of why traffic on highways tends to clump together in bunches, which we discussed in Why Do Dogs Have Wet Noses?

You correctly point out that bunching behavior on interstates is partly explained by slower cars in the passing lane, but you don't offer any reasons why they stay there. Several factors in rural interstate bunching need to be mentioned:

- Once you have a bunch, it tends to stay a bunch because passing is physically more difficult for the faster cars behind. Some drivers would rather tailgate than pass. Truck convoys are the prime example. They effectively change two lanes into one, and inevitably increase bunching. The faster cars have to be in the passing lane longer just to get around. . . .
- Cruise control is a mixed factor. It definitely contributes to extended time in the passing lane. Many cars will c-r-e-e-p around the slower car because they are unwilling to speed up slightly to complete their pass. Likewise, they are hesitant to go back into the right lane when passing a spaced string of traffic, because they may have to tap the brakes to wait for a faster car before they can pass the next car ahead. So instead, they continue passing a 63-mph string of traffic at 64 mph, blissfully ignoring the bunch growing behind them. But cruise control may also reduce bunching, by creating a disincentive to tailgate.
- Drivers with radar detectors, and other fast drivers, contribute to bunching. Cars will frequently speed up to tag behind faster cars (especially with radar detectors) because they assume that if there is a speed trap, the driver ahead will either slow down or will be the one ticketed.

The psychology of drivers is an elusive one, indeed, but few humans are as fragile as the expectant father. Sandra Stout of Colonial Heights,

Virginia, felt that we missed the boat in our discussion in When Did Poodles Roam the Earth? *of why you see folks boiling water during home deliveries in movies and television.*

Your answer was way off the mark. It has nothing to do with sterilizing things. I noticed that both of the experts you quoted were males, and you being male, the "sterilization theory" made sense. That is because the true purpose of the water boiling is for your gender.

When a baby is delivered at home, the husband, under normal conditions, becomes concerned about the amount of pain his wife is in and wants to help as much as possible. What he ends up doing is getting underfoot. So the midwife or female in charge will send the male, or in some cases the other children in the family, to boil some water so that he is out of the way but feels as if he is being helpful. That is why you never see the water—it never is used for anything.

More male bashing, heh. Doesn't anyone love us? Well, we guess Karen Friend of Baltimore, Maryland, loves us, sort of:

I'm a big fan of yours. Although I have no practical knowledge, I've read all your books and can consequently impress hordes of people at cocktail parties.

Gee, Karen, there's nothing you could possibly say that would make us prouder.

Speaking of pride, we have to eat ours, for we made a misstatement in When Did Wild Poodles Roam the Earth? *We stated that one of the reasons why horses might not vomit is because they must eat at a virtually nonstop pace to derive proper nutrition. We heard from veterinarian Robert E. Habel, one of the foremost ungulate specialists on the planet:*

The horse does not have to keep its stomach full; it has a capacious intestine and does not have to eat continuously, as thousands of trail riders could tell you.

My theory is that the main difference between the vomiters and the nonvomiters (other than alcohol consumption) may be in the brain, where the vomiting reaction center is located. Dogs and people may have evolved this protective mechanism because they swallow lots of nasty things (as you point out) that need to be vomited. Cows and horses don't.

DAVID FELDMAN

And while we are eating crow (but not vomiting it), may we apologize for a silly error in Poodles? In an offhand analogy in our discussion of why people don't wear hats as often as they used to, we contrasted the impact of John F. Kennedy's hatless inaugural with the popularity of the undershirt after Clark Gable flaunted one in It Happened One Night. We meant, of course, to say that Gable appeared without an undershirt and that sales of the apparel quickly plummeted (or so the legend goes). We were surprised that only two readers, Arnold Hecht of Greensboro, North Carolina, and Charles Raphael of Montreal, Quebec, wrote to nail us on what may be our most ridiculous mistake since we transposed the meanings of "diameter" and "circumference" in our first book, Imponderables.

Hmmm. Now we seem to be self-bashing. Let's escape to the comfort of hearing from some readers theorizing about perennial Imponderables. You still seem to want to talk about why there are dents on the top of cowboy hats, which we first discussed in Do Penguins Have Knees? Daniel Coppersmith of Mishawaka, Indiana, weighs in with an interesting theory:

> I have always believed that the dent was to allow rainwater to drain off the hat. If the hat were flat, water would stand on top of the hat and increase the chances of the water soaking in and leaking on the head of the cowboy. The front of a properly worn cowboy hat has a lip on the front brim. This keeps the water rolling off the top of the hat from splashing onto the face of the wearer.

We always thought the brim was more important for keeping the sun out of the eyes, and there's no particular reason why a cowboy hat couldn't have a rounded top. But since you didn't bash us, we're hardly going to insult you. Nor will we bad-mouth John A. Steer of Durham, North Carolina, whose surname lends him special qualification to theorize about cowboy hats:

> Here is another approach: How about convenience? In the days when cowboy hats were designed nearly all men, even cowboys, behaved as gentlemen should and tipped their hats on meeting and greeting ladies.

HOW DOES ASPIRIN FIND A HEADACHE?

In the East at that time, men wore derbies, homburgs, and even top hats. These all have stiff brims; thus, without a dent to grab hold of, they could still easily tip their hats. The cowboys' rough life required a soft hat that could be knocked back into shape when required—for some that may have been often. The dent was their hat handle.

We're almost through the Letters section, but there seems to be something missing. What could it possibly be? Oh, of course. A discussion of boots on the top of ranchers' fenceposts. It's with a slowly trickling tear down the side of one cheek that we announce that this is the first year since the publication of Why Do Clocks Run Clockwise? *that we received no new theories about the resons for their appearance. But at least Robert M. Brown of Bellevue, Washington, provided us with an exciting new sighting. Robert sent us a clip from his local paper, the* Journal American, *in which reporter Liz Enbysk profiles Warren Oltmann, whose boots are displayed on Highway 203 south of Carnation, Washington:*

> "If I can make one person smile per day I figure I've done something good," Oltmann figures. Besides, what else would you do with seven pairs of worn-out boots?

We feel the same way. If we can make one person smile per day, we're happy. Strike that. We'll settle for one living thing and/or one feline per day. We received this note from Catherine Greene, a ninth-grader from Silver Spring, Maryland:

> I adore your books, and so does my cat, Frances. She sits in my lap and pretends to read your books while I read them!

Better this way, Catherine, than if Frances read the books and you pretended to read them.

Having contended already in this book with the neverending debate about why we find one shoe on the side of the road so often, we are loath to open up the following can of worms. Still, we couldn't resist sharing this related conundrum, sent to us by Charlene Ingulfsen of Asheville, North Carolina:

DAVID FELDMAN

Why do I so often see loops of audio cassette tape beside the road? I've never lost a tape out the window of my car, but maybe that's the way others dispose of their tapes.

Something else I've noticed—I recently moved to North Carolina from Oklahoma. Loops of tape by the roadside aren't as common here as they were in Oklahoma and Texas. I wonder why. But I spent several months in Norway, and I often saw tape on the roadside in that lovely country as well.

Off the top of our head, Charlene, wouldn't it seem most likely that you are seeing the remnants of cassettes that were jammed in auto cassette decks? But do you expect us to know about the regional variations in audio cassette side-of-the-road dumping? Golly, do you think we are everywhere? Well, come to think of it, at least one reader, Ken Giesbers of Seattle, Washington, does think we're everywhere:

You live in New York City. HarperCollins Publishers are based in New York City. You conducted a survey of Philadelphia bakeries in response to the Imponderable in *When Did Wild Poodles Roam the Earth?* about seven layer cakes. So why do we send our Imponderables to Los Angeles? Are you omnipresent?

We've been reluctant to admit it until know, Ken, but yes indeed, we are omnipresent. It's hard work, being omnipresent, but we will stop at nothing to gather knowledge in our ever-vigilant fight to stamp out Imponderability. As a matter of fact, we have to sign off right now so that we can fight the good fight.

So have a safe and happy year, readers. And please behave: We can check up on you. Don't you remember? We're omnipresent.

Acknowledgments

Change is a constant, but the support and enthusiasm of the readers of Imponderables books is one of the few things I can always count on. Your letters are the lifeblood of this book, not only because you offer Imponderables and Frustables solutions but because your criticisms let me know where I've gone wrong, and your praise inspires me to keep working.

In the past year, I've tried to reply to your letters in a speedier fashion; most of the time, I have succeeded. Please be patient if it takes me a while to get back to you. Particularly when I'm on the road publicizing a book or in the throes of writing a new manuscript, I may have to slow down the correspondence. But rest assured I read every word of every letter I receive and still answer all mail that comes with a self-addressed stamped envelope.

It is with bittersweetness that I acknowledge my editor, Rick Kot, for all of his help over the last six years. Rick is leaving behind a trail of friends and admirers as he departs HarperCollins, and I'm at the top of that long list.

Rick's assistant, Sheila Gilooly, a gifted editor in her own right, has also flown the coop to pursue bigger and better things. Thank you, Sheila, for making my work not only easier but more fun.

Thankfully, all my other "main squeezes" at HarperCollins are still around to make it a wonderful place for an author. Thanks to Craig Herman for guiding my publicity for the past five years and to Wende Gozan for her indefatigable enthusiasm while booking my tour for *Poodles* and this book (this is her *Headache* as well as mine).

Every year, it seems the production schedule gets more hectic. Special thanks to the team that help make my prose coherent and the package attractive: Kim Lewis, Maureen Clark, Janet Byrne, Karen Malley, and Suzanne Noli.

Even the Grand Pooh Bahs at HarperCollins have been consistently gracious and supportive. Thanks to Bill Shinker, Roz Barrow, Brenda Marsh, Pat Jonas, Zeb Burgess, Karen Mender, Steve Magnuson, Robert Jones, Joe Montebello, Susan Moldow, Clinton Morris, and Steven Sorrentino. Connie Levinson and Mark Landau, and the entire special markets department, have been a constant source of creative ideas and friendship. And we can't even talk about the achievements of the Academic and Library Promotion Department (Joan Urban, Diane Burrowes, Virginia Stanley, and Sean Dugan)—after all, this is a family book. And a salute to all my friends in the publicity, sales, and Harper Audio divisions.

My agent, Jim Trupin, is like my Boswell—Tom Boswell, that is. Sorry, I couldn't resist a cheap joke, which is why Jim and I get along so well—I'm willing to listen to his clunkers, too. If Jim's my Boswell, then Liz Trupin's my Marion Ross, and my days have been happier since I've known her.

Kassie Schwan is one of the few illustrators I know who can make aspirin look interesting. Come to think of it, she's managed to make nine of my books look interesting. Thanks for your wonderful work.

Special gratitude is owed to friends in the publishing business who allow me to natter on about my problems and reciprocate by offering warm shoulders and sage advice. Thank you, Mark Kohut, Susie Russenberger, Barbara Rittenhouse, James Gleick, and all of my Prodigy pals, especially the Housewife Writers.

Let us now praise those whose research proved invaluable. Thanks to Sherry Spitzer, Judith Dahlman, Honor Mosher. David Schisgall, and Chris McCann for making my work so much easier.

Thanks to all my friends and family, who actually managed to tolerate me for another year: Jesus Arias; Michael Barson; Sherry Barson; Rajat Basu; Ruth Basu; Barbara Bayone; Jeff Bayone; Jean Behrend; Marty Bergen; Brenda Berkman; Cathy Berkman; Sharyn Bishop; Andrew Blees; Carri Blees; Christopher Blees; Jon Blees; Bowling Green State University's Popular Culture Department; Jerry Braithwaite; Annette Brown; Arvin Brown; Herman Brown; Ernie Capobianco; Joann Carney; Lizzie Carnie; Susie Carnie; Janice Carr; Lapt Chan; Mary Clifford; Don Cline; Dori Cohen; Alvin Cooperman;

Audrey Cooperman; Marilyn Cooperman; Judith Dahlman; Paul Dahlman; Shelly de Satnick; Charlie Doherty; Laurel Doherty; Joyce Ebert; Pam Elam; Steve Feinberg; Fred Feldman; Gilda Feldman; Michael Feldman; Phil Feldman; Ron Felton; Kris Fister; Mary Flannery; Linda Frank; Elizabeth Frenchman; Michele Gallery; Chris Geist; Jean Geist; Bonnie Gellas; Richard Gertner; Amy Glass; Bea Gordon; Dan Gordon; Emma Gordon; Ken Gordon; Judy Goulding; Chris Graves; Christal Henner; Lorin Henner; Marilu Henner; Melodie Henner; David Hennes; Paula Hennes; Sheila Hennes; Sophie Hennes; Mitchell Hofing; Steve Hofman; Bill Hohauser; The Housewife Writers; Uday Ivatury; Terry Johnson; Sarah Jones; Allen Kahn; Mitch Kahn; Joel Kaplan; Dimi Karras; Steve Kaufman; Robin Kay; Stewart Kellerman; Eileen Kelly; Harvey Kleinman; Claire Labine; Randy Ladenheim-Gil; Julie Lasher; Debbie Leitner; Marilyn Levin; Vicky Levy; Rob Lieberman; Jared Lilienstein; Pon Hwa Lin; Adam Lupu; Patti Magee; Rusty Magee; everybody at the Manhattan Bridge Club; Phil Martin; Chris McCann; Jeff McQuain; Julie Mears; Phil Mears; Roberta Melendy; Naz Miah; Carol Miller; Honor Mosher; Barbara Musgrave; Phil Neel; Steve Nellisen; Craig Nelson; The Night Owl Chat gang; Millie North; Milt North; Charlie Nurse; Debbie Nye; Tom O'Brien; Pat O'Connor; Terry Oleske; Joanna Parker; Jeannie Perkins; Merrill Perlman; Joan Pirkle; Larry Prussin; Marlys Ray; Joe Rowley; Rose Reiter; Brian Rose; Lorraine Rose; Paul Rosenbaum; Carol Rostad; Tim Rostad; Leslie Rugg; Tom Rugg; Gary Saunders; Joan Saunders; Mike Saunders; Norm Saunders; Laura Schisgall; Cindy Shaha; Pat Sheinwold; Aaron Silverstein; Kathy Smith; Kurtwood Smith; Susan Sherman Smith; Chris Soule; Sherry Spitzer; Stan Sterenberg; Kat Stranger; Anne Swanson; Ed Swanson; Mike Szala; Jim Teuscher; Josephine Teuscher; Laura Tolkow; Albert Tom; Matddy Tyree; Alex Varghese; Carol Vellucci; Hattie Washington; Ron Weinstock; Roy Welland; Dennis Whelan; Devin Whelan; Heide Whelan; Lara Whelan; Jon White; Ann Whitney; Carol Williams; Maggie Wittenburg; Karen Wooldridge; Maureen Wylie; Charlotte Zdrok; Vladimir Zdrok; and Debbie Zuckerberg.

Because Imponderables are questions with answers not easily found in books, we rely on the wisdom of experts in every imaginable field. Although we contacted close to 1,500 corporations, universities, foundations, professors, associations, and miscellaneous experts on everything from acrylic to yogurt, we thank here only the sources who led directly to the answers to the Imponderables in this book:

Morris Adams, Thomas Built Buses; Tony Aiello, California Beef Council; Bob Alter, Polaroid Corporation; Harry Amdur, American Photographic Historical Society; John Anderson, Borden's Glue; Carl Andrews, Hershey Foods Corporation; Joe Andrews, Pillsbury Brands.

Bill Baker, Recreational Vehicle Industry Association; Joseph P. Bark; Kim Barley, White Castle; Andrea Bean, ERIC; Kathie Bellamy, Baskin-Robbins; Elizabeth Berrio, Immigration and Naturalization Service; Susan Berry; Melissa Bertelsen, First Data Resources, Inc.; Jim Boldt, Great Northern Corporation; Al Brock, WKLX; Don Buckley, National Ice Cream Retailers Association; Robert Burnham, *Astronomy*; Russell Burns, American Racing Pigeon Union; Steve Busits, American Homing Pigeons Fanciers.

John Cahill, Fine Art Photography; Frank Calandra, Photographic Historical Society; Rick Campbell, NCAA; Jeff Carpenter, Washington State Superintendent of Physical Education and Health Education; Bob Carroll, Pro Football Researchers Association; Ellen Carson, Empire Berol USA; David Cerull, Fire Collectors Club; Lynn Chen, American Numismatic Association; Officer Claggett, Richmond, Virginia Police Department; Annette Clark, Scottish Heritage Association; Calvin Clemons, National Association of Writing Instruments; Linda W. Coleman, Bureau of Engraving and Printing; Mark T. Conroy, National Fire Protective Association; John Cook, Georgia Dermatology and Skin Cancer; Tony Crawford, Dallas Police Department; Todd Culver, Cornell University Laboratory of Ornithology; Kimberly J. Cutchins, National Peanut Council.

Sandy Davenport, International Jelly and Preserve Association; Harold Davis, FDA; Thomas Deen, Transportation Research Board; Georgeanne Del Canto, Brooklyn, New York Board of Education; Arthur Douglas, Lowell Corporation; Joe Doyle; Bill Dwyer, Federal Signal Corporation.

Merle Ellis; Kay Engelhardt, American Egg Board; Stuart Ensor, National Live Stock & Meat Board; Marcus Evans, GACCP.

Darryl Felder, University of Louisiana, Lafayette; Fred Feldman; Karen Finkel, National School Transportation Association; Sheila Fitzgerald, Michigan State University; Dan Flory, Cincinnati College of Mortuary Science; William Frank, Aluminum Company of America; Meryl Friedman, Mattel Toys.

Samuel R. Gammon, American Historical Society; Marsha R. Gardner, Hershey Foods; Brenda Gatling, United States Mint; Jay Gilbert; Joan Godfrey, Alpines International; Emmanuel Goldman, *Curriculum Review*; Ailette Gomex, California Pistachio Commission; Michael Goodwin, International Paper; Stanley Gordon, Bridge Division, Federal Highway Administration; Lee Grant, Agricultural Extension Service, University of Maryland; Tina Steger Gratz, American Dental Association; Robert Gray, Old Dominion Box Company; Gene Gregory, United Egg Producers.

Officer Hallock, Salt Lake City Police Department; Herb Hammond, New York Rangers; Paul Hand, Atlantic Dairy Cooperative; Darryl Hansen, Entomological Society of America; Charles E. Hanson, Museum Association of the American Frontier; Pat Harmon, College Football Hall of Fame; Ruth Harmon, Miller Brewing Company; Megan Haugood, California Table Grape Commission; John Bell Henneman, ICHRPI; Martin Henry, National Fire Protection Association; David Hensing, AASHTO; Billy Higgins, AASHTO; Janet Hinshaw, Wilson Ornithological Society; Bruce Hisley, National Fire Academy; Francis Hole; David Hoover; Ike House; John Howland, American Goat Society; Richard Hudnut, Builders Hardware Manufacturers Association; John Husinak, Middlebury College; W. Ray Hyde.

Peter Ihrke, American Academy of Veterinary Dermatology.

Simon S. Jackel; Sally Jameson, Braille Institute; Alison Johnson, Delta Airlines; Michele Waxman Johnson, Institute of Transportation Engineers.

Maggie Kannan, Department of Photographs, Metropolitan Museum of Art; Kelly Karr, American Meat Institute; Phil Katz, Beer Institute; V. Herbert Kaufman, SAE International; Carol Keis, Hanna-Barbera Productions; Glenda Kelley; Lynn Kimsey, Bohart Museum of Entomology; Anthony L. Kiorpes, University of Wisconsin-Madison School of Veterinary Medicine; Ben Klein; Phil Klein; Robin Klein, Pork Information Bureau; Don Koehler, Georgia Peanut Commission;

Richard Kramer, National Pest Control Association; Sharon Kulak, National Live Stock & Meat Board.

Catherine R. Lambrechts, Dean Witter Financial Services Group; Richard Landesman, University of Vermont; Michael de L. Landon, University of Mississippi; Christopher Landry, New Orleans Police Department; Gerald Lange, Alliance for Contemporary Book Arts; Michael Lauria; Kenneth Leavell, Du Pont; Thomas A. Lehmann, American Institute of Baking; Rafael Lemaitre, Museum of Natural History; Joe Lesniak, Door and Hardware Manufacturing Institute; Gene Lester, American Society of Camera Collectors; Barbara Linton, National Audubon Society; Jerome Z. Litt; Theodore Lustig, West Virginia University; Denny Lynch, Wendy's.

Steward MacBreachan; Alan MacRobert, *Sky & Telescope*; Judy Maire, National Association of School Nursing Consultants; Ed Marks, *The Ice Screamer*, Bob Martin, Scottish Tartan Society; Nancy Martin, Vermont Institute of Natural Science; John T. McCabe, Master Brewers of the Americas; Roy McJunkin, California Museum of Photography; Pat McKelvey, Wine Institute; Lisa McKendall, Mattel Toys; Carmen Miller, Helen of Troy Corporation; Patricia Milroy, McDonald's; Joseph Mitchell, University of Richmond; Randy Morgan, Cincinnati Insectarium; Rose Motzko, Walt Disney; Michelle Mueckenhoff, Dairy Council of Wisconsin.

Jean Naras, American Dairy Association; National Collegiate Athletic Association; Kevin Newsome, Newsome's Studio of Photography; James Nolan, Fibre Box Association; Human Numan, Z-100.

Richard O'Brien; Barnet Orenstein; Alberta Orr, American Foundation for the Blind; Betsey Owens, Virginia-Carolina Peanut Promotion.

Richard Palin, Loctite Corporation; Tonya Parravano, National Live Stock & Meat Board; Peanut Factory; Joan Peyrebrune, Institute of Transportation Engineers; Bob Phillips, American Racing Pigeon Union; Planters Corporation; Jay Poster, *Agronomy News*; Mary Potter, Mead Corporation; Bill Powell, Booth Memorial Medical Center; Gary Priest, San Diego Zoo.

Howard Raether; T.E. Reed, American Rabbit Breeders Association; Donna Reed, National Pasta Association; Carl Reichenbach,

Dixon Ticonderoga Company; Viva Reinhardt; Revlon, Inc.; John-Paul Richluso, American Association for State and Local History; Robin Roche, San Francisco Zoological Society; John R. Rodenburg, Federated Funeral Directors of America; Janet Rodowca, Fort Howard; Robert R. Rofen, Aquatic Research Institute; Grant Romer, George Eastman House; Officer Romero, Los Angeles Police Department; Mary H. Ross, Virginia Polytechnic Institute; Kate Ruddon, American College of Obstetricians and Gynecologists; Tonda Rush, National Newspaper Association; John Rutkauskas, American Society for Geriatric Dentistry.

Walter Sanders, Diners Club International; Richard Santore, Associated Funeral Directors Service International; Leslie Saul, San Francisco Zoological Society; Ray Schmidt; Robert Schmidt, North American Native Fishes Association; Paul Schofield, Discover Credit Corporation; Jim Schreier, Council on America's Military Past; Don Schwartz, Children's Hospital; Ira Schwartz, New York State Regents Advisory Committee; Norman Scott, Society for the Study of Amphibians and Reptiles; Samuel Selden; Arlene Sheffield, New York State Education Department; Ron Siebel, J.E. Siebel Sons' Company; John Simmons, American Society of Ichthyologists and Herpetologists; Charles Simpson, Texas A&M; Harry Skinner, Traffic Engineering Division, Federal Highway Administration; Philip and Shirley Smith; Bob Smith, Cytec; Bruce V. Snow; Stephen Snyder, Book Manufacturers Institute; Daniel Solomon, E&J Gallo Winery; Jeff Solomon-Hess, *Recycling Today*; Kent Sorrells, Altadena Certified Dairy; Dennis Stacey; Lynne Strang, Distilled Council of the United States; Robert Strawn, RVDA of North America; Joe Struble, George Eastman House.

Anne Tantum, American Association of Meat Processors; Thad W. Tate, College of William & Mary in Virginia; Farook Taufiq, Prince Company; Karl Torjussen, Westvaco Corporation.

United Airlines; USDA--Agricultural Research Service.

Pamela Van Hine, American College of Obstetrics and Gynecologists; Vanner Weldon, Inc.; Richard Van Iderstine, National Highway Traffic Safety Administration; Matthew J. Vellucci, Distilled Spirits Council of the United States; Ralph E. Venk, Photographic

Society of America; Rhoda Virgil-Madison, Detroit Police Department.

Larry Wallace, Monsanto; Roscoe Wallace, Monsanto; Steve Warren, MOR Media; James Weidman, Welch Foods, Inc.; Rebecca Weller, Fuller Brush Company; Vicki Wells, Miles, Inc.; Thomas Werner, New York State Department of Transportation; E.J. Westerman, Kaiser Aluminum and Chemical Corporation; Ron Whitfield, Marine World Africa USA; Steve Whitmire, Jim Henson Productions; Vann Wilber, American Automobile Manufacturers Association; Richard Wisniewski, University of Tennessee, Knoxville; Dori Wofford, Levi Strauss & Company; Wilton Wong, Images Unlimited Photography; Danny Wright; Jim Wright, New York State Department of Transportation.

Bruce and Janice-Carol Yasgur; Karen Yoder, Entomological Society of America.

And to the many sources who, for whatever reason, preferred to remain anonymous, our sincere thanks.

Index

Acrylic, virgin, 671–72
Actors, speed of speech of,
  241–43, 507
Address labels on
  magazines, 309
After-shave lotion, stinging
  and, 161–62
Age of majority, 21 as,
  624–25
Aging and effect on voices,
  24–25
Airlines
  chime signals on, 580–82
  inflation of oxygen masks
    on, 500–2
Aluminum cans,
  crushability of, 731–33
Ambidextrity in lobsters,
  3–4
Ambulances, snake emblem
  on, 144–45, 813–14
Angel food cake and
  position while cooling,
  617–18
Animal tamers and kitchen
  chairs, 583–85
Ants and separation from
  colony, 44–45

Appendix, function of,
  456–57
April 15, as due date for
  taxes, 330–33
Architectural pencils, grades
  of, 647
Area codes, middle digits of,
  372–73
Armpits, shaving of, 249
Art pencils, grades of, 647
Aspirin, headaches on,
  674–76
Athletics, Oakland, and
  elephant insignia, 14–15
Audio cassette tape on side
  of road, 824–25
Audiotape recorders, play
  and record switches on,
  327–28
Automobiles
  bunching of, on highways,
    821
  cardboard on grills of,
    188–89, 819–20
  clicking sound of turn
    signals in, 203
  cockroaches in, 577–78

Automobiles (*continued*)
elimination of side vents in, 13–14
fuel gauges in, 273
headlamp shutoff, 666–67
headlights and deer, 212–14
holes in ceiling of, 483
key release button on, 473
"new car smell," 367
oil loss after oil change, 814–15
position of brights/dimmer switch, 618–20
rear windows of, 447–48
weight of batteries, 405–6
winshield wipers, vs. buses, 602

Babies
blinking and, 158–59
sleep and, 56–57
Baby shrimp, peeling and cleaning of, 431
Badges, marshals' and sheriffs', 377–78
Bags, paper, jagged edges and, 117–18
Baked goods
seven-layer cakes, 80–81
unctuous taste until cooled, 151–52
Baked potatoes in steak houses, 127–29
Balsa wood, classification as hardwood, 389–90
Banana peels as slipping agents, 250–52, 532–33

Band-Aids, red tear strings on, 266
Bands, paper, around Christmas card envelopes, 203–4
Barbie, hair of, vs. Ken's, 578–79
Bark, tree, color of, 78–79
Baseball
dugout heights, 318
home plate, shape of, 435
"K" as symbol for strike out, 356–57
pitcher's mound, location of, 485
Baseball cards
wax on wrappers, 427
white stuff on gum, 426
Bathrooms
group visits by females to, 757–66
public, in supermarkets, 157
Batteries
automobile, weight of, 405–6
nine-volt, shape of, 104, 816–17
Bazooka Joe, and eye patch, 425
Beacons, police car, colors on, 709–11
Beanbag packs in electronics boxes, 201
Beer
in Old West, 321–22
and plastic bottles, 735–36
Belly dancers, amplitude of, 237–39, 506–7

Bubble gum
  baseball card gum, 426
  Bazooka Joe's eyepatch,
    425
  bubble-making
    ingredients, 424
  flavors of, 423–24
Bulbs, light
  halogen, 468
  high cost of 25-watt
    variety, 395
  and noise when shaking,
    350–51
Buses
  entry into, 328-29
  idling of engines on,
    724–25
  ridges on sides of, 475
Butter
  hardening after
    refrigeration, 392
  sticks, lengths of, 346
Butterflies, sneezing and
  coughing in, 655–56
Buttons, men's vs. women's
  shirts, 530, 797

Cable TV, volume levels of,
  381–82
Cadillacs, ducks on, 478–80
Caffeine, leftover, from
  decaffeinated coffee, 195
Cakes
  angel food and cooling
    position, 617–18
  reaction to loud noises,
    615–16
  seven-layer, missing layers
    on, 80–81

Calico cats, gender of,
  131–32
Cameras, black color of, 820
Can openers, sharpness of
  blades on, 176–77
Canadiens, Montreal, uni
  forms of, 816
Canceled checks
  numbers on, 123
  returned, numerical
    ordering of, 165–66
  white paper attached to,
    124–25
Cans, aluminum,
  crushability of, 731–33
Caps and gowns, at
  graduations, 99–102
Cardboard, on automobile
  grills, 188–89
Carpenters' pencils, shape
  of, 601
CAR-RT SORT on
  envelopes, 382–83
Cars
  batteries, weight of, 405–6
  holes in the ceiling of, 483
  key release buttons on,
    473
  and "new car smell," 367
  rear windows of, 447–48
Cashews, shells of, 539–40
Caskets, position of heads
  in, 8–9
Cassettes, audio, on side of
  road, 824–25
Cat feces, as food for dogs,
  35–37
Catnip, and effects on wild
  cats, 183–85

838

INDEX

Hairbrushes, length of handles on, 612–13
Hairs in mouth, gagging and, 650–51
Hairy ears in older men, 531–32
Half-moon vs. quarter-moon, 646–47
Halogen light bulbs, touching of, 468
Ham
  color of, when cooked, 589–90
  checkerboard pattern atop, 640–41
Hand positions in old photographs, 598–600
Handles vs. knobs, on doors, 722–23
Handwriting, teaching of cursive vs. printing, 608–11
Hats
  decline in use of, 227–31, 506, 807, 823
  dents in cowboy, 274, 310, 823–24
  holes in sides of, 430
Haystacks, shape of, 47–48
Headaches and aspirin, 674–76
Headbands on books, 700–1
Headlamps, shutoff of automobile, 666–67
Hearts, shapes of, idealized vs. real, 260, 524–25, 803–4
Heat and effect on sleep, 137–38
Height of elderly, 250

Helium and effect on voice, 412–13
Hermit crabs, "bathroom habits" of, 648
Hernia exams and "Turn your head and cough," 418–19
Highways
  bunching of traffic on, 821
  curves on, 695–96
Hockey
  banging of sticks by goalies, 690–91
  Montreal Canadiens uniforms, 469, 816
Holes
  on bottom of soda bottles, 187–88
  recycling of, in looseleaf paper, 679–80
  refilling of dirt, 622–23
Home plate, in baseball, shape of, 435
Honking in geese during migration, 682
Horses
  measurement of heights of, 364–65
  posture in open fields, 545
  vomiting and, 111–12, 822
Hospital gowns, back ties of, 436–38
Hot dog buns, slicing of, 465
Hot dogs, skin of, 358
Hotel amenities, spread of, 118–21
Houses, settling in, 32–34
"Hut," as football term, 40

INDEX

Lakes (*continued*)
ice formations on, 386–87
vs. ponds, 333–34, 815
Lane reflectors, fastening of,
402–3
Large-type books, size of,
439
Lasagna, crimped edges of,
365
Leg kicking during kissing,
770–71
Letters, 265–77, 539–52,
811–26
business, format of, 754
Levi jeans
colored tabs on, 59–61
origin of "501" name, 61
Liberal arts, origins of,
374–77
Light bulbs
air in, 199–200
halogen, 468
high cost of 25-watt
variety, 395
noise when shaking, 471
plinking by fluorescent,
351
Lighters, disposable, and
fluid chambers, 92–93
Lions, animal trainers and,
583–85
Lips, upper, grove on, 42–43
Lizards and eyes during
sleep, 715
Lobsters, ambidexterity of,
3–4
Looseleaf paper, recycling
of holes in, 679–80

Lotion, after-shave, and
stinging, 161–62

M&Ms, peanuts in plain,
265–66, 309–10
Macadamia nuts and shells,
386
Magazines
address labels on, 309
jumps in, 420–21
subscription insert cards
in, 461–62
Mail
CAR-RT SORT on
envelopes, 382–83
undeliverable, 317–18
Mailboxes and postmaster
general approval, 105–7
Mail-in refunds, vs.
coupons, 491–92
Mall, shopping , entrances,
doors at, 180–81
Marching, stepping off on
left foot when, 476–77
Margarine sticks, length of,
346
Marmalades, contents of,
140–41
Marshals' badges, shape of,
377–78
Matchbooks, location of
staples on, 173–74
Matches, color of paper,
174–75
McDonald's
Grimace, identity of, 747
"over 95 billion served"
signs, 745
straws, 745–46

McDonald's (*continued*)
wrapping techniques on
sandwiches, 746
Meat, age and doneness
preferences in, 534–35
Meatloaf, taste of, in
institutions, 243, 507,
809–10
Meats and doneness
preferences, 252–53
Men
dancing ability of, 218,
773–76
feelings of coldness, 218,
772–73
remote controls and, 217,
767–70
Menthol, coolness of, 496
Mickey Mouse, four fingers
of, 271
Milk
as sleep-inducer, 591
fat content in lowfat,
634–35
plastic milk containers,
635
in refrigerators, coldness
of, 308–9
single serving cartons of,
711–12
skim vs. nonfat, 633
skin on, when heated, 58
Milk cartons, design of, 416,
547
Milk cases, warnings on,
347–48
Mint, U.S., and shipment of
coin sets, 336

Mobile homes, tires atop, in
trailer parks, 163–64
Monitors, computer, shape
of, 129–31
Montreal Canadiens, uni
forms of, 469, 816
Moon
effect on lakes and ponds,
442–43
official name of, 323–24
quarter-, vs. half-, 646–47
Mosquitoes
biting and itching, 307–8
daytime habits of, 381–82
male vs. female eating
habits of, 494
Moths, reaction to light of,
21–23
Mottoes on sundials, 54–56
Movie actors, speed of
speech of, 241–43, 507
Muppets, left-handedness
of, 685–87
Musketeers, Three, and lack
of muskets, 603–4
Mustaches, policemen and,
219, 792–94

Nabisco Shredded Wheat
box, Niagara Falls on,
404–5
Nail polish and fingernail
yellowing, 703–4
National Geographics,
savings of, 533–34, 798
Necklaces, migration of on
body, 754

Putting, veering of ball toward ocean when, 107–8

Q-tips, origins of name of, 210–11
Quarterbacks and exclamation, "hut," 210
Quarter-moons vs. half-moons, 646–47

Rabbit tests, death of rabbits in, 643–45
Rabbits and nose wiggling, 477–78
Radio Shack and lack of cash registers, 469–70
Radio, lack of song identification on, 625–31
Railroad crossings and EXEMPT signs, 422–23
Rain, impending, smell of, 170–71, 598
Ranchers' fenceposts, boots on, 268, 551–52
Razors, men's vs. women's, 122–23
Rear admiral, origins of, 329
Recreation vehicles and wheel covers, 727
Recyclable plastics, numbers on, 155–56
Recycling of newspaper ink, 713–14
Red paint on coins, 691
Redshirting in college football, 620–22
Refrigeration of opened food jars, 171–72

Remote controls, men vs. women and, 217, 767–70
Restaurants
coffee, vs. home-brewed, 755
vertical rulers near entrances of, 669–70
Restrooms, group visits by females to, 217, 757–66
Rhode Island, origins of name of, 325–26
Rice Krispies, noises of, 548–49
Roaches
in automobiles, 577–78
reaction to light of, 20–21
Roads
blacktop, coloring of, 326–27
fastening of lane reflectors on, 402–3
vs. bridges, in freezing characteristics, 497
Robes, black, and judges, 190–92
Rodents and water sippers, 187
Roller skating rinks, music in, 274–75
Roman numerals on clocks, 541–42
Roofs, gravel on, 153–54
Rubble, Barney, vocation of, 747–48
Rubble, Betty, nonappearance in Flintstones multivitamins, 4–5

Rulers, vertical, in
restaurant entrances,
669–70
RVs and wheel covers, 727

Sacks, paper, jagged edges
and, 117–18
Salads, restaurant, celery in,
218, 781–83
Salt
in oceans, 453–54
and pepper, as table
condiments, 225–26,
505
Sand in pockets of new
jeans, 726
Scabs, itchiness of, 429–30
Schools, CPR training in,
605–7
Scotsmen and kilts, 683–84
Screen doors, locations of
handles on, 665
"Sea" gulls in parking lots,
198–99
Sea vs. ocean, 334–36
Settling in houses, 32–34
Seven-layer cakes and
missing layers, 80–81
7UP, origins of name,
313–14
Shampoos, lathering of,
348–49
Shaving of armpits, 249
Sheriffs' badges, shape of,
377–78
Shirts
buttons on men's vs.
women's, 797

Shirts (*continued*)
single-needle stitching in,
51
Shoes
of deceased, at funerals,
727–28
layers on, 363
on side of road, 245–48,
529–30, 795–96
Shopping malls, doors at
entrances of, 180–81
Shopping, female proclivity
towards, 754
Shredded Wheat, Niagara
Falls on box of, 404–5
Shrimp, baby, peeling and
cleaning of, 431
"Sic," as dog command, 355
Side vents in automobile
windows, 13–14
Sidewalks, glitter on, 734
Silica gel packs in
electronics boxes, 201
Silos, shape of, 549
Single-needle stitching in
shirts, 51
Skating music, roller rinks
and, 274–75
Skating, figure, and
dizziness, 337–39
Skyscrapers, bricks in, 102–3
Sleep
babies and, 56–57
drowsiness after meals
and, 138–39
eye position during, 146
heat and effect on, 137–38
"Slippery When Wet" signs,
location of, 741–42

Tunnels, ceramic tiles in, 135–36

"Turkey," origin of term, 269

Turn signals in automobiles, clicking sounds of, 203

Twenty-one as age of majority, 624–25

TWIX cookie bars, holes in, 28–29

Underarm hair, purpose of, 275–76

Uniforms
painters' whites, 17–19
surgeons, color of, 269

United States Mint and shipment of coin sets, 336

United States Postal Service (USPS)
and CAR-RT SORT on envelopes, 382–83
and undeliverable mail, 317–18

Upper lips, groove on, 42–43

UPS and shipment of coin sets, 336

Vegetable oil, vegetables in, 266

Vending machines, bill counting and, 271–72

Vent windows, side, in automobiles, 13–14

Video cassette recorders
counters on, 817–18
power surges and, 818–19

Videotape recorders
"play" and "record" switches on, 327–28
and storms, 484–85

Videotapes, rental, two-tone signals on, 448–49

Virgin acrylic, 671–72

Vitamins, measurement of, in foods, 148–50

Voices, elderly vs. younger, 24–25

Vomiting and horses, 111–12

Waiters' tips and credit cards, 707-9

Watches (timepieces), 271

Water
boiling, during home deliveries, 114–15, 821–22
manufacture of, 411–12

Water faucets, bathroom vs. kitchen, 548

Watermelon seeds, white vs. black, 398

Water temperature and effect on stains, 77–78

Water towers
height of, 395–97
in winter, 38–40

Weather
clear days following storms, 125
forecasting of, in different regions, 267–68
smell of impending rain, 170–71